© Lisa Lee

ABOUT THE AUTHOR

MICHAEL LARGO has been collecting statistics and information on the American way
of dying for more than a decade. He is the
author of three novels, and he lives with his
family in Miami, Florida.

For more information please visit:
www.FinalExits.com.

FINAL
EXITS

Also by Michael Largo

Southern Comfort

Lies Within

Welcome to Miami

The Illustrated Encyclopedia of How We Die

HARPER

NEW YORK · LONDON · TORONTO · SYDNEY

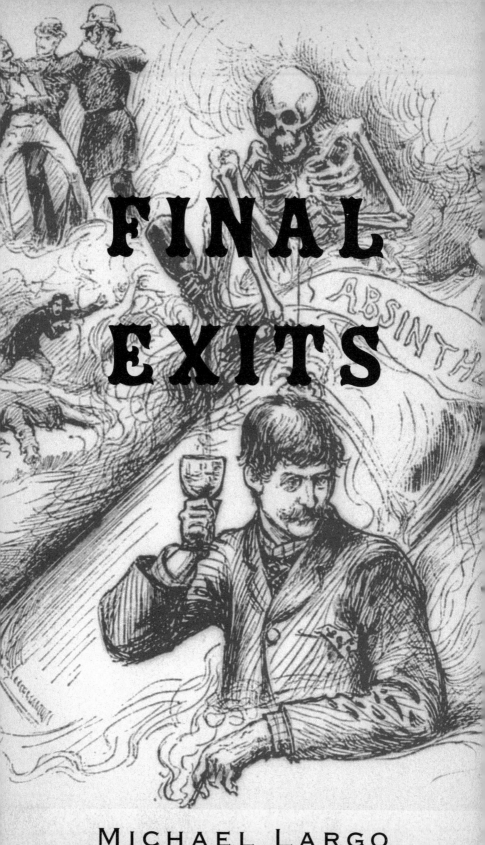

FINAL EXITS

MICHAEL LARGO

HARPER

Photographic credits follow page 468.

HarperCollins books may be purchased for educational, business, or sales promotional use. For information please write: Special Markets Department, HarperCollins Publishers, 10 East 53rd Street, New York, NY 10022.

FIRST EDITION

Title page illustration courtesy of the National Library of Medicine

Designed by Justin Dodd

Library of Congress Cataloging-in-Publication Data

Largo, Michael.
    Final exits : the illustrated encyclopedia of how we die / by Michael Largo.—
1st Harper paperback ed.
        p. cm.
    Includes bibliographical references.
    ISBN-10: 0-06-081741-0
    ISBN-13: 978-0-06-081741-1
    1. Thanatology—Encyclopedias. I. Title.
HQ1073.L37 2006
306.903—dc22   2006041217

06 07 08 09 10 DIX/RRD 10 9 8 7 6 5 4

Inspirational in life and death,
in loving memory
Dominick, Victoria, and Tom Largo

FINAL EXITS

INTRODUCTION

To die, kick the bucket, cross over to the other side, to meet the Maker, to be dead as a doornail, to get wasted, whacked, smoked, to sleep with the fishes, bite the dust, put on the wooden overcoat, or sleep with Jesus; whatever death is called, it's going to happen. In 1789, Ben Franklin wrote, "In this world nothing is certain but death and taxes." Death remains a certainty, but how do we die?

It is the enormous variety of the *how* that motivated me to research what became *Final Exits*. It seemed a puzzle that in 1700 there were less than one hundred causes of death described on death certificates, while today there are over three thousand. Of course, the medical aspect of how a person dies has remained the same since prehistoric times—the heart finally stops beating—yet many things that cause death have changed. With each advance in technology we discovered brand new ways to become deceased. As a student of anthropology and sociology, I saw how the connection in the variety of ways in which people met their destiny exemplified clearly how they lived. Thus, death becomes a benchmark of our culture, and I set out to gauge the rising water, to discover how it was we died before and how it is we die now.

Today, although we live longer, people are killed by everything, from cell phones, washing machines, and lawn mowers to the boundless catalog of man-made medicines. Changes in transportation, from the horse and buggy to space-craft, have vastly affected the landscape of death. Modern leisure activities, such as snowboarding and hang gliding, give new perspective to the human life span. Modifications and enhancements applied to age-old activities—from sex to warfare—prove there are yet new and astonishing ways to perish. This book unearths the facts on the most common ways to die, the strangest ways to go, and the fatal aberrations and oddities that marked the unluckiests' final exits.

Americans die everywhere, doing everything—2.4 million last year—though many could have enhanced their odds of survival if they knew the facts. It's surprising to learn how many people actually expired in a plane, an elevator, pushing through a revolving door, on skis, sleeping on a water bed, driving a taxi, at the end of a rope, while working behind the counter at a convenience store, while laughing, from hiccups, during or after divorce, while dancing in a nightclub, or while praying in church. The numbers and trends make clear how some activities are more dangerous than any of us would have believed. They also undoubtedly disclose the arbitrary though sometimes predictability of human fatality in a startling new way.

It took more than ten years to gather the multitudinous statistics on fatality into an informative, and, I hope, enlightening and entertaining book. But my interests in the causes of death go back to early childhood. When I was young, my father, an NYPD detective, occasionally took me from the comfort of our quiet Staten Island neighborhood into Manhattan where he worked. His spur-of-the-moment tours of the city were both exhilarating and scary. Instead of pointing out the typical sightseeing landmarks, my father offered comments about an ordinary looking street corner or a seemingly innocuous building; he knew the exact number of fatalities, murders, or mishaps that previously occurred at each of these places and would reveal small details to me. Although he intended these tours to be an education in the necessity of being cautious and alert, what struck me was that no one else, the pedestrians on the corner or the building's occupants, was aware of this past history. I thought a sign should have been posted—something to help it from happening again. Since then, I've been fascinated with the varied ways people have died and became an avid collector of strange stories, curious facts, and all things pertaining to our mortality. I wanted to make a definitive sourcebook on the way we die without being macabre, grim, or demoralizing.

What I have done here is count, record, and sift through the numbers to determine the actual things that kill people. This was not as easy as I first thought. There's still no standard in filling out death certificates; local, state, and national recording agencies are not wired together, and many times the attendant completing the required form at the bedside or at the morgue has a limited history of the person being duly pronounced. Besides, everyone seems to have special interest in the way the dead are tallied. Gun lobbyists put their spin on handgun fatalities. Some pharmaceutical companies, fad diet promoters, or certain plastic surgeons might stand to lose a lot of money if the true numbers are revealed. The bartering of body counts equals dollars; product improvements, the food we eat, the air we breathe at work, the roads we drive on, the clothes we wear—none of these issues will be made safer and less lethal unless the actual fatality numbers are known. Some special interests may not like the death tallies recorded here, but they are in fact the numbers I gathered from over fifty government agencies.

To get listed in this book a person had to be certifiably dead; being on life support or wishing they were dead wouldn't get them included here. I know that the dying part, right before death, is a sad and profound event. Ultimately, every death is a tragedy, and has to count for something. Those before us may be gone, but in this book they won't be forgotten. Instead, they'll instruct us, alarm us, titillate us, and sadden us with the way they went.

Although many of us avoid the subject, death is a potent element in our everyday life. We're not necessarily aware of it all the time, but it has infused our language. You'll be the death of me, dead man walking, dead presidents, drop-dead gorgeous, over my dead body, knock 'em dead, and until death do us part are some of the phrases used frequently in our daily speech. Even though death is most often the term used to describe a condition for which medicine has yet to find a cure, it's here to stay in all its various incarnations.

It's been said by many thinkers greater than I, from Kierkegaard to the Dalai Lama, that ignoring death leads to less prosperous living. Contemplation of our mortality can give a new perspective, and keep the importance of trivial things . . . trivial. Each day is truly a gift we must embrace with everything we have. Hug someone, smell a flower, kiss a tree. Sure, we all know we're going to die—it's in the contract—and in a healthy way we shouldn't overtly dwell on it. But if given a chance to increase the odds, an opportunity to avoid the randomness of the entire affair, would you take it?

There is something you can do to increase your chances for a healthy and long life: Read this book and understand how those who departed before you did indeed depart. Read it for your kids. I predict that those who buy this book will gain—at the minimum—an average of two extra years of life. My greatest hope is that the information I've gathered here might help save even one life.

So begin now and stay safe, be cautious. And let me give you one more bit of advice, which will suit you well when encountering the material you find here, or whatever may cross your path: "Never knock on Death's door. Ring the bell and run! Death hates that."

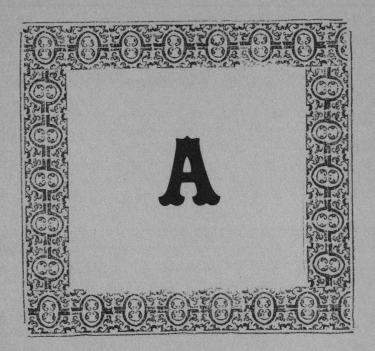

ABACTIO This is a medical term for abortion or premature labor induced by street drugs, herbal concoctions, or homestyle surgery. Regardless of one's opinions about the termination of unwanted pregnancy, the fact remains that it has been done since the onset of civilization. In Roman times, magic potions to dispel pregnancy were openly sold at market and persons knowledgeable about the theurgy of miscarriage were hired to recite incantations near a woman's swelling stomach. In the Middle Ages, the use of emetics, pastes, and physical maneuvers to stop pregnancy were

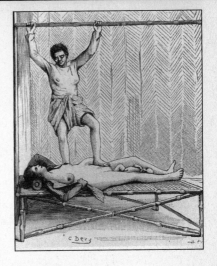

described in detail in medical literature (based on the translated writings of Galen, a Greek physician, circa A.D. 200) and used since the first medical school was founded in Salerno, Italy, in the eighth century.

Emma Goldman, a writer and human right's activist noted that, throughout history, prior to education and contraception, "Most women lived in continual dread of conception." For many wives of the late nineteenth and early twentieth centuries, getting pregnant was seen as a possible death sentence for either themselves or their unborn children.

For many women abortion was simply the most reliable form of contraception. To rid themselves of another pregnancy, women would massage their stomachs vigorously, jump off tables, throw themselves down flights of stairs and, when all else failed, resorted to the use of blunt instruments. Between 1850 and 1930 physicians and midwives offered a variety of remedies for "obstructed menses," prescribing recipes for mixtures often as lethal to the mother as it was to the embryo. Although it was illegal to sell or advertise

NOT AGAIN

During the seventeenth and eighteenth centuries, one in thirty childbirths ended in the mother's death from exhaustion, dehydration, infection, hemorrhage, or convulsions. The average female gave birth five to eight times in her life and with each birth she had a one in eight chance of dying. Colonial women referred to pregnancy as "one of the greatest earthly miseries."

contraception devices, the sale of these potions or "abortifacients" was acceptable.

In 1900 there were one hundred thousand abortions performed in New York City, and 17,300 deaths as a result of those procedures. Today, 1.3 million abortions are performed in the United States each year. Drug overdoses by girls under eighteen years old and "homestyle" abortions initiated by parents account for four thousand such terminations and 710 deaths, annually. However, those wishing to give up a child for adoption have to run a gauntlet of red tape and face ostracism. In 2003, U.S. couples adopted 20,099 children from other countries.

HOME REMEDY AWARD

Women were so desperate to get rid of pregnancy that they'd believe anything. Take, for example, this advice column from an 1880 rural newspaper, Nebraska Farmer: "To prevent conception, [a woman should] eat the dried lining of a chicken's gizzard [or] take gunpowder in small doses for three mornings. . . . A woman who wants to put an end to her childbearing must throw the afterbirth of her last baby down an old well or walk directly over the spot where the afterbirth was buried. [She should] drink a tea made from rusty nail water, or rub [her] navel with quinine and turpentine morning and night for several days: each of these remedies can induce abortion."

ABANDONMENT IN CARS In March 2001, a Texas mother left her five-month-old baby in his car seat while she went to work at a nearby restaurant. She reported to work at 10:00 A.M. and returned to the car at 3:00 P.M. She found the infant lifeless. During the day the heat inside the car had risen to 100°F. The distraught woman told police she must have forgotten to drop her baby off at the day care center.

In 2004, 298 children died when they were left alone in hot automobiles. According to a survey conducted by the National Safe Kids Campaign in 2002, ten thousand parents said they regularly leave children inside a running car for at least three minutes while attending errands. Although only one hundred

admitted to leaving the child in a car for thirty minutes or more, children left in unattended vehicles is becoming quite common. One woman confessed to leaving her three-year-old unaccompanied in a car for up to four hours each day because she had no access to child care. She would keep the window slightly open, park the car within sight of her office window, and provide the child with drinks and toys. However, during an exceptional hot August day in 2004, the child died of heatstroke.

LICENSE TO PARENT REVOKED

In October 2002, a father in Michigan left his two-year-old son in the car and went into a bar. The boy was not there when the father returned forty-five minutes later. During the next six days, while the child remained missing, snow and rain fell in the area. The child was found dead of hypothermia, exposed for too long to low temperatures, due to his father's senselessness.

FATALITIES OF CHILDREN IN UNATTENDED VEHICLES SINCE 1985: 2,780

A CORDYNIA Most people know mercury as the toxic shiny, silver white, liquid metal, sometimes dyed red and seen in a thermometer; they figure as long as they don't come into contact with the stuff they have no chance of getting, and dying from, acordynia—mercury poisoning. However, mercury is found in hundreds of common things we

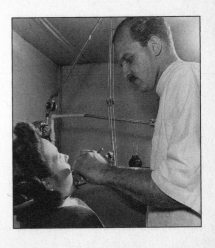

WHAT'S IN YOUR MOUTH?

Two-thirds of fillings used by dentists contain mercury. U.S. dentists put forty-four tons of mercury into patient's teeth each year.

use everyday from washing machines to motion-sensitive devices in your freezer, sump pumps, space heaters, and irons. The substance also is used in fluorescent and vapor lamps and in neon signs.

Power plants account for one-third (52 tons) of annual man-made mercury emissions in the country. All of these mercury vapors are easily transported through the atmosphere to land and water. Mercury is very soluble in water and gets quickly absorbed into the plankton levels of the food chain. It passes from little fish to big fish to us, virtually undiluted. That's why eating too much predator fish, such as swordfish, shark, and even canned tuna, causes mercury poisoning.

WHAT'S IN THAT FLU SHOT?

Another way mercury enters the body is through vaccines: The mercury-based Thimerosal is added as a preservative in adult and children's flu shots. From the first vaccines administered shortly after birth, mercury is injected into every child in America. The Journal of Mental Deficiency Research *reported on a study that found mercury in the hair samples of autistic children, raising the probability that the recent explosion of autistic children can be traced to mercury in vaccines. In 2004, the Immunization Safety Review Committee recommended the removal of mercury preservatives from children's vaccines after current stockpiles are depleted. Out of the 4 million people born each year in the United States, over twenty-four thousand will be autistic and another six hundred thousand children will be affected with mild to severe learning disorders caused by mercury that settles and disturbs brain cells. Before 1930, when Thimerosal was first added as a preservative in vaccines, the rate of autism was 1 in 20,000 births. Today, the rate is 1 in 144.*

6,530 PEOPLE ARE HOSPITALIZED AND FIVE HUNDRED DIE
FROM MERCURY POISONING EACH YEAR.

AGUE Genealogy buffs come across this cause of death so often, but we never hear of it in current times. By definition, "Ague"—pronounced EE-Goo—means chills, shakes, and fevers and according to old-time doctors, everyone died of it. Before 1920, a plethora of death certificates showed this as a cause. Back then it apparently made doctors appear very knowledgeable, especially when they didn't know exactly what was happening to the patient: "I'm sorry, his EE-Goo is too far advanced." It must have seemed more professional to ascribe a cause of death instead of the vague "malady," "unwellness," or "unknown sickness." Since then, at least five hundred diseases have been differentiated from this onetime catch-all killer—everything from an ordinary infection, or an abscessed tooth, to yellow fever. By looking at how the diagnosis of ague changed over the centuries, it's clear to see how science has advanced.

AGUE WAS RECORDED ON 319,334 DEATH CERTIFICATES
FROM 1850 TO 1920. (*See Also:* Postmortem/Death Certificates)

AIR BAGS Car air bag technology was originally developed to protect astronauts in crash landings of spacecrafts. The first crash-sensor air bag was invented in 1968 and was subsequently tested in some government vehicles in 1973. Air bags became a standard-issue feature in cars in 1990. An air bag senses impact and sudden deceleration and inflates at a speed of 200 mph, as fast as a shell fired from a sawed-off shotgun. While air bags do effectively save lives, they have also caused whiplash; eye injuries, including blindness; degloving (the outer layer of skin being peeled to the bone); quadriplegia; and death, by decapitation or otherwise. As air bag deaths mounted, warning labels got bigger. Scientists discovered, after contemplation of the most current data, that short people, children, and infants are more often affected.

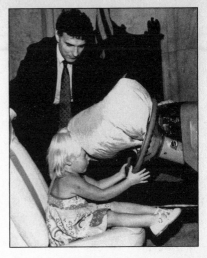

TOTAL FATALITIES FROM
AIR BAGS: 6,982

THE FINE PRINT

A thirty-two-year-old man, six foot, in good shape, and without health problems discovered the hard way that air bags can kill in an entirely new way. While he was driving home from a Halloween party in 1999, his car veered off the road on a slippery turn. The car's front end bumped to a halt against a wall, causing the air bag to deploy. Despite the relatively low impact, the police arriving at the scene found the man dead. They assumed drugs or an aneurysm were the cause of death, but awaited the results of an autopsy. It was discovered that the man had been sucking on a lollipop, picking through the Halloween candy, when his air bag inflated in his face. The explosive impact forced the candy, stick and all, to lodge in his throat, choking him to death. Since then, the fine print on the warning labels has encouraged drivers to avoid sucking on lollipops (eating) while driving.

AIR SHOWS Who doesn't love the roar of the jets and death-defying aerobatics? The last fatal performance in North America, in 1952, when twenty-eight in the audience died, prompted the initiation of a one thousand five hundred-foot minimum setback distance between the performing aircraft and the audience. According to Springfield Air Rendezvous, operators of extreme air shows, "The United States has achieved a complete elimination of spectator fatalities since the regulations were put in place more than fifty years ago." But it's not the same sterling safety record for the flyers of biplanes or turbo-charged jets: On average, five performer pilots die each year.

The most famous stunt pilots, the **Blue Angels,** perform intricate daredevil flying routines throughout the United States. There have been twenty-three fatalities among the navy's Blue Angels pilots since the group was formed in 1946.

SPECTATOR DEATHS AT AIR SHOWS:
1920–1999: 761

KING OF THE SKYWALKERS
Hollywood's first major stunt pilot was Ormer Locklear. He learned to play a good game of tennis on the wing of a flying plane, perfected the plane-to-plane transfer of pilots, and also did the first car-to-plane transfer, as seen in The Great Air Robbery *in 1919. One year later, he was called to simulate a nighttime crash and attached flares to the wings of his plane. He took the plane into a tailspin, but the movie lighting distracted him and he crashed for real. His death can be seen in the film* The Skywayman.

LOVE ME TENDER
June 26, 1996: While jumping out of a plane to promote the opening of a Boston nightclub, one of four Flying Elvises died when he was caught in a windstorm and blown out to sea.

ALCOHOLISM Heavy alcohol use changes people and makes them do all kinds of things. One incident that happened in a bar at Third Avenue in the Bronx, New York, not only shows the extremes of alcoholic transformation but how alcohol is often the silent partner in many deaths. In 1933, one heavy-drinking bartender heard about how a guy collected a lot of money when his wife died.

He decided he could do the same if he took out a life insurance policy on one of the regulars, an old stumblebum named Mickey M., an alcoholic apparently in the final stage of the disease. The bartender elicited the help of the bar janitor and together they paid for the policy, figuring they'd

have to wait only a few months before the old drunk kicked. After six months, and still no dead Mickey, they decided to accelerate the process. One night they told Mickey it was his birthday, and for the whole night drinks were on the house. They served him cocktails spiked with antifreeze, shoe polish, rat poison, and turpentine. But Mickey teetered out, only to return the next day looking for more. The bartender fed him a sandwich of rotten fish seasoned with a handful of carpet tacks, which Mickey seemed to enjoy, as he asked for another. A couple of nights later when Mickey passed out on his stool they dragged him out into the cold winter night. In a nearby park, they stripped him and poured water on him, sure he would freeze to death. When that didn't work, the bartender hired a muscle guy to throw Mickey out of a speeding taxi, to no avail. Finally, when Mickey refused to die, they held his head in the bar kitchen stove and turned on the gas. Death by gas, however, turns the body a bright red, and led to the conviction of bartender and bar janitor, who both died sober in the electric chair.

ALCOHOLISM AFFECTS FAMILY LIFE

The hardship a drinker causes leaves no one unaffected. Take the case of Grace McDaniels, a famous sideshow act, who started her career after winning an ugly woman contest. She had raw, meat-colored skin and a huge, protruding chin, set askew, making it nearly impossible for her to work her jaws. Her teeth were oversized and jagged, complemented by a tremendously bulbous nose and flapping lips. Soon after winning the contest she was hired by the circus and billed as "The Ugliest Woman in the World." Although she had the face of a mule, Grace was a kind and loving person; she attracted a surprising number of boyfriends vying for her favor. She married and, ironically, had a stun-

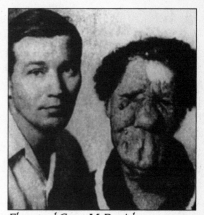

Elmer and Grace McDaniel

ningly handsome son. When the boy, Elmer, became older he forced Grace to let him be her manager. By then he was a full-blown alcoholic. He made Grace change her billing to "The Mule-Faced Woman" and claimed his mistreatment of her made her face uglier, which increased earnings. Grace endured this abuse for years until it was discovered that her son stole all the money she had saved through her lifetime of circus work, which broke her heart. She died in 1958 of cancer at age forty-five.

WAS UNCLE SAM AN ALCOHOLIC?

In the 1860s Dan Rice was America's most popular clown. Although he performed for audiences of all ages his friendship with Abraham Lincoln eventually earned him a position as Washington's unofficial court jester. Rice's clown costume and face paint was red, white, and blue: He wore a stars and stripes top hat and was considered the likely model for the stern-faced and somewhat angry Uncle Sam poster art. Although James Montgomery Flagg said he painted his own face into the poster art we familiarize as Uncle Sam, he used Rice's costume and perpetual demeanor as the model. Rice died penniless in 1900, at age seventy-seven, from the ravages of alcohol.

EXCESSIVE ALCOHOL CONSUMPTION CAUSES 78,490 DEATHS ANNUALLY.

In the nineteenth century, heavy alcohol drinkers were considered to be more flammable and were known to be involved in many unexplainable fires. Most of those deaths were due to the carelessness of the drinker and the impaired ability to respond and were most likely just slovenly cigarette smokers. (See Also: Smoking)

ALIEN ABDUCTIONS Although most abductions have occurred predominantly in rural areas to people with less-than-stellar SAT scores, the phenomenon was seriously studied by the U.S. government in the 1960s. A government panel, headed by physicist H. P. Robertson of the California Institute of Technology, examined UFO sightings in relation to possible dangers to national security and reviewed how enemies, contemplating an attack on the United States, might exploit the UFO craze and disrupt U.S. air defenses. It was decided that the topic should not be discussed since, as Robertson's report noted, even talk of UFOs might threaten "the orderly functioning" of the government and induce "hysterical mass behavior detrimental to constituted authority." However, this government policy has only instilled

devotees with an even greater zeal, spurring conspiracy theories and speculations of cover-up.

I BELIEVE, I BELIEVE

According to a recent Gallup poll, 100 million Americans think aliens have visited the earth. A somewhat smaller number of people believe aliens are actively seeking people for experimentation and terminal abductions. In the lexicon of UFO followers, a "terminal abduction" is a one-way ticket.

UFO analysts believe aliens crashed at Roswell, New Mexico, in 1947 and that the government has been secretly meeting with aliens ever since in an unknown location called Area 51. Devotees believe that one-third of the missing persons cases in America are unsolvable because the individuals have been abducted by aliens—not aliens across the border, but from outer space.

DATA COMPILED BY THE FBI LISTS 876,213 MISSING PERSONS REPORTS IN 2003. MORE THAN HALF WILL REMAIN MISSING AND 13,645 WILL BE FOUND DECEASED.

ALLIGATORS Once an endangered species, the prehistoric, powerful, and potent killing machine known as the American alligator is now flourishing to near precivilization population levels throughout the southeast and Texas. Incident reports of humans bitten by alligators have risen 63 percent since 2000. In the summer of 2004, a twenty-year-old woman died after an alliga-

tor bit off her arm during a late-night skinny dip in a lake at her grandparents' house in Fort Myers, Florida. In August that same year, a seventy-four-year-old woman, gardening near the bank behind her home, was bitten on the leg and arm by an alligator ten feet long, who dragged her into a Sanibel, Florida, lake, killing her. Just a month earlier, in that same community, a fifty-four-year-old female landscape worker was killed when a 12-foot, 457-pound alligator latched onto the woman's head as she bent to fertilize. In May 2006 a twenty-eight-year-old female was snatched, mid-step, while jogging in Broward County, Florida, and killed by a 400-pound one-eyed alligator.

Even when given plenty of time, it is a comfort for some to know that alligators do not prefer to eat humans whole. In July 2003, the gnawed body of a seventy-year-old man was found floating in a Venice, Florida, pond with an eight-foot alligator circling nearby. The man had been missing for days and was still 25 percent intact, only partially eaten by alligators. And in Stuart, Florida, a teenager, who had stolen a car and took refuge from the sheriff by hiding in a pond, was found five days later with only his abdomen and buttocks missing, proving that most alligators often choose only the fleshiest parts of human anatomy for consumption.

Between 1949 and 2006, Alabama, Florida, Georgia, Texas, South Carolina, and Louisiana all have recorded alligator attacks. Florida leads, with 248 reptile assaults.

WHERE HAVE ALL THE DUCKS GONE?

In New York, urban legends cite that alligators have emerged from toilet bowls and rumored to swarm in packs throughout the city's sewer pipes. Although no fatalities have been documented, in 1935 an eight-foot alligator was discovered living in the sewers and was taken from an East Harlem manhole. More recently, in June 2001, twenty-five people claimed to have spotted a two-foot-long alligator in Central Park. The NYPD was called and crime scene tape cordoned off the area. However, they had no success in capturing the tropical intruder, and the Central Park alligator is believed to be still at large. Under ideal conditions alligators can grow one to two feet every year. Future encounters with the Central Park alligator—now much bigger—are expected.

SINCE 1949 ALLIGATORS
HAVE ATTACKED
325 PEOPLE, KILLING 201.

ALZHEIMER'S DISEASE Previously, this disease was called "old age" or "senility." The most common form of dementia, Alzheimer's disease (AD) is a progressive, degenerative disease that attacks the brain, causing impaired memory, language, and motor skills as well as irritability and depression. First described by the German neuropathologist Alois Alzheimer * in 1906, this disease worsens with advancing age, although there is no evidence that it is caused by the aging process. In fact, it is not possible to confirm a person truly has Alzheimer's until their autopsy.

DID I DO THAT?
John James Audubon *(right)* spent his life exploring unchartered territories, propelled by an obsession to paint birds and wildlife. His meticu-

---

* Alois Alzheimer died in 1915 at age fifty-one of tonsillitis. Most of his study patients were elderly suffering from senility confined to an insane asylum in Frankfurt.

lously detailed paintings inspired laws to protect birds and their natural habitats. Today, Audubon is synonymous with bird conservation. In his later years he lived in New York City and suffered from Alzheimer's disease. He could not remember one bird he painted or tell the difference between a pigeon or a pig. Audubon died in 1851 at age sixty-five.

22,500 PEOPLE DIE EACH YEAR FROM ALZHEIMER'S DISEASE.

AMBULANCE CHASERS In the early part of the twentieth century, ambulance services were frequently operated by local funeral parlors. There was a slight conflict of interest; funeral-sponsored ambulances were known to take their time transporting the sick to the hospital. By the 1930s, most ambulance services were independent of funeral homes and competed to get the ill or injured to the hospital at record speeds. Many taxi drivers

were sought out by ambulance companies because they knew the roads, and without much training were plopped into the driver's seat of a large vehicle with a siren. There were 300 percent more head-on collisions and sideswipes of ambulances than any other commercial vehicle on the road in cities during the 1930s, 1940s, and 1950s. Today, most emergency medical technicians (EMTs) are part of the fire department, yet 60 percent of accidents still occur at intersections where ambulance drivers try to get away with a "rolling stop."

1,795 DIE AS A RESULT OF AMBULANCE CRASHES EACH YEAR.

AMNESIA People with amnesia appear physically normal and only know something is wrong because of extreme confusion and a sense of overwhelming vulnerability. With this condition the memory is not deleted; only the ability to access stored memories is malfunctioning. According to Ribot's *Law of Amnesia,* new memories die before older ones, the opposite of normal forgetting; thus, an amnesiac cannot use current events to bridge into past thoughts or learned behaviors. This is more than just forgetting your name. Memories—or the lack of them—can actually kill.

NOBODY HAD NOTHING

On September 3, 1998, "Richard Nobody" found himself walking around in the pouring rain and decided to pick up an emergency phone at a railway station. He asked if he had a wife, a career, and was eager to know what things he had interests in. Unfortunately, "Richard Nobody," as he was referred to by newspapers, was identified by an acquaintance, and was told he didn't have much: no friends, no wife, no immediate family, no house, and few possessions. Doctors believed he suffered from global amnesia, total memory loss associated with a recent traumatic event—which one, of course, Richard couldn't remember.

RED TIDE

In Maryland, in the summer of 2003, large groups of people living near the coastal communities around Chesapeake Bay developed amnesia. During the months of July and August unanticipated fatalities soared. Motorists set out in their cars and then suddenly forgot which was the brake pedal or the gas; green, yellow, and red blinking traffic signals made no sense; head-on collisions became epidemic. Others left their houses and couldn't remember where they lived. One amnesia-stricken man shot a neighbor who walked into the wrong house unexpectedly. Finally, biologists figured out that the amnesia was caused by microscopic organisms found in river estuaries during "red tide" blooms. Those affected had been in contact with the toxic excretions of these microbes.

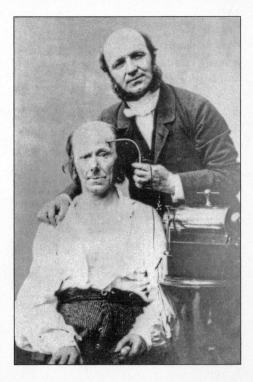

HIGH-VOLTAGE AMNESIA

In the 1950s, amnesia, selective or otherwise (and sometimes simple forgetfulness), was treated with electric shock therapy. In 1957, at the height of its use, 247 died from electric shock treatment administered with make-shift equipment by ill-trained practitioners. Today, electric shock therapy is called electroconvulsive therapy (ECT) and is used on fifty thousand people in the United States each year. Electrodes are strapped to the head and a current of 140–170 volts is blasted into the brain at one-second intervals to cause convulsions, in the hopes of returning the brain to normal functions. The side effects of this treatment usually cause more memory loss.

THREE HUNDRED DIE FROM THE EFFECTS
OF AMNESIA ANNUALLY.

AMUSEMENT PARKS The first amusement parks started in Europe in the 1550s and were called "Pleasure Gardens," filled with games, music, and the first amusement rides, including carved-out logs where revelers were sent down long, icy slides. In America, amusement parks were usually temporary, lasting only a few days or a week, like today's fun fairs or carnivals.

The first grand-sized amusement park, in the modern sense, was the 1893 World's Fair in Chicago. There, George Ferris introduced his 250-foot-high ferris wheel and LaMarcus A. Thompson set up the first roller coaster, the Switchback Gravity Pleasure Railway. Soon after, permanent amusement parks flourished, and by 1920 there were over two thousand parks across the country. With little or no regulation, fatalities and deadly mishaps were a common occurrence. Everything was made of wood so fire was a constant threat. In 1911, *Dreamland,* the first Coney Island amusement park, completely burned down. That year alone, 2,120 deaths at amusement parks, carnivals, and circuses were recorded.

HUMAN CANNONBALLS

Cannonball acts began to appear at carnivals after the Civil War. The first recorded human cannonball act was in 1871, when the exotic and beautiful Zazel was shot into the air. The Human Cannonball was the most dangerous carnival stunt, killing half of all the people who tried. (Most who ran away to join the circus were given a whirl in the cannon chamber.) Zazel (née Rose Ritcher) didn't last long. Within a year she broke her back and spent the rest of her life in an iron corset. In 1890, New York State passed the country's first law prohibiting people to become human cannonballs.

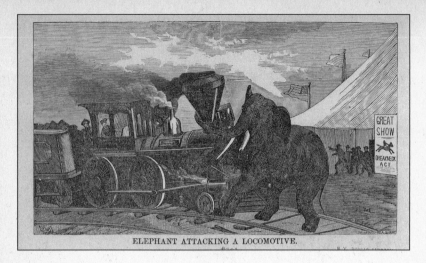

ELEPHANT ATTACKING A LOCOMOTIVE.

CROWDS GONE WILD

In 1916 a giant pachyderm was the mascot of a carnival in Erwin, Tennessee. One day, usually docile Miss Mary the Elephant went on an unexpected rampage and trampled and killed a man attending the park. The townspeople became enraged and demanded the elephant be put down. When the park owners refused, a group of vigilantes snatched the elephant from the amusement grounds and hauled her to a railroad bridge. They were determined to hang her for her crime. A crowd of five thousand gathered to watch the elephant hanged by a steel cable. On the first attempt the steel noose snapped, but on the second try Miss Mary met her fate.

NO ONE DIES AT DISNEYLAND

Despite the fact that millions have vacationed at Disney parks since 1955, almost no one has died at any of them. At least they weren't declared dead until they left the property, as it was in 1985, when a girl was crushed to death under the wheels of a tour bus in the Disneyland parking lot. She was pronounced dead on the scene by EMTs, although the death certificate bore the name of the nearest hospital as the place where declaration of death was certified.

Mark M. holds the honors as the first person killed at the "Happiest Place on Earth." In May 1964, Mark, age fifteen, undid his protective harness and attempted to stand on the Matterhorn Bobsleds. But his balance wasn't great and he fell out of the car to the track below. He died from internal injuries and was officially pronounced dead once off the park grounds.

In June 1973, Bob D., eighteen, of Brooklyn, and his ten-year-old brother hid out in the park after it closed. At Frontier Land they managed to stay on Tom Sawyer Island by climbing a fence that separated a fake burning cabin from the rest of the attraction. But after a few hours the

Chen P. was killed at Disney World one Christmas Eve when a mooring rope yanked a foot-long metal cleat from the hull of the Columbia, *the park's sailing ship, and whisked it into a crowd. His skull was pulverized by the nugget of flying metal. He was pronounced dead at Osceola Regional Medical Center, Kissimmee, Florida.*

stunt lost its appeal so they tried to swim across the river to get off the island. The younger brother did not know how to swim, so Bob hoisted his brother on his back. They got only halfway when he went under and drowned. The little Delaurtte doggie paddled to safety.

The two-mile per hour "PeopleMover," an electric tram running on elevated tracks, has had its share of fatalities. In August 1967, within two months after its opening, fifteen-year-old Nick Y. tried to change cars in transit, slipped, and was crushed, wedged between the tunnel wall and the train.

The first homicide at Disneyland happened in 1981 when Mel Y. was mortally stabbed in Tomorrowland. He was accused of touching someone's girlfriend, got into a scuffle, and was subsequently knifed.

KIDS RUN THE RIDES

Each year, 100 million people go through the turnstiles of amusement parks, with a resulting fatality rate of less than 3 percent of all paying customers. Although safety standards are measurably better than a century ago, there remain the odd deaths. The majority of serious accidents are registered by amusement workers, primarily under the age of eighteen. In 1999, for example, at the Lake Compounce amusement park in Bristol, Connecticut, a sixteen-year-old working as a ride attendant on the "Scrambler" stepped

GRANDMA AND REINDEERS
In 1993, a sixty-seven-year-old woman died when a sleigh ride tipped over at Santa's Village amusement park in East Dundee, Illinois. As the sleigh slid around the first curve, the horses began to speed up into a gallop, causing the sleigh to run off the track into a tree.

onto the ride before it had come to a complete stop. His legs got caught underneath the ride and he was dragged for quite a few more high-speed go-rounds. The loud heavy metal music and flashing lights that accompanied the attraction prevented the DJ operator from seeing the accident or hearing the victim's distress calls. (After his demise from internal injuries, park officials planned to reopen the ride later that night, but decided to wait until the following day out of respect for the victim.) Many workers meet their end, as OSHA reports indicate, through their own carelessness.

FUN FOR ALL AGES
Some of the safest-looking rides present a danger. On average, ten people die when sky ride gondolas come loose from their cables each year. For example, in 1978, three people were killed at Six Flags Mid-America after their gondola car fell from the park's Sky-

way ride. And in 1989, on the Swiss Sky Ride at the Texas State Fair, two gondola cars dropped eighty-five feet from the ride's cable to the ground, killing two and injuring seventeen below. Bumper cars kill two per season, as in the fashion of the eighteen-year-old female who was electrocuted after she fell onto the electrically charged floor of the ride at an Illinois park in 1981. Fires take at least fifty lives. In 1984 eight teenagers died in the Haunted Castle at Six Flags Great Adventure, New Jersey, when a lightbulb burned out in one of the rooms of the haunted house and a fourteen-year-old boy used his cigarette lighter to navigate through the darkness. The lighter had ignited the foam padding on the walls.

Log Fume rides account for another three fatalities per year. At one California park in 1993, a log rider became frightened and attempted to jump out of his seat as it approached the final incline. He lost his footing and fell into the rushing water between the log boat and the chute, ultimately becoming trapped underneath the boat for the duration of the ride.

Horseplay and general mischief account for about sixty deaths at amusement parks yearly. Take the 1994 kiddie ride incident at the Quassy Amusement Park, Middlebury, Connecticut. After the ride stopped, the attendant went to help a six-year-old boy raise the security bar on his seat. A group of teenagers, seeing the controls unattended, thought it would be fun to play a prank on the ride operator. They turned the ride back on, causing the boy to topple out of the car; he was dragged around the track until the attendant could race back to the controls. The teenagers were sent to counseling.

FROM 1900 TO 2000 THERE HAVE BEEN OVER
1.2 MILLION AMUSEMENT PARK–RELATED EMERGENCY ROOM INJURIES
AND 12,315 DEATHS.

ANABOLIC STEROIDS Steroids and other muscle-building performance substances are taken to build muscle, enhance performance, or improve appearance. These drugs, called "Gym Candy," "Pumpers," "Stackers," or "A's" are synthetic derivatives of the male hormone testosterone. Anabolic steroids were first formulated in the 1930s and given to soldiers in World War II to increase appetite and stamina—desirable on the battlefield. U.S. athletes began to use steroids in the mid-1950s, and by the 1960s their use pervaded all sports.

Prolonged use of steroids permanently damages the liver and can cause cancer, jaundice, bleeding, and hepa-

titis. Users have also reported feelings of paranoia and auditory hallucinations, uncontrollable violent feelings, and suicidal ideation. Although steroid advocates, ripe with testosterone, vehemently deny the drug's ill effects, since 1964 there have been 39,817 cases of steroid-related psychosis, many ending in suicide and homicide. In June 1997, the *International Journal of Sports Medicine* reported on a study of sixty-two power lifters and found that steroid users died at a rate five times higher than average. Generally, men on steroids experience shrinking testicles and baldness, and they may develop breasts. Steroids offer women the growth of facial hair, male-pattern baldness, and a deepened voice. Adolescents on steroids are assured to have their growth halted prematurely; yet recently there has been a significant increase in the use of anabolic steroids among eighth and tenth graders. Although steroids are banned by all professional sport teams, they are still easily obtained and consumed along with concoctions, such as a common hair-restoration pill, that mask their presence from drug tests.

Performance-enhancing drugs were used in the ancient Olympic Games (500 B.C.–A.D. 349). Concoctions of alcohol, stimulant herbs, and chewed leaves containing opiates were in widespread use. When the Olympic Games were revived in 1896, speedballs of cocaine, nicotine, and caffeine were consumed without inhibition. In 1896, six marathon runners died of heart attacks. Steroid use was banned in Olympic competitions in the 1980s, although accurate testing was not perfected until recently.

I JUST ASKED ABOUT THE WEATHER
According to the U.S. Department of Justice, 2003 saw an increase in "roid rage" homicides—111 steroid-induced brawls led to murder.

9,673 HAVE DIED FROM STEROID USE BETWEEN 1964 AND 2003.

A NIMAL HOSTAGES One twenty-eight-year-old woman, Janet S., believed life wasn't giving her what she deserved. One day she decided to do something dramatic to make people pay attention. On August 21, 1994, she stormed out of her apartment with a kitchen knife and her precious Siamese cat. She walked into a local grocery store in Gresham, Oregon, and set herself down on the floor in front of the manager's office. She then put the knife to the throat of the Siamese cat clutched in her arms. "Give me all the money or I'll do it," she screamed. "I'll kill this cat!" The manager stalled until the police arrived. When Janet saw the cops, she jumped off the floor and approached the police, screaming, "I'll kill this cat!" The police attempted to halt her with a squirt of pepper spray, but this only caused the cat to leap out of Janet's arms. With hostage gone, Janet went berserk. She raised the knife and lunged at the police. Unable to subdue her, the officers shot and killed the woman. (The cat eluded capture and was never seen again.)

TOTAL NUMBER OF POLICE-ASSISTED SUICIDES EACH YEAR: 413

A **NOREXIA** Anorexia is an obsession with food and its intentional limited intake, which produces a psychologically altered state. The medical community calls this a very secretive illness. Most of the 1 million people inflicted with anorexia do not see themselves as following an abnormal fasting regime. Instead, to many, it's a lifestyle they willingly choose, one that makes them feel victorious and in control.

Anorexia spiked in the female population in the 1890s, 1920s, and 1990s as each period's particular ideas about food, sex, love, and fashion changed. Today, girls make up 90 percent of the anorexia-related deaths among the young; however, an enormous percentage of elderly men die from it, too. Out of 10 million deaths in the United States over the last five years, only 20 percent of the deaths were overachieving females or teenage girls with distorted self-images. Most people who die from the disease are seventy or older. Some elderly anorexia starts due to limited funds to buy food, others lose the ability to taste, or feel worse after eating. For many, anorexia-related death is a result of depression and a passive form of suicide.

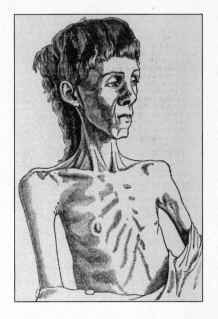

In the spring of 2003, a ninety-year-old Washington man simply stated to his family, "I don't feel like eating anymore, so I won't." By July he was admitted to the hospital and, although fed intravenously, he died—of pneumonia, according to the death certificate.

90,500 A YEAR DIE FROM ANOREXIA-RELATED CAUSES.

Anorexia was first diagnosed as a medical condition in the 1890s, but references to self-starvation appeared in medieval writings as early as A.D. 1300. On death certificates prior to 1920, anorexia was referred to as "consumption," which actually encompassed a wide list of mortalities that included everything from tuberculosis, cancer, or whenever a person physically wasted away.

A **NTHRAX** Five people were killed in the fall of 2001 by an unknown scientist who hoped to show the U.S. government how easy it was to launch a bioterrorist attack against the country. There were sixteen total anthrax

George Washington once got a case of skin anthrax
from wearing new wool underwear.

infections and ten cases of inhalation anthrax disease caused via powder sent in now-infamous envelopes.

Anthrax disease is caused by a germ, *Bacillus anthracis*. This is a prehistoric germ that has occurred naturally for tens of thousands of years in environments where herd animals graze, and is currently found in soil all over the world. In the 1700s and 1800s, wool workers frequently became infected with anthrax. It's also possible to get it from eating uncooked meat, although inhalation of spores is the most deadly.

There were eighteen cases of inhalation anthrax in the United States between 1900 and 1978, and 224 cases of skin anthrax infection between 1944 and 1994, primarily infecting people working with animal hides.

DISBURSEMENT DILEMMAS

Delivery of anthrax or other biological agents has always been the conundrum for the evil-minded. In 1972, an ecoterrorist group called R.I.S.E. tried to wipe out the human race with eight microbial pathogens, using aircraft to disperse the agents. Two of the planners fatally poisoned themselves, while the others fled to Cuba. In 1973, the Symbionese Liberation Army, hoping to incite a race war, used cyanide-tipped bullets to assassinate an Oakland, California, superintendent of schools.

CLEAN UP IN AISLE FIVE
Precise delivery of biological agents was perfected by the Tartars in the 1300s. They gathered bodies of plague victims and catapulted them into enemy fortresses. A diseased corpse hurtling over the wall was one sure way to get their attention.

SINCE 2001, FIVE DIED OF ANTHRAX.

ANTS In August 1998, a sixty-six-year-old nursing home resident in Jackson, Mississippi, taken outside to get some fresh air, was left unattended on the lawn in her wheelchair. Unbeknownst to her or her aide, the wheelchair had disturbed a nest, causing a colony of fire ants to swarm over her body and during the next hour she was bitten hundreds of times. The woman, who suffered from Alzheimer's disease, died two days later.

Venom from a single fire ant is minute; however, when an entire colony is triggered into a massive attack, the concentration of venom is toxic. Fire ants are insects that belong to the same order as bees and wasps. Many people are hypoallergic to even one bite. The venom contains several allergenic proteins that can mean trouble for sensitive individuals, causing chest pain, nausea, dizziness, shock, coma, or death.

FIRE ANT FATALITIES SINCE 1965:
4,289

A PHRODISIACS

Since Greek and Roman times people have been searching for a magical substance that will increase sexual prowess, or to make the unwilling suddenly not so. Although the powers of aphrodisiacs are more myth than fact, the allure to find that special, secret formula continues. People all over the world try certain foods and beverages, drugs, scents, lotions, or powders in a quest to acquire that elusive aphrodisiacal supremacy. Unfortunately, many are misguided and, in this delusional state, often ingest all kinds of things—at least once—with tragic results.

READ DIRECTIONS

In 2001, four men between the ages of twenty-eight and thirty-four, died in New York from topical aphrodisiacs they bought from a smoke shop. They thought the brown sugar–shaped cubes were to be dissolved in a cup of hot water and sipped like a tea, so they drank cup after cup. Originally intended to be made into a paste and rubbed on appropriate areas, the cubes contained bufadieno-lides, a naturally occurring cardioactive steroid. Instead of glowing with appeal, within thirty minutes the guys were suffering from severe vomiting and relentless diarrhea. A day later, they were all dead.

Six similar cases were reported in New York City between 1993 and 2002. All seven were men, ranging in age from seventeen to fifty-one, and they all met a gut-retching end after ingesting an aphrodisiac known as Chan Su, sold as "Rock Hard" or "Love Stone," which contains *Bufo bufo* (a common toad) venom. This is also the favorite (alleged) "aphrodisiac" used to spike drinks, as it does not need to be dissolved in hot water. This does not make the woman pass out, as do date rape drugs such as Rohypnol, though it usually does make the unsuspected user nauseous. Although the product is banned, it is still readily available.

KISS A FROG

In a recent survey, one in fifty college students admitted they might not kiss a frog, but would surely lick a toad if they found one. The toad that these aphrodisiac aficionados seek is the American native toad, *Bufo alvarius,* made more appealing since the U.S. Drug Enforcement Administration outlawed bufotenine, the toad's venom, found in any formulation, in the late 1960s. The U.S. law particularly states: "Toads may not be licked."

A decade earlier, in the 1950s, government researchers had injected bufotenine into inmates of an Ohio prison hoping to gain insights into schizophrenia and other mental disorders. Instead, according to the scientists' report in the May 18, 1956, issue of *Science,* the prisoners experienced hallucinations, nausea, chest pains, and turned "the color of an eggplant." They also became abnormally affectionate with one another and toward the researchers. This side effect most of all discouraged further U.S. studies with bufotenine, although unofficial research continues to this day.

Today, toad purists insist licking is worthless; they prefer to smoke a whole toad to extract the venom in a large version of a crack pipe.

If a toad-head can endure agonizing attacks of diarrhea, vomiting, tachycardia, and near systemic collapse, it's possible they'll experience hyperacuity of the senses, along with abundant energy and sexual stamina, without need for food or drink, which can last for three days.

THAT SOUNDS LIKE FUN
One anonymous experimenter posted his experience firing up a live venomous toad on TAC, The Ethnobotanical Society's Internet bulletin board: "First, I felt as if I was becoming a toad. I could feel myself changing into one. The next thing I felt was an overwhelming desire for cool water. I ran upstairs, stripping off my clothes as I went. I jumped in the shower and turned it on cold. All the while feeling like I was going to die."

SINCE 1958, THERE HAVE BEEN 1,925 DEATHS FROM
BUFOTENINE INTERACTIONS.

A LITTLE DAB'LL DO YA
"Spanish Fly" is the most historically widespread substance used to enhance sex. Extracted from a toxic beetle *(Lytta vesicatoria)* found in South America and parts of Europe, when swallowed it causes cruel gastrointestinal disturbances and ballooning of the kidneys. When the ground beetle powder is rubbed on the skin, fingered into the mouth, or applied to genitalia, the absorbed poisons can make the urinary tract burn, leading the desperate user to sense something different is surely going on down

there. If too much "Spanish Fly" is taken, the infected kidneys produce a cantharidin secretion, which increases the blood flow to the pelvic district and can result in a prolonged, burning erection. A mere 1.6 grams of the pulverized beetle powder—the weight of a dime cut in half—or 1,600 milligrams of liquefied "Spanish Fly" causes death within twenty-six hours.

6,613 HAVE DIED FROM "SPANISH FLY"
SINCE 1850.

BEFORE THE AGE OF QUICHE

Another old-fashioned sexual lubricant was the drink **absinthe,** a green, bitter liquor made of distilled wormwood herbs and other roots. Many artists and bohemians such as Van Gogh, Monet, Picasso, and Hemingway sang its praises as a potent aphrodisiac. The drink was highly addictive, however, and could cause blindness, cramps, nerve injuries, and mental disturbances. In 1879, *Harper's Weekly* wrote: "Many deaths are directly traceable to the excessive use of absinthe." In the late 1800s and early 1900s, 36 million liters of absinthe were sold annually.

ANOTHER IMPORTED FASHION.

ABSINTHE WAS BANNED IN 1915; DURING ITS HEYDAY,
NINE THOUSAND DEATHS EACH YEAR
WERE ATTRIBUTED TO ITS USE.

IN 2005, 208 TEENAGERS DIED FROM ECSTASY. AUTHORITIES EXPECT FATALITIES TO AT LEAST DOUBLE EVERY YEAR.

THE QUEST CONTINUES
*The new forbidden aphrodisiac is the drug **Ecstasy,** or other rave drugs. The party-inclined seek to stimulate sexual and romantic interaction with its use. Ecstasy affects the brain, altering its serotonin-releasing neurons. The high and sexual inhibitions one experiences is actually the result of the brain's shriveling.*

APPLE CIDER Apple cider lovers who seek out the nonalcoholic, pure, unpasteurized type are undertaking a dangerous swigging. In 1996, E. coli from apple cider killed thirty-four people. The Federal Drug Administration states that unpasteurized fruit juice sickens between sixteen thousand and forty-eight thousand people each year, despite warning labels.

TOTAL E. COLI DEATHS SINCE 1930: 182,904

APPLIANCES Kitchen appliances, such as dishwashers, refrigerators, and freezers, cause death every year, usually from electrocution arising from misuse or malfunction. Dishwashers sold from June 1991 through October 1992 have wiring in the door latch that can overheat and catch fire. Half a million of this type of dishwasher were sold and many are still in use.

Small appliances kill fifty each year: table fans (ten), electric beauty aids equipment, including curling irons and hair dryers (fourteen), television,* radio, and stereos (six). Most of these mishaps are caused by electrocution.

Early one morning in July 2002, a thirty-three-year-old man was cutting his lawn in a Dallas suburb while the grass was still moist with dew. He was tired of running out of gas when he used his old lawn mower and had decided to buy a new electric one that came with a long extension cord. But he was unaccustomed to flinging the cord aside. He ran over the power line and died from electrocution.

TOTAL NUMBER OF
APPLIANCE-RELATED DEATHS SINCE 1945: 20,532

ARSENIC POISONING Alchemists throughout history used arsenic to cast spells, simmer potions, and, quite routinely, to poison the unwary.

Arsenic is an element (As) found naturally in the earth's crust, water, soil, and air. Common household items such as tobacco smoke, laundry detergent, bone meal, seafood, beer, and even drinking water give us our daily dose of this very toxic substance. It's also used in manufacturing glass, rat and mice baits, and as an ingredient in weed killers.

* The **television** was Philo Farnworth's brainchild, when at age twenty-one in 1927, he experimented with what he called an "image dissector," by flashing light onto an etched glass plate. Its potential was quickly recognized and Farnworth was offered $100,000 by RCA, which he turned down. Others built on his idea and left the inventor of the television in obscurity. In 1957, he did appear on the TV program *I've Got a Secret* and received $80 and a carton of cigarettes after game show participants failed to guess his identity. Farnworth was more concerned with inventing than in the development of TV, and over the course of forty-four years secured three hundred patents for things such as enhanced vision for telescopes and infrared lights used in night vision devices. Doctors suggested he use alcohol to curb his hyperactive mind, unaware of the affect of ADD or ADHD, of which he possibly suffered. He ultimately died from the complications of alcohol abuse in 1971.

Throughout history, arsenic's easy availability made it the number one choice for poisoning. It can be added to foods without dramatically altering taste, making it a natural favorite for aspiring, nonconfrontational murderers. If dosed sparingly, arsenic accumulates and kills over time, without the target knowing what he is dying from. The recipient will have an upset stomach or a headache, but mild enough to attribute it to general malaise.

HELPFUL HINT!
People who believe they are being poisoned with arsenic should, if nothing else, add sulfur to their diet by eating a lot of onions and garlic. Sulfur slows down arsenic absorption in the body. Unfortunately, once arsenic seeps into the tissues, no treatment will be successful.

BLACK WIDOWS

Women prefer to murder using this quiet, less violent approach; those who've been caught killing with poison more than once are known as Black Widows. The two most infamous Black Widows of modern times were Marie Hilley and Nannie Hazel Doss.

Marie Hilley

Marie Hilley poisoned eight people, including her husband, daughter, and mother-in-law. Once a doting mother and loving wife, she suddenly felt trapped and began to feed arsenic to her family from 1979 to 1983. Eventually she was arrested and brought back to stand trial in the same small Alabama town that she considered too backward and had tried to escape by poisoning her way free. In 1987, while out on a three-day furlough from prison, she was seen wandering around the streets, picking through garbage cans. A few days later she was dead of hypothermia and was buried next to the husband she had murdered.

Nannie Hazel Doss, a sweet-looking woman, gave such a cheery confession to police after she was caught that the press nicknamed her "The Giggling Grandma." Between 1920 and 1954, in Oklahoma, Nannie had killed four husbands, two children, her two sisters, her mother, a grandson, and a nephew with arsenic. She said killing was a "cinch." Even though she collected life insurance on each of the dead, she was put in a prison for the mentally insane where she died of leukemia in 1965.

In 1850, at a July 4 celebration held at the Washington Monument, President Zachary Taylor sampled numerous covered dishes donated by citizens. He became very ill and died three days later. Arsenic was found during the examination of his exhumed remains in 1991 and it was believed he was murdered, although the original death certificate listed cause of death as "acute indigestion."

Women account for only 3 percent of all violent offenders in the United States, but commit 50 percent of all parental murders.

Belle Gunness placed ads in 1908 looking for a good honest man to marry. She enticed fourteen rich ones to her farm in Indiana, spiked their drinks with arsenic, and stole their wallets, before burning their bodies. She faked her own death and was never captured.

ARSENIC KILLS 2,315 IN THE UNITED STATES EACH YEAR.

ARSON One night in 1991 Julio Rodriguez went looking for his ex-girl-friend and found her bumping and grinding with another guy at the Happy Land social club in the Bronx, New York. Although Julio seemed unfazed, he came back an hour later with a few gallons of gasoline and two chains, one for the front door, one for the back. Eighty-six people died when he torched the place; only six survived, one of whom was his ex-girlfriend.

TOTAL ANNUAL DEATHS ATTRIBUTED TO ARSON SINCE 1965: 12,567

AUTOCASTRATION Throughout history many ancient cultures accepted this act of self-performed castration—removing of one's own

testicles—and even encour-aged it. In ancient China, the Middle East, and many Mediterranean societies the rich sought to hire the de-balled. Young male slaves of slight physique willingly cut away their testicles to escape the life of hard labor that the more masculine en-dured. The castrated, called eunuchs, were assigned to protecting and caring for the owner's harem, as it was believed that the castrated would not be at all inter-

ested in having sex. Hence, eunuchs often rose to esteemed positions within these cultures, becoming trusted servants and discreet confidants.

Throughout the ages eunuchs have been sought for theatrical purposes. In the 1500s Constantinople issued proclamations to let it be known that church choirs wanted eunuchs for their soprano vocal range (females were not permit-ted to sing), as they retained the highest angelic voices long after puberty. From the sixteenth through the nineteenth centuries, the Italian baroque operas of Rossini and Meyerbeer gave the *castrati* leading male heroic roles. Through the twentieth century even the papal choir gave places of vocal distinction to the castrated, the last of whom, Alessandro Moreschi, died in 1922.

Today, autocastration is performed by two distinct types of individuals: people suffering from acute psychosis and those wishing a sex change and are unable to go to doctors for professional surgery. Psychotics often view castration as the pinnacle of self-mutilation. In 2003, a twenty-six-year-old married man with a history of sexual abuse and pedophilic behavior dating from early adolescence, became very religious in an attempt to cure his problems. During the first five years of his marriage he had grown more irritable and paranoid, reported hearing sounds, displayed unpredictable violence, and was plagued by inappropriate mood swings. His obsession with religion became fanatical.

One day he went to an isolated field where, with a box cutter, he completely severed his scrotum at its base and then flung the testes thirty yards away into the bushes. After his body was found it was discovered that he had left his penis untouched. He died of blood loss.

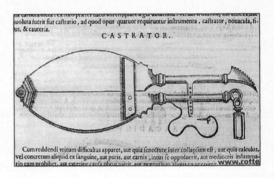

PROFESSIONAL CASTRATION

In the United States the concept of changing one's sex by castration was a well-guarded secret until 1952, when a ninety-eight-pound male G.I. became a woman. Although Christine Jorgensen *(below)* was not the first transsexual to undergo a physiological "change of sex," she was the first to tell her story to the media. She became a national sensation and for a while the idea of surgically changing sexes was in vogue. Some very wealthy men (including Aristotle Onas-

BEFORE   AFTER   TODAY

sis) "sponsored" sex change surgery. The downside of this "coming out" was an intense backlash by religious groups. Many teens, after attempting to fully emasculate themselves, went to the hospital for "patching up"; however, due to religious repercussion, they were treated as insane. They were sent to mental institutions, subjected to endless electric shock treatments, and even lobotomized if they didn't revert to acting the gender they were "supposed" to be.

Today, even with advances in surgery, people who feel they were born in the wrong body will often do anything they can to remedy it. This type of self-injury affects 10 percent of transgender teens.

TWELVE HUNDRED DIE EACH YEAR FROM AUTOCASTRATION.

AUTOEROTIC ASPHYXIATION Autoerotic asphyxia is achieved usually by hanging, strangulation, or suffocation. The lack of oxygen provides light-headedness, which allegedly magnifies sexual experience. More women than ever before are dying from "breath control play," believing orgasm is easier to achieve through asphyxia. Strangulation used to heighten sex is not new: References are found in medieval European documents and ancient Oriental sex guides; and it was commonly practiced by Eskimos and Yaghan Indians. Nowadays, simple neck restriction has been supplemented with drugs, stomach and chest squeezing, and even electrocution. In 2003, eight women died hanging naked from an electric rope contraption—which came with extra padding to prevent neck bruises or chafing—that was sold in exotic boutiques. (The self-rescue precautions were ignored.)

Officially, 1,214 people (predominately adolesecent males) died in 2004 attempting to constrict the blood flow to the brain during sexual activities. Even with more than one thousand known deaths, the number is probably much higher; masturbation asphyxiation is underreported because of the embarrassment of relatives.

SHRINK WRAP
Cellophane and plastic sheathing, a procedure called "cocooning," is now a favorite method to restrict airflow for optimal sexual experience. But it can be deadly. In 2002, a man in Portland, Maine, enclosed his body in plastic. He fashioned his cocoon with an airway using a small diver's snorkel. While engaging in masturbation, his teeth lost their grip on the snorkel mouthpiece and he died. When he was discovered, it was apparent he had made unsuccessful attempts to slice himself free with a knife.

A

UTOMATIC GARAGE DOORS New autoretraction devices have been installed on all garage door models and automatic gates since 1998; however, bizarre deaths still occur. In 2003, a Miami Realtor, showing a property with a driveway gate, reached between the slats of the gate just as it opened. To the horror of the prospective buyers, the Realtor was fatally trapped.

TOTAL DEATHS DUE TO AUTOMATIC GARAGE DOORS AND ELECTRIC GATES SINCE 1986: 3,113

AUTO RACING Street racing began from the moment cars were manufactured and turned loose on the roads. Today, race cars are sleek, technologically fine-tuned machines costing over $400,000, but the first cars used to race were beat-up versions of the typical family car, sometimes even rental cars, hastily modified for extra speed. During the fifty-five-year history of sanctioned auto racing, 260 people, including twenty-nine spectators, died at auto racing events per year.

FRONT ROW OR BLEACHERS

It doesn't matter where you sit at many auto races. In August 2005 a race car barreled into the stands at Mount Vernon Raceway, Illinois. At top speed it mowed a path through the crowd from the first row to the last line high up in the bleachers. Six were pinned under the car and two were killed.

February 18, 2000, seven-time Winston Cup champion Dale Earnhardt (forty-nine), "The Intimidator," died when he crashed in the final lap of the Daytona 500. His car collided with two other vehicles, before beelining straight into an outside wall. Earnhardt's seat belt failed to protect him in the crash.

THE KID DIVISION

Two hundred ninety-three children under the age of fifteen died racing go-carts between 2000 and 2002. More than half of the deaths were due to collision with stationary objects or other motor vehicles, and the second leading causes were from tip-overs, jumps, stunts, and entrapment.

DIE SITTING STILL

In December 2001, a twenty-one-year-old man was racing at 110 mph when he slammed into the back of a slow-moving car, killing its two passengers. One of them, however, happened to be his mother, who had been taking her seventy-two-year-old neighbor for a ride to get a glimpse of the season's Christmas lights. The mother and the neighbor were pronounced dead on the scene.

*On July 16, 1981, singer **Harry Chapin** (thirty-nine), known for his hit "Cats in the Cradle," died of a heart attack when a truck rear-ended his Volkswagen Beetle while waiting at a toll booth on the Long Island Expressway.*

IN 2003, 13,357 PEOPLE DIED FROM SPEEDING.

NEED FOR SPEED

Racing advocates say speeding is in the blood. Take the three young Amish men who had a late-night buggy race in the town of Leon, Pennsylvania, in 2002. They ran into a fourth buggy, leaving one horse dead.

AVALANCHE

By definition, an avalanche occurs when lots of material, such as snow, ice, rock, or soil breaks loose and slides at speeds of 200 mph or more. Every ten minutes an avalanche occurs somewhere in the world, yet with even the most sensitive equipment scientists are not capable of predicting when or where. More people are finding ways to reach the remote, less crowded areas of wilderness, thus increasing the frequency of death by natural entombment.

Although most avalanches only bury a few of the unaware at a time, there have been massive ones. The earliest known disaster was in 218 B.C. when Hannibal crossed the Alps to conquer Rome. Eighteen thousand soldiers, two thousand horses, and many elephants were buried alive under snow. In 1916, following almost the same unstable route as Hannibal, ten thousand U.S. and Allied troops were trapped and perished under a series of avalanches during a twenty-four-hour period. More recently, in 1962, tons of ice and snow slid down Huascaran Peak in Peru and killed four thousand people. In October 2005, a mudslide in Guatemala smothered one thousand four hundred.

COPTER BLADES AND AVALANCHES

On March 12, 1991, nine skiers were dropped on a slope by a backcountry helicopter service near Red Mountain Pass in Colorado. Moments later an avalanche occurred, killing the entire group.

THE TRAGIC SNOWBALL

The worst avalanche calamity in U.S. history, known as the "Wellington Snowslide," befell Wellington, Washington, on March 1, 1910. An enormous sheet of snow and ice broke loose from the Cascade Mountains and barreled down toward town, smashing into the railway station area at rush hour. The station building, three locomotives, carriages, rails, and other debris were swept away into an adjourning gorge 150 feet below. More than one hundred people were rolled into this humongous snowball and died.

The rapidity and unpredictability of avalanches make survival unlikely. The chances of endurance depend on rescue efforts. Eighty-five percent will live if dug out within fifteen minutes; chances decrease to 50 percent within thirty minutes, and 20 percent within one hour. After that, there's little hope.

IN THE UNITED STATES, ONE HUNDRED PEOPLE DIE FROM
AVALANCHES EACH YEAR, MOSTLY WHILE SNOWMOBILING,
SKIING, OR HIKING IN THE BACKWOODS.

When avalanches consist of soil but no snow they are called landslides. When the land begins to slide, 100 to 160 mph air blasts often precede the event. One was recorded in Yellowstone Park in 1996 strong enough to throw eleven campers fifty feet into the air, killing one.

IN THE UNITED STATES
LANDSLIDES KILL FIFTY
EACH YEAR.

MOON AN AVALANCHE

Those venturing into avalanche areas are encouraged to wear an avalanche beacon, sometimes called transponders or transceivers, that sends a signal to the rescuers. Experts also advise that if you see an avalanche of any kind approaching— including an avalanche of paperwork at the office—you should: Keep your mouth closed tightly, and turn away from the avalanche, trying to keep your backside to it.

DON'T RUSH ME

One morning in September 1997, a man was knocking back a few brewskies at a wayside bar near Port Angeles, Washington. Outside the plate glass window the sky looked clear; there hadn't been rain for weeks. Suddenly, the building shook and the walls shuddered. The few other customers and barkeep ran outside, saw what was happening, and kept on running. The one man at the bar paused, deciding to stay until he finished off the last of his perfectly good beer. He died when gravity tugged the hill above the bar down in a sixty-two-ton mudslide.

B

> Buy the farm: This phrase dates to World War II.
> When an American G.I. died, his soldier's insurance would allow
> his parents to pay off the mortgage on the family farm.
> By dying for his country, a soldier was also
> "buying the farm" for his parents.

BACKGROUND CHECKS When a high school girl hired a hit man to kill her boyfriend for breaking off their engagement, she never looked into the killer's credentials for his ability to follow instructions. The seventeen-year-old Los Angeles girl gave the hit man her boyfriend's address and her own, where the hit man was to come to collect payment after committing the deed. But, instead of breaking into her boyfriend's bedroom in the middle of the night, the hit man mixed up the addresses. He climbed through the girl's window and shot her.

EMPLOYERS KILLED BY EMPLOYEES
(FORMER AND CURRENT) IN 2004: 264

BAD WORDS In 1987, Texan Walter Mitchell killed his wife because she was about to say the words "New Jersey." At his trial, Mitchell's lawyer told the judge that there were others words that drove the man crazy. Mitchell was asked to cover his ears when his lawyer told the court that "Snickers" and "Three Musketeers" were equally inflammatory to the man. However, court-appointed psychiatrists and his previous rap sheet for domestic problems did not convince the jury of the man's insanity. (*See Also: Domestic Violence*)

BAGGY PANTS Every season a certain fashion seems to become popular with the hoodlum crowd. Sometimes, though, their clothing choices don't work in their favor.

PREFERRED HEADWEAR

An eighteen-year-old Tucson man knew the importance of dressing for the role. How hard could it be to rob a store? He knew the only thing you had to worry about were those security cameras. He had seen plenty of dumb guys caught because their faces were right there on the videotape. The wanna-be crook wasn't going to let that happen to him. He went to the local department store and asked the saleswoman in the lingerie department for panty hose, extra large and

In March 2002, in Orange County, Florida, three poker-faced hoods held up a local liquor store. They ran down the street, then back to their corner to divvy up the cash. The brains of the outfit, a nineteen-year-old, saw the cops approach. He told his gang to act cool and to hide their guns. He put his piece in his waistband, but the pants he wore were so baggy that the gun slid down his leg. When the gun hit the sidewalk, it discharged, firing a bullet through his groin, killing him.

extra durable. That night he went back to the same department store, ripped open the hose package, took a deep breath and tugged the thing over his head. He put the reinforced crotch section over his mouth and wrapped the legs many times around his neck, making a good knot; no one would ever see his face on film. As soon as he walked into the store, the alarm went off. A minute later he felt water; the overhead sprinklers went off. This was not what the man expected; he lost his cool and stumbled back. People were screaming and rushing out of the store—not because of the man, but because something had accidentally set the sprinklers off. Hours later the man was found under a display of bathroom robes, suffocated behind his mask. (*See Also:* Fashion)

DEATH OF PERPETRATORS DURING THE COMMISSION OF A CRIME SINCE 1990: 19,867

BALLOONS Marie Armant was the wife of American hot air balloon pioneer Jean Pierre Blanchard. Marie's balloon caught fire during a pyrotechnic stunt at an Independence Day celebration. She fell out of the basket and crashed through the roof of a house below, becoming the first woman to die an aerial death.

Today, ballooning has grown to be a big tourist business. There is also a booming new activity called sport ballooning, with numerous clubs that sponsor hot air balloon races and competitions.

Hot air aficionados call themselves "aeronauts" and do *not* answer to the pejorative "balloon head" moniker. At a recent ballooning festival in Albuquerque, New Mexico—the hot air balloon capital of the world—there were 1,019 balloons registered for festivities.

Midair collisions between balloons account for some serious accidents, but in a crowed sky, as it is at competitions, most balloon midair collisions are of the "kiss" variety, where there is little damage. Nine times out of ten, deaths were attributed to pilot error—for example, allowing the balloon to collide with power lines, or the pilot's inability to perfect the rapid descent technique when approaching an obstacle. On long, cross-country solo flights

most of the fatalities were due to running out of fuel. Ten percent of accidents were caused by equipment failure, malfunction, or lunacy.

THE MARTIANS ARE COMING

Large, colorful balloons are such a sight to encounter close-up that tragedies have occurred when they pass above the unprepared. It's usually in remote rural areas that balloons are mistaken for UFOs. In New Mexico, one incident involved a dog that barked furiously up at the sky. The dog's owner flew out of his cabin with a shotgun and pumped off a few rounds, killing one balloonist. Another balloon frightened a herd of cattle, causing a stampede, trampling ranch hands; one died of internal injuries.

THE LUNACY DIVISION

In 1995, three men decided to use their mountain-climbing gear to propel and dangle over the side of a hot air balloon as it sailed high above the patch-quilt farmlands of Illinois. The three adventures diligently prepared the ropes and attached the climbing straps to the balloon basket, taking all safety precautions possible. But as soon as the first guy jumped over the side, the mountain-climbing hooks and cleats severed the basket from the balloon. All three, clinging to the tumbling basket, fell to their deaths, the untethered balloon last seen passing the moon.

HOT AIR BALLOON CRASHES
IN THE UNITED STATES
AVERAGE THIRTY-FOUR DEATHS AND THIRTY SERIOUS
INJURIES PER YEAR.

BARBECUES For the last one hundred thousand years humans have eaten fire-cooked meals. Sitting three times a day in front of a smoking fire, and in the constantly smoldering environment of the cave, was the leading cause of non-accidental death for primitive man. Nevertheless, the tradition persisted and became America's favorite way to cook. At the 1793 ceremony for laying of

the cornerstone of the Capitol building, George Washington offered his guests a dinner of five hundred pounds of barbecued ox. President William Henry Harrison swayed thirty thousand voters by feeding them a massive barbecue in Virginia. Today, 77 percent of all U.S. households own a barbecue; in 2004 there were 740 million servings of barbecue food sold.

MOUTHWATERING AROMA

After his divorce, a fifty-eight-year-old man moved into a basement efficiency apartment in Staten Island, New York, in 1988. Determined not to let his diminished circumstances rob him further of the few things he enjoyed, he bought a small Hibachi charcoal grill. He set it up on the kitchen counter next to his hot plate and fired up the briquettes. However, he had forgotten how much smoke a sizzling steak made and quickly found himself engulfed in a toxic cloud. Instead of cursing his ex-wife for his plight, he just cranked open the small basement window and hoped for the best. After more than a month of this diet, he died of CO poisoning.

*In 1929, **Richard Evelyn Byrd** became the first person to fly over the South Pole, documented on* Newsreels, *making it the first media-covered exploration. On a subsequent Antarctic excursion he nearly died of carbon monoxide poisoning from barbecuing inside his tent. After years of exposure to barbecue fumes, he developed cancer and died in 1957 at age sixty-nine. **Briquettes** contain petroleum distillates and benzene, a known human carcinogen.*

BARBECUE COOKING CAUSED 203 INCIDENT-RELATED FATALITIES IN 2003. APPROXIMATELY FOUR THOUSAND INJURIES OCCURRED TO KIDS UNDER FOUR YEARS OLD.

BASEBALL According to the Consumer Product Safety Commission, 125,000 baseball and softball players under age fifteen were injured badly enough to seek treatment in hospital emergency rooms. The increase in baseball injuries and death has nothing to do with the actual game. Most Little Leagues don't let kids use wooden bats anymore and mandate the use of hi-tech alloy, graphite, and aluminum bats with pressurized air chambers. (Metal bats hit more home runs, and in order to standardize statistics, no other bat may be used.) A ball hit with a wooden bat travels at a maximum speed of 93 mph. A ball whacked with an alloy bat reaches a speed of 123 mph, giving the pitcher only four-tenths of a second to get

the glove up to protect himself. It is for this reason that, as the National Rifle Association is quick to point out, "baseball bats are used far more often to kill than semiautomatic rifles."

THE BEANBALL

YOU'RE OUT!
At Baker, Florida, on July 31, 1949, no one wanted to call a baseball game on account of rain and decided to play through a storm. A bolt of lightning struck the field, scorching a trench from first to second base, killing three players.

Since the beginning of the game, pitchers have tried to unnerve a batter by throwing a fastball close to the head. When they miss and hit the batter's head it's called a beanball. There have been thousands of hitters "beaned," with only a few deaths, most occuring before the mandatory use of helmets: In 1906, Thomas Burke of the New England League, Charles Pinkey in 1909 of the Central League, and Ray Chapman of Cleveland in 1920 were all professional players who were "beaned" and died.

IN 2002, THERE WERE 341 DEATHS FROM BASEBALL BLOWS TO THE CHEST, NECK, AND HEAD.

BASKETBALL Of all recreational sports, basketball ranks second in participation after baseball, but it has got the highest number of all injuries. In 2003, hospital emergency departments treated 653,676 people for basketball-related injuries. On sanctioned league basketball courts, sudden death is the number one killer; but in backyard setups and neighborhood courts, strangulation takes precedence: Kids doing the "slam dunk" get tangled up in the nets.

SINCE 1990, FIFTY-SEVEN YOUNG CHILDREN HAVE DIED DUE TO BASKETBALL NET ENTANGLEMENT.
(*See Also:* Sudden Death)

BATS On September 15, 1999, a bat flew into the house of a forty-nine-year-old California man. He chased it around until it flew out and didn't realize he had gotten bitten in the process, attributing his scrapes to the scuffle. The next day he began to hypersalivate, experiencing uncontrollable muscle twitching. He became confused and tried to bite his wife. After that, she took him to the hospital where he was placed on a mechanical ventilator. Within five days of initial contact with the bat he died of renal failure. In Utah, a forty-four-

year-old man, who liked to camp out-doors without using a tent, was bitten by a bat. For three weeks he had a sore throat, fever, chills, and weakness. He developed encephalitis from the bite of a silver-haired bat with rabies and died.

Since 1951 there have been twelve deaths directly attributed to rabid bats. However, in that same period, 8,312 died from histoplasmosis, a disease caused by inhalation of spores found in bat guano (excrement). It is advised not to handle bats without gloves.

BATTERY-POWERED VEHICLES Ride-on toys have caused 180 fires and twenty-two deaths since 1995. (In 1995, 10 million battery-powered *Power Wheels* ride-on cars and trucks were recalled due to faulty, over-heating wires.) In 2004, another ride-on toy was recalled after it was learned that a loose screw shorted out a battery wire; an eighteen-month-old California boy died from the fire caused by this wire short. Each year there are twenty-five fatalities from battery-powered golf carts. The government now requires golf carts that can reach 15 mph to be equipped with seat belts and windshields.

THERE ARE 1,134 DEATHS FROM NON-POWERED SCOOTERS
EACH YEAR; 90 PERCENT COULD BE PREVENTED
IF HELMETS WERE USED.

BEARS In 2002 in New Mexico, a ninety-three-year-old woman went downstairs into her kitchen when she heard pots and pans falling to the floor. She found a 275-pound black bear, which had busted the lock on the back door, helping himself to the food in the pantry. When the tough one hun-dred-pound lady tried to chase the bear out with a broom, the beast turned on her. She died "by mul-tiple bite injuries." Des-perate for food, black bears are getting bolder; these bear-human con-frontations are on the rise. In Colorado, bears are caught hanging out at malls and are seen regu-larly near schools. The American Bear Associa-tion claims that black bears have killed only forty people in the United States in the last one hundred years.

Tim Treadwell loved grizzly bears and they loved him, literally, because in the end, they ate every morsel of him. For thirteen summers Treadwell lived among the grizzlies at Alaska's Katmai National Park and Reserve to study bear behavior, documenting his encounters on homemade video. Treadwell knew the dangers—he once said, "If I show weakness, I'm dead. They will take me out, they will decapitate me, they will chop me up into bits and pieces"—but he persisted, even convincing a girlfriend to join him. In August 2003 his prediction came true; Treadwell and his girlfriend were killed and eaten by a grizzly. His story is told in Werner Herzog's documentary film Grizzly Man.

BETWEEN 1786 AND 1899, 143,983 PEOPLE WERE KILLED OR MAULED TO DEATH BY BEARS. FROM 1920 TO 2000 GRIZZLIES AND POLAR BEARS KILLED 1,682.

Daniel Boone, America's most famous pioneer, reportedly killed over ten thousand bears while he surveyed and settled the vast virgin wildernesses of Kentucky, West Virginia, and Missouri. Boone had set off into a hostile world without roads, toting only a flintlock musket and a knife. In 1820, at the age of eighty-six, he went on his final hunting trip near his home in St. Charles, Missouri, caught pneumonia, and died.

BEAUTY PAGEANTS The Miss America Pageant started in 1921 in Atlantic City, New Jersey, when a hotel owner wanted to come up with a gimmick to keep tourists in town after Labor Day. After he recruited dance girls, "lookers" who frequented the boardwalk—and even some hookers to spice up the beauty contest—the press sarcastically dubbed it the "real Miss America contest." The name stuck and the event persisted annually for over eighty years, eventually moving from Atlantic City to Las Vegas in 2006. Today, there are over three thousand pageants, two thousand for girls under twelve years old, attracting 250,000 participants annually. Some parents have been known to spend up to $12,000 to "beat the com-

petition" with the latest fashions and accessories. Often, the grand prize is no more than a trophy, but some beauty queens and their mothers will go to great lengths to secure the top spot.

I HAD NO MOTIVE

Barbara Dubois was a twenty-three-year-old finalist in the Yoknapatawpha County Literature Festival Beauty Pageant. In January 2004, the day prior to the final segment of competition, her body was discovered in her home. Soon after, Erma Webb, fifty-two, of Oxford, Mississippi, was arrested in connection with the murder. According to the Oxford Eagle, "Webb's daughter, Scarlett, was also a finalist in the pageant."

Until the 1996 murder of JonBenét Ramsey, a six-year-old beauty pageant champion, most of America knew little of this subculture. Her still-unsolved death, which some believe had to do with her winning streak, led to a national debate about the treatment and sexualization of young girls on the pageant circuit. Pageant mothers have a tendency to live vicariously through their children, and losing, or placing badly, is not acceptable. The government has laws to protect a child's health from smoking and drinking and provide education and safety, but not very much against manipulative adults.

Although only 1 percent of all those who participate in beauty pageants go on to further careers in modeling, the names of approximately forty-three hundred former beauty pageant participants show up in the obituaries each year—2 percent from murder or unexplained accidental death.

MISS CONGENIALITY

In 2004, the Miss Savannah Pageant was called off after the reigning queen was arrested for murder. Sharron Nicole Redmond, twenty-two, was charged with the murder of her boyfriend, whom she allegedly killed during an argument about another woman.

THE BEAUTY QUEEN KILLER

Serial killer Christopher Wilder (right) hung around the pageant and modeling circuits. He would attract young beauty queens with his camera, offering to take free pictures and advance their career. During the twenty years he was on the loose, he killed at least fifteen models and beauty queens, mostly in Miami, Florida. His reign came to an end soon after he killed a twenty-three-year-old Orange Bowl Princess and finalist in the Miss Florida Contest. The police cornered him and during the scuffle, a trooper's gun shot Wilder through the liver and groin; he died, permanently disqualified in 1984.

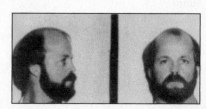

BEAVER FEVER *Animal House* and other college-life film fans might believe Beaver Fever is only an obsession with female "companionship," but it's actually the work of a parasite, called *giardiasis*. Hikers venturing into wilderness areas often pick up this parasite by drinking from what they believe to be the pristine waters of creeks and lakes. This water, however, is usually contaminated by droppings from infected animals, including beavers and muskrats.

Those plagued with Beaver Fever get stomach cramps, throw up at unusual times, and feel washed out. Beaver Fever is contagious and can pass from one Beaver sufferer to the next by sharing food or drinking from the same bottles. It usually only lasts a few weeks, but if left untreated it could be fatal. Beaver Fever is found all over the world but is more common in rural and wilderness areas.

Outbreaks of Beaver Fever occur periodically in college students attending campuses in the northern parts of the country. One fraternity, at Washington State University, became so frequently overwhelmed with Beaver Fever that failed grades and wasted semesters were epidemic.

2,130 DIE EACH YEAR
FROM UNTREATED BEAVER FEVER.

BED & BREAKFASTS There are over twenty-five thousand bed & breakfasts (B&Bs) operating in America. Over three hundred of these B&Bs claim to be haunted and offer not only a comfy bed but a close encounter with a ghost. When a B&B takes this tact to entice guests, it seems the more grisly their past, the better the bookings.

According to a recent Harris poll, 75 percent of Americans believe in ghosts. Twenty-eight percent of those surveyed believe it is possible to communicate with the dead. Ghost devotees note it's all in the ectoplasm; they claim this energy of the previously alive—whether it's benign or malevolent—is what lingers in the physical world. Although unlikely, it is possible that this ectoplasic energy can kill. Some believe that when a violent incident occurs, such as a murder, this malevolent ectoplasm force can regenerate and continue to kill at the exact location where the original death happened. In Quincy, Illinois, a pyromaniac ghost has been on the loose, setting unexplained fires all over town for over a hundred years. Certain streets in Manhattan still have higher-than-usual homicide rates, even neighborhoods that have been cleaned up from a more sordid time. For example, a restaurant on Barrow Street and a brownstone on Clinton Street continue to attract an unusual amount of crime even though the areas have vastly improved, as if marking the spot of previous violent deaths that occurred at these locations. Paranormal experts claim certain energy is just bad and believe it can cause fatalities in unknown ways.

REAL ROOM SERVICE

The San Carlos Hotel in Arizona is haunted by the ghost of a desperate woman dressed to the hilt for ballroom dancing who jumped to her death from the rooftop in 1928. She paces the halls, knocks on doors, and then runs. At The Lemp Mansion in St. Louis, a thirty-three-room mansion built in the 1860s by brewing baron William Lemp, guests can hear the

weeping and wailings of Lemp's family, all of whom met tragic ends, by way of suicide and murder. The McMenamins Edgefield B&B in Oregon was once the Multnomah County Poor Farm, and later a retirement home. This building is haunted by the destitute and old people whom, some say, are seen playing shuffleboard or trapped in an endless game of bingo. At The Myrtles Plantation in St. Francisville, Louisiana, an insomniac gets to test his sleeping skills knowing that the house was the site of ten murders and was built on an Indian burial ground.

In 1635, near the vicinity of Church and Vesey streets in Manhattan (then called New Amsterdam) sketchy records indicate that an Indian skirmish took place, in which as many as thirty natives and colonists died. In 1966, 164 buildings were demolished to build the World Trade Center on that exact location. A total of sixty died during its construction—more than any other office building in recent times.

BE GONE!

The Catholic Church, for one, has stepped up its vigilance in combating these lingering "evil" energies. In 1998, a new *Exorcism Handbook* was approved by Pope John Paul II. The document sets out a new and precise liturgical form for the rite of exorcism. This eighty-four-page booklet, available at church bookstores in the U.S., was published entirely in Latin, presumably the language demons understand. According to Father Jeremy Davies, co-founder of the two-hundred-member International Association of Exorcists, they have never been busier; the group performs at least one exorcism a week.

ALTHOUGH "KILLED BY GHOSTS" HAS NOT BEEN FOUND ON A SINGLE DEATH CERTIFICATE, THREE THOUSAND DIE EACH YEAR IN "UNEXPLAINED" FIRES. THERE IS ALSO A GROWING NUMBER OF UNSOLVED HOMICIDES IN THE UNITED STATES—5,213 IN 2003—THAT, DESPITE THE LATEST CSI TECHNIQUES, MIGHT HAVE ONLY ANOTHER, OTHER-WORLDLY EXPLANATION TO BLAME.

BICYCLES The first bicycle, called the penny farthing, had high, disproportionate-size wheels, the front much larger than the rear, so that a rider's feet couldn't reach the ground. Riding it was like riding a unicycle, which made keeping one's balance rarely possible; the contraption was notorious for causing accidents. Mark Twain, who learned to ride a high-wheel bicycle in the early 1880s, wrote of his numerous trips to the hospital trying to master it: "Get a bicycle. You will not regret it, if you live." Between 1880 and 1895, bicycle accidents, from falls and wagon collisions, caused 4,312 deaths.

NATIONAL DEAD CYCLIST MONTH

In 1869, forty years after the invention of the bicycle in France, bicycles became popular in the United States, when solid rubber tires replaced the iron wheels of previous models. By 1895, Chicago and other large cities put mailmen on bicycles. As soon as the car was invented, however, bicycle use declined rapidly and was relegated to a childhood activity. In 1962, a bicycling revival began, and by 1972 bicycles outsold cars in the United States. In 1975, over 75 percent of all bicycle traffic fatalities were youngsters. As of 1998, just 30 percent of all bicycle fatalities were still juveniles. Most fatal bicycle-car crashes occur in broad daylight,

FRIENDLY GHOSTS

Not to be confused with poltergeists— pure troublemakers—some ghosts can be helpful. A railroad intersection in San Antonio, Texas, was the site of a tragic accident in which ten schoolchildren and the driver were killed in the 1940s. Since then, any car stopped near this same railroad crossing has been pushed by unseen hands across the tracks to safety. Numerous drivers have tested this theory: Some have left the car in neutral, and some have turned off the engine twenty yards away from the tracks. Despite the incline and the bump of railroad tracks, the cars glide up and over, out of harm's way. One disbeliever dusted the back of her car with talcum powder. Once her car was pushed across, she got out to find many tiny handprints on the fender and two larger handprints, presumably the driver's, on the side door.

in good weather, with clear skies. June has the distinction of being the month with the greatest number of bicyclist fatalities.

Amelia Jenks Bloomer became a pioneer for women's rights because she wanted to ride a bicycle. It was impossible and ludicrous to do so, however, with the female fashion of the time, which consisted of rib-breaking laced corsets, layers of petticoats, and floor-length dresses. Bloomer, an active lecturer and writer, began to advocate women's wearing of pantaloons, which came to be called "bloomers." This style of garment was more comfortable, less sexualized, and got modern women ready for action. After an active life of riding bicycles and more, Amelia Bloomer died of pneumonia in 1894 when she was seventy-four.

ELEVEN HUNDRED PEOPLE ON BICYCLES COLLIDE WITH CARS AND DIE EVERY YEAR.

In Florida, a 2003 statewide survey found that bicycle fatalities had tripled since the new drunk driving statutes, which forced DUI-convicted alcoholics to ride bikes, were implemented.

BINGE AND PURGE Splurging on one piece of cake or an occasional candy bar is not bingeing. Eating three, four, or five pieces of cake and two pies—now that's bingeing, defined as eating for eating's sake, uncontrollably, even when hunger has long been sated. Bingers will, at the least, gain weight; at most, they can die from complications of obesity.

Bingers soon compensate for their feelings of guilt by learning the techniques of purging. This combination of bingeing and purging over a sustained period of time causes another set of medical

Stomachs have a tremendous capacity to hold an excessive amount of food and most people stop eating when they feel full. Tests on cadavers have shown that the average stomach will rupture when filled with four quarts of liquid. In 1985, a thin twenty-one-year-old model, after having starved herself to look good at a fashion shoot, ate wildly after finishing her assignment. The autopsy confirmed that her stomach exploded after she had eaten nineteen pounds of food in one sitting. A thirty-one-year-old Florida psychologist's death was documented in the American Journal of Forensic Medicine *in 1986. The woman was found dead in her kitchen surrounded by "an abundance of foodstuffs, broken soft drink bottles, and an empty grocery bag." There were six quarts of undigested hot dogs and broccoli in her ruptured stomach.*

problems, serious and fatal. No organ of the body remains unaffected by repeated purging. Purgers use self-induced vomit techniques, finger, spoon, or foul-tasting substance, laxatives and diuretics, to expel the food and the shame that eating excessive quantities have caused. They may also engage in extreme exercise, or go through periods of complete starvation.

Bingeing and purging was not always considered bad. The Egyptians practiced monthly purges in an attempt to remain healthy. The Romans had specially designed rooms, "vomitoriums," where one could vomit in order to eat again. Slaves were always in attendance, offering towels and beard combs; for Romans, fine dining and vomiting went hand in hand. The

practice went out of favor in the fourth century when overindulgence was seen as a sin of gluttony, in addition to the fact that excessive food supplies dwindled and people were concerned with eating what little food was available just to survive.

Eight million Americans suffer from binge-purge syndrome, the psychosomatic illness, known as *bulimia nervosa*. Death certificates reveal 960 deaths per year, although an additional 2,319 suicides resulting from this condition can be added to the list. Suicides among female sufferers occur more often during menstruation.

Terri Schiavo, the unlucky woman who became the focus of a right-to-death national debate in 2005, descended into a "persistent vegetative state" as a result of her constant purging. In 1990, her brain was starved of oxygen caused by abnormally low potassium levels. She then suffered cardiac arrest as a result of bulimia-induced hypokalemia (potassium imbalance) and went into a coma.

Many purgers also resort to drugs such as amphetamines to curb their cravings. Each year Americans take over 5 billion doses of tranquillizers and another 3 billion doses of amphetamines for dieting regimes. Approximately forty-eight-hundred people died in 2000 after unsuccessfully trying to find the right combination of uppers, downers, and diets.

LIQUID BINGE

Binge drinking has become widespread on many college campuses. According to the Harvard School of Public Health College's Alcohol Study, binge drinking is defined as "the consumption of at least five drinks in a row for men, or four drinks in a row for women." The body is only capable of metabolizing about an ounce of alcohol an hour. In 2002, at Cornell University, a drunken student died after binging when he fell into a gorge. In 2003, at Michigan State University, a student died from heart failure after downing two dozen consecutive shots of tequila. And in 2004, a Pennsylvania State University student died during his twenty-first birthday celebration from consuming four gallons of alcohol through a beer-bong apparatus.

TWENTY-FIVE THOUSAND DIE BECAUSE OF
ALCOHOL BINGEING EACH YEAR.

BINGO Casino lobbyists insist there is nothing wrong with a little wager, but a survey of nearly four-hundred Gamblers Anonymous members disclosed that 75 percent had contemplated suicide, and more than half had definite plans on how they would do it. The National Gambling Impact Study Commission reported on a 2003 case in Atlantic City, in which a sixteen-year-old boy attempted suicide after losing $6,000 on lottery tickets. And there was a middle-aged couple in Joliet, Illinois, who both committed suicide in 2004 after the wife accumulated $200,000 in casino debt.

Although women are far more likely to be addicted to gambling than men, it appears to be more dangerous for men: The total number of sudden cardiac deaths of elderly white men at or around casino tables within the last five years: 3,567

BLACK DEATH The bubonic plague started in China in 1330 and spread through Europe from 1347 to 1351, killing a staggering 25 million people, one-third of the civilized world's population. The disease originated from rat fleas. As the plague spread and killed with horrifying

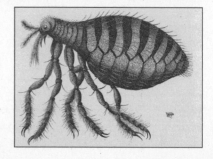

speed, Italian writer Boccaccio observed: "Its victims often ate lunch with their friends and dinner with their ancestors in paradise." Only when winter arrived, and the flea population died down, did the plague subside. Black Death outbreaks continued until the 1600s and proved to be one of the greatest catalysts for social and hygienic change.

FALSE ALARMS

In the 1700s colonists were ever fearful of the bubonic plague. Many other diseases, thought to be related to bubonic plague, were actually different and not contagious. One of these was Black Jaundice, now called Wiel's disease, an infection of the liver spread by bacteria in rat urine. Black Jaundice killed only a few at a time, but often got townships into a frenzy. Between 1750 and 1810, in the thirteen original colonies, 9,312 died from Black Jaundice, which was caused by a bacterium in rat urine that infected unprotected grain. Another misdiagnosed disease was Black Vomit that caused the sick to produce strange, dark upheavals. These people were quickly isolated and left to care for themselves, when in fact they were ill not from a bubonic contagion, but were sick with ulcers.

THE AMERICAN PLAGUE

In 1918 the United States experienced a sampling of what Black Death was like with the "Spanish Flu" epidemic. The infection would cause the lungs to fill with fluid, and victims would drown in their own bile. All across America people dropped dead on the street. Cars crashed as drivers died suddenly, without warning; the onset of symptoms to death was that rapid. One newspaper described how four women played cards together one evening and then, overnight, three of the women had died from influenza.

In just a few months, five hundred thousand Americans died from the disease which was believed to have originated in Spain. Recently, geneticists traced the flu's gene structure and discovered that the original host was a twenty-five-year-old soldier from Kentucky who had died at Fort Jackson, South Carolina, in September 1918. (His exhumed lung tissue indicated a mutated strain of flu, possibly acquired from chicken influenza, similar to SARS and bird flu today.)

Weeks later, hundreds of soldiers in the barracks where he died were shipped off to France. The Spanish flu killed 21 million people worldwide.

BLACKOUTS On November 9, 1965, at 5:15 P.M., the biggest electricity failure in U.S. history caused a thirteen-hour blackout in the Northeast. Eight hundred thousand people were trapped in New York City subways and elevators for over twelve hours. One hundred heart attack fatalities were recorded, which, Con Edison officials protested when faced with lawsuits said, would have statistically happened anyway. Only three deaths were directly related to the power outage, occurring when engaged machinery suddenly stopped.

Another blackout occurred in July 1977, lasting twenty-six hours, darkening primarily New York City. Ten of thousands poured from the ghettos and went on what *Time* magazine called "an orgy of looting." Arsonists set 1,837 fires and hurtled bottles and rocks at attending firefighters, injuring eighty and an additional 435 police while attempting to restore order. Two people died from looting and fires while thirty-nine other deaths were possibly attributed to the failure of back-up generators at city hospitals.

On August 14, 2003, at 4:11 P.M., the power went out throughout the Northeast, due to a distribution failure of an electrical grid. As a result, a forty-two-year-old Connecticut woman died in a fire sparked by a candle, a six-year-old died from falling down the stairs, and a fifty-eight-year-old man died of a heart attack while trapped in an elevator. Another two people were hit and killed by cars when traffic lights failed and cars did

BLACK DEATH: "I'LL BE BACK."
Black rats, bubonic flea hosts, are making a tremendous comeback all over the world, thanks to global warming with temperature changes similar to those of the Middle Ages. Between 1992 and 2002, bubonic plague killed 1,340.

*The electric **lightbulb** was Thomas Edison's illuminating idea. A master at both invention and promotion, Edison invented many other things, including the phonograph and the motion picture camera. He said, "Genius is one percent inspiration and ninety-nine percent perspiration." He died at age eighty-four, in 1934, from Bright's disease (inflammation of the kidneys); before doing so, however, he breathed his last gasp of air into a bottle. He had hoped his essence could be captured this way. The sealed bottle is still on display in Menlo Park, New Jersey.*

not stop at intersections. There were twenty-three cases of looting reported. Later, fifteen Ohio supermarkets sold meat that had been unrefrigerated during the blackout, spurring nineteen deaths in the area from E. coli and botulism poisoning.

BLOODLETTING In the 1700s doctors killed way more than they cured. Back then, even the most respected doctors believed that illness resulted from an imbalance in the body's four life-sustaining fluids, called humors: blood of the heart, yellow bile of the brain, phlegm of the liver, and black bile of the spleen. It was an accepted medical belief that draining significant quantities of blood from a patient would cure or prevent illness and return the body humors to a healthy, balanced state. Physicians routinely severed a vein, to drip an imprecise amount of blood (usually two to three pints) from a sick person into a bowl. When health did not return or the illness got worse, the sick were told to "be patient." It was said so often that a "patient" became anyone under a learned doctor's care.

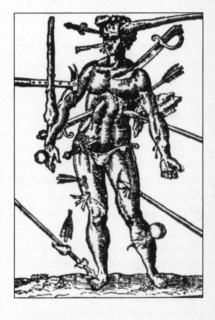

Bloodletting was practiced by the Egyptians over three thousand years ago and remained a medical tool for both Greek and Roman health practitioners. It reached its zenith in the eighteenth and nineteenth centuries. Medical quackery became rampant in the 1800s, so much so that by the beginning of the twentieth century any antique medical practice, bloodletting foremost, was shunned and ridiculed by the emerging modern medical establishment. The rise of faith in pharmacology to restore body imbalances became prevalent. Although bloodletting seems regulated

George Washington helped a neighbor whose carriage ran into a ditch during a storm. He came down with a sore throat, which grew worse. Physicians drained a pint of blood and made him drink a concoction of molasses, vinegar, and melted butter. They gave him an enema and then forced him to vomit. Heedless of Washington's protests, they repeated this three times, until he died soon after, at age sixty-seven, in 1799. Pneumonia was the official cause listed on Washington's death certificate.

to antiquity, other medical concepts abandoned at the turn of the twentieth century, such as hydrotherapy and the use of leeches, are regularly prescribed by today's physicians.

**BETWEEN 1795 AND 1910 THERE WERE 89,689
BLOODLETTING-RELATED DEATHS.**

BODY PIERCING Seven hundred thousand people got at least one untraditional piercing in 2004, adding metal studs to eyelids, nostrils, tongues, lips, belly buttons, nipples, and genitalia. Forgoing sterilization of equipment can leave the piercing enthusiast in danger of exposure to HIV infection and hepatitis B and C. Tongue studs can kill when they get infected from septicemia (blood poisoning) or toxic shock, or when the tongue-stud user swallows it, causing infection or choking.

Most metal jewelry inserted into hairy areas become germ magnets. It is not uncommon to see belly-button piercing oozing pus. Licking, sucking, and biting with a piercing can cause abnormal skin tearing or wounds that are difficult to heal. Other piercing-related accidents stem from studs and rings that catch on clothing—or when a disgruntled lover yanks off a nipple ring in a fight.

An eighteen-year-old woman in Long Island showed up at an emergency room in 2004 with a swollen tongue. She died from the infection that had grown around her gold stud. When a nineteen-year-old Oklahoma City man got into a minor car accident, the anchor from his Prince Albert piercing punched through the tip of the penis. The metal rod crossed over to his urethra, causing death.

STICKING YOURSELF
*Walter Hunt invented the **safety pin** in 1849 and sold his patent for what he called the "dress pin" for $400. Ten years later, while he labored to invent a new pin, he accidentally stuck himself. With no cure available against the simplest of infections, Hunt died of gangrene at the age of sixty-three. Nowadays sticking oneself with pins is the method of choice for creating homemade tattoos. In 2002, 75 percent of all criminals convicted of murder had at least one.*

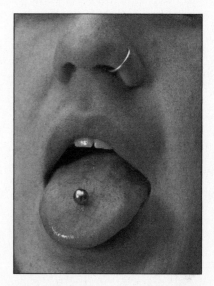

**SEPTICEMIA DEATHS CAUSED FROM
BODY PIERCING
SINCE 1990: 9,981**

BOILED AND BAKED

BDroughts and heat waves get little news coverage, yet heat kills more than floods, hurricanes, and tornadoes combined. Heat waves have been increasing, and to some this signals a malicious change in global climate conditions. Research has found that the elderly and very young, the obese, those with heart disease, or those on prescription drugs or drinking alcohol, die first in extreme heat conditions. However, even healthy individuals can perish in the heat if they take part in strenuous physical activities. The body ordinarily cools itself by sweating, but under some conditions perspiring isn't enough. If a body temperature rises too quickly, brain damage can occur when loss of

YEARS OF DUST

RESETTLEMENT ADMINISTRATION
Rescues Victims
Restores Land to Proper Use

potassium or electrolytes transpire rapidly, regardless of a person's general health. Excessive heat can result in other ailments that arise without warning, such as heatstroke, heat exhaustion, heat cramps, sunburn, and heat rash.

SKIN CANCER CAUSED 7,215
DEATHS IN 2003.

DO YOU PREFER GRILLED OR BLACKENED?

Way back in 1929 scientists had determined that exposure to sunlight causes cancer. However, not until the last part of the 1980s was UV and solar radiation exposure made a public concern. There are more than six hundred thousand new cases of nonmalignant skin cancer and 53,600 of the lethal melanoma skin cancer in the United States each year. Despite the alerts and sunscreens available, these numbers are rising; some now believe the ingredients in sunblocking lotions actually cause cancer. Nevertheless, it's a disease that is acquired by "lifestyle" factors, such as the notion that tanned

THOROUGHLY DEEP FRIED

One man in upstate New York was a jet fighter buff. He kept an eight-foot turbo engine from an F6 Phantom on a scaffold in his backyard and would fire it up occasionally to melt the snow. His neighbor, a sixty-three-year-old woman, would call the cops many times to complain about the roaring noise. In 1994, after a dozen complaints, the man was finally served a summons. Soon after, he invited the woman over for a cup of coffee to talk things over. When she came up his drive, he switched the position of the engine and stood ready. As soon as she got close enough he fired up the turbo and blasted the poor woman with the five thousand degrees heat, frying her instantly. After police hauled the man away, they wondered if it was necessary to make a chalk outline where the neighbor had died. Her body had already left a perfectly charred etching in the pavement.

is attractive. For various reasons, men are twice as likely as women to get skin cancer, which affects people of all skin colors and ethnicity.

BOTTOMING OUT Substance abuse leads many to die at the bottom, regardless of financial status or social class. By the end of the twentieth century, death from drug overdose had leveled at 14,500 incidents nationwide per year. Out of ten people who died, seven were male. More than half were white. And over 70 percent were thirty-five years or older.

END OF THE RAINBOW
Although excessive alcohol and street drug use guarantee an unpleasant death, many more die from the rainbow-colored assortment of prescription drugs. The best-selling drugs today are designed to increase levels of serotonin (the hormone that regulates mood swings), reduce pain, and boost energy. The number of children between the ages of six and twelve given serotonin-targeted drugs, or SSRI drugs (an abbreviation for Selective Serotonin Reuptake Inhibitors such as Prozac, Zoloft, Paxil, Luvox, Serozone, and Anufranil, to name a few) went from 41,000 in 1995 to 250,000 today. These types of drugs are powerful and mind altering, and 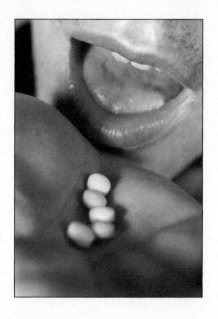 when pumped into kids after a period of time can impair development and regeneration of the liver, kidneys, and muscles. Many of these drugs can cause distorted sexual compulsions, criminal behavior, increase alcohol cravings, suicidal tendencies, and incite rages leading to domestic violence in individuals of all ages. It's hell to withdraw from antidepressants and serotonin-receptor drugs; detox and rehabilitation facilities are filled to capacity with people attempting to do so.

THE WINDFALL
In 1981, Joey C., age twenty-eight, an unemployed dock worker and a methedrine (speed) addict found a sack lying in the road. It had fallen from an armored car and contained over $1 million in unmarked bills. Instead of turning it in and receiving a $50,000 reward, Joey went on a cross-country spending

spree, high as a kite, leaving big tips and handing out hundred dollar bills like they were cigarettes.

Joey's run lasted a few months. He was arrested for theft and his lawyers argued that the windfall of money had made him temporarily insane. The authorities let him go free to become the unemployed dock worker and meth addict he once was. With no money to feed the progressed drug habit, Joey hung himself.

PRESCRIPTION DRUGS,
TAKEN AS DIRECTED,
KILL BY TRIGGERING ADVERSE
REACTIONS AND
SECONDARY ILLNESSES.
OVER 110,000 DIE ANNUALLY
FROM PRESCRIBED DRUGS.

BOTULINUM TOXIN This is derived from the bacteria *Clostridium botulinum,* which causes botulism. In pure form, botulinum toxin is the most poisonous substance known and is on the wish list of bioterrorists. Four grams of undiluted powder—the weight of a nickel—is lethal enough to kill 100 million people. The Food and Drug Administration approved botulinum toxin for cosmetic use in April 2002. The cosmetic versions of botulinum toxin, such as Botox, targets the neurotransmitters responsible for triggering muscle contractions, and in effect paralyzes the area injected, inhibiting the appearance of wrinkles. Usually,

SIDE EFFECTS WORTH NOTING

Although it's not certain that SSRI drugs cause violent behavior, there have been numerous cases of previously mild-mannered individuals suddenly turning malicious soon after taking the drugs. An Atlanta day trader lost money while on SSRIs and killed his family and others in a shooting spree before killing himself. New York City subways bomber Edward Leary was an SSRI user. In Iowa, a thirteen-year-old girl, also on these drugs, murdered her favorite aunt. A thirty-year-old man was on a serotonin-targeted drug when he killed a boy selling cookies door to door in New Jersey. Abbie Hoffman* was on an SSRI when he killed himself, although it was not proven that that was what led to his suicide.

---

* When Abbie Hoffman, the sixties radical, died in 1989, so did the period of history when some young people actually believed a Utopia possible. You can't ridicule a generation of dreamers that wanted no wars, no poverty, and equal rights for all. Currently, there are 35 million Americans dying in poverty, including 14 million children. In the 1960s, 30 percent of the babies born in the inner city had no fathers present; by 1995 that number reached 70 percent.

amounts ranging from 0.5 to 1.0 cc of the watered-down toxin—about one-half teaspoon—is injected into each area of the face. People with neuromotor disorders can develop seizures and breathing difficulties. Applications of the cosmetic versions of this toxin by hairdressers and such have added to its fatal misuse. Bootleg Botox imitations, which is more botulism than Botox, periodically floods the market and kills thirty people each year.

In 2004, 1.6 million Americans were shot with botulinum toxin and 1.1 million women had their lips enhanced with collagen injections. Breast enlargements numbered 246,000; breast reductions, 124,000. (See Also: Liposuction)

There have been 2,871 fatalities from botulinum toxin use since 1985.

Law enforcement, during a sting to find impostors in the cosmetic medical field, launched "Operation Frankenstein." They found hundreds of phony doctors performing cosmetic surgery behind beauty parlors. They also discovered that some legitimate doctors hired fake doctors deliberately to do assembly-line procedures such as tummy tucks, liposuction, and botulinum toxin treatments. The police found one man posing as a plastic surgeon who killed two clients, including a male champion bodybuilder that received women's breasts instead of pectoral implants. The impostors in the cosmetic field often use animal tranquilizers and kitchen utensils when offering cut-rate services.

BOWLING A Michigan man died after a fourteen-pound bowling ball was thrown from a passing car. His windshield didn't spare him. The bowling ball caused a head-on strike, killing him. Another bowling ball fatality occurred when one was dropped from an overpass, crashing through a passing car's rear window, scoring a direct hit to the passenger in the back seat. (*See Also:* Overpasses.) Other deaths are related to the environment of the bowling alley, as

some cater to a rowdy clientele or allow drug trafficking on the premises. In 1995, one such mix led to the Bowling Alley Massacre in Las Cruces, New Mexico, when three were murdered during a botched robbery attempt that authorities believe had to due with retaliation for a drug deal gone bad.

DEATHS AT BOWLING ALLEYS SINCE 1990: 2,102

BOXING Boxing has a scorecard of 1.3 deaths per one thousand participants, which the American Medical Association Council deems as safe as motorcycle racing on rough terrain. But according to the Federal Boxing Commission, only five hundred have died in the ring during sanctioned fights in the last hundred years.

In 1995, when boxer Jimmy Garcia died in the ring, officials were quick to point out that he had once sustained a head wound from a golf ball; they claimed it was that, and not the fatal punch, which caused the subdural hematoma that killed him.

Death can be expected in any contact sport. **Combative Sports,** such as judo and karate, have the same stats as boxing, but as opposed to the head-injury deaths common to boxers, many nonprofessional combatives die from internal bleeding. In 2001, a seventeen-year-old at a community karate competition in Illinois got a ruptured liver and died. A twenty-two-year-old suffered a burst pancreas and died from a karate kick to the abdomen in New Jersey in 2003. Most people assume the danger in karate and judo is from the possibility of strangulation, but since 1982, when the popularity of judo, for people of all ages, began to rise, no deaths have been directly credited to choking.

TOUGHMAN
Every year Toughman Competitions are open to the public. Often held at fairgrounds, anyone can get in the ring to fight an opponent, regardless of weight, size, or age, using anything but a weapon. In 2003, a twenty-four-year-old Sarasota, Florida, woman attempting to win the top prize—nothing more than a trophy and a Toughman jacket—died of hemorrhage. Four died in competitions in 2004, making a total of ten deaths in the short twenty-five-year history of the event.

Harry Houdini (right) *first had a career as a trapeze artist before he became the world's most famous magician. He had survived the high-wire and thousands of insane stunts. Sucker-punched by a jealous college student, Houdini developed a gangrenous appendix within a week, which became too serious for treatment. Houdini couldn't escape his hospital bed—he died on Halloween in 1926 at the age of fifty-two.*

BUILDING DEBRIS In 1989, one Chicago resident was kept awake at night by cats that congregated on the roof of his apartment building. He tried sleeping on the sofa, putting a pillow over his ears, and even taped cardboard and foam over the windows. But no matter what he did, he heard the cats howling during their mating season. It infuriated him that his wife could snore away through it all. After the third sleepless night, the man bought an air gun in the hopes of scaring the cats away from the ledges. When the cats started up that night, he

flung open the window, sat on the sill, and shot up toward the roofline. The cats quickly scattered in all directions. But in his success, a piece of rusted cornice broke loose and hit him in the head, knocking him from his windowsill perch to his death.

In May 1980, thirty-five people, including a Greyhound busload bound for Miami, plunged 150 feet to their deaths when a freighter slammed into a stanchion, knocking a one-thousand-foot segment of the Skyway Bridge into Tampa Bay.

Parts of buildings and other structures, including bridges, roofs, and overhanging decks, crumble to the ground, usually a piece at a time, killing 450 unsuspecting people every year. Twelve died at a party in Chicago in 2003 when a backyard deck pulled loose from a building. Another fifty-two died in Montana in 2004 when a deck collapsed at a casino. Deck collapses kill 250 per year. The worst (nonearthquake or noncriminal) structural failure in recent times occurred when the Kansas City Hyatt skyway, a suspended walkway connecting two buildings, broke apart in 1981, taking 110 lives.

PART OF THE DEBRIS

During the renovation of a historical building in Mississippi in January 2001, workers found the skeletal remains of a man who had been missing since 1985, lodged in an unused brick chimney. Papers in the man's wallet identified him to be Calvin Wilson, age twenty-seven. County Sheriff Tommy Ferrell said, "Wilson's criminal record shows he was a petty burglar, so the suspicion is that he was crawling down the chimney [as a means of entry] to burglarize the gift shop that was operating at this building during that period." Wilson got stuck inside the chimney and died there.

STRONG AS STEEL

Laminated safety glass, also known as auto glass, was invented in 1927. Safety glass achieves its elasticity with a thin film of plastic sandwiched between two or more pieces of glass. The plastic film helps to keep the glass intact when broken, hopefully minimizing injury from flying debris. Compared to normal glass, laminated designs are used in many high-rise buildings because they are hard to bust.

However, on July 9, 1993, a thirty-eight-year-old Chicago lawyer was showing an all-female group of visiting law students around the firm's new office suite in a downtown skyscraper. He joked that no matter how "hot" it got in there, the floor-to-ceiling windows couldn't open. He then began to demonstrate his knowledge of the window's strength and rammed his shoulder against the glass. But this time the safety glass gave way, and the man plunged twenty-four floors to his death.

BUNGEE JUMPING In April 1979, members of England's Oxford University Dangerous Sport Club were inspired after watching a film about "vine jumpers," and decided to hurl themselves, attached to a giant rubber band, off a bridge. This historic day in the progression of humanity marked the birth of the new worldwide recreational activity called bungee jumping. During the 1980s, bungee mania was brought to the

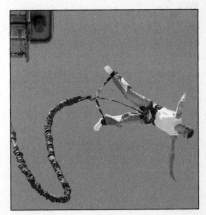

IT'S IN THE MATH

One man, a fast-food worker from Virginia, designed a homemade bungee cord that measured nearly sixty-eight feet in length for a leap from a seventy-foot railroad trestle. He wanted it close. Doing his calculations, he figured he had two feet to spare. Unfortunately, he forgot to compute how much the elastic band would stretch in ratio to the velocity of his own dead weight. His head collided with the concrete at the full force of gravity.

United States by brothers John and Peter Kockelman of California. Facilities quickly sprang up all over the United States, helping people jump from cranes, towers, bridges, and hot air balloons.

Bungee jumping must not be confused with **slingshotting**, the standard amusement park ride that launches the rider from the ground and flings them upward until they bounce to a halt.

The most famous bungee demise occurred during practice for the 1997 Super Bowl XXXI halftime show. Laura Patterson, forty-three, a former circus performer, suffered fatal head injuries performing a sixteen-person bungee jumping extravaganza. Needless to say, the segment of the show featuring bungee jumping was canceled by the NFL commissioner. Instead, they put a photo of Patterson on the Superdome scoreboard at the conclusion of the halftime show, without informing fans why.

Bungee jumpers can also experience temporary blindness, caused by blood vessels in the retina that burst under pressure. However, the Institute of Psychiatry reports that bungee jumping is twenty times safer than heroin.

LEAPS AND BOUNDS

Parkour is an extreme street sport in which a person runs through a city doing acrobatic leaps between roofs, over railings, up and over walls, down stairwells, and out of windows, trying to overcome any obstacle with a fluid grace and agility. Each major city now claims to have at least a one thousand-plus membership in this new activity. Two fourteen-year-olds in Baltimore died in 2003 trying to make a roof jump.

"SPORTING MAYHEM,"
A TERM FOR MANY EXTREME SPORTING ACTIVITIES,
INCLUDING BUNGEE JUMPING AND PARKOUR,
HAS APPEARED AS A SECONDARY CAUSE
ON 2,139 DEATH CERTIFICATES SINCE 1991.

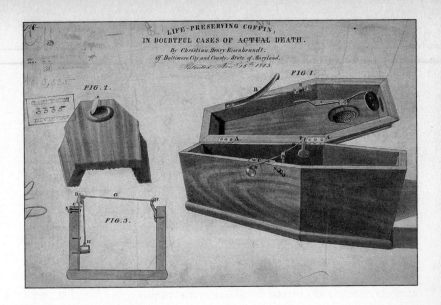

LIFE-PRESERVING COFFIN,
IN DOUBTFUL CASES OF ACTUAL DEATH.
By Christian Henry Eisenbrandt.
Of Baltimore City and County, State of Maryland.
Patented Nov. 15th 1843.

BURIED ALIVE Before there were scientific methods to accurately confirm death, such as the invention of the binaural stethoscope in the 1850s, premature burial was a common affair, so much so that people feared being buried alive more than dying. Physicians, short on available medical knowledge, or even a medical degree, periodically pronounced comatose or unconscious patients dead. In the 1800s fear of premature burial caused people to become fanatical. Citizen groups like the Society for the Prevention of People Being Buried Alive advocated for the deceased to be left in their caskets for days or weeks, if necessary, before being considered adequately dead to bury. In *Buried Alive,* published in 1895, the author, R. Franz, reported that seven hundred people were buried alive in a twenty-year period. During this time, many incidents of revivals were documented in local newspapers. The deceased would suddenly sit up or scream for help during funeral services, scaring the life out of family and friends. There were also reports of women giving birth inside their coffins and grave robbers prying open casket lids to find someone blinking in surprise. Because of all this hubbub, many people insisted on witnessing the beginning of rot before officially declaring their relative's death.

BATS IN THE BELFRY

The most popular contraption of the 1800s was the Bateson Revival Device, commonly known as Bateson's Belfry. A mini church bell was screwed to the exterior lid of a casket, on the end where the head would rest. The bell was attached to a cord through the coffin and strapped to the dead person's hand. Advertisements for the gadget guaranteed its effectiveness, "such that the least tremor shall directly sound the alarm." This product sold well and made inventor John Bateson wealthy. However, preoccupied to the point of psychosis over his own fear of being buried alive, he committed suicide in 1886 by soaking himself with linseed oil and setting himself on fire.

According to the *Thesaurus of Horror,* published in 1817, physicians were recommended to try the Sphincter Test to confirm death: "The test used by the Turkish physicians seems very simple and natural, for they never think a subject dead, or even hopeless, while there is any irritability or contractile power in the sphincter anus muscle." The test required a tube to be inserted into the mouth of the deceased. They would then squeeze on a balloon-like bladder, to force air in the throat. One lucky assistant held the nose and lips closed while another waited near the rear end. Death could be confirmed if the air blast shot out of the anus with a clap, the conclusion being that if the sphincter muscle had lost its contractability, the person, for all civilized intent, was gone.

WINTER SOLSTICE

In December 2003, a seventy-three-year-old man spent seven hours in a morgue freezer drawer before it was discovered that he was still alive. He had gone to the hospital with chest pains and subsequently sustained heart failure. After thirty minutes of unsuccessful resuscitation attempts the doctors sent him to the morgue. When his daughter arrived to retrieve his body for burial, the man opened his eyes and asked for a cup of hot tea. (The temperature in a morgue freezer is between 1 and 6°C.)

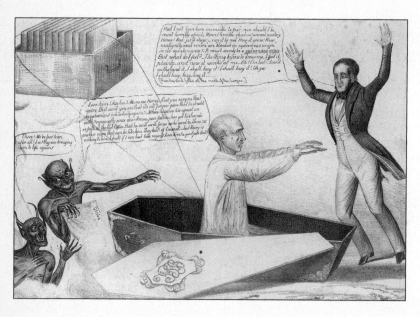

APPROXIMATELY 5,950 PEOPLE WERE BURIED ALIVE BETWEEN 1750 AND 1920.

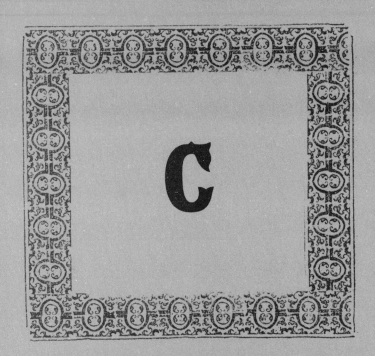

CANDLES Candles are responsible for 6,800 fires annually. Approximately 85 percent of all U.S. fire deaths occured in homes, caused primarily from unattended cooking, space heaters, candles, or cigarettes. Most of the fire-related deaths resulted from toxic fumes and smoke inhalation.

*Deaths caused by children playing with cigarette **lighters** have achieved a consistent average of two hundred per year, despite new "childproof" technology. Between 1988 and 2003, children under five caused 287 fires and sixty-five deaths, while playing with long-nose lighters, used to light charcoal, campfires, and stoves.*

IN 2004, THERE WERE 362,817 HOME FIRES IN THE UNITED STATES, WHICH TOOK THE LIVES OF 3,412 PEOPLE AND INJURED ANOTHER 17,100.

Every two hours a person in America dies in a fire.

CAPITAL PUNISHMENT The death penalty is one of the most controversial topics today, but throughout history, public executions were the biggest social events of the year and a great excuse to party. The uneducated and the elite would mingle to watch a fellow human die. Pastries, meats, fruits, souvenirs, and trinkets were hawked, similar to the fanfare surrounding a modern sporting event.

The total number of legal executions in America since colonial times exceeds 19,200. Most were convicted of murder; 1,086 were convicted of rape; and 1,300 were convicted for neither murder nor rape, but for slave revolt, piracy, adultery, witchcraft, theft, poisoning, sodomy, concealing birth, treason, espionage, counterfeiting, horse stealing, forgery, desertion, kidnapping, aiding a runaway slave, guerilla activity, or rioting.

From The Colonial Records of Pennsylvania, *written in 1693, about the hanging of a bargeman convicted of murder: "There were too few people there to make the affair enjoyable."*

Judicially condoned (non-lynching) hanging has claimed the lives of 13,350 people. Today, hanging is still an option as a method of execution in the states of Washington and Delaware. The last hanging, prior to the temporary suspension of the death penalty, happened in Kansas in 1965 when George York and James Latham were hung for murdering seven people while serving in the army. The last gala public hanging, of murderer Rainey Bethea, twenty-two, in 1936, was attended by twenty-thousand people. After the execution, souvenir hunters tore off pieces of her clothing.

Another well-attended multiple hanging was the Lincoln conspirators' execution. President Lincoln was assassinated on April 14, 1865, and by July 7 four were up on the gallows. Four thousand people, munching cakes and sipping lemonade, showed up for the execution of President Garfield's assassin, the legally insane Charles Guiteau, thirty-nine, in 1881. The largest multiple hanging in U.S. history occurred on December 26, 1862, when thirty-eight Sioux Indians were hanged simultaneously in Minnesota in retaliation for an attack in which hundreds of men, women, and children died.

The execution of women made men uncomfortable. One colonial-era legal scholar, William Blackstone,

In 1862, New Orleans gambler Bruce Mumford was convicted of treason and hanged for desecrating the American flag.

The very first condemned to death in North America was George Kendal, shot by firing squad for espionage in Virginia in 1608. The first North American hanging was one Daniel Frank in Virginia, 1622, for stealing, quartering, and eating a cow. The first public hanging was in 1630, in Plymouth, Massachusetts. John Billington, who arrived on the Mayflower, *was hanged for shooting another settler.*

GUILTY! GUILTY! GUILTY!
*Multiple hangings were sure to draw the largest crowds. Old West judge **Isaac Parker** (below) was the consummate "hanging judge." An impatient Bible-toting judiciary, he viewed all who stood before his bench as sinners. In his twenty-year career he presided over 13,400 cases and sent 161 to the gallows. (Intolerant of lawyerly wrangling or appeals, it seemed Judge Parker often left the judicial notion that the accused must be guilty "beyond a reasonable doubt" to be decided by a heavenly court.) In 1875, more than five-thousand came to watch three white men, two Indians, and one black man all hanged at the same time; Judge Parker had convicted them all of murder and was up on the scaffold to give the signal to release the trapdoor on which the men stood.*

noted: "As decency due to the sex forbids the exposing and publicly mangling of their bodies, their sentence is to be burned alive." Burning at the stake allowed women to keep their clothes on, while hanging, with all that twitching, was seen as very unseemly and unladylike. All the same, twenty-four women were hanged in Salem, Massachusetts, for witchcraft and adultery. After 1736, no one was legally persecuted for being a witch in the American colonies, and witchcraft was removed as a crime punishable by death.

AS OF 2005, A TOTAL OF 551 U.S. WOMEN HAVE BEEN EXECUTED, OF WHOM 505 WERE HANGED.

The youngest person hanged in America was twelve-year-old Hannah Ocuish, in 1789, for beating to death a six-year-old. A total of 159 juveniles have been executed in America.

THE ELECTROCUTING CHAIR.

The **Electric Chair** has taken 4,281; the **Gas Chamber**, 582; and **Lethal Injection** claimed another 918. Four pirates and seven slave revolters were **Hung by Chains** (wrapped in chains and hung from a tree at a crossroads). Twelve were executed for murder and adultery between 1712 and 1754 by **Breaking on the Wheel**. (A person was laid on the rim of a large iron wheel, spread eagle, naked, and tied to the spokes, then hoisted and left to the elements and scavengers.) Two persons were legally **Bludgeoned** (hit with clubs until dead): one soldier, Pichon Bartellemy, in Michigan in 1707; and one Indian by the name of Leather Lips in Ohio in 1810.

In America, sixty-six people (sixty-five of them escaped slaves) were executed by **Burning at the Stake**, ten in New York in the summer of 1741, and one (for witchcraft) in Illinois in 1779. Seven pirates were **Gibbeted** (covered in tar and then placed in a suspended iron cage at a crossroads and left to starve). One person was executed by **Pressing**.

In 1624, Richard Cornish, accused of "unnatural sexual relations," became the first man to be hung for a homosexual offense in America.

Since the Supreme Court reaffirmed the death penalty in 1976 there have been 6,943 persons put on death row and 1,022 have been executed: 854 were by lethal injection, 152 by electrocution, eleven by lethal gas, three by hanging (two in Washington State and one in Delaware), and two by firing squad (both in Utah).

GILES COREY'S PUNISHMENT AND AWFUL DEATH.

Giles Corey was executed by pressing in 1692 because he refused to say anything bad about a neighbor under investigation for witchcraft. The crazed townspeople of Salem tied him to stakes in the ground and laid a wooden pallet over his body. Boulders were placed on top of the pallet; interrogators asked a question, got no answer, and added another boulder. It was two days before Corey finally spoke. Tongue out of his mouth, eyes bulging, he said, "More weight," and died.

Just before he was electrocuted in May 1979, murderer John Spenkelink said: "Capital punishment—them without the capital get the punishment."

IN 2005, SIXTY WERE LETHALLY INJECTED, THE MAJORITY OF THEM IN TEXAS. IN CONTRAST, 2,419 WERE EXECUTED IN 2005 IN CHINA.

CARJACKING Carjacking is a theft of an occupied motor vehicle by force or threat of force. Of the 2 million vehicles stolen each year, forty thousand are by carjackings. Men are more likely than women to be victimized by carjacking. Forty-five percent occurred during the day in public garages or on streets less than twenty miles away from the victim's home. Handguns were used in 59 percent of successful carjackings.

TOTAL FATALITIES FROM CARJACKING SINCE 1990: 4,890

CARS In America there are 225 million passenger vehicles, one for every person over seven years old. Cars travel on 2 million miles of U.S. roads, enough concrete and asphalt to pave a six-lane highway to the moon. In the first quarter of 2004, Americans drove 624 billion miles, a road trip that could've taken them back and forth to Mars twenty times.

Future historians might be amazed that only about forty-three thousand Americans are killed on our nation's roadways every year. The minute-by-minute, mile-by-mile likelihood for potential crashes is astronomical; how many fender benders, sudden jamming of the brakes, or swerves onto the shoulder occur every moment? Too many to count. Barring close calls, the prospect of meeting random death in a car is a very real twenty-first-century phenomenon, and the most likely way accidental death will occur.

- ☠ Drivers under twenty-four are the only group more likely to die in a car than seniors.
- ☠ Four out of five car deaths occurred when the speed limit is under 40 mph.
- ☠ Fifteen thousand people die each year in alcohol-related car crashes.

The annual number of death in cars is still considered to be at an "acceptable" level. There are six times as many people driving now than there were in 1925, and 200 million fewer cars on the roadways. Even so, the chances of dying by car in the Roaring Twenties were twenty times greater than now. By 1938, traffic accidents had killed thirty-two thousand people in the United States, and by the mid-1950s the total death toll on U.S. highways surpassed the casualty figures for all U.S. wars combined. In 1960, when there were half as many cars about than today, 38,459 people died.

DRIVE TIME
The most deadly hour to drive Monday through Friday is from 4:00 to 5:00 P.M. Saturday has more fatalities than another day of the week. The fourteenth day of any given month has been, historically, the most lethal. Sunday morning between 12:00 and 2:00 A.M. is the most dangerous time on the weekend to be cruising.

Statisticians say if seat belts hadn't become mandatory and kids weren't put in car seats, or groups like Mothers Against Drunk Driving (MADD) didn't educate about the insanity of operating heavy machinery under the influence, the number of car deaths would easily exceed one hundred thousand today, not the mere forty-three thousand "acceptable" losses.

- ☠ 7,269 people aged sixty-five years or older die in motor vehicle crashes each year, twice as many men than women.
- ☠ The number of licensed drivers aged seventy years or older increases each year by nearly 50 percent.
- ☠ Half of the fatal crashes involving drivers eighty years old or older happened at intersections.

EVERY TWELVE MINUTES SOMEONE WILL DIE IN A CAR, AND EVERY FOURTEEN SECONDS A PERSON SUFFERS A DISABLING INJURY, FOR A TOTAL OF 8,800 LIFE-THREATENING ACCIDENTS PER DAY.

CAT BURGLAR A twenty-nine-year-old man bragged that he would make a great cat burglar. He was limber and had practice working for an air-conditioning company, sent into the tightest attics to repair air ducts. On his first attempt, he broke a small street-level window of a bank in Cincinnati. But while climbing through, he cut his hands and wrists on the wire-embedded glass. On top of that, the basement room he dropped into was empty and had no money or access to the safe. An hour later, failing to reach the window to climb back out, he finally used his cell phone to call 911 for help, but had already lost too much blood from his slit wrists, and died by the time the ambulance got there.

DEATHS DUE TO DELAYED MEDICAL CARE IN 2003: 310,867

CATCH-22 SYNDROME* This ailment holds the distinction as the only literary title to be listed as a cause of death. It occurs when the thymus fails to develop naturally during the eighth week of embryonic development, related to an anomaly in the chromosome 22q11. This horrible defect causes congenital heart problems, abnormalities of the large blood vessels around the heart, and disfigurement of facial structures. The parents of infants with Catch-22 syndrome are told that everything may seem fine, but could probably get worse; or the child may have something comparatively as minor as a chronic runny nose, or severe diaper rash, or—the major catch-22—they may fail to thrive altogether and become susceptible to sudden death. Most parents are baffled by the illogical set of possible outcomes and prefer to hear none of it. Most hope for the best and pray the newborn doesn't come down with a fatal case of Catcher in the Rye disease when older.

912 CATCH-22 DEATHS OF INFANTS OCCURRED IN 2003.

CELL PHONE ETIQUETTE In 2001 a businessman sat at a bar in Nashville while a game was on TV. When his cell phone rang, he answered and started talking—loudly. The other patrons sat patiently at first, as the bartender politely asked the gentleman to take the call outside. "Business," the man said, and kept on yakking, causing another customer to yell for the man to shut up. When the businessman gave the middle-finger salute, a third irate drinker cracked a beer bottle over the businessman's head, killing him.

HOMICIDES COMMITTED IN LICENSED DRINKING ESTABLISHMENTS SINCE 1965: 23,421

* Joseph Heller wrote the literary classic, *Catch-22* (1961), set in World War II Italy. The phrase "catch-22" has entered the English language to signify a no-win situation. Heller died in 1999 at age seventy-six of a heart attack.

CHEERLEADING It used to be just sis-boom-bah, rah-rah-rah, Go team!—with a bunch of high kicks and the occasional cartwheel. The pom-poms and cheers may still be a part of it, but today's cheerleaders aren't concerned with simply leading the crowd in cheer anymore. Cheerleading squads are now competing at a high level of gymnastics with stunts and tricks, doing daredevil routines that rival circus acts.

No longer tied to cheering the school team, most squads perform only for judges or for cable TV shows that follow the competitive cheerleading circuit. In the United States cheerleading is one of the fastest-growing activities for girls and young women. However, for many schools it's still considered a hobby and not treated as a sport requiring professional trainers or proper equipment.

Cheerleading started in Princeton in 1898 and was dominated by men in its early years. When large numbers of young men left college to fight in World War II, women took over the job. Today, 90 percent of cheerleaders are female.

Teams are often denied access to appropriate facilities that have soft mats and other safety-minded features; some have to practice in parking lots. The Con-

The main source of injuries results from the increased difficulty of stunts and the ever-increasing size of human pyramids cheerleaders try to form. During competitions, over forty stunts and difficult acrobatics have to be performed by a squad in three to five minutes.

THE PYRAMID
The Flying Wallendas (left) were the most famous modern-era trapeze artists. They perfected a seven-person pyramid on the high wire, despite one tragic human pyramid crash in 1962, in Detroit, when two performers died. The patriarch, Karl Wallenda, left the family circus act with Ringling Brothers to become a "skywalker," tiptoeing across cables strung between buildings and football stadiums. When he was sixty-five, he made a twelve-hundred-foot daredevil walk across the Tallulah Falls Gorge in Georgia and did headstands at a height of over seven hundred feet above the rocks. In March 1978, he died in Puerto Rico at age seventy-three by falling from a wire strung between two skyscrapers.

sumer Product Safety Commission now regards cheerleading as the most dangerous school activity in America.

For girls involved in sports, half of the catastrophic injuries occur on the sidelines, in cheerleading accidents. In 2003, there were twenty-five thousand hospital visits related to cheerleading injuries, involving ankle, shoulder, head, neck, and spine.

SINCE 1995, 782 CHEERLEADERS HAVE BECOME PARALYZED AND 123 HAVE DIED.

CHILD-BED FEVER This cause of death due to any complication, of either mother or baby during childbirth, occupied the most learned medical minds of the early colonial era, so much so that Dr. John Leake published a 319-page book in 1772 on probable methods to alleviate this rampant condition. Mothers died so frequently during birth—two hundred out of every one thousand births—that it wasn't uncommon for a man to marry one woman and end up being married to the woman's sister or cousin. So great was the loss of children that many chose not to name children until they had survived at least a year.

Most women relied on superstition as the only way to avoid child-bed fever. It was commonly thought that if a mother looked at a "horrible specter" or was shocked by a loud noise, her child would be disfigured. If it happened twice, she may die giving birth. If a hare crossed her path during the first three months of pregnancy, her child would suffer a cleft palate, or harelip. If a mother didn't want her child to become a lunatic or sleepwalker, it was advised that she not gaze at the full moon. And it was believed that if a mother had longings for another man, other than the baby's dad, it was thought these desires

PRACTICAL OBSERVATIONS

ON THE

CHILD-BED FEVER:

ALSO ON THE

NATURE and TREATMENT

OF

Uterine Hæmorrhages, Convulsions,

AND SUCH OTHER

ACUTE DISEASES,

As are most fatal to WOMEN during the State of PREGNANCY.

By JOHN LEAKE, M.D.

Member of the College of PHYSICIANS, London, And Physician to the Westminster Lying-in Hospital.

—Hinc videtur Medicus hac in re testis officio qui narrat, non judicat, fungi debere, ac partito singulas res quantumvis minimas notare; earum enim aliae statim ac perceptae sunt rectam curandi rationem ostendunt.   BAGLIV.

LONDON:

Printed for J. WALTER, Charing-Cross; T. BECKET and Co. Strand; R. BALDWIN, Pater-Noster-Row; and RICHARDSON and Co. Royal-Exchange.

SUPERSTITIONS TODAY
Despite advancements in technology, superstitions concerning birth persist. Many women think they should not take a bath while pregnant, fearing germs will enter the vagina and harm the baby in the womb. (Baths are, in fact, harmful in the first trimester when the water is over 100°F, because it can raise the body temperature and cause problems to the baby's development.) There's another lingering superstition that babies' nails should not be cut until after twelve months, otherwise the baby will grow up to be a thief. However, chewing their nails off is permissible.

could cause her to die giving birth or, at the very least, leave a purple birthmark stamped on her child's body.

A woman's peril giving birth didn't change much until about seventy years ago, when antibiotics and blood transfusions were introduced and made more readily available. In 1900, 90 percent of all births occurred at home, contributing to a death rate 65 percent higher than it is today. By 1940, more than half of all births took place in hospitals. With the ability to induce labor, the use of forceps, and the more-common practice of cesarean deliveries, a greater number of women survived childbirth, yet 40 percent still died from infections. By 1950, survival rate of medically supervised hospital births reached 90 percent.

In the past, child-bed fever occurred due to lack of medical advancements, technology, and prenatal care. Now there is a vast increase in survival rate—only seven out of one thousand births end in mortality of either mother or baby. Death today is due to increasingly low birth weights of infants or from unforeseen medical conditions that arise during labor.

IN 2003, 28,314 MOTHERS AND CHILDREN DIED
IN THE UNITED STATES OF WHAT WAS ONCE CONSIDERED
CHILD-BED FEVER.

CHINESE FOOD SYNDROME In 2003, a man was eating at a Chinese restaurant in Queens, New York, with his wife. The food was delicious, but even before he finished, the man began to sweat and, according to his wife, was acting "strange." The man knocked back his chair, fell onto a neighboring diner's table, crashing bowls of fried rice all over the floor, and ultimately ran from the restaurant into the street, where he was promptly hit by a city bus.

Although his demise was listed as a pedestrian fatality, the actual cause of death was Chinese Food Syndrome. This condition sometimes mimics a heart attack, causing chest pains, facial pressure, and burning sensations throughout the body. These symptoms are pharmacologic reactions to monosodium glutamate (MSG), a

popular white powder used to season food. The chemical glutamate exists naturally in the body as a neurotransmitter and helps protein synthesis. When natural glutamate is hydroiyzed during the manufacturing process for consumption, as it is in MSG, in order for it to dissolve quickly in saliva, it releases glutamate ions. In the MSG-intolerant, instead of aiding in the synthesis of proteins as natural glutamate does, it has a reverse reaction and forms brain lesions and can cause nerve cell damage. A 1995 FDA report concluded that asthmatics and people who can't tolerate large amounts of MSG may be at risk of death, which only trial and error, or eating MSG, will tell. Chinese restaurant advocates couldn't understand the flak and surely didn't want a disease named after their food. They subsequently conducted surveys and produced conflicting data. Some reports suggested that those who respond negatively to MSG were already delusional or perhaps would've died, no matter what they were eating. If you get a headache after eating MSG, pro-glutamate chefs dismiss it, saying it was probably the bad company you had for dinner and not the bad food that gave it to you. Although MSG is no longer used regularly, labeled as such, it is still found in many foods labeled as "hydrolyzed soy protein" and "natural flavoring(s)."

FOOD ADDITIVES KILLED 56,981 IN 2002.

DEADLY DELICACIES

Every weekend, in the back rooms of many of the best Chinese and Japanese restaurants, a select clientele gather secretly for a dangerous meal. This by-invitation-only dinner consists of vegetables smothered with the sweetest honey in the world, harvested from

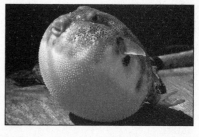

bees that use pollen exclusively from rhododendrons. A taste of this honey in its purified form contains enough toxins to send the risky dabbler into a coma. The

At age seventy-three President James Monroe officially died of tuberculosis in 1831. Without doubt, he was seriously infirm; however, it is believed that Monroe suffered his final seizure after brewing a deadly cup of tea that he made from poison mushrooms.

sauce of the main dish contains "Death Cap" mushrooms that look white and spongy, just like the ones in the supermarket, but if not cooked properly can poison and cause a rapid death. Fugu, the main entry, is the deadly dish that lures the gourmet. The expertly prepared fugu is the meat of the blowfish or puffer fish, which contains a deadly poison in its liver, bile, and eggs. One gram—the weight of a metal paper clip—of the toxin can kill three hundred people. It is the element of risk, as there's no antidote, which makes eating fugu so popular with these secret diners.

BETWEEN 2000 AND 2004, TWENTY-THREE FUGU CONNOISSEURS
DIED FROM BLOWFISH POISONING.

CHOCOLATE Americans consume 3 billion pounds of chocolate a year. Recent research has shown that chocolate is rich in naturally occurring compounds, polyphenols and flavonoids, which act as antioxidants. It's the sugar in chocolate that isn't good for you. Too much sugar causes imbalanced insulin production and diabetes. The U.S. Department of Agriculture (USDA) says sugar in small amounts is okay—35 grams, or eight teaspoons of sugar per day. One chocolate candy bar has around 20 grams of sugar. According to USDA data, sugar consumption in 2002 was 158 pounds per person. This is equivalent to about 237 grams or fifty teaspoons of sugar per day, 30 percent higher than 1992.

Sixteen million people have diabetes in the United States. Each year 24,000 people become blind because of diabetic eye disease; 38,000 people with diabetes undergo treatment for kidney failure; and 86,000 will need diabetes-related lower extremity amputations.

DEATH BY CHOCOLATE

When a nineteen-year-old diabetic got a job at a Hatfield, Pennsylvania, candy factory that specialized in making chocolate chips, he joked that being around all those sweets could be the end of him. Two months later, while mixing a twelve-hundred-gallon vat of liquefied chocolate, he lost his footing and fell into it. No one saw him fall and his body was not discovered until three days later, after a countless number of chocolate chips already sent to commercial bakeries had been baked into cookies from the mixture. Management told labor investigators that the new hire had previously been written up twice for unauthorized sampling.

**61,817 DIED IN 2003 OF
DIABETES-RELATED
COMPLICATIONS.**

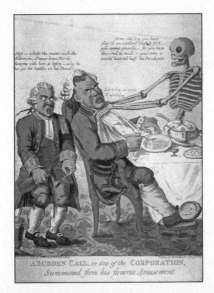

A SUDDEN CALL, or One of the CORPORATION, Summoned from his favorite Amusement.

CHOKING When President George Bush lost consciousness for a brief time in the White House after choking on a pretzel, many stand-up comics thought it was funny. In Hoboken, New Jersey, in 1999, a de-

Tom Dorsey, a big band leader, died in his home from choking in his sleep at age fifty-two in 1956. Jimi Hendrix died in 1970, age twenty-seven, choking on his own vomit. Tennessee Williams died in 1983 at age seventy-one when he choked on a bottle cap.

mure, sixty-one-year-old secretary, never got the chance to laugh. At a company dinner she began to gag on a fishbone; although coworkers tried the Heimlich maneuver numerous times, they were unable to dislodge it. They didn't know she had been prescribed drugs for nausea, which suppressed her ability to cough it back up. In a last desperate attempt to save the little lady, the boss of the company directed a big man from the receiving department to stand up on the table. The man grabbed the poor woman by the ankles, turned her upside down, and shook her, to no avail.

WHAT A GAG
In 1995, slapstick comedian Yves Abouchar, forty-five, choked to death on a custard pie that was thrown in his face. Apparently, he breathed in just as the pie landed and was suffocated by the artificial, cream-look-alike, foam rubber topping.

NUMBER OF CHOKING DEATHS
REPORTED AT U.S. RESTAURANTS
SINCE 1975: 11,931

CHRISTMAS DISEASE This disease was named after a ten-year-old orphan, Stephen Christmas, who had a different type of hemophilia than the more common form. The boy was the first known to have an unknown anti-coagulation factor, now called type B. Nevertheless, all hemophiliacs lack a clotting enzyme found in normal blood; they can bleed to death from a minor cut. Mention of hemophilia can be found in Jewish writings of the second century, which cite incidents of boys dying after simple circumcisions. Queen Victoria's son Leopold had hemophilia and passed it on throughout the royal bloodlines of Europe. As unfortunate as this condition is, it seems that researchers in 1952 had a bit of the Bah-Humbugs when they named the newly discovered strain "Christmas disease." If they really wanted to give the orphan boy a present, they could've called it Stephen's disease just as well.

CHRISTMAS DISEASE DEATHS SINCE 1955 DUE TO
COAGULATION DEFECTS AFTER INJURIES: 5,789
TYPE A HEMOPHILIC DEATHS PER YEAR FROM BLEEDING AND FROM
RECEIVING VIRAL INFECTED BLOOD TRANSFUSIONS: 1,680

CLEAN SWEEP In Washington, D.C., a twenty-nine-year-old woman was about to cross the street with her four-year-old daughter. She was intent on holding her little girl's hand while navigating a hand-pulled grocery cart. The moment the woman stepped from the curb she was swept under a large, motorized street sweeper. She was pulled down, then up, and into the whirling wire brushes; she was killed instantly. Her daughter was just about to be sucked under when the driver of the sweeper reached down and pulled the girl free. It took rescue workers over an hour to disentangle her mother's body.

COCKROACHES This insect ranks as the most hated pest in the history of mankind. Virtually unchanged in its 300 million year existence, the appearance of man has hardly affected cockroach evolution, offering them perhaps another item on the long and varied menu of things these creatures can eat. Cockroaches have no natural enemies and are practically indestructible, surviving comfortably at temperatures between 19 and 120°F. Flushing them down the toilet won't help because they can remain submerged for fifteen minutes without air. A cockroach can live off the glue of one postage stamp for a month and has the ability to lay eggs—thirty thousand from one female—two weeks *after* its head is cut off.

EATEN ALIVE

In 1798, a survey of ships found that cockroaches frequently gnawed the skin and nails of the men on board. According to entomologists Dr. L. Roth and Dr. W. Willis, one captain solved the problem by having the sailors wear gloves while sleeping "to prevent hordes of the insects from gnawing off their fingernails." Today's urban cockroaches have been known to chew the fingernails and devour the eyelashes of sleeping children. They are attracted to uncleaned faces and have even nibbled on the remains of food from unbrushed teeth. The cockroach usually prefers callused portions of adult hands and feet.

One study by scientists Rueger and Olson (1969) showed that bacteria and parasites spread by cockroaches lasted for many years: on cornflakes, 3.25 years; on crackers,

When cockroaches bite, they leave a mark that looks like a small pinprick. The bug has no venom and is deadly only because of the diseases it carries, which include polio, typhoid, and hepatitis. Cockroaches are also responsible for 65 percent of all food poisoning, spread through their feces and saliva, including salmonella poisoning and toxoplasmosis (a cause of congenital defects in unborn children).

COCKROACH ALLERGY

First identified as a disease in 1959, cockroach allergy is a severe allergic reaction that occurs when a cockroach crawls over the skin. A recent study by the National Institute of Allergy and Infectious Diseases (NIAID) showed that the combination of cockroach allergy and exposure to the insects exacerbates asthma-related illness among children in U.S. inner-city areas.

over 4.25 years; and on drinking glasses, over 3.67 years. When these researchers placed a mouse in a jar containing minuscule quantities of infected cockroach crap, the lab mouse died in one day.

4,657 DEATHS IN 1999 WERE ATTRIBUTED TO DISEASES TRANSMITTED OR CAUSED BY COCKROACHES.

Two other insects on the most hated list include the **housefly** and the lousy **louse.** Documented lice-control techniques exist from as long as four thousand years ago, but were obviously unsuccessful. Napoleon suffered defeat in Russia not from harsh winter conditions, but from typhus, a disease transmitted by lice. Over two hundred thousand of his five-hundred-thousand-man army died, in a six month period, during that invasion from lice.

Anne Frank died in March 1945 of typhus from lice-infested Bergen-Belsen, the concentration camp where she was imprisoned.

Five million people currently have lice. It's so widespread that schools have a "no-nit policy": If a child has lice nits (egg sacks) in the hair they are promptly dismissed, without discussion. Lice are parasites that suck blood and are about the size of a sesame seed. They have six barbed legs and can walk the length of a football field looking for a host. Besides spreading typhus, lice can also cause relapsing fever and trench fever and spread STDs. Pubic lice, commonly called **crabs,** are usually acquired during intercourse and, not too often, from public toilet seats.

The **housefly** is problematic because of its preference for crawling on garbage and excrement, then visiting humans and walking on their food. These insects are perfected carriers of lethal disease-provoking pathogens. The housefly specializes in transmitting—with the efficiency of a Typhoid Mary*— diarrhea, dysentery, typhoid, cholera, poliomyelitis, intestinal worms, eye infections, yaws, anthrax, and tularemia.

---

* Typhoid Mary Mallon was an Irish cook in New York in the early 1900s who moved from home to home as a private servant. When typhoid fever broke out, the city health officials traced the disease back to her. Although herself immune, she was a carrier. Doctors wanted to remove her gallbladder so she could carry on a normal life without jeopardizing others, but she refused and was isolated in a cottage on North Brother Island in the East River, between the Bronx and Queens, near Rikers Island. Quarantined for four years, she promised the authorities she would never cook again. Newspapers editorialized about her unfair treatment, forcing officials to allow her release, which they finally did in 1910. Five years later, when another outbreak of typhoid hit, Mary was found making homemade ice cream. Fourteen hundred people had died, and the public sentiment turned, now regarding her as a serial killer. She was returned to the cottage and lived in isolation. Eventually, she accepted her confinement, taking a job washing bottles in a bacteriology lab on the island. Before she died in 1938, Mary made extra money for herself selling baked goods and cakes to hospital employees on the grounds.

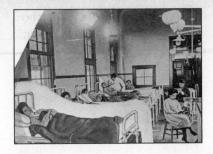

ALTHOUGH DEATH FROM COMMON HOUSEHOLD INSECTS HAS DECREASED IN THE LAST FEW DECADES DUE TO IMPROVEMENTS IN SANITATION AND CLEANLINESS, SINCE 1900, COCKROACHES, LICE, AND FLIES HAVE CONTRIBUTED TO THE DEATH OF 15 MILLION.

COMPETITIVE EATING Although obesity accounts for more than three hundred thousand premature deaths and is linked to the nation's number one killer, heart disease, competitive eating is another story. In the United States, public competitive eating contests are regulated by the International Federation of Competitive Eating (IFOCE). This group oversees the most noted events, such as the Nathan's hotdog-eating contest, held annually on July 4 in Coney Island since 1916.

Most competitive-eater deaths are attributed to the untrained. The IFOCE strongly discourages amateur participation and provides guidelines on how to increase food intake capacity with the "water method"—drinking water in quantities that expand the stomach—weeks before competition.

HEART ATTACK IS THE MOST FREQUENT DEATH FROM
RAPID OVEREATING: 8,189 SINCE 1965

COMPULSIVE DISORDERS According to The National Institute of Mental Health, 22.1 percent of Americans ages eighteen and older suffer from a diagnosable and thus manageable mental disorder in any given year including: depression (9.9 million); bipolar disorder and acute mania (2.3 million); schizophrenia (2.2 million).

Nineteen million people suffer from obsessive-compulsive disorders, including panic disorder, post-traumatic stress disorder, generalized anxiety disorder, or other phobias. Some of these disorders

make dying of the affliction a very bewildering affair. People with compulsive disorders often fear embarrassment or stigmatization and try to conceal their obsessions and rituals. Checking and rechecking, arranging and organizing, collecting and hoarding, or counting and repeating are a few of the compulsive ticks that could be maddening to both the afflicted and their next of kin. There are medications and treatments that effectively minimize these symptoms, but some people refuse to take them and ultimately die, confounded by the very action they believed would make them safe.

KILLER QUIRKS

A woman in Boise had a hand-washing compulsion. Many years previously, water had splashed from a public toilet into her eye, causing a bad infection. She washed her hands over one hundred times a day and absolutely refused to use any public facility, fearing she would go blind if she did. Homebound, washing and scrubbing, she eventually died of a skin infection from scrub-induced wounds on her hands that didn't heal.

Another man got the notion that only rats could protect him. He started with a pair, but within a year there were thousands in his house. He died from a disease transmitted by rat feces.

BRUSH, BRUSH, BRUSH

A Boston man feared dentists, so in order to avoid visits he began to brush his teeth more diligently. Eventually, he was scrubbing his teeth thirty times a day. When that wasn't enough, he began to gargle with cleaning fluids. In 1996, he died after swallowing ammonia.

Perhaps the most famous American to die at the hands of his unchecked obsession was **Howard Hughes** *(left)*. He was afraid of touching or breathing germs and had elaborate rituals for preparing food, and much more. But it wasn't always like that. When he was eighteen, he suddenly inherited a family fortune. With the money he went to Hollywood, started his own production company, and made hit movies. He became infamous for his womanizing and his eccentxtricities.

As he got older, his obsessions got worse. He stopped talking on the phone

"I am by nature a perfectionist, and I seem to have trouble allowing anything to go through in a half-perfect condition." —Howard Hughes

for fear that bacteria was transmitted through the lines, capable of infecting him. Hughes spent his entire time sitting naked in a white leather chair in the center of a large room called the "germ-free zone." Eventually, Hughes became a recluse. He managed not to be seen publicly or have his picture taken for twenty years. At the end of his life he didn't shave, trim his fingernails or toenails, or change his clothes until they fell off his body. He died in 1976 at age seventy-one, worth $1 billion. According to Dr. Raymond Fowler in the May 1986 issue of *Psychology Today,* Hughes died of heart failure and did not die in a plane accident as alleged. Howard Hughes was known for his love of aviation, but apparently it was speed he cherished most. FBI files of the autopsy report indicate Hughes had dozens of broken syringes in his arms and legs at the time of his death.

PEOPLE WITH COMPULSIVE DISORDERS ACCOUNTED FOR 9,816 DEATHS IN 1999.

CO-SLEEPING When children sleep in bed with their parents (usually between the two) it is called co-sleeping and is considered an unsafe practice. The cause of death written on certificates of children who are killed due to co-sleeping reads, "death due to overlay," but the scientific term is "Traumatic Compression." Many certificates offer additional clarification: "compressed beneath mother's body," "found under parent," or "accidentally rolled over by mother." In only 2 percent of the deaths was alcohol or drug consumption a factor.

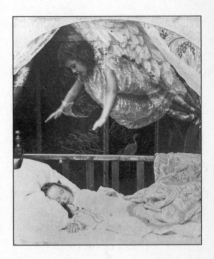

THE 2 PERCENT
In 1998, when a twenty-one-year-old woman had friends over for a drinking party in her apartment she let her two-year-old sleep on the couch next to her. One by one, her friends passed out in various places throughout the apartment. A heavyset female guest crashed out on the couch, between the mother and the child. The next morning, the boy was found deceased, his head buried under the drunk woman's thigh.

CHILDREN CO-SLEEPING WITH ADULTS ACCOUNTED FOR 1,557 DEATHS SINCE 1985.

CRAYONS In 1903 the first box of crayons sold for a nickel and had eight colors: black, brown, blue, red, purple, orange, yellow, and green. Now there are 120 colors. One hundred billion crayons have been used since 1903, which adds up to about 6.3 billion hours spent coloring annually.

In the last few years, crayons have been under attack for the toxins they might contain. Twelve jumbo crayons made in China, originally labeled "non-toxic," were found to have enough lead to present a poisoning hazard to young children who might eat or chew on the crayons. By the age of ten, the average child will use 730 crayons and eat less than two—usually the red or green ones.

In 2000 the U.S. Consumer Product Safety Commission published a study that found trace amounts of asbestos in two Crayola crayons and one Prang crayon. Larger amounts of "transitional" fibers, similar in appearance to asbestos, were also discovered. However, the amount is so minuscule that a kid would have to eat thirty-five hundred crayons a year to develop any asbestos-related disease. Crayon makers argued that if your child is consuming that many crayons, asbestos should be the least of your worries.

43,073 PEOPLE HAVE BEEN DIRECTLY KILLED BY ASBESTOS FOUND IN BUILDING MATERIALS SINCE 1979, 0 FROM CRAYON FIBERS.

CRUISE SHIPS Today's cruise ships are as big as small towns carrying as many as thirty-five hundred passengers happily out to sea. The $12 billion cruise ship industry literally bends over backward to provide every amenity a person could need, and then some, to try to make the experience a pleasant journey. However, the very same Pandora's Box of accidents that happen on dry land happens at sea. Slips and falls, food poisoning, falling objects, and medical emergencies are regular occurrences. Crime, too, doesn't get left behind. Most of the crime is theft, but there are more serious, deadly offenses being committed, usually by crew members. The ten homicides, 102 rapes, 1,345 heart attacks, and other fatalities that occur each year are almost never reported.

Many cruise ships are registered to foreign countries and are not required to report crimes to U.S. authorities—just read the microscopic type on the back of your ticket.

If you get seriously ill on the high seas, there are some cruise ships that aren't about to turn around. Maritime law does not require vessels to carry a

1914: *Empress of Ireland* collides due to fog with a Norwegian freighter in St. Lawrene River, killing 1,024.

1915: *Eastland* capsizes in the Chicago River; 812 dead.

1934: *Morro Castle* takes 134 in a ship fire off Asbury Park, New Jersey.

1956: *Andrea Doria* collides in dense fog with the *Stockholm* off Nantucket Island, Massachusetts, killing fifty-two.

doctor for passengers or to monitor the quality of medical care. Infirmaries are set up to handle sunburn and seasickness, and are often staffed by doctors who are not licensed in the United States. However, cruise ship companies aren't intentionally cruel and don't want people dying left and right—it's bad for business. In fact, death on today's cruise ships is fluff compared to the first two hundred years of U.S. marine travel. From 1750 to 1930, due to notoriously inebriated crews and unreliable equipment, travel by ship was the most lethal form of mass transit. Before 1820, all ships were wind powered, leaving passengers' survival to the whim of nature. Hurricane logs alone count 12,123 dead. When steamships arrived on the scene, the first models had crude boilers, which exploded regularly without warning. In 1823 alone, two thousand people died when the steam vessels were ravaged by explosions. In 1852, after seven disasters in a six-month period, Congress required engineers and pilots on steam vessels carrying passengers to pass certification and mandated an overhaul of the seriously corrupt Steamboat Inspection Service.

During the Civil War, thousands of sailors died at sea; the hope was that once the battles ended, the fatalities would stop. Yet the worst disaster was still to come. At the end of the war, Union soldiers released from prisons wanted to get home as fast as possible. The first ship leaving from

CAPTAIN HOOK ALIVE AND WELL

Besides exploding ships and perpetually drunk crews, passengers had to worry about pirates. One pirate, Nathaniel Gordon, was accused of killing at least three hundred on the open waters. When he was arrested at sea in 1859, two thousand people showed up for his hanging in New York City. Today, piracy is alive and well; the International Chamber of Commerce and the International Maritime Bureau counted 1,164 acts of piracy from 2000 to 2003, including 172 deaths and 502 cases of hostage-taking.

Vicksburg, Mississippi, in 1865 was the *Sultana (above)*, a side-wheel paddle steamship. It was registered to carry 376 persons including her crew, but in what was a near stampede, twenty-three hundred people rushed aboard. A day later, the steam boiler exploded. The soldiers, half-starved for months, were in no condition to swim. The wooden ship became an inferno and most men chose drowning to being burned alive. "The men who were afraid to take to the water could be seen clinging to the sides of the bow of the boat until they were singed off like flies." That day saw the death of 1,547. In an article published in *American Heritage,* one surviving eyewitness recalled: "On looking down and out into the river, I would see men jumping from all parts of the boat into the water until it seemed black with men, their heads bobbing up and down like corks, and then disappearing beneath the turbulent waters, never to appear again."

Another maritime tragedy that rocked the nation happened on a clear summer day in June 1904. The steamboat cruise ship *General Slocum* departed from Lower Manhattan and steamed leisurely up the East River, carrying 1,350 women and children en route to a Long Island picnic grove. By the time the ship reached 83rd Street, a fire had broken out, caused by a match thrown into a barrel of rags. The captain thought it insignificant—a prank of some sort from the immigrant quality of clientele he was forced to carry— and kept on sailing. By the time the 262-foot wooden *Slocum* reached 110th Street, the ship was engulfed in flames. Children, their clothes on fire, searched for their mothers. Many jumped into the river like "flaming torches tossed overboard." Finally, the captain grounded the ship on a rocky ledge, but left the stern in deep water.

Anna Frese, fourteen years old at the time, later testified during the Steam Ship Inspection Service inquest: "My mother told me to jump, but I could not get my hand off. It was baked on the rail with the paint. When I managed to get free I had to be careful to clear the paddle wheel, as people were being caught [in it] and died; so I tried to jump out far enough, and I struck a rock and broke all my front teeth."

The captain, with his hat on fire, beat his way through the crowd of immigrant women and jumped over the rails. The death count reached 1,021.

Cruise ships today may lack specialized medical care, but they do have plenty of life jackets and working lifeboats. After the *Titanic* sideswiped an iceberg, and 1,513 unnecessarily died due to a shortage of rescue boats, followed by the *Atlantic* (made by the builders of the *Titanic*), with 546 dead after hitting rocks near Nova Scotia, authorities forced cruise ship owners to take lifeboat seating capacity seriously.

Life jacket or not, twenty people jump off cruise ships each year and are reported missing, cause of death listed as "unknown." Some are found, but whether they jumped, were pushed, or slipped, only the sea really knows for sure.

ONE HUNDRED FIFTY DIE ON CRUISE SHIPS EACH YEAR FROM MEDICAL EMERGENCIES.
(*See Also:* Drowning)

WHAT HAPPENED TO "DOWN WITH THE SHIP"?

On October 15, 2003, the 310-foot **Staten Island Ferry,** *carrying its afternoon rush-hour capacity of over fifteen-hundred passengers from Manhattan, rammed into the Staten Island pier at full steam. The bow deck, crowded with commuters ready to bolt upon docking, had nowhere to run and no way to avoid the huge wooden pilings that splintered in an avalanche of falling logs and flying debris. Ten were killed, some torn in half and decapitated. Another thirty-four were injured. The assistant captain piloting the ferry ran home and later claimed to have blacked out; in February 2006 he was sentenced to 18 months in jail. That was the first bizarre death toll on the line since 1986, when a man with a samurai sword went berserk during a rush-hour ferry commute and fatally sliced two people and injured nine. Almost a hundred years earlier, a boiler on the ferry exploded as it prepared to leave Manhattan, killing 104.*

Poet and novelist **Hart Crane,** *though good with words, left without a final written note. While returning from a Guggenheim Fellowship in Mexico aboard the ocean liner Orizaba in 1932, he stood up on the rail and said, "Good-bye everybody!" He then jumped off the boat, into the churn of the propellers.*

More than two dozen people have gone missing on cruise ships since 2004.

CULTS A lot of groups are called cults, but few really make the grade. A real cult requires an absolute worship and devotion of a deity or godlike figure. A cult usually has a charismatic leader offering some unique spiel to get people to follow without question, until death. Doomsday, Armageddon, end of the world, the sky is falling—all are common prophecy themes that cult recruiters use to get membership numbers up in a hurry.

MIND CONTROL EXPERIMENT

Jim Jones, the son of a Klansman, declared himself a blended reincarnation of Jesus and Lenin when he started the **People's Temple.** He attracted thousands of followers by promising to lead them into salvation and save them from the impending nuclear holocaust. In 1977 he was forced to move his cult out of San Francisco to Guyana, South America, where he was certain to create a nirvana on earth at Jonestown.

Within a year, the families of cult members were worried and implored Congressman Leo Ryan to go to Guyana in 1978 to free anyone who wished to leave. Officially, he went to investigate alleged human rights abuses perpetrated by Jim Jones against American citizens at Jonestown. Shortly after Ryan arrived, a mob of cult members tried to hack him with machetes. Only slightly injured, Congressman Ryan quickly decided he was ready to leave, taking with him eighteen cult members who wanted to return to the States. Jones sent a brigade of loyal followers to the jungle airstrip. They gunned down Leo Ryan, three journalists, and one of the cult turncoats.

That evening, the reincarnated nut case ordered his followers to drink a purifying elixir—a bathtub filled with grape Kool-Aid, spiked with cyanide and tranquilizers. All nine hundred residents of Jonestown did what they were told; those who didn't were forced to drink or were shot. Infants received an oral dose by syringe. As the mass suicide progressed, ultimately tallying 909 dead, one cult member, who spit out her drink, grabbed a gun from a fallen guard and shot Jim Jones in the head. Two months later, Jones' killer allegedly slit the throats of her three children and then committed suicide. A year later, in 1979,

some other survivors of the People's Temple, Jeanne and Al Mills and their daughter Linda, were to start out on the lecture circuit, speaking about their cult experience, when all three were shot to death in their Berkeley, California, home. The Mills had devised a theory that Jim Jones was linked to the CIA, insinuating that the cult was allowed to flourish as part of a mind control experiment.

FAMILY TREE
David Koresh (né Vernon Howell) *(right)* was a failed rock musician who

studied the work of Jim Jones before he made his move to become the leader of the **Branch Davidians** in 1990, a radical offshoot of the Davidian Seventh-Day Adventists, a Christian sect formed in 1935. Like Jones, Koresh relished the limelight that being a cult leader brought. He, too, played on the doomsday prophecy, demanded unquestioning loyalty from his followers, and also enjoyed the self-declared sexual rights to every follower's wife. In 1993, when four ATF agents went to Koresh's cult compound to ask about the cache of heavy artillery he kept, a cult sniper killed them all. The Davidians refused to surrender and held out for fifty-one days. When the FBI decided to go in, a fierce shoot-out ensued. Koresh set the compound on fire, killing eighty-six cult followers. When the ashes settled, the dead inside the compound had expired from burns, smoke inhalation, suffocation, and self-inflicted gunshot wounds.

*The charismatic black leader of the **Church of Love** was Ben Yahweh (above), born Hulon Mitchell, Jr. He claimed to be a prophet, the "Son of the Son of God" from a lost Israelite tribe, and the only true Jew. He also preached that white people were devils. He sent his all black disciples, numbering over two-thousand strong, out to build a multimillion-dollar empire through prostitution and drugs, extortion, arson, and murder in the Miami area. He and sixteen of his inner circle were convicted in 1992 of killing at least fourteen white people and opposing blacks.*

THE TIDY CULT

Order of the Solar Temple, founded in 1984 by Dr. Luc Jouret *(left)*, was a less military-oriented cult, though no less deadly in the end. As the millennium approached, this apocalyptic cult convinced seventy-four people to commit mass suicide. Unlike most of Jim Jones' or Koresh's followers, the Solar Temple people were educated and from rich families. In a multimillion-dollar San Diego mansion, the cult members, ranging in age from twenty-six to seventy-two, shaved their heads, dressed in black pants, oversized shirts, and brand new black Nikes. They lay on their backs on cots and bunk beds throughout the mansion, their hands at their sides as if they were about to be beamed up, ready (as was posted on the cult's Web site called Heaven's Gate) to "shed their containers." They were, in fact, hoping to catch a ride on the spaceship that was concealed in the tail of comet Hale-Bopp. To die, they were given a choice of either pudding or applesauce, laced with a deadly dose of Phenobarbital. One shot of imported vodka was the chaser offered as their last earthly dessert.

When the bodies were found, the rented mansion was immaculately clean, trash bags taken to the street, toilet bowls disinfected, the lids down. Each dead cult member had a new $5 bill in his pocket and a small black suitcase under his cot. If they did, in fact, arrive safely on the spaceship hidden behind the comet, they did so without their bodies.

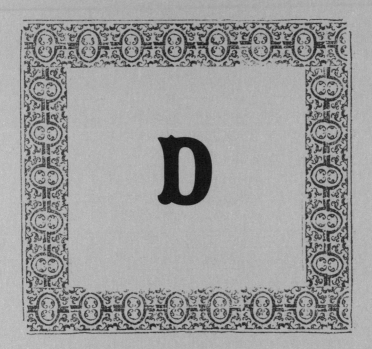

D

DANDY-WALKER SYNDROME

The name of this malady does not reveal how horrible it could be—no parents want to hear that their newborn baby is a Dandy-Walker. The Dandy-Walker syndrome is a malformation of the cerebellum (hindbrain), causing cardiac misshapenness, orthopedic and respiratory problems, as well as urinary abnormalities. Dandy-Walkers usually have large heads with bulging soft spots that make it very easy to damage their brain. If they survive, these babies may have weak neck muscles, poor head control and sporadic, jerky movements when walking. Fifty percent of babies with this disease die at birth, while others have lived up to fifteen to eighteen years with aggressive treatment. Regardless, Doctors Dandy and Walker, who isolated this disease, should have given this sad and serious condition a less jovial name.

Most of the date-rape deaths occurred as a result of drugs, such as GHB, Rohypnol and Ketamine, slipped into drinks: Ninety-two women reported this to be the case in 2002. According to the Justice Department, 883,000 cases of all types of dating assaults have been reported since 1999. Twenty-two percent of all homicides against females between the ages of sixteen and nineteen were committed by a dating partner, or someone they were dating.

12,129 DANDY-WALKER DEATHS SINCE 1965

DATING

When a date goes bad, it can go real bad, very fast. In 2003, one thousand female students at Pennsylvania State University were asked if they had experienced some form of sexual aggression; 50 percent said yes. Twelve percent of these acts were carried out by casual dates and 43 percent by steady dating partners.

ACCORDING TO THE
U.S. DEPARTMENT OF JUSTICE,
APPROXIMATELY THREE
WOMEN ARE MURDERED
BY THEIR BOYFRIENDS
EVERY DAY.

SEX—AND A LOT OF IT— IN THE CITY

Sex among New York City's singles was revealed in the now infamous "Preppie Murder Case" of 1986. Robert Chambers (left), a 6'6", two hundred-pound man admitted to having rough sex in Central Park with Jennifer Levin, which ultimately resulted in the death of the eighteen-year-old, 5'4", 130-pound woman. At Chambers' murder trial his lawyers insinuated that Levin so desperately wanted to have sex with him that he had to kill her to stop her. The two-year trial brought out diaries and videos describing how sex partners in the singles scene were changed as frequently as underwear. Chambers was sentenced to manslaughter and released from prison in 2004.

DEEP FRIED Rising from a depth of nearly ten thousand feet, waters that pass over magma chambers near the earth's core reach super hot temperatures of 400°F. These natural anomalies emerge through the surface as geysers, hot springs, bubbling mud pots, and steaming fumaroles. Yellowstone National Park has more of these geothermal wonders (thirteen hundred) than any other place on earth. Millions of tourists come to observe, and most keep their distance. But since 1870, a total of nineteen just had to get a bit closer—and boiled.

In 1981, a twenty-five-year-old man and a friend went to see the hot springs at Yellowstone. They left their dog in the truck and went for a closer look. But before they knew it, the dog escaped, ran ahead, and jumped into the hot spring. With surface water temperature above the boiling point, the dog began yelping, struggling to return to shore. Bystanders warned him not to go in, but the man felt he had to do something and refused to listen. He took two steps back, made a running leap, and dove headfirst into the boiling cauldron. He swam to the dog and grabbed it, but soon both went under. Only minutes passed before he emerged without the dog. His friend stepped into the water to lift him out, getting second-degree burns

on his feet. When the man was finally pulled from the geyser and took off his shoes, all of the skin on his feet peeled away. As he observed the wiggling skeleton bones of his toes, he said, "That was a stupid thing I did." Near the geyser spring, park rangers later

The U.S. Department of the Interior manages 83.3 million acres of national parks. In 2003, 211 people died in national parks while hiking, swimming, rock climbing, or crashing planes or other flying devices.

picked up two large pieces of skin shaped like human hands. By the time the ambulance arrived to take the man to the hospital, he was blind. He died two days later of third-degree burns.

FATALITIES FROM SCALDING SINCE 1965:

47,982

GOOD INTENTIONS, BAD TIMING

One couple went to Mount Rainier National Park in November 2001 to celebrate their first wedding anniversary, wishing to reconfirm their vows amid the natural Northwest splendor. Before they made it a mile into the wilderness preserve, a sudden gust of wind caused a huge hemlock tree to break loose. The tree dropped seventy-five feet off a cliff, landing directly atop the couple's SUV, instantly making the woman a widow.

More than 250 people have died in Yellowstone from hot springs, bears, bison, avalanches, exposure, and forest fires. *

DENTAL SCHOOL Out of twenty-nine thousand people a year who say "This job is killing me," nearly ten thousand really mean it and commit suicide. Of course, all kinds of people have taken their own life, affecting surviving family members in some ways more troubling than death by other causes, yet it's even more puzzling if the suicide appeared contented, successful, or, at least, employed. Experts say that job stress has increased to proportions not normally intended for the human psyche to handle. The average American professional usually works sixty hours a week and spends less than four days a year on vacation, completely unplugged. As the economy shifts and businesses downsize, a greater number of the employees spared the cut have to do that much more. In 2005, suicides numbered 31,655; there were more than one hundred thousand suicide attempts in addition to that.

* **Jim Bridger** was a mountain man who guided several expeditions to the Rocky Mountains area and discovered the Great Salt Lake in Utah. He was the first European to reach what is now Yellowstone Park and personally reported to President Ulysses S. Grant the uniqueness of that place, leading Grant to establish the land as the country's first national park in 1872. In his later years, Bridger became blind and rode around his Missouri farm on an old horse guided by his dog, Lassie. In 1881, at age seventy-seven, Bridger got lost and Lassie ran back to the farm to bring rescuers to where Bridger was holed up. Once rescued, Bridger was unable to shake a bad cold and died of pneumonia shortly after.

Pharmaceutical self-poisoning is the most preferred method of suicide by men and women in healthcare professions. Men in other occupations prefer guns, and women often use sharp instruments and liquid poison to commit suicide. Prior to 1950, the most preferred means to end one's life was the consumption of gasoline.

BEST JOB/WORST JOB

The data on which profession is most "dangerous" is shoddy, in part because suicides are often undisclosed. Most studies focus on a particular race, sex, or region; however, certain jobs do show up in numerous reports. Contrary to popular belief, dentists don't hold the top spot in professional suicides. The white male doctor, aged twenty-four to thirty-five, currently takes the lead. For blacks, jobs in protective service occupations such as security, crossing guards, and police top that list of suicide professions. For females, painters, sculptors, craft artists, and artist printmakers have the most successful suicide rates, followed by nurses.

On the West Coast, dentists have the second highest suicide rate, topped only by sheepherders and wool workers in the state of Washington. Dentists do it seven times more than the average worker. Researcher Steven Stack stated: "Dentists suffer from relatively low status within the medical profession and have strained relationships with their clients—few people enjoy going to the dentist." Sheepherders might be at risk because they have more than ample time on their hands and usually work alone. One researcher suggested that depression among sheepherders is due to loneliness and too much one-way conversation with their flock.

For nonprofessionals, reasons for suicide seem to be stress related, most often the result of a combination of boredom, repetition, and low self-esteem. The top suicides in the trades are:

1. **Painters/decorators**
   The preferred suicide method of painters is the ingestion of corrosive materials. This causes immediate burning in the mouth and throat, followed by intense stomach pain. Vomiting ensues, and an incredible thirst persists until the airways are choked closed, usually within a few hours.

2. **Carpenters**
3. **Retail sales assistants**
4. **Landscape workers**

5. Delivery drivers

In August 2001, one pizza delivery man had enough of "thirty minutes or free." He fastened a three-foot rod to the dashboard above the steering wheel of his car, intending to impale himself with it when he crashed into a utility pole. The metal rod missed the man's throat by inches, but the impact threw him against the steering wheel with enough force to kill him.

6. Security and law enforcement occupations
7. Welfare workers
8. Cleaners, window washers, road sweepers
9. Garage proprietors
10. Waitresses

The waitress category, like many aspects about suicide, is misleading. It is not the long-term food service worker who kills herself but usually the ones longing to break into another field, like the performing arts. The classic waitress demise belongs to **Lillian Millicent Entwistle** *(right)*, who had done some acting in New York before heading out to Hollywood. At first, she saw the Hollywood sign high on the hill as a symbol of hope, but after she failed to break into movies and seemed stuck in a waitress job, the sign became an unbearable, larger-than-life reminder of her rejection. In 1932, she scaled the fifty-foot letter *H* and committed suicide by plunging into the dark night below.

*Another actress who feared for her job and a return to a less-glamorous life was **Chris Chubbock**, a news anchor for Florida TV station WXLT-TV. On July 15, 1974 at 9:38 A.M. on her show* Suncoast Digest *she looked into the camera and said, "And now, in keeping with Channel 40's policy of always bringing you the latest in blood and guts, in living color, you're about to see another first—an attempted suicide." She pulled out a .38 from her handbag and shot herself in the head. According to the* Sarasota Herald Tribune, *the live news broadcast cut to commercial.*

OVER FIVE MILLION PEOPLE IN AMERICA HAVE ATTEMPTED SUICIDE AT ONE TIME IN THEIR LIVES.

DENTED CANS People who eat food from jars with loose lids, swollen or dented cans, or food left in opened cans can get food poisoning from the bacteria **botulism**. According to the U.S. Health Department Botulism Fact Sheet: "Classic symptoms of botulism include double vision, blurred vision, drooping eyelids, slurred speech, difficulty swallowing, dry mouth, and muscle weakness." Infants with botulism usually are constipated, appear lethargic, feed poorly, and have a weak cry and poor muscle tone. If left untreated, death is due to eventual respiratory failure. Sixteen infants die each year from "infant botulism" when fed pure honey.

SINCE 1975 THERE HAVE BEEN 24,811 BOTULISM FATALITIES OF INFANTS AND ADULTS.

DENTURES Every night, a fifty-four-year-old bus driver would rush through his route in order to catch a few winks in the back of his bus before he went home. He'd throw his head over the arm rest and snore up a storm. On September 28, 1992, his dentures dislodged while he slept, got caught in his throat, and gagged him to death. He had found such a good place to hide the bus, there was no one around to help.

DENTURE-OBSTRUCTION DEATHS, INCLUDING INCIDENTS DURING SURGERY SINCE 1965: 11,556

DILDO Dildo is from the Italian word *diletto,* meaning delight. In Texas, Georgia, Louisiana, Mississippi, Kansas, Colorado, and Alabama there are laws that make posession of "dildos, artificial vaginas, or any device designed or marketed as useful primarily for the stimulation of human genital organs" illegal; they can be bought in these states for educational purposes only. There are one thousand two hundred accidents reported annually in emergency rooms for treatment of conditions caused by misuse of mechanical dildos. Although dildos with flanged-collar bases are now decreasing accidents, as they prevent the devices from making deeper and dangerous penetration, misuse is reportedly painful. The Department of Justice lists no murders from dildos; however, one female, driving alone, was killed in a car crash on I-95 near Washington, D.C., in 2002, apparently distracted while using one while driving home. A small, lipstick-size stimulator, known as the "Pocket Rocket" was discovered in her vagina during autopsy, still engaged.

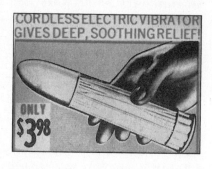

DOMESTIC VIOLENCE Each year four thousand seven hundred women are murdered. Six out of ten of these murders are motivated by love gone bad, at the hands of husband, ex-husband, boyfriend, relative, or acquaintance. Only 8 percent are killed by strangers.

The end of a relationship is the most harmful period. Women separated from their husbands are three times more likely than divorced women to get killed, and at twenty-five times greater risk than married women.

LOVE MISSING THE MARK
William Burroughs made his name as the renegade man of letters. He was the vagabond gentleman junkie, an anti-authoritarian who wrote the spooky novel Naked Lunch. *Burroughs tried to shoot an apple off the head of his second wife during a William Tell stunt reenactment in 1951. The bullet missed the apple and killed her.*

COPYRIGHT, 1877.   BY G.W. COOLIDGE.

The Tale of a Wedded Life.

SCENE V. MARRIED · HOME A LITTLE HELL.

HUSBAND-TO-WIFE HOMICIDES
SINCE 1990: 34,531

HOME DECORATING
Spouses predominately choose the home as the desired location to commit murder. Forty-nine percent of men prefer the bedroom, 35 percent the living room.

Women kill mostly in the kitchen, accounting for 91 percent of domestic homicide incidents.

DRINKING WATER In January 2000, a twenty-year-old army trainee guzzled twelve quarts of water, trying to make a clean urine specimen for a drug test. Shortly thereafter she endured fecal abandon, lost consciousness, and became confused; she died from swelling in the brain and lungs as a result of low blood sodium.

In March 2001, a nineteen-year-old Marine died from drinking too much water during a twenty-six-mile hike. Toward the end, he began vomiting and looked overly tired. Sent to the hospital, he went into a coma, developed brain swelling, and died the next day. In 1983, a forty-nine-year-old man, who feared that all food and medicine were poison to his body, believed that only pure spring water could flush it all out, and drank sixty-

There are about twenty cases in medical literature in which people were literally allergic to water. A twenty-year-old Vietnamese man living in California had the syndrome. Since the age of ten, if a drop of tap or seawater touched his skin, his skin would break out in hives, or white welts. From contact with water of any kind he developed a pounding headache and suffered severe respiratory distress. Getting caught in a rain shower was catastrophic, and proved fatal when he was caught in a thunderstorm in 1987.

four eight-ounce glasses of water per day. He eventually went into a coma and died of water on the brain, or "water intoxication."

DR. **DEATH** In botany, a Death Angel is a brilliantly white mushroom that looks picture perfect to eat. But under its white cap conceals spores of extreme poison and kills forty-two unsuspecting nibblers each year. In medicine, it's no less puzzling when a doctor hiding under a white lab coat is discovered to harbor evil intentions—more often than not, going undetected for years.

Dr. H. H. Holmes, real name Herman Mudgett, was kicked out of medical school but soon found a niche as a pharmacist, and later a drug tycoon. With his fortune he built a one hundred-room mansion with trap doors, false walls, and secret chambers. During the Chicago World's Fair in 1893, he rented rooms to visitors and then killed most of them, experimenting on their corpses. He said he killed 133, but twenty-seven bodies, mostly children, were found buried in his house. He preferred to kill by placing his victims in confinement until they starved to death. On Thursday, May 7, 1896, at 10:25 A.M., H. H. Holmes was hanged. They buried him face down, as the newspapers put it at the time, "hoping he would go straight to hell."

Dr. Frank Sweeney was a brilliant but twisted surgeon, believed to be the Cleveland Torso Killer. Sweeney dissected twelve vagrants in 1935 and left the bodies without heads all over town. Unique in serial killer cases, Sweeney killed both men and women by dissecting the limbs and heads with superior surgical skills. Although never arrested, once FBI agent Elliot Ness began an investigation, Sweeney checked himself into a mental institution. The crimes stopped soon after.

Genene Jones *(right)* was a twenty-seven-year-old vocational nurse who worked with terminally ill children. Traveling throughout Texas in 1984, she injected a heart medication, digoxin, into ailing infants, wanting to bring the children to the edge of death and back so she could be claimed their savior. At least forty-six didn't make it. She is in prison and eligible for parole in 2009.

Terri Rachals was a twenty-three-year-old intensive care nurse in Albany, Georgia, who allegedly killed twenty elderly patients with potassium chloride, which mimiced the effects of cardiac arrest. Newspapers in 1986 called her the "Murderess of the Century." She was sentenced to seventeen years in 1984.

Before his arrest in April 1987, **Dr. Donald Harvey** *(page 103, top)* killed at least twenty-three patients by injecting them with various lethal substances, including arsenic, cyanide, and petroleum-based cleanser. Some victims were chosen for occult ceremonies on his homemade altar. He was sentenced to life in prison.

Orville Lynn Majors, LPN, was on the nursing staff at an Indiana hospital. In only twenty-two months, 147 people died while he was on duty. He had injected epinephrine and potassium chloride to kill quickly and confuse the cause of death. In 1999, Majors was sentenced to life in prison.

Dr. Larry Ford *(center)* was a mild-mannered gynecologist in Irvine, California, who kept files on his female patients, complete with photos, personal effects, and medical records, under the floorboards of his house. He also had guns, ammunition, and explosives buried in his yard. In the refrigerator there were vials of botulinum, salmonella, and typhus. Ford dated many of the women in his files, and threatened to "ruin their lives" if any called off the affair; two surviving women came down with mysterious and serious neurological conditions that required brain surgery. How many people he killed is unknown. In 2001 he committed suicide shortly before his arrest for hiring a hit man to kill his business partner. There were indications the gynecologist had connections to the army's biowarfare program and to the CIA.

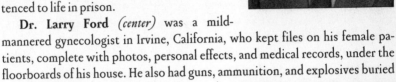

On January 12, 2004, **Dr. Harold Shipman** *(below)* hung himself in jail. In 2000 he had been convicted of murder and went from being a respected doctor to a known serial killer, responsible for the premature deaths of at least 215 patients in his care. Between 1975 and 1998, 887 of his patients died: 394 from natural causes, 172 from unknown causes, while the rest—215—were injected with pharmaceutical heroin. A onetime convicted drug addict himself, Shipman believed that allowing the terminally ill to die with one last tremendous heroin rush would be a painless and blissful way to end their suffering. He injected twelve thousand milligrams of dope into their veins, enough to kill three hundred of the hardest-core junkies with a single pop. Some observers surmised he turned from healing doctor to chief executioner because he had witnessed his mother dying slowly and painfully of

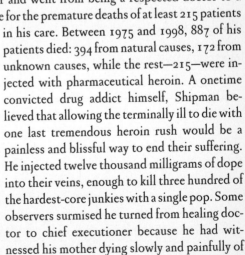

cancer. Nevertheless, he put to death not only terminally ill patients but others sufficiently ungrateful for his efforts as well as those who simply complained a lot.

DROWNING After car crashes, drowning is second on the list of injury-related fatalities for children under fifteen. Children under the age of one drown in buckets, tubs, and toilets. Kids, ages one to five, usually drown in swimming pools. Forty-two percent of all drowning deaths occur to people between the ages of fifteen and twenty-four in rivers and lakes. Nearly 50 percent of all adolescent and adult drowning deaths are alcohol related and usually occur during water recreation activities.

Other drowning deaths are unexplained. Take the case of actress **Natalie Wood** *(right)* who died during a trip aboard her yacht *Splendor* on Thanksgiving Day in 1981. She was last seen shortly after dinner by her husband Robert Wagner and actor Christopher Walken. The next morning, the yacht's life raft was found a mile away; Natalie Wood, dressed in a nightgown and down jacket was found floating dead beside it. Her death is still a mystery.

Media tycoon **Robert Maxwell** had a similar still-baffling sea demise. He was last seen alive on his yacht, *Lady Ghislaine,* at four o'clock in the morning in November 1991. The next day his ship sailed into port without him. Eventually, his naked body was found twenty miles away. Investigators deemed the cause of Maxwell's death as accidental or suicide, although the actual circumstances are still unknown.

Drinking played a part in Beach Boy musician Dennis Wilson's death in 1983. While diving from his fifty-two-foot yacht to retrieve a framed photo of his ex-wife he had just thrown overboard, he apparently suffered fatigue and drowned. Before he was buried at sea a few days later, an autopsy confirmed that he had been seriously intoxicated.

English romantic poet Percy Bysshe Shelley drowned while sailing in Italy in 1822. American poet Sara Teasdale, known for the book Rivers to the Sea, *drowned herself at age forty-eight in 1933. Virginia Woolf, a prolific author and feminist, filled her pockets with stones and drowned herself in a river at age fifty-nine in 1941.*

It doesn't take long to drown: A child can drown in twenty seconds and an adult can drown in sixty seconds. The most distinctive characteristic of drowning is the white foam that forms when mucus in the body mixes with water. This foam builds up in the mouth and windpipe, preventing air from entering.

ANNUAL U.S. DROWNING
FATALITIES: 12,756, NEARLY HALF
BETWEEN THE AGES OF
ONE AND FOUR

DUELING For the first two hundred years of American history, dueling was as common as apple pie. The tradition of two men settling their differences in a fight to the finish with sword or gun was passed on from primitive times. In the Middle Ages it was called "judicial combat." Sometimes two leaders would fight, or else send their best man as their replacement to determine who was "right," at first viewed as a less costly means than warfare. Soon, nobleman and commoner alike took up the practice, until there was a killing nearly every day. Eventually, to stem this outbreak of open murder, dueling gradually became acceptable only for the elite. If a commoner was found dueling, dead, alive, or slightly grazed, both winner and loser would be hanged. By 1777 an official code of dueling was published, outlining twenty-six rules of properly insulting, challenging, and squaring off to die. According to the rules of conduct, when a gentleman was insulted by another it was possible to offer an apology or receive lashes by the insulting aristocrat's own cane. But if a gentleman struck another, a duel must be fought. Refusal was an act of cowardice, followed by banishment from any honorable position in society. The probability of partaking in a duel was so great that dueling pistols, elaborately engraved weapons kept in lush, velvet-lined cases, became standard items in a man's haberdashery. According to Lawrence Kestenbaum's *Political Graveyard,* **seventeen politicians have died in duels.**

The most famous was the fatal duel between Founding Fathers Alexander Hamilton and Aaron Burr in 1804. Hamilton insulted Burr at a private party, offering, as historian Thomas Fleming noted, a "despicable opinion" about Burr's personal life. They had been political rivals for years, so when Thomas Jefferson put Burr on his ticket as vice president, Hamilton's verbal slight was seen as a political move. Hamilton's "opinion" could have been any minor insult. In the day,

*In 1845, at age seventy-eight, **Andrew Jackson** died of "consumption and dropsy from old wounds." Jackson had a bullet from another duel lodged in his chest for thirty-nine years.*

words that could lead to death included calling another gentleman a fornicator, madman, bastard, or a poltroon, a.k.a. coward. Hamilton, although successful in fourteen previous duels, died from Burr's gun. He was forty-one; Burr lived to age eighty-nine.

In reality, the chance of dying in a pistol duel was relatively slight. The guns often misfired and required a tremendous skill in accuracy to hit a man at forty paces. Most received flesh wounds and retained their honor.

Politicians found that forcing an opponent to a duel was a quick way to move up in the polls. Many times it worked.

The average gentleman had to withstand the stress of at least five duels during a lifetime. Even Abraham Lincoln once found himself in a duel, with Illinois auditor James Shields, after calling Shields "a fool, a liar, and smelly to boot." Lincoln chose a saber as the weapon, in the hope that his long arms would provide the advantage. He showed up on the riverbank, whacking at tree branches in preparation, but the duel never came to pass. Shields accepted the apology Lincoln offered.

The first law banning dueling and forbidding accepting a challenge to a duel was passed in 1838 in the District of Columbia. This forced politicians to go to Maryland to shoot each other. By 1858, twelve states had banned dueling, but it wasn't until the 1890s that the craze finally died down. When the twentieth century arrived, a man's honor came from making money; most could care less about verbal insults. If they did, lawyers and libel suits instead of pistols were used to uphold a person's good name. But as much as some believe that dueling is dead, every night in some bar across America there's a challenge to "take it outside" and settle the score the old-fashioned way. (*See Also:* Cell Phone Etiquette)

Political newcomer James Jackson, at age twenty-three, challenged the lieutenant governor of Georgia to a duel in 1780 and killed him. Jackson went on to become governor himself, as well as a congressman and senator.

Edgar Allan Poe (below) *challenged a newspaper editor to a duel after a bad review. Poe showed up but was too drunk to shoot.*

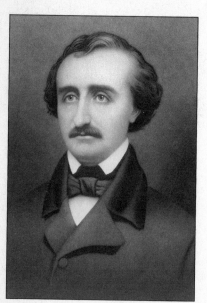

ONE WAY TO IMPRESS A WOMAN

The last formal duel occurred in 1959, when Barney Silva, a Los Angeles restaurant owner, and jazz musician Jack Sorin, could not agree about either's status with the same woman, so they resolved to settle it like men. The two met in Silva's living room, put their backs together, and marched off ten paces before firing at one another. Both died.

BETWEEN 1700 AND 1959,
FORTY THOUSAND PEOPLE DIED
IN DUELS.

DWARFISM Dwarfism is triggered by a genetic condition, resulting in short stature and disproportionate growth of the skeleton. According to Little People of America Inc., an organization with five thousand members (open to persons 4'10" or less in height) four hundred severely dwarfed children are born each year from parents of average height. Although any couple can have a child with dwarfism, a dwarf couple has an 80 percent chance of having an offspring with similar conditions. Symptoms that accompany dwarfism vary, but many have additional cardiac and respiratory ailments that dramatically shorten their lifespan. Others have internal organs that are abnormal or too small, making long-term survival difficult.

"SHE'S NOT ONLY MERELY DEAD. SHE'S REALLY MOST SINCERELY DEAD."
One hundred twenty-four little people appeared in the Wizard of Oz *(1939) as munchkins. The oldest surviving munchkin is actor Meinhardt Raabe. He played the coroner and celebrated his ninetieth birthday in 2005.*

MOST FAMOUS
General Tom Thumb (Charles Sherwood Stratton) *(right)* was born to normal-size parents in 1838. Tom was twenty-five inches and weighed fifteen pounds at eleven years old when P. T. Barnum put him in the circus, billed as a "General from England." Tom Thumb became a celebrity and traveled around the world, meeting leaders and royalty, including President Abraham Lincoln and Britain's Queen Victoria and Prince Albert. When Tom Thumb got married, he and his tiny bride, Livinia Warren, stood atop a grand piano to welcome two thousand guests. Tom Thumb died of a stroke at age forty-five on July 15, 1883. Over ten thousand people attended his funeral.

LITTLEST LITTLE PERSON
Lucia Zarate *(page 108, top)* was the smallest woman ever. She weighed only eight ounces and was seven inches long when she was born in 1863. She grew into an adult who measured twenty inches and tipped the scales at less than five

pounds. Dressed up in Victorian frills, Lucia was easily mistaken for a porcelain doll when she sat on an adult's lap. She was the highest paid sideshow attraction of her time, earning $20 an hour when twenty dollars was the average monthly wage. But despite the care she received to protect her fragile existence, she met her end while traveling on a train that stalled during a blizzard in the Rocky Mountains in 1890. There was no heat, and no matter how many quilts were draped over her, her small body couldn't stay warm. She stiffened like a toy statue and froze to death.

ISLAND OF HOBBITS

In 2004 archaeologists made a breathtaking discovery when they unearthed the remains of a hobbit-size culture that once thrived on the Island of Flores, Indonesia, populated by giant lizards and miniature elephants. Bones dating from ninety-five thousand to twelve thousand years ago indicate the existence of a sophisticated society of people no taller than three feet. Scientists are uncertain why they remained marooned on their secluded paradise for eons while our other, taller ancestors colonized the rest of the planet. What seems certain was the cause of their extinction: A volcano on the island erupted exactly twelve thousand years ago.

EARTHQUAKES Earthquakes are caused by shifting rocks and underground pressure and heat, which hasn't subsided since the planet was formed. Two hundred million years ago all the continents were joined in a huge landmass scientists call Pangaea. Earthquakes caused the continents to move apart to where they are today and, some say, until Pangaea is re-formed again, quakes will continue to rock the earth.

Thirty-nine U.S. states have ongoing earthquake activity. The USGS locates about twenty thousand earthquakes each year—about fifty per day. The earliest record of American earthquakes were stories Native Americans passed on to settlers, including one tale of a 1568 earthquake in the Connecticut area. The Pilgrims recorded a tremor occurring in 1638.

In 2002, a 5.2 earthquake hit the Ohio-Pennsylvania border and was felt in Illinois, Indiana, Michigan, New Jersey, New York, and southern Ontario, Canada, killing only one person when a chimney collasped. The most powerful earthquake ever recorded anywhere on the planet occurred in Chile in 1960, registering a 9.5. The second largest earthquake occurred in Alaska (9.2) in 1964, killing 130 people.

EARTHQUAKE FATALITIES INCREASING

According to seismic activity records kept by the U.S. Geological Survey (USGS), there have been over fifty major earthquakes between 2001 and 2005 that registered over 7 on the Richter Scale, which measures seismic waves and earthquake intensity. Although the number of earthquakes remains the same over the last twenty years, more people are dying with each one. Over two hundred fifty thousand deaths can be attributed to earthquakes during this study period. The most recent occurred on October 8, 2005, known as the northern Pakistan earthquake, and claimed 51,300 lives.

Earthquakes occurring in oceans create odd and unpredictable anomalies. **Tsunami,** the Japanese word for harbor wave, is a giant wave caused by underwater earthquakes. The worst was in 1946, when an earthquake in Alaska's Aleutian Islands sent a tsunami barreling to Hawaii, twenty-three hundred miles away. A half hour before it struck, people in the village of Hilo Bay thought that it was their lucky day. The water in the bay had miraculously receded more than two hundred feet along the flats, exposing ocean bottom never before seen. People grabbed baskets to harvest the multitude of fish flopping about. Then there was a roar: a wall of water 115 feet high was moving at 150 mph toward them. People raced back to the town like a scene from a Godzilla movie; 159 people were killed.

Another tsunami, which also originated from the Alaskan region in 1964, with a wave measuring 230 feet high, ultimately killed another 123. The 2004 Indian Ocean tsunami caused mass destruction of biblical proportions, killing over two hundred thousand. It is the fifth worst natural disaster, after the 1900 Galveston Hurricane, the San Francisco earthquake, the 1889 Johnson flood when twenty-two hundred died, and Hurricane Katrina in 2005. (See Also: Hurricanes)

The most destructive U.S. earthquake occurred on a cool spring morning on April 15, 1906, in San Francisco. The initial tremor killed only a few hundred but the resulting mayhem claimed many more. Nearly every structure in the city was made of wood, and fires soon erupted, causing building after building to burst into flames. People flooded the streets, scrambling desperately to save their possessions. Escape was blocked by people dragging steamer trunks, dining room tables, bedroom sets, and even grand pianos amid the flying embers and tumbling debris. Over three thousand died.

EATING LEAD Poverty brings with it irregular medical care and poor sanitary conditions in substandard housing areas. The risk of lead poisoning is primarily determined by the environmental conditions of the home; paint chips and lead dust from deteriorating paint are the most common causes of lead exposure in low-income housing units, particularly those built prior to 1946. Lead poisoning acts slowly, but has been determined to cause impaired reasoning and violent behavior. People of all ages can get lead poisoning, but children's smaller bodies absorb more lead than adults bodies do, and do more harm to children during developmental stages of growth. Living in substandard housing, 890,000 preschoolers in urban areas, especially in the Northeast and the

In 1990, a two-year-old Chicago girl was brought to a hospital for a low-grade fever and vomiting. She was discharged with prescriptions for antibiotics. However, her vomiting worsened, and she was brought back the same day. Five hours later she became unresponsive and lapsed into a coma. She died three days later. It was discovered that the girl's family had recently moved into an apartment constructed before 1920. A wall in the bedroom had numerous holes from which the girl had been seen dislodging and chewing on plaster.

Midwest, continue to be exposed to lead poisoning and have elevated blood lead levels.

In September 1999, a twenty-eight-month-old Wisconsin boy was brought to a hospital after four days of lethargy and reduced appetite. Although the child had no medical problems, his parents, unaware of the sources of lead poisoning, finally confided to the doctors that the child had been known to eat flaking paint. The boy developed seizures, became comatose, and died twenty-six hours later.

An advertisement in 1927: "There is no cause for worry when fingerprint smudges or dirt spots appear on a wall painted with Dutch Boy white lead . . . painted walls are sanitary, cheerful and bright."

TOTAL NUMBER OF DEATHS FROM LEAD POISONING
SINCE 1930: 49,212

EBOLA VIRUS One morning in 1967 a German monkey keeper who provided animals for scientific research had a slight headache and sensed a minor queasiness in his stomach. He began to bleed from every orifice, from his eyes, ears, nose, and sphincter. With a powerful burst of projectile vomit, ground-up parts of his internal organs, stomach, liver, and lungs flung fifteen feet across the room. No wonder Ebola virus is one of the most feared pathogens on earth; the guy had literally imploded. Called hemorrhagic fever, it's 95 percent fatal in humans, monkeys, gorillas, and chimpanzees. The virus was

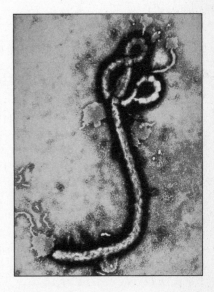

formally identified in 1976 when 430 people died in this most grotesque manner throughout villages along the banks of the Ebola River in the Republic of the Congo (formerly called Zaire). The virus had spread by the reuse of hypodermic needles, a common practice in Third World countries. The rapidity of its transmission and its startlingly quick incubation period of two days, with nearly zero signs of symptoms, made scientists around the world take notice. The virus had the potential to wipe out the entire human race within ninety days, and rapid containment was essential as the disease spread primarily through contact with body fluids. The infected dead could not be washed or handled; even the half dead had to be incinerated quickly.

MONKEY BUSINESS
Scientists in Italy, England, Switzerland, and the United States have been infected attempting to find cures for this resistant, snakelike virus. In 1989, in a

Maryland suburb, just footsteps from the White House, the United States had its closest call with mass infection. Four researchers became infected from doing research in a "monkey house" facility. Virus control was slow at first, until authorities set the timer: containment or "sanitary eliminination" for all involved. Luckily, the virus was stopped with only moments to spare. In 2000, new strains of Ebola were discovered—or, as some believe, manufactured. This new and improved Ebola virus is airborne and can spread as easily as the common cold. Millions could be infected with one sneeze.

GROUNDHOG DAY CANCELED

In June 2004, four people died in Wisconsin when they contracted the deadly **Monkeypox.** *This viral disease is similar to smallpox and is normally only transmitted by monkeys. However, it is believed that a Gambian rat, a rodent indigenous to African countries, escaped from a pet store and infected large portions of the prairie dog population, spreading Monkeypox quickly across the plains. Another six people in Illinois were fatally stricken with the pox in July 2004.*

SINCE 1976, ONE THOUSAND PEOPLE HAVE DIED OF EBOLA.

ECCENTRICS There were two formerly successful brothers in New York City, Homer, an engineer, and Langley Collyer *(below),* a lawyer/inventor, who decided that the quality of life outside of their brownstone was unacceptable. They became recluses in the heart of a bustling city, enjoying the company of only each other. In 1947, the police were called in to investigate the source of a horrible stench that emanated from their house and permeated the neighborhood. On March 21, when no one answered their knocks, the police kicked the door in. They found old newspapers piled to the ceiling, boxes, crates, and other contraptions from Langley's inventions in every room, leaving only small narrow passages to navigate. The stairs to the second floor were completely blocked off and required ladder access. The police found the body

of Homer Collyer, sitting on a chair with an empty cup in his hand, dead for only about ten hours. Years before, Homer had gone blind and was virtually paralyzed with arthritis. He had relied on brother Langley for nourishment and care. Langley, fearing thieves would one day want to get at his treasure trove of collected junk, had constructed elaborate booby traps strung from the ceiling. Langley's body was discovered under a huge mound of his booby trapped trash several weeks later; he had been dead for over a month. Homer had starved to death waiting for Langley to bring him some juice. Besides the bodies of the brothers, 120 tons of garbage was removed from the brownstone.

DEATHS OF SHUT-INS, RECLUSES, ANTHROPOPHOBICS, AND PERSONS WITH MIXED PERSONALITY DISORDER (MPD) SINCE 1950: 131,863

EJECTION The government has spent a tremendous amount on research to determine whether it's better to be ejected from a vehicle during an accident. Your tax dollars have helped discern that it is best to remain inside the car as much as possible. Since 1991, over 110,000 people have died in rollover crashes while driving sport utility vehicles.

Each year more than seven thousand people aged sixty-five years or older die in motor vehicle crashes; this number includes twice as many men than women.

ONE WAY TO CALL OFF AN ENGAGEMENT
On September 14, 2004, a Green Bay, Wisconsin, man threw his fiancée's eight-month-old daughter out of a car as he fled police. The girl, strapped to her car seat, was unhurt. The twenty-three-year-old man then continued to take police on a dramatic highway chase in his fiancée's car. He met a fatal end when the car crashed into an occupied patrol car and flipped over. In the rollover he was ejected and pinned under the vehicle. Later contacted, the woman reported her baby daughter doing fine, but was understandably upset about the money she wasted on a wedding dress.

Researchers determined one is 1.44 times more likely to be ejected from an SUV than a car, and fifteen times more likely to become airborne when not wearing a seat belt; half of all the annual auto crash deaths occur to the unbuckled. For every year of increased age, one is that much more likely to experience an ejection. This means that an eighty-nine-year-old who has been driving for seventy-one years has a 71 percent greater chance of going out that way.

IN 2002, OVER 9,500 PEOPLE WERE EJECTED DURING ROLLOVERS.

ELECTRIC KNIFE An elderly Utah man died of complications from an outpatient surgery performed near his anus. The man's backside area was prepped with antiseptic ointment that contained alcohol and other flammable substances. While the doctor was in the middle of removing a particularly difficult boil with an electric knife, the man passed a prolonged clap of gas. The combination caused a minor fire on the man's buttocks and genitals. Although the flames were promptly extinguished, infection set in, and the man, already in questionable health, passed away.

There are 7 million unnecessary outpatient surgery procedures performed in the United States each year, and a 17 percent chance something will go fatally wrong.

ACCIDENTAL DEATH CAUSED BY PHYSICIANS IN 2003: 120,000

DEATH BY ELECTRIC KNIFE: 1

ELECTROCUTION In 1881, Dr. Albert Southwick, a dentist and former steamboat engineer in Buffalo, New York, wrote a letter to Thomas Edison, describing how he witnessed a drunk man accidentally touch the terminals of an electric generator and die. When Edison needed ammunition to prove how much safer his DC (direct current) was compared with rival George Westinghouse's AC (alternating current), he recalled Dr. Southwick. A lot of money weighed in the choice of how electricity was going to be delivered to homes and businesses, whether it would be through an alternating current that varied cyclically in magnitude and direction, or direct

The first man to be executed in the electric chair was William Kemmler, on August 6, 1890, at Auburn State Prison in New York. The convicted murderer didn't die until eight full minutes after the switch was pulled. Since then, the method has been slightly improved. Now, two thousand AC volts are sent through three electrodes placed on the head in a tight-fitting cap, two are placed around the ankles, and two more at the wrists. The electrodes are attached to a saline solution-moistened sponge, so the skin won't burst into flames, and allow the current to disperse throughout the body equally.

current, where the direction of the current stayed constant. In an attempt to persuade in favor of his invention, Edison held public experiments in which horses, dogs, cows, and even one Coney Island elephant were electrocuted to death before a cheering crowd using Westinghouse's AC current. His DC current barely stunned the animals. To further his point, Edison hired inventor Harold P. Brown to design an electric chair to demonstrate how swiftly AC killed, reasoning that the public would choose his safer mode of electricity transfer after witnessing how lethal AC could be. After all Edison's efforts, Dr. Southwick was so impressed by Edison's AC demonstrations that he lobbied his friend, New York State senator David McMillan, to bring the electric chair issue to the state legislature, which eventually approved it as a tool for execution.

In 1999, a woman moved into her brand-new home in an Atlanta suburb. On the first night she reached up to change a bulb, unaware that the light fixture had been incorrectly wired; its polarity was reversed. She unintentionally touched the metal base of the bulb while it was in contact with the socket. She was promptly jolted across the room and later died in the hospital.

GO SOLAR

Today, the main source of electricity comes into American homes as alternating current since it is more cost-effective than DC current for long distance transmission. Installation and servicing of these lines kills sixty-six construction workers per year. In the last eight years, more than three hundred homeowners have died when attempting to install a TV antenna when it came in contact with an AC power line.

**FRAYED WIRES AND DAMAGED OUTLETS
CAUSED 411 DEATHS IN 2005.**

ELECTRONIC AIR FRESHENERS As Americans now spend 90 percent of their time indoors, there is a huge desire to create pleasant-smelling environments. In their quest for inspiring aromas Americans purchased 1 billion air fresheners in 2005. The problem, however, is that it's not actual pine forest, potpourri, or fresh-cut flowers one inhales, but methylene chloride and formaldehyde. A long recipe of chemicals most often found on the carcinogenic most wanted list, including this chemical concoction, produces tiny freshener molecules that are not easily exhaled, stick to hair follicles, and eventually enter the lungs. The average person breathes in about two heaping tablespoons of these "freshening" airborne particles each day. Air freshener gunk in the lungs captures this regularly inhaled dust, turning this trapped combination into lung tumors.

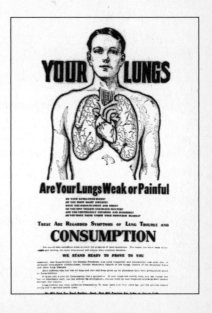

Many people worry about the outside polluted air coming into the home, so they purchase electronic air-filtering machines, which claim to ionize the air by emitting ozone. When the EPA conducted tests on the best-selling models it was discovered that the ozone-zapped air reached *higher* levels of pollution than before ionization, creating indoor vistas similar to

Indoor air is generally two to five times more polluted than that of the outdoors, but it can easily become a hundred times more polluted with the use of certain electronic air fresheners.

what could be inhaled in an urban area on a smoggy summer day. The indoor atmosphere of excessive ozone creates a powerful oxidizing environment, which sucks dry the body's antioxidants, such as vitamins C and E. The ozone-generating air fresheners are especially bad in a small bedroom with the door closed. Long-term exposure to ozone reduces lung capacity and aids development of asthmatic diseases.

In addition to cancer and asthma-related diseases, electronic air fresheners have caused 1,823 serious injuries and two hundred deaths since 1998. Forty-five cases of amputation, burns, scaldings, poisonings, body penetrations, and drowning were associated with these products.

ELECTRONIC PETS It's the occasional obsessed pet owner that drives with their dogs on their laps, paws to the steering wheel, head out the window. But now there's a new breed of pet that requires a whole other kind of care than Fluffy ever needed. If not attended to promptly for "cleaning" or "feeding," these robot dogs, cats, birds—really just electronic plastic eggs—can

"die." All the "training" is lost when the eyes flash two burial crosses or, in some models, two tiny tombstones. In Massachusetts, in 1999, a twenty-seven-year-old woman driver was distracted when she heard the beeping distress cry from her electronic virtual pet, dangling beside her ignition key. When the distress signals grew critical, indicating a weak battery, she attempted to press the small buttons in the demanding sequence needed to restore the electronic health of the creature. In doing so, she swerved off the road, careening into a group of cyclists. One bicyclist died instantly. At her trial for manslaughter, defense lawyers attempted to show the woman's emotional bond to the electronic egg, but were unable to convince the jury.

BATTERY FAILURE, PRIMARILY FROM BATTERY ACID, CAUSED 778 FATALITIES IN 2002.

ELEPHANTIASIS In 2001, when a Brooklyn nurse finished speaking to a rude patient on the telephone, she commented to a co-worker, "That guy has some balls." A few hours later, she had the surprise of her life when the man arrived at the clinic with a white sheet tied around his waist. The man carried a scrotum the size of a beanbag chair between his legs. The nurse couldn't do enough to help the man, dazed at the sight and at the man's unfortunate plight. The man had contracted lymphatic filariasis, commonly known as elephantiasis, while serving as a missionary in Africa five years before and until then had been previously too embarrassed to seek treatment.

This disorder is caused by parasitic worms carried by mosquitoes that inject the worm larvae into the bloodstream when it bites. The parasites then cause inflammation of lymph vessels and extreme enlargement of limbs, head, or torso. As blood flow is blocked due to this inflammation to the infected body part, the

limb, head, or genitals swell larger and larger until they reach grotesque proportions. Eventually, increased blood constriction causes gangrene and death.

Elephantiasis currently affects 120 million people worldwide and had claimed 40 million deaths since 1965. There are no vaccines available and few medicines to treat it. Early detection is the only chance to catch it. Most people believe the swell from a mosquito bite will eventually subside on its own and forgo medical care until it's too late.

NO ELEPHANT IN ELEPHANT MAN

John Merrick, known as the Elephant Man, was rescued from a life inside a sideshow cage by Dr. Frederick Treves, who described his patient as "deformed in body, face, head and limbs. His skin, thick and pendulous, hung in folds and resembled the hide of an elephant." Dr. Treves dubbed Merrick's condition "Elephant Man disease." Once treated as an ignorant savage, Merrick was quick to learn the manners and refinements of the Victorian Age, eventually entertaining royalty and becoming a sought after dinner guest. Cordially treated as a curiously trained monster, Merrick lived in the London Hospital, where he remained until his death in 1889. Long considered to suffer from "Elephant Man disease," or elephantiasis, Merrick suffered a much rarer disorder. After examining his skeleton, hospital records, and skin samples, a panel from the U.S. National Institutes of Health diagnosed Merrick's condition as Proteus Syndrome, a genetic disorder that causes abnormal growth and disfigurement, found in less than one hundred known cases.

243 AMERICANS DIED FROM OF ELEPHANTIASIS CAUGHT TRAVELING ABROAD SINCE 1995.

ELEVATORS You push the button, the door opens, and you get in. How the elevator works, what the cables are made of, or when it was last inspected is of no concern. Each year, people take 213 billion trips on elevators, escalators, and moving walkways, displaying perhaps the greatest example of society's blind faith in modern technology. When something goes wrong a simple "Out of Service" notice is posted, and the details are scrupulously concealed for the "good of the public."

Death certificates for people killed in elevators state that they were "caught in between," meaning wedged in elevator machinery counterweights, or between two cars, or between the elevator shaft or doorway and a car. People stuck in elevators have died after they forced open the door; many get cut in half trying to get out to a floor only partially accessible when the car suddenly began to move. Some try to escape through roof hatches and become entangled in the machinery.

LONGEST PLUNGE

In 1945, a B–25 army bomber got lost in the fog over New York City and crashed into the seventy-ninth floor of the Empire State Building. The engine ripped from the fuselage and crashed through the shaft of elevator number 6, severing all six cables that held aloft an elevator car stopped at the floor below. Inside that car was elevator operator Betty Lou Oliver, who then experienced the longest free fall of an elevator car before or since, plunging one thousand feet toward the subbasement. Witnesses recalled hearing the screams of a howling woman as the car descended, ending in a thunderous crash. When a crowd rushed below, they found a demolished elevator car and were shocked to find Betty alive among a pile of debris. She had been weightless in the fall and floated near the elevator ceiling. Although fourteen others died from the plane crash, somehow Betty survived, suffering a broken back and two broken legs. After six months of recuperation, Betty returned to her native Arkansas, where she resigned to stay firmly on the ground. (See Also: Empire State Building)

Most falls down lift elevator shafts are due to incompetence in operating manual door gates or by not checking to see if the elevator car is present when the door opens. Or, the door signals can malfunction and the car moves before everyone has exited. This is what happened to a welfare clerk in the Bronx, New York, in January 2002. He and three co-workers boarded an elevator, which began to rise before the door was closed. Sensing something amiss, the group pressed the button for the next floor. When it arrived, the door opened, but again started to close before all were off. The man attempted to straddle the doorway to allow his companions to exit by making an X with his body, using his arms and legs to prevent the errant door from closing. Despite his efforts, when the car began to ascend, he was promptly decapitated by the landing of the next floor.

Fifty-seven percent of the "fall deaths" are due to collapse of the floor of the elevator car. Many older elevators have rotted plywood floors or support brackets weakened by excessive overload; just the slightest load can send it tumbling below. That was the case in 2001, when an eighty-five-year-old Ohio woman entered an elevator alone. When the elevator reached the sixth floor, the woman fell down a shaft when the floor suddenly gave way.

Escalators kill primarily by strangulation and asphyxiation. In 1997, a thirty-seven-year-old man was found on his back, dead at the bottom comb plate of a subway escalator. The belt of his raincoat had caught in the downward moving steps and somehow managed to twist the coat about his body, choking him to death. Sixty people are injured every year when escalators suddenly accelerate and throw them to the bottom.

TAKE THE STAIRS

Flowing skirts, loose shoelaces, drawstrings, scarves, and mittens are items easily caught in escalators. Toes are the body part most often severed and entire steps have been known to collapse during transport. In 1996, one man fell up to his waist, his torso and legs dangling in the space below, when an escalator step broke free. He rode up the rest of the way trapped, struggling desperately to get out. Escalators generally do not shut off when jammed and continue until the emergency stop button is activated. The man was literally sawed in half by the relentless conveyor belt of the moving steps. He remained alive for two weeks after the incident.

SIXTY-FIVE ELEVATOR WORKERS
DIE ANNUALLY, DUE TO FALLING
OR BEING "CAUGHT BETWEEN."
IN 2004, 137 PEOPLE DIED
FROM INJURIES SUSTAINED
WHILE USING ESCALATORS
AND ELEVATORS.

EMPIRE STATE BUILD-ING The world's most famous urban icon is the 102-floor building in Manhattan, measuring 1,454 feet from sidewalk to the tip of its lightning rod. Completed on November 13, 1930, for a construction project that size it had one of the lowest death rates. Only six lives were lost, primar-

ily because Iroquois skywalkers—Native Americans known for agility and balance—were used for much of the high-rise work.

Ten thousand people visit the observation deck of the Empire State building every day. On February 23, 1997, a deranged man in his sixties opened fire into the crowd with a semiautomatic Beretta. He killed one Swiss tourist and injured six others before killing himself. That was the first—and so far only—incident of random shooting in the building's sixty-five-year history.

The day after Thanksgiving, 2004, a man, suffering from more than indigestion, climbed the security fence on the eighty-sixth floor observation deck and took a flying leap off. His brown hair turned white before he hit the roof of the sixth floor. He died instantly on contact, making him the thirty-second suicide jumper at the Empire State building since it opened in 1930.

TOTAL NUMBER OF PEOPLE WHO DIED AT THE EMPIRE STATE BUILDING: 2,110

ENTRAPMENT Cedar storage chests, specifically the models that automatically lock when closed, have suffocated 4,521 children since 1912. There are still 12 million of these chests in homes across America. Other common household entrapment deaths are caused by child **safety gates,** particularly the old accordion type that allows the child's head to get caught between the wooden slats; thirty-one deaths by head entrapment and subsequent strangulation were recorded between 1995 and 2000. **Playpens** that can collapse and fold

away for easy storage have killed fifteen children in the same study period. The top rails fold into a V, entrapping children accidentally. There are 12 million **old cribs** in use in America with slats too far apart or cutout de-signs in the headboard or footboard, which use loose-fitting mattresses, or are missing hardware. Infants can suffocate or get strangled when trapped between broken crib parts. Thirty-two deaths per year are caused by various models of old cribs.

RECLINER CHAIRS
This is not "coach potato" deaths, but suffocation and choking due to entrapment in footrests of reclining chairs. Since 1970, 2,880 children under four and three adults died when entrapped in the footrest of a recliner chair.

IN 2004, THERE WERE 122 CHILDREN KILLED BY ENTRAPMENT.

E PIDEMICS Contagious diseases spreading rapidly throughout large segments of a population has always been the dreaded scourge of mankind. In America, epidemics were met with the urgency of a house on fire. Municipalities mobilized ad hoc medical personnel to care for the sick, and enlisted enforcers to remove those suspected of illness from circulation, often without concern for due process or other civil liberties.

Dept. Pub. Health, Sanitary Div. F. 22

SMALLPOX

KEEP OUT OF THIS HOUSE

By Order of BOARD OF HEALTH

HEALTH OFFICER

Any person removing this card without authority is liable to prosecution.

In particular, yellow fever epidemics sent American cities into a panic more than two dozen times from 1700 to 1900. **Yellow fever** is a viral disease, initially transmitted to humans by mosquitoes, which remains silent in the body during an incubation period of three to six days, followed by fever, muscle pain, headache, shivers, loss of appetite, nausea, and vomiting. The person will seem to recover, when a week later the disease blooms and fever returns. The person turns yellow from jaundice, cramps up into a ball, and bleeds from the mouth, nose, eyes, and ears. After ten to fourteen days of this, when the kidney and liver are destroyed, the person dies.

1793: **In Philadelphia, 4,099 died of yellow fever** after sick sailors returning from the West Indies spread the disease. Mandatory quarantine for those suspected of infection was the only method of treatment available. In 1798 Philadelphia was hit by another yellow fever epidemic, killing another 2,085. This time, all but seven thousand had fled the city.

In 1803, yellow fever ravaged New York City because of one cabin boy on the ship *Zephyr,* returning from the Caribbean. In order to allow the cargo to be unloaded and for the passengers to set foot on land, the captain had to swear on a Bible that the boy died of worms. City officials, although suspicious, were reluctant to declare quarantine and disrupt the economically important seaport trade. In two years, fifty thousand citizens left the city and over two thousand died.

1832: **3,107 succumb to cholera in New York City.** Cholera is a waterborne disease, linked to poor sanitation and sewage. Back then, no one knew it came from water, food, or material infected by the feces of a cholera victim. Handling contaminated chamber pots, dirty laundry, or used bedsheets passed the disease along quickly. Cholera hit so suddenly that a man could be whistling as he walked to work at daybreak and be buried hastily by nightfall. The *New York Evening Post* described how pedestrians pitched and dropped on the streets "as if knocked down with an ax." Eighty thousand people fled the city to escape the disease.

1848: **Another 5,231 die of cholera in New York City.** Tens of thousands of Irish immigrants were packed into small, dilapidated tenements with garbage piled in the alleys, sometimes as high as the second-story window. Children played in streams of raw sewage. Newspaper editorials depicted the Irish moral character as the cause of the disease, befouled in poverty and ignorance, "exterminating themselves through drink, laziness, violence, criminality, and illegitimacy." Although the disease struck the predominately Irish Five Points Area, everyone was susceptible to cholera.

1853: **New Orleans gets hit with yellow fever, killing 7,784.** City officials knew the disease was endemic, recording the death of one hundred people per day within the first month, but refused to call for quarantine. The official silence was intended not to alarm the public or interfere with trade. Although the elite were quietly encouraged to leave the city, the general populace had no relief until the arrival of cooler autumn weather when the epidemic subsided.

In 1867, New Orleans had another epidemic and 4,012 died of yellow fever, transmitted by infected merchants arriving from Africa. That time, officials had the city of New Orleans quarantined. Trains were not allowed in or out. Poorer refugees trying to flee the plagued city were kept back by men with shotguns.

1879: **Yellow fever runs throughout the southern United States, taking 12,985.** In Memphis there were more than five thousand fatalities. Twenty-five thousand people left the city in a riotlike exodus. Five thousand sought shelters in "safe zones" that resembled concentration camps, which actually continued to spread the disease; standing water and unsanitary conditions in the camps increased the number of viral infected mosquitoes.

1916: **Across the United States seventy-five hundred die of polio and twenty-five thousand infants are infected.** Polio is a highly contagious infectious disease caused by viruses that live in the throat and intestinal tract. It's passed from human to human by fecal contaminated food and water. Septic tank contents infecting drinking water supplies were the primary cause of this outbreak and could be passed easily by simply shaking hands with an infected person or touching disease tainted doorknobs.

1949: Polio kills 2,811 and infects forty-three thousand children. In 1952 the disease took 3,899 lives and infected another fifty-eight thousand children. Parents were so frightened of this disease children were forbidden to enter swimming pools or drink from public water fountains. The crippling virus affects nearly 20 million people who got it in the 1950s and are still living today. Worldwide, over fifteen hundred new cases of polio are reported each year.

1981: AIDS epidemic begins. AIDS (Acquired Immunodeficiency Syndrome) is a virus that affects the immune system's T-cell production, a vital component needed to fight any variety of diseases the body may encounter. With deficient or malfunctioning T-cell production, for example, a simple cold will quickly turn into a fatal pneumonia. AIDS is transmitted by blood transfusions, sharing drug paraphernalia, and from unprotected sex. Over forty million are currently infected. The disease has claimed more than five hundred thou-

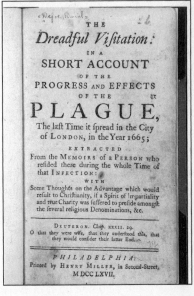

sand lives so far in the United States and more than twenty million worldwide. (*See Also:* Sexually Transmitted Disease)

1990: Hepatitis C becomes the "silent epidemic." People don't know they have it, sometimes until twenty years after infection. Hep C virus settles in the liver and destroys it. It is transmitted by blood transfusions, sharing toothbrushes with infected persons, and when drug users share needles or swap inhalation drug paraphernalia. There is no known cure for it, although experimental use of Interferon, a debilitating drug treatment, reportedly eliminates the virus from 20 percent of those who can endure the medication. Five million have Hep C, which eventually develops into cirrhosis and liver cancer; ten thousand die each year.

EUTHANASIA Euthanasia is mercy killing, the notion that one should be allowed to have a painless and peaceful death when life ultimately offers the prospect for neither. Today, the most active group advocating the "right to die" is the Hemlock Society, with almost twenty-five thousand members in seventy chapters across the country. According to their brochure, the group fields over twelve thousand calls a year on how best to terminate one's self with dignity. The Hemlock Society took their name from the poison hemlock tea that Socrates drank in 399 B.C., choosing in principle to die with dignity rather than to live with injustice.

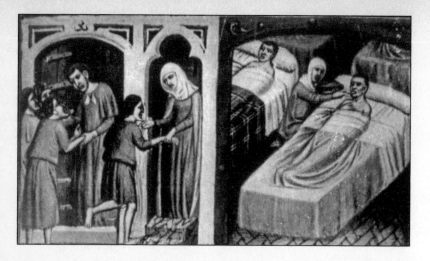

Advocates of euthanasia argue that mercy killing is the humane way to go. Throughout the history of warfare, numerous soldiers have put their dying comrades out of misery with a blade or a bullet, rather than leave them alone mortally wounded on the field. In frontier America, miles from any semblance of medical care, the prolonged illness of a loved one was shortened with a pillow over the face, or ended, as with injured horses, with a "lead gift" to the back of the head.

Euthanasia is a topic of hot debate; however, it's still illegal to commit suicide or to help one do it in every state except Oregon.

In January 2006, the U.S. Supreme Court upheld the constitutionality of Oregon's assisted-suicide law, paving the way for many other states to pass laws allowing the terminally ill to choose their endings.

In the 1990s, Dr. Jack Kevorkian (*right*) brought the issue of assisted suicide to the mainstream, becoming a staple for jokes on many a late-night talk show. He invented a machine called the Thanatron ("death machine" in Greek), rigged so a patient could pull a trigger on a trio of intravenous bottles hoisted above the deathbed. A timer starts a drip of saline solution to calm the patient and ends with a lethal dose of potassium chloride, which stops the heart cold in seconds. Kevorkian first displayed his

In 1930s Germany, euthanasia was a widely accepted practice. The Nazis expanded on this socially accepted idea by using the rationale promoted in a book by pre-Nazi psychiatrist Alfred Hoche, The Permission to Destroy Life Unworthy of Life. *The ill, malcontents, homosexuals, gypsies, and Jews, and all who fell under the Nazi's wide circle of hatred were deemed unworthy of living and deserving of death. More than 11,283,000 people were killed by the Nazi's practice of "euthanasia."*

device on the *Donahue Show* and later allowed an entire procedure to be aired on *60 Minutes* in November 1998, when he administered a lethal injection to a willing fifty-two-year-old terminally ill man. That got him nabbed. At age seventy-six, in March 1999, he was convicted of murder and sentenced to twenty-five years. At his trial he admitted to assisting in the deaths of 130 people.

In hospitals today, euthanasia is practiced all the time. Prior to surgery, doctors will ask if a patient would like to fill out a form, ordering doctors to cease what medical litigation documents call "heroic resuscitation" if the chances of returning to a normal life are slim. Each year, seventy-five thousand people are allowed to die amid a room of doctors and nurses who have been instructed not to take any aggressive measures to save their life. The "do-not-resuscitate" (DNR) patient is often given a morphine drip to make the remainder of his time as painless and peaceful as possible.

Since 1998, Oregon doctors have written 198 prescriptions for clear liquid Nembutal—a lethal dose of barbiturates—for terminally ill people; 128 of the deadly dosages were taken, but not all died painlessly or in peace. One man coughed and gagged due to an adverse drug reaction for thirteen minutes before exiting. Another vomited violently and took two hours to die, and one woman with impaired digestion lingered for fourteen hours before taking leave.

DO·NOT·RESUSCITATE ORDER

I request that in the event my heart and breathing should stop, no person shall attempt to resuscitate me.

This order is effective until it is revoked by me.

Being of sound mind, I voluntarily execute this order, and I understand its full import.

_____

(Declarant's Signature and Date)

An eighty-five-year-old New Hampshire woman was so troubled by the prospect of receiving medical care to keep her alive on life support that she tattooed a message to her would-be rescuers across her chest.

EXERCISE EQUIPMENT

Sales of treadmills, exercise bicycles, weight benches, and other apparatus to households reached $6 billion in 2005, displaying America's urge to get fit. Studies show most people use home exercise equipment for the first sixty days; shortly thereafter, they turn into clotheslines or as playthings for children. Unsupervised children can get caught in the back end of the treadmill where the belt goes around the roller. One exercise product, a rowing-type machine, had a defect that made the seat collapse during use, causing the user to fall abruptly, injuring many and killing two.

SINCE 1975, 4,399 HAVE DIED WHILE USING EXERCISE EQUIPMENT, TREADMILLS, ROWING MACHINES, WEIGHTS, STATIONARY BICYCLES, AND CROSS-COUNTRY SKI MACHINES.

FAD DIETS: The $33 billion weight-reduction industry claims to offer fast, safe, and permanent weight loss, but a survey conducted by Social Issues Research Center (SIRC) found that 95 percent of all diets fail. Desperate to lose the pounds, people are willing to try anything. But actually, popular diets like the "eat all the pork rinds, burgers, fried eggs, and bacon you want" food plans, originally developed in the 1940s for diabetics, can cause dehydration, electrolyte loss,

calcium depletion, weakness, nausea, kidney problems, thinning hair, and increased risk of heart attack. In 1997, a trendy liquid protein diet consisting of digested collagen with little or no essential substances added caused at least sixty deaths. Diet spokespersons always say there are no deaths from their regime; however, as accurate mortality figures on fad diets shift and disappear, malnutrition, uric acid poisoning, and unusual susceptibility to pneumonia are constants on the death certificates of fad diet followers.

A 1997 study by SIRC discovered that 80 percent of fourth grade girls have already been on some kind of fad diet.

DIET PILLS

Fen-phen, an appetite suppressant, killed sixty-two users in the 1990s before it was removed from the market. **Ephedrine** is another pill still aggressively marketed to enhance the metabolic system. Nothing more than an overpriced nervous system stimulant, ephedrine alkaloids cause heart attacks, strokes, paranoid psychosis, vomiting, fever, palpitations, convulsions, and comas.

Steve Bechler was a promising pitcher for the Baltimore Orioles. In 2003, the sudden death of this twenty-three-year-old athlete was originally blamed on heatstroke. It was later discovered that Bechler was battling a weight problem. The medical examiner report indicated the presence of ephedrine supplements in his blood.

IN 2004, AMERICANS INGESTED
3 BILLION DOSES,
WHICH LED TO FIFTY-FOUR DEATHS
AND ABOUT ONE THOUSAND
REPORTS OF
SERIOUS COMPLICATIONS.

NO CHANCE OF BECOMING A FAD

A popular urban legend cites the story of an obese man trying to lose weight who concocted a special homespun diet of nothing but beans for protein and cabbage for fiber. A month later, the man was found dead in his bed in his tiny unventilated apartment. Legend has it that after spending time in the room, four EMTs became ill, one severely enough to be hospitalized. Hank C. of Idaho might be the man to whom the urban legend refers, who died in 1991 from similar circumstances. The autopsy showed a high concentration of methane in the man's system. However, the coroner concluded that he died in his sleep not from breathing a poisonous gaseous cloud he himself had created—but from malnutrition.

TOTAL DEATHS FROM MALNUTRITION IN THE UNITED STATES LAST YEAR: 31,018

FALLING ASLEEP: According to the U.S. Department of Transportation, falling asleep at the wheel causes more than two-hundred thousand car accidents annually. As a result, products have sprung up to provide assistance to exhausted drivers who still want or need to get behind the wheel. Hearing aid–sized zappers that can be attached to the ear will send a jolt when the head nods or the chin touches the chest. There are CDs available with sequenced squeals and irregular loud beeps, as well as miniature alarm clocks that plug into the cigarette lighter. Some exhausted drivers employ home remedies: one truck driver constantly sucks lemons, while a traveling saleswoman shuts her hair in the sunroof so she'll be yanked back to consciousness when she dozes off. However, most experts suggest that a ten to fifteen minute off-road nap will increase the longevity of drowsy drivers and those who meet their wavering cars on the road. (*See Also:* Cars)

IN A CLOSE RACE WITH DRUNK DRIVERS, CHRONICALLY SLEEPY DRIVERS CAUSE MORE THAN FIVE THOUSAND DEATHS EACH YEAR.

FALLS: Most fatal falls occur when people are not climbing anything. Deadly falls are often caused by slipping in bathtubs or tripping over shoes. According to the CDC,

In a survey of licensed physicians in which anonymity was guaranteed, 42 percent confessed that they had most likely caused the death of at least one person because they had been too sleepy to make wise medical decisions or perform surgery to the best of their ability. According to the Institute of Medicine, ninety-eight thousand deaths occur annually from medical errors. Monday is the best day to have surgery: It's the day of the week with the lowest fatalities.

falls are the leading cause of injury and death for people over sixty-five. Regardless of age, white men have the highest fall-related death rates. In 1999, *The New England Journal of Medicine* reported that men, more than women, are affected by uneven floors, loose rugs, unstable furniture, and objects on floors; women have a greater ability to recall the location of objects than do men. Poor lighting and even poor eyesight also play a role in falls.

Since 1990, as many as two thousand people have been allegedly thrown off a roof, their deaths listed as possible homicides.

RISING ABOVE

Once a person climbs a ladder, age no longer comes into play. Neither does the height of the ladder. Each year, ladder use prompts hundreds of thousands of emergency room visits and workers' compensation claims. More claims are made due to falls off a three-foot stepladder while changing a lightbulb in an office, than from working on construction sites.

In the construction field, there is a greater chance for deadly falls from extreme heights. Annually, more than five-hundred workers tumble off scaffolds, ladders higher than thirty feet,

FALLING INSIDE A BARREL

Niagara Falls is an awesome waterfall: 1,076 feet across, one hundred fifty thousand gallons of water pour down per second, to the craggy rocks seventy-six feet below. Most of us stand and marvel, but a few wonder what it would be like to go over the edge and actually try it. Since 1829, fifteen people have attempted to go over Niagara Falls in everything from small oak and pickle barrels, inner tubes, kayaks, and canvas nets to a huge two thousand pound drum. Eight of these didn't survive. George Stathakis went over Niagara Falls in a two-thousand-pound barrel in 1930. The barrel became trapped at the bottom of the falls, behind the endless curtain of water for more than fourteen hours. By the time the barrel finally dislodged, he had suffocated inside his contraption. The most recent attempt, in 1995, ended unsuccessfully for Robert Overacker. He raced to the brink of the falls on his jet ski, planning to deploy a rocket-propelled parachute in midair. Unfortunately, his chute was not properly tethered to his back and he died.

over the edge of roofs, through sky-lights, or through rotten roof surfaces.

IN 2005, 12,400 FALLS RESULTED IN DEATH.

Allan Pinkerton, founder of the famous Pinkerton Detective Agency bearing the motto "We never sleep," tripped during his morning walk, bit his tongue, and died at age sixty-four of gangrene on July 1, 1884.

UP THE DOWN STAIRCASE

In 1996, a twenty-year-old man successfully broke into a real estate and insurance company office building in Huntington, New York. After spending the entire night trying unsuccessfully to crack open a six hundred-pound safe, he decided to pry the whole thing from the wall and take it with him. He managed to drag it to the stairs, but then scratched his head on how best to get it down the two flights to the back alley—push it, or slowly and quietly walk it down step by step? He decided to get in front and hold up the weight with his back. Within no time, he lost his balance; the safe promptly ran over him and dragged him down the stairs. The next morning he was found dead, flattened under the safe. He died not knowing that the safe he labored to steal was empty.

FASHION: Throughout the ages, when it comes to women's fashions, style has always beat comfort and form—even to the point of death. The stomach girdle was used by women as far back as 1800 B.C., in the Minoan era, to constrict their waists and amplify their busts. During the nineteenth and early twentieth centuries, the corset was essential to wear the fashion of the day: Victorian women displayed their higher social status through fragility, with a white powdery pallor and a cinched, corseted waist. Corseted women fainted and fanned themselves regularly due to lack of oxygen. Constricted by a corset, women's lungs didn't fully expand and their stomach and intestines were unable to function, making eating even more than a morsel of food an occasion to vomit. There were several reported incidents when girls died in torture, their livers pierced by their own ribs. Exemplifying the mores and desires of the time: *Gone With the Wind*'s Scarlet O'Hara had her waist tightened to an impossible eighteen inches.

Average women tried to have a perfect "hourglass" figure, even though men at the time claimed their ideal beauty to be the 1890s stage actress Lillian Russell, who weighed in at a full-figured two-hundred pounds.

BURN IT?

Since its first use, the brassiere has been the most controversial piece of underwear. Even its origin has garment historians' knickers in a twist:

Although earlier patents do exist, some say New York socialite Mary Phelps Jacob designed the bra in 1913. When the corset went out of style by the 1920s, erotic attention was transferred to the breasts. By the 1940s the modern bra became a standard. Some say it's good for women, some say it's bad. *Dressed to Kill* authors Sydney Ross Singer and Soma Grismaijer claim that wearing bras inhibits the balanced function of the lymphatic system in, on, and around the breast, and that this constriction allows for the buildup of breast toxins and increases the chances of breast cancer. The au-thors sampled 4,730 women and concluded that "women that go braless have a 21 times less chance of developing cancer."

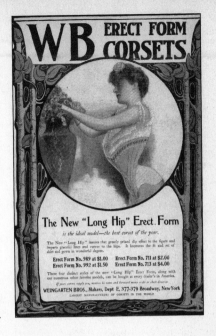

WB ERECT FORM CORSETS

The New "Long Hip" Erect Form

is the ideal model—the best corset of the year.

The New "Long Hip" insures that greatly prized slip effect to the figure and imparts graceful lines and curves to the hips. It improves the fit and set of skirt and gown in wonderful degree.

Erect Form No. 989 at $1.00   Erect Form No. 711 at $2.60
Erect Form No. 992 at $1.50   Erect Form No. 713 at $4.00

These four distinct styles of the new "Long Hip" Erect Form, along with our numerous other favorite models, can be bought at every dealer's in America.

If your corset supply you, mention his name and forward money order or check direct to

WEINGARTEN BROS., Makers, Dept E, 377-379 Broadway, New York

LARGEST MANUFACTURERS OF CORSETS IN THE WORLD

ELECTRIFYING FASHIONS

In 1999, two women, ages twenty-four and thirty-nine, were attending an outdoor function in a park when a sudden thunderstorm approached. Although there were taller objects around them, which should have been struck by lightning first, both women suffered a direct hit and died. Their misfortune could only be explained by the bras the women wore, fashioned for larger breasts, needing a heavier gauge of wire. (See Also: Lightning)

DYING FOR FASHION

In the 1920s the artist crowd liked to wear long, silk scarves, signifying the fashion of haughty elegance. On September 14, 1927, modern dance legend **Isadora Duncan** *(above)* rode in the passenger seat of a sporty Bugatti, her long flowing scarf flying in the wind. Things took a turn for the worse when the scarf got entangled in the spokes of the rear wheel. The driver kept whizzing along for a quarter mile before he looked over and saw Isadora dead from a collapsed larynx. Her death certificate read: "Accidental strangulation caused by a vehicle," and not the more accurate, "fashion roadkill." (*See Also:* Baggy Pants)

TOTAL DEATHS DUE TO ARTIFICIAL CONSTRICTION
SINCE 1850: 29,865

FEAR OF FLYING More than 612 million Americans fly in a commercial plane every year. When compared with all modes of transportation, traveling inside the cabin of a commercial airplane is still the safest, with a thirty-year average of only 1,451 fatalities per year.

Takeoff and landing are the most dangerous times and are responsible for over 95 percent of all accidents. Midair collisions happen less frequently. Mechanical problems or international sabotage or terrorism have also caused plane crashes since humans took to the skies.

COMPLETE LIST OF FATALITIES ON U.S. COMMERCIAL AIRPLANES SINCE 1945

1945. B-25 Bomber collides into the Empire State Building, leaving fourteen dead. (*See Also:* Elevators)

1947. At Fort Deposit, Maryland, an Eastern Airlines DC-4 goes down, taking fifty-three lives.

1951. Miami Airlines C-46 ditches into the Elizabeth River; fifty-six dead.

1951. An American Airlines plane crashes into homes in Elizabeth, New Jersey, killing seven on the ground and twenty-three aboard the plane.

BEST SEATS
When crashes do occur, for reasons known only to numerologists, passengers seated in row 23 survive most often.

1952. Again in Elizabeth, New Jersey, a National Airlines DC-6 falters and kills twenty-six.

1952. A stunt plane explodes during a Farnborough Air Show; pilot and twenty-eight spectators die. (*See Also:* Air Shows)

1955. A bomb on a United Airlines DC-6B kills forty-four.

1956. Midair collision over the Grand Canyon of a United Airlines DC-7 and a TWA Constellation; tally, 128 dead.

1959. American Airliner falls into New York's East River, claiming sixty-six lives.

1960. Northwest Airliner crashes after midair explosion over Tell City, Indiana; sixty-three perish.

1960. A United DC-8 and a TWA jet collide midflight over Brooklyn, killing 127 people.

1961. The crash-landing of a Sabena Airlines plane causes seventy-two deaths.

1962. During takeoff, an American Airlines jet falters into Jamaica Bay, New York, killing ninety-five.

1963. An Eastern Airlines DC-7 crashes during takeoff in Alaska and kills 101.

1965. Another Eastern DC-7 crashes taking off from Kennedy Airport in New York, killing eighty-four.

1971. In Juneau, Alaska, an Alaska Airlines aircraft crash-lands; 109 dead.

1972. Upon landing, a United Airlines 737 nosedives into a house and claims forty-five near Midway Airport in Chicago.

1972. An Eastern Airlines plane breaks into pieces in the Florida Everglades; 101 perish.

1975. Another Eastern jet miscalculates landing at JFK airport in New York and ends 296 lives.

1978. A private plane flies into a Pacific Southwest 737, causing 144 deaths over San Diego, California.

1979. At Chicago's O'Hare International Airport, an American Airlines jet fails to take off, killing 271.

1980. A holiday charter plane crashes, killing 138 on their way to Las Vegas.

1982. A Boeing 737 plummets into the Potomac River, taking seventy-eight.

1982. On takeoff at Kenner, Louisiana, a Pan Am jet crashes, killing 137.

1985. An Arrow Air DC-8 carrying 248 U.S. service personnel crashes in Newfoundland, killing all on board.

1985. In Reno, Nevada, a Galaxy Airlines plane crashes, causing sixty-four deaths.

Jack Gilbert Graham, a two-bit criminal, saw his mother as a big dollar sign and figured out how he would collect on her insurance. In 1955, when she came to visit him in Denver, Jack gave her a gift-wrapped box and made her promise not to open it until Christmas. She boarded the plane to go home, toting her gift, not knowing that she carried fourteen pounds of dynamite with a timer inside the box. The bomb exploded shortly after takeoff, killing forty-four people.

The worst ground incident occurred in 1977 when two planes, a Pan American jet, originating in Los Angeles, and a Dutch KLM 747, collided on the runway at Tenerife airport, in the Canary Islands, killing 583.

1985. A Delta jet goes down at Dallas–Fort Worth Airport; taking 126.

1985. Midwest Airlines falters in Milwaukee, killing twenty-seven passengers.

1987. In Detroit a Northwest Airlines plane crashes; 148 casualties.

1987. On its approach to Denver Airport, a Continental Airlines jet crashes and kills twenty-five.

On December 7, 1987, David Burke told his wife he was going back to work at the airport because he was rehired; instead he planned on getting even. He followed his ex-boss onboard a Pacific Southwest Airlines jet and repeatedly fired his gun in midflight. The plane crashed, killing all forty-three people onboard, including Burke.

1988. A Pan Am 747 explodes midflight due to mechanical problems just off the Northeast coast, instantly killing 248.

1988. Coming into Dallas–Forth Worth, a Delta 727 crashes, killing twelve.

1989. A United Airlines jet goes down in Sioux City, Iowa, claiming 110; 175 survive.

1989. An Eastern Airlines plane crashes in Miami, killing one and leaving forty-six survivors.

1990. An Eastern Airlines plane ditches in Cape Canaveral, taking one, leaving ninety.

1990. In Detroit, a Northwest Air DC-9 crashes, killing seven, leaving thirty-three survivors.

1990. In Los Angeles, a US Air plane crashes, killing twenty; sixty-three survive.

1991. Approaching Colorado Springs, a United Airlines plane crashes, killing all twenty onboard.

1992. A US Air jet crashes in Flushing, Queens, and kills twenty-four, leaving twenty-two alive.

1994. A US Air plane goes down in Charlotte, North Carolina; thirty-seven die, twenty survive.

THE PRESENCE OF ANGELS

On February 24, 1989, a forty-foot section ripped off the top of a United Airlines Boeing 747 flying one hundred miles south of Hawaii. Nine passengers were instantaneously sucked out and disappeared into the Pacific Ocean. The pilot and the other 328 passengers in this aerodynamically improbable aircraft attested to seeing a hand holding up the wings, ultimately bringing the craft to a safe landing.

1994. A US Air plane crashes in Aliquippa, Pennsylvania, taking 127.

1994. An American Eagle jet can't get lift at Roselawn, Indiana, and kills all sixty-four onboard.

1995. An American Airlines jet approaching Cali, Colombia, crashes and kills 152.

1996. A Valujet had combustible cargo that came loose and killed 105 over the Everglades, near Miami.

1996. A TWA jet goes down in Moriches, New York, taking all 242 passengers.

1997. A United Airlines 747 ditches into the Pacific Ocean, killing one, leaving 141 alive.

1999. An American Airlines plane, landing at Little Rock, Arkansas, takes ten lives.

2000. An Alaska Airlines plane crashes at Point Mugu Airport, Ventura County, California, killing all eighty-three onboard.

As a present for her seventh birthday, Jessica Dubroff was allowed to attempt to set a record as the youngest kid to pilot a plane across the United States. She died when her plane stalled shortly after takeoff from a Wyoming airport on April 11, 1996.

2001. An American Airlines jet is hijacked and flown directly into the north tower of the World Trade Center, killing eighty-one passengers, nine flight attendants, two pilots, and five terrorists.

2001. A United Airlines 767 is hijacked and flown directly into the south tower of the World Trade Center, killing fifty-six passengers, seven flight attendants, two pilots, and five terrorists. (2,749 death certificates related to the WTC attacks have been filed.)

2001. An American Airlines 757 is hijacked and flown directly into the Pentagon at Arlington, Virginia, killing fifty-three passengers, four flight attendants, two pilots, and five terrorists. One hundred twenty-five people were killed on the ground.

2001. A United Airlines 757 is hijacked at Shanksville, Pennsylvania, killing thirty-eight passengers, five flight attendants, two pilots, and four terrorists.

2001. An American Airlines jet crashes at Belle Harbor, New York, killing all 251 onboard and five on the ground.

WITH THE EXCEPTION OF THE 9–11 ATTACKS,
EACH YEAR APPROXIMATELY SIXTEEN PEOPLE
ARE KILLED ON THE GROUND
WHEN PLANES FALL FROM THE SKY.

FEED AND PET In 1993, a man took his son on a day trip to Moffitt Ranch, an exotic game preserve fifty-five miles northwest of San Antonio. They got out of the car to pet a nilgai, a large species of antelope. The antelope nibbled at their offerings like a calm, doe-eyed Disney movie pet until it suddenly remembered it was once a wild animal. With one swift switchblade slash of its sharp spiraled horns, the antelope sliced the man's leg, severing his femoral artery. The boy ran to call 911, but his dad lost too much blood to be saved.

ALL THE WEST GOING FOR MATTY.

FATALITIES AT WILD ANIMAL PRESERVES, SINCE 1975: 871

FIRE HOSES AND PRESSURE WASHERS

A fire hose shoots with the force of twelve hundred pounds of pressure per cubic inch—twenty times as powerful as the spray that comes out of a typical shower head. If that force of water were used to wash your hair, you would walk away with a more than perfect case of male-pattern baldness. However, this pressure is a good thing when it comes to fighting fires and is a relatively new concept in the long pursuit to save lives from rampant flames. Fire hoses were used as early as 4,000 B.C. Made of ox gut and attached to a big bag of water, firefighters would pounce or sit on the supply pouch to push the water to the inferno. For most of history the typical method of fighting fires was rarely successful—townspeople would fetch a bucket at a time from a cis-

tern or lake. Two Dutchmen invented the first prototype of the modern hose in 1673: a fifty-foot leather *"hoase"* sewn together by shoemakers. In America the first Dutch-type hoses were used in 1803 in Philadelphia. In 1825, the mayor of Boston convinced taxpayers that one hundred feet of hose could do the work of sixty men hauling buckets. This method in fact proved successful, and many municipalities across the country followed, adding hoses to the firefighter's arsenal.

From the 1800s to the 1930s, before building codes of any kind or other safety precautions were considered, chances of dying in a fire were always great and were cited as the most frequent cause of accidental death in America. Houses made of wood, without means of exit or egress, with nonelectric, liquid fuel as the source of lighting, and coal or wood ovens for cooking, caused over thirty thousand deaths per year. Today fire casualties are fewer, due in part to the fire hose and safety and prevention methods.

On August 29, 1884, a circus train ignited into flames as it traveled in the night through Colorado. A torch used for lighting inside the train had dislodged and set ablaze the sleeping car, where sixty circus workers rested. The fire blocked the exit door and all sixty perished, trapped inside the flaming car.

WORST FIRES

The Great Chicago Fire of 1871 started in a barn located at 137 De Koven Street, which some theorists believe was struck by a meteor. The fire ignited one closely built wooden house after another. Before the fire burned itself out, 17,876 buildings were turned to ash, leaving three hundred dead and one hundred thousand homeless. On the very same night in Peshtigo, Wisconsin, an unexplained fire, which some say was also caused by a meteor, destroyed eight hundred wooden buildings in that town, killing twelve hundred people.

On March 25, 1911, a fire broke out on the top floors of the Triangle Shirtwaist Company, a sweatshop in New York City. Five hundred women, many of them new immigrants, were crammed into the factory, which was equipped with only one exit door and no fire escapes. Within minutes, the trapped workers were clawing and scratching to get free. After 146 young women died in the fire, or from jumping out of windows to their death, reformers wanted this unnecessary loss of life to count for something. Legislation to improve conditions for the working poor was considered and eventually inspired many laws still in place today.

The Cocoanut Grove lounge was Boston's most popular nightclub, decorated to look like a tropical paradise with fabric palm trees draped in Christmas lights. On November 28, 1942, the place was packed with soldiers on holiday boogying with their sweethearts and sports fans hoisting

JUST THE THOUGHT OF FIRE

On September 19, 1902, two thousand people were assembled inside a Baptist Church in Birmingham, Alabama. Overcrowded as it was, some churchgoers got into a fistfight over a seat. When someone yelled "Fight!" a few people instead heard the word Fire, *which started a mad dash for the doors. Bonnets flying, prayer books tossed, the ensuing stampede killed 115 people, trampled and suffocated, without a puff of smoke in the air. (See Also:* Stampedes)

pitchers of beer in celebration of the local football team's victory. It was elbow room only for over two thousand people crammed in a place meant to hold half that. Just as the party was in full swing, a waiter used his lighter as a flashlight to change a burned-out bulb hanging from a palm tree. The fabric tree went up like a blowtorch, and a roaring fire spread quickly through the club. The side and rear exit doors were chained closed (so no one could sneak in and beat the cover charge), making the front revolving doors the only way out. In this scramble, 492 people died.

In the middle of the night on December 7, 1946, a fire broke out at the ten-story Winecoff Hotel in Atlanta, Georgia. The old building had only one staircase in the center, which turned into a fire funnel and quickly blocked the only way out for the three hundred guests. When the fire department arrived, their ladders were not long enough to reach the upper floors. People jumped eight flights down toward circular nets the firefighters held, but more missed the net than were saved. Bedsheets were tied into ropes, which burned as people lowered themselves to escape. In total, 119 guests died, hunkered at the windows awaiting rescue, huddled on the roof, sleeping in their beds, and on the ground where they fell.

EVERY YEAR, FIRES, BURNS, AND
SMOKE INHALATION RESULT
IN THE LOSS OF
THIRTY-SEVEN THOUSAND LIVES.

Fire hoses are not always used to put out fires; they also have a long history of use in riot control. Many other hoses are used for cleaning, some of which simulate the pressure of a fire hose when attached to a motor and pump. These home-style **pressure-washers** send out a needle-sharp spray of water that can strip the skin to the bone. They cause thirty-one hundred eye loss and deep lacerations each year.

HOLDING THE HOSE
For the men and women who step up to the blaze, the leading cause of on-duty fatalities is from heart attacks. In 2005, 106 firefighter deaths were attributed to overexertion and stress, motor vehicle crashes while responding to emergency calls, smoke inhalation or burns, and fatal traumatic injuries from falls or from being struck by objects. In 2000, three firefighters were murdered while on duty.

IN 2005, SIXTEEN DIED FROM ELECTRICAL SHOCK USING
PRESSURE-WASHER MACHINES.

FLESH-EATING VIRUS Many suppose flesh-eating viruses are something only seen in low-budget sci-fi flicks, but they are very real, spread quickly, and show up in all regions of the country. These new forms of flesh-gobbling bacteria have evolved into mutant strains that are increasingly resistant to antibiotics. In Texas, during the summer of 2004, forty were infected and eight died after one man went fishing at Lake Titicaca, Bolivia, and suffered a minor cut on his arm. The cut festered with Vibrio bacteria, and once he returned to the States it spread quickly to all he contacted. Pneumonia and heart failure followed within days. The skin of the dead looked as though it was burned by acid.

According to Dr. Loren G. Miller of the Biomedical Research Institute at Harbor-UCLA Medical Center, "[Flesh-eating viruses] is about as serious an infectious disease emergency as you can get." Diagnosis must be accurate the first time, as it was for a Buffalo police officer who nearly died from Escherichia coli, another type of flesh-eating bacteria. He contracted it 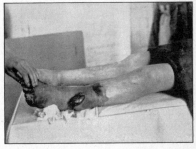 while searching through a trash can for evidence in the spring of 2004. One of the lucky ones, the police officer took only six months to recuperate in the hospital before returning to work.

However, even when caught early and treated with the correct antibiotics, chances of coming away unscathed are slim. Reconstructive surgery is almost always necessary. To save one New Haven high school football player's life from necrotizing fasciitis he caught from a skin chafe he received at practice, doctors had to amputate both of his legs and one of his upper arm muscles. Another New Jersey man, age forty-five, was killed by a tiny cut on his thumb nine days after contracting flesh-eating virus beta hemolytic strep A from rental tool equipment. Despite attempts to remove vast amounts of infected flesh, he died. In the spring of 2004, forty-seven people died in Tulsa, Oklahoma, and five nursing home residents in Gainesville, Florida, died from other strains of bacteria.

The only clue that some sort of flesh-eating virus has infected your skin is to check around a fresh cut. Look for small black dots to appear as the wound begins to heal.

DEATHS FROM VARIOUS FLESH-EATING BACTERIA
SINCE 1965: 34,833

WHEN ASPIRIN WON'T HELP
In 1998, an otherwise healthy twenty-three-year-old from Sheffield, Illinois, went to bed nursing a bad toothache. Three days later his family found him dead. An autopsy revealed that this tooth decay was actually a flesh-eating necrotizing fasciitis known as "galloping gangrene." The infection had spread rapidly to his neck and chest, killing him. The young man had a propensity for chewing on pens and not washing his hands, a typical way mouth-necrotizing fasciitis is spread.

FLYING COWS A motorist was killed in Vacaville, California, in March 1999, when a flying cow crashed through the windshield of his pickup truck. The eight-hundred-pound cow had been hit by a Mercedes-Benz, which hurtled the bovine into the path of the man's Toyota pickup.

Animals that wander onto highways and onto big city streets don't stand much of a chance, and rarely cause traffic fatalities, as dogs, cats, and squirrels are easily flattened and turned into roadkill. But it's a different story on rural roads. In the North Country, drivers suddenly encountering wild and domesticated animals are on the rise. Due to successful conservation efforts, moose, deer, and elk populations have increased and many of these large animals venture onto roadways. Between 1997 and 2003, there were 133 fatalities on country roads caused by deer and bear. Moose were the single greatest cause of animal-driver accidents in counties that bordered Canada during the last five years.

Hitting a moose, cow, or horse in a speeding car is like running into a guardrail. Out west, horses on roadways were the cause of forty-seven deaths, and cars careening into cows and steer killed sixteen people between 2000 and 2003.

PET-LOVING DRIVER SWERVES TO AVOID HITTING ANIMAL. . . . YOU KNOW THE REST.

The true number of deaths caused by car-animal incidents is difficult to pinpoint. In most fatalities that cite animal collision as the direct cause of death to a motorist, the animal had to be literally embedded in the grill or entangled in the bumper. However, it's estimated that

twenty times the number of driver fatalities could be attributed to near-misses. For example, in Washington State, a bus driver swerved to avoid a squirrel, causing the bus to hit a tree. The driver died and seven children on the bus were injured. In Pittsburgh, an unleashed and excited dog chased after every car that came onto its street. Mailboxes along the road were dented and downed by numerous cars swerving to avoid this brazen animal. Eventually, in a similar attempt to not hit this dog, two high school girls ran over a garbage can, lost control, and died in a head-on with a delivery truck.

The Fish and Game Department tracks moose-car collisions only when the moose is killed. In the last five years, 1,118 moose became roadkill. Morgues track human fatalities from colliding with moose; they report 561 deaths in the same period.

SINCE 1965, HORSES, COWS, AND
WILD ANIMALS
CAUSED 12,877 DEATHS.

FOOTBALL Each year, more than three hundred thousand football players are treated for injuries in hospitals. Repeated concussions and brain damage led to the majority of reported football fatalities; football is responsible for two hundred fifty thousand brain injuries in the United States. Ten percent of all college players get brain injuries, and 20 percent of all high school players wind up with some type of brain damage. When football became popular in America at the beginning of the twentieth century when fewer than fifty thousand played the sport, many games turned into a bloodbath. Back then, inflicting the most broken bones on an opponent was more important than gaining yardage. In 1905, 103 college athletes were killed on the field.

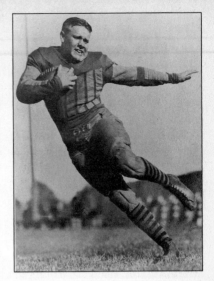

PROS NOT IMMUNE
Heatstroke, head injuries, and numerous undetected health-related variables can affect football players. Wide receiver Chuck Hughes of the Detroit Lions died of a heart attack in 1972 during a game against the Chicago Bears. At training camp in 1979 St. Louis Cardinals tight end J. V. Cain died of a heart attack. Korey Stringer of the Minnesota Vikings died of heatstroke during a training camp practice in 2001. San Francisco 49er lineman Thomas Herrion collapsed and died in the locker room after a game in August 2005. (See Also: Sudden Death)

TWENTY PEOPLE DIE ANNUALLY AS A RESULT OF FOOTBALL-RELATED INJURIES.

FOREIGN BODIES In 2004, twenty-nine people died from the insertion of a foreign body into the rectum. Death is usually listed as "coital trauma" from various causes. One death occurred from a person inserting an open deodorant bottle, and another from a curtain rod, which caused a rupture of the rectal membrane and death from rear end bleeding. Five others died that year from broomstick insertion, which caused perianal sepsis—infection from splinters or from inadvertently ingesting pieces of wood. Two died from chicken bone insertion, resulting in anal infection and rectal tearing. One perplexed individual sat on a soda bottle, which became completely engulfed inside his anus and pushed into his large intestine. He died when he tried to get it out using a coat hanger.

The insertion of small animals into the anus is a fairly common occurrence and, surprisingly, not a surprise to emergency room doctors. The average ER performs twenty small-animal-from-anus removals yearly. Animals most frequently "found" are gerbils or mice, and the occasional small hamster for good measure. The animals usually expire from suffocation but move around quite violently before doing so, often causing severe rectal bleeding.

DEATHS SINCE 1985 FROM RECTAL RUPTURES DUE TO INSERTION OF FOREIGN OBJECTS: 1,119

THE BEAST WITHIN

In July 2005 when emergency room doctors at the Enumclaw Community Hospital in Seattle began to exam a forty-five-year-old man wheeled in on a stretcher they realized he was already dead. The companion who brought him had bolted, which prompted authorities to hunt for the identity of the dead man and what caused his death. The trail led to a local farm, known on Internet chat rooms as the place to go to have sex with animals. It was discovered, by observing videos found on the premises, that the dead man regularly had intercourse with horses. According to the autopsy report, the man died of "acute peritonitis due to perforation of the colon." (See Also: Q-Fever)

FREE RENT A twenty-seven-year-old man lived on the third floor of his father's brick house in Park Slope, Brooklyn. He kept complaining to his father that the toilet was broken. After sending plumbers on three separate occasions over the course of a year, the father decided to go upstairs and see for himself what the problem was. While dismantling the bowl, the father reminded the son that he hadn't paid rent in eight years. An argument ensued and the father ended up clubbing his son to death with the toilet seat.

Tenant-landlord relationships can become strained when rent is unpaid, especially if the landlord lives in the same building. In March 2002, a tenant renting a room in Weehawken, New Jersey, fell three months behind in the rent. The irate landlord drowned his tenant in a bath and dumped the body in the marshlands. Defense counsel claimed the landlord was an alcoholic and suffered from depression.

Police in various parts of the country have begun to fine building owners if they have to go more than three times to the same apartment for the misdeeds of their tenants—no matter the reason—further exasperating landlords, who consider this an unreasonable financial hardship. If the landlord then tries to evict these tenants, the legal eviction process can take up to six to eight months of rent-free living before the undesirable occupants are finally forced to move. One New York landlord confronted late payers with a pit bull held on a flimsy leash. Another took the tact of removing all doors and windows on apartments of delinquent tenants. In March 2000, when one man new to the landlord business had a late payer, he, to say the least, lost it. He found it unacceptable that one twenty-year-old female tenant refused to pay rent. She blatantly informed him that she now owned the apartment, as she had spent money on improvements he had refused to make. So he hacked up her body and buried it in different locations.

SQUATTERS' RIGHTS

In July 2002, two squatters claimed a building in the Bedford-Stuyvesant area of Brooklyn, New York. The building had structural problems and the roof leaked, causing mold growth and lead paint to peel off the walls. Delon Lucas, eighteen, and Clarine Jones, twenty, considered themselves landlords and opened the barricaded door each evening for their business: They charged hourly rates to addicts who needed a place to shoot up or to homeless seeking shelter. Sometimes they put plaster dust in glassine packets and sold it as dummy bags of cocaine or heroin to suburbanites, or sold single cigarettes, called "a loosey," to the locals for a dollar apiece. When a thirteen-year-old boy came into the building to buy a cigarette they took his dollar and tried to send him away with nothing. An argument over the dollar broke out; the boy was found beaten to death and stuffed in a cardboard box. When police took both squatters into custody, each blamed the other for the killing. They said they were only trying to rebuild the community and felt unfairly discriminated against because they were squatters.

Earle Nelson was a preacher who specialized in killing landladies. He traveled the country and stayed in many boarding houses, preying on elderly women. He was hanged in 1928 for killing twenty-two.

HOMICIDES ATTRIBUTED TO PROPERTY RIGHTS SINCE 1965: 11,615

FROZEN TOILETS In January 1994, during an unexpected cold snap, a thirty-four-year-old New Mexico man was found on his toilet, frozen to death. The toilet in the apartment above had overflowed and water had been dripping on him all night. According to his girlfriend, the man had a history of sleeping on the bathroom floor, close to the toilet, or on it, whenever he had too much to drink. The man was discovered sitting rigid on the bowl encased in a thin sheet of toilet-water ice, icicles growing from his earlobes, ultimately dead of hypothermia.

The human body was designed to run smoothly at an internal temperature of 98°F. If body temperature decreases by as little as 2½ degrees, a person can die of hypothermia. Between 1979 and 1998 there were a total of 13,970 deaths attributed to hypothermia; men die of freezing three times more than women, due partially to men's greater propensity for risk taking in extreme cold.

The first warning sign of approaching hypothermia is shivering, followed by confusion and disorientation. When body temperature is 3 degrees lower than normal, the brain can no longer access memory. Speech becomes slurred and numbness, compulsive hand fumbling, and uncontrollable drowsiness occur.

Many of those who die frozen do so because of other problems. For example, in March 2001, a twenty-seven-year-old man was found dead in a remote area of Utah. The man was on a tractor that got stuck in the mud. It appeared he had worked feverishly to dislodge the vehicle. He got too wet and cold before he was able to free it and died of hypothermia. Another case involved a seventy-four-year-old woman with Alzheimer's disease. She wandered away from her nursing home wearing only a nightgown in Rhode Island in December 2003. There were two feet of snow on the ground, with the temperature at 15°F. She was last seen alive at 6:30 A.M. and was found dead three hours later in a ditch alongside the road.

Henry Hudson's death may prove that having rivers named after you doesn't mean much. Hudson died in 1611 when his men mutinied, forced him and his son into a small boat without food or provisions, and set them adrift in the wintry seas of St. James Bay in northern Canada; both died of frostbite.

Others die because they put themselves in harm's way. For example, on New Year's Eve in 1998, a twenty-three-year-old man decided to do a Polar Bear swim as a unique way to bring in the new year. He sawed a three-foot hole in the ice and invited his friends down to hang with him there at midnight. Despite the partying atmosphere, no one wanted to join him for the frozen skinny-dip. At 1:30 A.M. he stripped naked and jumped in headfirst. When he failed to resurface, his friends shone their headlights onto the ice, in the hope that he would see the lights and orientate himself to find the opening. The next morning, firefighters pulled the man's frozen body from the lake; he had only been two feet away from the exit hole when he died.

In February 2000, a fifty-year-old man was found dead in an alley behind a strip mall. At midday it had been 50°F, but dropped at night to 36°F. The transient's death certificate listed the cause of death as "hypothermia attributed to acute and chronic alcoholism."

FURNITURE A seven-year-old boy and a six-year-old girl visiting from the Midwest with their parents in 1993, stayed on the thirty-fourth floor of a New York City hotel. While the adults were in the exercise room, the kids looked out the window, and were amused at how high they were and how the people on the streets below looked like ants. At first they threw a few hotel pens out the window, and then an ice bucket. When none of the "ants" below seemed to notice, they upped the ante and tossed a chair down onto the street. Chan Chen, forty-one, visiting the city from Taiwan, was sightseeing when he was hit and killed by the piece of furniture that fell from above.

Millionaire Joseph Heer was still obsessed with money at age eighty-nine. Compulsively frugal, he hated more than anything to waste money on utilities, and had every heating device in the house strictly monitored by timers and usage gauges. One winter, after his power bill went up $3, he decided to cut off service rather than to be subjected to further outrageous power increases. In January 1986 he was found in bed, fully clothed, dead of hypothermia. In an envelope under his mattress, the police found $200,000 in cash.

WORST COLD SNAPS

1888: In Montana territories, Minnesota, Nebraska, Kansas, and Texas a sudden cold front brought a blizzard that caught kids walking home from school, killing 235 students. In March of that same year (long before the advent of weather forecasts) five feet of snow fell without warning on the East Coast and 400 froze to death.

1950: Billed as the "Storm of the Century," a blizzard with hurricane-force winds buried twenty-two states, downing power lines, stranding people in unheated homes, which took 383 lives.

1977: The Buffalo, New York, area was buried under snow, causing twenty-nine deaths.

1978: An East Coast freezefest killed fifty-four.

1993: A blizzard called a "Superstorm" hit the East Coast and took 270 lives.

1996: Snow and its rapid melting aftermath killed 187 in the Appalachians, the mid-Atlantic, and the Northeast.

THE WEATHER OUTSIDE IS FRIGHTFUL

When he was sixty-five, Renaissance man Sir Francis Bacon got an idea on how to preserve meat. To prove his theory, he purchased a chicken and tried to stuff the carcass with snow. The problem with his hypothesis was that the experiments could only be conducted during bad weather. During the winter of 1626 he ventured out during a blizzard to stuff more chickens and wound up becoming the stiff.

PEDESTRIANS KILLED BY FALLING OBJECTS SINCE 1945: 17,983

G

GANGS AND GANG WARFARE There are twenty-five thousand gangs in the United States, with 950,000 gang members in active status. Leaders of these groups have an endless supply of cheap labor to run illegal and outrageously lucrative operations. As anthropologist Joseph Campbell noted, "Boys everywhere have a need for rituals marking their passage to manhood. If society does not provide them they will inevitably invent their own." Gangs unite underprivileged youth and social outcasts with a fabricated sense of family loyalty and brotherhood, many times considering a killing or a crime spree as the rite of passage. Nearly all gangs are territorial and, in many instances, much more ruthless than other groups of organized crime. All-female gangs now make up about 15 percent of the criminal activity, but, male or female, the gang's primary business is illegal drugs.

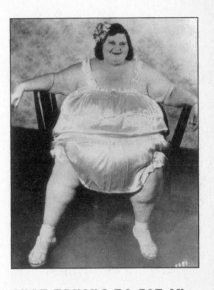

ROASTING MARSHMALLOWS

Sociologists recommend that youth join wholesome, extracurricular groups rather than seek peer approval from gang members. One man, a dedicated scout leader, was determined to turn a bunch of former gang members from East L.A. into good scouts and took them to the countryside on numerous camping trips. One night, while telling stories around the campfire and roasting marshmallows, one scout became upset, believing the scoutmaster's ghost story was in some bizarre way disrespectful of the boy's mother. After, the boy tried to snatch the toasting fork from another kid's hand. As the kid jerked it away, the metal prong (some say on purpose) somehow managed to get deeply embedded into the scoutmaster's neck, severing his jugular vein. The scoutmaster was DOA by the time the troop carried him out of the woods.

JUST TRYING TO FIT IN

In July 2004, gangs of fat women suddenly sprang up around the world, getting arrested in South Africa, England, and the United States. These women entered department stores in large numbers, intimidating the sales staff with boisterous behavior and bumping rumps. In the confusion they would shoplift huge quantities of small-sized garments, presumably for resale. Police have issued warnings to be on the alert for four or more plus-sized women hovering around petite clothing racks.

There are three hundred black gangs in Los Angeles County; the **Bloods** and the **Crips** are the most notorious. Another six hundred Hispanic gangs operate in Los Angeles County, along with a growing Asian gang force of about twenty thousand. New York leads the nation in gang membership, with twenty-four thousand.

The largest Chicago-based street gang, with members now in forty states, is the nearly all-black **Gangster Disciples.** Larry Hoover, the "Chairman of the Board" since the early 1970s, is currently serving a 140-year prison sentence for racketeering, conspiracy, and murder. He still runs the Gangster Disciples from behind bars and the group earns approximately $100 million annually from selling five-dollar bags of crack.

One evening in 1991, a couple visiting Los Angeles unknowingly drove into a part of town controlled by gangs. They had forgotten to turn the rental car's lights on, and gang members, fearing an attack by rivals, ran up to the car and fired ten rounds through the windshield.

Gangs identify themselves by wearing special colors and communicate with special hand gestures and handshakes. **The Vice Lords** use a "pledge of allegiance" to recruit new drug-runners and are organized like a corporation led largely by middle-aged career criminals. The gang sells millions of dollars worth of heroin and cocaine annually, keeping the morgues busy. In Chicago, Vice Lord territory, 389 homicides in 2003 were gang related.

The history of urban America is littered with the rise and fall of gangs. In the 1800s, New York City had vicious immigrant gangs roaming all the worst tenement neighborhoods of Five Points, near the vicinity of Park, Worth, and Baxter streets, and up to the Bowery. Sanitary conditions were deplorable and food was scarce and gangs formed so the destitute could survive. Dirty politicians such as Mayor William Tammany used the ruthless muscle of the Irish Five

SPECIAL HAND SIGN

In Washington, D.C., in April 2002, a woman was communicating in sign language with her fiancée as they drove to dinner, when another car carrying gang members approached the same stoplight. The gang thought the woman was flashing a rival's gang signs and shot her in the face. Neither the woman nor her boyfriend, both of whom were deaf, were gang members.

VIEW FROM THE "DEAD RABBIT" BARRICADE IN BAYARD STREET, TAKEN AT THE HEIGHT OF THE BATTLE BY OUR OWN ARTIST, WHO, AS USUATUE, WAS PRESENT AT THE FIGHT.

Points Gang to help win elections by threatening citizens to vote the right way (his way)—or else.

The **Swamp Angels** were orphan boys, some as young as five years old, who lived and operated in the sewer system. At night they would emerge from manholes and steal from storage yards and then stash their rich supply of goods in the cracks and crevices of the sewer tunnels.

Another New York gang was the **Dead Rabbits,** their name taken from the dead rabbit tied to the stick they carried as a lucky charm during street warfare. One leader was an Irish woman, Hellcat Maggie, who filed her teeth into fangs and wore long brass fingernails honed razor sharp. In one fight to the death in 1857, eight were killed when the Dead Rabbits fought the Bowery Boys. In a two-day battle on the streets of New York, in addition to the eight fatalities, one hundred were injured before the U.S. army was brought in.

From 1820 to 1850, the Natchez gang controlled a six-block section of New Orleans known as "The Swamp." Eight hundred murders in the area were attributed to the gang, which was noted for gambling and prostitution.

In 1851, there was a well-organized gang of Australian immigrants called the **Sydney Ducks** in San Francisco. The Ducks' favorite scheme was to start fires and then loot the neighboring stores while the police and firemen tended to the commotion. This gang's terrorism killed one hundred before twelve of the ringleaders were captured and lynched.

Another West Coast gang started during the California Gold Rush. In 1850, a law was passed prohibiting persons of Mexican descent from prospecting. As a result of being excluded from the action, shortly thereafter, Joaquin Murieta and his partner "Three-Fingered Jack" formed a gang of more than twenty Mexicans who began killing gringos and stealing their gold. They killed 133 before the U.S. Rangers were sent in to hunt them down. After the gang was ambushed, the Rangers put Murieta's head and "Three-Fingered Jack's" hand into jars to be displayed in San Francisco.

HELL'S FURY

*The **Hell's Angels Motorcycle Club** originated as a loose-knit bunch of guys on Hoggs and eventually became the organized crime syndicate it is today, with an intelligence network that rivals the CIA, operating throughout the United States, Canada, and Mexico. With "associates" in police departments across the country, in government offices, telephone companies, and attorney generals' offices, the Angels operate without subtlety and have no problem with the image they project, especially when dealing with those who've done them wrong. When one journalist wrote a derogatory article, he was shot in the back five times as he got into his car; one bar manager kicked a Hell's Angel drug dealer out of his establishment and was later beaten to death by three men outside his home; two prison guards were murdered to make a point on how Angels should be treated in prison. The Hell's Angels have two hundred chapters worldwide and eighteen hundred to two thousand members, double the club's membership of ten years ago. Sonny Barger, the founder, says the group is just a bunch of guys who love motorcycles. U.S. enforcement agencies believe otherwise and attribute at least three thousand murders to those who bear its winged skull logo.*

GANG ACTIVITY CAUSES
62 PERCENT OF ALL ASSAULTS,
52 PERCENT OF CHILD ABUSE
INCIDENTS, **68** PERCENT
OF MANSLAUGHTER CHARGES,
AND
49 PERCENT OF MURDERS.

GASTRIC BYPASS SURGERY With 61 percent of the American population now classified as overweight and more than 25 percent morbidly obese, sixty thousand people have opted to have their stomachs surgically reduced. The typical gastric bypass procedure attempts to reduce the size of the stomach and limit the amount of food the small intestine can absorb. Most surgeons prefer to cut and hand-sew the stomach, but staple guns are becoming popular, as the stapler is faster and leaves a neat row of staples. In 2003, a thirty-seven-year-old woman from Massachusetts died during a standard laparoscopic gastric bypass surgery when the staple gun malfunctioned. Staple guns are known to misfire and cause "leaks," commonly leading to rectal cancer or the need for a permanent colostomy, an opening in the abdomen for the drainage of stool.

Isaac Sprague, advertised by P. T. Barnum as "The Original Thin Man," was born a normal child and grew ordinarily until the age of twelve, when suddenly, due to a gastrointestinal disorder, he was unable to gain weight. (Sprague most likely had then-undiscovered Crohn's disease, which makes it difficult to eat large meals and less able to absorb vital nutrients.) When he died in 1890 at age forty-eight, from a weakened immune system and malnutrition, he stood at 5'4" and weighed fifty-one pounds.

33,722 PEOPLE HAVE DIED
DURING AND AFTER GASTRIC
BYPASS SURGERY SINCE 1994.

GEOGRAPHIC TONGUE
Some diseases and afflictions have such bizarre names that dying of them can be difficult to explain. A person with Geographic Tongue (GT) develops rough, swollen, and slimy areas on the tongue. Swelling can become severe and create problems speaking, chewing, and swallowing. Breathing eventually becomes difficult and complete blockage of the airway results. Most people with GT don't think it's serious, so they don't do anything about it until it's too late. Generally thought to be a result of emotional stress, or a reaction to an unknown allergy, once advanced, there is no cure. Although GT is not contagious, why the tongue develops a loss of papillae (tiny fingerlike projections on the surface of the tongue) and forms lesions is still poorly understood.

THIS DISEASE IS NOT ISOLATED TO ANY ONE GEOGRAPHIC
LOCATION OF THE UNITED STATES
BUT OCCURS INDISCRIMINATELY;
APPROXIMATELY 1,760 PEOPLE WITH
GEOGRAPHIC TONGUE DIE EACH YEAR.

G **IANTS** Ever since *Jack and the Beanstalk*, giants have been given a bad rap. Even in modern litera-

Between 1961 and 1980 there were 1,280 known giants, up from the period between 1886 and 1900, when there were 657 giants.

ture, Oscar Wilde continued the stereotype with "The Selfish Giant," referring to those who were excessively tall as ogres and brutes simply because of their size. In fact, most giants are gentle, if not seemingly clumsy in a world where everything is made for smaller people. Rarely a genetic abnormality, true gigantism becomes evident in childhood and is caused by a tumor in the pituitary gland, which secretes Growth Hormone (GH) in all humans. However, this anomaly stimulates the production of unregulated amounts of growth hormones, which enlarge the long bones and increase the size of muscles and organs, making children radically taller than others their age.

Today, giant children can be treated with medications that reduce hormone production levels to normal and relieve the pressure that the growing pituitary tumor exerts on the surrounding brain. It is possible for medicine to drastically reduce the population of giants throughout the world by treating this anomaly in children before long bones enlarge. If left untreated the child can die from ever enlarging organs and complications from broken and brittle bones. Gigantism, also called acromegaly, can develop suddenly in people in their forties. These people do not get taller, but their faces become elongated and

TALLEST MAN IN HISTORY

Robert Wadlow (below) *became a giant due to his overactive pituitary gland. Born an average eight and one-half pounds, he soon developed enormously, reaching fifty pounds by the age of one. At nine years old he was 6'2" and weighed three hundred pounds. He finally stopped growing when he was eighteen, reaching 8'11" and weighing 439 pounds. He wanted to have a regular life, go to college, and become an attorney, but it was hard to sit in school-sized chairs. For Robert, holding a small pen to write an exam was a challenge. When there was snow or ice on the ground his balance was precarious and he feared falling; typical of giants, his bones were so brittle that a stubbed toe could require hospitalization. He signed on with Ringling Brothers after dropping out of college during the first semester, but died at the age of twenty-two, in 1940, from an infection caused by a chafing leg brace.*

droopy and their teeth become more protruded and wildly spaced. Hands and feet of middle-aged giants become enlarged, soft, and moist and their body sweat becomes oily as the heart swells and the upper airways become obstructed. Older giants usually die from an enlarged heart or from an overgrown, blocked esophagus.

4,125 DIE OF GIGANTISM-RELATED COMPLICATIONS EACH YEAR.

GINGER ALE AND GANGSTERS

Vladimir M. was a waiter for a Queens, New York, nightclub who worked the weekend shift where Russian Mafia tough guys started hanging out. He spoke Russian and would throw around a joke or two with them to increase his tips. But one night, poor Vlad was too cavalier; he took an unfinished glass of ginger ale away from a gangster before the man was finished. The mobster was so insulted he had the waiter brought down into the basement. Vladimir was forced to drink two cases of ginger ale, one bottle after another poured down his throat, until he drowned.

Most consider organized crime to mean the Mafia, evoking images of Marlon Brando as the stately godfather Don Corleone, conducting his deadly business from the tranquility of an orange grove. Because of the movies, in the last fifty years America's fascination with the Mafia has changed from shock and horror to romanticism. Whatever the ethnic origin—Russian, Italian, Chinese, or Colombian—hanging with real-life wiseguys drastically reduces longevity.

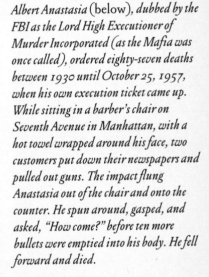

Albert Anastasia (below), dubbed by the FBI as the Lord High Executioner of Murder Incorporated (as the Mafia was once called), ordered eighty-seven deaths between 1930 until October 25, 1957, when his own execution ticket came up. While sitting in a barber's chair on Seventh Avenue in Manhattan, with a hot towel wrapped around his face, two customers put down their newspapers and pulled out guns. The impact flung Anastasia out of the chair and onto the counter. He spun around, gasped, and asked, "How come?" before ten more bullets were emptied into his body. He fell forward and died.

THERE'S NO SUCH THING AS THE MAFIA

The **Gambino** crime family, with 180 current members, is involved with narcotics, gambling, and car theft and has been linked to 934 murders. Top kingpin Carlo Gambino died of heart failure in 1976 at the age of seventy-four, the quintessential godfather, keeping court in the garden at his

Long Island mansion. His successor, Paul Castellano, who fancied himself more a businessman than a crime boss, was shot in front of Sparks Steak House in Manhattan. John Gotti, a.k.a. the Dapper Don because of his slick suits, had ordered the hit, and took over. Gotti, who once said, "You have to kill if you want to be on top of the hill," died in prison, a lot less dapper, in 2002 of cancer at age sixty-two.

The **Bonanno** crime family currently has 150 members and has hands in video porn, pizza parlors, street vendors, specialty coffee cafés, the Italian lottery, loan sharking, and narcotics. Linked to eight hundred murders, this family is known for brutal enforcement using baseball bats. The top Bonanno banana was Don Joe Bonanno; after a number of indictments, Joe retired in 1959 and died of a heart attack.

The **Genovese** crime family, with two hundred card-carrying members, is the most widespread and powerful, involved with labor, concrete, waste removal, narcotics, and gambling, and has been linked to fourteen hundred murders. Founding father Vito Genovese died in prison from heart failure at age seventy-two in 1969. In testimony against the Mafia, informant Joseph Valachi explained Genovese's reasoning and morality: "If you went to Vito and told him a guy was doing something wrong he would have the guy whacked. And then he would have you whacked for telling on the guy."

As a kid Vito's partner, **Charles "Lucky" Luciano** *(left)*, would charge weaker kids a fee to walk them to school so they wouldn't get beat up, and then beat them up himself if they didn't pay. So it was a natural progression that he grew up to specialize in the extortion-protection racket. He was so good at it that naval intelligence used his skills during World War II to protect New York harbors from Nazi saboteurs. Lucky narrowly escaped more than a dozen assassination attempts throughout his fifty years of crime and died of a heart attack in 1962 at age sixty-five.

There are one hundred members of the **Colombo** crime family, specializing in counterfeiting, cigarette smuggling, and bank fraud, as well as gambling, pornography, and loan sharking. Joe Profaci, who started the group, was a flamboyant, big Cadillac-driving, cigar-smoking boss who loved to have his picture in the papers. Linked to six hundred murders, he died at age sixty-five of cancer. All $200 million of his known assets simply vanished.

The **Luchese** family, with one hundred members, deals in waste management, the garment industry, construction, hijacking, narcotics, and gambling. Several of its members were portrayed in the movie *Goodfellas*. Linked to twelve hundred murders, the founder, Thomas Lucchese, died from a brain tumor at age seventy.

Frank Costello was at one time the most powerful crime boss America would ever see—he was instrumental in the creation of Las Vegas. After he was shot in the head and lived, he thought it best to retire. He died in his sleep at age eighty-two of heart failure.

IT'S JUST BUSINESS

The top mob guys rarely did the killing themselves, usually subcontracting the executions out to hit men. As more mafia hit men confess, the volume of brutal deaths attributed to these crime families seems to have been validated, but is still most likely under-recorded.

HANGING WITH THE WRONG CROWD

On February 26, 1990, Cornell Gunter (fifty-three) of the "Coasters," a group that sold 100 million records and was the first band to be inducted into the Rock & Roll Hall of Fame, was shot and killed while sitting in his car in Las Vegas by an unknown assailant. Another oldies singer, Bobby Fuller of the Bobby Fuller Four, was discovered dead at twenty-two in a similar fashion in 1966. Fuller was best known for his hit song, "I Fought the Law." Although neither death was confirmed to be mob related, they are assumed by many to be so.

Joey Fisher (a pseudonym) confessed in his autobiography, *Joey the Hit Man: The Autobiography of a Mafia Killer,* that he killed at least thirty-eight people in the last ten years, working as an independent contractor for many of the crime families. Sammy "The Bull" Gravano, who squealed on John Gotti, admitted to nineteen murders. Vincent "the Chin" Gigante (sometimes called the "Oddfather"), who walked the streets in bathrobes and pretended to be retarded whenever he was arrested, killed at least twenty-one for the Genovese family.

Richard "The Iceman" Kuklinski (above) was a killer-for-hire who allegedly murdered more than 125 people before his arrest in 1986. His activities make the worst serial killer look like an amateur.

ORGANIZED CRIME ACTIVITIES LEAD TO 4,196 MURDERS EACH YEAR.

GOING POSTAL The term *going postal*—now a synonym for workplace rage—was coined after an incident in 1986, in Edmond, Oklahoma, when postal worker Patrick Sherrill received a low score on his employee evaluation. Instead of returning to work and trying to improve flaws, he showed up with an AK-47, gunning for the supervisor. Sherill killed fourteen co-workers and injured seven bystanders.

OFFICE ROMANCE A NO-NO

Homicide is the leading cause of death for female office workers in America, most often the result of a romantic liaison gone bad. It's easier to get away from an obsessive former lover by changing apartments or other living arrangements than it is to find a new job.

There have been other incidents of violence at post offices, including a recent occurrence in Southern California in January 2006 when a female postal employee, out on medical leave for over two years, returned to the mail processing plant where she once worked to kill six former co-workers with a 9mm handgun. Although this has the distinction as the largest number of people murdered by a woman on the job, it still does not make the post office, as a workplace, more hazardous than any other. Any type of job, even dishwashing, can be dangerous. In March 2000, an enraged kitchen worker at a Key West, Florida, Marriott resort shot his supervisor in the back after the supervisor offered constructive criticism on the "proper method" of loading the dishwasher.

In 1955, psychiatrist and surgeon Walter Freeman, who created the lobotomy procedure, was beaten to death in his office by a patient who went berserk.

IN 2003, THERE WERE 677 WORKPLACE HOMICIDES BY SHOOTING, STABBING, AND FROM OTHER CAUSES, INCLUDING BOMBS. ANOTHER 220 WORKPLACE DEATHS RESULTED FROM PEOPLE WHO PURPOSEFULLY CHOSE WORK AS THE PLACE TO DIE, CAUSING FATAL SELF-INFLICTED INJURIES.

GOING TO SCHOOL Everyday, 52 million kids are rightfully encouraged to go to school. Since 1992, when the National School Safety Center (NSSC) began keeping fatality statistics in addition to attendance records, there have been 296 deaths during school hours. National Rifle Association Fact Sheets posted on the Internet cite a *Justice Institute* report from 2000, "School House Hype: School shootings and the real risks kids face in America," claiming that this is a small number of school-time fatalities, alluding to the notion that a student has as much chance of dying at school as he does from a falling comet.

On March 28, 1998, eleven-year-old *Andrew Golden* (below) *went to school dressed in army fatigues, armed with his grandfather's arsenal of seven guns, including rifles, revolvers, and carbines. He had a friend pull the fire alarm at Westside Middle School in Jonesboro, Arkansas, while he laid in wait. When the children and their teacher filed into the playground he opened fire, killing four girls and a female teacher.*

(Please note, however, there have not been 296 meteor-related deaths in recent years.) Between 1992 and 1999, out of 296 deaths, 172 were acts of students killing students, eighteen involving multiple homicides, the most notable in 1999 at Columbine High School in Colorado.

School fatalities include thirty suicides, five intervention deaths, and two unintentional firearm-related deaths. Most of these incidents occurred during "transition times," around the start of the school day, the lunch period, or the end of the school day.

The standard cafeteria folding table found in thousands of schools across the country weighs 350 pounds and stands about six feet tall when folded. Nine students have died after sustaining head trauma from stacked tables that fell on them, since 1980.

GOLF The most popular sporting activity for people over fifty is golf. The third and eighteenth holes are the most fatal, with 3,120 golfers dying, in a five-year study period, usually in the rough or in sand traps around those stations. Most deaths on the golf course are health related; only 2 percent are caused by golf clubs or golf balls.

In 1982, one thirty-five-year-old man, overly serious about his game, became angry when he made a bad shot. As he had done on many other occasions, he flung the club into the air. This time though, the club hit a tree, broke in half, and boomeranged right back at him, severing his jugular vein.

TEED OFF

A man died in 1998 when his brother hit him in the forehead with a 9-iron. New to the game, when he had heard his brother shout "Fore!" (a customary warning in golf that a player is about to swing), the man instead walked up to the tee. The man believed he was called to take his turn, and was fatally struck with the golf club.

GONE FISHING Commercial fishing vessels have the highest death rates of any water activity, claiming at least seventy lives a day. In the United States the fatality rate among fishermen is twenty-five to thirty times the total national occupational-related death rate. A number of factors are at play: equipment on fishing boats is often kept merely functioning, as economics prevent state-of-the-art improvements; dwindling fish supply makes the fishermen take more risks, heading further out to sea. In addition, hope and a dependence on luck to ride out bad weather usually contribute to their demise.

RECREATIONAL BOATING

Seventy million Americans enjoy recreational boating each year. More than seven hundred recreational boaters died in 2005 while afloat, half of them because they wore no life jacket. A quarter of them, life jacket or

Airboats *are flat-bottomed boats propelled by a big fan at the rear. In 2004, two died when the airboat* Swamp King *flipped in a Louisiana swamp. It carried sixteen tourists touring through the bayou looking for alligators when the drowning deaths occurred.* Swamp King's *Web site advertised that their airboats are "half ride and half tour and can make a 90-degree turn on a dime." The tour company plans to add the phrase "most of the time" in all future promotional material.*

not, died in fatal accidents relating to serious partying.

More than half of the recreational boating deaths happen while on lakes, ponds, reservoirs, and dams, when visibility is good, with a light wind blowing at 0–6 mph, and a water temperature of 70–79°F, on waters with waves less than 6 inches. On sailboats, head injury leads the list, while canoe deaths list hypothermia as the primary cause. On houseboats, carbon monoxide poisoning is the usual culprit; generators used to supply power for air-conditioning and lighting have exhaust vents beneath swim platforms at the back of the boat, which traps carbon monoxide and kills swimmers and boaters chilling out on board. And on personal watercraft, like jet skis, head trauma, usually from crashing into something, most often causes death.

ONE HUNDRED TWENTY-FIVE U.S. COMMERCIAL FISHING VESSELS SINK EVERY YEAR, KILLING APPROXIMATELY 310.

GUNS In the 1700s there was one musket for every four men. In 1865 there were seven hundred thousand weapons in the hands of citizens.* Today, Americans own 223 million guns. Forty-four percent of all U.S. households have at least one registered firearm.

A RETURN TO SILENCE

A man worked for a Yamaha watercraft distributor in Deerfield Beach, Florida. He tested jet skis and made sure they could achieve the highest speeds on a tourist-free lake, inhabited only by wildlife. A co-worker would stand on shore monitoring speeds with a radar gun. One morning in November 2001, the man got the jet ski up to 55 mph, with all systems a-okay. But when the co-worker looked up from the radar screen, the man was suddenly no longer aboard the craft. He had collided with a flying duck; being hit in the head by a ten-pound bird at such high speeds did as much damage as if he had been clocked in the head with a cinder-block. The cause of death: trauma by flying fowl.

---

* **Samuel Colt**, at age thirty-five, invented the **pistol with a revolving chamber**. He had worked as a sailor, and had spent long hours staring at the ship's wheel and used this principle to invent a gun that could shoot multiple bullets without reloading. He excelled at both invention and marketing and today would be considered a compulsive workaholic. In twelve short years, before he died of exhaustion at age forty-seven, Samuel Colt produced more than four hundred thousand Colt .45 revolvers. At his funeral in 1862, it was said of the Colt .45 that he invented: "God created man, but Sam Colt [the Colt .45] made them all equal."

THE RIGHT TO BEAR ARMS

In October 2001, a blind man in Michigan wanted to get a permit to carry a gun. Authorities hesitated. The man argued, however, that he had completed the required gun safety course and didn't have a criminal record or history of mental illness. Furthermore, Michigan's law does not specifically exclude people with disabilities from carrying a handgun, nor does it mandate shooting accuracy tests before issuing a handgun permit. He proved his point, so there's at least one blind man in Michigan packing.

VAN ZANDT, JACOBS & CO., 605 River St., Troy, N. Y.

The .25 Caliber COLT

(4-5ths Actual size of Pistol)

Hammerless!
Solid Breech!
Automatically Sa

Here Is Real Protection!

Automatic Grip Safety

This compact little COLT "Six-Shooter" is only 4½ inches long, weighs but 13 ounces, yet has the speed, accuracy and hard-hitting qualities that give confidence in an emergency.

Shoots metal-jacketed bullets as fast as the trigger is pulled; ejects the empty shells and reloads automatically for each shot.

Combined with these features is ABSOLUTE SAFETY FROM ACCIDENTAL DISCHARGE—the Grip Safety automatically locks the action until the trigger is purposely pulled—no worry on your part.

"You Can't Forget to Make it Safe!"

SEE THIS PISTOL AT YOUR DEALER'S. Write for free Catalog No. 85, descriptive of all COLTS in calibers .22 to .45.

COLT'S PATENT FIRE ARMS MFG. CO., Hartford, Conn.

HEAD BUTTS KILL MORE THAN MACHINE GUNS

Everyone has a head, but not many carry AK-47s around in public. Gun advocates believe this proves their point. The NRA, interpreting FBI data to further their cause, warns us that a head—when misused—is deadlier than a machine gun. In 2003, on an FBI data list of homicide methods, handguns were used to commit 6,790 homicides, and murder by machine gun totaled only fifty-eight. However, there were 925 people murdered by a head butt.

The FBI also has a category for murder when various sorts of guns, knives, hammers, fists, strangulation, fire, narcotics, drowning, poison, explosives, or head butts are not the cause—an additional 1,210 murderous means were recorded in the section called "other means."

IN THE "OTHER" CATEGORY

Take the case of a twenty-nine-year-old man from New Jersey. In March 2002, he invited his best friend, a thirty-one-year-old neighbor, over for some laughs. Things got out of hand, however, when the two started a spitball fight. The twenty-nine-year-old decided to bring out the heavy artillery and fetched the nail gun he used at his construction job, a tool capable of driving a nail through a four-inch board. He was only firing airbursts at first, but then thought it would be a scream to put some cigarette butts in the chamber. When those didn't achieve enough velocity, he added moistened wads of toilet paper behind the cigarette filters and aimed. The man couldn't stop laughing as his best friend fell down clutching his chest. Later, when charged with manslaughter, the man found out that three cigarette-fashioned bullets had penetrated his friend's rib cage directly above the heart, killing him.

THE MOST DEADLY CITIES

When it comes to keeping track of murder, the FBI breaks the nation's statistics into four regions: the South (42 percent), West (23 percent), Midwest (22.8 percent), and Northeast (19 percent). More specifically, the most murderous cities in 2004 were Chicago (448 homicides), New York

(570 homicides), and Los Angeles (hitting 518). Other cities on the top ten list: Washington, D.C.; Gary, Indiana; Compton, California; New Orleans, Louisiana; Detroit, Michigan; Baltimore, Maryland; Youngstown, Ohio; Richmond, Virginia; St. Louis, Missouri; and Atlanta, Georgia.

GUNS IN 2003 KILLED:
WHITE MALES, 4,785;
WHITE FEMALES, 1,962;
BLACK MALES, 5,350;
BLACK FEMALES, 1,095

UNINTENTIONAL DIVISION

Police knew who shot and killed John Hwilka in October 1998, but no arrest was made and the perpetrator never set foot in court. That's because the killer was a ten-pound poodle named Benji. Hwilka was demonstrating for his mother how to use a .45-caliber handgun—how to unload, load, and work the safety—when the dog came to John wanting a little attention. According to police who arrived on the scene, "The family poodle jumped on his chest, causing the gun to fire and killing him."

34,040 PEOPLE DIED FROM GUNFIRE IN THE UNITED STATES IN 2002. OF THESE FATALITIES, 54 PERCENT WERE DUE TO SUICIDE, 41 PERCENT RESULTED FROM HOMICIDE, AND 3 PERCENT WERE UNINTENTIONAL.

Guns in America kill more people in one week than during an entire year in all of Europe.

HAIR When one woman was little, she started a nervous habit of twirling her hair. Then she began putting the ends in her mouth. Eventually, she started to chew her hair and, ultimately, began to swallow it. Although she ate three meals per day in addition to her hair, she died at age twenty-one from starvation. At the autopsy a giant hairball (known as a *trichobezoar*) the size of a soccer ball was removed from her stomach. Hair, which is not digestible, prevented her body from receiving nutrients.

HAIRY FACES

Researcher Shah Ebrahim published his notions about shaving* in *The American Journal of Epidemiology* in 2003. He found that men who were clean shaven lived longer. Men who sported a few days' growth were "less likely to be married, had sex less often, and were more likely to smoke, have heart problems, and work in manual, blue-collar occupations than other men."

THE HUMAN STASH

The number of annual deaths from trichobezoar, also called pica, which is the ingestion of any nonfood item like dirt, forks, toothbrushes, burnt matches, or hair is 2,789. In February 2004, a Frenchman made headlines when, after his death, it was discovered he had eaten 350 coins—$650 worth—along with assorted necklaces and needles. During the last ten years of his life, his family had tried to keep coins and jewelry away from him, hoping that the desire to nibble currency and other silver items would pass.

HAIRY ALL OVER

Bearded ladies and dog-faced boys were sideshow standards. Excessive hair growth, called *hypertrichosis* or *hirsutism,* is caused by an overproduction of the hormone androgen found in the endocrine system. Fedor Jeftichew was one

---

* King Gillette looked in the mirror one morning and wondered how he was going to do it—shave his face, that is. He had a dull straight-edge razor but lacked the necessary strop belt or honing stone to sharpen it. Gillette's idea was to invent a disposable razor, and his marketing twist predicted his success; he gave away the razors to sell his blades. Fifteen years later, Gillette dominated the razor business. However, he lost most of his fortune in the stock market crash of 1929 and from the costs of battling relentless patent lawsuits infringing on his invention. He managed to hang on to one mansion until he died in 1932 at age seventy-seven from heart disease. His sons feuded over the house and eventually shaved it in half—they cut the family home down the middle to make two separate houses. Today, the Gillette Company is worth about $9 billion.

of many circus acts billed as **Jo-Jo, the Dog-Faced Boy** *(right)*. However, Fedor became the most famous hairy person in America after he signed with P. T. Barnum in 1884 at age eighteen and was advertised as half canine, half man: "Looks like a man, barks like a dog, and crawls on his belly like a snake." Although Fedor was born into circus life in Europe, he was never forced to act like a beast. When his father, also hairy and dog-faced, died suddenly, and left young Fedor to fetch for himself at age sixteen, he refused to bark or crawl on the ground as Barnum requested, claiming it "too rude." After he was dismissed from

the sideshow (replaced by another hairy man, Theodore Peteroff, billed as Jo-Jo The Dog-Faced Man), Fedor tried to shave his entire body every day, but instead ultimately chose to avoid people. With his diabetes unattended to, he went blind, and prowled the streets of New York, disappearing permanently at age twenty-two.

Another hairy boy was Stephen Bilgraski, called **Lionel the Lion-Faced Boy**. Born with six inches of fur covering his entire body, it was rumored that his mother, while pregnant with Stephen, witnessed his father being devoured by a lion. In the 1930s he became a big sideshow attraction in the U.S., but left the circus at the onset of World War II and returned to his native Poland to try and help his Jewish relatives escape. Stephen was captured immediately; his hair made it impossible for him not to be noticed. Because of his *hirsutism,* considered a genetic impurity by the Nazis, he was sent to the gas chamber and died at Auschwitz. (*See Also:* Euthanasia)

HAIRY AND UGLY

Throughout her sideshow reign (1850–1860), **Julia Pastrana** *(right)* was one of the most famous women in the world. In the nineteenth century, if you were called a "Julia Pastrana" it meant that you were ugly beyond words. Julia was 4'4", with black hair growing out of every pore of her body,

including her face. She had a long nose and huge ears and two rows of irregular teeth. Yet with all her fame and fortune, all she sought was love. When a failed singer by the name of William Lent asked her out on a date she jumped at the chance. Lent convinced her to leave the Barnum circus and join his touring act across the country. They married, even though it was obvious that Lent's intentions were not romantic, and Julia became pregnant a year later. She hoped desperately to have a normal child and for a chance at regular family life. However, in addition to being born hairy, the baby was seriously ill and didn't survive more than thirty-six hours. Julia had complications from the labor, but refused medical care, heartbroken as she was and died, in 1860, at twenty-eight years old. Playing the part of a devastated husband and father, Lent hired a mummification specialist to preserve Julia and the baby's bodies, which he displayed around the U.S. and Europe for many years. (Once believed lost, Julia Pastrana's mummy was discovered in 1990 in a box at the Oslo Forensic Institute, Norway.)

HALITOSIS Each year, Americans spend $2 billion on toothpaste, toothbrushes, oral-care gum, mouthwash, and breath mints, yet 90 million people still have chronic halitosis, known in the vernacular as really bad breath. Most of this odor originates from oral bacterium, which breaks down food particles left in the mouth. When in larger quantities, multiplying rapidly due to an abundance of lingering food (particularly protein), these bacteria release sulfur-

producing smells ranging from rotten eggs, feces, corpses, decaying meat to sweaty feet. Other foods such as onions, garlic, and coffee cause foul breath and linger in the body for up to seventy-two hours after ingestion. These foods' odors rise from the stomach and fill the lungs with a combination of gastric juices and partially digested foods. Garlic is so potent that it can be detected in the breath three days after rubbing it on your skin.

CLOSE TALKERS STAND BACK!
Many people who suffer from bad breath are often unaware, as it's considered impolite to broach this subject in public. However, halitosis does more than ruin relationships and keep people at a distance; it may also signify serious health issues, which, if left to fester, can decrease longevity. For this reason, some experts believe that reporting bad breath to the offending party might be considered a heroic act on multiple levels.

Ninety percent of bad breath can be curtailed with good oral hygiene: brushing three to five times a day and flossing will remove protein particles, eliminating the favored food supply of sulfur-emitting mouth bacteria. The other 10 percent of noxious fumes may be occurring due to stomach ulcers, the onset of kidney failure, or liver disease. Low-carb dieters who eat a lot of protein and develop serious halitosis are being warned by their bodies that organ damage is occurring.

Doctors specializing in the romantic field of halitosis spent an inordinate amount of time smelling and testing foul mouths to isolate a major cause of bad breath: an infection caused by *Helicobacter pylori*. This is a bacterium that cannot be eliminated by popping breath mints and could be spread to others by oral to oral transfer. This form of halitosis is a cancer-causing agent and can lead to gastroduodenal diseases, lymphoid tissue disease, and stomach cancer. With this, bad breath does not originate in the mouth, but rises from the stomach.

HALITOSIS APPEARED AS EITHER THE PRIMARY OR SECONDARY CAUSE OF DEATH ON 31,987 DEATH CERTIFICATES IN 2002.

HALLOWEEN What we know as Halloween is a combination of ancient holidays. The approaching winter prompted ancient societies to consider the possibility of death, as the weak and infirm rarely made it to spring; hideous masks were used to frighten off demons that brought about misfortune. The Celtic fire festival called "All Hallowtide" marked the end of harvest and the beginning of winter. When the Irish arrived in the 1800s they brought a version of Hallowtide already blended with other parts of Christian rituals such as "All Souls' Day," a day when Christians remembered all the souls stuck in purgatory.

SMELL THYSELF

Halitophobia is the fear of bad breath. One woman, whose college roommate kindly told her she had bad breath, developed a phobia that factored in her three divorces, and led to numerous missed opportunities in her career. (She refused to kiss her husbands on the mouth and would turn her head when conferring with co-workers.) Eventually, dread of her bad breath caused severe depression and suicidal contemplation. Following recommendations from a psychiatrist, the woman was examined by a halitosis specialist. It was discovered that she did, in fact, have reoccurring bouts of bad breath, which were caused by an entrenched bead she had jammed up her nostril as a girl. When the sinus doesn't drain, mucus builds and remains in the nasal passage, smelling really bad, especially when thick. The woman had the bead removed, and reportedly smelled like a rose garden.

Today, Halloween's about trick-or-treating and costume parties. It's also a time when child pedestrian deaths increase. Every year a total of 210 such deaths occur between 4:00 P.M. and 10:00 P.M., four times the pedestrian fatalities on any other given night. Sometimes, Halloween tricks also go wrong.

Another Halloween prank gone bad took place on a scary hayride in Alabama. An actor (hired by the company organizing the Halloween attraction), dressed as a gravedigger, was supposed to ambush the wagon as it went through the woods, leap up onto the ride amid the crowd nestled in the straw, and shoot a cap gun into the air. However, the actor, a twenty-two-year-old man, decided to use a real gun, figuring a .38 revolver would be much louder and authentic and would surely scare the life out of them. Unfortunately, he was correct; during his shenanigans he tripped on some hay

A REAL SCREAM
On Halloween 2000, a fourteen-year-old Chicago boy wanted to trick his friends into thinking he had hung himself from a tree. But the hidden plank on which he stood collapsed, causing the noose around his neck to tighten. For five minutes, as the prankster dangled, his friends laughed at how real his choking seemed, until it suddenly stopped.

and shot a thirteen-year-old girl in the head and wounded a seven-year-old. The local sheriff said of the actor, "He likely didn't mean to hurt anyone. He realizes he made a bad judgment call."

GIVE ME CANDY
The idea of "trick-or-treat" came from the Christian "All Souls' Day," when children would go from village to village asking for "soul cakes," or breads adorned with crosses. The more bread and currants children received, the better the chances their dead relatives had of getting out of purgatory. Sometimes children were encouraged by church elders to carve faces of lost loved ones on turnips or potatoes, creating bizarre caricatures, resembling modern jack-o'-lanterns. Today, children go from house to house filling their bags full of candy. Cautious parents often examine their child's booty for signs of tampered packages, apples with embedded razor blades, or unwrapped baked goods that may contain poisons or drugs.

Some lethal candy does slip through. Halloween night in 1970, in Detroit, a five-year-old boy lapsed into a coma and died of a heroin overdose. Examination of some of his Halloween candy confirmed it had been spiked with the drug. In 1974, in Houston, a man refilled Pixie Sticks candy with cyanide,

In 1996, an eleven-year-old girl in San Jose, California, collapsed after eating the cocaine-laced candy and cookies collected while trick-or-treating. In 2000, in San Francisco, over fifty trick-or-treaters were given little packets of marijuana covered with chocolate, made to look like miniature Snickers bars.

in an attempt to poison his neighbor's children who complained about his dog. Instead, his eight-year-old son got hold of one, ate it, and was dead by 10:00 P.M. Halloween night. In 1994, a three-year-old Connecticut boy died from cocaine poisoning from eating tampered Halloween candy.

NO SENSE OF HUMOR

In 1964, a suburban New York housewife who believed Halloween should be for small children and not teenagers sent a chilling message. When older kids came to her door, she would give them a package containing dog biscuits, steel wool pads, and arsenic ant-pesticide buttons all coated with chocolate. To the little kids she gave out untainted treats. Even though she thought she was clever, and clearly marked the teenager treat bags with skull and crossbones, one fed it to a young child, who subsequently died. During her trial she suffered a nervous breakdown and was sent to a mental institution for the criminally insane.

FROM 1998 TO 2002, 1,431 PEDESTRIAN DEATHS WERE DIRECTLY RELATED TO HALLOWEEN ACTIVITIES.

HANG GLIDING Twenty-five thousand people a year attach themselves to a nylon kite and jump off a cliff.

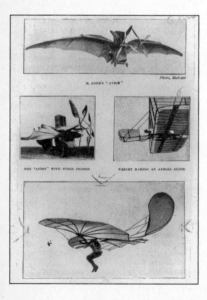

M. ADER'S "AVION" Photo, Malcoit

THE "AVION" WITH WINGS FOLDED

WRIGHT MAKING AN AERIAL GLIDE

Hang gliders have been around longer than airplanes. The Wright Brothers' first flights were made strapped to a glider, inspired by Leonardo da Vinci drawings, before coming to the final design of the airplane. In the 1960s, NASA engineer Francis Rogallo developed a super-large, kitelike model of a glider as a way to safely land returning spacecraft. Two other brothers, Bob and Chris Wills, formed in 1973 the first manufacturing company for hang gliders, and flew their "Wills' Wings" on three hundred-mile voyages. In 1977, Bob Wills crashed and died in a glider filming an aerial sequence for a film.

412 SUCCUMB TO THE FORCES OF GRAVITY WHILE HANG GLIDING EACH YEAR.

HAZING Initiation rituals are as old as humanity. There are many degrees of initiation, from lighthearted "roasts" to innocent horseplay. However, when the line is crossed from decency to hurtful behavior, the initiation becomes hazing. Although it has been banned in forty states, hazing is rampant in sports, student

organizations, marching bands, college fraternities and sororities, high schools, and in the military. Fifty-six percent of high school students and nearly 81 percent of all college athletes have experienced hazing.

OFFICIAL HAZING

When Shakespeare wrote "Cowards die many times before their deaths," he could have been penning a sonnet for military boot camps. Boot camps prepare recruits for the Brotherhood of Soldiering and for the hardships of combat. It can't be too easy, but sometimes it's too tough. The worst boot camp deaths occurred in 1956 on Parris Island. The drill sergeant yelled, "Anyone who can't swim will drown!" Heavily laden by their packs
and rifles, the young recruits headed into the river; six recruits who couldn't swim drowned. Even though this event forced the Marines to overhaul basic training techniques, new recruits still die from hypothermia, heat, and too-strenuous exercise, caused many times by previously undetected illnesses. A Defense Department report cited only fifty recruit deaths in a ten-year period; however, the actual figure is closer to ten times this amount.

TRUST IN US

In March 2004, a Masonic initiation turned deadly when a seventy-six-old-man killed a new member. Part of this secretive group's ritual ceremony requires new pledges to put their lives in the hands of their new brethren. The new member, a forty-seven-year-old Long Island man, knelt with his back to the altar, facing the assembled. The older member, holding a gun loaded with blanks, aimed above the younger man's head, intending to fire into stacked cans arranged on the altar. When he was arrested, the elder lodge man had two guns on him. He had not only missed the cans but mistakenly used the gun with real bullets. He hit the new man in the forehead, killing him instantly.

Humiliation is the key element in hazing, requiring the pledge to demonstrate submissiveness to elder members. Substance abuse plays a part in most college hazing, requiring excessive consumption of alcohol or drugs. (*See Also:* Binge and Purge.) Physical abuse is another mainstay for the hazer. A new hopeful may "voluntarily" suffer a minor "wedgie" or remain a few hours locked in a locker. Some have had to consume urine, rub "Icy Hot" on their testicles, or consume inordinate amounts of alcohol. In the drunken stupor of many of these initiation rituals, gang sex (with human and non-humans), is not uncommon. Rape and murder during the hazing frenzy happen every year.

The desire to belong and fit in leads young, desperate, and innocent pledges to submit themselves to the most illogical and dangerous circumstances, and no matter the reports, they never seem to learn. In 1978, a freshman at Northeastern was locked in a car trunk and told he would not be released until he drank two quarts of Jack Daniels. He died of alcohol poisoning that same night. In 1997 at Clarkson University, two freshmen were made to drink liquor from a bucket and were found dead, having choked on their own vomit. In 1999, at Monmouth College in New Jersey, five pledges had to dig six-foot graves on the beach; when the walls unexpectedly collapsed, one suffocated to death. In 2001, a Manhattan College pledge was driven to upstate New York on the coldest night of the year. The nineteen-year-old was abandoned, naked, on a rural road and died of hypothermia. In 2001, Florida A&M University was sued for $1.8 million after their marching band members, during an initiation, paddled their new tuba player so violently that the twenty-one-year-old died of kidney failure.

WHOSE EYE IS ON YOUR DOLLAR?

*Hazing is so ingrained in American culture that it's even represented on the currency. The hovering eyeball, the symbol for the secret **Order of the Illuminati**, known for deadly hazing rituals, is on every U.S. dollar bill. The Illuminati have been around for a thousand years and still exist. It is not, nor ever has been, a mere social club. The Illuminati is a highly structured organization of people in very high places from international banks, oil businesses, to all levels of government.*

Many presidents, including the Roosevelts, Kennedy, and both presidents George H. W. and George W. Bush have allegedly passed secret Masonic rituals. President Bush was in the Yale Skull & Bones Society, believed by some to be a steppingstone to the true Illuminati. The list of former "Bonesmen" consists of several prominent figures in contemporary American politics. Initiation purportedly required new members to dress as Don Quixote in order to learn the secret handshake and to run naked in the woods. Records of fatalities from these rituals are nonexistent; the "Bonesmen" take a vow to uphold "ambiguity and silence."

FIFTY DEATHS RESULT FROM HAZING ACTIVITIES EACH YEAR.

HEAD AND SIGNS Sticking your head out of a moving vehicle greatly increases the possibility of decapitation. Every year, 214 people learn this the hard way. Heads that hit telephone poles and stop signs at high speeds obviously do not fare well. While these impacts are usually the result of car accidents, a few are caused by not following some very simple advice, which nearly every child has heard: "Keep your head inside the window."

In 1996, a thirteen-year-old Minnesota boy leaned out of the bus window to call to his friends. At the same moment, the bus pulled out, causing the teen's head to crush against a tree. In 1994, a thirteen-year-old New Jersey girl stuck her head out of the bus and hit a utility pole. In 1988, a fifteen-year-old in New Hampshire, positioned to get a better view of a schoolyard fight, leaned out of the bus window and was beheaded by a street sign.

Decapitation by stop sign makes for gruesome endings and becomes the stuff of legends, offered as cautionary tales. However, the Headless Motorist urban legend does have basis in fact. In Atlanta in 2004, neighbors out for a walk

one Sunday morning found a headless corpse sitting in the passenger seat of a truck parked in a twenty-one-year-old man's driveway. When police arrived, they found the owner of the truck, in bloody clothes, asleep in his bed. It was discovered that he and a buddy had been out drinking. His friend's head was out the truck window when it came in contact with a utility pole support wire. The man drove the remaining twelve miles home with his headless friend next to him, apparently too wasted to realize why the conversation had suddenly stopped.

A French scientist was curious about how long consciousness remains after decapitation. When his curiosity (among other things) eventually got him sentenced to death by guillotine in 1754, the scientist instructed his assistant to carefully watch his face. Once his head was severed the scientist blinked to his assistant twenty times, signifying brain alertness for at least twenty seconds after the fact.

OTHER HEADLESS MOTORCYCLISTS

In rural Ohio, people gather during summer nights to watch a single headlight appear out of the darkness, crossing a bridge. Legend has it that this is the ghost of Elmore Waynecroft, whose motorcycle skidded on the wet pavement in 1954. Decapitated by a bridge cable, he somehow continued to drive the motorcycle another nine miles into town. (The actual distance Elmore continued to drive has not been verified, but that doesn't deter the crowds from gathering at the bridge.) In 1996, in Houston, Texas, a twenty-seven-year-old woman managed to continue driving her motorcycle for one hundred yards after she was decapitated by a panel of sheet metal that flew off the back of a truck.

There are 5 million registered motorcycles, which account for 10 percent of overall fatalities. Most fatal motorcycle accidents occur at intersections where riders try to make the turns at high speeds. Seat belts are a must for occupants of reinforced side-paneled cars, but easy riders like to let their hair blow free. The repeal of helmet laws has resulted in a 54 percent increase in fatalities. The woman who rode topless in 2000 to help repeal the Florida helmet law died in an accident two years later. She may have had her clothes on that day, but she wasn't wearing a helmet.

> IN 2005, 3,913 MOTORCYCLISTS DIED FROM
> HEAD IMPACT INJURIES.

HEATING PADS Dorothy M., age ninety, eased her aches and pains with a heating pad. For Christmas her nephew gave her a gel-filled pad that could be heated in the microwave. When the overheated sack of gel exploded, she suffered burns over 25 percent of her body, which led to her death. There are one hundred thousand of these pads in use.

> ONE THOUSAND TWO HUNDRED PEOPLE OVER THE AGE OF SIXTY-FIVE
> DIE FROM THE RESULT OF BURNS EVERY YEAR.

HICCUPS Hold your breath and count to thirty, put a cube of sugar under your tongue, or have someone scare you to death—these are just a few of the familiar home remedies used to alleviate hiccups. But for one man, who became the world record holder for the longest case of hiccups, nothing worked. Iowa farmer Charles Osborne remembered the day it started, when he lifted a pig to weigh it in 1922. Hiccups normally last a few minutes, but for Charles they lasted for sixty-eight years. He had two wives and eight children and, until he died in 1990, he endured forty spasms a minute, or 430 million hiccups in his lifetime.

Although the exact origin of hiccups remains a medical mystery, the noise is caused by air hitting the back of the voice box and by the irregular breathing it produces. Air that passes through the dome-shaped diaphragm muscle at the bottom of the chest, which involuntarily regulates breath, is disturbed from the normal rhythm. Eating too fast, stomach or throat irritations, or nervousness and unexpected excitement can result in hiccups. It is believed that when hiccups last for more than forty-eight hours something else is amiss; diaphragm tumors, kidney failure, pancreas disorders, and liver malfunctions are traced as the root of uncontrollable hiccups.

HICCUPS, NOTED AS "SINGULTUS" ON DEATH CERTIFICATES, HAVE ONLY BEEN REPORTED AS THE SECONDARY CAUSE OF DEATH FOURTEEN TIMES IN THE LAST TEN YEARS. PRIOR TO 1900, HICCUP DEATHS AVERAGED 3,245 PER YEAR.

HIDE-AND-SEEK Between 1945 and 1970 millions of freezers and refrigerators were made with lids or doors that latch closed, and have no mechanism to open the door from the inside. Children playing hide-and-seek have become trapped and suffocated—usually in less than ten minutes. Since 1988, twenty-seven children have died in discarded refrigerators with the doors still attached.

The family car can also be a dangerous place. Five young girls trapped themselves inside a car trunk while playing hide-and-seek in the summer of 1998 in Arizona. When the girls—sisters and cousins, ages two, three, five, six, and seven—were missing for no more than an hour the police brought in dogs to search the area. Soon after, all five were found dead of heat exposure. In Camden, Jersey, in June 2005, three boys ages five, six, and eleven were found dead in the trunk of a neighbor's car at whose home they were seen playing near five days earlier.

NEW JERSEY OBITUARY NOTICE: APRIL 15, 1896
"Miss Emma Fennelly died at Asbury Park on Tuesday of last week after suffering five days with hiccups. She was twenty-eight years old and had been sick for some weeks. On the Thursday before her death she was taken with the hiccups. The spasms of coughing continued for hours at a time with no intermissions. All sorts of remedies were tried, but the hiccups could not be stopped and they continued until her death. Brief relief was obtained by swallowing nine swallows of water without taking a breath, but the hiccups began again almost immediately. After the hiccups had continued a day the constant jarring of the internal organs caused intense pain and narcotics had to be administered to obtain relief."

After Janette Fennell was locked in her trunk by robbers, she led a campaign to have emergency releases installed inside car trunks. All cars built after 2001 are required to have them.

5,901 ADULTS AND CHILDREN HAVE DIED INSIDE CAR TRUNKS SINCE 1965.

HIT-AND-RUN When a motorist hits a pedestrian and flees the scene, it's filed as a "hit-and-run" incident. These drivers usually panic; have previous criminal records; or are drunk, afraid, or insensitive.

One of the cruelest incidents of hit-and-run occurred in Fort Worth, Texas, in October 2001, and defies motivation: A homeless man, Gregory Glenn Biggs, was struck by nurse's aide Chante Mallard's car with such impact that he became lodged in her windshield. It happened on a dark road, late at night. Instead of stopping, Mallard kept driving. With Mr. Biggs still stuck in the glass, she parked the car in her garage, turned the lights off, and went to bed.

When police arrested the twenty-five-year-old woman on charges of homicide, she admitted she heard Biggs' cries for help for two days before he finally died of blood loss and shock. In 2003, she was sentenced to fifty years for murder.

5,762 PEOPLE DIE FROM HIT-AND-RUN INCIDENTS EVERY YEAR.

HOLIDAYS Four hundred Christmas trees catch fire and holiday lights cause an additional five hundred fires. The National Christmas Tree Association reports 33 million natural, live-cut Christmas trees sold each year. Fire officials liken the drying of Christmas trees to a "bomb" in the middle of one's home. Christmas decorations that look like food are eaten by children and cause eighty-five deaths each season. Strangulation by holiday lights send thirteen hundred people to the emergency room each year. Gift wrappings thrown in  the fireplace burn irregularly, sending out dangerous sparks and producing a chemical buildup in the home, which has caused explosions. Twelve hundred people die in holiday fires started by gift wrappings each year.

OTHER HOLIDAY SEASON RED-ALERTS

- More people get food poisoning from holiday office parties when food is left exposed to warm room temperatures for longer than normal.
- **Holiday Heart Syndrome** prevails and more people die of cardiac arrhythmias (heart rhythm irregularity) due to alcoholic drinks, often combined with caffeine, chocolate, extra sugary desserts, and other assorted cold beverages.
- More infants and children are placed on adult beds during the holiday season sparking incidents of suffocation, strangulation, and entrapment.

W. C. Fields (right), *known for his nasal drawl and raw-looking purple nose, played on film and in life a misanthrope who loathed children, animals, and Christmas. One of his most famous sayings was, "I like children—if they're properly cooked." This consummate cynic drank heavily throughout his career despite being diagnosed with cirrhosis of the liver and eventual kidney failure. With his trademark straw hat, frayed gloves, and walking stick at his side, he died of pneumonia on Christmas Day, 1946, at age sixty-six, in the company of his longtime mistress, Carlotta. Ornery to the end, his supposed last words were: "Goddamn everyone in the whole fucking world and everyone in it—but you, Carlotta. Bring me another drink."*

On any given day, the national suicide rate is thirty-six per 1 million people. Suicide rates decrease on **Christmas Day** to twenty-nine per million and twenty-four on **New Year's Eve.** But on New Year's Day, with the prospect of returning to everyday life, the suicide rate jumps to forty-four per million. More people willfully kill themselves with car crashes during the holidays. There is also an increase in confrontations with police that end in the suicidal person's death during this season. (*See Also:* Animal Hostages)

HOME BIRTHS

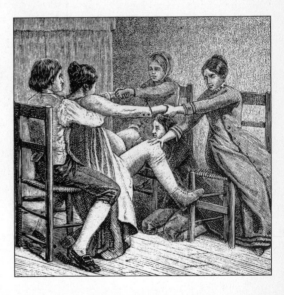

In May 1993 a California woman who preferred to do everything naturally, gave birth at home. She desired a peaceful setting reminiscent of when people lived in harmony with nature, and saw nothing wrong with allowing her two snakes, three dogs, and four cats to witness the event. After a successful delivery, the midwife, while tending to the mother, left the baby in a homemade cradle, swaddled in blankets. Unfortunately, one of the pythons had escaped its cage and proceeded to swallow the infant. It was not until the autopsy that the woman knew whether she had given birth to a boy or a girl. (*See Also:* Snake Handlers)

In general, midwives are skillfully trained and are qualified to use resuscitation tools, perform CPR, and administer epinephrine to an unresponsive infant, but most have little experience with pythons. A researcher for Childbirth Alternatives, Lewis Mehl, M.D., compared 1,046 home births and 1,046 hospital births. When common risk factors were taken into account, he found no difference in infant mortality rate. Midwife advocates claim the only risk of home birth is to obstetricians' and hospitals' income. Doctors say choose home birth with your

In October 2000, when a midwife practicing in the Northwest had a baby die when the umbilical cord wrapped around its neck, she was put on trial for manslaughter. In hospitals, where neonatal infections are four times as common as in home births, and lead to 30 percent more permanent birth injuries, deaths, more often than not, are simply added to the statistic roster.

eyes open and your fingers crossed. However, in 2002, the U.S. national infant mortality rose for the first time since 1954 to seven deaths per one thousand hospital births. That same year, Vermont, a state with the highest incidence of home births, had the lowest death rate for newborns.

IN 2001, HOME AND HOSPITAL BIRTHS HAD 38,180 INFANTS DIE AT BIRTH, OR WITHIN THE FIRST YEAR.

HOMELESSNESS *Taber's Medical Dictionary* lists "homelessness" in its encyclopedia of diseases and medical conditions. For the benefit of foreign medical students—perhaps so foreign they're from another planet—the prestigious text defines a homeless person as such: "Literally, a person who, by choice or circumstance, has no place that would be considered a home. The person may sleep in a regular place on the street, in an alley, on a park bench, or in a public place such as waiting room or subway car, but these locations cannot be classed as homes."

It's hard to count homeless people, because they try to stay hidden, living in vehicles or huddled on street corners, but according to the National Law Center on Homelessness and Poverty, there are seven hundred thousand people living out on the street on any given night. Half a million people try to get a bed in a shelter or eat at a soup kitchen each week.

"Homelessness does not exist if the homeless person sleeps on the street of his hometown." —Dan Quayle

Homicide and accidental injury are the leading causes of death resulting from homelessness. Most deaths occur during the first week of the month, the time when subsistence funds, if any, are allocated, much of which is used for drugs and alcohol. Forty percent of homeless people have a history of mental illness and 38 percent show signs of alcohol abuse. For homeless men between eighteen and twenty-four years of age, homicide is the leading cause of death. AIDS is the leading cause of death for homeless women, second to murder. Although single men count for more than 70 percent of the homeless population, a homeless woman has a ten times greater chance of dying on the streets than the homeless man.

HOMELESS EXTRAVAGANZA

The New Orleans Superdome became the world's worst homeless shelter after more than twenty-five thousand poor, homeless, frail, and forgotten citizens were hustled at the last moment into the sports stadium to escape Hurricane Katrina in August 2005. Surviving without air-conditioning or even fresh air in 90-degree heat, running water, food, or working toilets, the occupants festered, waiting for an alternative place to live for nearly two weeks. One hundred people reportedly died in the Superdome, mostly from heat exhaustion, one rapist was beaten to death by a mob, and one man committed suicide by throwing himself from an upper deck balcony.

54,300 DIE
FROM CONDITIONS STEMMING FROM
HOMELESSNESS EACH YEAR.

HOOKWORMS Vampires of the nematode species, hookworms live in the small intestines of nearly 80 million people on the planet. These parasites lay twenty-five thousand eggs a day, breeding worms that cling to the walls of the small intestine, sucking blood and causing fatal hemorrhages. Allowing an infected dog or cat to sleep in your bed, walking on carpets upon which dogs' butts have skidded, or strolling barefoot on sandy beaches where dogs are allowed to run are ways hookworms get into human bodies. Although the nematode is only about the size of a kernel of rice, the chewing mouth plates of

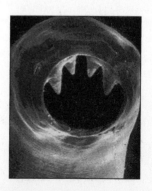

hookworms are ferocious. Many people carrying hookworms don't know it; twenty-five hookworms alive in the intestines will hardly cause ill affects. Hookworm disease first manifests itself as dry hair, dry skin, or the emergence of a potbelly. However, when the intestinal worm population increases to five hundred or one thousand, death is imminent. If caught early, medication can eliminate the parasite from the intestine, but anemia that the hookworm causes must be treated simultaneously for a better chance of survival.

Children with hookworms need blood transfusions in conjunction with parasite-eliminating medications.

The **tapeworm** is another parasitic worm that affects humans. A tapeworm can grow inside the large intestine to obscene lengths that surely top the charts, and ring the bell on the skeevy scale of grossest ways to die. Usually only growing to lengths of thirty feet, the tapeworm can live undetected inside a person for twenty years. Walking on soil contaminated with fecal matter or eating raw beef is a good way to pick one up. When the worm digs in and latches on with its teeth, making a home in the intestine, the infected person will experience abdominal discomfort, diarrhea, or constipation and vitamin B deficiency, anemia, and weight-loss results. If the worm gets very large it blocks the colon, causing fermentation and petrifaction of the stool. Toxins are produced that are absorbed into the bloodstream, resulting in death.

Up until the 1930s acceptable methods of removing tapeworms included starvation. The standard practice was to deny a patient food for three to five days and then place a bowl of aromatic soup at the open mouth of the tapeworm-afflicted individual. The hungry tapeworm, often twenty to thirty feet long and as thick as a thumb, was coaxed out of the intestine, inching up the throat toward the soup vapors. Doctors then grabbed the nematode from the mouth, tugging it hand-over-hand, plucking it from the infected person's body.

Today, doctors prescribe the less traumatic quinacrine hydrochloride (Atabrine) or niclosamide taken orally, causing the worm to relinquish its hold and pass, in parts, during normal bowel movements.

The largest tapeworm passed through the bowels by a human who did not die was 127 feet long, in India, in 1965.

SINCE 1985, 56,390 DIED OF TAPEWORM INFESTATION.

ULTIMATE WEIGHT LOSS

A woman wanted to shed a few pounds, so she ate pork tacos and added tapeworm larvae to the seasoning. She had read in the Weekly World News *(a great source for the latest bat-boy births) that after ingesting tapeworms people lost up to seventy-three pounds in one week. The article (published August 2004) stated that the fad to have your "own little diet coach deep down inside" was sweeping the country. Doctors at the Mayo Clinic found the* Taenia solium *parasite to be the cause of the woman's death in December 2004. This type of tapeworm, found in undercooked pork, causes severe pain, paralysis, as well as optical and psychic disturbances. Within days, while the larvae develop, permanent weight loss is achieved, although the resulting infection causes detachment of the retina, loss of consciousness, and ultimately death.*

HOOVER DAM The Hoover Dam is a concrete structure 1,282 feet across and 727 feet high. Built on the Colorado River between the Arizona and Nevada border, its construction began on December 31, 1933, lasted ten years, and at the time was the biggest dam in the world. Ninety-six deaths occurred during its construction, from heat prostration, drowning, blasting, falling rocks or slides, industrial accidents, and natural causes. Records originally cited 112 deaths; those unaccounted are believed to have fallen into the wet concrete, where they remain entombed today.

The **Brooklyn Bridge** is another man-made structure in which urban legend claims there are workers buried. The Brooklyn Bridge took thirteen years to build (1870–1883), and twenty-seven men died during its construction, but none actually ended up becoming part of the structure. Twenty-seven men also died during the construction of the **Bay Bridge** in San Francisco, and nearly eighty-two were killed during the construction of the **Golden Gate Bridge.**

STAY IN FORM

San Francisco's Golden Gate Bridge has always been a magnet for suicide jumpers— 169 people have leapt to their deaths into the open water 519 feet below. When a body hits the surface feet first, there are usually no broken bones; death is caused by internal concussions. Gary Erickson, a Marin County coroner, stated: "If you look at these people, they don't look like there's a whole lot wrong with them." Most bridge jumpers, however, hit the water in traditional "belly-whopper" fashion, which usually breaks the ribs, causing punctures to the heart, lungs, and major arteries, and death within a minute.

HORSE AND BUGGY

HORSE AND BUGGY Prior to 1915, the horse and buggy were the primary mode of transportation and a common cause of death. In one Chicago district in 1916, there were sixty-nine deaths: people were killed when their horse-drawn wagon was hit by a trolley car, when they were thrown from a wagon, from hitching a ride on a wagon, when they were kicked or bitten by horses, or from being trampled by a horse.

HORSE- AND HORSE-DRAWN–RELATED FATALITIES SINCE 1795: 193,912

CULTURAL SIDESWIPES

Forty horse-and-buggy fatalities still occur each year among the Amish population. Most incidents are caused when the horse-and-buggy is rear-ended or sideswiped by a modern motor vehicle. One such fatality occurred in September 2003 when Amish youngsters hurled tomatoes at cars that roared too close to their buggy. The operator of the buggy, a twenty-three-year-old Amish man, along with his companions, ran into a cornfield to hide from an angry motorist who had made a quick U-turn. The driver of the car randomly fired ten rounds into the seven-foot-high cornfield from the window of his car. He hit the twenty-three-year-old three times, who later died of multiple wounds to the chest.

HOTHEADS Men who are hostile and contemptuous of other people are 30 percent more likely to develop irregular heart rhythm *(arterial fibrillation)* and die of stroke or heart attack than men with less hostility. Hotheaded men who explode into boisterous outbursts have more heart flutters, causing the heart's two upper chambers to skip a beat and not pump out all the blood, allowing it to pool, form clots, and increase risk of stroke. These loudmouth men are 20 percent more likely to die from any cause than the quieter types, even more so than type A stress-driven, often rushed, and impatient personalities. Women, on the other hand, can be angry their entire lives and remain—at least heart-flutter-wise—unaffected.

HUNTING In colonial America, hunting was the primary sporting activity. The lower echelon hunted for food, while the upper class did it for sport, spending much of their time shooting deer, birds, or fox. Cockfighting and tying bears or bulls to stakes to be attacked by dogs were popular spectator sports of the day. Nearly 90 percent of the population engaged in some type of hunting. In 2003, 13 million people hunted, spending on average eighteen days a year in the pursuit of game. In the last ten years, hunting has declined by 7 percent, although there has been an increase in "wildlife watchers," those who hunt with only a camera lens or binoculars.

Big-game hunting remains steadfast in popularity. Deer season has the greatest number of true loyalists, drawing millions into American woodlands, dressed in camouflage and armed with high-powered rifles. The short open season and the limited availability of legal-size or trophy white-tailed deer puts pressure on many hunters; for many, the prospect of a

DON'T GET MAD, GET EVEN?

In 1948 Dr. Elaine Eaker of Boston University began a long-term study that followed the lives of three thousand people as they became adults. She found that it is better to bottle up anger than to let it out in a scream or tantrum. "It has to do with attitude and temperament," Eaker noted. The hostile and the angry not only made themselves and those around them miserable but their hearts were directly affected and they died sooner. It can be concluded that every ounce of unleashed rage takes away a few months from your life.

SERIOUS BUSINESS

Chai Vang (right) wandered onto private lands near Minneapolis in 2004, looking to hunt some deer. When other hunters, owners of the property, asked him to leave, he opened fire on the group, killing six and injuring three. Armed with an SKS 7.62-mm semiautomatic rifle, he kept firing as if he was in the Wild West, killing people one hundred yards away until he ran out of bullets. He was later arrested and pleaded guilty.

buckless season is unacceptable. During hunting season, hunters create problems for local residents. Fearing their animals will be mistaken for game, farmers paint in bold orange letters "COW" on the sides of their cows and label their barns in glowing orange: "Barn." Most hunting fatalities occur when a person, unmarked, is mistaken for a deer.

Carl Switzer, known as "Alfalfa" of The Little Rascals, *was shot to death in 1959 at the age of thirty-one. Switzer had tried to start a big game hunting expedition company after the acting roles dried up. He was shot by his partner over an argument of who-owed-whom fifty bucks.*

WEAR ORANGE

In December 2001, a Connecticut man killed his nineteen-year-old son when he mistook him for a deer while the two were hunting. Junior took off his orange vest to hide better in the brush, not knowing that deer are color blind. The man, hearing some rustling, fired twice, killing his son instantly.

FIFTY-SIX TWO-PARTY FATALITIES AND THIRTY-SIX SELF-INFLICTED HUNTING DEATHS OCCURRED IN 2003.

HURRICANES To be classified as a hurricane, a tropical, cyclonic storm system must have winds greater than seventy-five miles per hour. Hurricane categories relate to wind speed: Category 1 has winds 74–95 mph; a Cat 5 has maximum sustained wind speeds of at least 156 mph. The Galveston, Texas, no-name hurricane of September 8, 1900, claims the highest death toll, with over eight thousand dead due to flooding. The second worst storm occurred on August 29, 2005, when category 5 hurricane Katrina devastated the Gulf Coast from Biloxi, Mississippi, to New Orleans, killing more Americans than any other single natural disaster in over fifty years. The storm surge broke a five hundred-foot section of levee that kept the below sea level city of New Orleans dry, flooding the historic streets with up to twenty feet of surging water, causing fourteen hundred deaths.

OPENING THE BOOKS

The first American recorded hurricane happened in 1715 and lasted only one day. A convoy of twelve Spanish ships carrying gold, silver, and cocoa from Cuba got caught in a hurricane off the Florida coast on July 30. Eleven of the twelve ships bound for Spain sank; one thousand passengers, officers, and crewmen were killed.

NOT WHY, BUT HOW

The 65 million Americans who live on the Gulf and Atlantic coasts are warned by scientists to expect brutal hurricanes for the next thirty years. Each hurricane season, residents of coastal regions wait like sitting ducks for massive storms swirling in the ocean, with no means of shooting them down. Anxiety runs high as all TV coverage is preempted with hurricane whereabouts, intermixed with substories about lines for bottled water, gasoline, canned ravioli, and fights over jacked-up, pricey plywood.

In 2004, when Florida was hit by four major hurricanes, 106 died. Some perished as a direct result of hurricane disregard. A surfer out of Daytona Beach was lured to the surging waves for one last ride before the beaches were closed. Although it was quite possible he caught the ultimate wave, he was lost in rip currents and his body was never found. Another victim was a seventy-eight-year-old woman who went out in bad weather in search of her lost cat, Oscar, who had bolted when a window blew out just as the eye of a hurricane struck. She was hit by hurtling debris with Oscar's favorite treats in hand. Two others died while driving when a tractor-trailer lost control and ran over their car. Another curious guy, waiting for a bus, touched a downed power cable lying in a puddle and was electrocuted. An elderly woman refused to go to a shelter, staying put in her mobile home; when a tornado bred by the hurricane touched down on her exact address, the winds turned the trailer into a blender of splintered wood, mixing the poor lady with a flying water heater, tumbling stove, refrigerator, and kitchen sink.

Many others die during hurricanes from the change in barometric pressure,

LET'S DO IT

Two college girls headed off with their boyfriends on motorcycles in the blackness of night during the Labor Day storm of 2004 that hit the East Coast of Florida. The two motorcycles slammed into a tree that had fallen across the road.

which causes an epidemic of heart failures, such as it was in 2004 for one sixty-one-year-old Florida man who sought relief from the heat in his air-conditioned car after the power went off. Even though his car was running in his closed-in garage, it was the atmospheric change that killed him.

When hurricanes bring storm surges, with waves often as high as twenty feet, a vast amount of people die from floods, as it was for the 1900 Galveston Hurricane and Katrina in 2005. During Katrina the water rose so quickly through New Orleans that people died trapped in attics, or drowned as they attempted to swim to protruding rooftops in the hope of rescue.

Despite warnings that global warming or even "god's wrath" will bring more, bigger, and stronger hurricanes in coming years, approximately thirteen hundred new residents move into hurricane prone coastal regions every day.

In 2005 another storm, Cat 4 Rita, set its sights on the Gulf Coast. Since predictions for the exact path of a hurricane have a two-hundred- (plus or minus) mile margin of error, some nervous towns order evacuations too early. This was the situation in Houston, when 2.7 million people evacuated the city. One hundred thirty people died running away from the storm that never hit the populated portion of the Texas coastline. Stuck in traffic jams in sweltering heat caused more deaths than the wind, which killed five people when it hit the small Texas-Louisiana border town of Sabine Pass. Among the casualties were thirty elderly who, after being packed into an evacuation bus, died when their oxygen tanks caught fire. (See Also: Potluck Dinners)

U.S. FATALITIES FROM HURRICANES FROM 1940 TO 2005: 3,607

ICE CREAM

Ice cream has been around since the fourth century B.C. Roman emperor Nero (A.D. 37–68) had slaves run from the mountains for a constant supply of fresh snow and ice, which he mixed with goat milk and fruit toppings. In China, around A.D. 600, recipes using frozen milk and coconut were a dynasty favorite. After his voyages throughout China, Marco Polo brought back the formula for ice cream and sherbet prepared with salt and cream to his native Italy, and soon these treats became much-sought-after delicacies for European royalty. In America, the first ice cream parlor opened in New York City in 1776 and became a hangout for George Washington. (He spent $200 for ice cream during the summer of 1790, equivalent to more than $20,000 today.) Thomas Jefferson and Dolley Madison served it regularly to dignitaries visiting the White House and were delighted when guests believed the dessert to be poisoned. Prior to refrigeration, the taste of something so surprisingly cold and creamy, even during the middle of summer, was an unexpected sensation.

ICE CREAM WARS

Ice cream is big business. Although the national fleets of Good Humor trucks and the friendly ice cream man dressed in white are gone, the mobile ice cream vendor still roams the streets of America each summer. The new breed of independent ice cream man must fight to carve out a niche and will take extreme measures to protect his territory. In 2002, a New York City man murdered his cousin with a homemade sword in a dispute over an ice cream sales route. In 2001, in Philadelphia, the top ice cream man of the Humpty Dumpty Ice Cream Company was killed by competitors who tried to make it look like a botched robbery attempt. Ice Cream Wars go on each year and conflicts over vending routes account for 1,117 homicides since 1985.

YOU SCREAM, I SCREAM, SOME FALL DOWN

The lyric You Scream, I Scream, We All Scream for Ice Cream *was written by Howard Johnson and Robert A. K. King in 1928 to market the Eskimo Pie, the first chocolate-covered vanilla ice cream bar sold in the United States. America's love of ice cream hasn't changed; in 2003, Americans ate 1.4 billion gallons of ice cream. Unfortunately, the best-tasting scoop of vanilla ice cream has more than half the recommended daily allotment of cholesterol intake, a nutritional guideline suggested to avoid atherosclerosis, or hardening of the arteries. One million deaths each year are attributed to underlying atherosclerosis.*

MOST REQUESTED LAST MEAL

Clifford Bryson was scheduled to be executed for murder in Oklahoma in 2000. For his last meal he asked for a slice of German chocolate cake and a pint of ice cream. In fact, 96 percent of last meals granted to executed convicts include ice cream. When O. J. Simpson was found liable in the civil suit for the death of his ex-wife and Ron Goldman, he left the Santa Monica court and stopped to buy ice cream.

CROSSING CHILDREN

Although Ivan Pavlov, the Russian physiologist, worked with a German shepherd to demonstrate how dogs could be conditioned to salivate at the ring of a bell, he could have, instead, watched kids react to the sound of an approaching ice cream truck. According to the U.S. Department of Transportation, fatalities of children going to and from an ice cream truck "occur almost exclusively in residential areas, away from intersections, and generally happen as the child is leaving the vending vehicle."

Since 2001, 987 children were killed when buying ice cream.

EVERY DAY IS SUNDAE

An eight-year-old girl didn't like to be reprimanded. When her father scolded her and sent her to bed without her usual dish of ice cream, the little girl decided if she couldn't have dessert, no one should. As her father prepared to eat a piece of pie à la mode and a cup of coffee, she caused a disturbance to get him to leave the kitchen. While he was gone, she sneaked back in to drop ten rat poison tablets in her father's coffee mug. The man took one long swig, fell unconscious and eventually gagged on his own vomit. The girl claimed she didn't understand the seriousness of what she had done and was ordered by the judge to be released in the care of her mother. One month later, the girl tried the same technique on mom when ice cream was withheld, although less successfully, and was sent for intense counseling.

THE FACE BEHIND THE WINDOW

In more genteel times, no one cared who sold ice cream to children as long as it was cold. Now, some vendors are subject to extensive background checks to verify whether they are suitable to work with children or drive among them. It's not until any damage is done, however, that the public knows who is selling ice cream or why. In 1990, a Charlotte, North Carolina, man got a job as an ice cream man to be

near children. He was eventually arrested for selling poisoned ice cream. At the trial, nineteen children testified that he had chained them to a tree and force-fed them drugged Popsicles.

IMMERSION FOOT Some

people have to keep their tennis shoes and work boots in the garage or the back porch because the odor emanating from this footwear is potent enough to make people faint. This embarrassing foot odor, called *bromhydrosis*, is the first sign of Immersion Foot, a condition more commonly known as trench foot, which occurs when feet are subjected to cold and wet conditions for long periods.

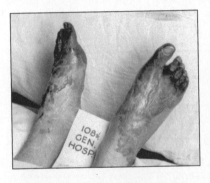

During the Korean War, five thousand U.S. soldiers died from trench foot, resulting from improperly kept footwear. During the Vietnam War, wet jungle conditions caused 4,130 to die from Immersion Foot and other infections classified as "jungle rot."

PAY LESS, PAIN MORE

Today, 3.5 million (noncombative) Americans get Immersion Foot without ever wearing army boots or traipsing through a jungle. Wearing shoes made from rubber, vinyl, or other synthetic materials does not allow the foot to "breathe" or dry out properly, creating mini-jungle conditions in the shoe. In addition to the knock-down odor, Immersion Foot sufferers develop extra layers of skin at the bottom of the foot that becomes thickened, macerated, and painful. Permanent damage to the circulatory system occurs, and death from blood poisoning or gangrene becomes more possible.

LOVE MAY BE BLIND, BUT IT CAN SMELL

In June 2003, in the middle of a Brooklyn street, a two hundred twenty-pound woman killed her boyfriend with a shoe. She was crazed that her boyfriend had decided to break up for what she considered a lame reason—her foot odor. The two came to blows; the woman got the upper hand, and pinned the man to the sidewalk by sitting on his chest. She then took off her size 12 high-heel shoe and clubbed him to death. The woman was arrested and charged with murder and the possession of a deadly weapon—her shoes.

SINCE 1950,
14,298 HAVE DIED FROM
IMMERSION FOOT.

For everyone, sexual intercourse intensifies the heart rate
as if you were suddenly running up a flight of stairs
carrying an eighty-pound sack of rice.

IMPOTENCE Rodney Dangerfield* said that when he took Viagra he "broke the chandelier." Overexertion is usually the primary cause of death when taking potency medications, during or just after sex.

Food and Drug Administration preliminary tests indicate that the chemicals known as selective inhibitors in erectile agent Viagra are relatively safe, as long as they're not mixed with nitroglycerin, a drug given to many heart patients. But many men don't care about the risks. Dr. William Steers, the University of Virginia's urology chairman said, "Men value sexuality over general health . . . They are going to take Viagra regardless of the consequences." Dr. Ira Sharlip of San Francisco, an impotence expert associated with the American Urological Association added, "I've had a lot of patients say, 'If I have to go, that's the way I want to go out.' "

DEATHS AMONG MEN AFTER
TAKING IMPOTENCE DRUGS
ARE AT
11,344 PER YEAR.

INDEPENDENCE DAY John Adams, the second U.S. President and a Founding Father, wrote to his wife Abigail, "We should always remember

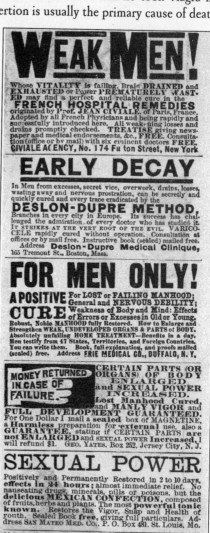

* Rodney Dangerfield (born Jacob Cohen), best known for his one-liners ("I don't get no respect"), died at age eighty-two from complications of heart surgery on October 7, 2004. For ten years Dangerfield suffered through numerous grave ailments, double bypass surgery, aneurysms, and an intracranial brain bypass operation in April 2003. In the last month of his life, he roused briefly from a coma, smiled at the doctors, and said: "I bought a cemetery plot. The guy said, 'There goes the neighborhood.' " (*See Also:* Laughing)

On July 4, 2005, fireworks killed eleven people. There were another eleven thousand visits to emergency rooms resulting from fireworks-related injuries.

that momentous day, the second of July. It ought to be solemnized with pomp and parade, with shows, games, sports, guns, bells, bonfires, and illuminations, from one end of this continent to the other, from this time forward forevermore."

Declared a federal holiday in 1941, Americans now celebrate Independence Day on the 4th of July with barbecues, picnics and parades, fireworks displays, and other enjoyable activities. It is also a time for backyard firecrackers, bottle rockets, cherry bombs, and other hazardous explosives. Pyrotechnics are associated with more than one thousand residential fires, costing millions of dollars in property damage and loss each year.

Boys under the age of fifteen are most often hurt, injured, and killed by fireworks. They love to throw lit firecrackers at each other or shoot bottle rockets at friends. Sparklers that sizzle at 1,800 degrees Fahrenheit tossed into a crowd have caused horrific burns, partial or total loss of sight, lacerations, and fractures.

Most fireworks deaths occur when trying to reignite a pyrotechnic dud. The now-shorter fuse on an explosive device that didn't work right the first time is the most dangerous.

"LIFE, LIBERTY, AND THE PURSUIT OF HAPPINESS"

*For the fiftieth anniversary of the Declaration of Independence, the government declared 1826 a "year of national jubilee." While across the country people celebrated The Fourth of July with real cannons and live bullets, two authors of the historic document died hours apart: **Thomas Jefferson** (right) succumbed to chronic digestive and urinary problems and diarrhea at age eighty-three. **John Adams** (left) died of pneumonia at age ninety.*

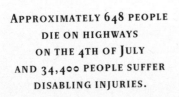

APPROXIMATELY 648 PEOPLE DIE ON HIGHWAYS ON THE 4TH OF JULY AND 34,400 PEOPLE SUFFER DISABLING INJURIES.

The July 4th holiday period is the third most heavily traveled on the nation's roads, after Thanksgiving and Christmas.

The greatest number of fatal accidents occur between 3:00 and 6:00 P.M. on July 4th.

INDIGESTION In 2001, a twenty-three-year-old man from Ocean City, Maryland, suffered from chronic heartburn. His friends told him he ate too fast and didn't drink enough fluids. One night, at a local Hooter's, the man was encouraged by his friends to wash down a basket of hot and spicy wings with a pitcher of beer. But instead of his regular bout of heartburn, he also got a bad case of burps. At first it seemed funny, but after a while his repetitive toad croaks got annoying, so he asked a buddy to punch him hard in the stomach to try to put an end to it. No one wanted to,

but a friend finally gave him one strong, stiff jab to shut him up. The man went outside for air and immediately collapsed on the sidewalk and died. It was later discovered that he was riddled with ulcers. Although the only medication he had ever taken was larger and larger doses of antacid, jalapeño-flavored wings, a stomach filled with beer, and a whack in the gut surely didn't help.

ALL YOU CAN EAT

Simple indigestion, called dyspepsia, is caused by eating too fast, too much, or foods that don't "agree" with the system. Although a burning sensation in the chest often follows, heartburn has nothing to do with the heart but is caused by stomach acids splashing up into the esophagus. Continued eating of spicy and greasy foods, mixed with a fair amount of stress, will lead to **ulcers,** unhealing open wounds at the junction of the stomach and small intestine. People who continue to gobble handfuls of antacid tablets to soothe what they believe is indigestion, but in fact are ulcers, increase the risk of fatal bleeding. Although in the U.S. remedies for gastrointestinal ailments tally sales of $2.5 billion each year, many doctors believe over-the-counter antacids temporarily disguise the problem, setting the stage for greater incidents of life-threatening stomach problems. (*See Also:* Over-the-Counter *and* Halitosis)

IN 2003, THERE WERE 850,000 NEW CASES OF PEPTIC ULCER DISEASE; 4,976 DIED.

INSOMNIA When the witches in *Macbeth* conjured the worst curse imaginable, they knew that denying sleep would be a wonderfully cruel joke to play upon the victim. It's commonly said that lack of sleep won't kill you, and insomnia, as a cause of fatality found on death certificates, is rare. However, there is one type of condition called **Sporadic Fatal Insomnia (SFI)** that makes for a bizarre and mortifying ending.

A forty-four-year-old California man found it increasingly difficult to fall

NUNCA DORMIMOS
REG. U.S. PAT. OFF.

WIDE AWAKE

asleep. Previously healthy, the man's family doctor downplayed his complaints, saying they were "all in his head." Four months went by with the man getting no more than one hour of shut-eye each night—safe doses of prescribed sleeping pills had no affect. He started to have trouble walking, lost weight, and burst into tears at the drop of a hat. His children were embarrassed to have him show up for events, and his wife canceled most couple-orientated social activities. Gradually, the man lost coordination and short-term memory, unable to sort dreams from reality. One year after his first sleepless night, his wife admitted him to a long-term care facility. Four months later, severely misdiagnosed and actually suffering from Sporadic Fatal Insomnia, he died. Recent research has begun to link SFI to abnormal brain proteins, responsible for wreaking havoc on sleeping patterns, known as circadian rhythms, and irreparably altering one normal body function after another.

OBSTRUCTIVE SLEEP APNEA, NARCOLEPSY, AND CHRONIC INSOMNIA AFFECT 30 TO 40 MILLION PEOPLE.

In 1997, four years after **Philip Taylor Kramer** *of the seventies rock band "Iron Butterfly" disappeared, his van was found at the bottom of a five-hundred-foot ravine in Malibu, California. Two hikers stumbled on the rusted wreck and found the skeletal remains of the former rock legend inside. Kramer's medical records indicated he suffered from extended sleeplessness, possibly from SFI, and was diagnosed with Dissociate Fugue. Authorities believe he intentionally drove himself off the cliff.*

TOTAL DEATHS SINCE 1960 ATTRIBUTED TO INSOMNIA: 21,756

INTERNET DATING Over a million people each day look for their soul mates in anonymous Internet chat rooms. These chat rooms have categories and headings that are intended to hook you up to people with similar interests, but almost beg the users to lie: "Thirty-something and self-made," "Forty and fit," "Fun-loving and Fifty." But the Net can entwine a sticky Web.

CREEPINESS FACTOR
Many of the thousand or more dating sites available on the Web attract a disproportionate share of

oddballs and an abundance of freaks. Take the case of the Internet dating fiasco that happened one night in San Antonio, Texas, in April 2000. An A&M University student headed out from his dorm room to meet a "very sexy" female named Kelly, whom he'd met in a chat room called "Looking for Love." The next morning the student's body was found in a ditch, with a bullet hole in his head. "Kelly" was actually Kenny Wayne Lockwood, an overweight, balding short-order cook. He pretended to be Kelly online to sexually molest his victims and had successfully deceived more than a dozen other young men into believing he was a woman. The A&M student had threatened to expose Kelly's real identity. Lockwood, while in jail and without access to his computer, committed suicide.

A forty-four-year-old multimillionaire divorcé, known for his gaudy jewelry and gullible nature, looked for dates on the Internet. He had personal ads on both Match.com and Matchmaker.com, despite his experience with a woman he met on a blind date who drugged him, stole his Mercedes, Rolex, and $71,000 worth of jewelry in 1993. In August 2002 his planned tryst with a woman he met online turned out even worse. He was found dead from a gunshot wound to the neck at a Best Western Hotel in Tempe, Arizona. The unknown assailant was never captured.

TOTAL INTERNET-RELATED HOMICIDES SINCE 1995:
442; RAPES: 2,194

JAIL BREAK States classify prison breaks differently and rarely report them nationally. In Florida, where older records could be obtained, there were 160 escapes in fiscal year 1998–1999, or one every other day. Over the last fifty years, 70 percent of escaped prisoners were recaptured alive, 15 percent were killed during capture or escape, 11 percent committed suicide, and 4 percent got away for good.

In 1850 there were only 6,700 people in the nation's newly emerging prison system. After the Civil War, there were 47,619 prisoners, and the percentage of black prisoners had grown from 0 to 33 percent. In 2005, there were 2,849,891 incarcerated persons living in America, costing taxpayers $41 billion. Prisoners sentenced for drug offenses constitute the largest group of federal inmates (61 percent). Female prisoners number 91,612.

Racist groups thrive in prisons throughout the United States, increasing chances of death behind bars to ten times higher than on the outside. Many prisons are overcrowded, making adequate medical care for AIDS, tuberculosis, and other chronic illnesses a challenge.

In 2003, 159 inmates were killed by other inmates, 6,750 were raped, and 2,354 correctional staff were injured seriously enough to require medical attention.

MOST FAMOUS ESCAPE
Alcatraz (below left), *also known as the "Rock," lies off the coast of San Francisco and once held the reputation as an escape-proof prison. However, during the years that the federal prison operated (1934–1963), thirty-six men tried to escape the island. Twenty-five were caught before they got a chance to jump into San Francisco Bay, six were shot and killed waist-deep in the tide, and two drowned. Frank Lee Morris and the two Anglin Brothers, as portrayed in the film, Escape from Alcatraz, were the only escapees never found.*

On June 11, 1962, Morris and his crew escaped, through a ventilator, leaving behind lifelike dummies in their bunks. The water temperature in the bay was 56 degrees on the night of their escape, and some believe they likely drowned in the notoriously strong current that surrounds the island. Although the FBI presumed them drowned, other lawmen figured that if the trio were ingenious enough to escape, they were capable of survival. The FBI continues to investigate annual sightings of Morris, from Spain to Argentina.

**THIRTY-FIVE HUNDRED PRISON
INMATES
DIE EACH YEAR.**

NO ONE GETS OUT

The bloodiest day inside a U.S. prison occurred in September 1971 when prisoners, some previously convicted of murder and rape, gained control of Attica prison in New York (below). "We are men, not beasts, and will not be driven as such," the prisoner leaders proclaimed. Twenty-nine prisoners and ten guards who were their hostages were killed by New York State troopers in their efforts to regain control.

NO LOOPHOLES

A North Carolina man was on top of the world, a self-proclaimed smart guy who made money by finding the loopholes in laws. He bought a $15,000 box of vintage imported cigars and took out an insurance policy, just like he did for his other valuables, protecting them against hazards, including fire. Once he finished smoking the two dozen cigars in the box, he filed an insurance claim, stating that the cigars had been "consumed" by fire. The insurance company took him to court but was ordered to pay the man his claim because his policy did not specify the exact nature of fire it covered or excluded. The man jauntily stepped into the bank with his check. However, the moment he cashed it, he was arrested, charged, and convicted of twenty-four counts of arson— one for each cigar. Unable to find a loophole, he was sent to prison for two years, where he meet his demise in an argument over a book of matches.

J AYWALKING A jaywalker is a pedestrian who crosses the street without regard for traffic regulations, when the light is red or outside of crosswalks. More than half of pedestrian fatalities are due to jaywalking, an illegal activity that, when enforced, will get the apprehended a ticket. Jaywalkers hit by cars are not seen as victims, but as lawbreakers. In New York City, when a driver hit an eighty-year-old woman who emerged from between parked cars near Central Park, he was arrested for driving without a license, not for the woman's death.

Many continue to jaywalk, seeing it as an act of rebellion. One self-proclaimed jaywalker stated after receiving a ticket that he was acting against the tyranny of automobile culture. Pedestrians must navigate along narrow sidewalks, street vendors, outdoor cafés, signposts, garbage cans, newspaper stands, and a large number of other people, which often makes spilling out into the street a necessary time-saving option, even if it's a fatal one. On rural roads where jaywalking is not the problem, the danger for pedestrians is sideswipes.

A ROAD LESS TRAVELED
Jerry Rubin was a social activist during the Vietnam War years, but left the political arena to become a successful entrepreneur. He made money in health foods and then the stock market. But he still had trouble following some rules, like waiting for the light to turn green. At age fifty-six, in 1994, he was killed by a car while jaywalking.

JAYWALKING FATALITIES SINCE 1990: 14,902

JELLYFISH All jellyfish are invertebrates—boneless blobs that invade U.S. beaches each year. The stinging capsules in their tentacles at first cause a mild local itch that often becomes severe burning with throbbing pain. Some jellyfish stings lead to cardiorespiratory arrest.

THERE ARE 1,918, MOST OF WHOM ARE CHILDREN, WHO DIE OF ALLERGIC REACTION EACH YEAR TO JELLYFISH.

WEAR A WET SUIT
A box fish or sea wasp, found primarily in the Pacific, is the deadliest marine creature. Just the slightest bit of its venom, ten times more potent than a cobra's, will cause death. Fifty-five die from sea wasp bites each year.

Starfish, cone fish, scorpion fish, sea urchins, and stingrays all have venom in their spines or tails that cause deadly allergic reaction in some people. Forty-five die each year from encounters with these creatures.

JOB'S SYNDROME In the Old Testament, Job's faith was tested by having to endure a series of misfortunes. One included body growths: According to the King James Bible, "Job was smote with sore boils from the sole of his

foot unto his crown." Because of this passage, doctors in 1966 thought Job's Syndrome was a good name to bestow on a condition wherein the afflicted are plagued with severe recurrent infections of both *Candida* (yeast) and staphylococci (spherical bacteria), which form as abscesses on the skin, in the sinuses, and in the lungs. Improper T-cell production is the cause of Job's Syndrome, which can be managed with an aggressive treatment of antibiotics. If the body builds resistance to medications the lungs eventually fill with fluid and airways close, causing death within a year after diagnosis. Although it's an inherited immune deficiency, manifesting predominately in red-haired, fair-skinned females, people of other coloring have been equally smote.

When a New York man was diagnosed with Job's Syndrome, he became irate. Acquiring the rare immune deficiency disorder was one thing, but as a practicing atheist he found it unacceptable to die of a disease with such religious connotations. He claimed his disease had little to do with a divine test as it had to do with deficient T-cell production. He planned to sue the AMA, citing separation of church and state, protesting that diseases with religious names have no place on public death certificates. Upon his death, his certificate cited as cause of death Buckley's Syndrome, a similar ailment with somewhat less biblical ramifications.

JOB'S SYNDROME FATALITIES SINCE 1999: 750

JUICE EXTRACTORS Squeezing juice from fruit would seem like a simple procedure. Since 1919 there have been 10,378 different contraptions offered to get the juice from an orange. Commercial units have swirling blades and powerful compression components, while home models have modified, though similar, designs. In 1998, one home juice machine company was fined $300,000 for selling forty thousand exploding juicers, which severed the fingers of twenty-three consumers and killed two. Other home devices with whirling blades include tree and leaf mulchers and snowplows.

JUNK COLLECTING "There's gold in them thar hills," Willy H. would say about the local dump in Van Nuys, California. He liked to show his neighbors all the wonderful and useful objects that could be made from things people threw away. One afternoon he was out flying a box kite that he had fashioned from discarded fabrics. Instead of buying a fifty-cent roll of twine, Willy guided his kite with a salvaged ball of fine aluminum wire. Things were working like a

EASY TO USE,
EASY TO CLEAN

In December 2004, a Deland, Florida, man was making wood chips for his garden. When the machine became clogged, he climbed on a ladder and tried to use a pitchfork to get it going without shutting it off. While doing so, he fell and landed headfirst into the machine. Police found his legs sticking out and concluded that the man died moments after falling into the mulcher.

READING AND
OPERATING MANUALS

Before William Bullock invented offset printing, every book or printed text was produced by hand. Bullock's press revolutionized printing and led to the mass production of the inexpensive "Dime Novel" as it allowed paper to feed on a continuous roll, and printed on both sides of the paper at once. In 1865, while working late in his shop, Bullock fell into one of the giant whirling rollers and was permanently put out of print.

charm until a gust of wind tangled the kite on a nearby power line. In a flash, a high-voltage electricity current traveled down the wire wrapped around Willy's hand and stopped his heart. (*See Also:* Eccentrics)

*Rock promoter **Bill Graham** (sixty), known for his rock 'n' roll shows at San Francisco's Fillmore Auditorium and New York City's Fillmore East, died October 25, 1991, when his helicopter hit an electrical tower in Vallejo, California.*

FATALITIES FROM POWER LINES SINCE 1985: 35,871

KABUKI MAKEUP SYNDROME

A rearrangement of the eighth chromosome, the genes of which are normally related to the inhibition of tumor growth and other blood disorders, causes this odd and visually striking ailment. Defined for the first time by Japanese doctors in 1980, the disease leads to permanent facial transformation that appears similar to that of actors in traditional Japanese Kabuki theater, known for its distinctive makeup style.

Previously, Kabuki patients were thought to have impish or elflike features for no other reason than genetics. Long and thick eyelashes, significantly arched eyebrows, flattened nose tips, and increasingly protruding ears develop in the afflicted. During the onset of Kabuki, teeth become widely spaced and irregular, and many doctors believe it to be a question of needing dentistry, not due to a disease. These facial changes, which are sometimes evident from birth but can develop during puberty or in adult women after giving birth, precede underlying heart abnormalities and an impending death by seizures. Until recently, men with Kabuki that had complexions similar to cosmetic masks worn by mimes* were left medically unobserved, considered to be eccentrics in perpetual makeup. Women with Kabuki were simply ignored as unschooled in the art of proper makeup use and were believed to pluck their eyebrows into arches on purpose. Hence, many with Kabuki went undiagnosed. Scientists are uncertain why

PERMANENT EYELINER

People do try to achieve the look of the perpetually made-up and get permanent makeup applied using a new technique, a form of tattooing, which creates lip or eye liners, or eyebrow colors. The type of ink used for permanent makeup has caused serious disfigurement, swelling, scarring, and respiratory fatalities.

---

* A famous mime performer, **Otto Griebling**, with a career spanning fifty years, was noted for juggling metal pie plates and other objects, performing in silence. In 1970, he had his larynx removed due to cancer, and pantomime became a way of life both in and out of makeup. He died in 1972.

the genes that cause this disease suddenly malfunction or rearrange in sequence for no apparent reason. The physical changes in a person's face cause no pain, although many psychological issues obviously arise. Since 1980, this previously unknown way to die has taken 3,750 lives.

THE SILVER SCREEN

Buddy Ebsen was originally cast to play the Tin Man in the Wizard of Oz, *but a few weeks into filming he got seriously ill, poisoned by the lead-based silver makeup and nearly died. He was replaced by Jack Haley. The makeup used on Haley was changed to aluminum-based, which allowed his wizard-awarded heart to keep ticking until he was seventy-nine years old. He died in 1978 of respiratory failure.*

For the 1964 James Bond film classic, Goldfinger, *Shirley Eaton, the actress who played a seductress (listed in the credits as "The Girl Covered Entirely in Gold Paint"), had to leave a patch of skin on her stomach unpainted to allow the skin to breath so she wouldn't die during filming.*

Skin is the body's largest organ. It eliminates body toxins and helps regulate body temperature; according to Life Extension *magazine, October 2003, "one square inch of skin contains 2,800 openings for sweat and oil glands." When the skin is entirely covered with paint, non-lead-based or otherwise, the lungs become incapable of oxygenating all cells and releasing toxins, which can cause a fatal metabolism imbalance within three hours.*

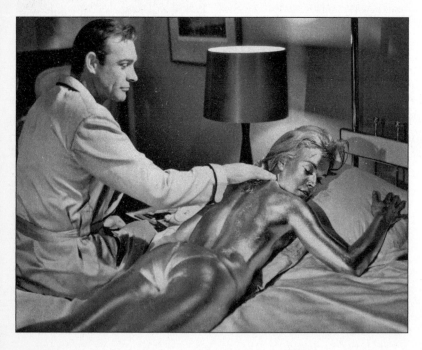

PUCKER-UP

According to *The Lipstick Indicator*, which measures lipstick purchases and other economic trends, women buy more lipstick when they have a pessimistic outlook. In the last four years, lipstick sales have skyrocketed; the average woman will use six pounds of lipstick in her lifetime. Today, there are more shades of lipstick than colors found in the biggest box of crayons, along with an endless slew of new products designed for no other reason than to beautify.

One government study, conducted by the Occupational Safety and Health Association (OSHA), identified more than 125 chemical ingredients in cosmetics believed to cause cancer and birth defects. Eight hundred eighty-four ingredients in personal care products such as perfume, skin creams, and shampoos were found to be potentially cancerous.

Rouge, or liquid foundation, caused 11,345 poison-related emergency room visits in 2002.

The FDA warns makeup users to be alert to allergic reactions that do not always appear as hives or skin rashes. Some allergic reactions are subtle and can come in the form of gradual mood changes. Certain types of depression may actually be an allergic reaction to the chemicals found in makeup. Scientists now believe that a number of psychotic mental illnesses are the result of allergies stemming from a woman's choice of makeup.

KILLER BEES Brazilian scientists imported African bees in 1956 in an effort to find a honeybee that could withstand tropical climates. Escaped specimens bred with local wild species and mutated into a killer bee. The new "Africanized" hybrid moved north, reaching Texas in 1990 and by June 2000, the bees were found in northeast Florida. As of June 2005 killer bees have been spotted in Nevada, Arizona, New Mexico, and California and on the East Coast from Georgia to New Jersey. Africanized bees are no more venomous than the common honeybee; however, this mutated variety is more aggressive, attacking a quarter mile away from the hive they are protecting. Most deaths from killer bees occur due to the sudden toxicity of multiple stings.

LOOKING FOR TROUBLE
In Texas, a man died after being stung forty times when he tried to knock down a giant nest with a rake. In January 2000, a seventy-nine-year-old Las Vegas man died when he was stung thirty times picking up the morning paper from his driveway. In March 2001, a swarm of two hundred killer bees enveloped a seventy-seven-year-old woman walking down the street, enticed by something in the bag she carried. The woman was stung over five hundred times.

**KILLER BEE FATALITIES
SINCE 1990: 179**

In 1999, a central Florida boy was attacked by a swarm of **yellow jack-**

ets, a territorial wasp that savagely guards its nest. The three-year-old was digging near the porch of his mobile home when his parents noticed the boy swatting at bees. The adults sprayed the boy down with a hose and dabbed on witch hazel. The bees had stung him fifty to seventy-five times on his face and head, and one hundred to one hundred fifty times on his body. Seven hours later, when the child stopped breathing, the parents called for an ambulance. "He had some bee stings, but he seemed to be all right," the boy's father said. If treated promptly with drugs such as epinephrine, those allergic to bee stings can be saved.

> HONEY BEES AND WASPS, PARTICULARLY THE YELLOW JACKET,
> CAUSE SIX THOUSAND DEATHS A YEAR.

KINKY HAIR DISEASE Kinky hair disease is due to a metabolic defect, a fatty acid buildup on the gray matter of the brain caused by improper copper metabolism. Copper, a trace mineral found in several enzymes and proteins, is essential for many bodily functions, particularly the absorption of iron needed for immune processes. When this mineral cannot be metabolized or expelled under normal body functions, it finds its way to the brain and gathers there. Kinky hair sufferers often feel cold when others do not, and in general

experience a prolonged sense of malaise, not as strong as depression but rather an unexplained melancholy and listlessness. But the most unfortunate physical outcome of this disorder is the acquisition of strikingly peculiar hair. Once-straight hair then becomes "kinky" or stumpy, snarled, meager, steely, and easily broken. Most people think their hair change is due to conditioners or shampoos and seek diagnostic tests too late. The hair turns white, ivory, or gray in color, which no amount of dye or highlights can cover. When copper cannot be metabolized, kinky hair patients actually are in the process of body metamorphosis; due to a lack of copper absorption, the essential structures of hair, brain, bones, liver, and arteries are changing.

The prospects for persons with kinky hair disease are not good as the body cannot function without adequate copper. Most affected persons die within the first decade after acquiring kinky hair.

1,563 DIED OF KINKY HAIR DISEASE IN 2004.

KISSING DISEASE

Evelyn Millis Duvall's 1956 book, *Facts of Life and Love for Teen-Agers,* cautioned that the first date is too soon for a goodnight kiss. This isn't just 1950s advice for the prim and proper. If your prospective love mate has a runny nose, a cough, or a splotchy red rash over his or her body, it might be better to forestall smooching until you see a blood test; jumping into a French kiss—that is, placing your tongues in each other's mouth— may be more than a bit of a risk in these infectious times.

Kissing disease, or **mononucleosis** (also known as the simpler "mono"), is a contagious viral infection, transmitted primarily by sharing saliva. The infection most often affects kissing-crazy and germ-spreading fifteen- to seventeen-year-olds, and causes fever from 102 to 104 degrees, red throats, swollen lymph glands in the neck, and swollen spleens. Repeated bouts of mono can lead to

cancer and are believed to be the lead- *If your nose itches, you will shake*
ing causes of Hodgkin's disease and *hands with or kiss a fool—old wives' tale,*
cancer deaths among that age group. *circa 1775.*
Those who had mono as a teenager are
advised to keep a strong immune system and boost T-cell production to offset
their greater propensity for cancer.

EPSTEIN-BARR VIRUS (EBV), CONSIDERED THE CAUSE
IN INFECTIOUS MONONUCLEOSIS, IS ATTRIBUTED TO
SEVEN THOUSAND DEATHS PER YEAR.
IF YOU ARE DIAGNOSED WITH ANY FORM OF EBV,
YOU, IN FACT, HAVE MONONUCLEOSIS.

LABOR DAY

The celebration of Labor Day began over 120 years ago in New York City on Tuesday, September 5, 1882, organized as a parade by union machinist Matthew Maguire to show worker solidarity. Twenty thousand workers marched up Broadway, chanting "Labor creates all wealth" and "Eight hours for work, eight hours for rest, eight hours for recreation!" But it was a relatively sedate protest parade followed by union family picnics and a firework display.

FREE LABOR WILL WIN

In 1894, President Grover Cleveland needed to get reelected and knew the populace was not too happy with his recent move against workers, sending twelve thousand National Guard troops to stop a railroad strike. As a last-ditch effort to win votes, he declared the first Monday in September a national holiday to honor labor, but lost the bid for reelection anyway. From 1920 to 1950 there were, at times, communist undertones to Labor Day celebrations that made entrepreneurs and the American capitalist government nervous.

Today, Labor Day is celebrated more as the last long summer weekend than as a tribute to workers. Some propose it should now be called Business Day, since only 15 percent of the work force is unionized, compared to 55 percent in 1950.

Labor Day ranks as the fifth busiest day for car travel. In the last ten years, 475 people died in car accidents on Labor Day. Fifty-two percent of these accidents were alcohol related. Another 425 people died staying put over Labor Day weekends, from falls or drowning or other incidents in the home. The Friday before Labor Day ranks as the second busiest day for air travel. Many vacation at U.S. beaches, which may attribute to increased shark fatalities. Twenty-five percent of all shark attacks occur on Labor Day.

LABYRINTH DISEASE

Some say trying to find a cure for any ailment requires persistence in getting through the maze of the medical system and will give you Labyrinth disease if you don't already have it. For those experiencing this illness, it is exceptionally hard to find a way out of its troubling side effects even with the best therapeutic treatment. Labyrinth disease is used to

KIM NOVAK W PODWÓJNEJ ROLI | JAMES STEWART
BARBARA DEL GEDDES W MROŻĄCYM KREW W ŻYŁACH ~ BARWNYM FILMIE

HITCHCOCKA

ZAWRÓT GŁOWY

TILT·A·WORLD

One thirty-one-year-old vertigo patient described his days as "living with a time bomb that has a random number generator on the timer. You never know when it's going to blow." Another forty-six-year-old compared his vertigo as being really drunk and getting stuck on the Tilt-a-Whirl, an amusement park ride, for hours at a time. The affects of this disease are so horrific that Alfred Hitchcock based an entire movie, the 1958 surrealistic masterpiece Vertigo, *around it.*

Vertigo can strike any time, so Labyrinth sufferers refrain from partaking in normal activities. Some become so affected by the illusion of spinning that they suddenly fall while standing or walking. These drop attacks, also called the "Crisis of Tumarkin" (named for British physician Arthur Tumarkin who studied the condition in 1936), can be lethal if the incident occurs at the wrong time, like when driving or when walking down a flight of stairs.

Sixty thousand people have some form of this disease and without medication will die within three years, although the cause of death is usually listed as

describe various forms of **vertigo** and is often called **Ménière's disease**, named after French physician Prosper Ménière who first described the syndrome in 1861. The cause of this disorder stems from a change in fluid quantity within the portion of the inner ear known as the labyrinth. The delicate membranes of the labyrinth channel that goes from the ear to the brain may have scar tissue or might be too narrow or too large from birth, which causes fluctuating fluid pressure to fill the inner ear. This disease could also be caused by a serious ear infection or a blow to the back of the head, injuring the cerebellum that regulates balance. Attacks of vertigo are disabling and often life threatening; without warning, the vertigo sufferer senses either that everything is spinning around them or that they themselves are spinning. Loud noises and busy places often aggravate attacks.

accidental. Some people with vertigo have dropped dead from heart attack or stroke, apparently overcome by an overwhelmingly dizzying episode.

**APPROXIMATELY FOUR THOUSAND PEOPLE WITH
LABYRINTH DISEASE DIED IN 2004.**

LATEX SENSITIVITY Every time one sixty-five-year-old man from Bar Harbour, Florida, walked into the dentist's office, he would break out in hives. For years, his wife called him a chicken for fearing the dentist and said his watery eyes and skin rashes were all in his head. When he clutched his chest and fell to the floor in his dentist's waiting room in 1996, paramedics arrived too late. He died of anaphylactic shock caused by an allergic reaction to rubber. It was later discovered that the air in the office was thick with fine molecules of latex dust from medical gloves and dental dams. The man had latex sensitivity before many knew what it was.

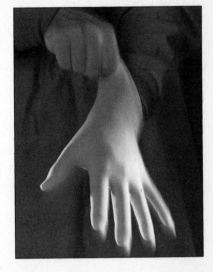

Latex sensitivity is an allergy to anything rubber, including medical gloves, condoms, birth control devices, first-aid gauze, bandages, pacifiers, baby bottles, maintenance gloves, balloons, balls, tennis racquets, pencil erasers, Halloween masks, elastic fabric, underwear bands, diapers, carpet backing, rubber mats, and paint. (Paint labeled "latex" actually contains no rubber or latex products.) Latex reactions usually become more severe if the person has recently eaten bananas, chestnuts, papaya, cherries, figs, passion fruit, peaches, or avocados, which contain many of the same proteins that cause latex allergies.

The body does not easily detoxify latex; the greater the exposure and the longer a person touches latex, the harsher the reaction. Healthcare workers and laboratory researchers, more than any other group, have rampant latex problems as they are required to wear medical gloves to protect themselves from diseases they come in contact with. At least 15 percent of all healthcare workers develop latex allergy, which can be a career-ending disability.

LEMONS INTO LEMONADE
One nurse in New Orleans sued the hospital when she experienced severe reactions from rubber gloves. She won a workers' compensation of $60,000 in 1997. After attempting to open a bakery, she went back to nursing a year later and once again sued again for symptoms of latex allergies, this time being awarded $75,000.

Hospitals are loaded with rubber and most medical equipment uses it in some procedure or another. Monitoring equipment, IVs, urinary drainage tubes, and oxygen supply masks are a few examples of rubber in use. Hospitals with recirculating air—compared to systems that bring in fresh air—have the greatest number of workers that suffer from latex reactions. In 2004, fourteen deaths were caused by patient reactions to the latex cuff and the lubricated rubber tube inserted into the rectum used in barium enemas.

GOT TO WEAR GLOVES

In 1847 Dr. Ignaz Simmelweis was a young doctor working in the maternity ward at a hospital in Vienna. No matter what he did, half of his patients died. At the time, doctors operated in their street clothes, and child-delivery rooms, like all other parts of hospitals, were filthy. Simmelweis gradually discovered that when he washed his hands before and after dealing with a patient that the infant and mother mortality rate dropped dramatically. He went on a vigorous campaign to get doctors and nurses to regularly wash their hands, but was met with hostility and ultimately dismissed from practicing medicine anywhere, blacklisted as an annoying pest. For fourteen years he lectured about unwashed hands as vectors of disease and eventually wrote a book, *Die Ätiologie, der Begriff und die Prophylaxis des Kindbettfiebers* on the subject in 1861. When the book received bad reviews, Simmelweis had a nervous breakdown and was committed to an insane asylum, where he got blood poisoning from attendants who didn't wash their hands; he died in 1865.

The first patent for rubber gloves was registered in 1878, declaring them a necessity for "surgical or other operations in which it is essential to protect the hands but still to retain delicate sensitivity." It was another forty years before surgeons regularly used gloves when operating.

SINCE 1995, RUBBER ALLERGIES
HAVE KILLED 3,976.

LAUGHING It's hard to get a straight answer to the question of what makes us laugh from research scientists who study laughter. However, they do know that the left side of the brain processes words in a joke or any statement and then sends them to the frontal lobes, a part of the brain that controls a person's affect, judgment, personality, and inhibitions. If the frontal lobes determine that something is funny, it sends signals to the motor cortex, a part of the brain that controls movement, causing laughter. People with a malfunctioning or damaged limbic system (the limbic system consists of the hypothalmus, hippocampus, and amygdale, a complex set of structures on both sides of the brain) have no emotions and cannot

laugh at anything generally considered funny.

Norman Cousins, longtime editor of *The Saturday Review,* was the first to document the positive effects of humor and laughter on the ailing in his book *Anatomy of an Illness,* published in 1976. Ten years earlier, Cousins was diagnosed with ankylosing spondylitis, a painful spine disease that ultimately results in a vegetative paralysis. When medical experts consulted their clipboards and gave him a one in five hundred chance of survival, Cousins laughed, mostly from shock. He did take the prescribed medications of the day, but also devised his own humor treatments. He found that fifteen minutes of vigorous laughter could help him have two hours of pain-free sleep. Blood tests showed his inflammation level was lower after each humor treatment. Cousins cured himself of that disease and lived until 1990, when he died of cardiac arrest at the age of seventy-five.

> *People with untreated heart disease are 40 percent less likely to laugh at funny situations, compared to people without heart disease.*

LAUGH LOUD AND SLOW
"Ha-ha," a typical laugh identified by a series of short vowel-like sounds, takes sixty milliseconds to pronounce and is repeated during laughter at continuous interims of two hundred milliseconds apart. If the laugh exceeds this speed, the brain will become starved of oxygen.

LAUGHING AT NOTHING
In 1999, a joke told in a Seattle bar started a thirty-five-year-old man on a thirteen-hour irrepressible laughing spasm. Doctors were unable to stop the man's laughter-induced convulsions and he eventually died of heart failure. Before he died, the man was asked what was so funny. Between gasps and hoots of laughter the man said: "There was something about an antelope. And shellfish. I remember a part about shellfish."

DO COMEDIANS LIVE LONGER?
Steve Allen: Born to vaudeville-comedian parents, Allen was known for his hysterical ad-libbed interviews with audiences and zany man-on-the-street televised interactions. He created the *Tonight Show* and wrote over four thousand songs and thirty-eight books. He died of a heart attack in October 2000 at age seventy-eight.

Abbott and Costello *(right):* Lou Costello (the short one) and Bud Abbott perfected wordplay comedy, such as the infamous 1940 "Who's on First?" skit, first seen in the movie *The Naughty Nineties*, in which Abbott tries in vain to explain to Costello that the baseball player on first base is in fact named Who. They were the first non-baseball players to be inducted into the Baseball Hall of Fame.

The duo first teamed up in 1936 and worked together for twenty years until money issues split up their act in 1958. A year later, Costello died from a rheumatic heart at age fifty-six. Abbott worked in a few small roles after his partner's death. He had epilepsy and a stroke, though he died of cancer in 1974, at age seventy-eight.

Roscoe "Fatty" Arbuckle *(below)*: Popular during the silent-movie era, "Fatty" Arbuckle was the original fat comedian: He weighed over three hundred pounds at the peak of his fame. In 1921, Arbuckle's career was destroyed when actress

Virginia Rappe was murdered in his hotel room after a reckless party. Accused of the murder, although eventually acquitted, Arbuckle never worked as a comedian again and died of a heart attack at the age of forty-six.

Lucille Ball: Known for her role as "Lucy Ricardo" in the classic TV comedy series *I Love Lucy,* Lucille Ball had labored in films for twenty years before that show became an overnight success. Besides being a comedic innovator, she was also a shrewd businesswoman, becoming the first woman to head a film studio. Lucy died in 1989 at age seventy-seven from a ruptured aorta after a surgical procedure.

John Belushi: Chubby, rubber-faced John Belushi died from a drug overdose in 1982 at the age of thirty-three. He was part of the original *Saturday Night Live* cast and starred in such movie classics as *Animal House* and *The Blues Brothers.*

Jack Benny: Bad violin-playing Jack Benny, respected for his comedic deadpan one-liners, died at age eighty in 1974 of cancer of the pancreas.

Milton Berle: A pioneer of television comedy, Milton Berle was known to a generation of Americans as "Uncle Miltie" from his long stint on *The Texaco Star Theater,* which debuted on the small screen in 1948. His jokes and comic skits bolstered the sales of millions of TV sets in homes across the country, making Berle one of the first stars of television history. The cigar-smoking Berle died from colon cancer at the age of ninety-three in March 2002.

John Candy *(right)*: At age forty-two, John Candy, a morbidly obese, lovable, and brilliant comedian, died of a heart attack while on location for what would be his last movie, *Wagons East.*

Johnny Carson: For thirty years (1962–1992) Johnny Carson was the comedic host of the *Tonight Show*. He had a quick wit and a gracious "everyman" charisma, which made him a staple on millions of bedtime TVs across America. His show was also the launching pad for many of America's now famous comedians. Carson, a lifelong cigarette smoker, died of emphysema at age seventy-nine in 2005.

Chris Farley: At thirty-three years old, the self-mocking overweight Chris Farley, known for his sweaty, frantic fall-down routines on *Saturday Night Live*, died of drug and alcohol bingeing.

Jackie Gleason *(right)*: Remembered best as Ralph Kramden on the 1951 TV show *The Honeymooners*, Jackie Gleason went on to be called "The Great One" by his peers in the entertainment industry. He died in 1987 at the age of seventy-one from cancer. *Honeymooners* co-star **Audrey Meadows** died of lung cancer in 1996 at age sixty-nine.

Phil Hartman: Comedian Phil Hartman was shot and killed by his wife, who had a history of cocaine abuse and mental problems, with a .38 revolver as he slept. He was forty-nine. After the police arrived, she killed herself. In his short but tremendous performing career, Hartman was a cast member of *Saturday Night Live*, as well as the voice of numerous characters on *The Simpsons*.

Laurel and Hardy: The official teaming of Stan Laurel and Oliver Hardy was created by a Hollywood movie studio and presented to the world in 1927 with the release of *The Second 100 Years*. They made their last movie and had their last laugh together in 1950. Oliver Hardy died in 1957 at age sixty-five, wasting away three months after a stroke. Stan Laurel, the skinny one of the comedy duo, made 182 motion pictures in his thirty-two-year career. He died of a heart attack at age seventy-five in 1961.

"If anyone at my funeral has a long face, I'll never speak to him again."
—Stan Laurel

Groucho Marx: The original wisecracking comic, Groucho smoked cigars, leered at women, and wiggled his bushy eyebrows into a fortune. He appeared in dozens of movies with his brothers, including *Duck Soup* and *Animal Crackers*, and hosted a quiz show *You Bet Your Life*, first on radio, then on TV, for over twenty years. At age eighty-six, with his young secretary-companion Erin Fleming at his side, he died from a stroke in 1974. (Erin Fleming committed suicide in 2003 at age forty-two.)

Tim "Kingfish" Moore: "Kingfish" started his career as a child street performer, shuffling and singing on sidewalks of Rock Island, Illinois. At age fifty he became George "Kingfish" Stevens on the popular—though now considered controversial because of its stereotypical portrayal of blacks—*Amos 'n' Andy* show. In 1959, at age fifty-nine, he died from pulmonary tuberculosis.

The Three Stooges *(above)*: Moe, Larry, Curly, and Shemp became the most successful comedy team in history by turning traditional slapstick comedy into a sadomasochistic hysteria. Children were warned by TV hosts, such as "Officer Joe Bolton," that the stunts the Three Stooges performed—like driving a ten-inch nail into someone's head—should not be tried at home. There were four primary comedians, three of whom were brothers: Moe Howard, Larry Fine, Curly Howard, and Shemp Howard. Curly died at age forty-eight from heart disease in 1952; Shemp had a heart attack in 1955 and died at age sixty; Moe died in 1974 at age seventy-seven of lung cancer; and Larry died in 1975 at age seventy-two of pneumonia in a nursing home.

Flip Wilson: Flip Wilson was the first black host of a prime-time variety show, *The Flip Wilson Show*. Between 1970 and 1974, it was the most popular show on television. Upon cancellation, he vanished from public life. In 1998, at age sixty-four, he died from liver cancer.

SEINFELD DISEASE

In 1997, a sixty-four-year-old Burlington, Massachusetts, man went to a doctor specializing in neuroscience at a laugh research clinic. The man complained of blackouts and spells of unconsciousness every time he watched *Seinfeld*. Anxious to discover a new laughing disorder, the researcher decided to observe the man at home, taking copious notes as Jerry and the gang went through their antics. As soon as the man went into a belly laugh, he gagged and fell headfirst onto the coffee table. Unfortunately for the researcher, hoping to coin a new syndrome, it was discovered that the man needed a triple bypass. His narrowed arteries, in conjunction with strenous laughter, cut off much-needed oxygen to the brain.

NO JOKE

What is surely no laughing matter is **Laughing Psychoses,** mental disorders that cause the afflicted to laugh for no reason. For most people, laughter is a sociably acceptable response to humorous stimuli, but for people with Laughing Psychosis, bursts of hysterical laughter at something not worth laughing at can be embarrassing and fatal. A person with this disorder begins to chuckle at odd times. As the disease progresses, they might wake up laughing, laugh themselves to sleep, burst out in a roar in a crowded elevator, or hoot uncontrollably at a funeral or at other equally inappropriate times.

Sufferers of laugh disorders have a buildup of disproportionate amount of amino acids in all four sections of their brain, causing the loss of contact with reality, inducing a laughing trancelike state. It's not exactly certain why the amino acid amounts affect how a person begins to see or hear things no one else thinks is funny, but many studies have found that a distortion occurs at the synapses of neurotransmitters. *A study at the Neuroscience Program at the University of Maryland found people are thirty times more likely to laugh in a group setting, and less probable to laugh at the same thing if alone.* These misfiring synapses cause an imbalance in the limbic system of the brain, as previously discussed, as well as the frontal lobes leading to confused judgment and nonexistent inhibitions. Drugs, such as dopamine, attempt to create a bridge that brings a person back to reality.

More women than men develop serious forms of laughing psychosis, usually between the ages of fifteen and thirty, most likely due to estrogen levels that affect the amino acids in the brain in different ways. Men in this age group are prone to self-induced laughing psychoses when subjecting themselves to acute toxicity from cannabis, acid, or speed. With each bout of hysterical laughter, more oxygen is cut off from the brain and more cells die, in turn, causing the

person to laugh at even less funny things. Elementary visual illusions and hallucinations and an unreal belief system are the causes of laughing to death.

DEATHS ATTRIBUTED TO LAUGHING DEMENTIA AND LAUGHTER AS A SECONDARY CAUSE NUMBERED 8,901 IN 2003.

LAUGHING GAS "Laughing euphoriants" are found in more than one-thousand household products, everything from vegetable cooking spray and furniture polish to deodorant. Laughing gas (N_2O) is extremely dangerous: It is used as a combustion catalyst in auto racing or as an oxidizer in semiconductor manufacturing, in air bags, and is added as a propellant in processed

foods such as whipped cream rechargers, or "Whip-Its," which are available at most large grocery stores and through restaurant supply outlets. Whip-Its, also called "poppers," are still sold in smoke shops and over the Internet. In 2004, over eight-hundred thousand children between the ages of twelve and seventeen practiced "huffing" in which the individual inhales nitrous oxide (N_2O) from a canister.

Nitrous oxide produces a sense of euphoria because it deprives the brain of oxygen. The effect is brief and causes slurred speech, poor balance, and puzzled thinking. Poked by a stick, a laughing gas user won't feel it; a fire alarm or police siren sounds no louder than a whisper. It's among the top five substances abused by adolescents because it's so easy to come by. Rave parties and concerts are typical places where nitrous oxide is available, often sold in "hits"—balloons inflated with N_2O.

The stuff is addictive because frequent users build up a tolerance and need more and more to get the initial laugh. By subjecting their bodies to chemicals and cutting off oxygen for extended periods of time, long-term addicts destroy their bone marrow and blood cells and poison the central nervous system.

The desire to get higher longer and faster often increases chances of death. The "huffer" seeks out confined spaces—a closet, a car, or simply puts a plastic bag over his or her head, not to lose one single molecule of the inhalant. The cause of death after inhaling is usually a heart attack. Laughing to death can occur very quickly, in only a matter of seconds.

**SEVEN HUNDRED DEATHS EACH YEAR ARE ATTRIBUTED
TO HOUSEHOLD INHALANTS.**

LAUGHING SICKNESS Laughing Sickness is actually the end result of prion disease, known as *spongiform encephalopathies,* caused by infected proteins and bacteria that enter the body from an outside source and turn the brain into a sponge. These laughing death diseases cause trembling, loss of coordination, and certain death. Other weird symptoms include mood swings, numbness, and incontinence. Eventually the mind is destroyed, similar to an Alzheimer's sufferer. As these diseases progress, a person can no longer walk without support. Chills and tremors get worse and the muscles jerk. The strangest part is the sudden outbursts of laughter and eerie howls of joy as the mind disintegrates.

One type of prion disease has become known as "Mad Cow," which killed eighty people in England. In America, the bovine "laughing brain" disease *(bovine spongiform encephalopathy)* is found in deer and elk in Colorado and Wyoming, endangering both hunters and the cattle that graze the same terrain. The deaths of twenty-five people known to eat the meat of wild animals were reported between 2001 and 2003.

In 1962, two social workers and three American humanitarian volunteers were fatally overcome by a bizarre version of laughing disease while stationed in Tanganyika, now called Tanzania, Africa. An outbreak of contagious laughter started among a group of school girls, aged twelve to eighteen. Sometimes these isolated fits of laughter alternated with bouts of uncontrollable crying. The laughter was contagious; it dispersed from one person to the next, eventually contaminating adjacent communities. The epidemic spread rapidly, and within days villages across the region were affected, becoming serious enough that schools were closed. The outbreak lasted for six months, killing more than nine hundred people and was believed to be caused by a spore of some sort that lay dormant in the environment.

**SINCE 1950, 2,892 AMERICANS HAVE DIED OF VARIOUS
LAUGHING SICKNESSES.**

LAWN DARTS Seventy-five children have been killed by lawn darts that punctured their skulls between 1965 and 1988, at which point the sale and production of lawn darts was banned. The Consumer Product Safety Commission cited the following, making lawn darts illegal: "The combined factors of weight, the narrow shaft, the speed that the dart travels at the time of impact and the thickness of the child's skull at the point of impact present

the risk." These observations and the fact that young children don't have the most accurate aim are the reasons for the ban. However, the dart board that uses smaller steel-tipped darts is still legal and found in many taverns throughout the U.S. Although no fatalities from these smaller darts have been reported since 1988, 139 people did lose at least one eye.

TOTAL DART FATALITIES OF ALL AGES SINCE 1950: 312

LAYING TRACKS 749,301 men were employed by railroads across America in 1890. That same year, the lack of safety conditions killed 2,675 and injured 41,142; all the same, the industry chieftains considered death or injury a product of the worker's own bad luck. There was no compensation for injuries or severance to the widows or families of the dead railroad worker. Companies denied responsibility and refused to install protective equipment. Sometimes, if relatives didn't make trouble, the rail-

road bosses would pay for a modest funeral—unless the worker was a Chinese immigrant. Some twenty thousand pounds of bones of Chinese railroad laborers were found buried across the country in shallow graves along the roadbeds and rights of ways.

INSTALLATION OF U.S. RAILROADS CAUSED 110,456 DEATHS.

LIGHTNING Lightning is a positive electrical charge that takes thirty seconds (at lightning speed) to travel from the negatively charged base of a rain cloud to the surface of the earth. A typical lightning storm lasts no more than thirty minutes, usually occurring during the summer months, in afternoons and evenings. Lightning can strike as far as fifteen miles from where it's raining and thundering; people have been killed by a bolt of lightning standing in the sunshine. Those who have been killed by lightning were usually taking cover under a tree or standing next to a telephone pole. Some were talking on their cell phones while leaning against a metal signpost or walking on top of metal sidewalk grates. If they were out in a park, they stayed on top of a hill or continued

pedaling on their metal bicycles. Those who were playing golf continued to handle metal clubs or didn't contemplate removing their spiked metal golf shoes. All these people felt the hair suddenly stand up on the top of their heads and did not realize they were about to suffer a direct hit by lightning. Those who sensed the static in their hair and managed to drop to their knees, hugged a car tire (or something rubber to ground themselves), dove for shelter, and removed jewelry were saved. Experts recommend staying indoors during lightning storms, although there are dangers there as well. Once inside, people who have died of lightning strikes continued to operate electrical appliances or wash dishes in metal sinks while lightning flashed outside. Twenty million cloud-to-ground lightning bolts occur in the United States each year. Eighty-four percent of lightning fatalities are male, with the majority of deaths occurring in July, on Sundays, Wednesdays, and Fridays, between 2:00 and 6:00 P.M.

FROM 1940 TO 2003, 9,007 PEOPLE WERE KILLED BY LIGHTNING IN THE UNITED STATES.

LIPOSUCTION This procedure, which vacuums fat from the human body, was first used in the 1970s, designed for people unhappy with their body contours. Today, it has become the most popular cosmetic surgery in the

United States, not only used for improving body shape but as a quick way for overweight individuals to remove unwanted pounds without dealing with issues of overeating. More than 410,000 procedures were performed in 2004 even when more than 90 percent of those who do it for weight reasons gained the pounds back within one year.

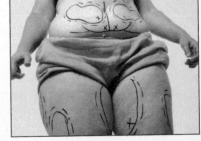

Between 1994 and 1998, when almost anyone, including untrained doctors and even cosmetologists were allowed to perform the procedure, one out of every one thousand people died during or shortly after liposuction. Now, as plastic surgeons primarily do it, the death rate has dropped to one death per three thousand. Practitioners point to the low number of death certificates that cite liposuction as a cause of mortality when discussing hazards (or lack thereof). However, they don't mention the new scientific-sounding term that appears on death certificates when a valuable income-producing and mostly unnecessary medical procedure such as liposuction causes a fatality. "Iatrogenic Causes" appears on the death certificates of many cosmetic surgery fatalities and probably explains the discrepancy between reported and actual deaths. "Iatrogenic" basically means any complication. It is the plastic surgery industry's attempt to keep mortality statistics in line and not upset the economic windfall that cosmetic procedures bring.

NEAR PERFECTION IS OKAY

Men, more than women, opt for liposuction. One fifty-year-old Michigan man was no slacker. This 6'2", 265-pound man worked out every day and was in tip-top shape, but the love handles, the small amount of flab on his lower back, prevented him from having the Perfect Body. He decided to let surgery help where exercise failed. While getting ten pounds sucked out he died from a pulmonary embolism. The same happened in 2004, when author Olivia Goldsmith, who satirized plastic surgery junkies in her bestselling book The First Wives Club, *died from anesthesia complications during a routine chin tuck.*

WORD GAME

Two hundred fifty thousand death certificates in 2004 cited "iatrogenic causes" as the primary reason for death, neatly circumventing the actual cause.

Here's the breakdown of the major reasons behind "iatrogenic causes" in that year:

- 12,000 deaths due to unnecessary surgery: Gallbladder removal for patients with negligible or no symptoms had increased by 50 percent to 5 million per year; 25 percent of hysterectomies (eight hundred thousand in 2004) had no medical justification; only 14 percent of the more than 1 million cesarean birth procedures were medically justified.
- 27,000 deaths due to medication errors in hospitals such as incomplete medical histories of patients, leading to life-threatening treatment and surgery performed on the wrong part, and even to the wrong patient, was reported over 350,000 times in 2004.
- 80,000 deaths due to infections after operations occurred in 2004.
- 106,000 deaths were attributed to non-error, negative effects of drugs prescribed to patients.

Other iatrogenic reasons included embolisms, internal blood clots, or a toxic reaction to anesthesia. Although these are risks with any surgery, the fact that liposuction is performed primarily for vanity's sake, and unnecessary to the actual health of the individual, makes it a bit sadder.

DEATH BY LIPOSUCTION SINCE 1970: 19,654

LITTER BOXES 64 million cats live in American homes with an estimated 50 million litter boxes. All cat owners must be aware of **toxoplasmosis**, a disease caused by a parasite that comes primarily from cat and sheep feces. Every year thirty-five hundred people die after coming in contact with the parasite while cleaning out the litter box (or the sheep stable) and then sit down to dinner without washing their hands.

**SINCE 1965,
THIS PARASITE HAS KILLED 39,781
CAT OWNERS.**

LOCKJAW "Step on a crack, break your mother's back, step on a line, you break your mother's spine." This classic rhyme teaches kids to look where they're going and, indirectly, also warns about stepping on harmful things, including rusty nails. Of course, avoiding sidewalk cracks does nothing to prevent spinal injuries, but getting a nail puncture, cut, or laceration could bring on extreme muscle rigidity, known as lockjaw or tetanus. Contrary to popular belief, it's not the rust that brings on lockjaw, but a microbe, *Clostridium tetani,* found in soil and common dirt, that affects the central nervous system. The spores lie dormant for up to forty years, ready to spring to life in the body's warm environment once it enters through an open wound. The toxins emitted by these germinating spores cause abdominal, back, and muscle spasms from the chest to the face. When this muscular rigidity sets in, there is little chance medicine can undo it, resulting in lung collapse and suffocation.

In the United States every child under seven years old is required to get a combined DTaP vaccine against diphtheria, tetanus, and whooping cough. This

TAKING IN STRAYS
An eighty-four-year-old woman loved animals and lived alone with more than thirty stray cats. When she died at her Stoneham, Massachusetts, home there was no one left to feed them. Police could not determine if she had died of natural causes or if her beloved cats had attacked her. Regardless, the police reported: "The body was in a semi-skeletal state. The cats were literally feeding off her."

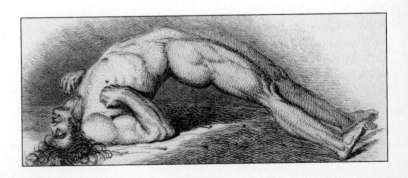

program has effectively reduced the U.S. death rate from 581 lockjaw deaths in 1947 to eleven deaths in 2003. (A booster is recommended every ten years throughout adulthood.) Before the vaccine was invented in the 1920s, tetanus killed thirty thousand people a year in the United States.

WORLDWIDE, 1 MILLION PEOPLE A YEAR GET TETANUS AND 270,000 DIE.

LOUD MUSIC At four o'clock one morning in June 2003, in a peach-colored, two-story building on Miami Beach, a man couldn't sleep. A birthday party was in full swing in the apartment below, with hard-thumping dance music, loud enough to rattle the windowpanes. Despite a city ordinance prohibiting music audible within one hundred feet of a residence after 11:00 P.M., the man knocked on his neighbor's door instead of calling police. When the partiers answered the door the man didn't bother to ask them to soften the music, instead, he just started shooting. He fired nine bullets into the crowded apartment, killing three revelers and wounding two. Defense counsel for the man cited "loud music" as the cause of the man's temporary insanity.

According to executives at major record companies, loud music is not dangerous, as long as there is no pain in the ears. Sound is measured in decibels (dB), defined as the loudness of sound in air as perceived by the human ear. According to Michael Lotke, M.D., a physician in the Deaf Access Program at Mount Sinai Hospital, hearing damage begins at 85 dB and the threshold for pain is 120 dB. A power tool generates 100 dB; listening to music through a stereo headset is registered at 110 dB; and any seat

"Dead as a doornail" has been used in literature since 1350, found in the work of Shakespeare and Dickens. A doornail was an oversized hook or spike used as a door knocker. When lifted, it fell back upon the door with its dead weight, giving us another term to signify a lifeless body.

FOR WAR NERVES

STOP NEEDLESS NOISE

Keep Fit - Keep Well - Keep Working

NO FUN IN FUNKYTOWN
The boom box, an oversized portable stereo, had its golden age from 1976 to 1985. Hot boom box summers filled urban streets with the 120+ decibel sounds of summer hits. The boom box era faded with the arrival of the Walkman; now there are many kinds of portable stereos, the most popular being the iPod. In 2005, people between the ages of fifteen and twenty-four who openly carried these devices on the street were eighteen times more likely to die by homicide during burglary attempts than those commuting in silence.

at a rock concert will send 120 dB of sound to your ears. At 160 dB the eardrum will rupture and any sound above this mark will create an air blast that causes death. At 200 dB the lungs will explode; very loud noise sends out ripples of pressurized air from the source and will create fatal embolisms in the hollow organs, such as the lungs and intestinal tracts. In World War I soldiers were found dead, without external injuries, after being too close to a bomb blast. Medical literature reports numerous deaths due to a loud or unexpected noise that caused a seizure or heart attack.

SECRET WEAPONS

The government has long known that sound is an effective weapon. Throughout history armies sought to unsettle the enemy with trumpets, drums, bugles, bagpipes, or sinister war cries. In 1989, the U.S. Army bombarded General Noriega with endless cycles of high-volume pop music when he was holed up in the Vatican Embassy in Panama. In Waco, Texas, the FBI attempted to drive the Branch Davidians a bit nuts with a 24-hour, 120-decibel barrage of golden oldies. In Iraq, during the first days of occupation in 2003, U.S. soldiers played heavy metal music at buildings occupied with snipers in an attempt to demoralize them. The government is currently developing new sonic weapons that will use the lower and higher frequencies not audible to the human ear. These sounds will be able to disorientate rioters or immobilize enemies with sonic-induced nausea. One spy supply company already offers an electronic device, "Sonic Nausea," which promises to give "headaches, intense irritation, sweating, imbalance, nausea, or even vomiting" for only $49.99 (two AA batteries not included). The company suggests hiding the device in an "inconsiderate neighbor's house [to put] an end to their late-night parties."

YOU ARE WHAT YOU HEAR

The effects of unrelenting loud noise on an unborn baby are not known, but it has caused miscarriages in animals. In 1992, the governor of Georgia gave free cassettes of classical music to all pregnant women, hoping that mind-stimulating symphonies would improve the state's literacy rate.

SHHH!

Any sound begins to damage the hearing when it is above 85 dB for a constant eight-hour period. The advent of high-powered music delivery systems has spawned a new generation of hearing impaired, with nearly one-third of all college students suffering from hearing loss. Many experts believe that constant exposure to even low levels of noise is unhealthy and creates stress. A study of noise at Los Angeles Airport in 2001 indicated that people living in close proximity to an airport seemed to have a higher death rate.

DEATHS ATTRIBUTED TO LOUD SOUNDS SINCE 1970: 34,831

LYME DISEASE Ticks are bloodsucking parasites, insects with two parts: a head to latch into the skin and a whole body capable of ballooning to the size of a silver dollar when filled with blood. In the last twenty-five years, different types of ticks and the diseases they carry have emerged as a significant cause of illness and fatalities in the United States. The most well known and common are deer ticks, which carry the bacterium *Borrelia burgdorferi,* known as Lyme Disease. Tick illnesses cripple the afflicted with recurring fevers, joint pains, depression, slurred speech, and weak legs. As the disease progresses, paralysis sets in and life on a ventilator can be imminent. To date there are no 100 percent effective treatments for tick-borne illnesses.

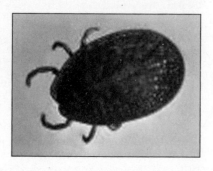

The tick and deadly bacteria it carries have been around for millennia, doing what parasites do: existing in the ecosystem to control population. Since 1977, when children living near Lyme, Connecticut, were discovered to have an odd form of arthritis, subsequently found to be transmitted by ticks, 621,918 people have been stricken by this disease. Ninety-five percent of these cases were from the states of Connecticut, Delaware, Maine, Maryland, Massachusetts, Minnesota, New Hampshire, New Jersey, New York, Pennsylvania, Rhode Island, and Wisconsin. In these prime tick states, many health insurance companies sneak into their policies a Sunset Clause, meaning that they will not provide coverage for treatment if you caught the disease from going outdoors after dark.

In addition to Lyme Disease, ticks cause Colorado Tick Fever, Masters' Disease, Powassan encephalitis, Relapsing Fever, Rocky Mountain Spotted Fever, tick paralysis, Query Fever, and Tularemia. The latter two are being developed as biowarfare agents.

SINCE 1900, TICK-BORNE ILLNESSES HAVE KILLED 1,133,871.

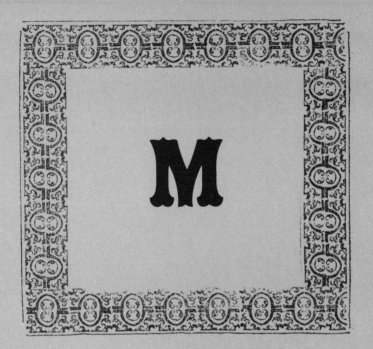

MALLS At the Crabtree Mall in Rhode Island, a fifty-nine-year-old man was sitting in the passenger seat while his wife, age fifty-three, cruised the parking lot in search of a free space. It infuriated him that his wife was a "circler," driving around and around until an open space was found. He insisted it was better to "stand by" and follow someone with packages heading to their car. A shouting match ensued, during which the man announced he was getting out and opened the door. As his wife circled more furiously, the man fell from the vehicle. He was caught under the wheel of another "circling" car and later died of internal injuries.

ANNUAL FATALITIES AT U.S. MALLS: 11,345

MARATHONS In the 1970s, Thomas J. Bassler, M.D., founder of the American Medical Joggers Association, ignited the running boom when he stated that a person trained to run a marathon would become immune to death by heart attack for at least a year. Since then, although his claim has proven to be false, scores of the ill prepared put their toes to the starting line.

Between 1993 and 2003, 41,867 fatalities were reported of people that ignored the warning signs such as chest pain, lightheadedness, fainting, and extreme breathlessness and died in their sneakers on the jogging trail or during other forms of exercise.

Strenuous exercise, including snow shoveling, causes twenty-five thousand deaths each year from sudden heart attacks. As the heart becomes stressed, pumping more blood faster, blood pressure rises and the arteries leading to the heart spasm. Exercising while angry or being too competitive produces aggressive emotions, which are more likely to trigger a heart attack. Sedentary people who throw themselves into a grueling workout are 107 times more likely to have a heart attack.

1,145 PEOPLE DIE EACH MONTH WHILE JOGGING.

MARIJUANA There are no known deaths from direct cannabis poisoning. Deaths while under the influence of pot are mostly grouped in vehicular fatalities.

MISSED OPPORTUNITIES CLASSIC

The secret syrup used in Coca-Cola was developed by pharmacist John Pemberton in 1886. He was wounded while serving in the Civil War in the Confederate Army, which, he explained, got him addicted to morphine and cocaine. Before Coke, he invented Vin Mariani, a cocaine-laced Bordeaux wine that flopped as a popular beverage due to its bitter aftertaste. His cola drink, which also contained cocaine, then considered a "medicinal" ingredient, was first offered for sale at an Atlanta soda fountain shop. However, it was unsuccessful and cost more for Pemberton to make than he earned. Ever desperate for money to feed his habit, Pemberton sold the cola formula to his bookkeeper, Frank Robinson, in 1887 for $1,750. Robinson thought up the soda's current name and marketed it as a tonic, thirst quencher, and pick-me-up. By 1890 Coca-Cola was America's favorite fountain drink. Pemberton died in 1888 from morphine addiction, virtually destitute. Today, the Coca-Cola Company is worth more than $58 billion and hasn't had cocaine as an ingredient since 1929.

Jim Fixx, author of the bestselling Complete Book of Running, *died at age fifty-two of a heart attack while jogging in 1984.*

MASCOTS Many teams and organizations have mascots, costumed actors dressed as an animal or object that is believed to bring good luck and boost fan loyalty and morale. Before 1950, most mascots were real animals, but as cartoon animation became ingrained in the American culture, life-sized caricatures of a team's mascot became a sporting staple. More than fifteen thousand people perform as mascots each year. Professional mascots earn anywhere from $60,000 to $100,000 a year with benefits, especially health insurance. To become a mascot you need to be part clown, part athlete, part stuntman, and be able to fall, tumble, cart-wheel, and repel off banisters and guardrails. In addition to unbearable heat—costume interiors usually reach 110 degrees despite ice vests and a small fan within the costume head—mascots have limited vision capabilities and often fall prey to overzealous opposing fans, obnoxious children, and excited drunks.

At the Big East hockey tournament in 2001, the Maine mascot Bananas was drop-kicked and whacked on the head with a hockey stick, suffering permanent brain damage. In that same year, Root Bear, the mascot of the Edmonton Eskimos, was trampled and severely beaten by an opposing fan after a winning game and carried from the stadium on a stretcher.

Sometimes mascots can have a mean streak and be overzealous and aggressive in their antics, which can bring on trouble. In 1988, Dodger manager Tommy Lasorda attacked Philly Phanatic, a fluffy, green, bearlike creature, after the mascot went through a skit using a doll of Lasorda as a punching bag. (In 1994, at the opening of a paint store, the same actor playing Philly Phanatic unintentionally broke a kid's back with a strong bear hug and was sued for $2.5 million.) The Miami Heat's Burnie pulled a female spectator by her legs from her courtside seat and dragged her halfway down the court in 1994. The forty-nine-year-old woman, wife of a local Supreme Court justice, had Burnie convicted of aggravated assault and later sued for $1 million. (Three years later, the same Burnie was coldcocked by NBA Hall of Famer Dolph Schayes, sixty-nine, when the mascot sprayed him with a water gun.)

Most fatal accidents occurred to mascots due to their limited field of vision through costume eyeholes. The most recent mascot death occurred at Disney World in February 2004, when Pluto was run over by a Snow Globe

IT'S MAGIC

In 2004, Snuff the Magic Dragon, mascot of the NBA's Orlando Magic, was grabbed in a choke hold and hung over the railing. The enraged and inebriated fan who assaulted Snuff, and later claimed that the mascot blocked his view, had to be subdued with stun guns. That same year, Pittsburgh Pirates outfielder Randall Simon stepped out of the dugout and hit a woman dressed as an Italian sausage with a bat. The Milwaukee Brewers' sausage mascot and a giant hot dog (also a woman), with whom the sausage traveled, were knocked unconscious. Simon was arrested and charged with assault. He was fined a mere $432 when he later said he was "just trying to be funny" and had no idea the mascots were women. Simon offered an apology and autographed bat to the injured sausage.

float. Javier Cruz, thirty-eight, who had played Pluto since 1996, tripped in front of the float and was crushed.

SINCE 1975, 1,765 MASCOTS OF ALL AGES, INCLUDING THOSE IN HIGH SCHOOL AND COLLEGE, WERE HOSPITALIZED AND TWENTY-ONE DIED.

MASTURBATION People who die while masturbating do so accidentally and not because they had hairy palms or warts on their fingers, went blind, or bumped into something with an erection and died of internal bleeding. In the 1950s straight-faced scientists claimed that even a single experience of masturbation could cause a boy or girl to fall into a vicious cycle of physical and mental deterioration, sure to bring about disability, insanity, and premature death. Since the first medical pamphlet about masturbation was published in London in 1715 *(Onania, or the heinous sin of self-pollution, and all its frightful consequences in both sexes considered)*, through the 1950s, masturbation was called the hidden plague and a "killer of youth." Death or disability can occur, however, when untested props are used. Recently, there were three cases of middle-aged men who died from electrocution while masturbating, somehow employing a hair dryer in their practices. Another one died from the inhalation of a zucchini, apparently swallowing it whole while masturbating. In 1980, an elderly man died of a heart attack while masturbating with a vacuum cleaner. *(See Also: Autoerotic Asphyxiation)*

3,761 DIE WHILE ENGAGING IN AUTOEROTIC ACTIVITIES IN THE UNITED STATES EACH YEAR.

TEAM LOYALTY
California Golden Bears offensive tackle Tarik Glenn (6'6" and 330 pounds) slugged and knocked unconscious Benny Beaver, the Oregon State University's mascot (a 5'9", 135-pound woman), after she tapped him on the shoulder with an inflated plastic hammer.

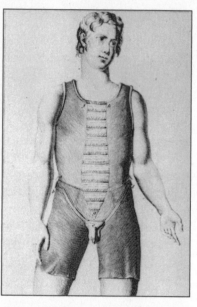

MENTAL RESEARCH In the 1920s, respected doctor Henry Cotton believed mental illness was caused by infection and recommended that physicians examine the deranged for infected body parts that could be removed to vastly reduce psychoses. He reasoned that by reducing infections anywhere on the body the mental capacity of patients would improve. Dr. Cotton claimed an 87 percent success rate and was hailed by the media as a pioneer. Using the power of his celebrity, New Jersey's Trenton State Hospital allowed him to order the extraction of eleven thousand teeth between 1919 and 1921. If the patient didn't get better, he would have other arbitrary parts of the stomach, bowels, or genitals removed; a random foot, hand, or leg had to go when treating the most stubborn. As a result, nearly all the patients at the mental hospital were toothless, and one-quarter were missing limbs. Eventually, after a number of anxious relatives complained, an inquest exposed a 45 percent mortality rate among those Dr. Cotton had treated, from surgical errors and worsening psychoses and suicide. When his methods were debunked, he dismissed his critics and stood by what he called his "extraordinary record of achievement." Dr. Cotton is now viewed by many as one of the most monstrous psychiatrists in American history.

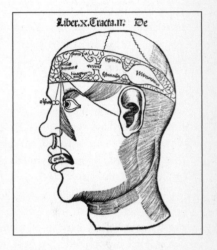

GUINEA PIGS 'R US

In 1932, in Macon County Alabama, the U.S. Public Health Service conducted The Tuskegee Syphilis Study, officially called the "Tuskegee Study of Untreated Syphilis in the Negro Male." Two hundred black men diagnosed with syphilis were denied treatment in order to observe their worsening conditions and understand how the disease spread within the body. All ultimately died of the disease. In 1950, the U.S. Navy, in an experiment to study how susceptible an American city would be to biological attack, sprayed a cloud of bacteria from battleships anchored in San Francisco harbor toward the city. Many residents succumbed to pneumonia-like symptoms and approximately two thousand died. In 1996 the U.S. Army, in a study to help understand possible disbursement methods and prevent biological attacks, dispensed *Bacillus subtilis,* a bacteria that causes dysentery, throughout the New York City subway system by dropping and smashing lightbulbs filled with the bioagent over ventilator grates. Diarrhea ran rampant, and was believed to have caused more than one thousand deaths, particularly in the elderly.

AGENT ORANGE

In the 1970s, chemicals called dioxins, the primary ingredient of Agent Orange, were tested on inmates in forty-two federal prisons across the country to see how it might affect combatants. Inmates were not informed what it was they were taking, although they were paid $100. Participants ingested seventy-five hundred micrograms of the toxic stuff—a dosage almost five hundred times more concentrated than Dow Chemicals requested for their product development study. The few inmates who complained about their illness such as loss of hair, diarrhea, and vomiting from the chemicals were given an additional $1,000 in their commissary account and radio privileges; this shut them up until they died within a few months from cancer. The exact number of dead has been "lost," as it is with most data from these studies, although estimates are at about one fifteen hundred.

KNOWN FATALITIES RESULTING FROM MEDICAL RESEARCH SINCE 1930: 50,345

METEORS Small meteors frequently enter the Earth's atmosphere and disintegrate, becoming "shooting stars." But not all do. Space rocks from the size of a basketball to a small car enter and break apart into pieces and hit the earth while still red hot. Over fifty thousand unexplained fires occur each year, which some believe are caused by meteors. There have been no confirmed incidents of any U.S. deaths by space rocks in recent decades (two occurred in Brazil in 1994), but scientists know the threat is real.

Researcher and physician Jesse William Lazear, who said, "I rather think I am on the track of the real germ," purposefully infected himself with yellow fever as part of an experiment to find a cure, and died in 1900.

Historically, every one thousand to ten thousand years a city is destroyed by something from outer space. A large meteor, similar to the Barrington Crater that hit Arizona fifty thousand years ago, measuring nearly one mile in diameter, will strike again and cause widespread damage and catastrophic death. If a meteor that size were to hit today, all living things within a one hundred miles of impact would be vaporized by its heat. A shock wave radiating out would reach

three hundred miles away in an instant, crumbling buildings as if they were made of sand. One thousand miles from meteor-ground-zero, a violent blast of rock, earth, and super-heated gas would roll over the countryside, wreaking unimagined devastation. The population of America would be reduced by at least 75 percent within an hour. Currently, NASA and other agencies are making plans to protect the United States from the inevitable large meteor impact scheduled to hit in 2029.

MICROWAVE POPCORN

People have been popping corn for four thousand years. The first known popping method was to bury it in hot sand until the kernels exploded. Today, popcorn is the nation's most popular snack food with 17.2 billion quarts consumed each year. In 2004, the EPA began to test popcorn vapors that were released from fully popped bags of microwaved popcorn. Popcorn factory workers and those at home who inhale microwave popcorn fumes on a regular basis got a rare lung disease from the combustion of dactyl, one of the ingredients in artificial butter flavoring.

TWENTY-FOUR DIED FROM INHALING POPCORN FUMES IN 2003.

MICROWAVES

In 1946, the microwave was invented by accident when a scientist working on ways to improve radar with a magnetron tube discovered the candy bar in his pants pocket had melted. In 1947, the first microwave was 5½ feet tall, weighed over 750 pounds, and cost $5,000. By 1976, the microwave oven had become more common in the kitchen than the dishwasher, "nuking" food in nearly 60 percent of U.S. households.

The microwave heats food's internal temperature by "vibrating" its molecules. Besides the few deaths caused by lunatics putting babies inside microwave ovens (three documented cases), there have been no known deaths recorded from harmful microwaves seeping out of failed oven doors; despite the lack of research, appliance manufacturer lobbyists deny that migraines and other cancer maladies are caused by microwaves.

Concern that heated carcinogenic toxins from plastic or "microwaveable"

containers can mix with your food remains another issue no manufacturer wishes to examine. Nevertheless, a microwave's tremendous power to alter the properties of a nuked specimen can't be denied. According to a November 2003 report in *The Journal of the Science of Food and Agriculture*, vegetables "zapped" the microwave lose 97 percent of all beneficial antioxidant nutrients.

One incident revealed a bizarre property of microwave ovens. A twenty-six-year-old man who wanted a cup of instant coffee placed a cup of water in the microwave. However, when he took the cup out, the water was not boiling. A few seconds later, the water in the cup suddenly "blew up" in his face, causing severe burns. Manufacturers refused to investigate the incident.

MICROWAVES IN CELL PHONE RADIO FREQUENCY

Studies show that a two-hour exposure to microwaves at the frequency emitted by cell phones kills rat brain cells. In addition to microwaves, mobile phones emit electromagnetic

fields and increase the temperature of the brain. Insomnia and memory loss from over-exposure to electromagnetic fields and cell phone frequency are the first signs of an overdose. More than 150 million people use cell phones every day, possibly creating a nation of people who can't sleep or remember much of anything.

**TOTAL DEATHS ATTRIBUTED TO MICROWAVES
IN THE ENVIRONMENT:**
1,457

MIGRAINE It's believed by some that Napoleon Bonaparte's short stature (he was 5'2") made him extra feisty, but it may have been something entirely different. Napoleon, who once said, "Anatomy is destiny," suffered from disabling bouts of migraine headaches.* His trademark stance, in which he held his hand inside his coat, may have been his desire to conceal that it was clenched in pain, coping with a migraine, rather than an attempt to present a regal posture.

Migraines are reoccurring head-aches that affect the lives of 28 million Americans. Migraines usually cause pain on one side of the head and are often accompanied by nausea and vomiting. As these attacks can last from several hours to several days, a migraine sufferer can become practically disabled and unable to perform even basic routines. The American Medical Association distinguishes a migraine from a tension, or cluster headache, classifying it as a neurological disorder; in other words, a migraine is a disease, the headache only a symptom. In a typical tension headache (usually the result of stress), blood vessels constrict and create a throbbing pain from lack of oxygen. The opposite occurs during a migraine: Cranial blood vessels expand, causing an inflammation of brain tissues. Due to reasons still unknown, this sudden blood vessel expansion (or *vasodilatation*) is often triggered by external events, such as sudden temperature change, bright lights, chemical smells, or perfume. Certain foods, such as chocolate, red wine, scotch, aspartame, aged cheese, and other foods containing nitrates and MSG, can bring on a migraine episode. More women sufferers

---

* Napoleon, Emperor of France, compared in greatness to Alexander the Great and Julius Caesar (who also suffered from migraines), died in a dark house, as a forgotten exile on Saint Helena Island, of stomach cancer at age fifty-one in 1821.

experience migraines on a regular basis, with the onset of the menstrual cycle. However, studies show that females who have sex and an orgasm during a migraine can raise their pain threshold, reducing migraine discomfort by 40 percent.

According to the American Academy of Pain Medicine, 150 million workdays per year are lost to migraines. Twenty-seven percent of all people under forty-five who have died of strokes did so as a result of migraines. Stroke is a term for any damage that follows interruption of the blood supply to the brain. People with migraines are at greater risk of stroke because during a migraine electrical activity in the brain cells are deceased and blood platelets get "stickier," more likely to form clots and block arteries.

HEADACHES AND HISTORY

Ulysses S. Grant, Robert E. Lee, Mary Todd Lincoln, President John F. Kennedy, and Elvis Presley suffered from migraines. During key Civil War battles, Grant numbed his migraines with alcohol, while Robert E. Lee sought rest and composure. Throughout the final engagement at Appomattox Station, Grant and Lee were both suffering from a severe migraine. Grant took another belt of bourbon and went on to become a war-hero president; Lee surrendered.

Mary Todd Lincoln was determined to endure her migraine for a night at the theater in 1865. She moved closer to her husband, put her hands in his, and asked, "What will [they] think of my hanging on to you so?" The president replied, "[They] won't think anything about it." A moment later he was shot in the back of the head by John Wilkes Booth.

President Kennedy didn't like riding in open motorcades because the bright sunlight triggered his migraines. All the same, Kennedy's brother Robert (who some say gave the president plenty of migraines over his pursuit of the

mob, Jimmy Hoffa, and Fidel Castro) suggested that the president ride through the streets of Dallas without the bulletproof bubble top, so he would have more contact with the crowd. President Kennedy was assassinated by two gunshot wounds to the head at age forty-six in 1963.

MIGRAINES KILLED A TOTAL OF
9,364 IN 2004,
MORE THAN THOSE MURDERED
WITH HANDGUNS.

Elvis Presley might still be alive if he didn't seek a plethora of remedies to medicate his migraines. His self-medication regime of painkillers, stimulants, and sleeping pills, seclusion, in addition to his diet of junk foods and peanut butter and banana sandwiches led to his premature death in 1977 at age forty-two. However, he probably would have suffered more migraines—or dropped dead on the spot—if he was alive when his daughter Lisa Marie married Michael Jackson. (See Also: *Toilet Time*)

MOBILE OFFICE In the good old days, driving distractions were simpler—reading a map or lighting a cigarette, women applying makeup, men shaving. Now, with the advent of the "mobile office," driver preoccupa-tion has soared to new heights. In addition to constantly talking on mobile phones—illegal while driving now in many states—people plug laptops, printers, and fax machines into their cars. Attachable laptop steering-wheel desks are sold for $39.99. (One mobile office accessory company advertised: "Join the thousands of mobile professionals on the road who use the Express Desk.")

LAPTOP-RELATED DISTRACTIONS KILLED
1,761 MOTORISTS IN 2004.

More and more cars are outfitted for comfort; social scientists are calling these technological advances "carcooning." Vehicles now often come equipped with surround-sound CD players, DVD players, video monitors, satellite TV, Internet access, dashboard video games, and navigation systems, confusing drivers as to where to focus their attention. Today, there's a booming business for custom shops

Forty-three thousand deaths and two-hundred thousand seriously disabling injuries are caused by human error while driving cars each year.

that specialize in illegally removing the steering wheel air bag and replacing it with a TV. Parents used to keep the kids occupied in cars by singing "The Bear Went Over the Mountain" and playing "I Spy." Now, each headrest can be equipped with separate TV screens and video game access. All this carcooning can lead to trouble: A family of five was killed when their SUV rolled over on I–75 in 2002 due to the distraction caused by an argument over movie choices.

6,415 DEATHS EACH YEAR
ARE ATTRIBUTED TO ELECTRONIC DEVICE DISTRACTION
WHILE DRIVING.

MOLASSES DROWNING On January 15, 1919, a tanker truck carrying 2 million gallons of frozen molasses parked at the junction of Commercial and Causeway streets in Boston exploded due to an unexpected rise in temperature. The molasses had begun to cook and created a volatile mixture of trapped gases. When the tanker ruptured, a tsunami of syrup three stories high engulfed buildings, an elevated train trestle, dozens of horses, and one cat. On warm summer afternoons, Boston residents can still smell the sweet aroma of goo that killed twenty-one people on that fateful day.

MOSQUITOES The mosquito is the sultan of germ warfare and has killed more people worldwide than the combined totals of all wars or catastrophes in history. Mosquitoes spread infection because, when they bite, blood from the last victim is pushed into the skin of the new one. New blood is sucked up, flowing into

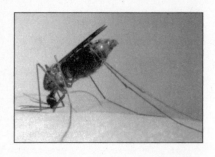

the mosquito "needle" by the process of capillary action. Even though mosquitoes pass bad blood to millions this way, health officials claim that mosquitoes cannot spread AIDS or hepatitis. Officials do admit, however, that mosquitoes are now spreading West Nile Virus, which causes encephalitis, or swelling of the brain. In 1999, when the disease was first detected, 398 people died. Since then, another forty have died from this disease, which has no cure.

During its two month lifespan, the female mosquito can inflict a thousand bites. Male mosquitoes suck plant nectar, not blood.

At the turn of the last century, about five hundred thousand cases of malaria transmitted by mosquitoes were reported. There are 176 separate species of mosquito currently abuzz in the United States. According to Joseph M. Conlon, a technical adviser at the American Mosquito Control Association, "Estimating mosquito populations, given their disparate breeding areas, would be an exercise in futility. The fourth generation of a pair of mosquitoes . . . assuming a 70 percent survival rate,

*On June 29, 1967, Actress **Jayne Mansfield** (above) died in a car crash. She was buzzing from a performance in Biloxi to make an appointment for a talk show appearance in New Orleans, when she was stopped dead by a mosquito truck spraying the road late at night.*

[they] would have produced a total of 49,843,353,164 mosquitoes—from just two mosquitoes, 14 weeks before!" The numbers of mosquitoes actually produced each year is staggering.

TOTAL MOSQUITO-RELATED DEATHS SINCE 1965: 10,726

Alexander the Great had conquered the world, but it was a little bug that got him: He died from a mosquito bite and suffered symptoms of a disease scientists now know as West Nile Virus. And Amerigo Vespucci, the mapmaker for whom North America was named, caught malaria from a mosquito while charting South America and died in 1512.

MUSIC BUSINESS Some say that musicians who died young had to give 100 percent for their art at a cost of their own life. Others say they just liked getting high. Jazz greats such as Charlie Parker, Miles Davis, John Coltrane, Thelonius Monk, and Bill Evans are all examples of artists who, although lost to substance abuse and mental difficulties, played some of their most beautiful music as they were dying.

In the last half of the twentieth century, the quest to become a popular musician offered the most egalitarian fast track to fame and immortality. On the other hand, the high stakes of the contemporary music environment often accelerated self-destructive tendencies.

OVERDOSE ROLL CALL
THE SEVENTIES

1970. **Jimi Hendrix,** a twenty-seven-year-old vocalist and guitar legend in his own time, overdoses on barbiturates in London, choking on his own vomit.

1970. **Janis Joplin,** a twenty-seven-year-old vocalist, dies of a heroin overdose.

1971. **Jim Morrison,** twenty-seven-year-old lead singer of The Doors, dies from alcohol and heroin abuse in a bathtub in Paris.

1971. **Duane Allman,** age twenty-four, of the Allman Brothers Band, dies while driving intoxicated on a motorcycle after a party.

1972. **Les Harvey,** age twenty-five, of The Stone Crows, performing while high, is electrocuted on stage.

RUSSIAN ROULETTE
Johnny Ace, an R&B singer, was twenty-five years old when he played the game backstage on Christmas Day, 1954, and died.
Terry Kath, age forty, member of Chicago, played with a loaded gun and lost in 1978.

1972. **Bobby Ramirez,** twenty-three years old, a member of White Trash, is beaten to death while trying to buy drugs.

1973. **Bobby Darin,** age thirty-seven, dies of heart failure while snorting cocaine.

1974. **Mama Cass,** of the Mamas & Papas, is thirty-two when she dies, not from choking on a ham sandwich, as some believe, but from a heart attack due to one too many crash diets.

1975. **Pete Ham,** age twenty-seven, of Badfinger, hangs himself after a drug binge.

1976. **Florence Ballard,** singer for the Supremes, is thirty-two when she dies from prolonged alcohol abuse.

THE EIGHTIES AND NINETIES

1987. **Will Shatter,** thirty-one, vocalist and bass player for Flipper—heroin overdose.

1988. **Hillel Slovak,** twenty-five, lead guitarist for the Red Hot Chili Peppers—heroin overdose.

1990. **Andrew Wood,** twenty-four, lead vocalist of Mother Love Bone—heroin overdose.

1991. **Johnny Thunders,** thirty-eight, vocalist for the New York Dolls—heroin overdose.

1993. **Stefanie Sargent,** twenty-two, guitarist for 7 Year Bitch—heroin overdose.

1994. **Kristen Pfaff,** twenty-seven, rock bassist for Hole—heroin overdose.

1995. **Jerry Garcia,** fifty-three, legendary singer of The Grateful Dead, dies from complications while trying to kick heroin.

1995. **Shannon Hoon,** twenty-three, of Blind Melon—heroin overdose.

1996. **Jonathan Melvoin,** thirty-four, keyboardist for The Smashing Pumpkins—heroin overdose.

1996. **Brad Nowell,** twenty-eight, lead singer of Sublime—heroin overdose.

*In 1979, **Sid Vicious** (below) of the Sex Pistols died of an overdose, while out on bail, four months after he stabbed his girlfriend, Nancy Spungen, to death in a New York hotel. Pathetically loyal to each other, Sid, age twenty-one, and Nancy, age twenty, became the image of the hardcore punk stars they portrayed, mixing sex, crazed violent aggression, and hard drugs—a ménage à trois that leaves no one standing.*

ASSORTED MUSICAL DEMISES, IN D-FLAT

Billie Holiday, blues singer, died in 1959 at age forty-four from liver disease, onset by alcohol and drug abuse. While dying in the hospital, police arrested her for possession of narcotics and kept a guard at her door until she died.

Hank Williams died at age thirty in 1953. The country singer mixed pills and drinks and had a heart attack combined with internal hemorrhaging.

Charlie "Yardbird" Parker, jazz legend, died from complications of heroin addiction, specifically liver disease, in 1955 at the age of thirty-five.

Dinah Washington, thirty-nine, "Queen of the Blues," overdosed on pills soon after marrying her seventh husband in 1963.

Sam Cooke, a thirty-three-year-old R&B singer known for the hit "Change Is Gonna Come," was shot by a hotel manager in 1964.

In 1994, fresh out of a rehab, **Kurt Cobain** (left), *twenty-seven-year-old rocker of Nirvana, is found in his Seattle home dead with a gunshot wound to his head. The autopsy shows there was 225 mgs of heroin in his blood, three times the amount needed for a lethal overdose. The most hard-core junkie would be immediately incapacitated after shooting that much dope, unable to hold a shotgun or fire it, which leads some to believe his death, although listed as suicide, has more sinister overtones.*

James Sheppard, thirty-three, of the Limelights was robbed and beaten to death in 1970 in Queens, New York.

King Curtis, a saxophonist on Buddy Holly and Andy Williams records, was stabbed to death by a derelict outside his West 86th Street apartment in Manhattan in 1971.

Gene Vincent, rock 'n' roll musician of the Blue Caps, known for the hit "Be Bop A Lula," succumbed to the fatal side of alcoholism in 1971 at age thirty-six.

Lee Morgan, thirty-three, jazz musician, was shot onstage by a jilted girlfriend in 1972.

Clyde McPhatter, of the Drifters, died at age forty in 1972 from complications of alcoholism.

Gram Parsons, twenty-seven, rock musician, onetime member of the Byrds, died of cocaine drug poisoning in 1973. His body was stolen after the funeral by a fan and taken to parties. Eventually, Parson's body was cremated and the ashes were scattered in the desert.

Jimmy Reed, R&B singer, was an epileptic who couldn't stop drinking alcohol, and often appeared onstage drunk. In 1976, at age fifty-one, while attempting a comeback, he died of respiratory failure.

Tim Buckley, rock vocalist, at age twenty-eight, died of a heroin and alcohol overdose.

Bing Crosby was seventy-six when he died during a strenuous game of golf in 1977.

John Lennon of the Beatles was killed at age forty by a deranged fan in front of a New York apartment building in 1979.

Samuel George, thirty-nine, known for the hit "Cool Jerk" was fatally stabbed during a family argument in 1982.

Marvin Gaye (left), *singer of "What's Goin' On," was forty-four years old when he was shot by his father. Gaye was addicted to cocaine and wished for death; some believe he forced his father into their final confrontation in 1984.*

Merle Travis, sixty-six, a country singer, died from complications of alcohol in 1983.

Felix Pappalardi of the band Mountain was forty-three years old when his girlfriend killed him with a knife in 1983.

Merle Watson, a guitarist known for "Pickin' the Blues" died from an accident on a tractor while he tended to his farm in 1985.

Walter Liberace was sixty-seven when he died of AIDS in 1987.

Keith Whitley, thirty-four, country singer, died of acute alcohol toxicity in 1989 from twenty shots of 100-proof liquor in a two-hour time span.

Art Porter, a jazz saxophonist, drowned at age thirty-five in 1989.

David Ruffin of The Temptations died in 1991 at age fifty from crack cocaine use.

Selena Quintanilla Perez, twenty-three, known simply as Selena, the Mexican-American Madonna, was shot by the president of her fan club in 1995.

Tupac Shakur, twenty-five, died from gunshot wounds suffered during a drive-by shooting in Las Vegas in 1996.

Christopher Wallace, twenty-four, known as the rapper Notorious B.I.G, was killed in a drive-by shooting in Los Angeles in 1997.

Jeff Buckley, a rising singer-songwriter, at age thirty, was drowned by the wake of a passing boat while swimming in a Tennessee river in 1997.

Layne Staley, thirty-four, lead singer of Alice in Chains died of a heroin overdose in 2002.

Lisa "Left Eye" Lopez, thirty, of TLC, died in a car accident in 2002.

Stephen Foster (right), *thirty-eight, composer of "Oh! Susanna," a national hit song in the 1850s, earned only $100 from its sale. He died penniless of alcoholism in the charity ward of a hospital in New York City in 1864.*

NARCISSISM This condition of total self-absorption was named after the character in a Greek myth, Narcissus, who fell in love with his own reflection in a pool of water and killed himself. A healthy amount of self-love is needed for survival, but when it becomes exceptionally exclusive it's considered a psychological personality disorder. According to the American Psychiatric Association, narcissism is considered a form of depressive illness, as the life of the typical narcissist is often rife with recurrent bouts of dysphoria, feelings of sadness and hopelessness, and anhedonia, the loss of the ability to feel pleasure.

When a narcissist is in full bloom, he may, in fact, achieve the success and adulation he desires. If he has enough money, his lack of empathy for anyone is ignored and considered an eccentricity. Celebrity narcissists may temporarily attain their fantasies of grandiosity and fame. However, when there is not enough recognition, unlimited success, or omnipotent power, the narcissist endures an ambitious, ruthless, and obsessive pursuit of gratification and dominance, which ultimately can never be achieved.

Narcissists often consider themselves to be sophisticated, perceptive, knowledgeable, judicious, scholarly, and astute, and often bestow some-

Lupe Velez (above) *was a gorgeous box-office sensation who made more than forty films from the 1920s until her death in 1944 at age thirty-six. As a star, she was meticulous about every aspect of her appearance and required a full-length mirror to be in her field of vision at all times. At Hollywood parties and events, she was known for making the most stunning entrances and equally dramatic exits. When she became pregnant she couldn't bear to look at herself in the mirror. Four months into her pregnancy, Lupe dressed in her best outfit, took a handful of sleeping pills, washed them down with liquor, and laid down to die, assured she'd make an attractive corpse. But she became nauseous, ran to the bathroom, and apparently slipped on the floor. She was found with her face submerged, drowned in the toilet bowl.*

times unwanted advice as a way to demonstrate their sense of unsurpassable superiority.

Like the Queen in *Snow White* who asks the magic mirror, "Who's the fairest one of all?" and then smashes the mirror when given an answer she doesn't want to hear, the narcissist often grows envious of others and seeks to destroy those who cause frustration. When fatal narcissism sets in, persecutory delusions are prevalent, and the deaths of themselves or others become imminent.

MANNERS AND ADVICE

Popular advice columnist Gilmore Polster was the longtime author of the "Gallant & Goofus" column in Highlights for Children. *Once the personification of rectitude, the retired solitary columnist's life—away from the adulation of fan letters—led to attention-seeking arrests for drug offenses and shoplifting. In Honesdale, Pennsylvania, in 1993, the sixty-three-year-old Polster was reportedly discovered dead in his apartment amid a sordid collection of smut magazines, overdosed on barbiturates.*

DEATHS FROM NARCISSISM AND RELATED DISORDERS
SINCE 1975: 13,983

In the 1960s, Gig Young, who also acted under the name Byron Barr, was the quintessential dashing and witty fellow, generally cast as the lighthearted bachelor pal who was more interested in fun than commitment. Offstage it was reported that he was thoroughly in love with himself. Although Young mostly played second banana to the lead, he did earn a supporting Oscar for his 1969 performance in They Shoot Horses, Don't They? *But by 1978, he was hardly recognized and could only land the occasional guest spot on TV. At age sixty-four, married only three weeks to his fourth wife, no longer a bachelor, witty, or lighthearted, he shot himself and his bride in their Manhattan apartment.*

NARCOLEPSY In 1999, Dan B., age twenty, was a member of the U.S. Marine Marching Band. As a tuba player he was expected to have strong legs and a durable back. Without provocation, the young man's knees would buckle under him and he would fall to the ground, sound asleep. He was re-assigned to playing lighter instruments, but his unexpected stumbling continued. Eventually Dan was demoted to playing the triangle, but there was no improvement, and he was finally discharged. It was then that he was finally diagnosed with narcolepsy.

In the United States, 293,000 people have narcolepsy, a central nervous system sleep disorder characterized by sudden episodes of muscle weakness or paralysis that resembles sleep. Many of these incidents are precipitated by laughter, anger, surprise, or stress.

Narcoleptics experience a life of constant sleepiness, despite the amount or quality of nighttime sleep. **Cataplexy,** a severe form of narcolepsy, afflicts sixty thousand people. These individuals suffer attacks that result in episodes of sudden sleep at any moment. The head drops and the jaw becomes slack while eating, talking, driving, and in other equally unsuitable situations.

A thirty-nine-year-old Maryland man knew he had narcolepsy, although he struggled to keep the information from his employer. On May 3, 1996, his co-workers threw him a surprise birthday party. Upon entering his office, he was greeted with noisemakers and screams of celebratory well wishing. The man promptly collapsed and fell into stage-4 sleep paralysis, from which he has yet to be revived. (See Also: Unconsciousness)

The narcoleptic is often stigmatized, perceived to be slow, constantly behind schedule, lazy, or lacking willpower. In fact, most narcoleptics are deemed totally disabled by age forty. There is no cure for this disorder, although a cocktail of stimulants, antidepressants, and mood-elevating drugs are prescribed. A new drug, Xyrem, the only FDA-approved treatment for cataplexy, has proven to be occasionally ef-

fective, although sixteen hundred emergency room incidents resulted from its use and sixty deaths due to fatal adverse reactions in 2004. Many people with these symptoms are reluctant to seek help; doctors are required to report even the mildest case of narcolepsy to the Department of Motor Vehicles, which will immediately issue a suspension of all driving privileges. Narcolepsy itself is not fatal, but fatalities have occurred when people fell asleep at the wrong time.

IN 2004, 1,550 NARCOLEPTICS DIED
IN ACCIDENTS.

NATIVE AMERICANS When Hernando de Soto explored Florida in 1540, he and his men spread a minor cold—previously unexperienced in the region—that eventually killed 75 percent of the native population. Now, Native Americans die from the diseases of alcoholism, tuberculosis, and diabetes, and from accidents, suicide, and homicide at rates seven times higher than other Americans. In 2004, the average lifespan for Native Americans was fifty-five years, younger than the life expectancy for residents of Bangladesh.

TOTAL NATIVE AMERICAN POPULATION IN 1700: 2.3 MILLION
TOTAL POPULATION IN 1900: 100,000
TOTAL POPULATIONS TODAY: 2.3 MILLION

NEEDLESTICKS There are 5.6 million workers in the healthcare industry, none of whom wish to be stuck with a needle containing blood-borne pathogens, including human immunodeficiency virus (HIV), hepatitis B virus (HBV), hepatitis C virus (HCV), and others. Between 450,000 to 550,000 needlestick injuries were reported in 2004; 57 healthcare workers contracted HIV after being stuck with a needle that punctured a latex glove. Another 137 healthcare workers got AIDS without being stuck by needles but by handling the bodily fluids of infected patients.

(*See Also:* Latex Sensitivity)

As of 2004 there were 23,473 active healthcare workers who have AIDS, including physicians, surgeons, nurses, dental workers, paramedics, technicians, therapists, and health aides.

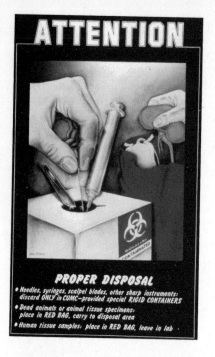

NEEDLESTICK DEATHS
SINCE 1985: 1,987

NEPHRITIS This is any type of kidney inflammation, which accounts for thirty-five thousand deaths per year and ranks as number nine in the top ten ways people die.

(*See Also:* Postmortem)

NONSTICK PANS Nonstick coated aluminum cookware with damaged or scratched surfaces emit toxic fumes when used. Fifteen hundred lung disease deaths have been directly attributed to these popular utensils. The fumes from these pans, coated with polymers made of flourine, carbon, and hydrogen, significantly add to unhealthy indoor air environments. Since smoke or carbon monoxide detectors do not register toxic cooking fumes, some avoid

NEPHRITIS IS HARD TO SEE

During the 1960s and 1970s, Jerome Rodale, at age seventy-two, was a celebrity on the talk show circuit who touted the secrets of growing old with vigor and style. The longevity guru declared, "I'm going to live to be one hundred, unless I'm run down by a sugar-crazed taxi driver." He was on the Dick Cavett Show *in 1971, tossing one-liners with Pete Hamill, when his head suddenly dropped to his chest as he let out one loud snore. Cavett, known for his wit, asked if Mr. Rodale was bored by the conversation. After a few chuckles, it was discovered that the longevity expert was, literally, a dead guest. Despite a change in lifestyle in his later years, Rodale's undiagnosed nephritis had caused a cerebral hemorrhage.*

death from scratched pots and pans by keeping parakeets and canaries in the kitchen—they expire promptly when a malfunctioning nonstick frying pan is in use.

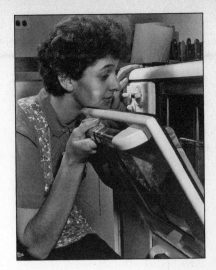

The biggest threat in the home lies with gas appliances like gas furnaces, stoves, dryers, and water heaters. In 2003, 1,250 people in the United States died from the "Silent Killer" carbon monoxide (CO) emitted by these necessary objects. The gas is odorless, colorless, and tasteless. Flulike symptoms—tightness in the chest, dizziness, fatigue, confusion, and breathing difficulties—are experienced shortly before death. It takes four to six hours of exposure for CO poisoning to kill, turning the dead body pink or bright red.

Vehicles running in an enclosed garage to "warm up" on cold mornings kill 207 each year.

DEATHS ATTRIBUTED TO INDOOR POLLUTANTS TOTAL 23,872 ANNUALLY.
(*See Also:* Electronic Air Fresheners)

NOSTALGIA Akin to homesickness, nostalgia was actually cited as a cause of death on certificates between 1766 and 1910. Reportedly, 31,987 people died from missing their loved ones, their home, or from a prolonged overwhelming melancholy. There is no way to know what the actual causes of these deaths were, although depression seems likely, which may have weakened immune systems and allowed for a greater susceptibility to disease. (*See Also:* Postmortem/Unexplained Illness)

NUCLEAR RESEARCH At a nuclear research facility in Los Alamos, New Mexico, in 1946, senior scientist Louis Slotin demonstrated to a team of scientists how to measure radioactive beryllium, the substance that shielded the more dangerous pluto- nium. While using a screw- driver to indicate small distances, his hand appar- ently flinched and caused the beryllium to ignite the plutonium into a criti- cal state. A "blue glow" instantly engulfed the room and all eight scien- tists and observers imme-

diately felt a heat wave travel through their bodies. The scientists received sufficient radioactive dosages, resulting in injuries and permanent disabilities. Slotin died within nine days, and two other scientists closest to the measuring demonstration died of radiation poisoning within two years. Five additional scientists present suffered for the remainder of their lives typical symptoms of overexposure to radiation, including weakness, loss of appetite, vomiting, and diarrhea.

TOTAL NUMBER OF FATALITIES AT NUCLEAR POWER PLANTS SINCE 1972: 2,877

THIS IS ONLY A TEST

*Although no one can argue with a policy of nuclear deterrence, fifteen thousand cancer deaths in the United States have been caused by **radioactive fallout** from Cold War nuclear weapons testing. According to a Department of Health and Human Services study published in USA Today in February 2002: "Twenty thousand nonfatal cancers among U.S. residents born after 1951 are linked to fallout from aboveground nuclear weapons tests that were conducted between 1951 and 1962, the year the testing was banned." The study found that lethal doses of radioactive particles dispersed from nuclear testing can last in the environment for one hundred years. Previous testing of nuclear weapons close to cities in New Mexico, Nevada, Atlantic City, New Jersey, and Savannah, Georgia, to name a few, may be linked to seventy thousand new cases of thyroid and prostate cancer each year.*

OBESITY A 350-pound, twenty-eight-year-old woman from Bastrop, Texas, had a long history of psychological problems. One evening in 1995 she called 911 and told the police to send the CIA over. Someone, she was certain, had been trying to kidnap her mother. When police arrived, they found the 110-pound, 48-year-old mother dead on the back porch. The woman told the police she had been sitting on her mother to keep her from being abducted. The excessive weight on the mother's back had smothered her against the floor.

John S., a former radio news anchor, weighed eight hundred pounds and hadn't left his Los Angeles home in three years until a small fire broke out. While the fire was burning, firefighters had to sledgehammer a hole through the wall and call for a forklift to get him free. He died later that day at Los Angeles County U.S.C. Medical Center from pulmonary difficulties.

William Taft, the twenty-seventh President (1909–1913), holds the distinction of being the largest president, weighing at times over 350 pounds. He brought oversized chairs and bathtubs into the White House, which he called "the loneliest place in the world." As a result of his tremendous size, Taft suffered gout, swelling feet, arthritis in his hands, and what he called "internal inflammation," severe indigestion that would keep him bedridden. His unsuccessful bid for a second term scored the worst incumbent defeat in presidential election history. He died at age seventy-two, in 1930, according to the death certificate, of "debility."

Born to normal-size parents, Robert Earl Hughes (left) caught a bad case of whooping cough at three months old that flipped the switch on his endocrine production. Due to glandular malfunction (now called an Endocrine Disorder)—regardless of how much he ate—he began to gain weight at an unprecedented rate. At six years old he weighed 203 pounds. When he was ten, he weighed 392 pounds, and by the time he was twenty-five he had reached 890 pounds. In 1956, at age thirty, Robert became the heaviest human on record at 1,069 pounds. His chest measured 124 inches; he wore a belt eleven feet long, and his arms measured forty inches around. When he was thirty-one years old he signed up with a traveling carnival

and was toted from location to location in a reinforced trailer truck that became his permanent mobile home. One wall was made of glass for people to observe him at his leisure. A year later, Robert gained even more weight and was unable to leave the trailer. When he caught measles he was too large to be taken to the hospital and soon developed a fatal uremia infection. After he died, in 1958, at age thirty-two, his body was placed in a piano case that was hoisted into the ground by a crane.

OBESITY AND PHYSICAL INACTIVITY ACCOUNT FOR MORE THAN ONE HUNDRED THOUSAND PREMATURE DEATHS EACH YEAR.

The Bermuda Triangle, a portion of sea from Miami to Bermuda to Puerto Rico, has been noted for the mysterious disappearances of at least twenty low-flying planes and more than one hundred ships. Although some scientists believe the unexplained disappearances are caused by methane hydrates—giant gas bubbles that arise from continental shelf shifts, which create aberrant atmospheric conditions—the Smithsonian Institution, in 1999, sponsored teams to search for giant squid as the most reasonable solution to this puzzle.

OCTOPUS AND SQUID Octopus have eight and squid have ten tentacles, each with hundreds of suction cups that have the sucking power to burst a man's artery, and have small, birdlike beaks used to inject venom into a victim. As recently as 2002, a 550-pound squid with fifty-foot tentacles washed ashore in Tasmania, and an octopus with thirty-foot tentacles was captured near New Zealand that same year. In deep ocean, octopus and squid have grown to monstrous dimensions with one hundred-foot-long tentacles. Large ocean fishing vessels have been attacked by these giant creatures all over the world. Although less than fifty of these creatures have been spotted in the past century, sailors once feared squid more than sharks. The squid was known to have pulled down entire boats and feed on the disorientated sailors struggling in the water. Researchers believe that unexplained deep-sea vessel sinkings and entire boat disappearances are the handiwork of squid.

MISSING SEA VESSELS WORLDWIDE SINCE 1795: 61,790

OIL RIG On July 6, 1988, an Occidental Oil rig platform exploded in the North Sea near Norway. A raging fire quickly set the entire platform ablaze. Most of the men died instantly in the initial fireball. One survivor said later, "I didn't have time to think it over. It was a case of fry and die or jump and try." The intense oil and gas heat melted steel hard hats right onto workers' heads. The rubber bottoms of work boots of the survivors who ran across the rig turned to glue before they dove into the water, which was covered with burning oil. One hundred seventy-three men died in the accident.

IN 2004 THERE WERE 599 FATALITIES IN THE OIL PRODUCTION INDUSTRY.

OLD AGE If you were born in prehistoric America you were an old man and likely to die by the age of eighteen. During Roman times life expectancy was twenty-five. In medieval England it was thirty-five. In New England, in 1789, it was expected that you would die by the age of thirty-eight. In 1900, in America, the average life lasted forty-nine years and 25 percent of the population never reached the age of five. In 1900, the leading cause of death was tuberculosis, accounting for one out of ten deaths;

today 54 percent of all people die from heart disease or cancer. By the end of the twentieth century, life expectancy reached its all-time high of 76.5 years for males and 79.9 for females. Today, 99 percent of babies born live long enough to go to kindergarten.

THE GOOD OL' DAYS
The philosopher Montaigne, in the essay "Of Age," written in 1575, observed: "To die of old age is a death rare, extraordinary, and singular . . . a privilege rarely seen."

IN 2005, 53 PERCENT OF ALL DEATHS OCCURED IN PEOPLE OVER SEVENTY-FIVE.

ORAL SEX When a woman receives oral sex (cunnilingus) air should not be blown into the vagina, as it can enter the bloodstream and create an embolism—an air bubble—that can kill the recipient in a matter of seconds. However, a full burst of air, as in blowing up a balloon, is required to achieve this. Pregnant women are at a slightly greater risk, as their term increases, when receiving this negative cunnilingus, due to increased blood supply to the pelvic area. Embolisms, in the vagina or rectum, not normally administered by oral sex, cause death.

In 2002, a Virginia woman using a carrot to obtain sexual self-excitement died from an air embolism. Other items that have caused air bubbles include, but are not limited to, soap-on-a-rope, a pumpkin, candles, batteries, and various appliances not designed for penetration. These odd or irregular shaped items allow more air in than out during the process, forcing trapped air pockets to escape into the bloodstream.

919 WOMEN DIE EACH YEAR OF AN EMBOLISM OBTAINED WHILE ENGAGING IN ORAL SEX AND REGULAR INTERCOURSE.

ORGAN SNATCHERS Forget pork bellies. The new cash commodity on the open market is organs—not the musical variety but human body parts. As surgical medical procedures advance and transplantation becomes routine, human organs are considered more valuable than gold. Brokers in this trade—licensed as medical consultants, who are more often black marketers—tout it as a win-win situation: The rich who can afford to buy get to live longer and the poor who supply get some much-needed cash. To the wealthy buyers desperately seeking a healthy organ, the brokers present their humble services as a near saintly act of humane kindness. To the homeless, debtors, refugees, undocumented workers, and prisoners who supply their organs, the brokers haggle, pay begrudgingly, and sometimes even steal a person's other parts during operations.

Many organ brokers generously offer travel accommodations to organ buyers. People seeking fresh kidneys are flown to Turkey or can be matched with an organ from a cache of waiting donors in rural Romania. One hospital in Manila is the prime destination for those seeking a new liver, harvested willingly from any number of families offering an offspring's organ to get them out of debt. One Nigerian doctor advertises on the Web, claiming he can get the transplant-seeker tourist nearly any body part desired.

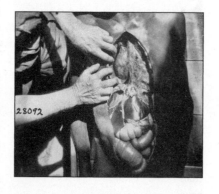

In 2002, a Miami, Florida, man, went to Venezuela for a cut-rate gastric bypass. He thought the seventeen-inch scar across his side had to do with the operation. Back in the States, he discovered that his left kidney had been removed.

Most brokers frown on parts harvested from cadavers and instruct their middlemen to bring them organs taken from the living, the cutting done in rooms reminiscent of back-alley abortion clinics.

The urban legend about a businessman who was enticed by a prostitute to go up to his hotel room and later woke up in a tub of ice with his kidney removed could not be confirmed. This method would not be practical and is entirely unnecessary: Organ sellers willingly sign up in many poor sections of American cities, namely Philadelphia and Newark, and receive approximately $3,000 per kidney, even though the trafficking of organs has been illegal in the U.S. since 1984. There is a serious shortage of organs available in the U.S. In order to increase organ procurement, Pennsylvania is considering legislation to pay poor families $300 toward "funeral expenses" if they allow the organs of a family member to be harvested after death.

An American was sentenced to death by a Philippine court for drug smuggling in 2001. At his sentencing he was given a choice: His death sentence would be commuted to life in prison if he agreed to "donate" one of his kidneys. In China, death row inmates aren't given the choice. In 2004, more than two thousand Chinese executed prisoners had every organ in their bodies removed and offered for sale on the transplant commodities market. In the United States, lethal injection or electrocution leaves organs unacceptable for donor programs. However, in May 2005 one U.S. death row inmate tried to use the ploy to have his execution postponed. It was discovered that the organ he wished to donate to his ailing sister was diseased.

DEATHS OF ORGAN DONORS SINCE 2001: 4,153

OUTER SPACE In 1958 the National Aeronautics and Space Administration (NASA) was created as a result of what science fiction writer Isaac Asimov called the "Sputnik crisis of confidence" in American technology and place in world power. NASA inherited objectives of the earlier National Advisory Committee for Aeronautics (NACA), which had been around since 1915 to research and develop anything that left the ground and stayed in the air.

An astronaut (derived from the Greek words meaning "space sailor") is a person who travels in space and though there are many people involved with NASA, there are fewer than four hundred Americans who have been in space. More than twenty astronauts have died in spacecraft or while testing experimental jets and rockets. The first major catastrophe occured on January 27, 1967. While on the launchpad, an electrical spark from a wire ignited the dense, pure oxygen in *Apollo I* and started a flash

fire. The cabin filled with smoke and flames that reached 2,500 degrees F. The only way out was an escape hatch, which had a design that required a delay of ninety seconds before it could be opened. Three astronauts, Virgil Grissom, age forty-one; Roger Chaffee, age thirty-two; and Edward White, age thirty-seven, died of smoke inhalation. Equally dramatic accidents included the January 28, 1986, tragedy when the *Challenger* space shuttle exploded on takeoff. All seven aboard died, including schoolteacher Christa McAuliffe, age thirty-eight, the first private citizen chosen for space flight. And on February 1, 2003, the space shuttle *Columbia* disintegrated as it returned from a sixteen-day mission, killing all seven onboard.

ROCKET SCIENCE

Robert Goddard was the quintessential U.S. rocket scientist. When he was a teenager, Goddard watched a fireworks display and decided to find a way to invent a man-sized bottle rocket. In 1926, he launched his first rocket, which lifted to only forty-one feet before it fell back to the Earth. Undaunted, Goddard perfected his rocket designs, which were used exclusively during the early stages of the U.S. space program. A soft-spoken man, never asking for money or accolades during his lifetime, he died of throat cancer at age sixty-three in 1945. When he died, the government gave his widow one million dollars.

OUT OF SPACE

Before astronauts were sent up in rockets, many tests were conducted with chimps. The first chimp to soar into outer space was Ham *(below)*. He traveled 155 miles through the heavens in 1961 before safely splashing down into the Atlantic. Unlike John Glenn, who was awarded a seat in the U.S. Senate, Ham was given an apple for his achievement. The astro-chimp was later housed at a zoo in North Carolina where he died at age twenty-seven of heart disease. The first chimp to orbit the globe was Enos, who died in 1961 shortly after returning to Earth. Other, less memorable, chimps were used to test whirling centrifuges and spacecraft ejection seats. In 1999, the U.S. Air Force decided to entirely rid themselves of monkeys. The 141 chimpanzees left over from the early years of the space program were not retired in style. Most were shipped off to AIDS research facilities, their fate unknown.

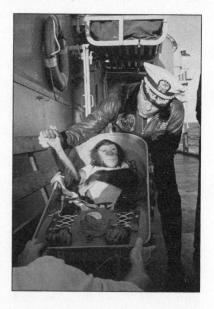

OUTLAWS (*See Also:* Westward Expansion) In 1934 America met a new kind of celebrity. That year, the country became captivated with the ex-

ploits of "Public Enemy Number One," **John Dillinger**, forever changing how the media portrayed outlaws. Dillinger started his career in crime at the ripe age of twenty with a botched stickup of a five-and-ten and was sent to jail. While behind bars he met guys who taught him how to rob the right way. Once out, his good looks, stylish hats, and agile leaps over bank counters brought him national fame and made him a newspaper favorite. However, after a year and a half of committing a string of successful bank robberies, things turned less romantic when, during one robbery, he and another of his eighteen gang of hoodlums killed two police officers. His arrest was a national event. Taken by plane to Chicago, he received a rock star welcome by a convoy of police and hordes of reporters. Dillinger joked with the beat reporters and posed for pictures before being put in a county jail to await trial. Even though he was guarded by fifty men, twenty armed citizens, and a battalion of National Guardsmen, Dillinger escaped, bluffing his way out using a wooden pistol and returned to robbing banks complete with his signature dramatic getaways. The police cornered Dillinger and his gang two or three times, but he always managed to escape, each time killing more cops and federal agents. With his face on wanted posters across the country, Dillinger had a plastic surgeon alter his face and change the tips of his fingers. Despite this, his true identity and whereabouts were discovered, and he was shot in the face and supposedly died in 1934. Although experts at the time claimed that what was left of the fingerprints were a match, some doubted it was really Dillinger, then thirty-one years old. He had a twenty-car funeral procession. Some believe the real John Dillinger was among the thousands in attendance.

IN TOTAL, THROUGHOUT DILLINGER'S NOTORIOUS CAREER, ELEVEN MEMBERS OF DILLINGER'S BAND OF OUTLAWS WERE KILLED, ALONG WITH SEVEN POLICE OFFICERS AND THREE FEDERAL AGENTS.

Around the same time, two other outlaws, **Bonnie and Clyde**, were rampaging across Oklahoma and Texas. Unlike Dillinger and his crew, this duo seemed to enjoy killing and mayhem more than robbery itself. Clyde Champion Barrow, twenty-three, and his companion, Bonnie Parker, nineteen, were no Depression-era Robin Hoods, as newspapers had first portrayed; they robbed from the poor and kept what little they got for themselves. Ray Hamilton, who committed crimes with Bonnie before Clyde showed up, said: "Bonnie and Clyde? They loved to kill people, see blood run. That's how they got their kicks. They were dirty people. Her breath was awful and Clyde never took a bath."

On April 1, 1934, Bonnie and Clyde were pulled over by two young highway patrolmen near Grapevine, Texas. As the officers approached the car, Bonnie and Clyde shot them dead. Two days later, the lovebirds killed another cop in

Miami, Oklahoma. Their day of reckoning came a month later, on May 23, 1934, when their car was ambushed by six police officers concealed behind roadside shrubbery in Louisiana. The police fired at least 167 shots from their machine guns. Bonnie and Clyde took fifty direct hits, dying on the scene. One policeman involved said: "We just shot the hell out of them, that's all. They were just a smear of wet rags."

DURING THEIR TWO-YEAR SPREE, BONNIE AND CLYDE COMMITTED THIRTEEN MURDERS AND SEVERAL ROBBERIES, NEVER NETTING MORE THAN $1,500.

*Lester Giles, né **Baby Face Nelson** (left), was the picture of a submachine gun–toting, Depression-era gangster; FBI head Edgar J. Hoover called him "a crazed killer with yellow eyes." Even though Baby Face killed four men during his criminal career from 1920 to 1934, robbing cars, private homes, jewelry stores, and banks, his mother still believed he could do no harm. After Baby Face was shot to death in a police ambush near Barrington, Illinois, she told reporters that her Little Lester had been a very attentive son and had never uttered a curse word in his life.*

OVERPASSES On November 22, 2002, just after midnight, a trucker driving through Nebraska heard something strike his cab. He then saw a black object crash through the windshield, ricochet into the sleeping cab, and then bounce back against the dashboard and explode. The "something" was a bowling ball dropped from above, and acted, quite literally, like a giant pinball. The man escaped unhurt, but two women driving a van three hundred yards behind him weren't as lucky. A second bowling bowl smashed their windshield and sent them both to the hospital. In 1994, an eight-month-old girl was killed in a similar episode in Jersey City, New Jersey.

Everywhere an overpass crosses a freeway, pranksters are lured to witness the effect of falling objects on passing cars. In 1990, a six-pound piece of concrete, no more than eight inches long, was tossed from an overpass in Cincinnati. It broke through the windshield of a forty-two-year-old man and struck him in the head, causing fatal injuries. His widow sued the Ohio Department of

Transportation and brought the case to the Supreme Court. At a cost of $26 million, protective fences were installed on the city's overpass bridges, as Ohio (Policy 1005.1) states, "to discourage the throwing or dropping of objects from bridges onto lower roadways and other property." In 2002, a Long Island man was killed when a frozen turkey was dropped onto his car, and in Yonkers, New York, in 2003, a forty-eight-year-old woman who had survived cancer died when a rock thrown from an overpass struck her through the windshield. Very few of these deadly pranksters are ever caught.

DESPITE THE MORE THAN $100 MILLION SPENT ON CAGES TO ENCLOSE AMERICA'S OVERPASSES, SEVENTEEN PEOPLE DIE EACH YEAR WHEN THEIR CARS ARE STRUCK WITH OBJECTS THROWN FROM ABOVE.

OVER-THE-COUNTER At one time "over-the-counter" meant getting a nonprescription drug dispensed by a pharmacist—over-the-counter—who told you how to take it. Today, over ten thousand medicines can be bought "off-the-shelf," with seldom a human in sight to offer even bad advice. Sure, a fine print encyclopedia of information is squeezed onto the box,

accompanied by booklets inside the carton, but 76 percent of literate people admit to never reading it. Why should they? If the medicine is in the pain reliever section of the drugstore, then it probably does the trick. No wonder 150,000 people in the United States are addicted to what the pharmaceutical business calls OTCs, an industry with $160 billion in U.S. sales in 2004.

No one is in a big rush to cure the common cold—not when there's $700 million to be made in annual cold and cough medication sales. Too-large doses of flu medications taken to treat sneezing, coughing, stuffy nose, aches, and fever can cause heart palpitations and respiratory failure. Nighttime cough medicines are most often abused and have replaced glue-sniffing among teenagers as the favorite way to get an easy high. Dextromethorphan (DXM) is found in cough medicines such as Robitussin. Use of this cough syrup has developed into cultlike devotion, with Web sites instructing teens on the proper way to "Robotrip." A couple of bottles will give the user a robotic gait (called "Robowalking"), mild hallucinations, and a generally zoned-out feeling. In large quantities it can decrease respiration and blood pressure and cause breathing to stop long enough for brain damage or death to occur. In 2004, when two seventeen-year-olds died in an Illinois town after a night of robotripping, law enforcement agencies requested pharmacies to make Robitussin a Behind-the-Counter (BTC) medicine, but met resistance from many short-staffed retailers. The makers of the drug urged people to take it only as directed and wished to keep the medicine where it is on the shelves—accessible to customers.

BETWEEN 1999 AND 2004
THERE HAVE BEEN 151
DXM-RELATED DEATHS.

With all this potential for abuse, today's drugstore medicines actually present only a fraction of the dangers that enticed the self-medicating infirm of one hundred years ago. Back then, most medicines actually delivered as advertised and often did *more* than alleviate aches and pains—they contained at least 50 percent either cocaine or heroin. The pharmaceutical industry began in earnest after 1805, after a twenty-one-year-old pharmacist, Freidrich Serturner, isolated an organic alkaloid compound from the poppy seed that had ten times the strength of regular opium. He called it morphine, named for Morpheus, the Greek god of dreams, which was soon used widely to treat a variety of aliments. By 1874 chemists at Bayer Pharmaceutical sought a less addictive substance than morphine and developed the first heroin, subsequently mass-producing all sorts of heroin-laced elixirs and medications, particularly their bestseller, *Heroin: The Sedative for Coughs*. Other pharmaceutical companies as well offered heroin, morphine, and cocaine in their products, which proved to guarantee sales not only because they relieved the pains of numerous ailments but were addictive as well. Regardless if the pain or ailment subsided, the false sense of well-being opiates induce caused these medications to be consumed without indulgence. In addition, the body quickly reaches a threshold of opiate tolerance, so that more of the drug is required each time to have the same affect of the previous dose.

Cocaine, first synthesized from coca leafs in 1855, was advertised as the spe-

BY THE HANDFULS
Pain relievers (called Internal Analgesics) come in acetaminophen (such as Tylenol), ASA (aspirin), and non-steroid anti-inflammatory drugs such as ibuprofen (like Advil). Thirty million people take these every day. Pain relievers cause 103,000 hospitalizations and more than sixteen thousand deaths per year due to allergic reactions and overdose. Acetaminophen, the leading OTC, known to cause acute liver failure if taken often and in large doses, caused the death of one hundred children in 2004. In 2005, a two-year-old North Carolina boy had the flu. He was given one teaspoon (500 mg) of adult Tylenol instead of 80 mg of infant drops as recommended. Due to the child's already lethargic condition, parents thought the flu and not the medicine caused his worsening condition and medical assistance was sought too late; the boy sadly died of liver failure within twenty-four hours.

Aspirin, taken for headaches, is recommended by some as a way to prevent heart attack and stroke. However, the American Association for Cancer Research found that people who took two or more aspirin a week had a 58 percent higher risk of pancreatic cancer. Pancreatic cancer kills thirty-one thousand in the United States each year.

cial ingredient in throat lozenges, "indispensable for singers, teachers, and orators," because it anesthetized the throat and provided the "pick-me-up that allow these professionals to hit their highest point." After Sigmund Freud advocated cocaine's benefits,

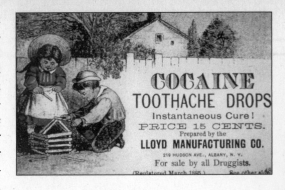

the drug flooded the market. However, death certificates from 1890 to 1912 show at least five thousand fatalities per year from cocaine use. In 1900, there were five hundred thousand people addicted to opiates, particularly morphine and heroin-laced medicines.

HACKSAW REQUIRED

Packaging of OTCs has become so sophisticated, with heated plastic seals and push-down tabs and backward-turning caps, that many medicine bottles seem to have been designed by seriously paranoid engineers. Before 1982, there was no such thing as "tamper-proof" packaging. That year Americans learned of a serial killer who emptied the contents of Tylenol capsules and replaced the white powdered medicine with cyanide, killing seven people in the Chicago area. Although the manufacturers were not to blame, the company took a major hit and decided to offer safer packaging as a way to re-boost sales. Regardless, some un-tamper-proof Tylenol bottles were again replaced with poison, causing more fatalities in 1986. Since then, the FDA has confirmed thirty-six fatal tampering incidents, including poisonings from Excedrin in 1986, Sudafed in 1991, and Goody's Headache Powder in 1992.

SEASICK

Dimenhydrinate, found in products like Dramamine, which effectively eases the ills of motion sickness and seasickness, has become another OTC teen favorite. This drug also has instructional Web sites, advising the potential abuser to start with two tablets and work their way up to eight to twelve tablets. This large quantity can provide a twelve-hour "trip" and create a "dream" state with hearing, visual, and olfactory hallucinations. This dosage will also cause incoherent speech, disorientation, delusions, depression, and amnesia. At least twenty-eight teenagers looking for a cheap trip with Dimenhydrinate products died between 2000 and 2004, and another 212 developed some form of brain damage that keeps them marooned on the perpetually rocking boat of their own dementia.

DESPITE THE SPACE-AGE PACKAGING,
FIVE THOUSAND DIE EACH YEAR DUE TO ACCIDENTAL POISONING
FROM PRODUCTS OR MEDICINES FOUND IN THE HOME
AND IN THE MEDICINE CABINET.

HERBAL BLISS

One million people in the United States take Chinese herbs and natural supplements each year and avoid OTCs altogether. The FDA, funded almost entirely by pharmaceutical companies, really dislikes herbal and alternative cures. More people die from inadvertently ingesting ornamental houseplants than herbal remedies each year— there were two deaths from herbs in 2004. In May 2004, Consumer Reports *listed twelve herbs and unregulated supplements that the novice user should avoid: androstenedione, comfrey, chaparral, germander, kava, bitter orange, organ extracts, lobelia, pennyroyal oil, scull cap, and yohimbe. These products are banned in many countries and if misused can cause cancer and liver damage.*

P

PARKINSON'S Parkinson's disease (PD) is a nerve disorder that causes the body to quake and shake uncontrollably. It's been known since 1817, when Dr. James Parkinson wrote a paper on "The Shaking Palsy." Parkinson's is not a disease of childhood and rarely affects anyone under forty, with most cases beginning at the onset of menopause for women and in the late fifties for men. Age generally deteriorates nerves in the brain that regulate muscle movement, but for those with PD the process accelerates and degeneration of the muscle-regulating nerves becomes severe. The causes of PD are often multifactorial, resulting from hereditary disposition or environmental factors. Researchers are tracing the origin of the hereditary form to a mutation that occurs within a chromosome which deals with the production of an amino acid responsible for producing dopamine, a chemical that transmits signals between nerve cells. Environmental factors that cause PD include exposure to magnesium in food or in drinking water, the use of synthetic heroin, as well as exposure to certain pesticides and wood preservatives. In 2004, 1.5 million Americans suffered from this disease. Death from Parkinson's is usually the result of falls or accidents.

18,653 PEOPLE WITH PARKINSON'S DISEASE DIED IN 2004.

PLASTIC MAKING Plastic was invented by Alexander Parkes in 1862 when he used an organic material derived from cellulose and discovered that, once heated, it could be molded and would retain its shape when cooled. Technology has improved the original formula, making plastic a substance that lasts forever and shows much versatility. It would be nearly impossible to go one day without touching a piece of plastic, as its uses are multitudinous.

But the making of plastics can get messy. Between 1947 and 1953, the Hooker Chemical and Plastics Corporation buried twenty-one thousand tons of industrial plastic waste near the Love Canal in upstate New York, named for the man who built it in 1892, William T. Love. In 1953, Hooker sold the land to the Love Canal school board for $1.00. At such a bargain, the town constructed a school and playgrounds on the land, uninformed of the toxic windfall below the surface. As early as 1958, children would run in from recess screaming, their feet burned by stuff seeping up from the ground. By 1978, 30 percent of the pregnant women in the Love

Canal district were having miscarriages, and 20 percent of the babies born had birth defects. Children routinely had seizures and kidney failure; babies, without rhyme or reason, died in their cribs. Adults in the town had migraine headaches and were told it was related to concerns about the faltering economy. Finally, in 1980, President Carter had the residents of Love Canal evacuated and began a government-funded cleanup. In 1990, the government told Realtors to sell the property again, claiming the abandoned land was safe. In 2004, the government declared Love Canal the cleanest neighborhood in America and although it was once hell for previous residents, for current occupants who got the newly constructed housing cheap, it was a real estate bargain. Since 1978, at least 212 former Love Canal residents have taken their own lives.

Julian W. Hill, the scientist who invented nylon in the 1930s, ultimately saw the downside of his invention, and said during a 1988 New York Times interview that "the human race is going to perish by being smothered in plastic."

DEATHS ATTRIBUTED TO TOXIC LANDFILLS OR DUMPING SINCE 1972: 15,660

THE P. COX FINE SHOES

P.COX
ROCHESTER.N.Y.
Mark.

SUPERIOR WORKMANSHIP
FIRST CLASS MATERIAL
EVERY PAIR WARRANTED.

PLATFORM SHOES The first platform shoes designed solely for fashion were used in the fifteenth century. Aristocratic ladies had them made of six- to twenty-four-inch blocks of wood to keep from stepping in the swill and sewage of the common streets. The higher the heel, the richer the woman. If a lady wore two-foot-high shoes she could afford to hire more escorts to help her keep stable as she made her way across the cobblestones.

In the disco seventies, platform shoes fit into the flamboyance of the era, especially while attempting a *Saturday Night Fever* split. The platform shoe fad died when disco became passé but has since gone through a stiletto-heeled revival. Twisted ankles, fractured bones, bruises, and scraped knees are common injuries to any novice platform or high-heel wearer. Longtime use of high heels and raised shoes affects the calf muscles and Achilles tendons and invariably cause shortening of height. One woman who practically lived in five-inch high heels eventually found that her ankles were permanently locked. The overindulging stiletto wearer can also develop "ankle equines," a horse-hoof gait that contrasts the sexy sway high heels were desired to provide. Recent deaths have prompted warning labels to be placed on platform-combo-high-heel shoes over eight inches high.

FOOT-RELATED FATALITIES SINCE 1975: 18,983

PLAYGROUNDS In 2004, 79 percent of all playground fatalities occurred at public facilities. Hanging ropes, untied shoelaces, dog leashes, and clothing strings that got entangled in the equipment caused 50 percent of the deaths. Falls, equipment tip-over, equipment collapse, and swing impact also caused deaths.

*Backyard **trampolines** are becoming more popular in suburban neighborhoods. In 2003, 37,500 children were treated with injuries obtained while trampolining; eleven deaths occurred. Falls from trampolines due to general horseplay or while attempting acrobatic stunts were the most frequent cause of death, followed by landing on the neck while practicing somersaults.*

BETWEEN 1990 AND 2000, 147 CHILDREN UNDER AGE FIFTEEN DIED IN SITUATIONS INVOLVING PLAYGROUND EQUIPMENT.

POISONOUS SPIDERS Fear of spiders—arachnophobia—crosses all class distinctions. The well-dressed have been known to kick off heels, hike up skirts, and leap onto a desk at the sight of a Daddy Longlegs traversing the office floor. Entomologists say that there is nothing to fear: Even though there are over fifty thousand different types of spiders, only

In 1999, a passenger became "a fashion fatality" in a car crash when the driver, a twenty-five-year-old female wearing platform shoes, could not hit the brakes adequately. That same year, a twenty-four-year-old woman was found dead in her car. She had apparently fractured her skull when she tumbled over in her five-inch platform shoes. Embarrassed, she told her friends to go ahead into the party. They thought she remained behind to clean herself up in the car, but she had actually died of a brain hemorrhage.

a few are poisonous and, on average, only kill fifty people a year in the United States. Death comes predominantly from two spiders: the brown recluse spider and the more famous black widow.

The black widow is common in the southern and southwest United States, although it has also been found as far north as Canada. The adult male black widow is black with a red or reddish orange hourglass mark on its lower abdomen. Females are smaller and less colorful, but strong enough to kill and eat the male shortly after mating. Black widow venom is fifteen times more poisonous than a rattlesnake's and takes about ten hours to spread throughout the entire body, at which point the most severe pain has already begun. The abdominal throbbing can be so great that people think they have a burst appendix. The muscles cramp and the involuntary processes needed for breathing become strained. The elderly, children weighing less than thirty pounds, and those with weak immune systems are most likely to develop respiratory paralysis and die within one to twelve hours (depending upon an individual's hypersensitivity to the venom) of receiving a black widow bite.

The brown recluse spider has violin-shaped markings on its head. The brown recluse's native habit was Nebraska and eastern Texas but can now be found throughout the Midwest and Southwest regions of the U.S. When the recluse bites, it causes deep skin ulcers, which are occasionally fatal. It likes to hide in drawers, shoes, and under car visors or in glove compartments. In 2003, a healthy sixty-nine-year-old Kansas man felt a stinging when he put on his loafers. Later, he found a small brown spider smashed between his toes. Two days later his toe swelled and soon after he developed fever, chills, nausea, vomiting, and muscle aches. The man eventually died of hemolytic anemia, a condition that destroys red blood cells. Less than 3 percent of people need skin grafts after suffering a brown recluse bite and even fewer have fatal hypersensitivity to its venom, but there is no way to know if you are allergic until you're bitten.

WHAT'S COOKING
In 1983, three latchkey boys in Louisiana, aged eight to thirteen, died shortly after eating homemade soup. Their mother had left instructions to take the pot of soup she had prepared from the refrigerator and reheat it for dinner. Earlier that morning, however, she had placed a box of unpacked groceries on the shelf in the refrigerator next to the soup, not knowing that inside bags of fresh produce lurked a dozen or more black widow spiders. Experts believe the spiders had sought the warmth of the soup pot and drowned. The boys heated the soup, mixing the spider venom thoroughly throughout the broth, causing respiratory failure in all of the brothers later that night.

THERE ARE ONLY EIGHT VERIFIABLE DEATHS FROM BROWN RECLUSE SPIDERS FOUND IN MEDICAL LITERATURE SINCE 1965. HOWEVER, MORE THAN EIGHT HUNDRED DEATH CERTIFICATES CITE HEMOLYTIC ANEMIA, OR ALLERGIC REACTION TO AN "UNKNOWN" INSECT BITE, WHICH IS MOST LIKELY THE BROWN RECLUSE'S.

POLAND'S SYNDROME First described and medically documented in a cadaver examined by Dr. A. Poland in London in 1841, this is a genetic anomaly in which the child is born with webbed fingers. As with many birth defects that occurred throughout history, this physical deviation was once considered a sign of something evil. In 1635, in Salem, Massachusetts, Margaret Cooke gave birth to a child with these abnormal hands and was subsequently convicted of witchcraft.

Today, children born with Poland's Syndrome have support groups. One young woman born with the disorder can play the violin (with a prosthetic cuff attachment for the bow) and uses a recently invented "fork attachment" for eating. However, due to insensitive peers, teenagers with this syndrome are at a greater risk for drug abuse and suicide.

RELATED POLAND'S SYNDROME FATALITIES SINCE 1970: 6,587

MAKING THE BEST OF IT

Francesco Lentini *(right)* was born with an extra leg with a nearly developed foot growing from the base of his spine like a tail. Growing up he was a sullen boy who felt he was the victim of a cruel cosmic joke. His parents placed him in a home for disabled children where he met kids far worse off than he; some were without legs and couldn't play soccer with the advantage he had. Lentini said, "From that time to this I have never complained. I think life is beautiful and I enjoy living it." He worked in many sideshows, billed as the **"Three-Legged Wonder."** He died of heart disease, in 1966, at the age of seventy-eight.

MAKING THE WORST

"The Lobster Man" Grady Stiles (below) *was born in 1932 with his fingers and toes fused together, which made his hands and feet look like lobster claws. The genetic oddity, called* ectrodactyly, *had been passed down in his family's genes for at least five generations. Stiles and his wife had baby after baby, all born with the lobster-like condition. He had them added to his sideshow act, "The Stiles' Family Show" that traveled to county fairs and carnivals, upping the ante he required from promoters. The children born without clubbed hands and feet were allegedly done away with at birth. Grady was a raging, violent alcoholic and wife beater who had a close call with the electric chair after he killed his daughter's boyfriend when the man attempted to take her from the family business. In 1992, his wife hired a hit man; "The Lobster Man" was found executed with three shots in his head.*

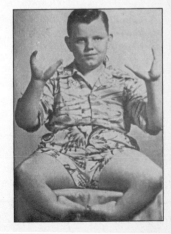

POLICE TRAINING In 2002 a group of fifteen New York City police officers practiced terrorist assault training in abandoned and partially destroyed buildings, rigged with pop-up targets to simulate a more realistic setting. A forty-four-year-old man with an arrest record for loitering and vagrancy happened upon the remote police training site. While the officers were on break, he climbed into a building and hid. When he heard them coming back to the site, he jumped up and yelled "Boo!" Seventy-three shots were fired at the man, sixty-three of which made lethal contact.

FATALITIES FROM LAW ENFORCEMENT AND SECURITY TRAINING ACTIVITIES SINCE 1975: 985

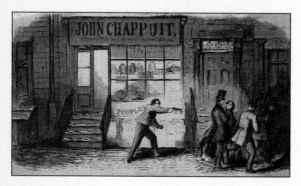

Dating back to the first law enforcement fatality in 1792, when NYC deputy Isaac Smith was shot and killed while attempting to arrest a drunk, more than fifteen thousand police in the U.S. have died on duty between 1792 and 2004. Prior to September 11, 2001, when more than seventy New York City police officers died at the World Trade Center, the deadliest episode in law enforcement history occurred on November 24, 1917, when nine Milwaukee police officers were killed after anarchists planted a bomb at their station house. According to "Fallen Heroes Report" released annually by the National Law Enforcement Officers Memorial Fund, 154 officers died in the line of duty in 2004: seventy-two from miscellaneous accidents such as unintentional discharge while cleaning firearms, fifty-seven from shootings, fifty-one from auto wrecks, twelve while attending traffic stops or while helping at accident scenes, nine in motorcycle accidents, eleven from job-related illnesses, three in aircraft accidents, three from drowning, three from bombs, two from falling, one from being beaten, one from being struck by a falling object, and one from being electrocuted. Eight of the dead on duty were female.*

POLICE CARS

The Ford Crown Victoria, with its big V–8 engine, is an interceptor car favored by police departments across the country. However, since 1983, eighteen officers have died while sitting in this model waiting to catch speeders or drunk drivers. When the car is rear-ended it has been known to experience fatal fuel tank explosions.

POTLUCK DINNERS

In 1988 when a San Diego man with terminal lung cancer was told he had no more than two months to live, he said what he was going to miss most was his own funeral. So he threw a memorial service for himself. More than three hundred friends and family, including dozens of grandchildren, attended his potluck memorial dinner. As the guest of honor, sitting at the head table in his wheelchair, he removed his oxygen mask to enjoy one last cigar. While hacking up some phlegm, a burning cigar ember fell into the gas tank, igniting it. The man died two days later from the injuries he received from the explosion.

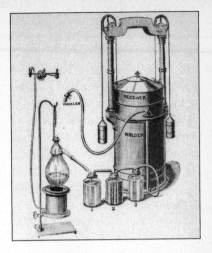

Some medical supply companies give out red alert cards with the warning: "Oxygen In Use. No open flames, smoking, matches, or candles to be used."

DEATHS FROM PORTABLE OXYGEN CANISTERS SINCE 1985: 8,876

CONSIDERATE FAREWELL

In 1991, in Columbus, Ohio, a thirty-five-year-old man was seriously in debt. Financially, he admitted, he was finished. With the last money he had, he bought a casket and a few cases of booze and set up fifty chairs. When his guests arrived at the party, they thought he was pulling a flamboyant practical joke and encouraged him to get into the casket to try it out for size. He good-naturedly obliged, pulled out a shotgun he had hidden in the coffin, stuck the barrel in his mouth, and pulled the trigger.

PROSTITUTION

The oldest profession is also one of the most dangerous. When the first attempt to count the number of working prostitutes was conducted in New York City in 1880, fifty thousand women over the age of fourteen were employed as such, among the general population of 1.2 million. Prostitutes accounted for 40 percent of all botched abortion deaths, and for 50 percent of the known deaths from syphilis in 1900.

In 1997 there were 762,200 women in jail, most of them for drug possession or prostitution charges—a 400 percent increase since 1980. A study published in the *New York Times* in 1998 found that serious psychiatric illnesses resulting from exposure to physical danger are more common among prostitutes than among troops who have weathered combat. Recent research indicates that female prostitutes have the highest rate of death by murder of any population of women ever studied. Two hundred thousand women between the ages of twenty-six and thirty-nine were arrested for prostitution in the United States in 2004.

Prostitutes come from all social backgrounds. In Chicago, a street-by-street survey conducted by the Chicago Coalition for the Homeless counted 1,000 street prostitutes, 2,000 escorts working with an agency, another 170 working in massage parlors, 1,275 practicing prostitution via exotic dancing, and 11,500 women who barter sex for drugs. Each year 50,000 women and young girls are trafficked into the United States from Latin America, Southeast Asia, and the former Soviet Union to work as prostitutes.

FROM 1989 TO 2000, CRACK-ADDICTED STREETWALKERS IN NEW YORK CITY INFECTED 1,572 CUSTOMERS WITH HIV WHILE PROVIDING FELLATIO WITHOUT CONDOMS.

PURSE SNATCHING In July 1988, a chronic mugger snatched a purse outside Madison Square Garden in New York after a heavy metal concert. A group of young "headbangers" saw what the man had done and began to chase him with a vengeance. He ran ten blocks but couldn't shake the outraged mob. He finally found shelter in a trash compactor behind a department store. He made himself as comfortable as possible, giving his pursuers plenty of time to give up. He must have fallen asleep, because he was still there the next morning, when the compactor was switched on and he was crushed.

DEATH FROM REFUSE COLLECTION, PROCESSING, AND DISPOSAL EQUIPMENT SINCE 1965: 1,333

Q-FEVER Q-Fever, originally called Query Fever (possibly referring to the questionable means of acquiring it), is disease from a bacterium, *Coxiella burnetii,* now understood to be transmitted to humans by sheep, goats, and other herd animals. Sheep can live with this bacteria in their systems, which occurs naturally throughout the world, but humans cannot. Transfer of this bacterium from sheep to humans requires extremely close contact with the animal. The most direct way to contract Q-Fever is to be amorously involved with sheep, although only 2 percent of the people infected with Q-Fever have admitted to these practices. Scientists believe the number of people sexually involved with sheep is probably much higher, although they cannot keep accurate records as doctors are not required to report this disease or how it was transmitted. To belie suspicion on how exactly a Q-Fever sufferer developed his malady, some reports now indicate the infection may be contracted from barnyard dust that had been contaminated with sheep placental material, birth fluids, and excreta.

Early, often ignored symptoms of Q-Fever include chills, sweats, non-productive cough, and queasy stomach. However, prolonged close contact with sheep can lead to more life-threatening conditions such as hepatitis and endocarditis, a heart valve disorder. (*See Also:* Foreign Bodies)

In December 2004, a South Carolina man was arrested for allegedly having sex with a sheep used in a nativity scene. He was charged with cruelty to animals. Authorities did not report whether he had Q-Fever.

SIXTY-FIVE PERCENT OF PEOPLE WHO ACQUIRE Q-FEVER FROM SHEEP THROUGH UNORTHODOX MEANS EVENTUALLY DIE: 2,302 SINCE 1995.

Chronic Wasting Disease (CWD) is a more serious condition acquired from wild animals and usually only found in people who come in exceptionally close contact with elk, bison, or deer. In many aspects it is similar to Mad Cow Disease, belonging to the spongiform encephalopathies category of aliments. In 2003, three Wisconsin hunters, allegedly looking to bag a buck, came down with an encephalitis-like brain disease apparently only transmitted by a doe. As the hunters had not gutted the doe or eaten its meat, which are the usual ways this disease is transferred to humans, officials were baffled by the eerie coincidence that all three hunters caught the disease. Unfortunately, the three hunters' brains turned into a soft mass before they were able to enlighten researchers on the exact means of transmission. (*See Also:* Laughing)

QUACKS Since it's so difficult to become a doctor, many bypass professional training and opt to buy credentials off the Internet. Currently, impostors choose to become doctors more than any other occupation, followed by registered nurses, massage therapists, pharmacists, and dentists. A complete set of diplomas and transcripts for these professions can be bought for $250. There are at least ten thousand unlicensed doctors in the United States currently treating patients. Another 1,781 licensed doctors lost their right to practice in 2004 and yet found a way to stay in the medical field.

THE DOCTOR.

Although John Roland Brown had his doctor's license suspended in 1984, he still continued to make money with the scalpel and was well known in the sex-change circles. He performed amputations for customers who had "apotemnophilia," the fetish of getting sexual gratification from the removal of a limb. Brown was paid $10,000 to amputate the leg of a healthy man, who later died of gangrene while recovering in a hotel room. Brown was arrested in 2002 and charged with murder.

DEATH BY
UNLICENSED
DOCTORS SINCE
1970:
14,891

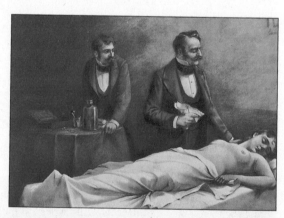

Horace Wells was the first doctor to use anesthesia in medical procedures in the 1840s. After his arrest for inappropriate behavior with two sedated female patients, Well anesthetized himself to death with chloroform.

QUALITY TIME After he was legally separated from his wife, one thirty-five-year-old man didn't get to see his kids as much as he would have liked. He was determined not to let the emotional quicksand of the situation interfere with maintaining a bond with his two children and planned educational and fun adventures for each weekend that he spent with his two little ones. One afternoon in September 2001, he intended to teach them about archery and drove them out to an old farm field, owned by his friend, that was safe for practice. As soon as he set up the target, however, he took one step and suddenly vanished. He had walked on the lid of a cesspool, which caved in and swallowed him up. Rescue workers were brought in, but it was a few hours before they found his body.

TOTAL DEATHS FROM CESSPOOLS/SEWERS SINCE 1965: 9,334

QUINSY Early English medical records from the 1400s show that any abnormality involving the neck and throat was called Quinsy. In the early 1900s, more than fifty thousand death certificates cited Quinsy as the reason for a person's final adieu. Today, it is only used to describe a peritonsillar abscess, a pus wad that grows behind the tonsils caused by severe untreated tonsillitis or recurrent throat infections.

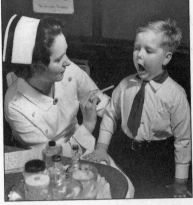

"Quinsy" comes from the Greek term for dog collar. Many of the dead Quinsy patients one hundred years ago actually had diphtheria, which caused these enlarged bull-sized necks and had nothing to do with pus caused by tonsillitis. Diphtheria (*Corynebacterium diph-*

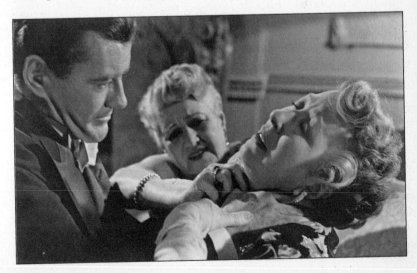

theriae) is a bacterium that festers in soft mucus tissues and causes the infected person's throat to close little by little. The disease was also referred to as "The Strangler," because those dying of it felt as if hands were clenched around their neck. Not until the 1880s was diphtheria bacteria isolated as the cause of this fatal throat aliment. It took another fifty years before a vaccine was offered in 1929 that made the body's immune system trigger the production of its own diphtheria toxin. Between 1796 and 1930, over 150,000 people were infected annually with contagious diphtheria, passed quickly through sneezes and coughs, leading to more than thirteen thousand deaths every year. Diphtheria has been nearly wiped out in the United States; only forty-one people have died of it in the last fifteen years. Today, tonsil-related deaths are caused by removing them.

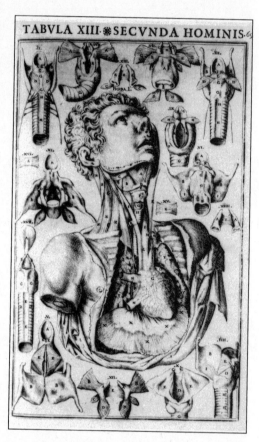

TABVLA XIII · ❋ SECVNDA HOMINIS.

BRIBED WITH UNLIMITED ICE CREAM

Starting in the 1950s one million kids a year had their tonsils removed, serving as the pediatric surgery du jour for nearly two decades. In 2004, 286,000 children under fifteen had their tonsils removed, prescribed mainly as a way to treat recurring ear infections; 6,340 died, mostly as a result of anesthetic complications and hemorrhage.

RABBITS In March 2002, a Santa Rosa man stopped to observe a fluffy rabbit on the neighbor's lawn. He thought it was an escaped Easter Bunny and lowered his hand to pet it. Suddenly, the small, gray jackrabbit lunged and dug its choppers into the man's wrist, breaking the skin. The man turned and ran but the angry jackrabbit pursued and chased him. In the meantime, two other jackrabbits emerged from the woods and joined the assault. Even though city officials could not determine whether the rabbits had rabies, the man was subjected to six rounds of rabies vaccine shots.

When it comes to death by teeth, man's best friend wins the prize. There are 53 million dogs in America that bite eight hundred thousand people seriously enough to seek medical treatment every year. Twenty people die from dog bites annually, mostly children. The highest risk breeds for fatal biting are pit bulls, Rottweilers, German shepherds, huskies, Alaskan malamutes, Doberman pinschers, chows, Great Danes, St. Bernards, and Akitas. All dog breeds are capable of carrying rabies.

In New York, a fifty-four-year-old man was bitten on the thumb by an unvaccinated puppy. Four months later he was delirious, frothing at the mouth, and wildly agitated and died of cardiac arrest. Rabies can take from a few days to over four months before symptoms are noticed, but death usually occurs from three to thirty days after exposure. Dogs, cats, cattle, horses, bison, elk, sheep, skunks, raccoons, foxes, coyotes, bats, and muskrats have all tested positive for rabies and bite approximately fifteen hundred people every year. Rabid or not, anyone bitten by a wild animal or dog that doesn't have veterinarian-provided medical records should be subjected to an arduous regime of rabies vaccines.

RABIES IS AN ACUTE VIRAL INFLAMMATION OF THE BRAIN. THERE HAVE BEEN 2,890 HUMAN DEATHS FROM RABIES IN THE UNITED STATES SINCE 1980.

RAT-BITE FEVER From head to rear, the average urban rat body is about nine inches long, in addition to its slithering snakelike tail that is over ten inches in length. Drip-dry, an adult rat weighs about a half pound.

Since the beginning of civilization, rats have been man's nemesis, known to

carry at least seventy diseases. Killing rats is a losing battle because of their ability to breed so quickly. A female rat is ready to give birth when it's two months old and can get pregnant every three weeks, producing six to twelve rat pups each time. In New York City, in 2003, there were twelve rats for every person, or 96 million rats, running through buildings and the subterranean network of tunnels and pipelines below the streets.

In 2004, 317 people were bitten by rats in New York City; 1,781 people were bitten by other New Yorkers.

Most rat bites treated immediately with antibiotics are not fatal. However, in 2003, the CDC posted a warning about the emergence of Rat-Bite Fever, a disease that kills twenty-five thousand a year in Asia, after three healthy women in the U.S. died within twelve hours after a rat bit them. A thirteen-year-old in Colorado died in 2004 from rat-bite fever after he was bitten by his pet hamster. Despite the name, rat-bite fever in the United States is usually transmitted by lab rodents, gerbils, hamsters, and mice.

12,987 PEOPLE DIE EACH YEAR
FROM RAT-BORNE DISEASES.

RAW MEAT *Listeria* is the name of the bacterium that spreads like wildfire even in refrigerated foods, causing nearly 30 percent of food poisoning deaths. It is found in soil and sewage and contaminates a

variety of foods, including raw meat, raw vegetables, and some processed cold cuts and soft cheeses. One in five who consume *Listeria* will die.

LISTERIA FATALITIES IN 2004:
30,890

WHEN IT'S NOT THE MEAT BUT THE COMPANY YOU KEEP

When a young man from Iowa argued with his uncle over who should get the dark meat at their family's Thanksgiving dinner, the uncle took out his .22-caliber rifle and pumped four dark bullets into his ungrateful nephew.

At a July 4 celebration in 1850 at the Washington Monument, President Zachary Taylor sampled many of the covered dishes donated by citizens. He became very ill, possibly from food poisoning of the Listeria *variety, and died three days later. Many historians had their doubts and exhumed his body in 1991. Arsenic was found during the autopsy and it was believed he was murdered, although the original death certificate stated "Acute Indigestion."*

WHAT'S IN THAT SCHOOL LUNCH?

The National School Lunch Program was created by Congress over fifty years ago as a "measure of national security, to safeguard the health of children." Twenty-seven million meals are served during each school day. According to the USDA, which buys millions of pounds of ground beef for distribution to schools, day care centers, homes for mentally disabled, and other institutions, salmonella and E. coli are still prevalent, causing over five hundred deaths each year. Young children are among those most vulnerable to food poisoning bacteria.

TOTAL FATALITIES TRACED TO SCHOOL LUNCHES SINCE 1980: 27

RECORD BREAKERS Desperately seeking to see his name in the *Guinness Book of World Records*, Robert L., twenty-seven, died trying to climb to the top of five borough bridges in four hours when he lost grip of a Brooklyn Bridge cable and tumbled five hundred feet to the street. His name appeared only in his obituary.

Another record breaker was Doug Danger, who beat Evil Knievel's best by jumping twenty cars. In 1991, Doug zipped over forty-two cars (251 feet) and finally got his name in the *Guinness Book of World Records* for the farthest jump ever completed. The record has yet to be surpassed, even though two record seekers have died trying to do so.

Every year, more and more people climb mountains, but getting to the top isn't enough. To break a record you have to be fast, do it solo, walk backward, or, as one man attempted to do, with no hands. (The man had previously lost both hands from frostbite in another climb.) And little mountains don't count. It has to be the biggest; Mt. Everest, at 29,028 feet, will surely get those in pursuit of greatness noticed and more than 180 Americans have died attempting to scale it. There are 120 bodies still frozen on its various points.

In 2000, a nineteen-year-old from Jamaica, Queens, decided he wanted to do something important with his life. He searched the Guinness *record book and contemplated challenging titles held in best sack racing, brick carrying, underwater rope jumping, and sprinting up flights of stairs. After a few exhausting tries at these, the feat he attempted to beat was the pogo stick jumping distance record: an athlete held the* Guinness Book of World Records *title for traveling 23 miles in 12 hours 27 minutes on a pogo stick in June 1997, at Queensborough Community College Track. Unfortunately, the nineteen-year-old only made it onto the U.S. Department of Transportation's non-motorized vehicle fatalities list (Pedestrian Synthesis Report) while pogoing across a busy street.*

AVERAGE ANNUAL DEATHS OF OFFICIALLY SANCTIONED RECORD SEEKERS SINCE 1920: 33

RESTAURANTS Emergency room records from five states show that the majority of people—60 percent—admitted for food poisoning had eaten the tainted food at a restaurant. However, after a complete analysis of all data, it emerged that far more people poison themselves from their own cooking, but home cooks are not likely to file a report against themselves. In 2004, the Centers for Disease Control reported an all-time high in food poisoning: Seventy-six million Americans suffer food poisoning each year; five thousand die from it. (*See Also:* Raw Meat)

WHEN YOU'RE ON THE MENU

Giovanni da Verrazzano discovered New York Harbor in 1524. He described the inhabitants of New York City at the time: "The people are almost like unto the others, and clad with feather of fowls of diverse colors. They came towards us very cheerfully, making great shouts of admiration." But Verrazzano didn't get the same welcome when he sailed south to the Caribbean and anchored off Guadeloupe. There, in 1528 at the age of forty-three, he was placed in a boiling cauldron and eaten while still fresh.

NATIVES of the CARIBEE ISLANDS feasting on Human Flesh.

AMERICAN CANNIBALS

In the winter of 1874 Alfred Packer killed five prospectors with a pick ax and then ate them. He was sent to prison for his misdeeds—the only person in America ever convicted of cannibalism. But he was released on a technicality: He had become a vegetarian in prison and, once released, made a living selling autographed photos of himself before he died in 1899 from ulcers.

Another incidence of cannibalism occurred in 1846, when eighty-seven people of the ill-fated Donner party tried to migrate across America. George Donner and several other families had joined together to make a subsequently unsuccessful attempt to cross the Sierra Nevada Mountains in California during winter. Some survived by eating the people in their group who had died. Only half made it out alive.

RESTLESS LEG SYNDROME Restless Leg is a neurological disorder that makes the afflicted move their legs and sometimes arms involuntarily. Most single people, or people who usually sleep alone, don't know how seriously they have the syndrome, as most sufferers in the early stages only jerk their legs during sleep. If cohabitation begins and the person with RLS sleeps next to another, the seriousness of the disorder becomes apparent. At the very least, both the Restless Leg sufferer and his or her partner suffer from sleep deprivation. As the condition progresses, uncontrollable leg and arm flailing can occur throughout the day.

The first mention of this uncontrolled limb movement syndrome was found in the writings of seventeenth-century anatomist Dr. Thomas Willis. Now there are nearly 1 million knee-jerk prone individuals in the U.S. In 2005, studies by venerable research institutions, sufferers explained that restless leg sensations feel "like Coca-Cola bubbling through [my] veins" and "like maggots crawling through [my] limbs." The RLS Foundation Web site recommends the restless leg afflicted not fight the urge to kick: "If you attempt to suppress the urge to move, you may find that your symptoms only get worse." Some sufferers find respite only in movement. One California man who had this disorder found relief when walking: In 1982, he left his house and didn't stop walking for 2^1/2 years. Recently, a plethora of autopsies performed on Restless Leggers point to an iron deficiency as the most probable cause. In the end—in addition to a life of sudden kicks and flaying arms—the inflicted die of anemia or end-stage renal disease.

IN 2003, 74,116 PEOPLE DEVELOPED END-STAGE KIDNEY
OR RENAL FAILURE, 5 PERCENT OF WHICH WERE ATTRIBUTED
TO RESTLESS LEG SYNDROME.

REVOLVING DOORS There were 12,231 injuries involving revolving doors alone in 2004. One eighty-year-old man tried to enter a midtown Manhattan revolving door with his walker. Trapped inside, he suffered a stroke and could not be reached in time for revival. Another incident involved a six-year-old boy, who got his head caught between a revolving door panel and the wall of the revolving door chamber, with a fatal outcome. A thirty-seven-year-old woman was hit in the ankle so hard with a fast-moving revolving door that her anterior tibial artery ruptured and she died of internal bleeding.

SINCE 1970 MECHANICAL DEVICES, INCLUDING REVOLVING DOORS,
ESCALATORS, AUTO LIFTS, AND AUTOMATIC DOORS,
HAVE CAUSED 7,491 FATALITIES.

RICE CAKES A New Year's custom for Japanese Americans is to eat *mochi,* a gooey rice cake served grilled and wrapped in dried seaweed. In 2003, fifty-six elderly people died and 125 others were hospitalized after choking on these gooey treats over the New Year's holidays in the United States. Twelve others were in a coma. Every year, mochi gets lodged in many traditionalists' throats, but it's usually the elderly who die.

TOTAL ASPHYXIATIONS
ATTRIBUTED TO RICE CAKE EATING
SINCE 1965: 1,601

Chewing gum was invented by John B. Curtis in 1848. He'd seen Indians chew the sap from spruce trees and labored over a Franklin stove to develop the right formula. He endured a variety of bitter concoctions before he opened State of Maine Pure Spruce Gum Company, the first commercial chewing gum factory in America. An avid chewer and sampler of his new product lines, he died from asphyxia caused by a lump of gum stuck in his throat.

MORE THAN TWO THOUSAND EIGHT HUNDRED PEOPLE DIE EACH YEAR FROM CHOKING, YET ONLY THREE HUNDRED DIE FROM CHEWING GUM, USUALLY CHILDREN UNDER THREE YEARS OLD.

RIOT ACTS When the Constitution was drawn, the Founders made freedom of speech and the right to assemble peaceably number one in importance. Striking workers, women suffragists in long skirts*, antiwar protesters, civil rights advocates, and even the KKK have taken to the streets to espouse their cause. The earliest protests in the United States often turned into riots.

---

* Women's suffrage protests were nearly always peaceful, led by the movement's founders **Elizabeth Cady Stanton** and **Susan B. Anthony**. In 1895, Stanton published *The Women's Bible,* a study of sexism in the Old Testament, and believed organized religion contributed to ill will toward women. She was also productive in winning property rights for married women, equal guardianship of children, and liberalized divorce laws so that women could leave abusive marriages. She lived to the age of eighty-seven, dying of heart failure in an apartment in New York City that she shared with two of her grown children in 1902. Susan B. Anthony was the organizational genius behind protests, described as the "Napoleon" of the suffragist movement. She died at eighty-six years old, also of heart failure in 1906.

Stanton and Anthony

The first civil rights protest happened in 1811, when five hundred slaves led by Charles of the Deslonde plantation in Louisiana threw down their tools and secured weapons. They marched to New Orleans with a goal to free all slaves, but the protest turned violent when non-slaves were killed and plantations were set on fire along the way. Ten miles from the city, chanting "Freedom or Death!" they were met by U.S. government troops. Over two hundred died in what was called the **Slave Riot.** Fifty-six of the protest leaders were hung and their heads were displayed along the Mississippi River to discourage further unrest.

In 1810 there were 1.2 million slaves in the United States. Life expectancy was 16.5 for males and 19.5 for females.

In 1831, another slave, Nat Turner of Virginia, began to organize a protest after he had a dream in which he heard the words, "The last shall be first." More than one hundred slaves joined Turner, who waited until the eclipse of the sun before beginning the protest. It wasn't long before the group went from protesting to murdering, killing whites indiscriminately: 24 children, 18 women, and 13 men. Turner's group also savagely beat the blacks who refused to support them on their march. Troops dispersed and captured most of the protesters alive. Turner, one hundred revolters, and an additional forty believed sympathizers were hung.

In January 1837, fires destroyed wheat supplies, which caused the price of flour to go to $15 a barrel, increasing the cost of a loaf of bread by one penny. At the time, the economy was in shambles; people were starving and freezing to death and many could not afford one penny more. New Yorkers assembled with placards and chants: "Bread! Meat! Rent! Fuel! Their prices must come down!" In what became known as **The Bread Riots,** mobs of thousands sacked stores and warehouses, strewing the streets with flour and wheat. Thirty-four people were killed before the police could restore order.

*In 1863, President Lincoln passed the nation's first draft law, inciting the **Draft Riots** by including a clause that allowed a person to be excluded if he made a payment of $300 or hired a replacement. For any working man this amount was an impossible sum, affordable only to the rich. Instead of raging against the lawmakers, rioters blamed the Emancipation Proclamation, considering the Civil War as a fight against slavery, and nothing more. In retaliation, the whites attacked free northern blacks, lynching and burning hundreds. In New York alone, one thousand were killed during protests, which lasted four days, making it the deadliest riot in American history.*

The worst **labor riot** was the Great Railroad Strike of 1877 when seven hundred thousand workers seeking better wages went on strike in twenty-six states. In Baltimore, the state militia fired into a boisterous crowd of strikers, killing eleven and leaving forty wounded. Andrew Carnegie's adviser, Thomas Scott, requested that strikers be given "a rifle diet for a few days." As a result, the War Department formed the National Guard to control future disorder. Another fatal labor riot happened in 1937 on Memorial Day, when police confronted striking Republic Steel workers and their families, killing ten and wounding 211.

Racial Riots took place throughout the 1960s, all relating to the civil rights movement. In 1965, six days of rioting in the Watts section of Los Angeles left thirty-four people dead and over one thousand injured. In Chicago, two were killed and sixty-five injured from rioting in 1966. In 1967, Newark riots left twenty-three dead, and on the same day in Detroit, related riots killed forty-three. Seven thousand people were arrested but not before thirteen hundred buildings were destroyed and twenty-seven hundred businesses were looted.

During the Vietnam Era there were several **anti-war protests** that turned into riots when too many people got involved and emotions got out-of-hand. In May 1970, at Jackson State College in Mississippi, the National Guard fired four hundred shots at a dormitory, killing two students, wounding twelve. A few weeks before, antiwar protestors also faced the Ohio National Guard at Kent State and thirteen students were shot and four died. Two of the dead students were not attending the anti-war rally but were on their way to class.

The **L.A. Riots of 1992** started after four Los Angeles police officers, seen in a nationally televised video beating motorist Rodney King, were acquitted of all charges. Thirty-six hundred fires erupted and four thousand National Guardsmen were called in. After several days, the violence left $1 billion in damages and fifty-five people dead.

ROAD DEBRIS Mattresses, home furnishings, building materials, cut timber, pipes, and concrete blocks tied to the roofs of cars or overloaded into pickups come loose and create unexpected road debris obstacle courses for drivers. Vehicle parts can fall off at any time: Blown

A man in Washington, driving with his window rolled down, experienced the fright of his life. A pebble caught under the tire of a passing car shot out with the velocity of a bullet. It broke the lens of his sunglasses, causing enough of a distraction for him to crash and die.

tires and tire treads, driveshafts, bumpers, hoods, magnetic signs, and brake parts have all contributed to fatalities. At 65 mph, even small debris can be deadly.

In Wichita, Kansas, a thirty-six-year-old woman was driving her regular school bus route when a pipe fell off a plumbing truck, bounced down the highway, and smashed through the bus windshield, killing her. The bus careened off the road and injured thirty children. In Florida, a long metal bar the size of a spear pierced through the windshield of a car driving on the Interstate highway.

On November 19, 1998, film director **Alan Pakula,** *age seventy, known for* To Kill a Mockingbird, Sophie's Choice, *and* The Pelican Brief, *died on the Long Island Expressway when a metal pipe smashed through his windshield and killed him instantly.*

The bar went through a thirteen-year-old girl's chest and pinned her to the seat. In Fredericksburg, a man was killed after a cooking grill bounded out of the back of a pickup truck, starting a chain reaction pileup of five cars that shut down northbound Interstate 95 for three hours.

1,413 PEOPLE DIE EVERY YEAR ON THE ROAD DUE TO ROAD DEBRIS.

ROAD RAGE The combination of traffic congestion, more miles driven, daily stress and anger, and the human tendency to fight for territorial rights has caused drivers to be assaulted with everything from guns to water bottles, sloppy hamburgers, and used diapers. Potential road-ragers like to tailgate as they believe they'll get the car ahead of them to speed up. They like to move into your lane and the very lane space you occupy. They like to yell, smash their steering wheel, swear, use hand gestures, and honk their horns.

DURING THE LAST SEVEN YEARS, OUT OF ALL 290,000 PEOPLE WHO DIED IN TRAFFIC ACCIDENTS, 45,200 OF THOSE DEATHS ARE DIRECTLY RELATED TO AGGRESSIVE DRIVING.

RODEO Cowboy athletes in this sport die in greater numbers on their way to a rodeo event than riding a bucking bronco or holding onto a raging bull. A typical pro-rodeo cowboy travels one hundred thousand miles to different events each year, flying in small planes, rain or shine, landing wherever the ground looks fairly level. Or they drive, concussion or not, hauling trailers in pickup trucks with bald tires. During the actual rodeo event, 21 percent of

the one thousand men who participate will get blows to the head and
shoulders and sustain facial injuries.

THAT'S REAL BULL

*In May of 1994, a forty-three-year-old
man from Buckhead, Georgia, and some
friends decided it would be cool to get their
pictures taken with a small herd of bison
during their trip out West. They climbed
over the fence and stood fifteen feet from
the herd. While posing with their backs to
the animals, one charged. His pals
escaped, but the man suffered a horn
puncture—a couple of tons of charging
pressure—into his back and died.*

**IN 2002, TWENTY-EIGHT RODEO
BULL RIDERS SUFFERED
TRAUMATIC BRAIN INJURY
AND THREE DIED.**

ROLLER COASTERS According to Japanese neurological research,
riding in roller coasters increases the risk of blood clots on the brain and
further brain injury. But enthusiasts,
say it's not the ride, it's the rider. In
1980, a twenty-six-year-old Missouri
man was killed because he slunk down
in the roller coaster car, hoping to get
another free go-round. The operator
thought the train in which the man
was hiding was empty, and shifted the
track to divert the train into a service
area. The service area track had low

clearance, and the twenty-six-year-old got his head crushed between the back of
the seat and an overhead wooden beam.

In 1985, a twenty-nine-year-old man was killed on the "Cyclone" roller
coaster in Coney Island, Brooklyn,
when he stood up to do the wave and
got clocked on the head by a crossbeam. Another incident on the "Cyclone" happened in 1988, when a
twenty-six-year-old roller coaster
maintenance worker, who always rode
the last car in the train on his lunch
breaks, stood up as the car began its
pitch down the first hill. He was
promptly ejected and dropped thirty
feet to a crossbeam of a lower section

*In 1981, a twenty-year-old park
employee, who had an "I'd rather be
surfing" bumper sticker on his Pinto
station wagon, was doing a test run on the
"Rolling Thunder" roller coaster at Six
Flags Great Adventures in New Jersey
when he fell off the ride and died.
Investigators concluded: "The employee
may have assumed an unauthorized
riding position that did not make use
of safety restraints."*

of track and died. In 2002, a twenty-four-year-old California man went into the restricted area of the Great America Theme Park, climbed a six-foot fence, and went beneath the "Top Gun" roller coaster to retrieve his hat. He was hit in the head by the leg of a passenger dangling from the speeding ride, and died, just before he was able to grab his favorite cap. And, in May 2004, an obese man was unable to secure the safety harness around his wide girth on the Boston "Superman" roller coaster. He flew three hundred feet to the ground, faster than a speeding bullet, to his death.

FATALITIES ON ROLLER COASTERS SINCE 1965: 265

CHEAPER THAN REPAIRS
*In New York, amusement parks must pay a $25 permit fee for each kiddie ride and allow one inspection per year. In New Jersey, amusement park riders take comfort knowing that any fatality will be investigated by the State Labor Department. Amusement park operators in many states who are in violation of the Carnival/Amusement Ride Safety Act when a death occurs will be charged with the maximum fine of $1,000. For some, the occasional death is cheaper than maintenance. (*See Also: *Amusement Parks)*

SAND AND SURF Some people go to the beach and never get into the water. But even then, a few manage to find a way to die. A twenty-one-year-old man on a Hatteras Island, North Carolina, beach, sat at the bottom of a nine-foot-deep hole he had proudly dug in the sand when, without warning, the wet sand walls collapsed, swallowing him. A crowd of fifty tourists gathered to try to dig him free with toy shovels and their hands. A backhoe was eventually brought in, but by the time he was excavated he could not be revived.

2004 BEACH FATALITIES: 3,876; 90 PERCENT OF THESE WERE CAUSED BY SWIMMERS TRAPPED IN RIPTIDES.

SCORPIONS Scorpions are poisonous arthropods, characterized by an elongated body and a segmented tail that is tipped with a venomous stinger. These creatures, which have remained unchanged for 400 million years, are found in deserts, grasslands, forests, and even under rocks on snow-covered mountains. In Texas, in 1999, a woman and her lover were on trial, accused of attempting to kill the woman's husband by placing a scorpion in his bed. (The husband died in 2001 when the brakes on his car were tampered with.)

TWENTY-SIX HUNDRED HAVE DIED IN NORTH AMERICA FROM SCORPION STINGS IN THE LAST SIXTY-FIVE YEARS.

SEA DIVING Every year three hundred thousand people take the plunge scuba diving; 140 don't come up in time and die. The most common cause of death in experienced divers is an embolism, air bubbles that escape through small tears in the lungs, caused by ocean pressure, that block an artery. Another problem for divers is when they go down too deep and attempt to come up too fast, and die of Decompression Sickness, or the bends. Standing on dry land, normal atmospheric air exerts fourteen pounds of pressure per square inch against the body, while at thirty-three feet below sea level the pressure rises to double what the

body normally experiences. The air we breathe consists of 80 percent nitrogen, 19 percent oxygen, and 1 percent argon, and under normal pressure the nitrogen will remain as it usually does in the bloodstream, doing no harm. Excessive underwater pressure forces nitrogen out of the blood, escaping in the form of tiny bubbles, to block capillaries and stop the blood from flowing properly. In effect, underwater pressure agitates the blood like a shaken can of soda. Scuba gear (Self-Contained Underwater Breathing Apparatus) puts more nitrogen in the blood, making it even more dangerous. Divers returning to the surface too quickly will die of brain damage and heart attacks if not placed in a decompression chamber immediately. The decompression chamber returns the body to normal pressure and forces the radical nitrogen back into the blood and stops it from fizzing. People that free-dive and do not take in extra nitrogen from scuba gear never get the bends.

THIRTY-THREE PEOPLE DIE EACH YEAR FROM DECOMPRESSION SICKNESS.

THE FIRST BENDS

*James Buchanan Eads, designer and builder of the **Eads Bridge** in St. Louis, invented the first decompression chamber in 1874 out of necessity. His bridge plans called for supports to be placed one hundred feet below the surface of the Mississippi River. He used boxes with a slide-away floor filled with compressed air to send down workers, who dug at the river bottom with hand tools. These men were essentially diving without gear in a box filled with air that was subjected to extreme pressure, unknowingly forcing the air's nitrogen to bubble out of their veins. When they were brought up rapidly, workers suffered excruciating cramps and chest pains. Through trial and error, and the death of fourteen laborers, the safe rate of ascent and the gradual return to normal pressure was established.*

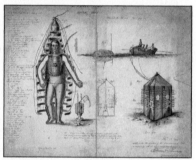

Once underwater, divers often encounter **barracudas.** These fish have 178 sharp, cutting teeth in two parallel rows, travel in large schools, and have been known to grow up to seven feet long. A swimmer's dangling bracelets will make them charge. Two people are killed by barracudas each year in U.S. waters.

Sea Lions have a playful reputation, but the males are very territorial and attack during mating season. In the last ten years, five people have been savagely bitten and drowned when they got too close to these creatures.

Moray Eels look like six-foot alien worms. They have razor-sharp teeth that kill four spearfish divers each year from bites that cause profuse bleeding. Every year nineteen people die from eating highly toxic moray eel meat that they mistake for other edible eel species.

Sharks cannot be ignored by anyone who goes into the sea. There are 350 different types of shark, of which thirty have been known to kill humans. Prehistoric in their random savagery, great whites, tiger sharks, bull sharks, oceanic white-tip sharks, and mako sharks often pursue people as prey, attracted by splashing, shiny jewelry, contrasting colored swimsuits, and tan lines (especially on the soles of the feet). In marine areas where there's a steep drop-off, sharks attack at high speeds, and the targets never see it coming. According to the University of Florida, home of the International Shark Attack File, there were sixty-one unprovoked attacks in 2004. Between five and fifteen people are killed by sharks each year in U.S. waters.

Sharks are most likely the cause of death for people who are considered lost at sea. Because no remains are found, however, these deaths are not added to the shark attack count. There are more than twelve thousand people classified as missing at sea worldwide.

On July 30, 1945, the battle cruiser USS Indianapolis was sunk by a Japanese torpedo in the middle of the South Pacific Ocean. Nine hundred men jumped overboard and survived the initial attack, only to become subjected to the worst shark massacre in modern times. The battleship was on a secret mission, delivering components needed for the coming Hiroshima atom bomb, a campaign so clandestine that other ships in the navy didn't even know the Indianapolis was missing. For five days, sailors bobbed on the open seas in life vests, fighting hypothermia, starvation, and saltwater dementia. Sharks came during the second day at dawn, tearing through sections of sailors, feeding upon their dangling legs in a frenzy. The sailors' blood brought more sharks. Many of the sailors' bodies toppled over, eaten thoroughly up to the bottom of their life vests. Defenseless to what lurked below, the sailors could do nothing but wait for the deadly jaws to return. By the time the survivors were rescued, fortunately spotted by a passing U.S. navy ship, a total of 580 men had been devoured.

SERIAL KILLERS Referred to by law enforcement as "Infamous Assholes," there have been four hundred known cases of serial killers since Jack the Ripper. According to Dr. Eric Hickey, professor at Fresno State Criminology Department, 88 percent of serial killers are male, 85 percent are Caucasian, and the average age when they claim their first victim is usually around 28.5. Typically, the serial killer is an underachiever, a troubled youth, and in the opinion of many, ultimately incapable of creating anything but destruction. The killer must first complete three separate murders that are spaced by a duration of time specialists call "the cooling-off period," which can vary from a few days to years, and must have a particular method to their killings, before their behavior is considered "serial."

The first record of an American serial killer rampage was that of two cousins **Big Micajah** and **Little Wiley Harp**. (They were legally named Big and Little.) They left their New Jersey home as young men in 1775, heading south to become overseers of slaves in Virginia. When job openings proved scarce, they joined a gang of outlaws that roved the North Carolina countryside, raping farmers' daughters, pillaging livestock and crops, and burning farmhouses. They admitted to killing forty. Once captured, Big and Little's heads were hung from an oak tree.

In England, during colonial times, killers were not simply hung, but were donated, while alive, to barber-surgeons for educational purposes, for medical research, and as a practical deterrent to copycats.

Carl Panzram *(right)*, America's most unrepentant serial killer, was an alcoholic by the age of nine, and grew up to be an arsonist and sodomizer. He mugged randomly and beginning in 1900, killed ten in the U.S., another dozen or more in Europe and South America, and six men in one day during his brief stay in Africa. Before he was hanged in 1930 at age thirty-nine, he spit in the executioner's face and said,

"Hurry up you bastard, I could kill ten men while you're fooling around!"

Albert Fish *(left)*, the Brooklyn Vampire, killed sixteen people throughout the 1920s and claimed to eat parts of his victims. He was caught and electrocuted in 1934.

Edmund Kemper *(right)*, was the "Coed Killer" who roamed highways across America seeking out hitchhikers, giving 150 women their last ride. His rampage started in the mid-1960s after he killed his mother and his mother's friend. He had a high IQ, yet enjoyed mutilation and necrophilia. He was sentenced to life in 1975 and currently helps the FBI with its serial killer profiler program.

The **Zodiac Killer** murdered five in San Francisco in 1969 and sent parts of a bloody shirt and twenty-one letters to local newspapers, in which he wrote, "This is the Zodiac speaking," and stated, "Hunting humans was the most exciting of all sports." The killings stopped, although the letters kept arriving until 1974. The killer has never been captured.

Dean Corll, known as the Candyman, was an electrician who tortured and murdered twenty-seven boys in Houston through the early 1970s. He attracted his victims by throwing drug parties at his house. He was killed in

1973 by a teenager he had recruited for help during a typical torture gone bad.

John Wayne Gacy *(left),* tortured and gagged his victims to death. He killed thirty-three boys in Chicago between 1972 and December 1978 and buried them in the crawl space under his house. A building contractor, he was a family man who loved children and visited hospitals dressed as Pogo the clown. He was executed by lethal injection in 1994.

"Son of Sam" **David Berkowitz** *(right),* who killed six lovers in parked cars in the late 1970s throughout New York City, said he did so because he was seeking revenge on a mother who abandoned him. At many of the crime scenes he left misspelled notes for the police describing himself as Sam, son of Papa Sam, or Satan, who supposedly gave Berkowitz killing instructions through a neighbor's dog. Berkowitz was sentenced to 365 years in prison.

Henry Lee Lucas *(left),* a scraggy drifter and alcoholic, earned the bulk of his income by providing sexual favors to strangers. Obsessed by bestiality and sex, he said he heard voices in his head, but the voices didn't keep him from studying books on police procedures on how best to plant misleading clues and evade capture. He partnered up with Ottis Toole in 1977 and went on a cross-country death odyssey, preying on hitchhikers and women with car trouble, robbing, raping, torturing, and murdering. The duo confessed to and recanted up to six hundred murders, but it's believed the number is closer to forty. Ottis Toole died of cirrhosis of the liver while in prison. Lucas spent time watching his favorite TV programs in prison for fifteen years before he was killed by lethal injection on March 21, 2001.

Known as the Hillside Stranglers, **Kenneth Bianchi** and **Angelo Buono, Jr.,** killed twelve women while posing as police detectives in Los Angeles between October 1977 and February 1978. They both got life in prison. Buono was found dead of heart failure in his cell on September 21, 2002. In 2006, Bianchi was still in prison in Washington.

Between 1974 and 1978, **Ted Bundy** *(right)*, disturbed by his impotence, would feign a broken arm or other acts of innocence and lure brunette women to their deaths. He killed thirty and was given the electric chair in 1989.

From 1979 to May 1981, **Wayne Williams**, a black man, killed twenty-seven young black boys in Atlanta. In 2006, he was still in prison.

Between 1978 and 1991, **Jeffrey Dahmer** killed seventeen boys and kept their body parts in the refrigerator for eating. In 1992, while awaiting execution, he was killed by another inmate. He was found dead with a sharpened broom handle stuck in his eye.

Aileen Wuornos was a prostitute who killed seven men in Florida in the late 1980s and early 1990s who had picked her up on the highway. Originally sentenced to the electric chair, she got the needle in October 2002.

Between 1974 and 1991 **Dennis Rader** *(left)*, known as the BTK serial killer, which stood for his method (Bind, Torture, Kill), murdered at least ten people in Wichita, Kansas. During his crime spree he sent misleading letters to police, but halted correspondence in 1991. Apparently wanting to be captured, Rader sent letters again with incriminating evidence in 2004. In 2005, the former city inspector, Cub Scout leader, and church-council president was sentenced to ten life sentences.

Richard Ramirez *(right)*, the Night Stalker, broke into homes in California, made women declare their love to Satan, and then killed them, thirteen in total in 1989. When asked to describe himself, he said, "Asshole—and proud of it." He received nineteen separate death sentences. In 2006 he remained on death row, selling his autographs over the Internet.

SEXUALLY TRANSMITTED DISEASE

To wear or not to wear—a condom, that is—remains the question that still carries the weight of a Shakespearean soliloquy in bedrooms across America. It's the scary list of sexually transmitted diseases that makes the question easier to answer. In the heat of things, it's not always easy to make metaphysical decisions,

> King Mongut of Siam, circa 1860, considered the world's greatest lover, had nine thousand wives. His last words before he died of syphilis were "I only really loved the first seven hundred."

but it's sex among consenting adults that has caused more deaths than any other type of human-to-human contact—even more so than murder.

From the beginning of time, people realized there were unexpected consequences from sex. Some believed too much pleasure must have a price, and sought ways to lower the odds. The earliest condom was displayed in Egyptian artwork, circa 2600 B.C., showing a man with an arc of erection sheathed in a material presumably made from an animal hide. In A.D. 1500, Dr. Fallopius published a book about his experiment on eleven hundred men using his invention of a linen penis sheath, which he claimed successfully stopped the spread of infections.

In the 1700s, the famous lover Casanova stated he made love to 122 women in one year using the linen condom and avoided acquiring a disease or conceiving a child.

Linen gave way to rubber in the 1840s, soon after Charles Goodyear discovered a way to vulcanize rubber plants and stretch the material into all shapes and sizes. By 1861 there were advertisements in the *New York Times* for "Dr. Power's French Preventatives," but this was yanked after the Comstock Law of 1873 made it illegal to sell birth control devices, and the U.S. Postal Service was ordered to confiscate condoms sold through the mail. Before the 1930s, when the thinner, flexible latex was developed, condoms were made of a thick rubber, smelled like a tire, and were not lubricated. Condom use peaked in the 1950s but lost popularity with the advent of the birth control pill. When the AIDS epidemic began to spread in the 1980s, condom use was back in style.

The number one sexually transmitted disease, which has killed more humans than any other over the last five thousand years, is **syphilis.** Caused by a micro-

The condom brand Ramses honors the great pharaoh Ramses II, who fathered over 160 children.

scopic, spiral-shaped bacteria, it is transmitted by sexual contact or through mucus membranes. This ugly-sounding disease was named after a shepherd in a Latin poem who went nuts in the latter stages of infection. In the sixteenth century, English chronicler John Stow described it as such: "A mysterious epidemic, hitherto unknown, which had struck terror into all hearts by the rapidity of its spread, the ravages it made, and the apparent helplessness of the physicians to cure it." (Sounds like AIDS today, doesn't it?) Historically, many people are not aware that they have syphilis, as it mimics symptoms of so many other diseases.

In old death records, syphilis showed up mostly as bad blood or pox; only within the last one hundred years has the disease become directly associated with sex. In fact, in the 1880s men believed having sex with a virgin would cure it. In that era, if you had syphilis you were considered a victim of Darwin's natural selection and worthy of elimination from the breeding pool. Those who contracted it were thought to be weak and selected for judgment. Before the discovery of penicillin, fifteen thousand people died each year from the disease and many more were committed as a result of the dementia it caused. By 1920 there were three hundred thousand patients in insane asylums in the United States; 45 percent suffered

*Icon of American gangsters, **Alphonse "Scarface" Capone** (below), killed 412 former associates and potential witnesses. Beginning in Chicago in 1925 at age twenty-six, with only a fourth-grade education, Al Capone created an empire of gambling, bootlegging, prostitution, dance halls, and other rackets that earned $6.5 million a week. He lived like a tyrannical king; with a snap of his fingers all his desires were fulfilled, including those by his harem of prostitutes. During this period he contracted syphilis. In 1932, Capone was sent to prison for eleven years on charges of tax evasion. By the time of his release he was clinically insane. He died in 1947, drooling, ranting, and shriveled, quite unglamorously, at age forty-eight.*

from some form of sexually acquired dementia. Syphilis destroys the brain and is linked to brutal crime. Several Jack the Ripper suspects had syphilis, among them Queen Victoria's grandson, Prince Albert Victor, who, many believe, committed several London murders during his fits of dementia.

In 2004, thirty-two thousand new cases of syphilis were reported in the

United States, dramatically up from previous decades when new incidents were negligible. The CDC believes a syphilis comeback is pending, along with the latest sexually transmitted disease, **chlamydia,** with 3 million new cases occurring annually. Chlamydia, named for the bacterium *Chlamydia Trachomatis,* causes urethral infection, kidney problems, and swollen and tender testicles. In women it can kill by causing ectopic pregnancies.

The true epidemic of our times is AIDS, transmitted predominately by unprotected sex. HIV infection was first recognized in 1981 and has since killed a total of 501,669 in the United States. There are now 1,185,000 Americans living with HIV; hopefully, this makes the decision whether or not to use a condom less complicated.

IN 2004, AIDS KILLED 18,017 IN THE U.S., INCLUDING 17,934
ADULTS AND ADOLESCENTS, AND EIGHTY-THREE CHILDREN
UNDER AGE THIRTEEN. BETWEEN 2000 AND 2004, 942 DIED OF SYPHILIS
IN THE U.S., AND ONE HUNDRED THOUSAND WOMEN
BECAME INFERTILE AS A RESULT OF CHLAMYDIA AND 716 DIED.

SIAMESE TWINS Conjoined twins result when the embryo begins to split in two, but halts for some reason during the process. The condition occurs in one of every two hundred thousand births, and 60 percent of conjoined twins are stillborn or die within a day. In the last five hundred years, only six hundred unseparated, conjoined twins have lived past the age of twenty.

The most famous conjoined twins were Chang and Eng, the original Siamese twins. P. T. Barnum hired them for his sideshow when they were seventeen

years old. Joined from the chest to their hips, they stayed on the circus payroll for ten years before they had enough of the exhibition life. They then became farmers in North Carolina, changed their name, and were known as the Bunker Brothers. They married local girls in a double wedding ceremony and went on to father eighteen children. In 1874, at the age of sixty-three, Chang Bunker caught bronchitis from working in the fields and died. Eng stood helplessly by and died a few hours later.

The oldest female conjoined twins were Millie and Christine McCoy, born into slavery in North Carolina in 1851. As infants they were sold to showman J. P. Smith for $30,000, but were soon kidnapped by a rival sideshow promoter. When Smith regained possession of the twins when they were four years old, he decided to return them to their mother. The girls were subsequently educated by Smith's wife and

The McCoys

learned to speak five languages and composed operatic songs. They eventually toured with P. T. Barnum and were billed as "The Two-Headed Nightingale." In 1912, at age sixty-one, Millie died of tuberculosis; seventeen hours later, Christine died.

Today, conjoined twins are separated soon after birth, which often results in the death of the weaker twin. In the United States, two sets of conjoined twins still survive: Ronnie and Donnie Galyon, born in 1952 in Ohio, who are joined at the stomach; and Lori and Reba Schappell, born in 1961 in Pennsylvania, who are joined at the head.

IN 2004, NINETY-EIGHT CONJOINED BIRTHS WERE RECORDED WORLDWIDE AND THREE SEPARATED TWINS SURVIVED.

The first attempt, recorded in medical literature, to separate conjoined twins occurred in 1134. Two girls, known as the Biddenden Maids, were born in Kent, England, but both died during a separation attempt when they were four. There have been approximately two hundred attempted surgical separations of conjoined twins, and only fifty-three of one of the twins lived. There are three cases where both twins survived into adulthood.

SICK BUILDING SYN-DROME Before air conditioning, when buildings had working windows, no one died from Sick Building Syndrome. Now, poorly ventilated buildings are rife with everything from black mold, pollen, virus, bacteria, and biological concoctions of all stripes. Leaky roofs, dripping air ducts, and sweating plumbing pipes create pockets of stagnant water inside walls, on suspended ceiling tiles, or on carpets—the perfect breeding ground for numerous nasty organisms. Pigeons and bird droppings also enter the interior breathing space of a building, making it sick. People living or working in sick buildings can themselves develop illnesses. Some acquire a persistent cough, muscle aches, and may develop tightness of chest, fever, or chills.

The first notion that a building's air could be deadly occurred at a war veteran's convention of the American Legion in 1976. Before it was discovered that a bacterium lurked in the air ducts, two hundred men got seriously ill and thirty-four died within ten days. Twenty-five thousand new cases of Legionnaires' disease, now called legionellosis, show up every year. More than fifty thousand people annually are directly affected by Sick Building Syndrome, a term used to describe any ailment as a result of occupying a maleficent structure, dramatically decreasing their longevity.

Asbestos is a naturally occurring mineral, which looks like a crystalline, fibrous serpentine rock. Over two thousand years ago the Greeks and Romans discovered the fiber-resistant properties of asbestos and learned to weave its fibers into napkins and tablecloths, which they cleaned by throwing them into a fire. During the Middle Ages, Marco Polo was shown garments made from asbestos fibers that were resistant to flames. But its use went out of popularity until the 1890s when a huge deposit of asbestos was discovered in Quebec. The fibers extracted from the minerals were once again hailed as a wonder product. Asbestos, derived from the Greek word for "inextinguishable," was a substance promoted as a way to save lives from fire. Between 1890 and 1970, 250 million tons of asbestos were used in building products, sprayed on walls, used in air ducts, mixed in cements, added to floor tiles, and used as pipe covers; nearly every building constructed before 1975 had some type of asbestos in it. Even though manufacturers of asbestos have known of its dangers since the 1920s, its use was continued because it was cheap filler and bound well with all kinds of building product ingredients—and also because the manufacturers didn't tell their consumers about the risks. Once the dangers were revealed, industry lobbyists focused on asbestos' fire-retardant qualities and assured the public that the fibers, once inhaled, were no different than dirt. However, long-term exposure to asbestos fibers causes mesothelioma, lung, and gastrointestinal cancer. In 1989 the Environmental Protection Agency established an asbestos ban and phase-out program, but it was overturned by the U.S. Court of Appeals in 1991. It is still used today in many products such as vinyl-asbestos floor tiles, pipe coverings, roofing paper, automobile transmission components, and brake linings. Asbestos has been related to the death of 230,000 people in the United States from 1979 to 2004.

SICK BUILDING SYNDROME APPEARS ON MANY DEATH CERTIFICATES
AS HYPERSENSITIVITY PNEUMONITIS, AN INFLAMMATORY
LUNG DISORDER: 19,392 HAVE DIED SINCE 1991.

SIDEWALK CAFÉS Many major city planning and zoning departments don't like sidewalk cafés. Health risks for consumers include car and bus soot and carbon monoxide contamination of food and open beverages. Flies and other insects flock to uncovered sidewalk cafés and spread foodborne illnesses with impunity. Petty theft and robbery increase and vehicular accidents to both pedestrians and patrons become more probable. In theory, for a restaurant to get a sidewalk permit it must maintain a width of eight feet of "passable sidewalk" for pedestrians, and isn't supposed to use chairs or tables made of metal or anchored with lead weights, nailed, bolted, screwed in, or cemented to the sidewalk. Presumably, this requirement for the use of light-weight plastic tables and seating is designed to minimize carnage when chairs go flying.

Every twenty-four hours in the United States a car loses control and goes up onto a sidewalk. It's a matter of statistics that when and where a sidewalk café is filled with latte sippers it will at some point get hit. In July 2004, a Los Angles man drove his car up onto a sidewalk and barreled full speed ahead for three blocks, apparently mistaking the gas pedal for the brake. The eighty-six-year-old drove his maroon 1992 Buick LeSabre through three sidewalk cafés and side-swiped a gaggle of window shoppers along the way. Thirty-two people were injured and another eight died on the scene.

Experienced sidewalk café diners know to be vigilant and fan their food often to prevent flies from landing. They also never keep their back to the traffic.

FOUR-LEGGED DRIVERS

In September 2004 a pickup truck plowed into an outdoor sitting area of an ice cream store in Arkansas. The driver of the 350 Ford was a dog. The pet was left unattended in a running vehicle and apparently knocked into the stick shift. Once the truck was in gear, it picked up speed, rolling down a hill; four were injured and one died.

*On March 29, 1999, **Countess Vera Tolstoy**, ninety-five, granddaughter of famous Russian novelist Leo Tolstoy, died in a car crash when she drove off the road and onto the sidewalk in New Smyrna Beach, Florida.*

NO HORSE SENSE

In 2002, in rural Pennsylvania, two men on horseback galloped through a crowded picnic area of a tavern. Luckily, no one was seriously injured. When arrested, the field sobriety test indi-

LOOK BOTH WAYS

In October 1991, a man deliberately drove his pickup truck through the outdoor seating section of Luby's Cafeteria in Killeen, Texas, and didn't stop until he crashed through the restaurant's plate glass window, instantly killing a whole booth full of diners. The driver then got out with his gun and killed twenty-three more and wounded twenty before he shot himself. A survivor, who hid inside a dishwasher for nearly fifteen hours after the incident was over, was asked by TV news reporters for her comments. She said, "Sometimes looking both ways isn't enough."

cated that both men were extremely drunk. When the two went to trial a year later, the charges against the men for drunk driving were dismissed. "A horse is a horse, of course, of course," the justice ruled, quoting from the 1960s TV sitcom *Mr. Ed,* a show about a talking horse. "The state's drunken-driving law applies to vehicles and doesn't apply to horses."

TWO HUNDRED FIFTY PER YEAR DIE WHILE DINING AT AN OUTDOOR CAFÉ.

SINKHOLES One morning in 1981, a woman looked out her window in Winter Park, Florida, and saw her full-grown thirty-foot oak tree get sucked into the ground. Then a car parked on the street vanished before her eyes. Before the sinkhole stopped swallowing things up, her house was gone, as were parts of two neighboring houses, five cars, a camper, and a string of telephone poles. The hole wound up eight stories deep and had swallowed up an area the length and width of a football field. Miraculously, no one was killed.

Movement below the surface of the ground, subterranean springs, or unpredictable geological shifts cause sinkholes. This phenomenon happens suddenly, without warning. The greatest damage from sinkholes occurs in Florida, Texas, Alabama, Missouri, Kentucky, Tennessee, and Pennsylvania.

In April 2006 a twenty-seven-year-old man in Sacramento, California, was standing in his kitchen when a sinkhole opened up and swallowed him. Three days later his body was retrieved from a thirty-feet-wide by 20-feet-deep abyss.

In a Florida region four miles inland from the Gulf of Mexico and about forty-five miles north of Tampa, at least eighteen sinkholes hit the area each year, almost all on Thursdays. To date, the Sunshine State has had a total of forty-six fatalities and numerous injuries attributed to these events.

During the past thirty years, almost 350 sinkholes have mysteriously appeared in and around Harrisburg, Pennsylvania. That's an average of twelve per year, but the year 2000 broke the record with thirty-two sinkholes reported in the spring alone. Some believe the sinkholes materialize because of mining, although the mines are located fifty miles away.

King Kong–size sinkholes, such as the Winter Park incident above, are the exception. The average sinkhole size is three to four feet across and four to five feet deep, therefore making sinkholes usually fatal to only one unsuspecting person at a time.

SINKHOLE FATALITIES SINCE 1930: 2,531

> According to U.S. geological data, for reasons unknown, most sinkholes seem to occur on Thursdays.

SITTING IN COACH Many airlines have added something new next to the vomit bag in the seat pouch: a laminated card with suggested in-flight exercises. This seemingly altruistic heath tip is a way to preempt further class action lawsuits levied against airlines for providing cramped seating spaces on their planes. More than five hundred people died from sitting in coach between 1999 and 2003 as a result of deep-vein thrombosis (DVT), in which a blood clot, formed in immobile legs while sitting prolonged in cramped spaces, climbs up the leg and blocks arteries leading to the lungs. This condition does not develop exclusively on planes, however, and can occur when anyone is stationary and confined for any length of time. Reporter David Bloom, age thirty-nine, died of DVT in Iraq in 2003 while sitting cramped in a tank for days at a time.

IN 2004 THERE WERE 1,727 DEATHS AS A RESULT OF
DEEP-VEIN THROMBOSIS.

SKY SURFING The first successful parachute jump out of a balloon occurred in France in 1876, but started in earnest in World War I with barnstormers, U.S. infantrymen who got into the heat of battle by jumping into it from a plane, landing anywhere close by, sometimes on a barn. During World War II, modern parachuting was perfected, and recreational competitions began in America in the early fifties. There are currently thirty thousand members in the National Skydiving Association (USPA), making a combined 2,440,000 jumps in 2004.

Sky surfing combines parachutes and snowboards and is part of a new group of extreme sports. This and other hybrid sporting activities achieve even greater risk and adventure and kill 120 each year. One experienced skydiver plummeted fifteen thousand feet to his death when his emergency parachute became entangled with the surfboard to which he was strapped. He hit the ground at about 90 mph.

A study of extreme sports participants by psychologist Dr. Bruce Ogilvie found risk takers to be "success oriented, strongly extroverted, above average in abstract ability and superior in intelligence." The report concluded that 94 percent are emotionally stable.

THIRTY PEOPLE DIE PER YEAR
FROM STRAIGHT—NON-EXTREME—
SKYDIVING.

SLEEP TERRORS Soon after falling asleep, people who suffer from "night terrors" act as if they're awake, rousing out of bed with sudden and uncontrollable fright. They scream, sweat, act confused, get a rapid heart rate, and hyperventilate. Some seem to be caught between a dream state and reality, and see spiders and snakes or strange people in the room. One individual died, in Akron, in 1976, when he jumped out of bed and then set the sheets on fire to kill the imaginary crawling insects. Most people with sleep terrors have no memory of their actions the next day.

Thirty percent of U.S. adults have some form of sleeping disorder. Five million take prescriptions for sleep-phase syndrome disorders.

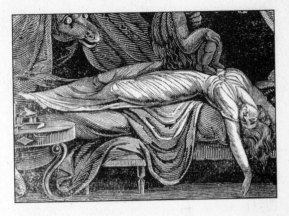

SINCE 1975, 65,982 PEOPLE HAVE DIED FROM ACTIVITIES DURING SLEEP TERRORS AND OTHER SLEEPING DISORDERS OTHER THAN INSOMNIA.

ONDINE'S CURSE

When polled, most people would prefer to die in their sleep. For centuries, scientists have wondered what causes an otherwise healthy person to go to sleep one night and never wake up. Recently, researchers have focused on neurotransmitters in the brain stem that control breathing: A person can suddenly hyperventilate without reason and die, not able to to control their breath. Some believe that the amount of involuntary breaths each person is arbitrarily allocated in life becomes "used up." The phenomenon is so baffling that researchers called the condition Ondine Syndrome, *named for a water nymph in a European fairy tale. Ondine was a beautiful and magical nymph who gave up her immortality to give birth to a child by the man she loved. However, once Ondine began to age as mortals do, the man started to look for younger nymphs. When Ondine found her unfaithful husband with another, she pointed her still-magic finger at him and said, "You swore faithfulness to me with every waking breath." Helping him to keep his promise, Ondine cast a spell to put him to sleep, during which he lost his breath and died.*

SLEEPWALKERS Habitual sleepwalkers harm themselves attempting to do normal activities, while still asleep; many sleepwalkers open locked doors, climb out windows, and operate appliances carelessly. A rancher in Wyoming, in 1977, sleepwalked out of bed, put on his slippers, and grabbed a saddle. He climbed over a fence that corralled a vicious bull—not the one that held his horse—and was gored to death. A twenty-one-year-old man sleepwalked out of his Northeast dormitory in 1982 and was found dead, tumbling naked in an industrial clothes dryer. A sixty-four-year-old grandmother from Cincinnati, a lifelong sleepwalker, was out in the middle of the night, in a storm, vacuuming the lawn when she was struck by lightning.

There have been at least twenty legal defenses that have used sleepwalking as a rationale for murder. In 1981, Steven Steinberg, of Scottsdale, Arizona, was accused of stabbing his wife Elena twenty-six times with a kitchen knife. Steinberg didn't deny the fact that he killed her, but claimed he did it while sleepwalking. He walked away (fully awake) a free man.

In 1997, another Arizona man, forty-three-year-old Scott Falater, tried to use the sleepwalking defense when he was accused of murdering his wife. He was seen by a neighbor holding his wife's head under water in their backyard pool. Falater had also stabbed his wife forty-four times. Falater's problem was that he had gone beyond the typical disassociated behavior common in most sleepwalkers: He had put on gloves before committing the crime, changed his bloody clothes afterward, and hid the murder weapon. The jury decided his actions were too complex and sent him to jail.

MIDNIGHT SNACK

*One woman in Rhode Island in 1986 died from sleep eating, known as **Night Eating Syndrome**, or NES. Despite following a restrictive diet that was essential for her health during the day, she gained two hundred pounds in three months. She was finally found out when her husband discovered her lifeless body at the kitchen table the next morning with every box and can from the pantry and refrigerator opened and empty before her.*

DEATHS ATTRIBUTED TO ACCIDENTS WHILE SLEEPWALKING SINCE 1975: 5,366

SMOKING Everyone has heard of the perils of smoking, yet 48 million people still do so, primarily because of its physical effect. Nicotine, the substance in tobacco that produces a good feeling and mild, euphoric sensation, got people's attention from the beginning. The tobacco plant, indigenous to America, was long known to natives as a potent herb, with evidence of its cultivation on the continent dating from 6,000 B.C. Natives used it as a medicine for toothaches, chewed leaves for endurance, and smoked them to dispel evil spirits. From 1617 to 1798, tobacco was the colonies' most valuable export. People smoked it in pipes, chewed it, or used it as snuff. When cigarettes were invented

Lucy Page Gaston was the first person in America to rally against cigarette use and founded the Chicago Anti-Cigarette League in 1899. A journalist who once started a magazine to endorse clean living, she launched vigorous anti-smoking campaigns and coined the slogan, "Ban the coffin nail." Although she successfully had fourteen states virtually outlaw cigarette use, many people were turned off when, lacking medical proof of tobacco's dangers, she said simply that cigarettes "were the work of the devil." Ironically, Lucy died of throat cancer in 1926, positively not from smoking, and more likely from chanting protests.

SNAKE HANDLERS Although it's a misdemeanor in many states to handle poisonous snakes in public, the law is rarely enforced when it's done so for religious practices. Snake-handling congregations believe the Bible commands them to do it as evidence of their faith: If a person is bitten, it indicates

and mass produced in the 1880s, more people took up the use of tobacco. In 1900, the average smoker lit up nine hundred cigarettes per year; in 2002 the average smoker lit up 7,300 cigarettes per year. Additives in modern cigarettes increase the health dangers and allow nicotine to enter the bloodstream more quickly. Many doctors encourage patients to stop smoking and aid their struggle with withdrawal by prescribing any variety of anti-depressant and mood-stabilizing medications, some say substituting one harmful substance with another.

In 2003, a Florida man was so hooked on cigarettes that even with his neck wrapped in gauze from throat surgery to remove cancer caused by his three-pack-a-day habit, he couldn't quit. Because he was too weak to flick a cigarette lighter, he lit a strip of paper on the stove. His bandages caught fire and, being too infirm to extinguish it, his house burned down and he died.

ALTHOUGH NOT ALL OF THESE FATALITIES WERE CAUSED BY CIGARETTES, THERE WERE 120,000 LUNG CANCER DEATHS IN 2003.

the presence of some hidden sin. John Wayne "Punkin" Brown, Jr., of Parrottsville, Tennessee, was the most prominent leader of the traveling snake-handling churches in the Southeast who handled snakes for seventeen years. His wife died in 1995 during a service in Middleboro, Kentucky, after receiving a bite from a timber rattler. On October 3, 1998, the good "Punkin" was preaching in Alabama when a newly captured three-foot rattlesnake sank its fangs into his fingers. Despite having built up antivenom from seventeen previous rattler bites, this serpent proved lethal to Brown. Medical attention was delayed, as churchgoers thought the preacher's twitching and convulsions were part of the ceremony. He died shortly thereafter.

A forty-five-year-old man from Seattle was a nonreligious snake handler who just loved reptiles. He gave lectures and demonstrations, attempting to dispel the public's fear and "gross misunderstanding" of snakes. In 1998, he was in his hotel room handling a deadly Egyptian cobra, preparing for the day's show, when it bit him. He, more than anyone, knew he had only minutes to survive. He ran out into the street screaming, "Egypt! Egypt!" but people had no idea what he was talking about, and he died.

ANNUALLY, SEVENTY-THREE PEOPLE DIE DURING RELIGIOUS SNAKE-HANDLING CEREMONIES.

Every year over 150,000 Burmese pythons are imported into the United States to be sold as pets, but more than half are eventually released into the wild. These snakes can grow up to thirty feet and have insatiable appetites, eating whatever is in their sights, with little regard if the object eaten is digestible. In the Everglades, in October 2005, a ten-foot python tried to swallow an eight-foot alligator and exploded. In 1996, a New York man tried to feed his thirteen-foot reticulated python a live chicken, but somehow managed to become the meal instead. The same thing happened in Colorado in 1998 when a man's twenty-foot python swallowed him whole. The

THEY CAN'T BE HOUSEBROKEN

Seven hundred people each year are injured by pet snakes, and 212 die. In 2001, in Pittsburgh, a mother left her eight-year-old daughter quietly watching TV on the couch when she went out to the store for a short time. While she was gone, the family's ten-foot pet Burmese python got out of its cage. When the mother returned, she discovered the snake completely wrapped around her daughter. All pythons, pet or not, kill by curling themselves around their prey and squeezing until their victims are asphyxiated. The girl was incognizant and had no pulse when paramedics arrived. She died later that night at Children's Hospital of Pittsburgh.

snake died when the suffocated man became an impassible, huge bulge in the dead snake's body.

FATALITIES AS A RESULT OF SNAKES SINCE 1965: 13,102

SNEEZING Fifty million Americans just sneezed. A sneeze, technically called an involuntary oversensitive reaction of the immune system, is usually caused by irritation to the mucus membranes of the nose or throat.

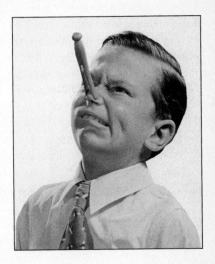

The typical sneeze shoots out of the nostrils at 90 mph and disperses more than 16 million germs over a radius of twenty-five feet. However, when sneezing is a reaction to infirmities other than the common cold, the rate, frequency, and velocity of sneezing can vary. Most sneezing caused by colds can last two to three days, averaging one hundred to two hundred sneezes. According to the *Guinness Book of World Records*, the longest sneezing fit was endured by Donna Griffith in 1981. She sneezed for 971 consecutive days, hearing "God Bless You" over 3 million times. Griffith apparently suffered from an unknown allergen.

Sneezes caused by allergies can be triggered by nearly anything, including pollen, dust, animal dander, mold, latex, or food. Violent sneezing caused by allergic reactions can fracture a person's ribs or burst blood vessels in the eyes. Many post-op patients are advised to have antihistamines on hand to prevent incidents of prolonged sneezing; sneezing fits after surgery caused 394 deaths in 2003.

The first sneeze triggered by food allergies causes more serious problems and should be considered a warning that the body is in trouble. Food allergies can kill within twenty-minutes, causing respiratory failure, inadequate blood

SNEEZING IN PUBLIC

"God Bless You," used as a polite term offered when someone sneezes, is accredited to St. Gregory, who would bestow the short and sweet blessing upon plague victims who had a small chance of survival once sneezing began. (Gregory died in A.D. 390 of pneumonia at the age of sixty.) However, during the Spanish Flu epidemic of 1919 in the United States and abroad, a person was not offered a "God Bless You" or even a "Salud." Sneezers were routinely sought out by police, arrested, and placed into jails as a desperate effort to quarantine the illness.

circulation, and a choking sensation called anaphylaxis. Approximately ten thousand people a year have an anaphylactic shock reaction, and 750 die, 150 of them adolescents allergic to peanuts. But for most of the 50 million Americans that just sneezed again, a sneeze is just a sneeze, and, on a positive note, one good, forceful "achoo" is said to produce one-tenth of an orgasm.

SNIPERS Charlie Whitman, a former marine and married man, set up his rifle and tripod in the clock tower at the University of Texas one morning in August 1966. Within ninety minutes he killed fourteen people and injured dozens more before he shot himself dead.

The horror of a sniper attack is its randomness; snipers usually don't know who they are killing, picking victims by chance. In the fall of 2002, the Washing-

ton, D.C., area was under siege by the actions of the Beltway Snipers. Six victims within a twenty-five-mile radius were killed indiscriminately within the first twenty-seven hours. For the next twenty-three days all outdoor activities including football games, jogging, and picnics were abandoned; gas stations were covered in giant tarps to conceal patrons, and shoppers getting the essentials zigzagged and ran as they went to and from supermarkets. Another three people were injured and three more were killed before the two men responsible were taken into custody. Motivated by a plot to extort $10 million from the U.S. government, John Allen Muhammad *(above)*, thirty-two, and his nephew Lee Boyd Malvo, seventeen, drove around the city and shot people with a rifle aimed through the punched-out hole of a car trunk. Muhammad was sentenced to death and Malvo received life without the possibility of parole.

THERE HAVE BEEN 514 SNIPER HOMICIDES BETWEEN 1965 AND 2004.

SNOWBOARDING The snowboarder uses a larger version of the skateboard to attain downhill speeds exceeding 50 mph. The main cause of death for snowboarders occurs when participants encounter a tree-well. In areas where the snow is so high that it covers treetops, the snow around the tree is loosely packed, causing the unsuspecting snowboarder to sink into it, and suffocate. In the history of U.S. skiing there has not been one death from falling

down into a tree-well; skiers can "kick out" and get themselves situated into a position to breathe until they are rescued. That's not the case with snowboards, because the apparatus that holds the feet in place on the board makes it difficult to detach quickly, so the boarder is pulled under the snow like an anchor.

545 PEOPLE HAVE DIED SNOWBOARDING SINCE 1999.

IN 2004, THERE WERE THIRTY-SIX SKIING FATALITIES.

SPECTATORS In 1989, a woman disrupted a baseball game at Shea Stadium. Reportedly inebriated, she shimmied up the foul pole, jumped 120 feet to the playing field, and died. In 1996, at the opening game, a San Francisco 49er football fan celebrated the team's victory by pushing a metal trash bin on wheels to the highest point of the stadium ramp and riding on top as it sailed down the aisle. The bin flipped over the barrier between the fans and the field, causing this overly enthusiastic individual to fall forty-two feet to his death. In March 2002, a thirteen-year-old hockey fan was killed by a deflected puck, the first recorded in hockey league history.

U.S. SPECTATOR DEATHS SINCE 1900: 5,988

SPERM ALLERGY When partners click, it's attributed to

WINTER WONDERLAND
242,000 skiers, ice skaters, hockey players, sledders, tobogganers, and snowmobilers will require hospital emergency room treatment for injuries this year.

Sixty percent of ski deaths are due to collision and 72 percent from head injuries. Michael Kennedy (in 1997) and Sonny Bono (in 1998) died when they skied into a tree. Most deaths occurred on slopes classified as "intermediate," since people take more risks on slopes they consider less challenging. Most skiing deaths occur to men under thirty-five years of age.

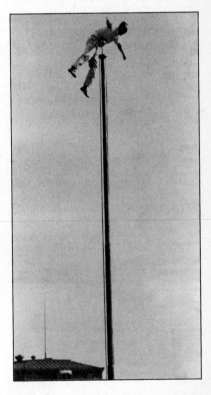

good chemistry. But starting in 1958, medical records list women who died from bad chemistry—they were allergic to sperm. One such newlywed died a year after her marriage. Her husband said: "It all started a year ago when we married. She choked, gagged, and got ill, very sick after we had sex without using condoms." The couple did not relate their unprotected sex to her reaction; they thought maybe it was his cologne or the detergents they used to wash the sheets. In 2001, she was rushed to the hospital after sex but died en route. The twenty-three-year-old woman was allergic to the protein in sperm, which triggered her immune system to overreact. Death from sperm allergies starts with swelling around the eyes, sneezing, nasal congestion, vomiting, and diarrhea. When there's too much sperm, a woman's airways swell so much that she actually dies from lack of air.

SPERM ALLERGY FATALITIES
SINCE 1958: 415

STOPWATCHES EVERYONE
Normally, sperm is ejaculated at a speed of 29 mph.
At speeds any lower than that, conception may be difficult, and a woman wishing to conceive will need to augment her partner's lackluster ejaculation by adjusting into a position that will enhance gravity and momentum. If the sperm ejaculates at speeds higher than 30 mph (some men have sperm that accelerates to 45 mph) women can experience uterine soreness, apparently from the ricochet effect of the sperm off the walls of the uterus. No deaths have been recorded from high-speed sperm.

SPONTANEOUS COMBUSTION In 1979, while walking home on a cold day in January, a professor of mathematics at the University of Nashville suddenly experienced a burning pain in his left leg. When he looked down, he noticed a flame shooting out of his kneecap. He reportedly informed a colleague about the incident, who convinced the professor it was probably imaginary, perhaps due to the stress of starting a new semester. Later on, while grading papers, the professor apparently ignited fully and turned to ash.

Scientists who study the phenomenon of spontaneous human combustion (SHC) usually hear the sounds of distant snickering emanating from the academic community (as do those who study UFOs). Nevertheless, there is a body of smoldering research documenting this unpleasant way to die. It's believed that extreme stress could set a human being ablaze.

The classic case of human combustion is that of Mary Reeser, a St. Petersburg, Florida, woman, who burst into flame in her apartment in 1951. Known in the press as "The Cinder Woman," all that was found of Mary was her leg and slippered foot *(right)*. The overstuffed chair she sat in was burned, but nothing else in the room was damaged. And as it is with all SHC deaths, the floor around where Mary had been was covered with a gelatinous, foul-smelling, oily yellow liquid.

In most human combustion deaths, family members in other parts of the house hear no sounds, or cries for help; usually the only sign that something is wrong is the foul smell after the fact. One witness thought his mother-in-law was burning kielbasa on the stove again before he discovered her to be a victim of SHC. Eighty percent of the known cases are female because, as the FBI investigation report on the Mary Reeser case noted (reported in 1951 by Jerry Blizin of the *St. Petersburg Times*): "Women burn hotter and quicker than men, because proportionally, women carry more fat."

There is no way to know if an individual is prone to self-ignition. Researchers who dismiss the SHC affair offhandedly suggest a way to avoid burning from the inside out: During extremely stressful periods it is recommended to drink plenty of water and have a fire extinguisher close by.

TOTAL NUMBER OF DEATHS POSSIBLY ATTRIBUTED TO SPONTANEOUS COMBUSTION: 215

Dr. Dougal Drysdale of Edinborough University in Scotland writes: The idea that the body can burn like a candle isn't so farfetched at all. In a way, a body is like a candle inside out. With a candle the wick is on the inside, and the fat on the outside. As the wick burns, the candle becomes molten and the liquid is drawn onto the wick and burns. With a body, which consists of a large amount of fat, the fat melts and is drawn onto the clothing, which acts as a wick, and then continues to burn.

In 1976, a New Jersey building contractor was driving past one of his construction sites. As he waved to his workers, he suddenly burst into flames. At first it was thought he was on the wrong end of a mob hit until it was discovered that his body was burned more severely than one that has been caught in a normal fire. In spontaneous human combustion cases, the hands and feet are usually untouched by fire, whereas the torso is completely destroyed, the bones flash-fired completely to ash. The man's body had turned to ash, but the Armani suit he wore was left untouched by the fire.

SPRING BREAK During a six-week period every year, 1.5 million college students set out to have fun and relax during spring break. The majority head to five top locations: Panama City, Florida; Daytona Beach or Fort Lauderdale; Cancun, Mexico; and Colorado ski resorts. Approximately five hundred partyers die each year in DUI accidents and from fatal accidents from falling drunk off balconies, ski accidents, drowning, and alcohol poisoning. Another 106 will be paralyzed from diving into shallow ends of pools; 489 will be raped; and at least ten will spend many years in foreign jails.

NOT PART OF THE PACKAGE PLAN

In 2003, a twenty-one-year-old woman was sentenced to five years at Mexico's Ensenada Prison for using a friend's credit card, which her friend, it was learned, had stolen, to pay a spring break hotel tab. More than three thousand Americans are in Mexican prisons, which have a 25 percent higher fatality rate than those in the U.S. In Mexico, drug possession of any amount, even one joint, brings at least one year in jail, and anyone over sixteen is tried as an adult. One Mexican jail survivor said most American female prisoners in Mexico do their sentence "on their backs," a euphemism for rape at the hands of police and prison guards.

GONE WILD

U.S. liquor companies also head to the spring break destinations, employing bikini-clad hostesses to hand out promotional T-shirts, hats, and buttons. According to the *Journal of American College Health*, otherwise sensible students seem to go wild on spring break. On average, men have eighteen drinks per day and women have ten. Half the men and 40 percent of the women drink until passed out. Half of the women have unplanned sex and 53 percent of all sex—planned and unplanned—is unprotected.

STAGE FRIGHT It's human nature to analyze the most conspicuous. That's why stage fright is an anxiety almost everyone has experienced at one time or another; no one wants to be dissected by the crowd. Dry mouth, tight throat, shaky knees, and nausea are typical symptoms experienced when a person is set to speak before an audience. According to the Advanced Public Speaking Institute, the most experienced public speaker can overcome stage fright by the simple and scientific method of "envisioning the audience in their underwear."

After examination of over 1 million death certificates, not one person has died of stage fright. However, the inability to get off the stage once the limelight fades can be fatal. Literally dying onstage is decidedly more conspicuous than any stage fright in its extreme. In 1943, fleshy, owl-faced **Alexander Woollcott** was one of the highest paid critics in America and a viper-tongued celebrity of his time. During a live radio show, he had a heart attack, motioned for his interviewees to keep talking, and waited until he was off the air to die.

Carmen Miranda *(right)* was a flamboyant "lady in the tutti-frutti hat," who wore outlandish tropical costumes and gyrated in a caricature of eroticism and sensuality. During World War II she was very popular, appearing in films with Bing Crosby, Betty Grable, and Judy Garland, but by the mid-fifties her act was considered passé. In 1955, at the age of forty-six, she planned a big comeback. She got a spot on the popular *Jimmy Durante Show,* came out kicking and dancing in her full fruit headdress, but had a heart attack and died during the on-air performance.

Tyrone Power was the picture of masculinity, and one of the most famous leading men of Hollywood from the 1930s through the 1950s. He died from heart failure while filming a fencing scene in 1958 at the age of forty-four.

Nelson Eddy was a handsome, singing sweetheart during the 1930s. At the time, he was the highest paid singer in the world and starred in fourteen hit Hollywood musicals. By the 1960s he played to the golden oldies crowd, doing one-night stands on the nightclub and lounge circuit. He died what he loved doing best, though not to a packed crowd. At sixty-nine years old, in 1967, while performing

for seniors at a morning show in Palm Beach, Florida, he suffered a cerebral hemorrhage onstage and died.

Irene Ryan *(left)* was in her late fifties when she became famous as the cantankerous and wiry "Granny Clampett" on TV's *Beverly Hillbillies.* She was a dedicated actor who set up trust funds and scholarships to help starting thespians. When she was seventy-one, and knew she had a brain tumor, she still performed on Broadway. During a rendition of *Pippin,* in 1973, she suffered a stroke onstage and died.

Dick Shawn, known for his zany movies such as *It's a Mad, Mad, Mad World,* had a bizarre, stream-of-consciousness nightclub routine, with quirky and unpredictable characterizations. During a performance of a comedy skit at a San Diego college in 1987, he fell down and died of a heart attack. People clapped for five minutes, believing it was part of the act.

Redd Foxx worked his way out of Saint Louis poverty by laughing and telling jokes. He considered himself the funniest dishwasher on earth, and was regarded by others as the Jackie Robinson of comedians, known best for his role on the TV sitcom *Sanford and Son.* In 1991, on the set of *The Royal Family,* a new sitcom he was to appear in, he had a heart attack, dying at the age of sixty-nine.

The ukulele-playing, falsetto crooner with long, frizzy hair, Herbert Khaury, known as **Tiny Tim** *(right),* died at age of sixty-four of a heart attack while performing his hit "Tiptoe Through the Tulips" at a Minneapolis fundraiser in 1996.

FINAL CURTAINS
A few other performers brought the meaning of stage fright to new heights when the stage they acted on became deadly.

Vic Morrow *(below),* Bronx-born tough guy, was a hero to many boys growing up in the 1960s. He played the brave Sergeant Chip Saunders in the hit TV series *Combat!* (1962–1967) and was the highest paid television performer of the time, earning $5,000 per week. But by the 1970s he got little work, due to his reputation as a hard drinker. Lonely and despondent in 1982, at age fifty-three, Morrow jumped at the chance to appear

in Steven Spielberg's film adaptation of the classic TV series *The Twilight Zone.* The boys who loved him in the sixties were now old enough to make movies; Morrow was certain he could resuscitate his career in mainstream films. For a scene in the movie, he waded across the Santa Clara River carrying two Vietnamese children. A helicopter, intending to land close by crashed beside them, its propeller blade whirling like a horrific *Dice-o-Matic.* All three actors were killed; Morrow and one of the children were decapitated. The film was made and paid tribute to the actor's last performance.

Brandon Lee, son of martial arts star Bruce Lee, was killed on the set of the movie *The Crow* when a stunt with a .44 magnum went wrong. The tip of a dummy bullet lodged in the chamber and discharged with the same force as a real bullet, killing him at twenty years old.

The *Poltergist* horror series is associated with four odd deaths during or soon after its production. Dominique Dunne, who played the older daughter in the film, was choked to death by her ex-lover. Heather O'Rourke, the little blond girl who played Carol Anne, died from a mysterious blood infection. Julian Beck, who played the "good spirit" in *Poltergist II* developed stomach cancer and died shortly after filming. Will Sampson (best known as the tall "mute" Indian in *One Flew Over the Cuckoo's Nest*), who played Taylor, the "bad spirit" in *Poltergist III*, died during routine surgery.

During the filming of the movie *The Exorcist*, nine people died who were in the film or were closely associated, including Jack MacGowran who played Burke Dennings. At one point the entire set burned down mysteriously, delaying production for six weeks.

Anthony Wheeler, a struggling actor, was happy to have landed a part in live theater, albeit a low-budget production of *Jesus Christ Superstar*, in 1997. Playing Judas, one scene required that he hang himself from a scaffold, which he did twenty times with authentic drama. But, one night, the trick noose stayed tightened and he was unable to loosen himself after the curtain fell. The audience of more than six hundred knew something was wrong when Wheeler appeared, still hanging and dead for real, in the next scene.

THE FRIGHT OF STAGE EXCLUSION

Long after they overcame stage fright, when faced with the inability to find work and hear the sounds of fading applause, many have staged their own last performance.

Clara Blandick was Auntie Em in *The Wizard of Oz*. She was on the set for only one week and was considered an insignificant player, billed last in the film credit below Pat Walsh, the head flying monkey. In 1962, at eighty-one years old, nearly blind, living in a cheap, rundown Hollywood apartment, she took sleeping pills, tied a plastic bag over her head to speed up the process, and died.

A supermodel by nineteen, **Margaux Hemingway** *(right)*, was a fixture at the ultra-cool Studio 54 in the late 1970s. There, she took to drinking and drugs with a vengeance, even more so after her flavor-of-the-month, flash-in-the-pan movie career was over. In her heyday, she had held the most lucrative modeling contract awarded to date, but ended up dismayed, impoverished, living in a small apartment over a garage in Santa Monica. At age forty-one in 1996, she killed herself by overdosing on Klonopin almost thirty-five years to the day after her grandfather, Ernest Hemingway, committed suicide.

Ray Combs hosted the game show *Family Feud* for six years, replacing original host Richard Dawson in 1988. By 1996, at forty years old, depressed, half a million in debt, and involved in his own marital feuds, he hung himself with bedsheets in his hospital room at Glendale Adventist Hospital, despite a seventy-two-hour "suicide watch."

R. Budd Dwyer was a politician who, like actors, learned to play to the camera. After he was convicted of conspiracy, mail fraud, and racketeering for taking a $300,000 bribe while he was the Pennsylvania state treasurer, he called a press conference in his office. With cameras running, playing the role of the unjustly accused, Dwyer distributed his twenty-page press statement, fielded a few questions, then placed the barrel of a .357 revolver in his mouth and shot himself.

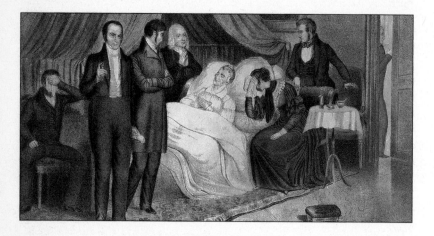

WE'LL SHOW THEM STAGE FRIGHT
William Henry Harrison was reelected president in 1840. At age sixty-nine, some thought he was too old to handle the job. To show he had stamina and was a skilled orator and public speaker, he persisted and delivered a nearly three-hour speech during the March inaugural celebration, despite a driving, freezing rain. Harrison caught a cold and died thirty-two days later, becoming the first U.S. president to die in office.

STALKING Eight percent of American women and 2 percent of American men will be stalked in their lifetimes—that's 1.4 million American stalking victims every year. The majority of stalkers have been in relationships with their victims, but a high percentage were just acquaintances, neighbors, friends, or co-workers.

Francis Patrick Doyle, an eighty-year-old Kansas man, became the good neighbor type of stalker. Even at his ripe old age, love and rejection did something to his hormones. When Marguerite Bacher's husband died, longtime friend Francis was there to aid the widow. He drove her places, helped with household chores, and had a key to her house. One year later Marguerite went to her sixtieth high school reunion and ran into a former boyfriend, Lawrence Kubik, who hadn't lost a bit of his charm. At age seventy-seven, Marguerite and Lawrence started a whirlwind romance and were married within six months. Francis offered his best wishes, but he quietly seethed and began to stalk the newlyweds. One night in November 1998 he used his old key to enter their house and hid behind a chair, baseball bat in hand. He waited until after midnight, then bludgeoned poor Lawrence to death. He just bunted Marguerite a few times, but when she didn't appear pleased with what he had done, Francis knocked her unconscious. After he called 911, the police found him sitting in the chair with a bloody baseball bat; he told them the couple had been already beaten when he arrived, and that he was there—as he had done so faithfully—to help. Francis was convicted of first degree murder, despite defense tactics that claimed he was too mentally impaired, suffering from erotomania.

In classical times it was believed that unrequited love caused mental disorders. In the 1600s it was often referred to as Old Maid's Psychosis. Today, erotomania refers to a psychological syndrome in which a person believes another is secretly in love with them and communicates messages of affection through code. It is also considered to be a person's obsessive pursuit to regain love lost.

Erotomania was the cause of the 1980 murder of diet guru Dr. Herman Tarnower, the creator of the Scarsdale Diet. When he dumped his lover, headmistress Jean Harris (below), for a younger model, Ms. Harris promptly drove to his home with a loaded gun and shot him five times. After her arrest, Harris insisted she had gone to the doctor's house to commit suicide in his presence. The gun, she claimed, went off by accident when Tarnower struggled to take it away from her. Harris was sentenced to life imprisonment, but was set free in 1993, the recipient of a pardon by then-New York Governor Mario Cuomo.

DELUSIONAL LOVE

For more than ten years, **Margaret Mary Ray** was the dangerously persistent celebrity stalker of cerebral funny man and *Late Show* host David Letterman. Ray believed she and Dave were soul mates. She stole his Porche in 1988, spied on his Connecticut home through binoculars, and was arrested more than half a dozen times for stalking. In 1998, at age forty-six, she committed suicide by kneeling in front of an oncoming train.

EROTOMANIA, STALKING, AND
OBSESSIVE LOVE–RELATED DEATHS
IN 2004: 3,890

STAMPEDES In February 2004, 244 Muslim pilgrims died in Mecca in a stampede during a devil-stoning ritual, wherein participants hurl rocks, pebbles, and shoes at pillars in a symbolic gesture to repel evil. The worst religious stampede occurred in 1990, when 1,425 died in a pedestrian tunnel during that year's pilgrimage to Mecca. In August 2005, someone yelled "suicide bomber" during a religious procession in Iraq, causing 950 to die in a stampede.

In the last one hundred years in the U.S., 8,123 have died during "panic" stampedes, defined as hysteria due to mass claustrophobia, the fear of being closed in without an escape route.

The actual cause of death during a stampede stems from asphyxiation, when those trapped in the melee are literally smothered under a sea of humans. Others are crushed or suffer broken necks.

The worst U.S. stampede happened on December 30, 1903, at Chicago's Iroquois Theater *(right)*. Proper gentlemen in top hats and ladies in frills turned wild in a mad dash for the door when smoke was spotted onstage, and 602 died. The most recent U.S. stampedes both occurred in February 2003, twenty-one people died in Chicago at the E2 nightclub trying to exit from the second floor. Security guards allegedly used pepper spray on a patron, which resulted in a rush for the stairwell. At the Station, a Rhode Island nightclub, a heavy metal band used fireworks at the beginning of their show. Within minutes, fire engulfed the soundproofing foam behind the stage and quickly

spread, darkening the club with a thick, black smoke. Unable to find the way to the exits, one hundred died. The band's tour manager, responsible for igniting the pyrotechnic display, was sentenced to ten years in prison in February 2006.

STOWAWAYS Five people per year stowaway on planes and die. Airlines, in addition to encouraging passengers to purchase tickets, attempt to educate potential stowaways on the dangers of this mode of travel by displaying signs in many airports. Most potential stowaways believe that once they hide in any part of the plane they're ready to go, but popular options, such as wheel wells and baggage areas that are not pressurized, offer limited oxygen and extremely cold temperatures. On February 20, 2001, a U.S. Airways jet flew from London to San Francisco. Shortly after it landed, a mechanic spotted what he thought was a hydraulic leak near the wheel well. Instead, he discovered the leak to be dried blood from the body of a man frozen to death.

DYING TO GET IN

Five thousand foreigners attempt to make unauthorized entry into the United States each day via the Canadian or Mexican borders and at airports without valid documents. About four thousand of them are apprehended. In 2003, 369 people died due to exposure or drowning while crossing the treacherous U.S.-Mexico border. Migrants are subjected to robbery and rape by criminals who ambush them at known border-crossing points. In January 2000, thirty-two Mexicans stuffed inside a box truck (a truck with a boxlike cargo area that sits on the frame, separated from the cab) died when it fell into a canal in Texas. Another forty-four Mexicans crammed into a semi-trailer truck died of hypothermia and starvation in 2001 in the Arizona desert. Each had paid $500 to a smuggler, who abandoned them locked inside. In Seattle, in 2001, ten dead Chinese stowaways and fifteen others dehydrated and starving were found in an airtight container on a cargo ship originating from Hong Kong. Many of the dead were elderly and disease-free, but had succumbed to the rigors of the two-week voyage inside the windowless 9- by-36-foot steel box. The ones who survived were stuck secretly with the dead bodies for seven days or more. All survivors were eventually deported.

SUBWAYS On average, forty-two people are killed annually in the path of oncoming subway trains throughout the U.S. Some trip, slip, or fall, and a few are pushed. In 1999, one deranged man, who pushed an unwary woman off the subway platform at 23rd Street in New York City, explained it was "her turn" before he sat down on a bench and waited for police.

A forensic student taking a sample from a seat in a NYC subway car found a smorgasbord of nastiness, including human and rodent excrement, human semen, and a horde of chicken bones, sucked clean, under one seat.

SURF CITY

Others have died perched on the four-foot-wide top of a four hundred-ton subway car as it takes off at 30 mph. They keep an eye out for signal signs and fast-approaching tunnels, which typically give only a few inches of top clearance. In 2003, five thrill-seeking teenagers died while riding on top of New York City subway cars.

SUDDEN DEATH Sudden death while playing sports occurs 136 times per year. Attributed to "cardiac concussion," usually as a result of a sudden, hard blow to the chest, it can occur during any sport but is more common while playing basketball or football. The average age when sudden death occurs is seventeen.

Other causes of sudden death for high school and college athletes include overexertion, dehydration, or from previously undetected heart ailments.

Sudden death in **chess** requires that your piece be sacrificed if you make a non-capturing move, which makes for a quick and harrowing game. Participants who play chess professionally are quite serious, and tournaments have been known to be great stress inducers. Numerous world-class chess pros have died of heart attack or stroke during tournaments, including Ed Edmundson (sixty-two), Paul Keres (sixty-four), Paul Leonhardt (fifty-one), Vladimir Simagin (forty-nine), and Frank Marshall (sixty-seven). Stress aside, competition can kill: One chess pro's sudden death was attributed to poisoning by a rival.

MAKING WEIGHT

In December 1997, three healthy college wrestlers in three different states died while trying to make a weight-class qualification. A typical regime for a wrestler of any age trying to qualify for competition can include fasting, the use of laxatives, emetics, diuretics, fluid restriction, self-induced vomiting, hot rooms (boiler rooms), hot boxes, saunas, steam rooms, and vapor-impermeable suits. In the hours preceding the official weigh-in, all three wrestlers prompted dehydration through extreme perspiration (while wearing rubber-lined sweat suits) and died suddenly as a result of serve electrolyte imbalance, a by-product of hyperthermia. Since then, The National Collegiate Athletic Association has prohibited these practices; however, athletes can't get on the mat if the scale disqualifies them, and still persist in using these tactics.

POLITICAL SUDDEN DEATH

*In 1923, at age fifty-seven, President **Warren G. Harding** died mysteriously while working at his desk in the Presidential Suite at the Palace Hotel, San Francisco. At the time, Harding was implicated in the Teapot Dome scandal, an investigation into monetary irregularities in the Veterans' Bureau. The president was not only accused of overlooking his attorney general's corrupt dealings but newspapers also discovered he had a mistress and an illegitimate daughter. Although officially Harding died suddenly of a heart attack, some believe the president died from poison, administered by himself or his wife. No autopsy was performed, and by order of his wife, Harding's body was embalmed within the hour of his death.*

TALK SHOWS When Ralf Paintz convinced his ex-wife to appear with him on *The Jerry Springer Show*, she thought the program was going to feature their reconciliation. Instead, she encountered Panitz in front of the audience ranting "Jerry! Jerry! Jerry!" with a new wife he had secretly married. The hitch was that Paintz, although divorced, still spent many nights over at his ex-wife's house, even after he was re-married. Furious, to the delight of the program's producers, the humiliated ex-wife demanded Paintz come over and get his belongings or she would throw them in the trash. She then stormed off the stage, laughed at by the audience and cursed at by Paintz's new wife. Hours after the episode aired, Paintz showed up at his ex-wife's house. More heated words were exchanged, and the argument escalated to violence. Upset about having to move his possessions, Paintz choked and beat his ex-wife to death. The son of the dead woman sued the show, alleging the program had "created a mood that led to murder." A spokesperson for *The Jerry Springer Show* claimed that neither the show nor its producers were responsible.

LIFE IMITATING RERUNS
In Rochester, New York, a clothing store owner, age fifty-three, would do anything to not go out of business. In 1994, he asked his friend to help him collect insurance money by staging a robbery. The two watched endless reruns of Columbo *and other cop shows on TV while drinking scotch in the back office to learn how police operate. They knew they had to make the crime look authentic. The next evening, the store owner produced a gun and told his friend to shoot him in the arm. After a few more whiskeys and* Kojak *episodes, the friend obliged, aimed the gun, and pulled the trigger. But firing a loaded gun wasn't as easy as it seemed on TV. The friend missed the man's arm, shooting him once in the chest, and killed him.*

HOMICIDES AS A DIRECT RESULT OF TALK SHOW, GAME SHOW, AND REALITY TV PARTICIPATION SINCE 2001: 13

TAXIS AND TRUCKS There are two-hundred thousands taxi drivers in the United States. 95 percent of cab driver deaths occur while the meter is running, 75 percent of the time from a gunshot to the back of the head. Since 1990, taxi drivers and chauffeurs have accounted for 865 homicides on the death meter.

The first pedestrian death in the United States was caused by a taxi. It happened in New York City, in 1899,

when sixty-eight-year-old Henry Bliss stepped off a streetcar and was run over by a taxi on the corner of Central Park West and 79th Street.

August 16, 1949: **Margaret Mitchell,** *age forty-eight, wrote her one and only book, the wildly popular novel* Gone With the Wind, *before she was thirty years old. While en route to see a movie with her husband, a cabdriver rammed into her as she stood on the curb, killing her instantly.*

There are three million truck drivers in America. Approximately 852 truck drivers die every year when their rigs jackknife or overturn.

THAT'LL TEACH 'EM
At a Georgia truck stop, two truckers got into an argument. One got so steamed he pulled out his hunting knife and stuck it into the tire of the other guy's truck. "Now, that'll teach ya," he said, just as the pressurized air from the punctured tire propelled the knife back into his own throat, killing him.

THANKSGIVING Thanksgiving is an American tradition that started with the Pilgrims and Native Americans, even though they only had one Thanksgiving dinner on September 21, 1621. There were no similar feasts there-

after until Abraham Lincoln declared it a national holiday in 1863. Franklin Roosevelt assigned it to the fourth Thursday of November in 1939.

The four-day holiday kills 550 people on the roadways each year. Pound for pound, car for car, it's the increased volume of traffic that provides the boost in carnage, and not the quality time spent with relatives.

The day after Thanksgiving is called "Black Friday" not from the increased number of funerals but because retailers generate enough revenue to put their ledgers "into the black."

Thanksgiving has more alcohol-related traffic fatalities than any other weekend during the year, including New Year's Eve and New Year's Day combined. It's the kickoff to the annual drunk driver "Killing Season," from Thanksgiving through New Year's Day, when more than four thousand alcohol-related traffic fatalities occur each year. Fifteen percent of people who never drive after drinking do so during this season. Women are 30 percent more likely than men to drive after drinking one or two drinks during this period.

In addition, there are more incidences of cooking fires on Thanksgiving. Add to that the 13 percent of turkeys left to defrost improperly that become contaminated with salmonella, and there are 1.3 million illnesses and an additional five hundred deaths a year.

ANNUAL AVERAGE HOLIDAY ROSTER OF CAR ACCIDENT DEATHS FROM 1995 TO 2003

New Year's Eve: 149
New Year's Day: 163
Super Bowl Sunday: 105
St. Patrick's Day: 151
Memorial Day: 348
Fourth of July: 212
Labor Day: 529
Halloween: 201
Thanksgiving: 503
Thanksgiving to New Year's Day: 4,398

THRIFT STORES A U.S. Consumer Product Safety Commission study of thrift stores and 301 bargain outlets found a large number of hazardous products offered for sale. Fifty-one percent of the stores sold discontinued children's jackets or sweatshirts with nonsecured or stitched-in drawstrings at the waist or neck. Twelve percent of the stores sold cribs once recalled because they caused strangulation and suffocation. Recalled, defective car seats also found their way to thrift store racks, as did an abundance of recalled toys, such as toy basketball nets, long known for random strangulation. Twenty percent of the stores sold hair dryers that did not protect against electrocution. These stores also sold halogen lamps without wire guards and playpens with protruding hardware and loosely secured top rails.

Twelve million bean bag chairs that were recalled found their way to dollar stores. Thirty-six children suffocated in 2003 on the small pellet foam used to fill the bags; there were also nineteen fatal injuries reported from the zippered model of the bean bag chair.

Halogen Floor Lamps give off so much light and heat that the bulb can ignite flammable materials. The filament of a halogen bulb reaches 2,000 degrees Celsius and can fry an egg in thirty seconds. Forty million units are still in homes and annually cause approximately 270 fires and nineteen deaths a year.

THYROID DISEASE The thyroid is a butterfly-shaped gland located at the front of the neck that acts as the chief regulator of all organ functions. An imbalance in the rates of metabolism can wreak havoc anywhere in the body. Thyroid disease begins with inflammation of the gland, sometimes called Hashimoto's disease (named for Japanese physician Hashimoto Hakaru who identified it in 1912), referring to the condition when the immune system in effect attacks the thyroid gland, leading to hypothyroidism (underproduction of thyroid hormones). When the thyroid overproduces hormones it is called hyperthyroidism, or Graves' disease, named after Robert James Graves. These imbalances trigger fibromyalgia (chronic muscle pain and fatigue), lupus, endometriosis (growths around the uterus and pelvic cavity), irritable bowel syndrome, nodules, and cancer. However, thyroid disease is often misdiagnosed and not revealed to be the source of problems until too late. Symptoms of thyroid malfunction include weight gain or loss, loss of interest in sex, feeling cold or hot, constipation, bulging eyes, brittle nails, and hair loss. Thyroid disease is the eighth leading cause of death for women between fifteen and sixty-four. Exposure to radiation, overindulgence of soy products, overconsumption of undercooked goitrogenic foods, such as broccoli, brussel sprouts, and cabbage, or insufficient iodine in the body can trigger thyroid disease.

In 2005, the life expectancy for an American female was 80.67 years, compared to 48.1 years in 1900, when the infectious diseases pneumonia, influenza, and tuberculosis were the leading causes of death for women.

Today, cancer is the disease American women say they fear the most, but **heart disease** is still the number one killer, taking more lives than cancer, car accidents, and diabetes combined—approximately 475,500 American women each year. **Cancer** is the second deadliest, with lung cancer the leading cause of cancer deaths among women in 2004. This has replaced breast cancer: There are 183,000 new cases of breast cancer each year; 46,000 women die of breast cancer annually. The third leading cause of cancer deaths in U.S. women is colon cancer, affecting over twenty-eight thousand women.

EACH YEAR, 270,000 WOMEN OF ALL AGES DIE FROM ALL CANCERS.

TOASTER Between 1926 and 1930, housewives across America were dropping like flies. The cause of death: electrocution. The source: home appliances—in particular, the new pop-up toaster. The early designs didn't always work with hand-sliced bread of varying thickness, leading the frustrated cook to use a fork to fish it out. Electrocution by toaster killed 3,213 people, enough to lead to the one of the country's first product warnings, which was included in every box.

In 2004, a fast-food worker with eighteen months' experience was in charge of the close-up routine. After damp-mopping the floor for five minutes, he plugged a toaster into a floor outlet, and promptly received what turned out to be a fatal shock.

BAD PRODUCT HALL OF FAME
In 2003, a record-breaking 344,717 new patent applications were filed. In 2004 over nineteen hundred of these new products were manufactured, distributed, and then recalled after they proved unsafe. There were 9,876 deaths from bad products. For example, home-use air pumps have killed 377 people since 1965. In March 2003, a new model was recalled when the glass on the gauge, under pressure, exploded and embedded in a man's neck, severing his artery and killing him.

A New Jersey woman filed a wrongful death suit against Kellogg and Black & Decker for the fatal fire that spread through her home when a Pop-Tart burst into flames inside her toaster oven. Later, she admitted to placing the pastry in the toaster, taking the kids to school, and returning twenty minutes later to a flaming Pop-Tart and toaster.

BETWEEN 1985 AND 2004, 224 PEOPLE WERE KILLED BY TOASTERS.

TOILET TIME Unlike other human endeavors like dancing or painting works of art, the time one spends sitting on a toilet has not earned as much print. The average female will sit on the bowl for two hundred hours each year—the equivalent of five, forty-hour workweeks—while the male will sit on his throne for a total of three workweeks in the same pursuit. The time and surroundings in which toilet hours are spent have coincided with advancements in civilization: The more advanced the society, the more leisure time, and thus more time to spend contemplating life in the loo. However, the actual process of bowel movements hasn't changed since the first cavemen sought shelter behind a bush, clutching a handful of the softest leaves.

Today, the most prevalent hindrance to productive toilet time is constipation, prompting over 2.5 million to visit the doctor and spend more than $300 million on laxatives each year. Constipation for a week or more will not result in death, unless there is a serious cause, such as blockage from scar tissue or undetected intestinal growths. Most deaths while sitting on the toilet occur from attempting the **Valsalva maneuver.** Scuba divers employ a version of this technique to clear out water that got into air lines, but the inexperienced sitting on the toilet have less luck in performing it successfully. The Valsalva maneuver is an attempt to forcibly push out the contents of the bowels while keeping the mouth and nose closed. The barometric pressure in the lungs can get out of balance, causing the compressions that pump blood through the heart to malfunction. In other words, the aggressive pusher dies instantly of a heart attack.

A GOOD PLACE TO GO
In 2002, an eighty-six-year-old man was found dead, sitting on the toilet. Police entered the premises by force when neighbors called complaining of a bad stench. Dates on prescription medicines found next to his body indicated the man had died over a year before.

**THE KING WAS ON
HIS THRONE**
Elvis Presley was found dead on the toilet, ultimately dying of a heart attack while employing the Valsalva maneuver. His last words: "I'm going into the bathroom to read."

**1,213 DIE
FROM COMPLICATIONS CAUSED
BY AGGRESSIVE PUSHING DURING
TOILET TIME EACH YEAR.**

USE A PLUNGER

In December 2004, a Pennsylvania man died while attempting to unclog a toilet. The blockage was so bad he decided to dump two bottles of liquid drain cleaner into the bowl at the same time. The sixty-nine-year-old man staggered back and fell unconscious from the fumes. The death certificate indicated chlorine gas poisoning was the cause of death and did not mention his toilet, or the blockage he had previously produced, as the secondary cause.

TOOTHACHE New studies have correlated tooth decay to heart disease, proving that bacteria from the mouth can enter the bloodstream and become trapped in the heart. Since antibiotics and dental care have improved, fatalities from infected teeth and gums are rare; however, throughout most of history, bad teeth was a leading cause of death.

The first dentists in Greece, documented by Hippocrates in 400 B.C., extracted teeth by holding a chisel held against the base of the tooth and pounding around it with a hammer. Ancient Chinese dentists used their hands to remove teeth and were honored with the title of dynasty-sanctioned "tooth pullers" if they were able to yank a nail from a piece of wood with their fingers. As recently as World War II, a person was considered medically unfit for service if he didn't still have two-thirds of his natural teeth. Today, most tooth-related fatalities are a result of dental procedures gone awry.

In Oklahoma City, a jury recently awarded $1.3 million to a thirty-three-year-old man for the brain damage he suffered at the hands of his dentist. The dentist had hooked up the man, his last patient of the night, to nitrous oxide. Somehow, he forgot about the patient, still under the gas, and locked the office and went home. The next morning when the dentist returned to work, the man had been under anesthesia for ten hours.

FROM 2001 TO 2005,
812 DEATHS OCCURRED
IN DENTIST CHAIRS.

Nathan Mayer Rothschild was the richest man in the world
at the beginning of the twentieth century.
He died in 1915 from an abscessed tooth,
which nowadays can be cured by a $10 antibiotic.

TOOTHPICKS Sherwood Anderson, an American writer, confessed that he wrote better under the influence of "strong drink." While attending a fancy cocktail party in 1941, apparently warming up for a writing session, he knocked back the bourbon. A tray of hors d'oeuvres were presented and, during an important discourse, he grabbed a miniature frankfurter with a toothpick. Without a thought, he put the mini hot dog in his mouth, and swallowed the whole thing, toothpick and all. Too embarrassed to make a fuss, or too many sheets to the wind to notice, he ordered another drink to wash it down. A week later, while traveling on an ocean liner, he died of peritonitis, an inflammation of the stomach, caused by the toothpick.

DEATHS FROM TOOTHPICKS SINCE 1900: 17,903

TORNADOES A typical tornado will occur without warning on a sunny afternoon. Within minutes the sky turns a sinister green, gusts of wind shoot up, throwing around handfuls of leaves and dust clouds. The sky will then split open in a torrential downpour, often followed by golf ball–sized hail. Rain and ice pour from low black clouds, as if emptied from a dump truck. A few seconds later, there is a spooky stillness. Then it appears, in the near horizon: a massive funnel at least a mile wide; there's nowhere to go, no possible way to escape.

The United States is the tornado capital of the world. A tornado's whirling winds have exceptional force, with recorded speeds exceeding 250 miles per hour. These funnel-shaped clouds move in narrow paths and bring nuclear-like destruction: Houses blown apart from the inside out, farm animals and body parts strewn about, apparently imploded from the force. Meteorologists classify the most memorable tornado-storm occurrences as Tornado Outbreaks. The most relentless outbreak, dubbed the Super Outbreak of April 3, 1974, lasted sixteen hours and moved across thirteen states, producing 148 separate

tornadoes before the storm system was through. This outbreak injured five thousand and killed 315.

Meteorologists speak nostalgically of the Super Outbreak. However, there was another outbreak that took even more lives. The Tri-State tornado of March 18, 1925, lasted only 3½ hours but caused 1,442 deaths. In that one outbreak, storms developed in Kentucky, Tennessee, and Alabama, leaving behind a wide swath of wet and wind-pounded graves.

The twentieth-century's accurate record keeping doesn't end with those losses. Another notable storm produced ten tornadoes near Tuscaloosa, Alabama, on March 21, 1932, taking a total of 330 lives. On Palm Sunday, April 11, 1965, an outbreak of fifty tornadoes in the Great Lakes region took 256 people.

MORE THAN EIGHT HUNDRED TORNADOES ARE REPORTED IN THE UNITED STATES EACH YEAR, KILLING 150 ON AVERAGE.

TOUPEES In 1981, a fifty-four-year-old Detroit man was newly divorced and wanted to get into the disco scene. One night he felt his toupee shift from all the wild gyrating on the dance floor. He ran into the bathroom and went into a closed stall, got out his bottle of special glue, and applied it extra liberally. Sitting on the toilet with the wig on his knees and an open bottle of glue between his legs, he decided to light a cigarette. The fumes exploded, causing serious complications, from which he died two weeks later.

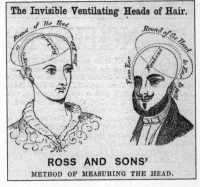

The Invisible Ventilating Heads of Hair.

ROSS AND SONS'
METHOD OF MEASURING THE HEAD.

FATALITIES FROM FLAMMABLE PRODUCTS SINCE 1975: 39,981

TOYS Small toy parts, balloons, and small swallowable balls lead in toy-related deaths. Between 1995 and 2003, 174 children died while playing with toys. In 2003, seventeen children died, five of those from choking: One choked to death on the antenna ball on a toy caterpillar, one on half of a spherical toy, another choked on a building block, another on a marble, and one swallowed a button eye from a large, stuffed bear.

TRAIN TRACKS In 1998, one man from Hornell, New York, was hit by a train as he walked on the tracks, talking on a cell phone—he didn't hear the whistle. A twenty-seven-year-old from Burlingame, California, sat on the edge of a station platform and thought there was enough space for the train to go by without hitting him; he miscalculated. A twenty-two-year-old man, of Berkeley Springs, West Virginia, played a game of chicken with his friends to see who could stand the longest on the tracks in front of an oncoming train. He won the game, but lost his life.

TEXT MESSAGING

In June 2005 Tara McAvoy, who had been deaf since birth, was crowned Miss Deaf Texas in an annual event that started with the first pageant in 1962, an offshoot of the national (then called) Deaf-Mute Convention, inaugurated in 1880.

Sadly, in March 2006, the eighteen-year-old beauty queen took a shortcut from her home to her mother's place of employment across railroad tracks near Austin, Texas, when she was fatally clipped by a train's snowplow. The teen, walking only one foot away from the tracks, had been preoccupied exchanging text messages with friends and family when the train approached and sounded the horn. After the train conductor realized the whistle and blast was getting no response, he activated the emergency brake, but couldn't stop the train in time.

YOU CAN'T BEAT THE TRAIN

There are currently eight commercial railroad companies in the United States, operating twenty thousand locomotives pulling half a million freight cars, along 150,000 miles of tracks. A typical 150-car freight train needs at least a mile and a half to come to a full stop when it's traveling at 50 mph. Every year, 650 people die in automobiles that try to beat the train as the gate falls or drive around a train crossing gate when it's down.

SEVEN HUNDRED PEOPLE WALKING ON OR NEAR THE
RAILROAD TRACKS DIE EACH YEAR.

UMBRELLAS In 2002, a Georgia man died when a large pool umbrella he had set up in his backyard was dislodged by a strong wind and sent cartwheeling toward him at the other end of his property, impaling him through the neck and chest. The man managed to drag himself into the kitchen to call 911 with the open umbrella still speared into his chest. When the police arrived, they thought he had been attacked. He died at the hospital later that evening.

TOTAL INJURIES FROM ALL TYPES OF UMBRELLAS SINCE 1975: 19,867; TOTAL FATALITIES: 91

L'ESSAI D'UNE POMPE.

— Tenez, voyez la force du jet... Du premier coup je vais culbuter ce monsieur qui ne s'attend à rien et qui n'est pas mon confrère.

PARAPLUIE PISTOLET.

— Ah! mon Dieu, quel malheur!... je voulais lui offrir la moitié de mon parapluie, et voilà que je lui ai brûlé la cervelle en plein estomac!

UNCONSCIOUSNESS Everyone has experienced unconsciousness when asleep. The average, healthy fifty-year-old, for example, has spent at least one-third of his life, or twenty years, unconscious. Unconsciousness outside of sleep can lead to premature fatality. (*See Also: Sleepwalkers.*) Degrees of unawareness range from syncope (fainting) to deep stupor and, ultimately, to the comatose state, derived from the Greek word for "deep sleep." In a coma, the central nervous system shuts down and allows the organs to function independently of each other. In other words, coma is the maximum level of oblivion. Fifty percent of comas are due to head trauma; the other half are the result of infectious disease, drugs, electrocution, or from exposure to gases.

Without care, the average coma patient would last no more than ten days; however, with life support and

Your "Home Sweet Home" sign needs a warning label. In 2003, 29,500 fatalities happened in the home. The leading causes of death were from solid and liquid poisoning: Five thousand people died from household cleaners, paints, drugs, and medicines. Falling down stairs and slipping on wet floors, icy steps, or in bathtubs claimed the lives of 9,300 people, mostly over the age of sixty-five. From 2002 to 2003, more than half of all home deaths occurred during leisure activities.

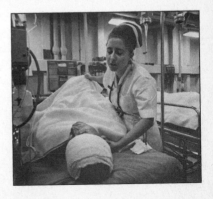

dedicated care the comatose can remain alive for decades. If, or what,
they may be thinking, no one knows.
The problem with someone in a coma,
other than the obvious, is that it is im-

*When a person goes into a coma, the
initial medical care costs are
approximately $199,000, and then an
additional $90,000 a year for life.*

possible to predict whether he or she will come out of it; no one can know, with
100 percent certainty—without an autopsy—whether the person is truly brain
dead.

HOW MUCH TIME LEFT?

Dr. Joanne Lynne, director of the Center to Improve Care of the Dying at George
Washington University Medical Center studied two thousand coma deaths and
found that most doctors gave inaccurate predictions on how long a person
might live: 20 percent, after being told that they had two months to live, died
the very next day. In most other incidents, doctor's predictions scored a 50-50.
Regardless—proving it's all arbitrary—once in a coma, even with care, a person
will usually die within two months.

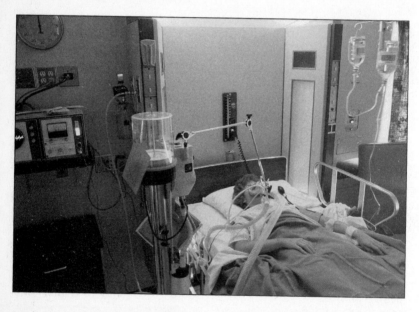

The exceptions spur advocates opposed to ending life support for any reason. Of course, every case is individual and depends upon the extent of life support needed. For example, some need a ventilator to help them breathe; others
just require intravenous nourishment and catheter for the disposal of waste.
Nevertheless, only occasionally do comatose persons suddenly revive after
many years. Patricia White Bull, mother of four, was in a coma for sixteen years
after complications from giving birth. One day in 1999, while a nurse was making her bed, Bull suddenly sat up and said, "Don't do that." She later left the hospital completely recovered and resumed a normal life with her children.
Another case involved Terry Wallis, who went into a coma after a car acci-

dent one Friday the 13th in 1984. Nineteen years later, on another Friday the 13th in 2003, he suddenly opened his eyes and spoke. He asked his mother to bring him a Pepsi and then wanted to speak to his grandmother, who had died years earlier while he was in the coma. He was able to recite the grandmother's telephone number from two decades past. Terry had regained consciousness in the exact same time slot where his mind had shut down.

IN 2003, EIGHTY THOUSAND PEOPLE WERE IN A COMA; 68,981 OF THOSE HAD DIED BY 2004.

LOCKED IN

During a locked-in or "waking" coma, a person is not in a deep sleep but completely awake, with a nearly full functioning brain. However, they are unable to speak, move, or react normally to stimuli and usually keep their eyes closed and locked. Five thousand patients each year fall into a waking coma on the operating table as a result of anesthesia failure. Inadequate anesthesia may cause the patient to feel the pain of surgery without the ability to signal to the doctors, move, or communicate. In some incidents, individuals in these circumstances have died of fright.

UNISEX The word *unisex* was first introduced in the 1960s by hair salons that served both men and women, but the blurring of gender lines goes back further than that. In the 1700s it was common for men to wear garments adorned with feminine frills and lace and don various wigs for different occasions. However, the true claim on androgyny belongs primarily to the hermaphrodite, a person born possessing genitalia of both sexes.

Hermaphrodites don't like the term and prefer to label their situation as a "sex differentiation disorder." Nowadays, children born with both male and female genitalia are given tests to see which of the sex chromosomes—XX or XY—are more prevalent in the blood. After they are assigned a gender, surgery is usually performed to enhance the chosen sex. Many hermaphrodites are unaware that they have even undergone surgery to enhance their more prevalent gender, determined strictly by chromosome count. In the 1970s, prior to surgical modifications, one individual described how he was given both a girl's and a boy's name on two differ-

ent birth certificates that were not recorded until he developed further, to see if one genitalia became more physically predominant at about six months of age. In this case, even though male was his assigned gender, and he was raised as a boy, he began to develop breasts at puberty. As it was for this person, true hermaphrodites often suffer from psychological gender confusion—with or without surgery—primarily because they were assigned the wrong gender. Hermaphrodites who have openly lived as both male and female number less than four hundred in medical literature.

Societal treatment of those with sex differential disorders hasn't changed much since 1838, when Herculine Barbin published a memoir, *Memoirs of a French Hermaphrodite*. Although Herculine had both sex organs, she was raised in a convent as a female. She described a life of abuse and intolerance, considered a freak of nature, doomed to a life trapped in a sexual masquerade. Barbin did switch her gender to male at age twenty-four and lived as such until her suicide six years later, after which her genitalia were removed and sketched for future physicians to study.

Bobby Kork
?
2691-1

Bobby Kork *(right)* was the most celebrated "half and half," as he/she was referred to in the 1940s sideshow circuit where Bobby found employment. His sexual anatomy was divided equally from head to toe, right down the middle. On the right side, Bobby was a man, with a short haircut and half a mustache. On the left, Bobby was a female with long hair, smooth skin, and one fully developed breast. Below the belt Bobby had full male and female genitalia. But personality-wise, testosterone ruled. If he was called a freak, he'd bust a nose. After work, he was a nightclub junkie and had numerous affairs with beautiful women. He died of food poisoning in 1950 at age forty-two.

SIXTY-FIVE THOUSAND CHILDREN ARE BORN WITH INDISTINGUISHABLE
REPRODUCTIVE ORGANS EACH YEAR.

The average life span of a hermaphrodite is forty-nine years.

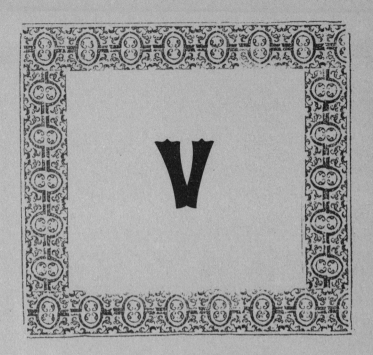

VALENTINE'S DAY Valentine was a Roman Catholic cleric executed on February 14, 270. His crime was marriage: As a priest, he had defied the orders of Emperor Claudius II, a fierce general, who preferred his soldiers unwed, and continued to marry young lovers in secret. While in jail, Father Valentine befriended the jailer's daughter, a beautiful, young blind woman. Legend has it that Valentine performed a miracle by restoring her sight. Before he was executed, the dedicated cleric sent a loving note to the jailer's daughter and signed it "From, Your Valentine." (Father Valentine was canonized a saint in A.D. 350.) Ever since, the date of his execution for bringing couples together commemorates love. Even Shakespeare recognized the holiday in *Hamlet*, at a time when English women believed that the first man they saw that day would ask for marriage within a year.* Other historians suggest it was the weather and not the saint that kept love in mind during February; it would have been beneficial, in those days without heat, to have a warm body close by during the coldest month of the year.

Today, "From Your Valentine" is duplicated on $937 million worth of greeting cards; another $100 million is spent on candy and flowers each year. With all this attention focused on love it is no wonder that many who do not have it become agitated and depressed and act irrationally.

* In the 1500s, if a loved one committed suicide on Valentine's Day, or any other day, a household's entire property was immediately forfeited to the Crown.

IN LIEU OF FLOWERS

Clara and David Harris got married on Valentine's Day in 1993. Ten years later, Clara (right) confronted her husband, leaving the same hotel where their wedding ceremony was held, with a much younger mistress. Acting on what the defense later described as "sudden passion," Clara ran over her husband three times with her Mercedes in the parking lot. On Valentine's Day in 2004, she was sentenced to twenty years in prison.

Failed expectations of Valentine's Day cause more engaged and steady couples to separate than any other occasion. On Valentine's Day, 1993, one Miami woman was so convinced that her longtime boyfriend would propose that she tore through the box of candy, frantically squashing chocolates in the hope of finding an engagement ring. When none was found, she grabbed a kitchen knife and stabbed him twice in the chest. Today, to avoid feelings of rejection, 15 percent of American women send themselves flowers on Valentine's Day.

ANNUAL SUICIDES THE WEEK BEFORE AND AFTER VALENTINE'S DAY: APPROXIMATELY 2,900

VALENTINE'S DAY: IT'S A MASSACRE

On Valentine's Day in 1929, Al Capone sent Machine Gun McGurn to a warehouse at 2122 North Clark Street in Chicago in order to kill Bugs Moran, a rival bootlegger. Seven men were lined up against a wall and executed; Bugs not among them, having escaped. The most brutal massacre in gangster history

eventually brought Capone down. For three decades, the bricks with 414 bullet holes that made up the wall against which the seven were lined up has been offered for sale as a "unique" Valentine gift. There have been no buyers to date.

VEGETARIANS   In 2005, there were 4.8 million noninstitutionalized people in the United States who ate vegetables exclusively, excluding all meat, fish, poultry, and eggs.

There are many types of vegetarians; the list of categories goes from the noncommittal vogue-tarians (who only say they are when in the company of other vegetarians) to vegans (who eat only nonanimal foods that fall from trees or plants).

TOO LITTLE, TOO LATE

In Homestead, Florida, in 2004, vegan parents Joseph and Lamoy Andressohn were charged with aggravated manslaughter when their malnourished five-month-old daughter died. The child weighed only six pounds and was fed only wheat grass, coconut water, and almond milk. The state also removed from the vegans' custody their four other children, who were only allowed to eat uncooked organic fruits, vegetables, and nuts.

Eating more vegetables is medically sound common sense, with many benefits; it's the extreme variants of these regimes that can cause unexpected fatalities.

COURAGEOUS ENEMAS

Organic coffee enemas are recommended by some alternative experts as a way to achieve an intestinal system–cleansing flush and to prevent many forms of cancer.

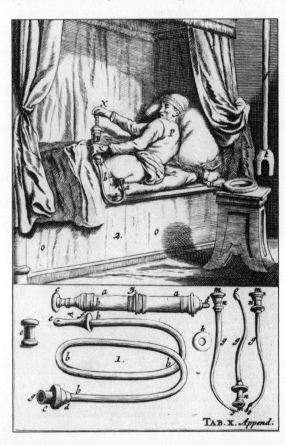

TAB. X. *Append.*

Directions suggest best results are gained when the coffee is inserted into the anus warm, caffeinated, and black, without cream or sugar. In 2003, two Seattle women died following the advice of wayward coffee enema gurus. One woman self-administered twelve coffee enemas, one each hour during the night. The other gave herself four coffee enemas every day for a week. Their deaths were attributed to fluid and electrolyte imbalance.

Many new vegetarians are, in general, open-minded and attempt to seek healthier food alternatives outside the mainstream. However, as with anything, when one is too open-minded the risk is in taking bad advice.

Another vegetarian's death caused outrage among the loyal. When one man who had been a vegetarian for four and a half years died of Mad Cow disease at the age of twenty, many pro-vegetable advocates claimed he must have gotten the tainted prions from Jell-O. Close friends of the deceased vouched that he never snuck a burger into his diet plan and could have only acquired the disease from the milk he regularly added to his gelatin. It was a relief, not to the dead man's family, but to vegetarians, the milk industry, and Jell-O lovers, when the coroner* said: "I am satisfied that it is more likely than not that [the man] contracted this disease prior to 1990 before he became a vegetarian through eating some form of contaminated beef product, such as beef burger."

VENDING MACHINES In 1976, the soda machine in a dark church basement in Providence, Rhode Island, looked like an easy way for one nineteen-year-old to get some spending money. When he failed to pick the lock on the coin box, he decided to rock the machine back and forth, hoping to free at least a few dimes. Frustrated, he went at it with greater abandon, until the whole thing toppled over and crushed him.

KILLED FROM RECKLESSNESS DURING VANDALISM SINCE 1965: 25,980

SMASH AND GRAB

This concept seems like a fairly easy way to get what you want without paying. In 1992, one man in Boston thought he could lift a few bottles of expensive cognac on display behind a liquor store's window. The store's surveillance camera captured him cupping his hands around his eyes to get a closer look at the bottle display. He looked around, left the camera's field of vision for a few minutes, and then returned with a cinder block. Standing a couple of feet from the window, he hoisted the block over his head, and threw it as hard as he could at the glass. The window, made of Plexiglas, bowed, but didn't break, causing the cinder block to bounce right back and hit the man squarely in the head. The video showed him twitching on the ground at first; then he lay still in a pool of blood, his death his own doing.

---

* In England, a very unpopular man was the tax collector, called a crowner, whose duty it was to collect the tax due when someone died. To many, the crowner had a seemingly unnatural ability to show up before the body was cold. Over time, the word *crowner* became *coroner*, referring to the person who investigates deaths that are not due to natural causes.

VIDEO GAMES Video game usage is underreported: Most only confess to six hours per week, but like an alcoholic who says he had a couple of drinks, a "couple" often means way more than two. Parents minimize the effects video gaming has on children who spend an inordinate amount of free time at the controller; some say it helps hand-eye coordination or that it keeps their kids safe at home. In 1967, children watched TV for two hours per day, but by 2002, many spent five hours a day watching TV, on the Internet, or playing video games. In 1970, when video games were introduced, only 13 percent of kids played them weekly. In 2002, 95 percent of all teenagers said they played at least one video game per week. Many experience moodiness and withdrawal symptoms when denied video game leisure time. The onset of video game addiction begins when players demonstrate poor hygiene, slumping grades, and become isolated, replacing human contact with video

KIDS SAY THE DARNDEST THINGS

In September 2003, two brothers, age fourteen and sixteen, had spent many days playing Grand Theft Auto. *Scolded to get out of the house, the two took shotguns down to Interstate 40 near Newport, Tennessee, and fired at passing cars. After they killed one man and caused numerous car crashes, they told police they were inspired by the video game. After the tragedy, Rockstar Games, a leader in the $7 billion video game industry due to* Grand Theft Auto's *success, pointed to the "M" rating on every box. You're supposed to be at least eighteen years old to play the game.*

X-BOX MURDERS

In August 2004, a twenty-two-year-old man and three teenagers broke into a vacation house on Daytona Beach and set up a place to have a long summer party. When the owners of the house, living in Maine, sent their granddaughter to check in on the house, she found six people living there. She had the squatters removed and took the clothing and X-box the squatters left behind to the three-bedroom rental house she shared with friends. The squatters found out where the granddaughter lived and kicked open the front door in the middle of the night. Armed with baseball bats, they systematically beat and stabbed the granddaughter and her five roommates, ages eighteen to thirty-four, while they slept. The murderers were apprehended because the only thing they took when they were done was the X-box.

game characters. Some obsessed players develop carpal tunnel syndrome, high blood pressure, increased heart rate, and seizures.

Although proponents for video games say decades-long exposure to violence will not alter the ability to differentiate between right and wrong, judges across the country are accepting "video game violence" insanity pleas for defendants of all ages charged with serious crimes. Eighty-five percent of all games on the market in 2005 were rated "extremely violent."

GOOD GRAPHICS, REAL AUDIO

Flash-pattern, a term once used to describe the pattern of firefly luminescence, is now a warning issued on video games. Some individuals have flash-pattern sensitivity and could experience a seizure if overtired, sleep deprived, or prone to epileptic tendencies. In 2003, the video game *Pocket Monster* caused stress, fatigue, and hyperventilation to many who played it, and sent at least one hundred children into epileptic-like seizures. Although there have been fifty known deaths from this phenomenon, video game manufacturers claim this could have happened anyway, especially if the victims were already epileptic.

Game manufacturers also point to the hidden values of some of these new high quality games. In March 2004, three burglars broke into a house in Galveston, Texas, holding the babysitter and the three children she was watching at gunpoint. In another room, a video game's realistic crime scene and authentic audio began to play a police siren. The robbers paused and heard the video: "This is the police, you're surrounded." Nervous already, the burglars thought it was the real police. They bolted from the house, scared away not by a security system or a pit bull but by a video game.

VIGILANTES For one hundred years starting in 1865, vigilantes executed by hanging, without trial, 4,730 black people and 293 whites. To a vigilante mob, any alleged offense could warrant a death sen-

In 1955, fourteen-year-old Emmett Till left Chicago to spend the summer with his relatives in Money, Mississippi. Unaccustomed to the segregation practices of the South, Emmett, on a dare from his buddies, whistled at a white woman in a grocery store. Later that night Emmett was snatched from his bed, beaten and mangled, before he was dumped into the Tallahatchie River. His mother brought the boy's body back to Chicago and held an open casket funeral. The visible brutality became a rallying point at the start of the civil rights movement. Although two men confessed to killing the boy, they were never convicted.

tence, including: grave robbing, suspicious behavior, sneaking into a girl's room, preaching, associating with a white girl, arguing with a white man, using inflammatory language, taking part in a railroad strike, unwilling to aid a lynch posse, writing a brazen letter to a woman, making moonshine during Prohibition, being a foreign laborer, abusing one's spouse, and making prank phone calls. Many became victims of mistaken identity; anyone who *looked* similar when the person the mob was after could not be found was subject to a lynching.

VOLCANOES On the scale of natural disasters that take human lives, volcanoes are way behind earthquakes, floods, tsunamis, and hurricanes. During the last five hundred years, two hundred thousand people have been killed by volcanoes from only 105 eruptions. There are few active volcanoes in the United States.

Mount Saint Helens, a volcano in Washington State, fatally erupted on May 18, 1980, at 8:32 A.M. The plume rose thirteen hundred feet into the air, darkening towns eighty-five miles away. The initial eruption of lava, at a temperature of 600° F, rocketed at a speed of 650 mph. Avalanches, earthquakes, and fires followed as a result of the blow and sixty-two people were killed. This wasn't another Mt. Vesuvius—the Italian volcano that caught two thousand citizens of Pompeii on August 23, in the year A.D. 79 by sur-

BRING IT ON
One craggy individual, eighty-four-year-old Harry Truman, refused to leave a mountain lodge he owned, determined not to abandon his house and two dozen cats. He was sure he could outsprint whatever Saint Helens threw his way; a week later rescuers found him and his cats inside his lodge, buried under thirty feet of ash.

prise, freezing their bodies where they stood into ash-covered statues. Scientists knew Mount Saint Helens was due to erupt and had almost entirely evacuated the surrounding areas.

Another person, close to the volcano on purpose, was volcanologist Dave Johnson. He stayed at his observation camp, with a few of his staff, less than six miles from the volcano. Each member of his expedition group disintegrated within ten minutes of the initial eruption. Another person known to have been going toward the volcano rather than running away from it was *National Geographic* photographer Reid Blackman. He was eight miles from the volcano when the lava blew. He dashed to his car for cover, but the windows smashed and he died, in the driver's seat, ignition key in one hand and a camera in the other, buried to his shoulders in ash.

KODAK MOMENTS

Many hikers get the desire to look down into an active volcano and snap a picture. However, anywhere within one hundred yards from the blowhole is known as "the death zone." The terrain is unstable, the temperatures are extreme, and puffs of toxic fumes and gases are regularly emitted without warning. Sometimes small boulders are coughed up and temporarily block the blowhole, so that a hiker may even be standing on it without knowing. John Seach, a volcanologist, warns hikers: "You will be killed if you stay there long enough. Limit your time in this area to minutes, if you approach it at all." Other experts suggest people stay far away and use a zoom lens.

PIED PIPER

In 1933, a nineteen-year-old student committed suicide by jumping down the active crater of a volcano on Oshima, Japan. For reasons unknown, his actions inspired many others; 311 students jumped into the lava during the following three-month period.

SINCE 1976, EIGHTY-SEVEN HAVE DIED AFTER SUCCUMBING TO VOLCANO CURIOSITY.

WAR When it comes to dying, warfare changes all the rules. Killing is not murder according to the Rules of Engagement, and whatever is necessary to ensure victory and survival is permitted. By 2003 America had been in eleven wars, spent over $3 trillion on the battlefield, and lost 651,234 lives during direct conflict and 243,931 in war-related activities, including preparation for warfare and illness as a result of the conflict.

The first military confrontation, the **War for Independence,** originated from a discussion about freedoms and taxation that escalated to warfare in April 1775. In the first battle, at Concord, Massachusetts, 90 American colonists and 275 British died. Eight years later, in April 1783, when Congress officially declared an end to the war, more than 217,000 colonists had served in the army at a time when the population was under 3 million.

Colonists used rifles that fired one shot at a time and had to be reloaded by hand; some had only knives, swords, bayonets, or home-fashioned weapons. In contrast to the British who had superior forces with unlimited arms and ammunition, colonists had to melt statues and silverware to make bullets. Cannons were also a part of the artillery used by both sides, but then they had smooth-bore barrels, which meant the cannonballs didn't spin and were not very accurate. The cannon had to be loaded after each shot, which required the soldier to stand exposed to the enemy and push down a bag of gunpowder before dropping another cannonball down the barrel. Round cannonballs would scuttle along the ground, harming anyone they hit. Artillerists aimed so that the ball passed through as many people as possible, attempting to knock down their targets like a line of standing dominoes. The cannonball in this period had no explosive charge, but had the velocity to decapitate or knock a leg off at the knee. Soldiers leapt, dodged, and hopped, keeping an eye on the bouncing ball. Colonists devised the use of cylindrical canisters stuffed with scrap metal fragments, which they fired from cannons when closer to the British infantries, hoping to cause blindness or other wounds that led to gangrene, thereby eliminating the combatant from the next showdown.

4,435 DIED ON THE **AMERICAN** SIDE OF THIS WAR, FEW ON THE BATTLEFIELD, THE MAJORITY FROM INFECTIONS AND DISEASE.

"I ONLY REGRET THAT I HAVE BUT ONE LIFE TO LOSE FOR MY COUNTRY."

Nathan Hale became one of the most famous heroes of the American Revolution, an example of American liberty and patriotic spirit needed for recruitment. At the beginning of the conflict, Hale, at age twenty-one, was captured and interrogated by the British commander-in-chief, General Howe. Howe tried to bribe Hale into joining the British side, offering him a prestigious position as an officer in the king's infantry. When Hale refused, he was tried as a spy and hanged. He held onto his patriotic spirit to the end, when he spoke these last words: "I regret I have but one life to lose for my country."

The **War of 1812** was also fought against the British and established American independence from England once and for all. The British military campaign was primarily directed at Canada and concerned the continuing hostilities between France and Britain. The British armed the Native Americans with unlimited firepower and encouraged their fight against American pioneers. The British also stopped and searched American ships and developed plans to capture Baltimore and New Orleans. This war forced America to become a naval power, as most battles were fought at sea using cannons. Many deaths were the result of fire on burning ships and by drowning. Smoothbore cannons were still in use, but Americans improvised to inflict greater damage: The shot was heated

to furnace-red, causing fires once embedded in a wooden hull; or cannonballs were hollowed out and filled with gunpowder and a fuse. Sailors on the receiving end were assigned to sprint across the deck to grab this fuse bomb like a hot potato and toss it over the side.

286,730 U.S. MILITARY FOUGHT IN THIS CONFLICT AND 2,260 DIED.

The first War on Terror was called the **Indian Wars,** which lasted from 1817 to 1898 and related directly to American growth and westward expansion. It was a bloody war of skirmishes and raids, in which citizens and settlements on both sides were fair game. Peace treaties were made and broken, usually by the U.S., causing Indian tribes, even once former enemies, to band together to fight the ever-growing U.S. military presence and colonial sprawl. It was a war ultimately about real estate and retaliation. Unlike other military conflicts, the U.S. kept sketchy and partial records of its actions against native tribes. Officially, the U.S. military used 106,000 soldiers in the Indian Wars and recorded a total of one thousand U.S. military soldiers killed. However, the true casualties for both sides, including combatants and civilians, exceeded one hundred thousand, and if the actual dates for Indian Wars reached back to the 1600s the total deaths would tally more than a million.

Colonists familiar with European warfare techniques, such as army marching against army on a battlefield, encountered for the first time no-holds-barred, guerilla warfare. The Iroquois, for example, had been at constant war with other Native American groups before the first settler arrived, and were used to close hand-to-hand combat and surprise attacks. Every Iroquois male was trained to be immune to pain. Their captives and prisoners of war were forced to run a gauntlet and had fingernails pulled out and their limbs hacked off. Then they were either decapitated or roasted alive and eaten.

The most famous battle of the Indian Wars was **Custer's Last Stand** at Little Bighorn, Montana. In late 1875, more than ten thousand Sioux, Blackfeet, and Cheyenne Indians left their reservations, livid over treaties the U.S. had broken and gathered in Montana under warrior Sitting Bull to fight for their lands. The Indians spotted 210 of Lt. Cl. George Armstrong Custer's men coming toward their village and sent Sioux chief Crazy Horse and his band of warriors across the river to ambush him. When Custer *(right)* found himself surrounded he ordered his men to shoot their horses and fashion a wall with the carcasses, but they rendered scant shelter against bullets and an endless barrage of arrows. Within

an hour, Custer and his men were annihilated in one of the worst Indian War military disasters. After their victory, the Indians stripped the bodies and mutilated all the uniformed soldiers, believing that the soul of a disfigured body would walk the earth for all eternity. For some reason, Custer's body was stripped and cleaned, but was not scalped or mangled. Custer was wearing buckskin instead of the typical blue uniform, so the Indians may have thought him to be an innocent and not a soldier.

Custer's exact last words are unknown, since not one U.S. soldier survived. However, before he set out to launch a surprise attack on Sitting Bull's village he was overheard saying, "I think we'll catch them napping."

The **Mexican War,** from 1846 to 1848, stemmed from America's annexation of Texas, and was primarily about who owned the water rights of the Rio Grande. Many American teenagers and young men volunteered for duty, looking for romantic military and heroic adventures. But most of them died from heat, dust, and insect bites. Battle records claim 1,173 U.S. deaths, but the war was mostly fought in the countryside, and through disease and informal fighting, the total was more in the range of 11,550 U.S. deaths and more than 30,000 on the Mexican side.

The most famous clash associated with the Mexican War, the battle of the Alamo, actually took place ten years prior, when Texans fought for independence from Mexico. Mexico did not want to give up Texas and sent General Santa Ana with an army of six thousand to squash the rebellion. Gathered in San Antonio at the Alamo, an old mission turned into a fort, were 188 men, including frontier legends Jim Bowie, a master knife thrower; sharpshooter and frontier legend Davy Crockett; as well as James Bonham and William B. Travis. For fifteen days the defenders of the Alamo held off Santa Ana's massive troop, before all 188 inside the mission garrison were killed.

The **Civil War** lasted for four years, from 1861 to 1865, and engaged 30 percent of the population. There were 22 million people living in the North and 9 million living in the South, 4 million of whom were slaves. It was a time when no one living in America was immune from the intimacy of death and dying:

	UNION	CONFEDERATE
Soldiers:	2,213,400	1 million
Cost (today's dollars):	$27 billion	$17 billion
Combat fatalities:	140,500	74,500
War-related deaths:	225,000	60,000

More than two hundred thousand blacks fought for the Union, and thirty-eight thousand died, the majority from varied diseases, including sunstroke.

Once a battle began, death was furious and brutal. The Battle of the Wilderness exemplifies this type of warfare. For two full days, from May 5 to 7, 1864, Union soldiers fought the Confederate at extremely close range. Witnesses described how the endless barrage of bullets literally sawed trees in half. The heavy gunfire eventually set the brush ablaze, killing the wounded and fit alike. One survivor wrote: "Ammunition trains exploded and the dead were roasted in the conflagration; the wounded dragged themselves along with their torn and mangled limbs, in the mad energy of despair, to escape." When the smoke cleared, twenty-five thousand from both sides were counted dead on the battlefield.

The first soldier killed in the Civil War was Luther A. Ladd, a nineteen-year-old volunteer from Massachusetts, shot by a sniper as the Union marched into Baltimore, on April 19, 1861. On May 26, 1865, the last soldier killed in the Civil War was nineteen-year-old John J. Williams of Indiana. Although Confederate soldiers knew of Lee's surrender on April 9, 1865, many troops in Texas, Arkansas, and Oklahoma continued to fight. During the very last confrontation of the war, at Palmito Ranch in Texas, the Confederates won, killing 110 Union soldiers, Williams their final mark as they retreated.

SIDE BUSINESS
Before the Civil War, no bodies in the U.S. or abroad were embalmed. The need to ship back dead soldiers to their families prompted Dr. Thomas Holmes to develop a technique in which blood was replaced with an arsenic-based liquid. Arsenic, deadly to the living, proved in Dr. Holmes' mixture to be a great preservative for the dead. After the war, Holmes opened a drugstore in Brooklyn and found sales were brisk for two of his homemade formulas: his own recipe for root beer, and the embalming fluid he invented. To attract customers to linger for a sip of soda he displayed the embalmed head of a young woman in the storefront window. Although referred to today as the "Father of Embalming," Holmes requested not to be embalmed when he died. After his death in 1900, during building renovation, twenty embalmed corpses were found buried in the pharmacy's basement.

In the postwar climate of hatred and revenge, **Robert E. Lee** was indicted after the war for treason. Indiana Congressman George W. Julian demanded that Lee be arrested and hanged as soon as possible, but Lee, who encouraged reconciliation on both sides, was never brought to trial and the matter was dropped without fanfare. In 1870, at age fifty-six, he died of heart disease.

Harper's Magazine wrote, "Lee personified what was best of a bad cause."

Stonewall Jackson (right), the South's best general and in whom the Confederates put all their hope of victory, was mistakenly shot by his own men on May 2, 1863. Doctors then amputated his left arm, but fever set in and he died at age thirty-nine eight days later. Soldiers had taken the amputated arm and buried it near a battlefield to bring them good luck, but it was eventually exhumed in 1929 and reburied closer to home at Jackson's family plot in Spotsylvania, Virginia.

The **Spanish American War** took place in a three-month period in 1898 and centered on America's desire to oust Spain's colonial rule from the Caribbean (Cuba and Puerto Rico) and from the Pacific (Guam, Hawaii, and the Philippines). American Imperialist yearnings for strategic locations on both shores also played a part. Three hundred thousand U.S. military were called to duty for both the Caribbean and Pacific fronts, of whom 387 died in direct battle and another 2,059 in related incidents, primarily from tropical diseases. Six billion

dollars were spent on this endeavor. "Remember the Maine" became the war's slogan, referring to the U.S. ship that exploded in Havana Harbor on February 15, 1898. Most of the war's casualties occurred during this incident, with 260 U.S. naval personnel wounded and killed. It still has not been determined whether the destruction of *The Maine* was an inside job or sabotage, but it was the main impetus for the U.S. to enter the revolutionary war already in progress between Cuba and Spain. The U.S. navy outnumbered the few ships Spain sent to defend Cuba and Puerto Rico and mostly fled from the battlefield by the time Teddy Roosevelt and the "Rough Riders" reached San Juan Hill. Congress had formerly declared war on Spain in April 1898 and by August of that year Spain accepted the peace proposal, ultimately relinquishing many of its former colonies to the U.S.

The U.S. tried to remain neutral during **World War I,** believing it was Europe's affair, but was drawn into the conflict when German U-boats sank the American vessel *Lusitania* off the coast of Ireland in May 1915, killing 1,201 people onboard. Congress didn't officially declare war on Germany until December 1917 and soon after sent nearly 5 million U.S. military into battle. Fifty-three thousand were killed on the front and another sixty-three thousand from disease. Influenza and diarrhea affected nearly everyone, more than mustard gas or machine guns. Hand grenades, machine guns, aerial bombing, and chemical warfare were introduced as new ways to kill. The Great War brought mass devastation and suffering and was thought to serve as an example to end all wars.

The last American soldier was killed as the armistice was being signed on November 11, 1918, at 11:00 A.M. A messenger tried to flag down **Private Henry Gunther** with news that the war had ended, but he had just charged at a German machine gun nest on foot with a fixed bayonet. The messenger waved the paper over his head and shouted that the war was over, when Gunther was shot in the left side of his head and died at 11:01 A.M.

Sergeant Alvin York *(below)* was deemed America's greatest hero. From humble origins, born in a log cabin in Tennessee, he went to war and was reported to have silenced thirty-two enemy machine gunners and captured 132

prisoners with only seven men left in his
unit. Hollywood, Broadway, and advertisers
courted him by offering huge advances, but he
refused. Ten years later, he caved in and was
seen everywhere, even in a major motion picture. In 1951, the IRS accused York of tax eva-
sion and went after him with a full frontal
attack. By this time, however, the old war
hero was destitute, and three years of pressure from the IRS caused York to suffer a heart
attack, keeping him bedridden. The IRS still
persisted, until 1961, when President John F.
Kennedy ordered the matter closed and called

the IRS's actions a national disgrace. York died in 1964 of heart disease.

World War II lasted from 1940 to 1945. Sixteen million U.S. military were
sent to war. 291,557 died in battle and 113,489 died from war-related actions
and illnesses, tallying a close second to lives lost in the Civil War, but many more
World War II vets came home seriously wounded: 670,844. There are still seventy-eight thousand missing in action.

America's involvement in the war began with the first Japanese bomb
dropped on Pearl Harbor on December 7, 1941, at 7:49 A.M. It smashed through
the roof of a barracks complex, killing thirty-five men eating breakfast there.
The surprise attack killed a total of 2,388, including thirty-four pairs of brothers. Angered by the death of a friend at Pearl Harbor, the five Sullivan brothers
of Iowa enlisted and requested to serve together on the *U.S.S. Juneau*. Less than
a year later, their ship was hit by a torpedo, killing four of the brothers on impact; the fifth brother was eaten by sharks. Their deaths led to changes in U.S.
military policy, not allowing family members to serve together in the same unit
or ship.

The average age of men who fought
in World War II was twenty-six. Eighty
percent of the personnel involved
were reported to have never fired a
gun or killed an enemy during the war.
The largest battle in U.S. military history took place at the end of the war
and lasted for six weeks, from December 1944 through January 1945: The
Battle of the Bulge assembled six hun-

*The most decorated soldier was **Audie
Murphy** (right), who was credited with
killing 240 enemies, and returned to
write an autobiography,* To Hell and
Back. *He died in 1971 at age forty-seven
in a plane crash.*

dred thousand Americans during the coldest, snowiest weather in the Ardennes Forest on the German-Belgian border. There were 61,000 Americans wounded, 23,554 captured and 19,000 killed, most in the first three days.

The **Korean War** started in 1950 and ended in stalemate in 1953. It cost the taxpayers $263 billion. Nearly 6 million military personnel were involved, of which 33,866 died in combat and twenty thousand died from war-related illnesses like trench foot. (*See Also:* Immersion Foot.) This war pitted the United States, South Korea, and their U.N. allies against North Korea and the Chinese Communists, and had more to do with containing the spread of communism than about North and South Korean territory. In this campaign, dubbed the Forgotten Victory, more than five thousand U.S. soldiers died due to frostbite. Eight thousand one hundred men have yet to be located.

The **Vietnam War** lasted for eleven years, from 1964 to 1975, and this time pitted the United States, South Vietnam, and their U.N. allies against North Vietnam and the Chinese communists. It cost taxpayers $346 billion. Nine million U.S. military were involved, of which 47,410 died in battle and forty-two thousand died from related-war activities. Nine thousand veterans killed themselves within five years of their return from overseas. The average age of death to all U.S. combatants was twenty-three. Amputations and crippling wounds were 300 percent higher than during World War II. There remains fifty-five servicemen missing in action.

Soldiers in Korea and Vietnam fought in the first wars with uncertain boundaries and unclear directives. Anyone could be an enemy—destitute children approaching for candy or old women asking for help could be strapped with explosives. Jungle terrains concealed booby traps and made each step an endless walk through a horror house rigged with murderous pop-ups.

Vietnam vets encountered fragment mines, devices activated by trip wires just a few centimeters above ground. Often mounted on stakes or tied to trees and undergrowth, these mines shot out a barrage of metal fragments at

After the war is another story. Thirty percent of the 697,000 U.S. Gulf veterans are afflicted with unexplained illnesses, including brain malfunctions that radically alter personality, and others that even affect children born to male and female veterans after the war. Fumes from burning oil fires, nerve gas, or the vaccines administered to troops in anticipation of biological and chemical attacks might be the cause. Timothy McVeigh who blew up the Murrah Federal Building in Oklahoma in 1995, killing 168 people, was a Gulf War veteran; so was one of the Beltway snipers, who killed thirteen with an accomplice in 2002 (See Also: Snipers), as well as the failing Arizona nursing student, Robert S. Flores, who killed four in October 2002. They were all on the ground during Operation Desert Storm.

PUTTING THE MIND THROUGH BOOT CAMP

The military now tries to prepare soldiers for the psychological effects of warfare, training them to shift instantly from high-alert battle mode to dealing fairly with civilians, without unnecessary force. But it doesn't always work: In July 2002, four soldiers, three just returning from Afghanistan, each based at Fort Bragg in North Carolina, killed their wives. Two wives were shot, one was choked, and one was stabbed to death. All four murders took place off the base, within a two- to four-week period. Two of the soldiers soon after shot themselves, and the two remaining were charged with murder. Military spokesmen assured the press that any link between the killings and the affect of the men's time in Afghanistan was purely coincidental.

two times the speed of bullets. Physiological damage suffered by soldiers during this war was unequal in scope to any other that American soldiers had seen.

The **Persian Gulf War,** fought in 1991 to liberate Kuwait from an Iraqi annex attempt, lasted just forty-three days and cost $61 billion; 1.2 million U.S. military were deployed, of which 148 died in battle and 121 died from accidents. Eighty-eight thousand tons of bombs were used.

The **War on Terror** began after Islamic militants declared a holy war against the United States and crashed two planes into the World Trade Center in New York City, one into a field in Pennsylvania, and another into the Pentagon in Washington on September 11, 2001. The 2,998 people who died, although not classified as typical casualties of war, were issued death certificates citing the cause as "terrorism involving an assault (homicide)." The first phase of the war called "Operation Enduring Freedom" involved U.S. military action against the Taliban and Osama bin Laden's al Qaeda forces in Afghanistan at a cost of $600 million during its first twenty-five days in October 2001 and another $66 billion by 2006.

BY MAY 2006, 291 U.S. MILITARY DIED IN BATTLE AND AFGHAN WAR-RELATED ACTIVITY.

IRAQI WAR

For the first time in U.S. history, a war was launched for preemptive reasons. The United States acted on information that Iraq harbored weapons of mass destruction and attacked the country on March 19, 2003. No weapons were found. By May 1, 2003, the U.S. had completely occupied the country and President Bush declared an end to major combat operations. However, a tremendous cache of arms, sophisticated enough to shoot down U.S. helicopters and indiscriminately ambush military vehicles, remained in the hands of insurgents. Once again, U.S. soldiers were assigned to fight a war against unclear enemies, making it extremely dangerous and psychologically damaging.

BY MAY 2006, 2,447 AMERICAN MILITARY HAD DIED, 37,198 WERE SERIOUSLY INJURED, AND $400 BILLION HAD BEEN SPENT AND/OR ALLOCATED.

WATER BEDS Between January 1994 and December 2004, eighty-three children died in water beds, sixty-eight due to airway obstruction. Infants were found lying facedown on the soft, impermeable surface of the water bed. Eleven died because they had become wedged between the mattress and the water bed frame after they rolled or moved in

WHAT IS IT GOOD FOR? ABSOLUTELY NOTHING! *R&B singer Edwin Starr* (below), *who served in the army for three years, won a Grammy for the most successful antiwar song of all time, "War." He died at the age of sixty-one in 2003 of a heart attack.*

their sleep. During that same period, 296 children younger than two years old died on adult beds, including standard twin, queen, and king-sized beds, wedged between the mattress and the wall, headboard or footboard, or entrapped at the neck by railings or an adjacent piece of furniture.

WEDDING DAY

There are six thousand weddings every day around the country. Most people hope for good weather and fair times ahead. However, every year some couples mark the occasion as their first and last as husband and wife.

Another wedding day mishap happened in South Carolina in 1992. The best man ran out onto the runway to moon the newlyweds as they departed the ceremony in a small private plane. But he misjudged distance, keeping his pants down too long, and was killed as the couple's getaway plane taxied to take off.

THE COMPATIBILITY TEST

In Port Jervis, New York, in 1999, a newly married couple got into a drunken fight right after their wedding reception. The groom didn't like the way his bride had danced with his cousin, accusing her of allowing his cousin's hands to linger just a bit too long on her ass. Neighboring hotel guests heard shouting from the honeymoon suite, and a crash, as the groom fell out of the window with stab wounds in his chest. The bride was found knifed to death in the room.

Bunk Beds caused fifty-seven entrapments from railings and from reasons mentioned above, as well as fall deaths. Fifty-five were children under three years old.

HONEYMOONS TO DIE FOR

In 1989, a thirty-three-year-old man and his new wife were married at City Hall in New York City. To make the day special they drove up to Niagara Falls, but after the long drive the man's nerves were on edge. They soon got into an argument and he became irritated by his new wife's high-pitched whine. He grabbed her mouth and put her in a headlock to try to keep her quiet. She resisted, and rightly so, but somehow during the scuffle the man broke her neck and she died instantly.
Distraught at the loss of his new bride, he leaped over the rail into the roaring falls.

After marriage, many young couples move in with the in-laws, a new arrangement that can prove to be stressful under any circumstances. One twenty-two-year-old Dallas man came to live at his new mother-in-law's house right after his 1981 Texas wedding. Within hours, police were called to the residence. The man told the authorities he killed his mother-in-law by accident. He claimed to have hacked her to death in the garage because he mistook her for a large raccoon trying to take a piece of his leftover wedding cake.

In A.D. 453, Attila the Hun took time off from pillaging and plundering to get married to his seventh wife. After a feast of barbecued yak and many calfskins of wine, Attila retired to the bridal tent with his newest bride, Ildico, a young, Germanic woman known not only for her beauty but also for her powerful right jab. When he was found dead the next morning with a nosebleed (left), some said Attila was poisoned, but others believe that the fierce warrior not only liked it rough in battle he liked it the same way in bed—his new wife was capable of inflicting her own measure of pain. Although Attila had long suffered from a deviated septum, making him prone to nosebleeds, it's believed that he ultimately died that night from rough sex and too much wine.

KISSING COUSINS

When people whose bloodlines are too close marry—for example, cousins marrying cousins—their offspring have an exceptional high mortality rate. The phrase "Inborn error in metabolism" is recorded on these death certificates, which is the nice way of saying "bad genes."

TRY, TRY AGAIN

When Glynn Wolfe *(left)*, who held the *Guinness Book of Records* title as the world's most-often married man, died at the age of eighty-eight in Redlands, California, none of his twenty-nine wives wanted to claim the body. Although he had nineteen children, forty grandchildren, and nineteen great-grandchildren, it took two weeks for a son, from wife number 14, to finally show up to bury him.

WESTWARD EXPANSION The year 1849 marks the beginning of mass migration into the western states. When news that gold was for the taking in the riverbeds and hills of California, many decided it was time for a change of scenery. The term "Gold Rush" was no exaggeration; between 1848 and 1849 San Francisco's population grew from eight hundred to eighty-six thousand. In total, more than five hundred thousand people went to look for gold.

THEY MADE THE MAPS
THAT GOT THEM THERE

Meriwether Lewis and William Clark were commissioned in 1803 by Thomas Jefferson to explore the uncharted western regions of America. They were given $2,500 and embarked on a four-year adventure. Lewis put a lot of his own money into the project to make it work, but when he returned, the new administration in Washington refused to pay his debts. Lewis (top, left) became an alcoholic and committed suicide at age thirty-five in 1809. William Clark (bottom, left) took over the task of publishing the expedition's journals and was eventually named Superintendent of Indian Affairs. His job was to remove all the Indians he had met along his journey. Clark died of pneumonia in 1838 at the age of sixty-eight.

FREE LAND—AND LOTS OF IT

From 1841 to 1861, three hundred thousand easterners, enticed by the prospect of acquiring and owning as much free land as they could work and cultivate, went via covered wagon through the Oregon Trail, in groups ranging from fifty to three hundred people. Many died along the way or settled wherever they wished, usually when the grueling journey could be suffered no more. The trip from New York City to the Pacific Ocean took five months and cost, in today's equivalent, $5,000. The death rate was high, most succumbing to diseases, including scurvy, smallpox, tick-borne fever, cholera, or harsh environmental conditions. For example, in 1850, more than two thousand healthy people were dead by the time the wagon trains reached Wyoming three months

ORPHAN TRAINS

In the 1850s New York City was overrun with orphans. The police routinely arrested beggars, sometimes as young as five years old, and put them in jails with adult criminals. Between 1851 and 1929, one hundred thousand children were sent by train to rural areas of America and were then cleaned up and put on a stage to be chosen by farmers needing cheap labor. One child wrote how his teeth were examined "by old dirty hands," and others spoke of abuse that would be hard to fathom today. More than 50 percent of the children ran away and at least thirty thousand died from disease.

later. During that same year, eighty-six were recorded as drowned while attempting to forge across treacherous rivers. Wagon masters gave no refunds for death. Historian John G. Mitchell wrote for *National Geographic:* "20,000 people died on the Oregon Trail between 1841 and 1859—an average of ten graves for every mile."

When people think of the Old West stories of gunslingers, lawless justice comes to mind. At the beginning of the War on Terror when President Bush said he wanted Bin Laden "Dead or Alive," it evoked images of the tumbleweed streets of Dodge City, when men were men and the bad got dead. But, in reality, the Old West was wildly safer than a night stroll through many urban areas today. The true gunslinger era followed a twenty-year period after the Civil War, when veterans accustomed to guns and killing became cowboys, moving cattle from Texas grasslands to towns with railroads. Dodge City, Abilene, Hays City, Wichita, and Ellsworth, among others, became the "Sodoms of the plains," where men, money, alcohol, and brothels mixed, nearly always causing trouble.

The average age a gunslinger outlaw died was thirty-five, either from a shoot-out or from hanging. Lawmen lived longer, a third of them reaching the age of seventy years old. But about 40 percent of all gunmen, good, bad, or ugly, died of natural causes. It was common for gunslinger outlaws to become lawmen when no one else wanted to be sheriff, which greatly increased their longevity. The occupations of some of the deceased gunfighters included: law officers, mostly deputies; cowboys turned criminals; ranchers; farmers; cattle rustlers; and hired guns or bounty hunters. Unlike duels, which primarily had to do with upholding honor, many gunfights were crime related: bringing those wanted for crimes to justice, retribution for stealing cattle, or farmers trying to reclaim stolen land. Street gunfights peaked between the years 1895–1896, with forty-three fatalities during that period alone, and then quickly tapered off.

FATAL GUNFIGHTS FROM 1860 TO 1909

Texas: 159
New Mexico: 84
Kansas: 73
Oklahoma: 63
Arizona: 59
California: 21
Colorado: 20
Missouri: 17
Wyoming: 16
Utah: 9

HOW BAD WERE THE BAD?

Cherokee Bill (né Crawford Goldby) was an average gunslinger with six kills, and the great ability to coin phrases. "This is as good a day to die as any," he said when finally led to the gallows on March 17, 1896. When the executioner asked if he had any other last words, he remained pissed off to the end: "I came here to die, not make a speech."

Billy the Kid *(right)*, born Henry McCarthy in Brooklyn, claimed to have killed twenty-one men by the age of twenty-one. But he wasn't that good of a shot, and actually murdered only four. Billy the Kid was killed in December 1880 by Sheriff Pat Garrett (a former gunslinger who promised to bring law and order to Lincoln County, Nebraska). Two shots did him in: one in the mouth, which broke Billy's buckteeth and shattered three vertebrae in his neck, and another bullet in his heart.

Jesse James *(below)* was the picture of the Old West desperado, a handsome, witty American Robin Hood, who stole from the rich and was kind to the poor. For sixteen years he robbed banks, trains, and stagecoaches. He killed at least eight men, many of them Pinkerton agents looking for him. (Pinkerton was a national detective agency hired by banks and the government as private security.) When the price on his head rose to $10,000, a gunslinger, named Bob Ford, became a bounty hunter and went out looking for him. In 1876, Ford found James, age thirty-five, straightening a picture on the wall at a house James rented in St. Joseph, Missouri, and shot him thirty-two times. Ford was signed up to write a book, *How I Shot Jesse James* but marketing efforts couldn't dissuade people from considering him anything other than the assassin of a folk hero.

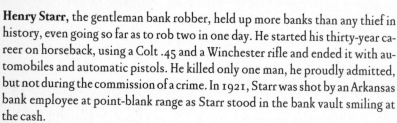

Henry Starr, the gentleman bank robber, held up more banks than any thief in history, even going so far as to rob two in one day. He started his thirty-year career on horseback, using a Colt .45 and a Winchester rifle and ended it with automobiles and automatic pistols. He killed only one man, he proudly admitted, but not during the commission of a crime. In 1921, Starr was shot by an Arkansas bank employee at point-blank range as Starr stood in the bank vault smiling at the cash.

Ben Thompson, born in England, spent his early years in frontier America beating up bullies who made fun of his drunken father, and became the gunslinger with the most kills to his credit. He was truly a quick draw and deadly accurate, feared by lawmen, and was reported to have killed more than twenty. In 1884, when a bar owner refused to shake hands with Thompson, he pulled out his pistol but was shot by three other gunslingers the bar owner had hired for protection. He died with nine bullets in his back.

HOW GOOD WERE THE BEST?

Wyatt Earp, an icon of the Old West lawman, was described by fellow marshal Bat Masterson as "a quiet unassuming man, not given to brag or bluster, but at all times and under all circumstances, a loyal friend and an equally dangerous enemy." Earp was involved with law enforcement for only six years and eventually ended up in California, working in Hollywood as an adviser on westerns during the silent movie days. He died at the age of eighty, in January 1929, of heart failure. It is believed Wyatt Earp killed no more than three men.

"Doc" John Henry Holliday was described by his associate Wyatt Earp as "the most skillful gambler, and the nerviest, fastest, deadliest man with a six-gun I ever saw." "Doc" was a dentist, but just as he started his practice he came down with tuberculosis. Unable to practice dentistry due to his illness, he went out West, earning $40,000 a year from gambling, killing six in the process. On the run from the hangman's noose, he came to Tombstone, Arizona, and was recruited into law enforcement, killing a few more in the O.K. Corral shoot-out in 1882. Five years later, he went to Glenwood Springs, Colorado, a famous health resort, for his worsening tuberculosis. On the morning of November 8, 1887, with whiskey glass in hand, he said, "This is funny," and died. "Doc" is believed to have killed at least ten men.

James Butler "Wild Bill" Hickok *(right)* was an Indian fighter and marshal. He became a legend in his own time, when in 1865 he killed a gambler in the street at high noon, and the gunfight was written about in *Harper's Weekly*, thus creating the stereotype of the Old West gunfight recalled in dime novels, TV, and movies. When asked by journalist Henry Morton Stanley how many men he killed, Bill threw back a shot of whiskey and said, "I suppose I have killed considerably over a hundred." "What made you kill all those men? Did you kill them without cause or provocation?" "No, by heaven I never killed one man without good cause." Records indicate Bill killed no more than twelve. In 1876, he was shot from behind and killed while playing poker, holding two pair of aces. In poker, a pair of aces is still called a dead man's hand.

WORKING In 1912, twenty-one thousand American workers died from accidents on the job. In 1913, the Bureau of Labor Statistics stepped up to see exactly what was happening and counted twenty-three thousand indus-

trial deaths among a workforce of 38 million—that was eighty-seven people who died each day. Today, the workforce is 130 million, with fifty-nine hundred accidental deaths a year, or twenty-two people each day who punch in but don't punch out.

Many fatal labor accidents are attributed to carelessness and inattention to the dangers at hand. Such was the situation for a Frito Lay repairman, age thirty-four, who while working the lonely nightshift in 2000, fell through the two-foot opening in the top of a fifteen-foot vat of unheated cholesterol-laden vegetable oil and drowned. Co-workers said he had been light-headed since he started a no-carb diet.

Carelessness caused one twenty-seven-year-old worker to die at Sea World, Florida, when a twenty-ton killer whale dropped on him. The whale was harnessed to be lifted by crane and transferred to another tank. The worker swam under the whale to inspect the fastening, when another employee operating the crane hit the release instead of the lift switch.

In California, a winery worker was found dead after stumbling into an enormous, twenty-three thousand-gallon stainless steel vat of red wine. While taking level measurements through a hatch at the top of the container, the thirty-one-year-old man overextended his reach, slipped, and drowned before he could be rescued.

A Brink's armored car guard, riding in back to protect the money, fell to the floor of the truck when the driver suddenly braked. A palette of boxed coins stacked to the ceiling—$10,000 worth—toppled over and crushed him to death.

GET A JOB
Although working is sometimes hazardous, unemployment is far more dangerous. Working at a paying job has been proven to be positive for one's well-being and self-esteem, which improves a person's chance of living longer. Suicide among the unemployed is ten times higher than for those who have either a full or part-time job. There are currently 2 million unemployed workers in the United States. (See Also: Dental School)

DEADLIEST JOB
Construction equipment operators, fabricators, and laborers, when combined, have the largest number of fatal work injuries (approximately 2,118 per year) of any occupational group.

Lumberjacks, who prefer to be called timber harvesting specialists, are included in the construction industry. Lumberjacking is the most dangerous job in America. There are more than five hundred thousand people employed in the U.S. forestry industry. Of that approximate total, 120,000 men and 353 women are sent each day into woods accessible by only dirt roads, given heavy machinery, and instructed to fall as many trees as possible in the shortest amount of time. The combination of rough work, the need to fill quotas, falling trees, and chainsaws killed 211 tree cutters last year. Another 24,589 suffered injuries requiring hospital care. In the mills, which produce everything from toilet and tissue papers to two-by-fours, there have been 121 deaths stemming from nasal cancer.

One Pennsylvania construction worker literally took matters into his own hands. Lagging behind schedule, the man was buzzing quickly along with the power saw when his hand got in the way. His entire left hand was cut off at the wrist and fell into the sawdust like a glove. The pain was so unbearable, he reached for the nail gun and shot himself in the head at least a dozen times with one-inch nails.

OCCUPATIONAL DISEASES
860,000 people a year are sick of work—or, more precisely, get sick from work. Occupational diseases cover a broad spectrum of activities and exposure levels, thereby making

an accurate record of work-related illnesses a challenge. A hundred years ago, work was work and you were happy to get a paycheck regardless of the dangers. However, basic chemicals like lead in paint, asbestos in walls, and DDT to spray bugs, once thought safe, over time have proven deadly. In 2005, 4.7 million workers were exposed to chemicals known to cause various deadly illnesses. For example, 470,000 Americans work with questionable levels of radiation seeping into their bodies, and 340,000 routinely handle potentially toxic metalworking fluids. In other words, workers today unknowingly partake in unregulated experiments to determine which chemicals will kill tomorrow.

DEATH FROM OCCUPATIONAL DISEASES: 60,300 EACH YEAR

MISCELLANEOUS DANGERS TO RADIATION TECHNICIANS

On November 13, 1974, nuclear technician and whistle-blower **Karen Silkwood** (right), *outraged about numerous spills, leaks, and mislaid plutonium at the power plant at which she worked, was coincidently killed in an automobile accident on her way to a meeting with a* New York Times *reporter and an Atomic Energy Commission official.*

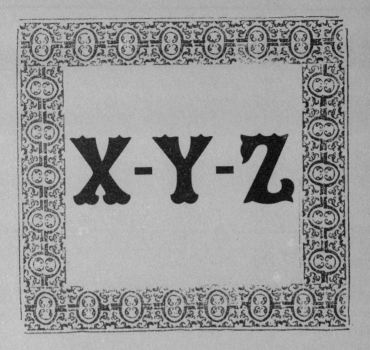

X-RAY Every time you get an X-ray, radiation, measured in millirems (mrems), enters the soft tissue of your body and remains there nearly forever. A typical dental X-ray shoots 2 mrems into the head, neck, and thyroid gland. A chest X-ray delivers 20; a CAT scan, 200. In addition to medical X-rays, naturally occurring radiation enters the body from environmental sources, adding another 60 mrems per year. It's been proven that people who are exposed to more than 10,000 mrems of radiation in their lifetime, from whatever source, will develop cancer.

Others quickly saw the benefits of Rontgen's invention and tried to make their own invisible rays, soon understood to be caused by shortened wavelengths of electromagnetic light. Thomas Edison and his assistant Clarence Daly *(above)* dove headfirst into his emerging science of imaging technology. They gave numerous public demonstrations of their version of the X-ray machine, happily showing the illuminated bones of their own bodies. Daly used his hand repeatedly as the subject to fine-tune the apparatus. He discovered quickly that the light beams made "burns" on his skin. But these were not like ordinary wounds, and before long the blemishes turned cancerous. Within a year, the cancer spread throughout his body, and in 1904 Daly became the first American to die from X-rays. Distraught over the loss of his intelligent companion, Edison, himself suffering a wandering left eye and growths in his stomach, abandoned any interest in radiology. For the rest of his life, Edison refused to be X-rayed for any reason.

Despite the dangers, the medical community seized upon the opportunity to use X-rays for a glimpse inside the body. Tuberculosis, a deadly killer of the time, could be detected early when doctors viewed the disease's development in the lungs. However, many of the X-ray technicians were dying. Not until 1934 were attempts made to issue guidelines for safe levels of exposure. Lead, the only readily available substance X-rays cannot penetrate, began to be employed as shields.

Today, the power and danger of X-rays are the same as they were one hundred years ago. Even with lead protection and other usage guidelines in place, the moment an X-ray enters the body, cell physiology begins to change. Many cells die immediately and gene mutation begins even after moderate exposure. When DNA fails to synthesize, rapid cancerous growths are inevitable.

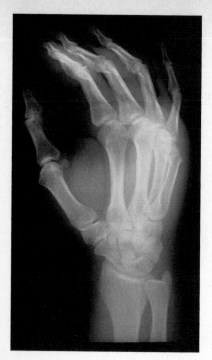

TWENTY THOUSAND A YEAR
DIE DUE TO
RADIATION EXPOSURE.

YAWNING Reading about yawning increases yawning. Seeing another person yawn does the same. According to child psychologist John Piaget, people become susceptible to "yawning contagion" by the age of two and few can build up immunity, no matter how hard they try. For centuries medical doctors saw no harm in yawning, believing it was either a reflex to increase oxygen supply or to expel excessive carbon dioxide. Yet with vast research dollars expended in so many other areas, the real cause of a yawn remains a mystery.

One man, Dr. Robert Provine of the University of Maryland, has spent his life studying this tired but true subject and is considered the world's leading expert on the yawn. When he

William Rontgen accidentally invented the first X-ray machine in 1895. While attempting to see how far an electric current would travel in a vacuum (cathode), he noticed that something odd happened when he produced this new altered light beam. He aimed the light beaming through the cathode at a wooden door six feet away and was stunned when he could see what was behind it. He immediately called his new device an X-ray machine— X, standing for something unknown to science. Some unorthodox historians say he fired his new light beam at a passerby on the street to see what women were wearing under their petticoats. But, being an experienced researcher, William returned to more serious tests and fixed one end of his electric cathode device to photograph plates and began to develop film images of what he discovered. At first, he experimented on inanimate objects inside of boxes before using his wife Bertha as a subject. The first X-ray of a human is a picture of Bertha's hand. Soon after she became ill and remained in seclusion for nearly the remainder of her life, finally dying of cancer in 1919. Four years later, Rontgen died of cancer of the intestine.

supplied pure oxygen to yawning test patients, the yawn did not stop, somewhat dispelling the notion that yawning signals a need for oxygen. He conducted further tests to see if a person yawned from boredom and found that more subjects yawned watching thirty minutes of white static on a TV screen than they did from viewing a rock music video. Science is moving closer to understanding the yawn, and very well might find it to be a remnant of humanities' "collective unconscious," a term Carl Jung coined to describe information empirically understood since before birth, perhaps somehow transmitted in the genes. Monkeys, chimps, and many other animals, including fish, yawn. Some new research points to the idea that the yawn signals to oneself (and others) that the time to rest is approaching. The yawn may very well be the first attempt at a universal language.

YAWN TO END ALL YAWNS

According to a story reported in the Melbourne Herald Sun *in July 1999, one man died when a hippo yawned. A circus clown, a dwarf named Od (né Hito Maka, age thirty-four), jumped off a trampoline just as a hippo, waiting to perform in the next act, yawned. The man landed square in the animal's mouth, which opened to a span of four feet. The hippo's involuntary gag reflex caused Od to be instantaneously swallowed whole. The one thousand-plus spectators who witnessed it continued to applaud wildly until common sense dictated that there had been a tragic mistake. Attempts to force the hippo to regurgitate the body were not successful.*

Today, medicine looks at the yawn suspiciously only if it occurs in excess. Sleep apnea, overmedication, and hidden heart aliments are diagnoses made for the excessive yawner.

IN 2004, YAWNING WHILE DRIVING CAUSED FOURTEEN HUNDRED DEATHS.

ZOOFATALISM This is a psychological disorder in which the afflicted get dangerously close to zoo animals or keep wild animals as pets against better judgment. In May 1998, a Chicago gas station mechanic told his coworkers he was going out to the local tavern after work. Worried by his failure to show up at the bar or to return home, his friends began scouring the city for their colleague. The next day's newspaper ran a story about an unidentified man mauled to death by the local zoo's Bengal tiger, after he apparently climbed into the tiger enclosure shortly after dark. The article described the shredded pieces of clothing found, prompting the co-workers to believe it was their missing friend. Once the men positively identified the mutilated remains as their co-worker, one friend said, "The whole thing is very weird—we cannot figure it out at all. Maybe he was being chased by someone and ended up in the zoo."

At an Illinois fairground, one nineteen-year-old tiger keeper was mauled to death when he climbed on top of a cage full of circus tigers, pulled down

his pants, and started to defecate. The angry tigers latched onto his ankles and ate him, a piece at a time, as they pulled him through the cage. Since 1999, prospective zoo employees have been subjected to psychological testing.

In 1993, a twenty-three-year-old woman was killed by her boyfriend at the zoo. Knowing his temper, she decided to go to his job to tell him of her decision to break up, hoping a public place would elicit a more civilized response. The boyfriend seemed to take the news okay. He checked his watch and asked her to wait around for ten minutes while he fed some animals. "You have to see the lions eat. They devour 103 pounds [the woman's exact weight] of raw meat in one gulp." Figuring she could give him at least ten more minutes of her time, she allowed him to lead her into a room with a slide panel, where she could observe the lion feeding. After he left her alone, she decided on her own to open another window panel and saw a group of people. Just as she was about to yell and warn the onlookers that the lions were about to come out, she realized she was on the wrong side of the glass. Another door opened and two African lions raced into the pen. The woman lingered for a week in the hospital before dying of internal injuries.

FATALITIES BY ZOO ANIMALS SINCE 1965: 1,570

POSTMORTEM

DEATH CERTIFICATES Recording a person's death dates back to church records of eleventh-century England. In America, information on birth, marriage, and death have been kept since 1632 by ministers and trustees of different townships and churches. In most southern and western states, notation in the family Bible was the only recording made. Until the 1800s, many rural localities didn't keep regular records; time-recorded causes of death were often ambiguous, haphazard, and lacked standardization until the end of the nineteenth century.

UNEXPLAINED ILLNESS Between 1766 and 1910, many causes of death that appeared on death certificates seem arcane or random. As most diseases were not classified as they are today, reasons for death often reflected the caregiver's attempt, or those present at death, to describe the demise the best they could. *(See Also:* Ague.) For example, during the 1800s, **Commotion** was listed as a cause of death on 21,542 certificates, perhaps related to head injuries or concussions, or used to describe how a person's head was jostled or struck.

Domestic Illness was recorded on 153,190 death certificates and seemed to be the 1800s politically correct way to describe some sort of mental deterioration, often attributed to old age. Clues from death certificates that mention "bedridden," "hasn't been out for years" point to the possibility that Domestic Illness was cited for deaths from depression, Alzheimer's, or Parkinson's before those diseases were identified, or for any stroke victim who was subsequently required to stay at home *(See Also:* Alzheimer's Disease and Parkinson's). This cause of death disappeared entirely by 1905 with advances in psychiatry and other medical specialties.

Dry Bellyache appeared on 48,933 certificates between 1822 and 1890; its symptoms are very similar to lead poisoning.

Ecstasy was found on 19,388 death certificates dating from the 1790s to the 1880s and was used to describe a person who had lost the ability to reason; it was considered much more violent and dramatic than Domestic Illness. For much of the 1700s and 1800s mentally ill persons were confined to prisons and subjected to inhumane conditions. Lacking prisons or other institutions, many rural and pioneer communities chained violent psychotics to any object until they died. Any form of mental illness wherein the person acted wild and agitated and needed to be chained to a tree or a pillar was said to result in death caused by Ecstasy.

Flux of Humour was used frequently and cited on 187,453 certificates between 1750 and 1850. It usually referred to an unknown incurable imbalance somewhere in the body *(See Also:* Bloodletting). After 1850 it mostly defined circulation problems and blood diseases. Today, there are hundreds of illnesses that would have once been called Flux of Humour, including high blood pressure, diabetes, and hardening of the arteries.

Milk Leg, now known as postpartum thrombophlebitis, was an infection that caused a woman's legs to swell after giving birth, and signaled the onset of infection and death. By the 1930s it was discovered to be caused by blood clots and embolisms that were treated with massage and aspirin. Today, anticoagulant drugs are prescribed to eliminate the problem.

Puerperal Exhaustion was written on death certificates to describe death while giving birth. *(See Also:* Child-Bed Fever)

Cancer appeared on 48,982 death certificates between 1820 and 1865. This was not what we use to describe cancer today, but referred only to signs of external tumors. It was a medical term borrowed from the Latin word meaning crab, and described crablike veins that surrounded a body protrusion or abnormal growth. Today, this might be melanoma tumors, a cyst, or an untreated infection.

Other reasons for death could be even less medically imprecise, such as those found on death certificates of the 1880s:

"Died suddenly. Nothing serious."
"Don't know the cause. Died without aid of physician."
"Don't know cause. Had never been fatally ill before."
"Lack of ambition."
"Worn out."
"Visitation of God."

FEAR OF DYING

In colonial times the dying did not go gentle into that good night. Religious beliefs so instilled a fear of Hell that entire segments of society lived life as if under a state of siege. When Cotton Mather, a famous Puritan minister and scholar, was about to die in 1723, it was observed that he "lay feeble and sore, broken upon his deathbed and faced his life's end with desperate fear and trembling." Mather, who had spent a lifetime giving powerfully graphic "fire and brimstone" sermons, was tormented by thoughts that he, too, may be sent to Hell.

When eighteen-year-old John Tappin was about to die in Boston in 1673, he wailed not at his pain but from the thought of Hell. Although he had been a hard-working, religious child, he confessed that "his hardness of heart and blindness of mind" destined him to eternal damnation.

(as appearing on death certificates)

1. **Convulsions.** *This was written as a cause of death due to any demise by gagging, from epilepsy to food caught in the windpipe.*

2. **Fever.** *Any death caused by high body temperatures, regardless if it was the plague or a bad cold.*

3. **Chrisomes infant.** *The death, for any reason, of a baby under three months, including stillborns.*

4. **Aged.** *The death of any person over fifty years old, and were probably the result of heart attacks and other coronary ailments.*

5. **Teeth.** *Death from infections of the teeth and gums.*

6. **Small pox.** *Any fatal disease that caused marks or skin rashes.*

7. **Dropsy:** *Death after there was swelling or retention of water anywhere in the body, due to circulation disorders. Swollen feet and legs and fainting spells associated with the ailment led to the origin of its name.*

8. **Grip of the guts:** *A death when a person clenched their stomach and died in pain, most likely from unknown ulcers, cancer, or food poisoning.*

9. **Tissick.** *This was a death preceded by a cough, everything from what we know today to be pneumonia to lung cancer.*

10. **Measles.** *This death was mostly attributed to children and encompassed many childhood illnesses, from actual measles to tonsillitis, although the doctors then had no knowledge of precise causes or diagnosis.*

BY THE NUMBERS In the United States, the first semblance of governmental tracking of death and disease took place with the creation of the Marine Hospital Service (MHS) in 1798. This government agency was designed to take care of seamen exclusively, who were a vital part of the New Republic and necessary for prosperous trade and national security. Over time, the MHS, which became the Public Health Service (PHS), was called on to do more than care for sick sailors. It took over the responsibility of supervision of national quarantines, conducting medical inspections of immigrants entering through major seaports, and prevention of the interstate spread of disease.

Before 1850, vital statistics were not generally recorded. A person died and was buried. Not until 1893 did the Public Health Service start the "Mor-

TOP TEN WAYS PEOPLE DIED IN 2005

1. Heart disease
2. Cancer
3. Brain malfunctions
4. Lung diseases
5. Accidental death
6. Diabetes
7. Pneumonia and flu
8. Alzheimer's
9. Nephritis
10. Infections

bidity and Mortality Weekly Report"; it took until 1905 before a majority of the states in the country participated. The PHS kept detailed records on seaman deaths and epidemics, but did not communicate data with the Census Bureau, such that no singular, national database on death was kept until World War II, when it was needed to monitor critical civil defense activities during wartime as there was a serious shortage of doctors and hospital supplies. As anyone searching for information on their ancestor's genealogy knows, documents are bafflingly scattered. (The National Archive has over 4 billion records.)

During World War II, the Census Bureau formed a data collection division, intended as a way to gather different agencies' death statistics into one place, called the Bureau of Vital Statistics, which published the "Current Mortality Sample" to study death trends on a national level. The Bureau of Vital Statistics coerced funeral directors to send in death certificates in a timely manner by refusing to issue burial permits until death certificates were exchanged at the local registrar. From this effort grew the National Center for Health Statistics, which has kept the records on U.S. vital statistics ever since.

At the outbreak of the Korean War in 1950, the threat of biological warfare created a rush to train epidemiologists to watch out for alien germs. Records had to be kept, and so the Centers for Disease Control (CDC) was created. Once an insignificant branch of the Public Health Service, today the CDC tracks extensively how people die. This agency is an institution synonymous around the world with public health.

Now it's possible in the United States to obtain a death certificate, or proof of death (that is, who died and the date of death can be obtained immediately), but the true cause of an individual's demise often floats in the limbo of giant databases in over a hundred government agencies, committees, and research groups until it finally lands at the Bureau of Vital Statistics, sometimes three to five years after the fact.

CADAVER ENCOUNTERS Many of the first people who inhabited North America did not actually bury the dead. They preferred exposing the cadavers, arranging the bodies in trees, on platforms, or set off in canoes. The first colonists in North America, particularly the Roman Catholic missionaries,

preferred burials within a fortified settlement on consecrated church grounds. All deceased were buried facing east, with their arms crossed over the chest, wrapped in a shroud held with a Christian brass pin. After contact with Europeans, Native American cultures adopted other practices, such as constructing gable-roofed wooden shelters over graves and marking them with crosses. Archaeological records show that no dead were buried in coffins on American soil until the English arrived.

But where to bury and what should be done with the body has not always been clear. It's still possible to bury the deceased in the home garden, if an attorney could be found to cite the Garden Law Act of 1880. The dead are considered "clinical waste," and since the 1970s, the Environment Protection Agency has regulated what happens with cadavers which makes it very difficult "to push up the daisies" in your own backyard. Even so, it's

It would cost approximately $500,000 in legal fees and taxidermy costs to have Uncle Buck pose on his favorite recliner for eternity.

BEFORE AND AFTER
In the 1930s Dr. Carl von Cosel ran a tuberculosis clinic in Key West. When he was fifty-six, he fell in love with Elena, a beautiful twenty-two-year-old patient. When she died he couldn't bear to be without her and stole her body from the local mausoleum. After attempting numerous experiments at resuscitation, he preserved her body eerily close to how it was at the time of death. Carl dressed Elena in silk stockings and various gowns. He slept with her as his wife for seven years until her family discovered the body missing. Although the statute of limitations for his body snatching crime had run out, so he could not be charged, he agreed to return Elena to the family plot. Carl did manage to snatch Elena's body once more. He moved out of town, and slept with her every night for another fourteen years until he died in 1952.

still possible to have someone kept close after death. It's not entirely illegal to preserve the entire body aboveground—even stuffed, life size, if so desired—as long as the relative of the deceased proves before the court that they're not entirely insane for wishing to do so.

Today, 75 percent are still buried underground and 25 percent are cremated. In Europe, the numbers are reversed, more preferring incineration to decomposition.

Today it's still possible to be useful as a cadaver—not as revered as ghoulish Dr. von Cosel's Elena but as a donated cadaver for medical students fumbling through anatomy and dissection courses. Parts of cadavers are regularly traded through an organ donor program, but they carry anonymity, which is not the case for a whole body offered for study.

Today, different states have different guidelines regarding cadavers. The EPA recommends that authorities be contacted immediately; some states require notification within forty-eight hours, and others give you five days. After that, keeping a cadaver on the Q.T. without a permit could subject you to a misdemeanor.

A popular legend purports that Marilyn Monroe's body, preserved by elaborate embalming, is currently kept in a secret room somewhere in Beverly Hills.

MESSING WITH CADAVERS

During an excavation of Ben Franklin's London house, ten skeletons were discovered buried in the basement. It is believed that Franklin let his friend Dr. William Hewson, a pioneer anatomist, hide the bodies there. In the 1700s, the dissection of humans for any purpose, including study, was prohibited, and the only way to get fresh cadavers was from grave robbers. Getting caught with a cadaver was a serious crime and punishable by death. Dr. Hewson died at age thirty-four of blood poisoning after cutting himself while dissecting a rancid corpse.

Ben Franklin's role in the illegal experimentations, or if he had knowledge of the burials, are unclear. Franklin did live in the house from 1757 to 1762 and again from 1764 to 1775, the time period from which the bones are dated.

Einstein's brain had been preserved like pickles in a glass container for years and transported across the country for research. *

WHERE ELSE?

In May 2004, a Spokane, Washington, man called police to ask what he should do with the fifty-nine-year-old woman in his freezer. The man had been the woman's caregiver and told police she had died more than a week prior, stating he placed her in the chest-sized freezer "to protect her whole dignity," which made absolutely no sense to anyone. The police could not remove the body because it was frozen among foodstuffs and instead had the entire freezer transported to the morgue. The man was not arrested for any crime, although he was sent to the local hospital for psychological evaluation.

---

* Albert Einstein was a physicist and mathematician who won a Nobel Prize for the theory of relativity. He died in 1955 at age seventy-six when an aorta in his stomach exploded. He requested that his body be cremated and his brain be removed for study.

BURIAL AT SEA In January 2002, a commercial fisherman in Maine hauled in his net and found a coffin. The police were notified and investigated the casket markings. They located the funeral home and found that the coffin was from a military burial at sea two years prior. The coffin was returned to its resting place, at the bottom of the Atlantic Ocean.

The military has strict regulations for burial at sea. If a navy officer wishes to go to "Davy Jones' locker"—maritime slang for ocean graveyard—the navy requests signed approval from next of kin, a sanctioned burial permit, and a copy of the death certificate. The deceased is then placed in a regulation metal casket, along with at least one hundred pounds of rock or sand inside, for ballast. Additionally, at least ten two-inch holes are drilled in the sides so the casket will take on water properly, sink, and stay sunk. It is required that whole body burials take place where the water is at least six hundred feet deep. Each one must be reported to the Environmental Protection Agency.

A modest funeral currently costs over $10,000. Classic wood coffins are making way for new, sleek, airbrushed designs depicting whatever interest the deceased had in life. There are bright coffins that resemble race cars and others that are painted in patriotic hues or with religious symbolism. The Cleveland Caskets Company even has one model that looks like a wrapped package, bearing a big label: RETURN TO SENDER.

No permit is required to scatter cremated ashes at sea. If entire urns are dropped into the ocean they must be made of biodegradable material and have enough weight to descend to the bottom. All ash scattering must be at least five hundred yards from shore.

POTTER'S FIELD A potter's field is a graveyard for the unknown, unclaimed, and stillborn. The term was first used in the Gospel of St. Matthew, which cited that Judas' body was taken to a potter's field, where strangers to the community or those unwanted by family were buried.

Hart's Island is perhaps the most famous potter's field in the U.S., located between the Bronx and Long Island. Purchased by New York City in 1868 from the Hunter family of the Bronx for $75,000, it has the distinction as one of the least memorable places to rest for all eternity. At this potter's field, the dead are placed in large trenches dug by prison inmates who are paid $24 a day for their

JOHN DOE

Every day, at any city morgue, there are at least a few toe tags that read John Doe, identity unknown, race, color, or national origin, a guess. Unclaimed bodies can remain at the morgue for a varied length of time at the discretion of the coroner, depending if a crime was involved or if leads on locating a family member seem promising. Otherwise, four to six weeks is the standard time the unclaimed body will remain in a refrigerated drawer. For one month in 2001 the body of John Doe case #92-0024 lay in a chilled locker at the Oregon's Marion County Coroner office. The coroner advertised in the newspaper in an attempt to locate next of kin. The man was finally found to be Henry Haones, born June 10, 1932, when a former social worker called to ask the coroner what limited information he had. The autopsy determined that Henry, age sixty-nine, had died of hypothermia complicated by pneumonia. Henry had a key, a pack of cigarettes, and $27 in cash, but even after identification no family came forward to claim him. He was sent to Butteville Cemetery, the northwest corner of which is used as a potter's field, and buried at taxpayer's expense.

labor. According to the NYC Department of Corrections, which maintains Hart's Island, babies are placed in "shoebox-sized coffins stacked five high and twenty across," while adults in larger cardboard cartons are piled "three high, two across" for a total of 1,650 bodies per trench. Amputated body parts—legs, arms, and organs from area hospitals—are also buried there in smaller boxes simply labeled "refuse." Each year as many as five thousand unidentified souls are entombed into cardboard coffins, which the city buys for the rock bottom price of $54 apiece.

SINCE 1869, MORE THAN 750,000 HAVE BEEN BURIED ON HART'S ISLAND.

OSCAR WINNERS

HOW TO LIVE LONGER

Social status has proved to be a verifiable factor in life expectancy. Poorer segments of the population—most often without access to quality education and occupation—are more affected by illness than wealthier segments. A recent study of the life span of Oscar winners indicates that success may also play a part in extending life. A study published in May 2001 in the *Annals of Internal Medicine* considered all 762 actors and actresses who had ever been nominated for an Academy Award. As a control, the researchers studied performers of the same sex, age, and relative wealth who were in the same films but not nominated for their roles. The study concluded that peer recognition and success prolonged the lives of the winners by an average of 3.9 years. Other studies indicate that success, social status, and recognition boost the immune system. A study of baseball players inducted into the Hall of Fame also points to this conclusion.

FLICK, CLEVELAND

SWITCH HITTERS LIVE LONGER

Elmer Flick, an outfielder, lived longer than any other Hall of Fame inductee. He was born January 11, 1876, in Bedford, Ohio, and died January 9, 1971, in Bedford, Ohio, at the age of ninety-seven. He batted left- and right-handed, although he threw with his right hand only. Elmer Flick played major league

Players inducted into the Baseball Hall of Fame outlived their contemporaries by an average of 6.9 years.

ball for thirteen seasons and ended with a .345 batting average. He was elected to the Hall of Fame in 1963, which at age eighty-seven seemed to give him a second wind.

Ross Youngs was the youngest Hall of Famer to die. He was born April 10, 1897, in Shiner, Texas, and died October 22, 1927, in San Antonio, Texas, at the tender age of thirty. He batted right, but threw only with his left hand. Youngs hit over .300 for seven consecutive seasons and recorded a career average of .322. A kidney disorder ended his career in 1926. His tragic story swayed voters to induct him into the Hall of Fame posthumously in 1972.

DON'T WRITE POETRY?

After examining all Nobel, Pulitzer, and all other major award recipients in poetry, it was discovered in a study conducted by Dr. James Kaufman of California State University in 2003 that poets have a life span fifteen years below average. The life expectancy of a poet today is sixty years of age.

WHAT IS DEATH?

IN THE EYE OF THE BEHOLDER

One modern definition of death was formulated by a Harvard Medical School committee in 1968. It was decided that a person was legally dead when irreversible cessation of all brain functions, including those of the brain stem, occurred. The committee devised a test to determine reaction to stimuli: If there was no spontaneous muscular response, no respiration, and no reflexes of any kind, and if a flat electroencephalogram, indicating the absence of electrical brain activity, was recorded, then the person was dead. The Harvard team recommended that this condition persist for twenty-four hours before issuing an official declaration of death.

Today, a person in a coma can be hooked up to machines, their body kept alive for decades. Fear of being buried alive has been replaced by the worry that you're kept alive when you're not—when death, a permanent cessation of functioning, has arrived.

Of the 2.4 million deaths in the United States each year, experts believe that at least half could have been prevented, or at least prolonged, if the individual had chosen a different lifestyle.

EPITAPH

The epitaph is the final comment, summary, or commemoration for the deceased engraved on a tombstone. In ancient Egypt, the tombs (sarcophagi) of the elite were carved with hieroglyphics that told the story of the person's life, depicting passed events, both real and embellished, yet they probably still provide the most extensive written history of the period available today. The Greeks and Romans kept up the practice, inscribing battles, victories, and conquests the well-to-do and notable dead achieved in life. Frescos and sculptured profiles of the deceased were also painted and engraved on markers and burial vaults, which gave status to their descendants, while the commoners often received no more than a pile of stones over their graves. In colonial America, the gravestone etcher was a busy man and the best often consulted the dying in advance in order to take down messages the soon-dead wished to leave for eternity. Ben Franklin, who died at the age of eighty-four of debility on April 17, 1790, wrote his own epitaph, which is engraved on the stone found at Christ Church Cemetery, Philadelphia:

"I shall be once more in a new and more beautiful edition,
corrected and amended by the Author"

For the less prolific, epitaph engravers had plenty of stock messages on hand. These are the most popular found throughout colonial graveyards during the 1700s:

> Pause, stranger, when you pass me by,
> For as you are, so once was I.
> As I am now, so will you be.
> Then prepare unto death, and follow me.

> We all have a debt
> To nature due
> I've paid mine
> And so must you.

As with the above, tombstones during that period were embellished with skulls and bones, intended to silently admonish the living to live righteously or else. At the time graveyards were often on the front lawns of churches or on main streets that people passed regularly. In 1733, one Concord, Massachusetts, family saw an opportunity and had their father's tombstone placed on a street corner near their family-run inn; their father's grave may very well be the nation's first billboard:

> Beneath this stone, in hopes of Zion,
> Doth lie the landlord of the Lion;
> His sons keep on the business still,
> Resigned unto the heavenly will.

Early American epitaphs, as with those of the Egyptians and Romans, were also used as a sort of mini-obituary, describing how the person came to meeting their maker. This is one for a man who died in 1745:

> He got a fish bone in his throat
> and then he sang an angel note.

(*See Also:* Choking)

Another man, who died in 1748 of overeating in Virginia, was immortalized with the following epitaph:

> Here lie the bones of Joseph Jones
> Who ate while he was able.
> But once overfed, he dropt down dead
> And fell beneath the table.
> When from the tomb, to meet his doom,
> He arises amidst sinners.
> Since he must dwell in heaven or hell,
> Take him—whichever gives the best dinners.

(*See Also:* Competitive Eating)

For a man who died during a yellow fever epidemic in Philadelphia in 1790:

> Grim death took me
> without any warning.
> I was well at night,
> and dead in the morning.

(*See Also:* Epidemics)

This epitaph was found in Enosburg Falls, Vermont:

> Here lies cut down like unripe fruit,
> The wife of Deacon Amos Shute:
> She died of using too much coffee,
> Anny Dominy—eighteen-forty.

(*See Also:* Vegetarians/Courageous Enemas)

Sometimes, epitaph engravers seemed to have a bit too much fun describing the cause. Here is one for Anna H., who died in 1938 in Schenectady, New York, presumably from a fall.

> Here lies the body of our Anna
> Done to death by a banana
> It wasn't the fruit that laid her low
> But the skin of the thing that made her go

(*See Also:* Falls or Foreign Bodies)

Another tongue-in-cheek epitaph in a Moravian cemetery, New York:

> Wherever you be,
> Let your wind go free.

For holding it in,
Was the killing of me.

(*See Also:* Toilet Time)

Of course epitaphs also described how a person lived.

Rebecca Freeland
1741
She drank good ale,
good punch and wine
And lived to the age of 99.

By the late 1800s various new technologies were already causing deaths and were noted on gravestones. Here is one for a woman who died from a fire caused by a kerosene lamp. Before companies were held liable for false advertising, this was another way to get back at the manufacturer of a faulty product for all eternity:

Ellen Shannon
Who was fatally burned
March 21, 1870
by the explosion of a lamp
filled with "R. E. Danforth's
Non-Explosive Burning Fluid"

(Girard Cemetery, Pennsylvania)
(*See Also:* Fire Hoses and Pressure Washers)

Harry Edsel Smith
Looked up the elevator shaft to see if
the car was on the way down.
It was.
(Albany, New York, 1914)

(*See Also:* Elevators)

One executed man who apparently rustled sheep for a living had this final note:

Here lies the body of
Thomas Kemp.
Who lived by wool
and died by hemp.

(*See Also:* Capital Punishment)

When Americans moved westward a new sense of poetic justice appeared in epitaphs.

Here lies Lester Moore
four shots from a .44
No Les—no more

(Lester Moore was employed as a station agent for Wells Fargo Company in Naco, Arizona, and died during a robbery in 1888.)

Dan Slater
1845–1867
Hung for stealing horses that didn't exist
Here are the people responsible for this

(Under the inscription are names of the six jurors who convicted him, presumably buried in the same grave.)

Here's one of a man who followed bad advice and entered town believing it clear of bounty hunters in his pursuit:

Here lies the body of Arkansas Jim.
We made the mistake,
But the joke's on him.
(Boot Hill Cemetery,
Tombstone, Arizona)

Here lays Butch,
We planted him raw.
He was quick on the trigger,
But slow on the draw.
(Silver City, Nevada, 1878)

Toothless Nell (Alice Chambers)
Killed 1876 in a Dance Hall brawl.
Her last words: "Circumstances led me to this end."

(*See Also:* Westward Expansion)

When the final words attributed to a person's life are chosen by a disgruntled bereaved, the epitaph becomes truly the ultimate last word.

Tom Smith is dead, and here he lies,
Nobody laughs and nobody cries;
Where his soul's gone, or how it fares,
Nobody knows, and Nobody cares.

(From Oconto Falls, Wisconsin, cemetery, circa 1876)

Beneath this stone my wife doth lie
Now she's at rest and so am I.
(Baltimore Cemetery, 1910)

Anna Wallace
The Children of Israel wanted bread
And the Lord sent them manna
Old clerk Wallace wanted a wife
And the Devil sent him Anna
(Bibbesford, England, 1799)

Here lies
Ezekial Aikle
Age 102
The Good
Die Young.
(East Dalhousie Cemetery,
Nova Scotia)

One adulterous husband in Atlanta, Georgia, got these final words posted on his grave:

Gone, but not forgiven

And a not-much-loved wife in New Hampshire got this:

Tears cannot restore her
—therefore I weep.

Some used the epitaph as an opportunity to talk back to the living. On one hypochondriac's grave found in Littleton, Colorado, who died in 1979, the message is clear:

I told you
I was sick!

The Pennsylvania tombstone of a twenty-seven-year-old who died in 1984 has a marijuana leaf etched on the headstone above the words:

Hi!
Stay High.
Bye!

(*See Also:* Marijuana)

In the end, some people just run out of words. This epitaph on a Chattanooga, Tennessee, stone from 1954 sums it up:

Here lies Ned.
There is nothing more to be said—

SOURCES

National Center for Statistics and Analysis (http://www-nrd.nhtsa.dot.gov/)

The National Center for Health Statistics (http://www.cdc.gov/nchs/)

National Safety Council (http://www.nsc.org/)

American Association of Poison Control Centers (http://www.aapcc.org/)

Centers for Disease Control and Prevention (http://www.governmentguide.com/)

Environmental Protection Agency (http://www.epa.gov/)

Journal of the American Medical Association (http://www.jama.ama-assn.org/)

U.S. Consumer Product Safety Commission (http://www.cpsc.gov/)

National Institutes of Health (http://www.nih.gov/)

The World Bank Group (http://www.worldbank.org/)

The National Archive (http://www.archives.gov/)

National Institute on Aging (http://www.nia.nih.gov/)

National Council on Alcoholism and Drug Dependence (http://www.ncadd.org/)

Bureau of Labor Statistics (http://stats.bls.gov/)

Administration for Children and Families (http://www.acf.dhhs.gov/)

United States Census Bureau (http://www.census.gov/)

FEDSTATS (http://www.fedstats.gov/)

World Health Organization (http://www.who.org/)

Arthritis Foundation (http://www.arthritis.org/)

U.S. Food & Drug Administration (http://www.fda.gov/)

National Rifle Association (http://www.nra.org/)

National Highway Traffic Safety Administration (http://www.nhtsa.dot.gov/)

American Cancer Society (http://www.cancer.org/)

National Cancer Institute (http://www.cancer.gov/)

American Heart Association (http://www.americanheart.org/)

President's Council on Fitness (http://www.fitness.gov/)

U.S. Treasury (http://www.treas.gov/)

Federal Bureau of Investigation (http://www.fbi.gov/)

U.S. Department of Justice (http://www.usdoj.gov/)

National Kidney Foundation (http://www.kidney.org/)

National Safe Kids Campaign (http://www.safekids.org/)

U.S. Agency for HealthCare Research (http://www.ahcpr.gov/)

National Center on Sleep Disorders (http://www.nhlbi.nih.gov/)

U.S. Department of Agriculture (http://www.usda.gov/)

National Center for Education (http://nces.ed.gov/)

National Science Foundation (http://www.nsf.gov/)

U.S. Fire Administration (http://www.usfa.fema.gov/)

U.S. Department of Defense (http://www.defense.gov/)

U.S. Department of State (http://www.state.gov/)

United States Historical Society (http://ushs.org/)

U.S. Immigration and Naturalization Service (http://www.ins.usdoj.gov/)

National Archive of Criminal Justice Data *(NACJD)* (http://www.icpsr.umich.edu/
NACJD)

MMWR: Morbidity and Mortality Weekly Report (http://www.cdc.gov/mmwr/)

National Organization for Rare Disorders (http://www.rarediseases.org/)

American College of Obstetricians and Gynecologists (http://www.acog.org/)

*Barlett's Familiar Quotations: A Collection of Passages, Phrases, and Proverbs Traced to Their
Sources in Ancient and Modern Literature.* Little, Brown; 17th Edition, 2002

Encyclopedia of Drugs, Alcohol, and Addictive Behavior. New York: Macmillan, 2001

Handbook of Nursing Diagnosis, 6th Edition, J. B Lippincott Co.

The Oxford Dictionary of Quotations. Elizabeth Knowles, ed., Oxford University Press;
5th Edition, 1999

Physician's Desk Reference. 40th Edition, Medical Economics Company

The Popular Medical Encyclopedia, Fishbein, Morris, ed. Doubleday, 1948

Principles of Anatomy and Physiology, 7th Edition, HarperCollins

Statistical Handbook on Violence in America. Phoenix, AZ: Oryx Press, 2004

BIBLIOGRAPHY

Introduction: "Knock on death's door," from *Doctor, Doctor*. Directed by Robert Belinger, writing credits: Paul Attanasio, Neena Beber, et al., 1989.

Abactio: "One of the greatest earthly miseries," quoted in Reed, James. *From Private Vice to Public Virtue: The Birth Control Movement and American Society Since 1830*. Basic Books, 1978; DeBartolo, Carmack S. "Women and Family Planning: Historical Perspectives for Genealogical Research." *National Genealogical Society Quarterly*, June 1996; Faragher, John Mack. *Women and Men on the Overland Trail*. New Haven: Yale University Press, 1979, 123; Riddle, J. M. *Contraception and Abortion from the Ancient World to the Renaissance*. Harvard University Press, 1994; Goldman, Emma. *Anarchism and Other Essays*. New York: Mother Earth Publishing, 1911.

Abandonment in Cars: Guard, A., Gallagher, S. "Heat-related deaths to young children in parked cars: an analysis of 171 fatalities in the United States, 1995–2002." *Injury Prevention*, 2005, 11:33–37; "Child Dies When Teen Leaves Her in Hot Car." *Associated Press*, August 29, 2004; McLaren, Catherine, M.D., Null, Jan, CCM, Quinn, James, M.D. "Heat Stress From Enclosed Vehicles: Moderate Ambient Temperatures Cause Significant Temperature Rise in Enclosed Vehicles." *Pediatrics*, July 2005, vol. 116, no. 1.

Acordynia: Lockitch, G., et al. "Significant Levels of Mercury in Autistic Kids." *Journal of Mental Deficiency Research* 32:169–181; Wecker, L., Miller, S. "Trace element concentrations in hair from autistic children." *Journal of Mental Deficiency Research*, 1985 March, 29 (Part 1):15–22; "Vaccines and Autism." *Institute of Medicine (IOM) Report Immunization Safety Review*, May 2004; "MERC Concern: Mercury awareness for Michigan citizens." Michigan Department of Natural Resources, 1993; "Toxicological Profile for Mercury." U.S. Department of Health and Human Services, Agency for Toxic Substances and Disease Registry, March 1999, Division of Toxicology, Atlanta, Georgia; Skare I., Engqvist A. "Human exposure to mercury and silver released from dental amalgam restorations." *Environmental Health*, 1994, 49:384–394.

Ague: Boyd, Robert. "Another Look at the Fever and Ague of Western Oregon." *Ethnohistory* 22, 1975:135–54; Anto,

J. M., Sunyer, J., and Kogevinas, M. "Environment and health: the long journey of environmental epidemiology at the turn of the millennium." *Journal of Epidemiology*, 2000, 49–60; Ackerknecht, Erwin H., M.D. *A Short History of Medicine*. New York: The Ronald Press Company, 1968; Appleby, A.B. *Health and Disease in Human History: A Journal of Interdisciplinary History Reader.* Cambridge, Massachusetts: MIT Press, 2000.

Air Bags: Kahane, C. J. "Evaluation of the effectiveness of occupant protection: federal motor vehicle safety standard interim report # 208." Washington, D.C.: U.S. Department of Transportation, National Highway Traffic Safety Administration, June 1992: DOT–HS–807–843; Kahane, C. J. "An evaluation of child passenger safety: the effectiveness and benefits of safety seats." Washington, D.C.: U.S. Department of Transportation, National Highway Traffic Safety Administration, 1986: report no. DOT–HS–806–890; O'Brien, Catherine. "Automakers argue less forceful air bags would save lives." Associated Press (AP), June 1997; Madlung, A. "The Chemistry Behind the Air Bag: High Tech in First-Year Chemistry." *Journal of Chemical Education*, 73 (4), 1997; "National Highway Traffic Safety Administration: Air bag-related injuries." *Annals of Emergency Medicine*, 2003; 42:285–286.

Air Shows: Springfield Air Rendezvous (http://www.springfieldil.com/airshow/); Bilstein, Roger E. *Flight in America 1900–1983.* Johns Hopkins University Press, 1984; Leary, William M., ed. *Aviation's Golden Age: Portraits from the 1920s and 1930s.* Iowa City: University of Iowa Press, 1989.

Alcoholism: "Insurance Murder Charged to Five." *New York Times*, May 13, 1933, 28; "Four Men to Die for Bronx Killing." *New York Times*, October 20, 1933, 38; Bourne, P. G., Fox, R., ed. *Alcoholism.* McGraw-Hill, 1980; Gomberg, E. L., et al., ed. "Alcohol: Science and Society Revisited." *Health Science Publications*, 1982; National Institute on Alcohol Abuse and Alcoholism (NIAAA) Fact Sheet 2004: http://www.niaaa.nih.gov; Parker, Mike. *The World's Most Fantastic Freaks.* London, 1997; Hamlyn, Dan. *Step Right Up!* Harper & Brothers, 1951; Carlyon, David. *Dan Rice: The Most Famous Man You've Never Heard Of.* PublicAffairs, 2001.

Alien Abductions: Nakaya, M., Blum, Howard. *Out There: The Government's Secret Quest for Extraterrestrials.* Simon & Schuster, 1990; Haines, Gerald K. "CIA's Role in the Study of UFOs, 1947–1990." *Studies in Intelligence* 1, no. 1 (1997): 1–28, reprinted in *Intelligence and National Security* 14, no. 2 (Summer 1999):26–49; Bryan, C. D. *Close encounters of the fourth kind: alien abduction, UFOs, and the conference at MIT.* Penguin, 1996; Matheson, Terry. *Alien abductions: creating a modern phenomenon.* Prometheus, 1998.

Alligators: Ross, C., ed. "Crocodiles and Alligators." New York: Facts on File, 1989; Conant, Roger. *Reptiles and Amphibians: Eastern and Central North America.* Boston: Houghton Mifflin, 1991; *Herp Herald*, newsletter of the Gainesville Herpetological Society 18(3):6–7; "Alligator Attack Fact Sheet." The Fish and Wildlife Conservation Commission (FWC), updated on 7/22/05.

Alzheimer's Disease: Shriver, Maria. "What's Happening to Grandpa?"

Center for Health Information, WT 155 .S561, 2004; Sabiha, Khatoon, Ph.D. "Aberrant Guanosine Triphosphate-Beta-Tubulin Interaction in Alzheimer's Disease." *Annals of Neurology*, August 1989, vol. 26, no. 2; Alzheimer Association (www.alz .org); Ford, Alice. *John James Audubon, A Biography*. Abbeville Press, 1988.

Ambulance Chasers: Elling, R., Guerin, R. *Ambulance Accident Prevention Seminar Student Workbook*. New York State Emergency Medical Services Program publication. December 1988; Harry L. Smith, M.D. *Memoirs of an Ambulance Company Officer*. Doomsday Press, 1940; Hansen, Arlen. *Gentleman Volunteers: The Story of the American Ambulance Drivers in the Great War*. Arcade, 1996; National Highway Traffic Safety Administration: Injury Survey 2002–2003: (http://www.injurycontrol.com); "Ambulance Crash-Related Injuries Among Emergency Medical Services Workers." United States, 1991–2002, *Morbidity and Mortality Weekly Report*, February 2003.

Amnesia: Adams, R. D. *Principles of Neurology*. McGraw-Hill, 1997: 429–430; Eustache, F., Desgranges, B., Petit-Taboue, M. C. "Transient global amnesia: implicit/explicit memory dissociation and PET Assessment of Brain Perfusion and Oxygen Metabolism in the Acute Stage." *Journal of Neurology and Neurosurgery Psychiatry*, September 1997, 63(3):357–367; Anderson, D. M. "Toxic red tides and harmful algal blooms: a practical challenge in coastal oceanography." *Review of Geophysics* (Suppl.), 1995, 1189–1200; Vargo, G. A. "Alkaline phosphatase activity in the red-tide dinoflagellate, Ptychodiscus brevis."

Journal of Experimental Marine Biology and Ecology, March 2004, Ecol. 6:251–264; Levine, Peter. *Victims of Cruelty: Somatic Psychotherapy in the Treatment of Posttraumatic Stress Disorder*. North Atlantic Books, 2000.

Amusement Parks: Maranian, Matt. *Los Angeles Bizarro*. St. Martin's Griffin, 1997; Adams, Judith A. *The American Amusement Park Industry: A History of Technology and Thrills*. Twayne, 1991; Kyriazi, Gary. *The Great American Amusement Parks; A Pictorial History*. Citadel Press, 1976; Mangels, William F. *The Outdoor Amusement Industry*. Vantage, 1952; Price, Harrison. *Walt's Revolution! By the Numbers*. Ripley Publishing, 2004.

Anabolic Steroids: Taylor, W. N., Black, A. B. "Pervasive anabolic steroid use among health club athletes." *Annals of Sports Medicine*, 1997, vol. 3, no. 3, 155–159; Terney, R., McLain, L. G. "The use of anabolic steroids in high school students." *American Journal of Diseases in Children*, 1998, vol. 144, 9–103; Tricker, R., O'Neill, M. R., Cook, D. "The incidence of anabolic steroid use among competitive bodybuilders." *Journal of Drug Education*, vol. 19, no. 4, 313–325; Van Raalte, J. "Perceptions of anabolic steroid users." *Journal of Applied Social Psychology*, 1993, vol. 23, 1214–1225; WHO Task Force on Methods for the Regulation of Male Fertility 1990, "Contraceptive efficacy of testosterone-induced zoospermia in normal men." *Lancet*, vol. 336, 955–959.

Animal Hostages: Foote, William PhD. "Police Assisted Suicide Probed." *Forensic Echo*, vol. 2, Issue 8, 1999; Brenner, S. W. "Undue Influence in the Criminal Law: A Proposed Analysis of the Criminal Offense of Causing Suicide." *Albany Law Review*

47 (1982):64; Dupont, Randolph, Cochran, Sam. "Police response to mental health emergencies." *Journal of the American Academy of Psychiatry Law*, *28*:338 (2000); "Mental illness frequently deepens tragedy of police shootings." *Seattle Post-Intelligencer*, May 25, 1994.

Anorexia: Suzanne Abraham. "Afraid to Eat: Children and Teens in Weight Crisis." *Healthy Weight Publishing Network*, 1997; Hornbacher, Marya. *Wasted: A Memoir of Anorexia and Bulimia.* HarperFlamingo, January 1999; Cassel, C. K. "Geriatric abdominal pain." *Geriatric Medicine,* 1997, 138–145; Inouye, S. K., et al. "A Multicomponent Intervention to Prevent Delirium in Hospitalized Older Patients." *New England Journal of Medicine*, 1999, 34:669–676; Brumberg, Joan Jacobs. *Fasting Girls: The History of Anorexia Nervosa.* New American Library, 1989.

Anthrax: *Anthrax: Safe working and the prevention of infection.* Health and Safety Executive (HSE), Health and Safety Series Booklet HS(G) 174, HSE Books; Cherniack, M. G. "Diseases of unusual occupations: An historical perspective." *Occupational Medicine Review*, July-September 1992. vol. 7, no. 3, 369–384; Kligman, E. W., Peate, W. F., Cordes, D. H. "Occupational infections in farm workers." *Occupational Medicine Review,* July-September 1991, vol. 6, no. 3, 429–446; "U.S. Army Chemical Corps: Anthrax and bacillus anthracis." Chemical Corps, Technical Library, 2002; *Encyclopedia of Terrorism.* Combs, Cindy C., Slann, Martin, eds. New York: Facts on File, 2003.

Ants: Hoffman, D. R. "Reactions to less common species of fire ants." *Journal of Allergy and Clinical Immunology*, No-

vember 1997, 100 (5):679–683; Ownby, D. "Pediatric anaphylaxis, insect stings, and bites." *Immunology and Allergy Clinic of North America*, May 1999, 19 (2): 347; Goddard, J., Jarratt, J., de Castro, F. R. "Evolution of the fire ant lesion." *Journal of the American Medical Association*, November 1, 2000, 284(17):2162–2163.

Aphrodisiacs: Camphausen, R. C. *The Encyclopedia of Sacred Sexuality: From Aphrodisiacs and Ecstasy to Yoni Worship and Zap-lam Yoga.* Inner Traditions, 1999; Wilson, R. A. *Sex & Drugs: A Journey Beyond Limits.* New Falcon Publications, 1983; Abel, J. J., Macht, D. I. "The poisons of the tropical toad Bufo agua." *Journal of the American Medical Association*, vol. 56, 1531–1536; Allen, E. R. and Neill, W. T. "Effect of marine toad toxins on man." *Herpetologica*, 1956, 12:150–151; TAC, The Ethnobotanical Society (http://www.entheogen.com/entheolinks.html); *The Sonoran Dessert Toad*: http://www.bufoalvarius.org/tripReports.htm; Lynch, Emma. "A review of the clinical and toxicological aspects of traditional (herbal) medicines." *Expert Opinion*, 2005, vol. 4, no. 4, 769–778; Schivelbusch, Wolfgang. *A Taste of Paradise: A Social History of Stimulants.* Pantheon Books, 1992.

Apple Cider: "Unpasteurized Fruit Juices: A Potential Health Risk." Ministry of Health Services, Health File #72, March 2000, "Warning Labels Required on all Untreated Juices," Food and Drug Administration, Alert, P98–25, September 1998.

Appliances: U.S. Consumer Product Safety Commission (CPSC): *Recall-Bulletins (1965–2005).*

Arsenic Poisoning: Ginsburg, Philip. *Poisoned Blood.* Scribner's/Warner,

1998; "Arsenic in Drinking Water," *National Academy of Sciences*. National Academy Press, 1999; Godfrey, Donald. *Philo T. Farnsworth*. University of Utah Press, 2001; *Encyclopedia of Criminology and Deviant Behavior*. Taylor and Francis, 2001; Kelleher, Michael D. *Murder Most Rare: The Female Serial Killer*. Dell/Random House, 1998.

Arson: Nicholas, Faith. *Blaze: The Forensics of Fire*. St. Martin's Press, 2000; U.S. Fire Administration (USFA) http://www.usfa.fema.gov.

Autocastration: Myers, W. C., Nguyen, M. "Autocastration as a presenting sign of incipient schizophrenia." *Psychiatry Service*, 2001, 52:685–686; Heriot, A. "The Castrati in Opera." Secker and Warburg, London, 1956; Blacker, K. "Four Cases of Autocastration. Arch." *General Psychology*, 1963, 8:169–176; Hoyer, N. *Man into Woman: An Authentic Record of a Change of Sex*. Popular Library, 1953; Devor, Holly. "Cross Dressing, Sex, and Gender." *Journal of Sex Research*, August 1993, vol. 30, no. 3; Minyard, F. "Wrapped to death. Unusual autoerotic death." *American Journal of Forensic Medical Pathology*, June 1985, 6(2)151–152.

Autoerotic Asphyxiation: Jenkins, Andrew P., Ph.D. "When Self-Pleasuring Becomes Self-Destruction: Autoerotic Asphyxiation Paraphilia." *Journal of Health Education*, March 2000; Ernulf, K. E., Innala, S. M. "Sexual bondage: A review and unobtrusive investigation." *Archives of Sexual Behavior*, December 1995, 24(6) 631–647; Blanchard, R., and Hucker, S. J. "Age, Transvestitism, bondage, and concurrent paraphilic activities in 117 cases of autoerotic asphyxia." *British Journal of Psychiatry*, September 1991, 159, 371–377; Gowitt, G., and Hanzlick, R. "Atypical autoerotic deaths." *American Journal of Forensic Medical Pathology*, June 2002, 13(2).

Automatic Garage Doors: *Holmes Safety Association Bulletins 2000–2005*, Falls Church, Virginia; "Garage Door Openers Are Not Toys,": U.S. Consumer Product Safety Commission, Washington, D.C., 1998.

Auto Racing: Osmar, Harold. "Where They Raced," *Osmer Pub.*, 2000; "Go-Cart/Fun-Kart Related Injuries and Deaths," 1996–2003: U.S Consumer Product Safety Commission, Washington, D.C.

Avalanche: "Snow Avalanches: A Handbook of Forecasting and Control Measures." Forest Service, Department of Agriculture. January 1961. *Agriculture Handbook No. 194* Library of Congress, Department of Agriculture 18899; Handl, Leo. *Snow and Avalanche Manual*. Wagner University Press, 1955; *Landslide and Debris Flow (Mudslide) Report*. National Disaster Education Coalition, Washington, D.C., 1999.

Background Checks: *FBI Law Enforcement Bulletins, 1999–2005* (www.fbi.gov/publications); "Fact Sheet: Workplace Violence." Health and Safety Bulletin American Federation of State, County and Municipal Employees, AFL-CIO, Department of Research, 2003; Paterson, B. "Standards for violence management training." *Security Journal*, 2000, vol. 13, no. 4, 7–17; Hassett, Kelly. "Woman charged in murder-for-hire scheme." *Utica Observer-Dispatch*, December 21, 2002.

Bad Words: *See Domestic Violence*.

Baggy Pants: Tucson Police Department Crime Analysis Unit. *Annual Crime by*

Beat, 1995; Rights of Crime Victims, *Washington Post*, June 29, 1998, A14; Bureau of Justice Statistics and the Federal Bureau of Investigation. *National Incident-Based Reporting System, 1997–2005.*

Balloons: "The first air voyage in America, Blanchard balloon voyage." Penn Mutual Life Insurance Company, Philadelphia, 1943; *Hot Air Balloon Accidents*: http://www.hotairballoon accidents.com; National Transportation Safety Board: *Hot Air Balloon Accident Reports 1995–2005.*

Barbecues: Lolis, Eric. *Cornbread nation 2: the United States of barbecue.* Chapel Hill, University of North Carolina Press, 2004; Lovegren, Sylvia. Barbecue. *American Heritage*, vol. 54, June 1, 2003; Food History Pamphlet Box, Library of Congress. 36–44., E171.A43; "Prehistoric barbecue." *Discover*, vol. 10, March 1989, 14–15.; CDC: *Injury Book Fact Sheet: CO poisoning, 2001–2005*; Adams, Harry. *Beyond the Barrier with Byrd: An Authentic Story of the Byrd Antarctic Exploring Expedition.* Donohue & Co., 1932.

Baseball: Consumer Product Safety Commission: *Baseball Safety Fact Sheet, 1999–2005;* Nemec, David. *1001 Fascinating Baseball Facts.* Publications International Ltd., 1994; *National Electronic Injury Surveillance System of the United States*: Consumer Product Safety Commission; Gormacker, M. "American Academy of Pediatrics: Risk of injury from baseball and softball in children." *Pediatrics,* April 2001, 107(4): 782–784.

Basketball: *National Electronic Injury Surveillance System of the United States*: Consumer Product Safety Commission; "Sports Fact Sheet." *Orthopaedic Surgery Associates and Institute for Preventative Sports Medicine*, Ann Arbor, Michigan.

Bats: Anderson, L. J., Nicholson, K. G, Tauxe, R. V., Winkler, W. G. "Human rabies in the United States, 1960 to 1979: epidemiology, diagnosis, and prevention." *Annual Internal Medicine*, May 1984; CDC: "Human death associated with bat rabies." *Morbidity and Mortality Weekly Report* January 23, 2004; 53(2):33–35; Warrell, M. J. "Human deaths from cryptic bat rabies in the USA." *Lancet,* 1995, July 8; 346(8967):65.

Battery-Powered Vehicles: U.S. Consumer Product Safety Commission: *Recall Alerts, 1990–2005* (www.recalls .gov).

Bears: Shelton, James. *Bear Attacks: The Deadly Truth.* Pallister Publishing, 1998; Brown, Gary. *The Great Bear Almanac.* Lyons and Burford, 1993; Aron, Stephen. *How the West Was Lost: The Transformation of Kentucky from Daniel Boone to Henry Clay.* Baltimore: Johns Hopkins University Press, 1996; Ebert, Roger. "Grizzly Man." *Chicago Sun Times*, August 12, 2005.

Beauty Pageants: Karnoutsos, Carmela. "New Jersey Women: A History of Their Status, Roles, and Images." *New Jersey Historical Commission,* 1997; Banet-Weiser, Sarah. *The Most Beautiful Girl in the World: Beauty Pageants and National Identity.* University of California Press, 1999; Watson, Elwood. "Miss America Pageant: Pluralism, Femininity, and Cinderella All in One." *Journal of Popular Culture* 34, no. 1 (2000):105–126; Ballerino, Colleen. *Beauty Queens on the Global Stage: Gender, Contests, and Power.* Routledge, 1995; Shackelton, Kelly. "Pageant Finalist's Mother Arrested." *Oxford Eagle*, April 2, 2004; Buchanan, Edna. "South Florida's

Crimes of the Century Riveted the Nation." *Miami Herald*, September 15, 2002.

Beaver Fever: "Giardiasis (Beaver Fever)." Ministry of Health Services, Health File—no. 10, February 2000; Addiss, D. G., Davis, J. P. "Epidemiology of giardiasis in Wisconsin. Increasing incidence of reported cases and unexplained seasonal trends." *American Journal of Tropical Medicine and Hygiene*, 1992, 47:13–91; Lengerich, E. "Severe giardiasis in the United States." *Clinical Infection Digest*, 1994; 18:760–763.

Bed & Breakfasts: Cohen, Daniel. "A Natural History of Unnatural Things." *McCall's*, 1971; Guiley, Rosemary Ellen, ed. *The Encyclopedia of Ghosts and Spirits*. Checkmark Books, 2000; "Mexicans Confront Satanism with National Meeting of Exorcists." *Catholic News Agency*, September 2, 2004.

Bicycles: Corey, Shana. *You Forgot Your Skirt, Amelia Bloomer*. Scholastic Press, 2000; Sharp, Archibald. *Bicycles and Tricycles*. Reprint of the 1896 edition, Cambridge, Massachusetts: MIT Press, 1977; Herlihy, David V. *Bicycle: The History*. Yale University Press, 2004; National Highway Traffic Safety Administration (NHTSA): *Classification of Motor Vehicle Traffic Accidents (ANSI D16.1–1989–2005)*.

Binge and Purge: Cahalan, D. "American Drinking Practices: A National Study of Drinking Behavior and Attitudes." Rutgers Center of Alcohol Studies. Monograph No. 6, New Brunswick, NJ: *American Journal of Psychiatry*, 1986; 143:838–845; Hohlstein, L. A., Smith, G. T., and Atlas, J. G. "An application of expectancy theory to eating disorders: Development and validation of measures of eating and dieting expectancies." *Psychological Assessment,* 1198, 10, 49–58; Duncun, D. F. "Chronic drinking, binge drinking and drunk driving." *Psychology.* 80:681–682, 1997; Wechsler, et al. "Harvard School of Public Health College Alcohol Study: Binge drinking by American college students." *American Psychiatric Association*, 1994. *Diagnostic and Statistical Manual of Mental Disorders* (4th ed.). Washington, D.C. American Psychiatric Association; Timby, N., Eriksson, A., Bostrom, K. "Gamma-hydroxybutyrate associated deaths." *American Journal of Medicine*, 2000; 108:518–519; Curfman, G. D. "Editorial: Diet pills redux." *New England Journal of Medicine* 337:629–630.

Bingo: Barthelme, Frederick. *Double Down: Reflections on Gambling and Loss*. Houghton Mifflin, 1999; American Gaming Association: "Statistics on Gaming at National and State Levels," 2003; National Gambling Impact Study Commission, National Opinion Research Center: "Extensive study on gambling behavior, problems and attitudes," 1999; *Gamblers Anonymous*: http://www.gamblersanonymous.org/.

Black Death: Brown, David. "Spanish FLU: It All Started in Kansas." *Washington Post Weekly Edition*. March 23–30, 1992: vol. 9, no. 21; "Spanish Flu Found in Barracks." *Rolling Stone*, January, 22, 1998; Robert S. Gottfried. *The Black Death: Natural and Human Disaster in Medieval Europe*. Free Press, 1983.

Blackouts: "The Great Blackout: Its Meaning for the Future." *U.S. News & World Report*, November 22, 1965, 40–42, 85–86; Rosenthal, A. M., ed. *The Night the Lights Went Out*. New American Library, 1965; Baldwin,

Neil. *Edison: Inventing the Century.* Hyperion, 1995; Haberman, Clyde. "Night of Terror." *Time* magazine; July 25, 1997.

Bloodletting: Wanjek, C. *The Roots of Bad Medicine: Misconceptions and Misuses Revealed.* John Wiley, 2002; Ackerknecht, Erwin H. *A Short History of Medicine.* The Johns Hopkins University Press, 1982; Appel, Toby. *Bloodletting Instruments in the National Museum of History and Technology.* Smithsonian Institution Press, Washington, 1979; Seigworth, Gilbert. "Bloodletting Over the Centuries." *New York Journal of Medicine*, December 1980, 2022–2028.

Body Piercing: Armstrong, Myrna L. "A clinical look at body piercing." *RN* magazine, September 1998; Hollis, D. G., Weaver, R. E., Riley, P., eds. "Streptobacillus moniliformis: Identification of unusual pathogenic gram-negative aerobic and facultatively anaerobic bacteria." U.S. Department of Health and Human Services, 1984; Petroski, Henry. *The Evolution of Useful Things: How Everyday Artifacts—from Forks and Pins to Paper Clips and Zippers—Came to Be as They Are.* Vintage, 1994.

Boiled and Baked: McNab, Alan L. "Climate and Droughts." National Oceanic and Atmospheric Administration, 1991; Hirschboeck, K. K., Muller, R. A. "Floods, droughts, and the jet stream." *American Association for the Advancement of Science*: 15–20 February 1990, New Orleans, Los Angeles; "Burning issues: press conference report." *American Academy of Dermatology*, May 2, 1994; WHO, World Health Organization: "Protection Against Exposure to Ultraviolet Radiation," Report: WHO/EHG/ 95.17, Geneva; National Center for Victims of Crime: *Analysis Data Reports, 1995.*

Bottoming Out: Norden, Michael. *Beyond Prozac: Antidotes for Modern Times.* Regan Books, 1996; Allan, T. R., et al. "Selective serotonin reuptake inhibitors in the treatment of mood disorders in primary care: depression and premenstrual syndrome." *Connecticut Medical Journal*, April 1996, 60(4):215–219; "Methamphetamine Abuse and Addiction." National Institute on Drug Abuse, April 1998.

Botulinum Toxin: Borodic, G. E., Ferrante, R. "Histologic assessment of dose-related diffusion and muscle fiber response after therapeutic botulinum A toxin injections." *Journal of Movement Disorders*, January 1994, 9(1):31; Brin, M. F., Lew, M. F., Adler, C. H. "Safety and efficacy of NeuroBloc (botulinum toxin type B) in type A-resistant cervical dystonia." *Neurology*, October 22, 1999, 53(7): 1431–1438; Abrahamsson, K., and Rieman, H. "Prevalence of Clostridium botulinum in semipreserved meat products." *Applied and Environmental Microbiology*. 1971, 21(3):543–544; Institute of Medicine: *CAM report, Quackwatch 2001–2005.*

Bowling: Romo, Rene. Unsolved "Cruces Killings Revived." *Albuquerque Journal,* February 10, 2003; "Bowling Hazards." Weiss & Associates, P.C., Newsletter, 2004; *Bowling Proprietors' Association Newsletter,* BPA, March 2005.

Boxing: Beaussart, M., and Beaussart-Boulenge, L. "Experimental study of cerebral concussion in 123 amateur boxers by clinical examination and EEG before and immediately after fights." *Electroencephalography and Clinical Neurophysiology*, vol. 29, 529–530; Bellotti, P., Chiarella, F., Domenicucci, S., and Lupi G. "Myocardial contusion after a professional boxing match." *American Journal of Cardiology* 69, 1992, 709–710; Pieter, W. and Zemper, E. D. "Injury rates in children participating in taekwondo competition." *The Journal of Trauma*, 1998, 43, 1:89–95; De Lillo, Lucia. "Blagojevich bans Toughman competitions," *Medill News Service*, January 14, 2004.

Building Debris: Creighton, Peter. *The First Book of Skyscrapers*. Franklin Watts, Inc., 1964; "The American Society of Civil Engineers: 1996–2005 Annual Report Card for America's Infrastructure," The American Society of Civil Engineers; Cain, Louis P. "Historical perspective on infrastructure and U.S. economic development." *Regional Science and Urban Economics*, vol. 27 (2):117–138; Dimeo, J. "The agony of the street." *American City and County*, 2003, 106(6):56–62; "Skeletal Remains Found." *Natchez Democrat*, January 2001.

Bungee Jumping: Harris, M. "The ups and downs of bungee jumping editorial." *British Medical Journal* 1992, 305(68):1520; Vanderford, L., Meyers, M. "Injuries and bungee jumping." *Sports Medicine*, 1995–20(6): 369–374; "Cord too long in bungee jump." *New York Times*, July 2, 1993, A-11; Rohter, L. "Bungee jumping death in Michigan leads to ban and a fight in Florida." *New York Times*, July 18, 1992, A-5; Lim, P. "Bungee jumping's unencumbered cord gets tangled." *Wall Street Journal*, August 11, 1992, B-2; "Youth, 19, killed in bungee test jump." *Boston Globe*, August 3, 1992, 12–23.

Buried Alive: Taylor, Troy. *Beyond the Grave*. Whitechapel Productions, 2001; Bondeson, Jan. *Buried Alive: The Terrifying History of Our Most Primal Fear*. W. W. Norton, 2002; Ramesland, Katherine. *Cemetery Stories: Haunted Graveyards, Embalming Secrets, and the Life of a Corpse After Death*. Harper Paperbacks, 2001; Mitford, Jessica. *The American Way of Death Revisited*. Vintage, 2000; Walker, George Alfred. "Gatherings from graveyards (1839), passim." Report from the Select Committee on Improvement of the Health of Towns (Parliamentary Papers 1842 (x), no. 327), London; J. Saunders, *London Burials*. Charles Knight, ed., London (1841–1844), vol. IV, 161–174.

Candles: "Hazard Report on Candle-Related Incidents." U.S. Consumer Product Safety Commission, 1998–2005; *U.S. Fire Administration*: www.usfa.ferna.gov.

Capital Punishment: Banner, Stuart. *The Death Penalty: An American History*. Harvard University Press, 2002; Dow, David R., Dow, Mark, eds. *Machinery of Death. The Reality of America's Death Penalty Regime*. Routledge, 2002; *Death Penalty Information Center*: www.deathpenaltyinfo.org; "Capital Punishment Statistics, 1865–2004," Bureau of Justice Statistics, Department of Justice; Culpin, Christopher. *Crime and Punishment Through Time*. HarperCollins, 1997; Hill, Frances. *The Salem Witch Trials Reader*. Da Capo Books, 2000; *National Death Penalty Archive (NDPA)*: http://www.albany.edu; Palmer, Louis, J., Jr., *Encyclopedia of Capital Punishment in the United States*. McFarland & Company, 2001.

Carjacking: U.S. Department of Justice's Bureau of Justice Statistics: "Report on carjackings in the U.S., 1992–1996, 1997–2004." (NCJ171145)

Cars: Flink, James J. *The Car Culture.* Cambridge, Massachusetts: MIT Press, 1975; *National Highway and Traffic Safety Administration*: http://www .nhtsa.dot.gov.

Cat Burglar: CDC: "Ambulatory Health Care Data, 1990–2002"; FBI: "Uniform Crime Reporting (UCR) Program 1929–2003."

Catch-22 Syndrome: Ammann, A. J, Wara, D. W., et al. "The Catch-22 syndrome and the fetal alcohol syndrome." *American Journal of Diseases in Children*, October 1982, 136(10): 906–908; "DiGeorge Syndrome (Catch-22): Congenital absence of the thymus and its immunologic consequences: concurrence with congenital hypoparathyroidism." White Plains, NY: March of Dimes-Birth Defects Foundation, 1968: IV(1): 116–121.

Cell Phone Etiquette: FBI: "Uniform Crime Reporting (UCR) Program 1929–2003"; Hill, Erica. "Cell phone etiquette 101." *CNN Headline News*, October 29, 2003; Ehrenreich, Barbara. "From Stone Age to Phone Age." *The Progressive*, September 1999, 17.

Cheerleading: Chappell, L. R. *Coaching Cheerleading Successfully.* Champaign, Illinois: Human Kinetics, 1997; *Suite com 101:* www.suite101.com; "Taking Care of Injuries.": www.i5ive .com/article.cfm/cheerleading/ 34022, retrieved, August 2001; "Cheerleading Fun Facts." www .cheerleading.about.com: retrieved November 2004; Peters, Craig. *Chants, Cheers, and Jumps.* Mason Crest Publishers, 2003.

Child-Bed Fever: Leake, John. *Practical Observations on the Child-Bed Fever: Also on the Nature and Treatment of Uterine Hæmorrhages, Convulsions, and Such Other Acute Diseases, as are Most Fatal to Women During the State of Pregnancy.* London: Printed for J. Walters, [et al.], [1772] Reprinted, London, Sydenham Society, 1949; Lorie, Peter. *Superstitions.* Simon & Schuster, 1999; Levy, J. "Maternal Mortality and Mortality in the First Month of Life in Relation to Attendant at Birth." *American Journal of Public Health*, 13, 1923, no. 2, 88–95; Borst, C. G. *Catching Babies: The Professionalization of Childbirth*, 1870–1920, Harvard University Press, 1995.

Chinese Food Syndrome: Baylock, Russell, M.D. "Chinese Restaurant Syndrome." Health Press, 2001; Morgan, M. R., Fenwick, G. R. "Natural foodborne toxicants." *Lancet*, December 15, 1990; 336(8729):1492–1495; Drouin, M. A., Herbert, M., Karsh, J., Mao, Y., and Yang, W. H. "The monosodium glutamate complex: assessment in a double blind, placebo-controlled, randomized study." *Journal of Allergy Clinical Immunology*, 1995, 757–762; Diamond, S., Prager, J., Freitag, F. G. "Diet and headache. Is there a link?" *Postgraduate Medicine*, 1986, 279–286; CDC: "Tetrodotoxin poisoning associated with eating puffer fish transported from Japan—California, 1996." *Journal of the American Medical Association*, June 5, 1996, 275(21):1631; Field, J. "Puffer fish poisoning." *Journal of Accident Emergency Medicine*, September 1998, 15(5): 334–336.

Chocolate: Tomaso, E., M. Beltramo, Brain. "Cannabinoids in Chocolate." *Nature,* August 1996; Coe, Sophie. *The True History of Chocolate.* Thames and Hudson, 1996; Centers for Disease Control and Prevention: "The Economics of Diabetes Mellitus, Abstracts 192–298; Fatal Facts Accident Reports—1990–2002"; Occupational Safety and Health Administration Office of Training and Education's *Training Resources:* http://www.osha.gov.

Choking: CDC: "Choking Hazards Fact Sheet, 2001"; *Morbidity and Mortality Weekly Report* (1965–2003): "Fatal choking-related incidents"; Conway, David. *Gone Before.* Edmonton, 2000; Schessler, Ken. *This Is Hollywood: An Unusual Movieland Guide.* Redlands, California: Ken Schessler Publishing, 1993.

Christmas Disease: Biggs, A. S. "Christmas disease: a condition previously mistaken for haemophilia." *British Medical Journal*, London, 1952,2:1378–1382; Brettler, D. "Clinical manifestations and therapy of inherited coagulation factor deficiencies." *Hemostasis and Thrombosis: Basic Principles and Clinical Practice, 3rd ed.* McGraw, 1994, 169–83.

Clean Sweep: Cashman, John R. "Hazardous Materials Emergencies: Response and Control," Sanitation Manufacturers Association, 1983, Site Emergency Response Planning. Washington, D.C.; "American Trucking Association's Emergency Action Guides." *U.S. Chemical Materials Agency*, 1986, Washington, D.C.; Russell, E. R., et al. "Risk Assessment/Vulnerability Validation Study, vol. 2: 11 Individual Studies." Washington, D.C.: U.S. Department of Transportation, June 1999.

Cockroaches: Millikin, Larry E. *Flies, Lice, Mites, and Bites. Current Diagnosis.* vol. 9. W. B. Saunders 1997; Roth, L. M. and Willis, E. R. "The Biotic Associations of Cockroaches." Smithsonian Miscellaneous Collections, 1960, vol. 141. Smithsonian Institution, Washington, D.C.; McKittrick, F. A. "Evolutionary studies of cockroaches." Cornell University Agricultural Experimental Station 389:1–197, 1964; *Infectious Diseases Society of America (IDSA)* http://www.idsociety.org; Bourdain, Anthony. *Typhoid Mary: An Urban Historical.* Bloomsbury USA, 2001.

Competitive Eating: *International Federation of Competitive Eaters:* www.ifoce.com; *Association of Independent Competitive Eaters*: http://www.competitiveeaters.com.

Compulsive Disorders: Drosnin, Michael. *Citizen Hughes.* Bantam Books, 1985; Fowler, Raymond D. "Howard Hughes: A Psychological Autopsy." *Psychology Today*, May 1986; *Diagnostic and Statistical Manual of Mental Disorders.* American Psychiatric Association (DSM-IV), Washington, D.C., 1994; Keks, N.A., Kulkami, J. "Treatment of Schizophrenia." *Medical Journal of Australia* Aust 1989–151: 462–467; Rappoport, M. D., Judith. *The Boy Who Couldn't Stop Washing.* Penguin Books, New York, 1989; Foster, Constance. *Funny You Don't Look Crazy.* Dilligaf Publishing, Ellsworth, Maine, 1993; Roy, C. "Obsessive-Compulsive Disorder: A Survival Guide for Family and Friends." Obsessive Compulsive Anonymous, New Hyde Park, New York, 1993.

Co-Sleeping: Collins, K. A. "Death by overlaying and wedging: a 15-year retrospective study." *American Journal of Forensic Medical Pathology*, 2001, 22:155–159; Klonoff-Cohen, H., Edelstein, S. "Bed sharing and the sudden infant death syndrome." *British Medical Journal* 1995, 311:

1269–1272; Pharoah, P. "Bed sharing and sudden infant death." *Lancet*, 1996, 347:2.

Crayons: "Baja Products Announce Recall of My First Crayon-Balls and My First Crayon-Ball Activity Sets." Release #05-153, U.S. Consumer Product and Safety Commission, April 2005; Schmeider, Andrew. "Major brands of kids' crayons contain asbestos, tests show." *Seattle Post-Intelligencer*, May 23, 2000; Dykstra, Peter. "Crayon makers, government: No evidence of asbestos threat in crayons." *CNN Environment & Technology Unit*, May 25, 2000.

Cruise Ships: "Death on the Dark Water: The Story of the Sultana Disaster in 1865." *American Heritage*, October 1955; "Diarrheal disease on cruise ships, 1990–2000: The impact of environmental health programs." *American Journal of Preventative Medicine*, April 2003, 227–233; Glass, Roger I. "Disease Transmission on Cruise Ship." *Emerging Infectious Diseases*, January 2005; Maxtone-Graham, John. *The Cruise Ship Phenomenon in North America*. Cornell Maritime Press, 2005; "Increase fight against piracy." *American Shipper*, vol. 41 (1999) nr.8, 57; "U.S. Civil Service Commission: Information Concerning Examination for Entrance to the Steamboat Inspection Service" (Washington, D.C.: Government Printing Office, 1910); "Report of the United States Commission of the Investigation upon the Disaster to the Steamer General Slocum." U.S. General Slocum Disaster Investigation Commission, October 8, 1904. (Washington, D.C.: Government Printing Office, 1904); Weissenstein Michael. "Staten Island Ferry Accident Kills 10." Associated Press, 10-15-03.

Cults: Dafoe, Stephen. "The Fires of Sirius: The Solar Temple." *Templar History Magazine*, Fall 2002, vol. 2, no. 1; Samways, Louise. *Dangerous Persuaders. An Expose of gurus, personal development courses and cults and how they operate*. Penguin Books, 1994; Samples, Kenneth. *Prophets of the Apocalypse. David Koresh & Other American Messiahs*. Baker Books, 1994; Layton, Deborah. *Seductive Poison. A Jonestown Survivor's Story of Life and Death in the People's Temple*. Aurum Press, 1999; McCormick, Mary. *Hearing the Voices of Jonestown*. Syracuse University Press, 1998.

Dandy-Walker Syndrome: Wolpert, S., Haller, J. "The value of angiography in the Dandy-Walker syndrome and posterior fossa extra-axial cysts." *American Journal of Roentgenology*, June 1970, 109; Russ, P., Pretorius, D. "Dandy-Walker syndrome: a review of fifteen cases." *American Journal of Obstetric and Gynecology*, August 1989, 161(2):401–406; Ecker, J., Shipp, T. "The sonographic diagnosis of Dandy-Walker and Dandy-Walker variant: associated findings and outcomes." *Prenatal Diagnosis*, April 2000, 20(4):328–332.

Dating: Sugarman, D. B., Hotaling, G. T. "Dating violence: prevalence, context and risk markers." Pirog-Good, M. A. and Stets, J. E., eds. *Violence in dating relationships*. New York: Praeger, 1989, 31–32; Fitzpatrick, D. and Halliday, C. "Not the Way to Love: Violence Against Young Women in Dating Relationships." *Cumberland County Transition House Association*. Amherst, NS, 1999; "Preventing Dating Violence: Making Waves." *Premier Issue*, Winter 1998; Wolfe, Linda. "Wasted: The Preppie Murder." Backinprint.com, retrieved, November 2000; "Violence by Intimates: Crimes by Current or Former Spouses, Boyfriends, and Girlfriends." U.S. Department of Justice Report, March 1998; Centers for Disease Control and Prevention: "Costs of Intimate Partner Violence Against Women in the United States," April 2000; Bureau of Justice Statistics Crime Data Brief: "Intimate Partner Violence, 1993–2001, February 2003."

Deep Fried: U.S. Department of Interior: "National Park Service Fatality Investigation Reports: 1985–2003" (pkfl267); "Yellowstone is a wilderness filled with natural wonders that are also potential hazards." http://www.yellowstoneonline.com/yellowstoneonline/html/danger.html., retrieved February, 2005.

Dental School: "Mortality of Dentists: 1968 to 1972." Bureau of Economic Research and Statistics, *Journal of the American Dental Association*, January 1975, 195; Rich, C., et al. "Suicide by Psychiatrists: A Study of Medical Specialists Among 18,730 Physician Deaths During a Five-Year Period, 1967–72." *Journal of Clinical Psychiatry*, August 1980; "National Occupational Mortality Surveillance database." Mortality Rates and Causes Among U.S. Physicians, Frank, et al., *American Journal of Preventive Medicine*, 2000, vol. 19, no. 3; McCleary, R., Chew, K., et al., "Age and Specific Cycles in United States Suicides, 1973–1985." *American Journal of Public Health*, 1991, 81: 1494–1497; "Regional variations in suicide rates— United States 1990–1994"; Centers for Disease Control and Prevention, August 29, 1997: *Morbidity and Mortality Weekly Report*, 1997, 46 (34): 789–792; Anderson, R. N., Smith,

B. L. "Deaths: leading causes for 2001." National Vital Statistics Report, 2003, 152(9):1–86.

Dented Cans: CDC: "Infant botulism— New York City, 2001–2002." *Morbidity and Mortality Weekly Report* 2003; 52: 21–24; Angulo F., Getz, J. Taylor, J. P., et al. "A large outbreak of botulism: the hazardous dented can." *Journal Infectious Disease,* 178:172– 177; Shapiro, R., Hatheway, C., Swerdlow, D. "Botulism in the United States: A clinical and epidemiologic review." *Annuals of Internal Medicine*, 1998, 129: 221–228.

Dentures: "Surveillance for Dental Caries, Dental Sealants, Tooth Retention, Edentulism, and Enamel Fluorosis— United States, 1988–1994 and 1999– 2002," *Morbidity and Mortality Weekly Report.* Centers for Disease Control and Prevention, August 26, 2005, vol. 54, no. SS-3.

Dildo: Findlay, Heather. *Freud's "Fetishism" and the Lesbian Dildo Debates.* Feminist Studies 18, 1992, 563–579; Barbach, Lonnie Garfield. *For Yourself: The Fulfillment of Female Sexuality.* New York: Doubleday, 1975; Barker, Tara. *The Woman's Book of Orgasm: A Guide to the Ultimate Sexual Pleasure.* Citadel Press, 1998.

Domestic Violence: Curcio, William Thomas. *Domestic Abuse, Sexual Trauma, and Welfare Receipt: The Prevalence, Effects, and Implications for Poverty Theory.* Rutgers University, 1999; "Domestic Violence: The Law and You." Trenton, New Jersey: Division on Women, Office for the Prevention of Violence against Women, 1995; O'Dea, Colleen. "Safe at Home? Justice Advances for Domestic Violence Victims." *New Jersey Reporter* 25, no. 3, 1995, 14–19; Berry, D. B. *Domestic Violence Sourcebook.* Los Angeles:

RGA Publishing Groups, 1995; "Myths and Realities: A Report of the National Commission on the Insanity Defense." American Psychological Association, January 9, 1996.

Drinking Water: U. S. Environmental Protection Agency: "2004 Edition of the Drinking Water Standards and Health Advisories." (EPA# 822R04005); Sebastian, C. S., Sinha, D. "Serum sodium stabilizing effect of enalapril after standard water load in a patient with a history of self-induced water intoxication." *Biological Psychiatry*, July 19, 1995, (4):655–663; Backer, H. D., Shopes, E. "Exertional heat illness and water intoxication (hyponatremia) in hikers." *American Journal of Emergency Medicine*, October 1999, 17(6): 532–539.

Dr. Death: "Angel of Death Euthanasia Toll May Never be Known." Reuters, March 14, 2002; Dalrymple, Theodore. "Attack of the Killer Nurses: A Look at a Curious Phenomenon." *National Review*, May 28, 2001; Lane, Brian. *The Encyclopedia of Serial Killers*. New York: Berkeley, 1995; Lucy, David. "A Review of the Role of Roster Data and Evidence of Attendance in Cases of Suspected Excess Deaths in a Medical Context." *Law, Probability and Risk*, 2002, 1, 141–160; Scott, Gini Graham. *Homicide: One Hundred Years of Murder in America*. Los Angeles, CA: Roxbury Park, 1998.

Drive Time: National Center for Statistics and Analysis: "Fatality Analysis Reporting System." (FARS) 1990–2002.

Drowning: Nemiroff M. J. "Near-Drowning." *Respiratory Care* 1992; 37 (June): 600-8; Smith D. *Water rescue: basic skills for emergency responders*. St. Louis, MO: Mosby, 1994; *Drowning: New perspectives on intervention and prevention*. Boca Raton, FL: CRC Press LLC, 1999; U.S. Coast Guard, Department of Homeland Security. Boating Statistics [online]. 2003. [cited 2005 Aug 24]. Available from URL: www.uscgboating.org/statistics; Lambert, Gavin. *Natalie Wood: A Life*. London: Faber and Faber, 2004; Webb, Adam. *Dumb Angel: The Life & Music of Dennis Wilson*. Creation Books, 2001; Davies, Russell. *Foreign Body: The Secret Life of Robert Maxwell*. London: Bloomsbury, 1995.

Dueling: Fleming, Thomas. *Duel: Alexander Hamilton, Aaron Burr and the Future of America*. Basic Books, 2000; Baldick, Robert. *The Duel: A History of Dueling*. London: Spring Books, 1970; Lawrence Kestenbaum's *Political Graveyard*: www.politicalgraveyard.com.

Dwarfism: Saxon, Alice. *P. T. Barnum: The Legend and the Man*. New York University Press, 1989; *Little People of America, Inc. (LPA)*: www.lpaonline .org.; Adams, Jonathan. "An Island of Hobbits." *Newsweek*, November 2004; Patton, R. G. "Short stature associated with maternal deprivation syndrome: disordered family environment as cause of so-called idiopathic hypopituitarism." *Endocrine and Genetic Diseases of Childhood and Adolescence*, 2nd ed. McGraw, 1975, 77-87.

Earthquakes: Eiby, G. A. *Earthquakes*. New York: Van Nostrand Reinhold, 1980; Bolt, Bruce A. *Earthquakes*. New York: W. H. Freeman, 4th ed. 1999; U.S. Department of the Interior: *U.S. Geological Survey Hazards*: www.usgs.gov.

Eating Lead: Fergusson, J., Malecky, G., Simpson, E. "Lead foreign body ingestion in children." *Journal of Pediatric Child Health*, December 1997, 33(6):542-544; Mowad, E. "Management of lead poisoning from ingested fishing sinkers." *Archives of Pediatric Adolescent Medicine*, May 1998, 152(5): 485; Amann, Dick. "The Lead Poisoning of America's School Children." An Action, Programmed Studies, Inc. Stow, Massachusetts, 1991; Pesce, John. "The Lead Paint Primer." Star Industries, Inc., Melrose, Massachusetts, 1987.

Ebola Virus: Amblard, J., Obiang, P., Edzang, S. "Identification of the Ebola virus in 1994 [letter]." *Lancet*, January 18 1997, 349(9046):18; Jaax, N., Davis, K. J., Geisbert, T. J. "Lethal experimental infection of rhesus monkeys with Ebola-Zaire virus by the oral and conjunctival route of exposure." *Archive of Pathology and Laboratory Medicine*, February 1996, 120(2):140–155; Takada, A, Kawaoka, Y. "Pathogenesis of Ebola virus infection: recent insights." *Trends in Microbiology*, July 1998, 6(7):258–259; Breman, J. G. "Monkeypox: an emerging infection for humans?" Scheld, W.M., Craig, W.A., Hughes, J.M., eds. *Emerging Infections* 4. Washington, D.C.: ASM Press, 2000, 45–76.

Eccentrics: Lidz, Franz. *Ghosty Men: The Strange But True Story of the Collyer Brothers, New York's Greatest Hoarders: An Urban Historical*. Bloomsbury USA, 2003; "Homer Collyer, Harlem recluse, found dead at 70." *New York Times*, March 22, 1947; Agras, M. W. *Panic: Facing Fears, Phobias, and Anxiety*. W. H. Freeman, 1985; Beck, A. *Anxieties and Phobias*. Basic Books, 1985; *Mental Health Statistics*: www.mhsip.org; CDC: National Center for Health Statistics: "Advance Data No. 360." June 23, 2005.

Ejection: "Advanced Glazing Research Team: Ejection Mitigation Using Advanced Glazing: A Status Report." National Highway Traffic Safety Administration, November 1995: NHTSA Docket 95–41 GR; "Advanced Glazing Research Team: Ejection Mitigation Using Advanced Glazing, Status Report II," National Highway Traffic Safety Administration, August 1999: NHTSA Docket 95–41 GR; Zagaroli, Lisa. "Agency quietly rejects stronger glass standard." *Detroit News*, March 3, 2003.

Electric Knife: Filkins, J. A. "With no evil intent: the criminal prosecution of physicians for medical negligence." *Journal of Legal Medicine*, 2001, 22: 467–499; Shah, S. "A survey of prescription errors in general practice." *Pharmacology Journal*, 2001, 267: 860–862; *Medical Malpractice Statistics:* http://www.medicalmalpractice.com/National-Medical-Malpractice Facts.cfm.

Electrocution: Friedel, Robert. *Edison's Electric Light: Biography of an Invention*. Rutgers University Press, 1987; Dyer, Frank. *Edison, A Biography*. McGraw-Hill, 1959; Jaffe, R. H. "Electropathology: a review of the pathologic changes produced by electric currents." *Archives of Pathology and Laboratory Medicine*, 1928, 5:839; "Analysis of Construction Fatalities." Occupational Safety and Health Administration Data Base 1989–2002.

Electronic Air Fresheners: "Safety Topics: Methylene chloride." Occupational Safety and Health Administration, Washington, D.C., December 2003; Mason, Mark. "Full-Scale Chamber Investigation of Air Freshener Emissions." *Journal of Environmental Science and Technology*, 2004; Sarwar, Golam, Olson, D. A., Corsi, Richard L. "Indoor Fine Particles: The Role of Terpene Emissions from Consumer Products." *Journal of Air and Waste Management*, 2004, 54:367–377.

Electronic Pets: Alvisi, A. and Narduzzo, A. "Playstation and the Power of Unexpected Consequences." *Communication and Society*, December 2003, vol. 6, issue 4, 608–627(20); Aarseth, E. "Computer Game Studies." *Game Studies*, vol. 1, issue 1, July 2001; Johnson, M. "Living Dangerously: Driver Distractions at High Speeds." *Traffic Injury Prevention*, March 2004, vol. 5, issue 1, 1–7.

Elephantiasis: WHO editors. "Lymphatic Filariasis: Diagnosis and Pathogenesis." Bulletin of the World Health Organization 71, March/April 1993, no. 2, 135–141. Treves, Fredrick. *The Elephant Man: A Study in Human Dignity*. Acadian House, 1995. Howell, Michael and Ford, Peter. *The True History of the Elephant Man*. Harmondsworth: Penguin, 1980.

Elevators: Armstrong, David. "Escalator accident injures." *Boston Globe*, February 22, 1996; "ASME Standards Committee on Elevators and Escalators, 2002." American Society of Mechanical Engineers 17.3; "Safety Code for Existing Elevators and Escalators." New York: American Society of Mechanical Engineers; "Risky ride: A special report on elevator and escalator safety." *Boston Globe*, May 23, 1996; CPSC. 2001: Consumer Product Safety Alert: "Escalator Safety. Elevator Accidents." *Engineering News*, 1887, vol. 18, 141; "Elevator Accidents." *Engineering Record*, 1904 vol. 50, 355; Brake, Alan G. "Up, Down, Across: Elevators, Escalators, and Moving Sidewalks." *Architecture*, 93, 2004.

Empire State Building: Goldman, Jonathan. *The Empire State Building Book*. St. Martin's Press, 1980; Tauranac, John. *The Empire State Building*. Scribner, 1995; Fletcher Banister, Sir. *A History of Architecture*. Charles Scribner's, 1975.

Entrapment: Krug, E. G., Dahlberg, L. "America: where kids are getting killed." *Journal of Pediatrics*, 1998, 132(5):751–755; Sleet, D., Bonzo, S. E. "An Overview of the National Center for Injury Prevention and Control at the Centers for Disease Control and Prevention." *Injury Prevention* 1998–2003, 4(4):308–312; Centers for Disease Control and Prevention: "Entrapment involving children—United States, 1987–2004." *Morbidity and Mortality Weekly Report* 2004; 47(47):1019–1022.

Epidemics: Powell, J. H. *Bring Out Your Dead: The Great Plague of Yellow Fever in Philadelphia in 1793 Philadelphia*. University of Pennsylvania Press, 1993; "Cholera" quote from *Evening Post*: Haskell, Charles, "Reminiscences of New York by an Octogenarian 1816–1860." New York: Harper & Brothers, 1896; Hoehling, A. A. *The Great Epidemic*. Boston: Little Brown & Company, 1961; Coffey, Michael, ed. *The Irish in America*. New York: Hyperion, 1997; Homberger, Eric. *Scenes from the Life of a City: Corruption and Conscience Old New York*. Yale University Press, 1996; Bres, P. L. J. "A century of progress in combating yellow fever." Bulletin of the WHO 64.6 (1986), 775–786; "Jesse William Lazear." *Alabama Journal of Medical Science* 9.1 (1972), 102–114; Coleman, William. *Yellow Fever in the North: The Methods of Early Epidemiology*. Madison, Wisconsin: University of Wisconsin Press, 1987; Sass, Edmund J. *Polio's Legacy*. University Press of America, 1996; Liang, T. J., Rehermann, B. "Pathogenesis, natural history, treatment, and prevention of hepatitis C." *Annuals of Internal Medicine*, February 15 2000, 132(4): 296–305. Editorial on Irish from: Hachey, Thomas E., Hernon, Joseph M. Jr., and McCaffrey, Lawrence J. *The Irish Experience: A Concise History*. New York: M. E. Sharpe, 1996.

Euthanasia: Humphry, Derek. "Oregon's Assisted Suicide Law Gives No Sure Comfort in Dying." *New York Times*, December 3, 1994; Barnard, C. *Good Life, Good Death—a Doctor's Case for Euthanasia and Suicide*. Prentice-Hall, 1980; Kevorkian, J. *Prescription: Medicine*. Prometheus Books, 1991; McLean, S. *Death, Dying & the Law*. Dartmouth, 1996; Egan, Timothy. "Oregon's Assisted-Suicide Law Threatened by a Technicality." *New York Times Service*, November 19, 1997; "Do Not Resuscitate" (Sample Form): University of Michigan Health System.

Exercise Equipment: Worrell, T. W. "Factors associated with hamstring injuries." *Sports Medicine*, May 1994, 17(5):338–345; Goldner, R. "One hundred eleven thumb amputations." *Microsurgery* 1990: 11(3):243–250; Weiland, A. "Replantation of digits and hands: analysis of surgical techniques and functional results in 71 patients with 86 replantations." *American Journal of Hand Surgery*, January 1977, 2(1):1–12; "Summary Health Statistics for the U.S. Population." National Health Interview Survey, Centers for Disease Control and Prevention, 2003.

Fad Diets: Popkess-Vawter, S. "Overeating, Reversal Theory, and Weight Cycling." *Western Journal of Nursing Research*, 1998, 20, 67–83; Harper, Angela. "Atkins and Other Low-Carbohydrate Diets: Hoax or an Effective Tool for Weight Loss?" *The Lancet*, 2004, 364.9437; Thomas, C. D. "Nutrient balance and energy expenditure during ad libitum feeding of high-fat and high-carbohydrate diets in humans." *American Journal of Clinical Nutrition*, 2005, 55, 934–942; "Emergency Medical Service Reports, 1999–2002." Idaho Health and Welfare; "USDA coordinated nutrition research program on health and nutrition effects of popular weight-loss diets." The United States Department of Agriculture, January 10, 2001; Fox, Kate. "Mirror, Mirror: A Summary of Research Findings of Body Image." *Journal of Social Research Institute*, 1997.

Falling Asleep: Bonnet, M. "We are chronically sleep deprived." *Sleep*, December 1995, 18(10):908–911; Russo, M., Thorne, D., et al. "Sleep deprivation induced Balint's syndrome (peripheral visual field neglect): a hypothesis for explaining driving simulator accidents in awake but sleepy drivers." *Sleep* 1999; 22(Suppl 1):327; Mikulincer, M. "The impact of cognitive interference on performance during prolonged sleep loss." *Psychological Research*, 1990, 52:80–86; Mitler, M. M. "Two-peak 24-hour patterns in sleep, mortality and error." *Sleep Research*, 1990, 19:399; Weinger, M. B., Ancoli-Israel, S. "Sleep Deprivation and Clinical Performance." *Journal of the American Medical Association*, 2002, 287:955–957.

Falls: Alexander, B. H. "The cost and frequency of hospitalization for fall-related injuries in older adults." *American Journal of Public Health*, 1992, 82(7):1020–1023. Petrie, Francis. *Roll Out the Barrel: The Story of Niagara's Daredevils*. Boston: Mills

Press, 1985; American Geriatrics Society, et al. "Guideline for the prevention of falls in older persons." *Journal of the American Geriatrics Society,* 2005, 49:664–672; American Academy of Pediatrics: "Falls from heights: windows, roofs, and balconies." *Pediatrics,* May 2001; Tinetti, M. N. "Preventing Falls in Elderly Persons." *New England Journal of Medicine,* May 1, 2003, 348: 1816–1818.

Fashion: Broby-Johansen, B. *Body and Clothes.* Faber & Faber, 1968; Carter, Ernestine. *20th Century Fashion.* Eyre Methuen, 1978; Boucher, François. *20,000 Years of Fashion—The History of Costume and Personal Adornment.* H. N. Abrams, 1967; Singer, Sydney Ross, Grismaijer, Soma. *Dressed to Kill: The Link Between Breast Cancer and Bras.* ISCD Press, 2002; Blair, Frederika. *Isadora: Portrait of the Artist as a Woman.* McGraw-Hill, 1986; Devin D. "Women hit by lightning." *Odds and Ends Magazine,* November 1999.

Fear of Flying: "Airline Report (JTS), vol. 7, no. 2/3, vol. 8, no. 1." *Journal of Transportations and Statistics,* U.S. Department of Transportation: Transportation Service Index TSI, 1976–2003, Bureau of Transportation Statistics; Cobb, Roger. *The Plane Truth: Airline Crashes, the Media, and Transportation Policy.* Brookings Institution Press, 2003.

Feed and Pet: U.S. National Park Service: Animal Statistics Summary, "GRTE," August 2004; Olney, P. J. S. *Creative Conservation: Interactive Management of Wild and Captive Animals.* New York: Chapman & Hall, 1994; "Biological Report B–282." U.S. Department of Interior, Fish, and Wildlife Service, 1996.

Fire Hoses and Pressure Washers: Ditzel, Paul C. *Fire Engines, Firefighters: the Men, Equipment, and Machines, from Colonial Days to the Present.* New York: Crown, 1976; Cowen, David. *Great Chicago Fires.* Lake Claremont Press, 2001; Allen, Troy. *Disaster.* Castle Books, 1974; Gess, Denise. *Firestorm at Peshtigo: A Town, Its People and the Deadliest Fire in American History.* Henry Holt, April 2003; "On-Duty U.S. Firefighter Deaths Reach Ten-Year Peak." *National Fire Protection Association,* 2004.

Flesh-Eating Virus: McCarthy, James S. *Parasitic Diseases of the Skin. Current Therapy,* W. B. Saunders, 1996; Hopkins, JoAnn, et al. "Genome of the bacterium Streptococcus pneumoniae (galloping gangrene) strain R6." *American Society for Microbiology,* 2001, vol. 183, 5709–5717; Dr. Loren G. Miller quote: Johnson. Linda A. "Dangerous Super Bugs Worry Doctors." Associated Press, September 14, 2004.

Flying Cows: "Collisions Between Large Wildlife Species and Motor Vehicles In Maine" (Interim Report) Executive Summary, Maine Departments of Inland Fisheries and Wildlife, December 2002; Forman, T. T. *Road Ecology.* Island Press, 2004; "General Technical Report JNT–84 U.S. Impact of Backcountry Recreationists on Wildlife." U.S. Forest Service, 2003.

Football: Clarke, K. S. "Epidemiology of athletic head injury." *Clinical Sports Medicine,* January 1998, 17(1): 1–12; Mueller, F. "Fatalities from head and cervical spine injuries occurring in tackle football: 50 years' experience." *Clinical Sports Medicine,* January 1998, 17(1):169–82; Neft, David. *The Football Encyclopedia: The*

Complete History of Professional Football from 1892 to the Present. St. Martin's Press, 1994.

Foreign Bodies: Seow-Choen, F. "Anal Fistula." *British Journal of Surgery,* 1992, 79:197–205; Weigelt, J. A., Thal. E. R. *Operative Anal Trauma Management,* 1st ed. Stamford, Conn: Appleton & Lange, 1997; National Center for Health: *Vital and Health Statistics Series 23, no. 24* (12/04); Colman, I., et al. "Utilization of the emergency department after self-inflicted injury." *Academic Emergency Medicine,* 2004; 11(2): 136–142; Sullivan, Jennifer. "Trespassing charged in horse-sex case." *Seattle Times,* October 19, 2005.

Free Rent: Saville-Smith, K. *2004 National Landlord Survey—Preliminary Analysis,* Center for Research, Evaluation and Social Assessment, September 2004; Robinson, Leigh. *Landlording: a handy manual for scrupulous landlords and landladies who do it themselves,* 6th ed. El Cerrito, California: ExPress, 1992; Ilka, Douglas. "Program helps landlords work problems out with tenants." National Center for Community Policeing, September 1996.

Frozen Toilets: Hirvonen, J. "Some aspects on death in the cold and concomitant frostbites." *International Journal of Circumpolar Health,* April 2000, 131–136; Danielsson, U. "Wind-chill and the risk of tissue freezing." *Journal of Applied Physiology,* December 1996, 81(6):2666–2673; Danzl, D. F. "Accidental hypothermia." *Wilderness Medicine.* 51–103; Keatinge, W. R.: "Hypothermia: dead or alive?" *British Medical Journal,* January 5, 1991, 302(6767):3–4; Miller, James. "Blizzards." *Encyclopedia Americana,* ed.

Lawrence T. Lorimer. Birmingham: Grolier, 1996, 82; Collins, K. *Hypothermia: The Facts.* New York: Oxford University Press, 1983.

Furniture: Bingham, C. "Adolescent problem behavior." *Journal of Adolescent Research,* 2004: 19(2):205–223; Demetriades, D., et al. "Traumatic deaths: Prevalence and association with type and severity of injuries." *Journal of the American College of Surgeons,* 1995: 687–692, 2004; "Pedestrian Facilities in Work Zones." U.S. Department of Transportation, Federal Highway Administration: B.02.02.06, 2002.

Gangs and Gang Warfare: Campbell, Joseph. *The Power of Myth.* Doubleday, 1988. Meade, Michael. *Men & the Water of Life: Initiation & the Tempering of Men.* Harper, 1993, Ottenberg, Simon. *Boyhood Rituals in an African Society: An Interpretation.* University of Washington Press, 1989; Wall, Kathleen. *Lights of Passage: Rituals & Rites of Passage for the Problems & Pleasures of Modern Life.* Harper, 1994; "Violence by Gang Members: 1993–2003." Justice Department Statistics, National Crime Victimization Survey data: NCJ 208875; "Homicide Trends in the United States: 2002 Update," *British Journal of Surgery,* NCJ 204885; Wethern, George. *A Wayward Angel: The Full Story of the Hell's Angels by the Former Vice-President of the Oakland Chapter.* Lyons Press, 2004; Aubury, Herbert. *The Gangs of New York: An Informal History of the Underworld.* Thunder's Mouth Press, 2001.

Gastric Bypass Surgery: Lichtenstein, Gary. "The Year Book of Gastroenterology." C. V. Mosby Publishing Co. December 15, 2004; O'Brien, A.,

Smith, A. "Prospective study of a laparoscopically placed, adjustable gastric band in the treatment of morbid obesity." *British Journal of Surgery*, 1999, 86(1):113–118; MacLean, L.D., et al. "Stomach ulcer after gastric bypass." *Journal of American College Surgery*, 185z:1–7, 1997.

Geographic Tongue: Eidelman, E. "Scrotal tongue and geographic tongue: polygenic and associated traits." *The Journal of Oral Surgery, Oral Medicine, and Oral Pathology*, November 1976; Patrikakos, G. "Benign migratory glossitis or geographic tongue: an enigmatic oral lesion." *American Journal of Medicine*, December 15, 2002, 113(9):751–775.

Giants: Thomson, Rosemary Garland, ed. *Freakery: Cultural Spectacles of the Extraordinary Body*. Atkinson, 1938; Freda, P. U. "Current concepts in the biochemical assessment of the patient with acromegaly." *Growth Hormone and IGF Research Society,* August 2003, 13(4):171–184; Fitzgerald, Paul. *Gigantism & Acromegaly: Handbook of Clinical Endocrinology*. Appleton & Lange, 1992.

Ginger Ale and Gangsters: Schecter, Harold. *Deranged: Stories in the New York Daily News and the New York Post*. Pocket Books, 1990; *Encyclopedia of Organized Crime in the United States,* Westport, Connecticut: Greenwood Press, 2000; Abadinsky, Howard. *The Mafia in America: An Oral History*. Praeger, 1981; Kelly, Robert J., et al. *Handbook of organized crime in the United States*. Greenwood Press, 1994; Maas, Peter. *The Valachi Papers*. Putnam, 1968; Fisher, Joey. *Joey the Hit Man: The Autobiography of a Mafia Killer*. Thunder's Mouth Press, 2002.

Going Postal: Lane, Brian. *The Encyclopedia of Mass Murder*. Headline Book Publishing, 1994; Dart, Bob. "Study Calls 'Go Postal' Stereotype Mere Myth." *Atlanta Journal-Constitution*, September 2000; Kaufer, Steve. "Workplace Violence: An Employer's Guide." *Workplace Violence Research Institute,* 2001.

Going to School: "Stolen Van, Stolen Guns and Five Stolen Lives; Jonesboro's Day of Tragedy Ended With the Words: 'Grandpa, I Took Your Guns,' " *New York Times*, March 29, 1998; "Youth violence: A report of the Surgeon General." United States Public Health Service. Office of the Surgeon General. (2004) Washington, D.C.: Author. HQ 799.2 .V56 U561 2004; Capozzoli, T. K. *Kids Killing Kids: Managing Violence and Gangs in Schools*. Boca Raton, Florida: St. Lucie Press, 2000; "National School Safety Center's Report on School Associated Violent Deaths. An in-house Report from the National School Safety Center." (NSSC), June 2003, Westlake Village, California; Donohue, Elizabeth, et al. "School House Hype: School shootings and the real risks kids face in America." *Justice Policy Institute*, 2000.

Golf: Grossman, Peter. *The Everything Golf Book*. Adams Media Corporation, 1996; Towle, Mike. *The Ultimate Golf Trivia Book*. Rutledge Hill Press, 1999; U.S. National Weather Service: "Day by Day Lightning Casualty Statistics, January 1, 1980 through December 31, 2004." National Weather Service, Pueblo, Colorado.

Gone Fishing: U.S. Coast Guard: http://www.uscgboating.org/statistics/accident stats.htm; Backus, A. "Wearing flotation could save your life." *Commercial Fisheries News*, 2001, 28(7):6B; Dotter, E. and Backus, A. "The Price of Fish—Our Nation's Most Perilous Job Takes Life and Limb in New England." *Alicia Patterson Foundation*, 2005.

Guns: "Benji dog killed owner." *Scripps Howard News Service*, October 15, 1998; Yonover, Neal. *Crime Scene USA.* Hyperion, 2000; Sugarman, Josh. *National Rifle Association: Money, Firepower & Fear.* Washington, D.C. National Press Books, 1992; Reza, A., et al. "The epidemiology of violent deaths in the world." *Injury Prevention*, 2001. vol. 7, 104; "Nonfatal and fatal firearm-related injuries—United States, 1993–1997, 1997–2003": *Morbidity and Mortality Weekly Report.* Centers for Disease Control and Prevention, vol. 48. 1999—vol 64 2003; FBI: "National Crime Victimization Survey (NCVS) 1987–2004"; Boothroyd, Geoffrey. *Guns Through the Ages.* New York: Sterling Publishing, 1962.

Hair: Bogdon, Robert. *Freak Show: Presenting Human Oddities for Fun and Profit.* University of Chicago Press, 1988; Penzel, Fred. *The Hair Pulling Problem: A Complete Guide to Trichotillomania.* Oxford University Press, 2003; Drimmer, Frederick. *Very Special People.* Amjon Publishing, 1973; Fitzsimons, Raymond. *Barnum in London.* London: Geoffrey Bles Ltd, 1969. "Jo-Jo dog faced boy sideshow act at dime museums and circuses." *Chicago Tribune*, February 2, 1904; Binder, B. J., Goodman, S. L. "Pica: a critical review of diagnosis and treatment." *The Eating Disorders*, 1988, 331–44; Ebrahim, Shah. "Shaving & Longevity." *American Journal of Epidemiology*, 2002, 156:1100–1104.

Halitosis: Rosenberg, M. "The science of bad breath." *Scientific American*, 2002, 286 (4):58–65; Eli, R., et al. "Self-Perception of Breath Odor." *Journal of the American Dental Association*, 2001, 132:621–626; Williams, M. "Helicobacter pylori: from the benign to the malignant." *American Journal of Gastroenterology*, November 1999, 94(11 Suppl):S11–16.

Halloween: Linton, Ralph. *Halloween Through Twenty Centuries. Great Religious Festivals Series.* New York: Schuman, 1950; Santino, Jack. "Halloween in America: Contemporary Customs and Performances." *Western Folklore* 42 (1983) 1–20; Limburg, Peter R. *Weird! The Complete Book of Halloween.* Bradbury Press, 1989; "Halloween Safety Fact Sheet, 1997." National Center for Victims of Crime; Murray, Howard. "Scary Scams." *Chicago Tribune*, October 29, 1999.

Hang Gliding: Carlson, Shawn. "Using a Kite as an Experimental Platform." *Scientific American*, 2000, vol. 283, no. 3, 98–99; Welch, A. *Soaring hang gliders.* London: John Murray, 1981.

Hazing: Springmeier, Fritz. *Bloodlines of the Illuminati.* Ambassador House, 2002; Nuwer, Hank. "Unofficial Clearinghouse to Track Hazing Deaths and Incidents." (http://hazing.hanknuwer .com); Sutton, Anthony. *Skull and Bones, Secret Societies: An Introduction to the Order.* Veritas Publishing, 1988; Nuwer, H. *Wrongs of Passage: Fraternities, Sororities, Hazing, and Binge Drinking.* Bloomington: Indiana University Press, 1999; Robbins, Alexandra. *Secrets of the Tomb: Skull and Bones, The Ivy League, and The Hidden Paths of Power.* Little, Brown, 2002; Sutton, Antony. *America's Secret Establishment: An Introduction to the*

Order of Skull & Bones. TrineDay, 2002; Woodward, Bob. "Bush Opened Up to Secret Yale Society." *The Washington Post,* August 7, 1988.

Head and Signs: Doyle, William. *The Oxford History of the French Revolution.* New York: Oxford University Press, 1989; "US: Statistical Abstract of the United States," 1992, 112th ed. Government Printing Office; Scott, Beth. *Haunted Heritage: A Definitive Collection of North American Ghost Stories.* Tor Books, 2003; "Headless Body in Topless Bar." *New York Post,* 1982; "Scrap Metal Decapitates Woman." *Houston Chronicle,* December 20, 2001; Gorner, Peter. "Professor Shines a Little Light on the Source of Bizarre Tales." *Chicago Tribune,* September 10, 1986; "Man with Louisville ties decapitated in Georgia crash." *Courier-Journal,* August 31, 2004; Kraus, J. F. "Motorcycle crashes: Injuries, rider, crash and vehicle characteristics associated with helmet use." *Journal of Traffic Medicine,* 1995, 23(1):29–35. Wilde, Robert. "Does the Head of a Guillotined Individual Remain Briefly Alive?" (http://europeanhistory .about.com).

Heating Pads: Turner, D. G., Leman, C. J. "Cooking-related burn injuries in the elderly." *Journal of Burn Care Rehabilitation,* 1999, 10:356–359; "Deaths among the elderly in the home." *Fire Journal,* March 2003, 19–22.

Hiccups: *Guinness Book of World Records.* New York, Sterling Publishing, 1993; Anthony, T. R. "On temporal structure of human hiccups: ethology and chronobiology." *International Journal of Chronobiology,* 1978; 5(3): 477–492; "Death from Hiccups Obituary." Retrieved from Distant-Cousins.com, *Archive of Genealogical Data,* November 2004.

Hide-and-Seek: Centers for Disease Control: "Fatal car trunk entrapment involving children—United States, 1987–1998." *Morbidity Mortal Weekly Report,* 1998, 47(47):1019–1022; "Traffic Safety Facts 1998." Washington, D.C., National Highway Traffic Safety Administration, 1999: 208; Bonnie, R. J., et al. *Reducing the burden of injury: advancing prevention and treatment.* Washington, D.C., National Academy Press, 2004, 319; Ott, Dwight. "3 Boys Found Dead." *Philadelphia Inquirer,* June 25, 2005.

Hit-and-Run: Grossman, D. C., Hart, L., Rosenblatt, R. "From roadside to bedside: the regionalization of trauma care in a remote rural county." *Journal of Trauma,* 1995, 38(1):14–21; Solnick, S. "The hit-and-run in fatal pedestrian accidents: victims, circumstances and drivers." *Accident Analysis and Prevention,* 1995, 27(5):643–649; "Ft. Worth Driver Lets Pedestrian Die in Garage." *Star-Telegram,* March 9, 2002.

Holidays: Maas, R.P. "Artificial Christmas trees: how real are the lead exposure risks?" *Journal of Environmental Health,* 2004, 67 (5):20–24; The National Council for Suicide Prevention (NCSP): http://www.ncsp.org/; U.S. Consumer Product Safety Commission (CPSC): "Holiday Decoration Safety Tips for Avoiding Fires and Injuries," Release # 02-056; U.S. Fire Administration: "Holiday Tree Fire Hazards # FEMA 024"; Monti, Carlotta. *W. C. Fields and Me.* Prentice-Hall, 1971.

Home Births: "Gracious Births." *Midwifery Today,* Winter 1994, No. 32, Mitford, Jessica. *The American Way of Birth.* Dutton, 1992. "What Midwives Want From Their Clients." *The Birthkit,* Spring 1995, vol. 2, no. 5;

Declercq, Eugene, PhD. "The Transformation of American Midwifery: 1975 to 1988." *American Journal of Public Health*, May 1992; "Trends in Characteristics of Births by State: United States, 1990, 1995, and 2000–2002." National Vital Statistics Report, vol. 52, No. 19. 152 pp. (PHS) 2004-1120; "Baby Eaten By Python." *The New Straits Times*, April 8, 1998; Mehl, Lewis. "Scientific research on childbirth alternatives and what it tells us about hospital practice." *National Association for Parents & Professionals for Safe Alternatives in Childbirth, 21st Century Obstetrics,* 1978, vol. 1, 171–207.

Homelessness: *Taber's Cyclopedic Medical Dictionary*, edition 17, F. A. Davis Company, 1993; Shinn, Marybeth. "Homelessness: Abstracts of the Psychological and Behavioral Literature, 1967–1990." *Journal of American Psychological Association*, December 1991; Henslin, J. M. *Homelessness*. Garland Publishing, 1993; "Practical Lessons." National Symposium on Homelessness Research, Washington, D.C.: U.S. Department of Housing and Urban Development. U.S. Department of Health and Human Services. Paper copy; 1999; Fosburg, L. B., Dennis, D. L., eds. "NCH Fact Sheet #1." National Coalition for the Homeless, September 2002.

Hookworms: Albonico, M. "Hookworm infection and disease: advances for control." *American Thoracic Society*, 1997: 33:567–579; Schantz, P. M. "Tapeworms." *Gastroenterology and Clinical Association of North America*, 1996, Sep: 25(3):637–653; Siebold, Louis. "Tapeworm Remedies." *American Journal of Pharmacy*, 1884 vol. 56; "Tapeworm Diet Sweeps Hollywood! 50-foot Parasites Are Latest Weight-Loss Craze." *World Weekly News*, August 31, 2004.

Hoover Dam: Stevens, Joseph E. *Hoover Dam: An American Adventure.* University of Oklahoma Press, 1988; Green, S. W. *The Complete History of the New York and Brooklyn Bridge: From Its Conception in 1866 to Its Completion in 1883.* New York: S. W. Green's son Publisher, 1883; Roach, Mary. "Don't jump!" Salon.com. Retrieved February 9, 2001.

Horse and Buggy: "Superintendent of Police's Annual Report." Chicago Department of Transportation, 1916; Rittenhouse, Jack D. *American Horse-Drawn Vehicles.* New York: Bonanza Books, 1967; "Wheels Led the Way: Horse-Drawn Vehicles, Plain and Fancy, 1820–1920." Yakima Valley Museum (January 1973); "Driver shoots and kills man after Amish throw tomatoes at his car." *Dayton News*, September 2, 2003.

Hotheads: Rathore, S. S., Berger, A. K., et al. "Acute myocardial infarction complicated by atrial fibrillation: prevalence and outcomes." *Circulation*, March 7, 2000, 101(9):969–974; "Study Cautions Quick Tempered Men." *Star-Telegram*, March 1, 2004.

Hunting: Taylor, Dale. *Everyday Life in Colonial America.* F & W Publications, 2002, "National Survey of Fishing, Hunting, and Wildlife-Associated Recreation." Annual Reports: 1955–2004. U.S. Fish & Wildlife Service; "Deer Hunting in the United States: An Analysis of Hunter Demographics and Behavior." Addendum to the 2001 National Survey of Fishing, Hunting, and Wildlife-Associated Recreation (Report 2001-6) 2004; "Five hunters killed in Wisconsin woods." CNN.com, retrieved November 22, 2004.

Hurricanes: Elsner, James. *Hurricanes of the North Atlantic: Climate and Society.* Oxford University Press, 1999; Dunn, Gordon. National Weather Service: WBTM SR 38: "Florida Hurricanes." November 1967 (PB 182 220); Sugg, Arnold, et al. National Weather Service: NWS SR 56: "Memorable Hurricanes of the United States Since 1873." (April 1971:COM 71 00610); Eliot Klienberg, "Hurricane season 2004: The year Florida's luck ran out." *Palm Beach Post*, November 29, 2004; Emmanuel, K., "Warm Seas Fuel More Destructive Storms." *Nature*, July 31, 2005; Treaster, Joseph B., and Zernike, Kate. "Hurricane damage 'enormous.' " *New York Times*, August 31, 2005; Zarin, D. "The Superdome: Monument to a Rotten System." *Out of Bounds Magazine*, September 5, 2005.

Ice Cream: "The History of Ice Cream." *Journal of International Association of Ice Cream Manufacturers* (JAICM), Washington, D.C., 1978; Ornish, D., Scherwitz, L. W., et al. "Intensive lifestyle changes for reversal of coronary heart disease." *Journal of the American Medical Association* 1998, 2800:2001–2007; Cobb, V. *The Scoop on Ice Cream*. Little Brown, 1985; Funderberg, Anne. *Chocolate, Strawberry, and Vanilla: A History of American Ice Cream*. Popular Press, 1996; Shoyeb, Jacqueline. "Who's selling ice cream?" *The Arizona Republic*, August 21, 2004.

Immersion Foot: Fiorillo, L., Zucker, M., Sawyer, D. "The pseudomonas hot-foot syndrome." *New England Journal of Medicine*, August 2, 2001, 345(50); Curtis, Rick. *The Backpacker's Field Manual*. Random House, 1998; Zucca, M., et al. "Gram-negative bac-

terial toe web infection: a survey of 123 cases." *Journal of the American Academy of Dermatology*, October 2001; "New York City woman charged after killing boyfriend with her high-heeled shoe." Associated Press, June 8, 2003.

Impotence: Hellstrom, W., ed. *Handbook of Sexual Dysfunction.* American Society of Andrology, chapter 14, 70–74; Holmes, S. "New treatment for erectile dysfunction." *British Journal of Urology International*, 2003, 91: 466–468.

Independence Day: Lott, John R. "Igniting a Controversy: Big-government vs. fireworks." *National Review,* July 1, 2005; "Injury Visits to Hospital Emergency Departments: United States, 1992–2003." National Center for Health Statistics. Vital Health Statistics 13(131); Giblin, James. *Fireworks, Picnics and Flags.* Clarion Books, 1983.

Indigestion: Adson, D. E., Mitchell, J. E. "The superior mesentric artery syndrome and acute gastric dilation in eating disorders: A report of two cases and review of the literature." *International Journal of Eating Disorders,* 1198, 21, 103–114; Brandon, S. "An epidemiological study of eating disturbances." *Journal of Psychosomatic Research,* 24, 253–257; Soll, A. H. "Medical treatment of peptic ulcer disease." *Journal of the American Medical Association,* February 28, 1996. DA-19960410(8):622–629.

Insomnia: Morin, C. M., et al. "Nonpharmacologic treatment of chronic insomnia." *An American Academy of Sleep Medicine Review,* December 15, 1999; Spencer, R. S, Will, R. G. "First hundred cases of Sporadic Fatal Insomnia: retrospective case note review of early psychiatric and neurological features." *British Medical Journal* June 22, 2002: 324(7352); Fiorino, A. S. "Sleep, genes and death: fatal familial insomnia." *Brain Research Review*, October 1996, 22(3).

Internet Dating: "Computer Crimes and Computer Related or Facilitated Crimes." Statement of Charles L. Owens, Chief, Financial Crimes Section, Federal Bureau of Investigation, March 19, 1997. "Cyberstalking: A New Challenge for Law Enforcement and Industry." A Report from the Attorney General to the Vice President (August 1999); "Online Victimization: A Report on the Nation's Youth by the Crimes Against Children." Children Research Center, Washington, D.C., June 2000; Maher, Heather. "Online and Out of Line: Why Is Cybercrime on the Rise, and Who's Responsible?" ABCNews.com., retrieved June 2005; O'Brien, Kimberly. "Man guilty in Internet sex case." *The Roanoke Times*, May 8, 1999.

Jail Break: Florida Department of Corrections: "98–99 Annual Report"; Deutsch, Michael. "Twenty Years Later—Attica." *Social Justice*, 1991, 18(3):13-25; Bosworth, Mary. *U.S. Federal Prison System*. SAGE Publications, 1st ed., June 2003; Campbell, Bruce. *Escape From Alcatraz*. Ten Speed Press, 2004; Henderson, Les. *Crimes of Persuasion: Schemes, scams, frauds.* Coyote Ridge Publishing, 2000.

Jaywalking: Landersman, Jay. *Jaywalking*. Weidenfeld and Nicolson, 1993; "Jaywalking Crackdown Blames Victims: Why Are Cops Chasing Pedestrians Instead of Dangerous Drivers and Scofflaws." *Transportation Alternatives*, August 24, 1995.

Jellyfish: Edström, A. *Venomous and Poisonous Animals*. Malabar, Florida: Krieger Pub. Co., 1992; Halstead, B. *Poisonous and Venomous Marine Animals of the World*. Princeton, New Jersey: Darwin Press, 1988.

Job's Syndrome: Bannatyne, R. M. "Job's syndrome, a variant of chronic granulomatous disease." *Journal of Pediatrics*, 1969; Hensley, T., et al. "The face of Job." *Journal of Pediatrics*, August 1998, 133(2):303-305.

Juice Extractors: Braddock, R. J. "Processing technologies of citrus juice." *Abstracts of Papers of the American Chemical Society*, 2001, 222:41-AGFD; Cameron, R., et al. "Effect of juice extractor settings." *Journal of Agricultural and Food Chemistry*, 1999, 47(7):2865-2868; Morann, James. *Printing Presses: History and Development from the Fifteenth Century to Modern Times.* University of California Press, 1975; "Man Killed After Falling into Mulcher." Deland, Florida (Associated Press), December 1, 2004.

Junk Collecting: OSHA: "Construction Fatalities Data Abstract." (3351. 2004); "Preventing Electrocutions Near Overhead Power Lines." Department of Health and Human Resources (NIOSH) Publication No. 91-110; Office of the Fire Marshal and the Electrical Safety Authority Case Studies, July 2003 (EBS. 03.09.01).

Kabuki Makeup Syndrome: Angelogolou, M. *A History of Make Up*, London: Studio Vista, 1979; Armstrong, L. Further delineation of Kabuki syndrome in 48 well-defined new individuals. *American Journal of Medicine*, December 2004, 22;132A(3) 265-272; Vaux, K. K. "Developmental outcome in Kabuki syndrome." *American Journal of Medicine*, November 2004, 2;132A(3) 263–264. Advance Monthly Retail Sales (Lipstick Indicator) U.S. Bureau of Censuses, Department of Commerce: CB05-112; FDA Alerts Consumers About Adverse Events Associated with "Permanent Makeup." Report T04-20, July 2, 2004, Current Intelligence Bulletins, 1992–2003. (GT-67) National Institute for Occupational Safety and Health (NIOSH); Craig, W. J. "Topical Use of Tea Benefits Skin Health." *Life Extension*, August 27, 2003, 51(18):5307–5314.

Killer Bees: "Boy stung by yellow jackets." *The St. Petersburg Times*, October 4, 1998; "Bees sting man about 150 times." *Galveston County Daily News*, June 7, 2003; "Africanised 'killer' bee chronology." *Shield Insect Journal*, July 2003; Free, J.B. *Bees and Mankind*. Boston: Allen & Unwin, 1982; Nichol, J. "Bites & Stings: The World of Venomous Animals." New York: Facts On File, 1989; Landau, Elaine. *Killer Bees: Fearsome, Scary, and Creepy Animals*. Enslow Publishers, 2003.

Kinky Hair Disease: Brownstein, J. N. "Oral manifestations of kinky hair syndrome." *Journal of Clinical Pediatric Dentistry*, Summer 2001, 25(4): 317–322; Harris, E., Qian, Y. "Genes regulating copper metabolism." *Molecular Cellular Biochemistry*, November 1998, 188(1–2):57–62; Oshio, T., Hino, M., et al. "Urologic abnormalities in Menkes' kinky hair disease: report of three cases." *Journal of Pediatric Surgery*, May 1997, 32(5): 782–784.

Kissing Disease: Tosato, G., et al. "Epstein-Barr virus as an agent of haematological disease." *Clinical Haematology*, March 1995, 8(1):165–99; Pereira, M. "EB virus antibody at different ages." *British Journal of Medicine*, November 29, 1969; Aldrete, J. S. "Spontaneous rupture of the spleen in patients with infectious mononucleosis." *Mayo Clinic Proceedings*, September 1992, 67(9):910–912; Duvall, Evelyn Millis. *Facts of life and love for teen-agers*. Association Press, 1956.

Labor Day: Ansary, Mir Tamim. *Labor Day (Holiday Histories)*. Heinemann, 2001; Mink, Gwendolyn. *Old Labor and New Immigrants in American Political Development: Union, Party, and State, 1875–1920*. Cornell University Press, 1986; Nicholson, Philip Yale. *Labor's Story in the United States*. Temple University Press, 2004.

Labyrinth Disease: Ishiyama, G., Ishiyama, A. "Drop attacks and vertigo secondary to a non-meniere otologic cause." *Archives of Neurology*, 2003, 60(1): 71–75; Tumarkin, A. "The otolithic catastrophe: a new syndrome." *British Medical Journal*, 1936, 1:175–177; Baloh, R.W. "Drop attacks with Menière's syndrome." *Annals of Neurology*, 1998, vol. 28; Thomsen, J. "Placebo effect in surgery for Menière's disease: nine-year follow-up." *American Journal of Otology*, July 1989, 10(4):259–261.

Latex Sensitivity: Kay, A. B. "Allergy and allergic diseases." *New England Journal of Medicine*, 2001, 344(1):30–37; Mäkinen-Kiljunen, S., Reunala, T. "Cross-reacting allergens in natural rubber latex and avocado." *Journal of Allergy and Clinical Immunology*, 1995, 96:167–173; Bubak, M. E., et al. "Allergic reactions to latex among health-care workers." *Mayo Clinic Proceedings*, 2002, 67:1075–1079; Semmelweis, P. "Die Aetiologic, der Begriff und die Prophylaxis des Kindbettfiebers." Pest-Wien-Leipzig, 1861. Reprint translated into English by F. R. Murphy, 1941.

Laughing: Bernstein, D. K. "Development of Humor Implications for Assessment and Intervention." *Topics in Language Disorders* 6.4, 1996; Cousins, Norman. *Anatomy of an Illness*. Bantam Books, 1981; Alexander, L. *Origin and Mechanisms of Hallucinations*. Plenum Press, 1970; Gajdusek D. C. "Unconventional viruses and the origin and disappearance of kuru (Laughing Psychosis)." *Science*, September 2, 1977, 197(4307):943–960; Gibbs, Wayt W. "Side Splitting." *Scientific American*, January 2001; Oderman, Stuart. *Roscoe "Fatty" Arbuckle: A Biography of the Silent Film Comedian*. McFarland and Company, 1994

Laughing Gas: McGarvey, E. L., Clavet, C. G. "Adolescent inhalant abuse: Environment of use." *American Journal of Drug and Alcohol Abuse*, 1999, 731–741; Young, S. J. "Inhalant abuse and the abuse of other drugs." *American Journal of Drug and Alcohol Abuse*, May, 1999; Kurtzman, T. L., et. al. "Inhalant abuse by adolescents." *Journal of Adolescent Health*, March 2001, 28(3):170–180.

Laughing Sickness: Gibbons, R. V., Holman, R. C. "Creutzfeldt-Jakob Disease in the United States: 1979–1998." *The Journal of the American Medical Association*, 2000; 284, 2322–2323; Holman, R. C., Khan, A. S. "Epidemiology of Creutzfeldt-Jakob Disease in the United States, 1979–1990: Analysis of National Mortality Data." *Neuroepidemiology*, 1995, 14: 174–181; World Health Organization Fact Sheets, November 2004 (http://www.who.int).

Lawn Darts: "Consumer Product Safety Commission Bans Lawn Darts." CPSC Document #5053; Rodriguez,

J. O. "Prevention and treatment of common eye injuries in sports." *American Family Physician*, April 1, 2003, 67(7):1481–1488.

Laying Tracks: Robertson, Donald. *Encyclopedia of Western Railroad History*. Caxton Press, 1998; Daniels, Rudolph. *Trains Across the Continent: North American Railroad History*. Indiana University Press, 2000.

Lightning: Fontanarosa, P. B. "Electrical shock and lightning strike." *Annuls of Emergency Medicine*, February 1993; Uman, Martin. *All About Lightning*. Dover Publications, 1987; Curran, E. Brian, et al. "Lightning Fatalities, Injuries, and Damage Reports in the United States From 1959–1994. National Severe Storms Laboratory, National Oceanic and Atmospheric Administration; "Statement on Lightning Safety Awareness and Recommendations for Lightning Safety—2002." American Meteorological Society: http://www.lightningsafety.noaa.gov/.

Liposuction: Stewart, James. *Blind Faith: How the Medical Establishment Let a Doctor get away with Murder*. Simon & Schuster, 1999; Phillips, D. "Increase in U.S. medication error-deaths between 1983 and 1993." *Lancet*, 28, February 1998; vol. 351, 643–644; "Deaths associated with liposuction: case reports and review of the literature." *Journal of Forensic Science*, January 2002, 47(1):205–207; "Consumer Reports on Health." Consumers Union of U.S., Inc., March 1998.

Litter Boxes: Reese, R. E. Betts, R. F. *A Practical Approach to Infectious Diseases*. Little, Brown, 1996; Fiery, Ann. *The Complete and Totally True Book of Urban Legends*. Running Press Books, 2001.

Lockjaw: Sanford, J. P. "Tetanus—forgotten but not gone." *New England Journal of Medicine*, March 23 1995, Lee, H. C., Ko, W. C. "Tetanus of the elderly." *Journal of Microbiology and Immunological Infections*, September 2000; 33(3): 191–6.

Loud Music: "Hearing Impaired Substance Abusers." *ALMACAN Newsletter*, April 1983; Sataloff, R. T. "Occupational Hearing Loss." Marcel Dekker, Inc. Publications, 1993; "American Academy of Otolaryngology Committee on Hearing and Equilibrium on the Medical Aspects of Noise." *Journal of the American Medical Association*, 1979, 241; Florentine, Mary. "On the Behavioral Characteristics of Loud-Music Listening." *Ear & Hearing*. December 1998; 19(6):420–428; Muller, Judy. "Sonic Bullets to be Acoustic Weapons of the Future." ABCNEWS.com, retrieved March 12, 2003; Locke, Michael, M.D. "Hearing Impairment." eMedicine.com, August 14, 2004.

Lyme Disease: Barbour, A.G. *Lyme Disease: The Cause, the Cure, the Controversy.* The Johns Hopkins University Press, 1996; Burgdorfer, W. "How the discovery of Borrelia Burgdorferi came about." *Clinical Dermatology*, July–September, 1993 11(3):335–338; Hanrahan, J. P., et al. "Spirochetes isolated from the blood of two patients with Lyme disease." *New England Journal of Medicine*, 1983, 308:740–742.

Malls: Aronson, Stanley M., M.D. "Grandma, her shiny buick, and the marketplace." *Journal of Rhode Island Medical Society*, September 2003; Duany, Andrés, Plater-Zyberk, Elizabeth. *Suburban Nation: The rise of sprawl and the decline of the American Dream.* North Point Press, 2000; "Traffic Safety in the New Millennium: Strategies for Law." National Highways & Safety Administration: DOT HS 809 758, 1998.

Marathons: Franklin, B. A., Bonzheim, K. "Snow shoveling: a trigger for acute myocardial infarction and sudden coronary death." *American Journal of Cardiology*, 1996, 77:855–858; Bassler, T. J. "More on immunity to atherosclerosis in marathon runners." *New England Journal of Medicine* 299:301, July 27, 1978; Kolata, Gina. "Runners' lore doesn't hold water." *New York Times News Service*, April 14, 2004; Frere, Jennifer A., et al. "The Risk of Death in Running Road Races." *The Physician and Sports Medicine*, April 2004 vol. 32, no. 4.

Marijuana: Zimmer, Lynn. "Marijuana Myths, Marijuana Facts." Lindesmith Center, 2001; Mittleman, M. A. et al. "Triggering myocardial infarction by marijuana." *Circulation*, 2001, 103:2805–2809; Singh, G. K. "Atrial fibrillation associated with marijuana use." *Pediatric Cardiology* 2000, 21:284; Hayes, John. "Dr. John S. Pemberton (inventor of Coca-Cola)." *Nation's Restaurant News*, February 30, 1996.

Mascots: Sahadi, Jeanne. "Six-Figure Jobs for Spring Training." *Money*, February 22, 2005; Kava, Brad. "Behind the Bright Lights." *Mercury News*, September 3, 2004; Peters, Jessica. "No compassion necessary for mascot-assaulting Simon." *The Stanford Daily*, July 17, 2003; Sports Illustrated Staff. "A history of bizarre mascot incidents." *Sports Illustrated*, July 10, 2003; Mussenden, Sean. "Disney Float Kills Costumed Worker." *Orlando Sentinel*, February 11, 2004.

Masturbation: Adams, Karl. *Marathon Masturbation.* Chatsworth, California: Helios, 1979; Bechtel, L. S.,

Westerfield, C., Eddy, J. M. "Auto-erotic fatalities: Implications for health educators." *Journal of Health Education*, 2001, 38–42; Dietz, P. E., O'Halloran, R. "Autoerotic fatalities with power hydraulics." *Journal of Forensic Sciences*, 2:1996, 359–364; Dietz, P. E., "Autoerotic asphyxia in the United States." *Journal of Forensic Sciences* 40(4):574–581. "Killer of Youth," quoted from Tiisot, Samuel-August. *Onania, or the heinous sin of self-pollution, and all its frightful consequences in both sexes considered.* London, 1715.

Mental Research: Vankin, Jonathan. *The 60 Greatest Conspiracies of All Time.* Citadel Press, 1997; McCarthy, Coleman. "The Consequences of Covert Tactics." *Washington Post*, December 13, 1987; Clorfene, Liane Casten. "Anatomy of a Cover-Up: The Dioxin File." *The Nation,* November 30, 1992; Scull, Andrew. *Madhouse: A Tragic Tale of Megalomania and Modern Medicine.* Yale University Press, 2005; McCarthy, C. R. "Historical background of clinical trials involving women and minorities." *Academy of Medicine.* September 1994, 69(9): 695–698. National Library of Medicine; Lederer, Susan. *Subjected to Science: Human Experimentation in America after the Second World War.* Johns Hopkins University Press, 1995; Jones, James H. *Bad Blood: the Tuskegee Syphilis Experiment.* Collier Macmillan, 1981; Rutz, Carol. *A Nation Betrayed: The Chilling True Story of Secret Cold War Experiments Performed on Our Children and Other Innocent People.* Fidelity Publishing, 2001.

Meteors: Aherns, T. J., O'Keefe, J. D. "Large impact craters on the Earth." Abstracts for the international workshop on meteorite impact on the early Earth, LPI Contribution, 1990, vol. 746, 3; Ceplecha, Z. "Influx of interplanetary bodies onto Earth." *Astronomy & Astrophysics*, 1992, 263: 361–366; Ward, S. N. "Asteroid impact tsunami: A probabilistic hazard assessment." *Icarus*, 2000, 145:64-xx; Tate, Jay. "Avoiding collisions." The Spaceguard Foundation. *Space Policy*, 2000, 16:261–265.

Microwave Popcorn: Armour, Stephanie. "Is butter flavoring ruining popcorn workers' lungs?" *USA Today.* September 6, 2002. Moy, Chelsi. "Yatsko widow sues for 'popcorn lung.'" *Great Falls Tribune,* July 17, 2005.

Microwaves: Bass, Gordon. "Radar: Is Your Cell Phone Killing You?" *PC/Computing*; December 1999; Marcus, Alan I., Segal, Howard P. *Technology in America: A Brief History.* Harcourt Brace Jovanovich, 1989; Sumnu, G. "A review on microwave baking of foods." *International Journal of Food Science and Technology*, 2003, 36, 117–127; Garcia-Viguera, C. "Phenolic compounds content in edible parts of broccoli inflorescences after domestic cooking." *Journal of the Science of Food and Agriculture*, 2003, vol. 83(14).

Migraine: Gardner, K. "The genetic basis of migraine: how much do we know?" *Canada Review of Neurological Science*, November 26 1999; Sacks, Oliver. *Migraines.* Vintage, 1999; et. al. Migraine: "It's Not All In Your Head." *Journal of Heath*, Vol. 2 No. 3 March, 1993. Staff eds. "Picasso joins the list." *Headache News Newsletter*, American Council for Headache Education, September 2000; Benson, Michael, ed. *Who's Who in the JFK Assassination: An A-to-Z Encyclopedia.* Citadel Press, 1993; Hersh, Seymour. *The Dark Side of Camelot.* Back Bay Books, 1998.

Mobile Office: Bahls, Steven C., Bahls, Jane Easter "Dead Man's Curve." *Entrepreneur*, July 2000; "Even No-Hands Cell Phones in Moving Vehicles Hazardous: Researchers Point to Distraction of Conversation Itself." *Insurance Advocate*, February 26, 2000, 43; Royal, D. "National Survey of Distracted Driving." National Highway Traffic Safety Administration, 2003, Report # S 03-0833.

Molasses Drowning: Puleo, Stephen. *Dark Tide: The Great Boston Molasses Flood of 1919*. Beacon Press, 2003; Boston Duck Tours, Boston, Massachusetts: oral history: July 2004.

Mosquitoes: White, William, Jr., White, Sara Jane. *A Mosquito is Born*. New York: Sterling Publishing, 1978; Reese, Ron. *Mosquito*. Utah: Aro Publishing Company, 1975; Huang, Kevin. "Malaria." *Insecta Inspecta World*, 1999; Beasley, D. W. C., Davis, C. T., et al. "Molecular determinants of virulence of West Nile virus in North America." *Archives of Virology*, 2004; 18:35-41; Noble, Elmer R., Noble, Glenn A., Schad, Gerhard A. MacInnes, Austin J. *Parasitology*. London: Lea & Febiger, 1989; Joseph M. Conlon, American Mosquito Control Association: correspondence September 2003.

Music Business: Corvette, Nikki. *Rock 'N' Roll Heaven: The Deaths and Lives of Musical Legends from the Big Bopper to Kurt Cobain*. Boulevard Books, 1997; Katz, Gary J. *Death By Rock & Roll: The Untimely Deaths of the Legends of Rock*. Carol Publishing Group, 1995; Pike, Jeff. *The Death of Rock 'N' Roll: Untimely Demises, Morbid Preoccupations and Premature Forecasts of Doom in Pop Music*. Faber and Faber, 1993.

Narcissism: Parish, James Robert. *Hollywood Celebrity Death Book*. Pioneer Books, 2002; Golomb, Elan. *Trapped in the Mirror: Adult Children of Narcissists in Their Struggle for Self*. Quill, 1995; Freud, S. "Three Essays on the Theory of Sexuality (1905)." *Standard Edition of the Complete Psychological Works of Sigmund Freud*, vol. 7. London: Hogarth Press, 1964; Million, Theodore. *Personality Disorders in Modern Life*. John Wiley, 2000; Crowe, Dominic. "Gallant of 'Goofus and Gallant' Fame Dead." *Arts & Entertainment, The Rail, #15, 2002*.

Narcolepsy: Aldrich, M. S. "Diagnostic aspects of narcolepsy." *Neurology*, 1998, 50(2 Suppl 1):S2–S7; US Xyrem Multicenter Study Group. "Sodium oxybate demonstrates long-term efficacy for the treatment of cataplexy in patients with narcolepsy." *Sleep Medicine*, 2004, 119–123; Benbadis, S. R. "Daytime sleepiness: when is it normal? When to refer?" *Cleveland Clinic Journal of Medicine*, 1998, 65:543–549; Roth, B., et al. "A study of 124 narcoleptics: clinical aspects." *Archives of Neurology and Psychiatry*, 1988, 139(4):41–51.

Native Americans: Shoemaker, Nancy. *American Indian population Recovery in the Twentieth Century*. University of New Mexico Press, 1999; Nardo, Don. *The Indian Wars*. Lucent Books, 1991; Jackson, Robert H. *Indian population decline: the missions of northwestern New Spain, 1687–1840*. University of New Mexico Press, 1995.

Needlesticks: Hanchett, Marilyn, R.N. "A new approach to needle safety primary prevention." *Managing Infection Control*, March 2002; Bierman, Steve, M.D. "Needlestick injuries." *Compliance Magazine*, February 2003;

"Updates: transmission of human immunodeficiency virus (HIV) and hepatitis B virus (HBV) in the health-care setting." *Morbidity and Mortality Weekly Report*, June 29, 2005/50 (RR-11).

Nephritis: Grande, J. P. "Mechanisms of progression of renal damage in lupus nephritis." *Lupus*, 1998, 7(9):604–610; Duley, I. "Understanding and Living with Autosomal Dominant Polycystic Kidney Disease." *Journal of Polycystic Kidney Research Foundation*, 1995; Greene, Wade. "Guru of the Organic Food Cult." *New York Times Magazine*, June 6, 1971.

Nonstick Pans: Burros, Marian. "Is there an extra ingredient in nonstick pans?" *New York Times*, August 20, 2005; U.S. "Urged to Put Warning Labels on Non-stick Cookware." *Reuters*, May 15, 2003; Wrenn, K. "Carbon monoxide poisoning during ice storms: a tale of two cities." *Journal of Emergency Medicine*, July-August 1997, 15(4).

Nostalgia: Anspach, Carolyn Kiser. "Medical Dissertation on Nostalgia by Johannes Hofer, 1688." *Bulletin of the History of Medicine*, 2 [1934] 376–391; Jackson, Stanley. *Melancholia and Depression: From Hippocritic Times to Modern Times.* Yale University Press, 1986.

Nuclear Research: Libby, Leona Marshall. *The Uranium People.* Charles Scribner's Sons, 1979; Rhodes, Richard. *The Making of the Atomic Bomb.* Simon & Schuster, 1986; Eisler, Pete. "The fallout of nuclear fallout." *USA Today*, January 21, 2005.

Obesity: Fiedler, Leslie. *Freaks: Myths and Images of the Secret Self.* New York: Simon & Schuster, 1978; Arrigo, Bruce. *Punishing the Mentally Ill: A Critical Analysis of Law and Psychiatry.*

State University of New York Press, 2002; Coletta, Paolo Enrico. *The Presidency of William Taft.* University Press of Kansas, 1973. Townley, Bruce. "Morbidly obese man." Retrieved from: http://asylumeclectica.com., October 5, 1999.

Octopus and Squid: MacKenzie, Debora. "Seismic surveys may kill giant squid." *New Scientist*, September 2004; Puente, Maria. "Testing Waters to Learn More about Giant Squid." *USA Today*, February 1, 1996; Holger, Jannasch. "Life at the Sea Floor." *Nature,* April 1995; Brookesmith, Peter, ed. *Creatures from Elsewhere: Weird Animals That No-One Can Explain.* London: Orbis Publishing, 1984; Conniff, Richard. "Clyde Roper Can't Wait to be Attacked by the Giant Squid." *Smithsonian*, May 1996, 126–136.

Oil Rig: Greenhouse, Steve. "165 Feared dead from oil rig blast." *New York Times*, July 8, 1988; Frieman, Fran Loucher. *Failed technology: true stories of technological disasters.* New York: ITP, 1995: Urquhart, Frank. "Offshore oil industry warned it needs to move faster to improve safety." *The Scotsman,* August 2005.

Old Age: Montaigne, Michel de. *The Complete Essays of Montaigne.* Trans. Donald Frame Stanford. Stanford University Press, 1965; Litton, Robert Jay. *The Broken Connection: On Death and the Continuity of Life.* New York: Simon & Schuster, 1979.

Oral Sex: Blue, Violet. *The Ultimate Guide to Cunnilingus.* Cleis Press, 2002; Weidman, Susan. "They Say It's Not Sex; But experts call it an oral sex epidemic." *Lilith*, January 2004; Orebaugh, S. L. "Venous air embolism:

clinical and experimental considerations." *Critical Care Medicine*, August 1992, 20(8)1169-1177.

Organ Snatchers: Rother, Larry. "The Organ Trade: A Global Black Market—Tracking the Sale of a Kidney on a Path of Poverty and Hope." *New York Times*, May 23, 2004; Stamatis, George. "Blacks and poor more likely to be organ donors than receivers." *Medical News Today*, December 7, 2004; Kaserman, David L. *US Organ Procurement System.* American Enterprise Institute Press, 2002; "Illegal Trade in Human Organs." National Human Rights Commission: D.O.No.11/5/2001-PRP&P; de Castro, L. D. "Human organs from prisoners: kidneys for life." *Journal of Medical Ethics*, 2003, 29:171-175.

Outer Space: Asimov, Issac. *How We Found Out About Outer Space.* Fitchenryl and Whiteside, 1977; Fox, Mary. *Inventors and Inventions: Rockets.* Benchmark Books, 1996; Murray, Bruce. *Journey Into Space: The First Three Decades of Space Exploration.* W. W. Norton, 1990; NASA history: http://history.nasa.gov/.

Outlaws: Cromie, Robert. *Dillinger: A Short and Violent Life.* McGraw-Hill, 1962; Nash, Jay Robert. *Bloodletters and Badmen.* M. Evans and Company, 1995; Borus, Daniel H., ed. *These United States—Portraits of America From the 1920s.* Cornell University Press, 1992; Treherne, John. *The Strange History of Bonnie and Clyde.* Cooper Square Press, 2000. Ray Hamilton quoted from: Henderson, Jordon, et al. "The Inside Story of the Killing of Bonnie Parker and Clyde Barrow." *True Detective Mysteries Magazine*, November 1934.

Overpasses: Reddig, Mark H. "Bowling ball strikes, but trucker is spared." *Land Line Magazine,* November 2004; TranSafety, Inc., "Ohio DOT Negligent in Failing to Install Fencing on Freeway Overpass in a Timely Manner." *Road Injury Prevention & Litigation Journal*, November 1997.

Over-the-Counter: Horn, J. "Pharmacology of over-the-counter analgesics used for the treatment of headache." *Headache,* 1994; Singh, G. "Complications of Prescription and Over-the-Counter of Nonsteroidal Anti-Inflammatory Drugs: A View from the ARAMIS Database." *American Journal of Therapeutics*, 2000; Morgan, H. Wayne. *Drugs in America: A Social History, 1800–1980.* Syracuse University Press, 1981; Burak, L. J. "College students' use of widely advertised medications." *Journal of American College Health*, 2000, 49(3):118-121, Gzesh, Jennifer. "Cough syrup ingredient deadly." *Daily Illinois News*, August 23, 2004; Beck, Melinda, Agrest, Susan. "Again, a Tylenol Killer." *Newsweek*, February 24, 1986; Consumers Union Staff Editors. "Dangerous Supplement Still at Large." *Consumer Reports*, May 2004; "Acetaminophen Toxicity in Children." *American Academy of Pediatrics*, October 2001, vol. 108, no. 4, 1020–1024.

Parkinson's: Raskin, S. A, Borod, J. C. "Neuropsychological aspects of Parkinson's disease." *Neuropsychology Review*, September 1990, 1(3):185-221; Mosley, Anthony, D.M.D. *The Encyclopedia of Parkinson's Disease.* Facts on File, 2004.

Plastic Making: Fenichell, Stephen. *Plastic: The Making of a Synthetic Century.* New York: HarperBusiness, 1996; Deegan, J., Jr. "Looking Back at Love Canal, New York USA." *Environmental Science Technology*, 1987, 21(4): 328-331, Paigen, B., et. al. "Prevalence of health problems in children living in the Love Canal, Hazardous Waste and Hazardous Material." Environmental Protection Agency: 1985, 2(1):23-43; Moyers, Bill. *Global Dumping Ground.* Seven Locks Press, 1990; Ember, Lois. "Love Canal Cleaned Up." *Chemical & Engineering News*, March 19, 2004.

Platform Shoes: Rossi, W. A. *The sexlife of the foot and shoe.* Krieger Publishing, 1993; Meyerson, Mark. *Foot and Ankle Disorders.* W. B. Saunders, 2000; Steele, Valerie. *Shoes: a Lexicon of Style.* London: Scriptum, 1998; Ledger, Florence E. *Put Your Foot Down: a Treatise on the History of Shoes.* C. Venton Publishers, 1985; Getzlaff, J. A. "Platform shoes get the boot in Osaka." Salon.com, retrieved February 16, 2000.

Playgrounds: Weintraub, Rachel. "Playing It Safe: The Sixth Nationwide Safety Survey of Public Playgrounds." *U.S. PIRG Reports*, June 20, 2002; Phelan, K. J., et al. "Trends and patterns of playground injuries in United States children and adolescents." *Ambulatory Pediatrics*, 2001, 1(4), 227-233; Tinsworth, D., McDonald, J. "Special Study: Injuries and Deaths Associated with Children's Playground Equipment." U.S. Consumer Product Safety Commission, February, 2001.

Poisonous Spiders: Royston, H. *The Book of Spiders.* Eagle Editions, 1998; Langley, R. L. "Deaths resulting from animal attacks in the United States." *Wilderness Environmental Medicine*, 1997; 8:8–16; Boyer, Hassen L. V. "Spider bites." *Wilderness Medicine: Management of Wilderness and Environmental Emergencies*, 1995, 1769–1786; Vetter, R. S., Barger, D. K. "An infestation of 2,055 brown recluse spiders (Araneae: Sicariidae): implications for bite diagnoses in nonendemic areas." *Journal of Medical Entomology*, November 2002, 39(6): 948–51; Sams, H. H., et al. "Nineteen documented cases of Loxosceles reclusa envenomation." *Journal of the American Academy of Dermatology*, April 2001, 44(4):603–608.

Poland's Syndrome: Jay, Ricky. *Jay's Journal of Anomalies.* Farrar, Straus and Giroux, 2001; Norman, Tom. *The Penny Showman: Memoirs of Tom Norman "Silver King."* G. B. Norman-Noakes, 1985; Marks. M. W., et al. "Management of deformity in male patients with Poland's syndrome." *Plast Reconstr Surg*, April 1991, 87(4): 674–678; Rosen, Fred. *Lobster Boy.* Pinnacle Books, 2002.

Police Training: Cunningham, W. C., Taylor, T. H. *The Hallcrest report I: Private security and police in America.* Butterworth-Heinemann, 1991; Pearsall, Susan. "To Shoot, or Not to Shoot? Now, Decide in 2.9 Seconds." *New York Times*, July 18, 1999; "Census of Fatal Occupational Injuries: Operating Manual 1992–2002." U.S. Department of Labor, Bureau of Labor Statistics; "Fallen Heroes Report." National Law Officers Memorial Fund, 2004. NLEOMF: Washington, D.C; Floyd, Craig W. "Deputy Sheriff Isaac Smith: America's First Law Enforcement Fatality." *NLEOMF Newsletter*, August 3, 2000.

Potluck Dinners: Church, Barbara. "Flawed regulator blamed in oxygen-tank fire." *The Chief*, May 1, 1999; Suarez-Penaranda, J. M., et al. "Planned Complex Suicide: Unusual Suicides by hanging and gunshots." *American Journal of Forensic Medicine & Pathology*, March 1997, 18(1): 104–106.

Prostitution: Bullough, Vern L. "Making It Work: The Prostitutes' Rights Movement in Perspective." *Journal of Sex Research*, February 1, 1994; Adams, G. "Sex in Old New York." *American Mercury*, 1941, vol. 52; Adler, Michael. "The Terrible Peril. A Historical Perspective on the Venereal Diseases." *British Medical Journal*, 1980, vol. 2, 201–212; Zuger, Abigail. "Many Prostitutes Suffer Combat Disorder, Study Finds." *New York Times*, August 18, 1999; "Prostitution: A Violent Reality of Homelessness." *Chicago Coalition For Homeless Study*, May 23, 2001.

Purse Snatching: Metro Datelines: "2 More Held in Death of a Suspected Thief." *New York Times*, March 29, 1988; "Fatalities by industry and event." U.S. Department of Labor. CFTB 0155 Table A-1: 1965–2003.

Q-Fever: Nesterov, Andrey. "After sex with sheep, don't kill the animal!" *Pravada*, April 4, 2004; Levy, P. Y., et al. "Coxiella burnetii: report of 15 cases and review." *Clinical Infectious Disorder*, August 1999, 29(2):393–397; "Man gets probation in animal molesting case at Charleston Nativity Scene." *Charleston Daily Mail*, July 23, 2003; Freinhar, J. P. "A prevalence study of bestiality (zoophilia) in psychiatric in-patients, medical in-patients, and psychiatric staff." *International Journal of Psychosombology*, 1991, 38(1–4): 45–47; Fauber, John. "Families left to ponder connection after deaths of three participants." *Milwaukee Journal Sentinel*, July 20, 2002.

Quacks: Siwolop, Sana. "That Quest to Enhance Beauty Can Leave Scars." *New York Times*, July 14, 2002; Wills, Larry. "Dr. Fake: The phony degree industry is exploding in Nevada and beyond." *Las Vegas Mercury*, January 1, 2004; Bruno, Richard L., Ph.D. "Devotees, pretenders and wanna-bes: Two cases of (Apotemnophilia) Factitious Disability Disorder." *Journal of Sexuality and Disability*, 1997, 15:243–260.

Quality Time: Powell, Morgan. *Plugging Cisterns, Cesspools, Septic Tanks, and Other Holes.* Kansas State University Press, 1998. Weishuhn, Larry L. "There's No Place Like Home: Abandoned Outhouses." *Progressive Farmer*, October 2002; Sussman, Charles. "Death Highlights Cesspool Danger." *New York Post*, September 5, 2001.

Quinsy: Cowan, D. L., Hibbert, J. "Acute and chronic infection of the pharynx and tonsils." *Scott-Brown's Otolaryngology*, 5th ed., McGraw-Hill, 1997; Scheidemandel, Heinz, H. E., M.D. "Did George Washington Die of Quinsy?" *Archives of the Journal of Otorhinolaryngology*, September 1976; (102), 519–521, Starr, Paul. *The Social Transformation of American Medicine.* Basic Books, 1982; Middaugh, J, M.D. "Side Effects of Diphtheria." *American Journal of Public Health*, March 1979, vol. 69, no. 3.

Rabbits: "Jack rabbits attack walkers in Sonoma County: man bitten, woman forced to evade jack rabbit." Associated Press, March 29, 2002; Brogan, T., et al. "Severe dog bites in children." *Pediatrics*, 1995; 96, 950; Krebs, J. W., et al. "Rabies surveillance in the United States during 1999." *Journal of American Veterinary Medical Association*, December 15, 2000, 217.

Rat-Bite Fever: Cunningham, B., et al. "Rat bite fever in a pet lover." *Journal of American Academy of Dermatology*, February 1998, 38:330–332; Richter, C. P. "Incidence of rat bites and rat bite fever in Baltimore." *Journal of the American Medical Association*, 128: 324, 1945; Holden, P. "Rat Bite Fever—an occupational hazard." *Canadian Medical Association Journal*, 91:78–81; Sullivan, Robert. *Rats: Observations on the History and Habitat of the City's Most Unwanted Inhabitants.* Bloomsbury, 2005.

Raw Meat: Taege, A. J. "Listeriosis: recognizing it, treating it, preventing it." *Cleveland Clinical Journal of Medicine*, June 1999, 66(6): 75–80; Mishu, B., et al. "Outbreaks of Salmonella enteritidis infections in the United States, 1985–1991." *Journal of Infectious Diseases*, 1994, 169:547–552; Ferllini, Roxana. *Silent Witness: How Forensic Anthropology is Used to Solve the World's Toughest Crimes.* Firefly Books, 2002; O'Meara, Kelly Patricia. "School Lunches Causing Illness." *Insight Magazine/The Washington Times,* April 4, 2000.

Record Breakers: "Man Dies Trying to Set Record Scaling Brooklyn Bridge." Associated Press, April 3, 1999; Gould, Philip J. *The Book of Alternative Records.* Metro Books, 2004; *Guinness World Records 2006.* Guinness, 2005; "Pedestrian Synthesis Report (1997)." U.S. Department of Transportation, Federal Highway Administration.

Restaurants: Mead, Paul S., et al. "Food-Related Illness and Death in the United States." Centers for Disease Control and Prevention, September 2004, vol. 5. no. 5; Martinage, Moria. *Cannibal Killers.* St. Martin's Paperbacks, 1993; Pennington, Piers. *The Great Explorers.* J. G. Ferguson Publishing Company, 1979.

Restless Leg Syndrome: Bonati, M. T., et al. "Autosomal dominant restless legs syndrome maps on chromosome 14q." *Brain*, 2003, 126(Pt 6):1485–1492; Trenkwalder, C., et al. "Positron emission tomographic studies in restless legs syndrome." *Movement Disorder*, 1999, 14(1):141–145; Restless Leg Syndrome Foundation: http://www.rls.org/.

Revolving Doors: Laeger, U. "Crush accidents in mechanical revolving doors." *Journal of the National Library of Medicine*, January 2, 1989, 151(1): 33; Yang, Jean. "Revolution & Evolution: A Discourse on Revolving Doors." *The Harvard Independent*, November 11, 2004; Bull, Charlotte. "Company sentenced after worker crushed to death." *Journal of Occupational Safety and Health Service*, August 15, 2002.

Rice Cakes: "Japanese choke on New's Food." Associated Press, January 2, 1999; "New Year's Mochi Death Toll Mounts." *Mainichi Daily News* (English version), January 3, 2005; O'Flynn, P. "Fish bones and other foreign bodies." *Clinical Otolaryngology*, June 1993, 18(3): 231–233; "Choking deaths," *Morbidity & Mortality Weekly Report*, vol. 54, No. 34; Karling, J. S. *The Great American Chewing Gum Book.* Chilton Book Company, 1942.

Riot Acts: Barry, Kathleen. *Susan B. Anthony: A Biography of a Singular Feminist.* New York University Press, 1988; Banner, Lois W. *Elizabeth Cady Stanton: A Radical for Woman's Rights.* Little, Brown, 1998; Headley, Joel Tyler. *The Great Riots of New York, 1712–1873.* Bobbs Merrill, 1970; Genovese, Eugene D. *From Rebellion to Revolution: Afro-American Slave Revolts in the Making of the Modern World.* Louisiana State University Press, 1979; Katz, William Loren. "The New York City Draft Riots of 1863." *New*

York Amsterdam News, 94, 2003; Yearley, Clifton K., Jr. "The Baltimore and Ohio Railroad Strike of 1877." *Maryland Historical Magazine*, September 1956, 61, no. 3; Knopf, T. A. "Race, Riots, and Reporting." *Journal of Black Studies*, 1974, 4:303–327; Dean Albertson, ed. *Rebels or Revolutionaries? Student Movements of the 1960's.* Simon & Schuster, 1975; Gooding-Williams, Robert. *Reading Rodney King—Reading Urban Uprising.* Routledge, 1993.

Road Debris: Scopatz, Robert A., Ph.D., et al. "Longer Combination Vehicle Safety Data Collection." *AAA Foundation for Traffic Safety*, July 2005; D'Aniello, Dana. "Road Debris Causes 25,000 Crashes a Year." Associated Press, September 7, 2004.

Road Rage: Joint, Matthew. "Road Rage." *AAA Foundation for Traffic Safety*, April 26, 2002; Daw, J. "Road rage, air rage, and now 'desk rage.'" *Monitor on Psychology*, July/August 2001, 52–54.

Rodeo: "Cowboy Up! One Hundred Years of Rodeo." *Journal of Nevada Historical Society*, May 2001; Haney, C. Allen. "Rodeo injuries: an examination of risk factors." *Journal of Sport Behavior*, December 1999, vol. 22, 443–466; Royce, Lee. "Where the buffalo roam . . . keep your distance." *Sports Afield*, September 2001.

Roller Coasters: Adams, Judith A. *The American Amusement Park Industry: A History of Technology & Thrills.* Twayne Publishers, 1991; Larkin, M. "Are amusement park rides bad for the brain?" *The Lancet Neurology*, 2002, 1(5):274; "Deaths and Injuries Associated with Amusement Rides." U.S. Product Safety Commission, 1972–1993: 1993–2003; Costanza, Jared.

"Ride Accidents (http://www.ride accidents.com/).

Sand and Surf: Maron, M. "Sudden Death and Other Risks Associated With Dry-Sand Beach Holes." *Journal of the American Medical Association*, 2001: 285, 964; Moir, C., M.D., et al. "Accidental Burials in Sand: A Potentially Fatal Summertime Hazard." *Mayo Clinical Proceedings*, 2004, 79: 774–776.

Scorpions: Greenfeld, Lawrence A. "Women Offenders." Bureau of Justice Special Report, December 5, 1999; Amitai, Y., et al. "Scorpion sting in children. A review of 51 cases." *Clinical Pediatrics*, March 1985, 24(3); Buchanan, P. "Death from Centruroides scorpion sting allergy." *Journal of Clinical Toxicology*, 2001: 39:561–562.

Sea Diving: Philip, R. B., et al. "Hematology and blood chemistry in saturation diving." *Undersea Biomedical Research*, December 1975, 2(4): 233–49; Uzun, C., et al. "Alternobaric vertigo in sport SCUBA divers and the risk factors." *Journal of Laryngology and Otology*, November 2003, 117(11); Dorsey, Florence. *Road to the Sea: The Story of James B. Eads and the Mississippi River.* Pelican, 1998; Fenner, P. J. "Venomous marine animals." *Spums*, December 2004, 34(4): 196–202; Newcomb, Richard F. *Abandon Ship! Death of the USS Indianapolis.* Holt, 1958; Gilbert, Carter R., "Annual Reports." International Shark Attack File (ISAF): American Elasmobranch Society and the Florida Museum of Natural History.

Serial Killers: Hickey, Eric, Ph.D. *Serial Murderers and Their Victims*, 4th ed., Wadsworth Publishers, 2005; Newton, Michael. *The Encyclopedia of Serial Killers.* Checkmark Books, 2000; Lane, Brian, Gregg, Wilfred. *The Encyclopedia of Serial Killers.* Berkeley, 1995; Schechter, Harold. *Depraved: The Shocking True Story of America's First Serial Killer.* Pocket, 1994.

Sexually Transmitted Disease: Chevallier, Eric. *The Condom: 3000 Years of Safer Sex.* Puffin Books, 1995; Tone, A. *Devices and Desires: A History of Contraceptives in America.* Hill and Wang, 2002; Hayden, Deborah. *Pox: Genius, Madness, and the Mysteries of Syphilis.* Basic Books, 2004; Bergreen, Laurence. *Capone: The Man and the Era.* Simon & Schuster, 1994; Fielding, R., et al. "Sexually transmitted infections: implications for prevention and control." *Clinical Infectious Disorders*, 2004, 39:533–538. Stow, John. *Annales of England.* London, 1592, reprinted by Offices of the Society, London, 1910.

Siamese Twins: "Chang and Eng Bunker Papers." Inventory (#3761) Manuscripts Department, Wilson Library, University of North Carolina at Chapel Hill; Watt, H. "Conjoined Twins: Separation as Mutilation." *Medical Legal Review*, 2001, 237–245; Beardsley, Laura E. "Body Doubles: Siamese Twins in Fact and Fiction." Mutter Museum, Philadelphia, Spring 1995.

Sick Building Syndrome: Goldman, R. "Problem buildings: building-associated illness and the sick building syndrome." *Occupational Medicine*, 1989. "Recognition and Management of Health Effects Related to Mold Exposure and Moisture Indoors." Center for Indoor Environments and Health: U.S. Environmental Protection Agency, September 30,

2004; Amsden, G. W. "Treatment of Legionnaires' disease." *Drugs*, 2005, 65(5); Bowker, Michael. *Fatal Deception: How Big Business is Still Killing Us with Asbestos.* Touchstone, 2003.

Sidewalk Cafés: "Reclaiming the Sidewalks." *Transportation Alternatives* (TA), October 2004; "Boxed In on the Sidewalks of New York." *TA Bulletin*, June 9, 2004; Heineman, Hannah. "35 Hospitalized After Market Mayhem." *Santa Monica Mirror*, July 23, 2004; Rugeley, Cindy. "Blood Bath in Killian." *Houston Chronicle*, October 17, 1991; "Drunk rider ruling stirs scorn." BBC News, September 24, 2004.

Sinkholes: Ehgartner, B. L. "Mine-induced Sinkholes Over the U.S. Strategic Reserve." Report SAND95-1661C. Sandia National Laboratories, Albuquerque, New Mexico, October 1995; Schmidt, Walter. "Geologic and geotechnical Assessment for the Evaluation of Sinkholes." Florida Geological Survey Open-File Report 72, 1997; Beck, B. F., Sinclair, W. C. "Sinkholes in Florida." Report No. 85–86–4, FSRI/UCF, U.S. Geological Survey, 1995.

Sitting in Coach: Ball, Kay. "Deep vein thrombosis and airline travel—the deadly duo." *AORN Journal*, February, 2003; Ramzi, D.W., et al. "DVT and pulmonary embolism Diagnosis." *American Family Physician*, June 15, 2004, 69(12); Battaglio, Stephen. "NBC reporter Bloom dies in Iraq." *New York Daily News,* April 7, 2003.

Sky Surfing: Dwiggins, Don. *Bailout: The Story of Parachuting and Skydiving.* London: Crowell-Collier Press, 1969; Krulewitz, Josh. "Generation Ex: Extreme Games." *American Fitness,* September, 1994; Ogilvie,

Bruce. "Clinical Issues in Sports Medicine." *Sports Medicine*, March 1, 2001, vol. 31, no. 3.

Sleep Terrors: Chervin, R. D., et al. "Sleepwalking and sleep terrors: what triggers them?" *Pediatrics*, January 2003, 111(1); Siegel, J. M. "Why we sleep." *Scientific American*, November 2003, 289(5); Young, T., et al. "The occurrence of sleep-disordered breathing (Ondine's Curse) among middle-aged adults." *New England Journal of Medicine*, April 29, 1993, 328(17): 1230–1235.

Sleepwalkers: Hublin, C., Kaprio, J., Partinen, M. "Prevalence and genetics of sleepwalking: a population-based twin study." *Neurology*, January 1997, 48(1):77–81; Zucconi. M., et al. "Nocturnal paroxysmal arousals with motor behaviors during sleep." *Journal of Clinical Neurophysiology*, November 1997, 14(6):513–522; Robin, G. "Evolution of the Sleepwalking Defense: Welcome to the Twilight Zone of Mental Illness, Psychiatry, and the Law." *Journal of Contemporary Criminal Justice*, August 13, 1997: 224–235; Allison, Kelly C. *Overcoming Night Eating Syndrome*. New Harbinger Publications, 2004.

Smoking: Gately, Iain. *Tobacco: A Cultural History of How an Exotic Plant Seduced Civilization*. Grove Press, 2003; Tate, Cassandra. *Cigarette Wars*. Oxford University Press, 2000; "Cigarette Smoking-Attributable Morbidity—United States." *Morbidity and Mortality Weekly Report*, September 5, 2003.

Snake Handlers: Norris, R. L. Jr. "North American Venomous Reptile Bites." *Wilderness Medicine: Management of Wilderness and Environmental Emergencies* 1995, 3:680–709; Brown, Fred. *The Serpent Handlers: Three Families and Their Faith*. John F. Blair Publisher, 2000; Kimbrough, David. *Taking Up Serpents: Snake Handlers of Eastern Kentucky*. Mercer University Press, 2002; "Pet python kills girl by coiling around neck." Associated Press, August 27, 2001.

Sneezing: Neugut, A., et al. "Anaphylaxis in the United States: An investigation into its epidemiology." *Archives of Internal Medicine*, 2001, 161 (1):15–21; Ray, N. F., et al. "Healthcare expenditures for sinusitis in 1996: contributions of asthma, rhinitis, and other airway disorders." *Journal of Allergy and Clinical Immunology*, 1999, 103 (3 pt. 1):408–414; Sampson, H. A. "Peanut Alergy." *New England Journal of Medicine*, 2002, 346:1294–1299; Vogue, Adalbert. *St. Gregory The Great*. St. Bede's Publications, 1969.

Snipers: National Violent Death Reporting System (NVDRS): CDC, 1985–2003; "Reported Sniper Attacks, 1982–2001": FBI, Summary of Uniform Crime Reporting System; Lavergne, Gary M. *A Sniper in the Tower: The True Story of the Texas Tower Massacre*. Bantam, 1997; Boorstein, Michelle. "Malvo Gets Two More Life Terms." *Washington Post*, October 27, 2004.

Snowboarding: Fact Sheet: "NSAA Report on Skiing/Snowboarding Safety 1992–2002." National Ski Areas Association, Lakewood, Colorado; Machold, W., et al. "Risk of injury through snowboarding." *Journal of Trauma*, 2000, 48:1109–1114, Koehle, M. S., et al. "Alpine ski injuries and their prevention." *Sports Medicine*, 2002, 32:785–793.

Spectators: Handwerk, Brian. "Sports Riots: The Psychology of Fan Mayhem." *National Geographic*, June 20, 2004; "Teenage girl dies after getting hit in the head." Associated Press,

March 20, 2002; Sugar, Bert. *The Baseball Maniac's Almanac.* McGraw-Hill, 2004; Brown, Adam. *Fanatics!: Power, Identity and Fandom in Football.* Routledge, 1998.

Sperm Allergy: Tsang, K. Y. "Evaluation of Transfer Factor potency and Prediction of Clinical Response." *Immunomodulation: New Frontiers and Advances,* 115–130. Plenum Press, 1984; Bernstein, Jonathan A. M.D. "Prevalence of Human Seminal Plasma Hypersensitivity Among Women." *Annals of Allergy and Asthma Immunology,* 1997-78:54–58; Bernstein, J., et al. "Is Burning Semen Syndrome a Variant Form of Seminal Plasma Hypersensitivity?" *Obstetric Gynecology,* 2003, 101:93–102.

Spontaneous Combustion: Arnold, Larry E. *Ablaze!: The Mysterious Fires of Spontaneous Human Combustion.* M. Evans and Company, 1996; Randals, Jenny. *Spontaneous Human Combustion.* Barnes & Noble, 2003; Harrison, Michael. *Fire from heaven: A study of spontaneous combustion in human beings.* Methuen, 1978; Blizin, Jerry. "The Cinder Woman." *St. Petersburg Times,* August 9, 1951.

Spring Break: Weschsler, Henry, et al. "College Alcohol Use: a Full or Empty Glass?" *Journal of American College Health,* May 1999 vol. 47, no. 6; "Spring Break in Mexico Fact Sheet, 2004." Mexico Embassy of the United States: U.S. Dept of State; Leinwand, Donna. "Alcohol-Soaked Spring Break Lures Students Abroad." *USA Today,* January 5, 2003; Naimi, T, et al. "Binge drinking among US adults." *Journal of the American Medical Association,* January 1, 2003.

Stage Fright: Hoff, Ron. *I Can See You Naked.* Andrews McMeel Publishing, 1992; Advanced Public Speaking Institute: http://www.public-speaking.org/; Schrof, Joannie M. "Why everyone gets stage fright." *U.S. News & World Report,* 126.24 June 21, 1999; Jarvis, Everett G. *Final Curtain: Deaths of Noted Movie and T.V. Personalities.* Carol Publishing Group, 1995; Parish, J. R. *Hollywood Celebrity Death Book.* Movie Publisher Services, 1993; Stern, M. F. *Celebrity Death Certificates.* McFarland & Company August 2003; Floethe, Steve. "News Anchor Commits Suicide." *Sarasota Herald Tribune,* July 15, 1974.

Stalking: Brewster, Mary P. "Needs of Former Intimate Stalking Victims." U.S. Department of Justice, National Institute of Justice: Washington, D.C., 1998; Mullen, Paul E., Pathe, Michele, Purcell, Rosemary, Stuart, Geoffrey W. "A Study of Stalkers." *American Journal of Psychiatry,* 1999, 156:1244-1249; "Syllabus by the Court: State of Kansas vs. Francis Patrick Doyle," No. 84,814. Supreme Court State of Kansas, January 25, 2002; Bruni, Frank. "Behind the Jokes, a Life Of Pain and Delusion; For Letterman Stalker, Mental Illness Was Family Curse and Scarring Legacy." *New York Times.* November 22, 1998; Sontag, D. "Clemency Given Jean Harris Leaves 3 Others Wondering." *New York Times.* January 1, 1993.

Stampedes: *Chronology—The worst stampedes of the 21st century.* Rueters, August 21, 2004; "Four men charged with manslaughter in Chicago nightclub stampede that killed 21." *Associated Press,* September 24, 2003; Brandt, Nat. *Chicago Death Trap: The Iroquois Theatre Fire of 1903.* Southern Illinois University Press, 2003.

Stowaways: "Man found dead in plane wheel well." *Reuters,* October 24, 2004; Fenner, Austin. "Stowaway's body parts rain down." *New York Daily News,* June 8, 2005; Ellingwood, Ken. *Hard Line: Life and Death on the U.S.-Mexico Border.* Pantheon, 2004; Davidson, M. *Lives on the Line: Dispatches from the U.S.-Mexico Border.*

Subways: Worth, R. "Woman Is Pushed Into the Path of No. 6 Train." *New York Times.* November 16, 2001; Barnes, J. "Second Murder Trial Opens in Subway Shoving Case." *New York Times,* March 4, 2000; Stevenson, Jed. "Another Death in Subway Surfing." *New York Times,* November 21, 2003.

Sudden Death: Futterman, L. G., et al. "Sudden cardiac death in athletes." *American Journal of Critical Care,* July 1999, 8(4); Anderson, R. "Commotio cordis. When sudden death isn't a sporting term." *Emergency Medical Service,* July 2003, 32(7); Litsky, Frank. "Collegiate Wrestling Deaths Raise Fears About Training." *New York Times,* December 19, 1997; Pandolfini, Bruce. *Pandolfini's Chess Complete: The Most Comprehensive Guide to the Game, from History to Strategy.* Fireside, 1992; Dean, John W. *Warren G. Harding.* Times Books, 2004.

Talk Shows: Scott, Gina G. *Can We Talk?: The Power and Influence of Talk Shows.* Insight Books Inc., 1996; Bronstad, Amanda. "Insurer blocked from passing buck on fees for Jenny Jones case." *Los Angeles Business Journal,* December 13, 2004; "Talk-show guest slain, police seek ex-husband and new wife." CNN.com, July 26, 2000; Albrecht, W. Steve, et al. *Fraud Examination and Prevention.* South-Western Educational Publications, 2003.

Taxis and Trucks: Lyman, S., Braver, E. R. "Occupant deaths in large truck crashes in the United States: 25 years of experience." *Accident Analysis and Prevention,* 2003, 731–739; Cohen, B., et al. "Mean Streets: Pedestrian Safety." Environmental Working Group, Inc., 1997–2003; Lueck, Thomas J. "Safety Issue Is Stressed by Cabbies in Bias Effort." *New York Times,* November 11, 1999.

Thanksgiving: Polacsek, Michele. "MADD Victim Impact Panels and Stages-of-Change in Drunk-Driving Prevention." *Journal of Studies on Alcohol,* 2001, vol. 62; "Thanksgiving Holiday Period Traffic Fatality Estimate, 1990–2004." National Safety Council; "Annual and New Year's Day Alcohol-Related Traffic Fatalities—United States, (1982–1990)–(1991–2002.)" *Morbidity and Mortality Weekly Report.*

Thrift Stores: "CPSC Study of Hazardous Products in Thrift Stores, Annual Reports, 1997–2002." Hazardous Analysis Division, U.S. Dept. of Consumer Safety.

Thyroid Disease: Arem, Ridha. *The Thyroid Solution.* New York: Ballantine, 1999; DeGroot, Leslie. "Graves' disease and the Manifestations of Thyrotoxicosis." *Thyroid Manager,* December 10, 2003; Mokdad, Ali H., et al. "Actual Causes of Death in the United States." *Journal of the American Medical Association,* 2004, 291:1238–1245.

Toaster: Cowan, Ruth Schwartz. "The industrial revolution in the home: household technology and social change in the 20th century." *Technology and culture,* January 1976 vol. 17; Cohen, Daniel. *The last hundred years, household technology.* Evans, 1982; Chowdary, R., et al. "Electrocution associated with consumer products." CPSC, 2001.

Toilet Time: Lambton, Lucinda. *Temples of Convenience—and Chambers of Delight.* Pavilion Books, 1998; Hart-Davis,

Adam. *Thunder, Flush and Thomas Crapper.* Trafalgar Square Publishing, 1997; Meyers, S., et al. "Choroidal hemorrhage after Valsalva's maneuver." *Ophthalmic Surgery*, May-June 1995, 216–217; Oludiran, O., et al. "Morbidity and mortality from bowel injury." *African Journal of Reproductive Health*, December 2003, 65–68; Lahr, C. *Shining Light on Constipation: Rectal Descent, and Other Colon, Rectal, and Anal Problems.* Sunburst Press, 2004; "Elvis Aron Presley, Case 77-1974." Report of Investigation by County Medical Examiner. Office of the County Medical Examiner, Memphis, Tennessee.

Toothache: *Hippocrates.* "Dental 1, case 4." Translation: W. H. Jones. London: W. Heinemann, 1923, 1:193–195; Blake, J. B. "Dental history." *Journal of American College of Dentists*, 1961; "*Mark Macsenti v. Jon D. Becker, D.D.S.*": January 22, 2001, nos. 98–6485, 99–6012. The U.S. District Court for the Western District of Oklahoma.

Toothpicks: Weber, B. *Sherwood Anderson.* University of Minnesota Press, 1964; Wilcox, C. M., et al. "Spontaneous bacterial peritonitis. A review of pathogenesis, diagnosis, and treatment." *Medicine* (Baltimore), November 1987, 447–456.

Tornadoes: Grazulis, T. P. *The Tornado: Nature's Ultimate Windstorm.* University of Oklahoma Press, 2001; Burt, C. *Extreme Weather: A Guide and Record Book.* W. W. Norton & Company, 2004.

Toupees: "Extremely Flammable Spray Grade Contact Adhesive." Data Sheet Commercial Item Description A-A-1936A Type. Report WA 980/1981. Polymer Institute, Brno; "Fire Investigation Report." Chicago Fire Department (CFD) March 14, 1981.

Toys: McDonald, Joyce. "Toy Related Deaths and Injuries, Calendar Year 2000." CPSC Memorandum, November 5, 2001; "NEISS Data Highlights—2003." Consumer Product Safety Review 7.2 (Fall 2004).

Train Tracks: "Railroad and Grade-Crossing Injured Persons by Victim Class Reports" BTS-NTS, 1994–2003. National Highway Traffic Safety Administration (NHTSA). National Association of the Deaf. Miss Deaf America Pageant. (http://www.nad.org) Plohetski, Tony. "Authorities say Miss Deaf Texas struck by train's snowplow." Austin American-Statesman, March 14, 2006.

Umbrellas: Tinetti, M. E., et al. "Risk factors during leisure activities among elderly persons living in the community." *New England Journal of Medicine*, 1999; Graves, E. J. "1999 Summary Report: (Higgins General Hospital, Breman, Georgia)," National Hospital Discharge Survey. Advance data from vital and health statistics; no. 185:1–12.

Unconsciousness: Joanne Lynn, M.D., et al. "Relationship Between Predictions of Prognosis and Their Treatment Preferences." *Journal of the American Medical Association*, June 1998, vol. 29; Arrillaga, Pauline. "Mom begins slow recovery from a 16-year-long coma." *Detroit News*, March 12, 2000; Carey, B. "Inside the Injured Brain, Many Kinds of Awareness." *New York Times*, April 5, 2005; "Man speaks after 19-year silence." CNN, July 8, 2003; Rendell-Baker, L. "The Mount Sinai Hospital's role in the development of anesthesia safety standards." *Mount Sinai Journal of Medicine*, 2002, 12–17; Fox, Gary D. "The lost lesson of Terri

Schiavo." *St. Petersburg Floridian*, October 26, 2003.

Unisex: Dreger, A. D. "Hermaphrodites and the Medical Invention of Sex." Harvard University Press, 1998; Yajima, A., et al. "Molecular Biologic Analyses of Tetragametic chimerism in a True Hermaphrodite with 46,XX/46,XY." *Fertility and Sterility*, January 1995, vol. 63, no. 1; Foucault, Michel. *Herculine Barbin*. Pantheon, 1980; "Bobby Kork. Collection Number: 7652." Division of Rare Manuscript Collections: Cornell University Library.

Valentine's Day: Bulla, Clyde Robert. *St. Valentines Day*. Crowell Company, 1965; Attwater, Donald. *Avenel Dictionary of Saints*. Avenel Books, 1981; "Harris gets 20 years for Mercedes murder." CNN, February 14, 2003; Ruth, David E. *Inventing the Public Enemy: The Gangsters in American Culture, 1918-1934*. University of Chicago Press, 1996.

Vegetarians: Figueras, Tere. "Raw-Food Vegetarians Ate Steak, Report Says." *Miami Herald*, July 22, 2003; "Mad cow victim was a vegetarian." Associated Press, August 28, 2003; "Coffee Enema Doctor Sentenced." Associated Press, April 20, 2000; Reay, D. T. "Death related to coffee enemas." *Journal of the American Medical Association*, 2003, 244:1608–1609.

Vending Machines: Butler, Daniel. *America's Dumbest Criminals*. Rutledge Hill Press, 1995; Sevilla, Charles M. *Disorderly Conduct: Excerpts from Actual Cases*. W. W. Norton & Company, 1999; Federal Judicial Caseload Statistics, Federal Bureau of Investigation 1976–2002, 16–051216-6.

Video Games: Young, Kimberly S. "Internet addiction: A new clinical phenomenon and its consequences."

American Behavioral Scientist, December 2004: 48,4,402; Hauge, Marney R., et al. "Video game addiction among adolescents." *Society for Research in Child Development*, December 2003; Mansfield, Duncan. "Grand Theft Auto makers fight $246M lawsuit." *USA Today*, November 11, 2003; Davis, Rose. "The Xbox murders." *New York Daily News*, August 9, 2004; "Robbers scared off by Playstation game get jail time." ABC News, December 14, 2004.

Vigilantes: Crawford, Theron Clark. *An American Vendetta; a Story of Barbarism in the United States*. Clarke and Co., 1888; Cunningham, Dan. "The Horrible Butcheries of West Virginia." *West Virginia History Journal*, 1946//25–44.Arc 1; Ginzberg, Ralph. *100 Years of Lynchings*. Loneer Books, 1962; Whitfield, Stephen J. *A Death in the Delta: The Story of Emmett Till*. The Free Press, 1988.

Volcanoes: Simkin, T., and Siebert, L. *Volcanoes of the World*. Geoscience Press, 1995; Carson, Rob. *Mount St. Helens: The Eruption and Recovery of a Volcano*. Sasquatch Books, 1990; Perry, Ronald W. *Citizen Response to Volcanic Eruptions: The Case of Mt. St. Helens*. Irvington Publishers, 1983; Seach, John "Volcano Live": http://www.volcanolive.com/html.

War: Jessup, John E., ed. *Encyclopedia of the American Military*. Charles Scribner's Sons, 1994; Burg, David F., ed. *The World Almanac of the American Revolution*. Scripps Howard Company, 1992; Beirne, Francis F. *The War of 1812*. Dutton, 1949; Levenson, Dorothy. *Homesteaders and the Indians*. Franklin Watts, 1971; Utley, Robert M. *Frontier Regulars: The United States Army and the Indian, 1866–1891*. Macmillan, 1973; Carter,

Alden R. *The Mexican War: Manifest Destiny*. F. Watts, 1992; Ainsworth, Fred C., Brig. Gen., Kirkley, Joseph W. "The official records of the Union and Confederate armies." U.S. War Department, Washington Government Printing Office, 1897: Series I, vol. 3, 1881, Series IV, vol. 2, 1900; Mayer, Robert G. *Embalming: History, Theory, and Practice*. McGraw-Hill, 2000; Quote from "Battle of Wilderness" *Harper's Weekly*, June 4, 1864; Goldstein, Donald M. *Spanish-American War: The Story and Photographs*. Potomac Books, 2000; Gray, R. *Chronicle of the First World War*. Facts of File, 1990; Adams, Michael C. C. *The Best War Ever: America and World War II*. Johns Hopkins University Press, 1994; Aid, Matthew M. "American Commitment in the Korean War." *Intelligence and National Security* 15:1, 2000; Karnow, S. *Vietnam: A History*. Penguin, 1997; Atkinson, Rick. *Crusade: The Untold Story of the Persian Gulf War*. Boston: Houghton Mifflin, 1993; Elliston, J. Lutz, C. "Hidden Casualties: An Epidemic of Domestic Violence When Troops Return from War." *Southern Exposure*, 31.1, 2003.

Water Beds: Nakamura S., et al. "Review of hazards associated with children placed in adult beds." *Archives of Pediatric Adolescent Medicine*, October 1999, 153:1019–1023; Kirrchner, J. T. "Deaths Associated with Small Children Sleeping in Adult Beds." *American Family Physician*, March 2000.

Wedding Day: DeJarnette, Margaret. "Wedding Stories: Tales From Three Couples." *New Orleans Magazine*, January 1, 2000; de Vos, Gail. *Tales, Rumors and Gossip*. Libraries Unlimited, 1996; Fiery, Ann. *The Complete and Totally True Book of Urban Legends*.

Running Press Books, 2001; Baden, Michael M., M.D. *Unnatural Death*. Ballantine Books, 1990; Howath, P. *Attila: King of the Huns: The Man and the Myth*. Carroll & Graf, 2001.

Westward Expansion: Whalen, John. *The Big Book of the Weird Wild West*. Factoid Press, 1998; Donnelly, Clarence Shirley. *The Hatfield-McCoy Feud Reader*. McClain Printing Co., 1971; Forbes, Malcolm. *They Went That-A-Way: How the Famous, The Infamous, and The Great Died*. Simon & Schuster, 1988; Wellman, Paul. *A Dynasty of Western Outlaws*. University of Nebraska Press, 1986; Lamar, H. R., ed. *The New Encyclopedia of the American West*. Yale University Press, 1998; Pendergast, Tom. *Westward Expansion: Primary Sources*. Gale, 2001; Cook, Jeanne F. "A History of Placing-Out: The Orphan Trains." *Child Welfare* 74(1), January/February 1995, 181–197; Nichols, George Ward. "Wild Bill Hickok," *Harper's Weekly*, February 1867; Hickok quote: Stanley, Henry Morton. *St. Louis Missouri Democrat*, April 1867.

Working: Hunting, K., et al. "Occupational Injuries among Construction Workers." FACE Report 2004; Newman, L. S. "Occupational illness." *New England Journal of Medicine*, 1995, Frumkin H. *Carcinogens. Occupational Health: Recognizing and Preventing Work-Related Disease*. Little, Brown, 1995; Brown, Bradford. "Selected Occupational Fatalities Related to Logging as found in Reports of OSHA Fatality/Catastrophe Investigations: Profiles of Work Injuries and Illnesses." OSHA Citations in SIC 2421: Sawmills and Planning Mills; *The Cutting Edge Chainsaw Safety Handbook Practical Methods and Procedures for Safe Power Saw*

Operation. Forest Products Accident Prevention Association; Bronfenbrenner, Kate. *The Killing Of Karen Silkwood*. Cornell University Press, 2000.

X-Ray: Berrington, A., et al. "100 years of observation on radiologists: mortality from cancer and other causes 1897–1997." *British Journal of Radiology*, 2001, 507–519; Bettyann, K. *Naked to the Bone: Medical Imaging in the Twentieth Century*. Perseus Books, 1998; Keen, W. W. "The Use of the Rontgen X-rays in Surgery." *McClure Magazine*, May 1896, vol. 6; Tselos, George D. "New Jersey's Thomas Edison and the Fluoroscope." *New Jersey Medicine* 92, November 1995.

Yawning: Provine, Robert R. "Contagious yawning and infant imitation." *Bulletin of the Psychonomic Society* 27, March 2, 1989, 125–126; Provine, Robert R. "Faces as releasers of contagious yawning: An approach to face detection using normal human subjects." *Bulletin of the Psychonomic Society* 27. 3, May 1989, 211–214; "Hippo Eats Dwarf." *Grapevine, Pattaya Mail: Melbourne Herald Sun*, July 25, 1999.

Zoofatalism: Reade, L., Waran, N. "The modern zoo: how do people perceive zoo animals?" *Applied Animal Behavior Science*, 1996, 47:109–118; Ramsden, Matt. "Tigers' victim identified as co-worker." *Dispatch*, May 13, 1998. Stabbins, B. "Top 20 Homicides of the Year." U.S. Department of Justice FBI Report, 2000. FBI, Supplementary Homicide Reports, 1976–2002.

Postmortem: Death Certificates: Sperry, Kip. *A Guide to Family History and Historical Sources*. Brigham Young University, 2005; Silverman, Kenneth. *The Life and Times of Cotton Mather*. Harper & Row, 1984; Sperry, Kip. *Reading Early American Handwriting*. Genealogical Publishing Company, 2003.

Unexplained Illness: Allderidge, Patricia. "Hospitals, Madhouses and Asylums." *British Journal of Psychiatry*, 134[1979] 321–334; Berrios, German E. *Obsessional disorders during the nineteenth century: terminological and classifactory issues*. London, Tavistock Publications, 1985; Garrison, Fielding H. *An Introduction to the History of Medicine*. W. G. Saunders, 1929; Brown, Edward. *Creating Traumatic Emotional Disorders before and during World War I*. Athlone Press, 1995; Nutting, J. *The Poor, the Defective, and the Criminal*. Mason Publishers, 1902; Scull, Andrew, ed. *Madhouses, Mad-doctors and Madmen: The Social History of Psychiatry in the Victorian Era*. University of Pennsylvania Press, 1981; Bordley, James. *Two Centuries of American Medicine 1776–1976*. W. B. Saunders, 1976; Leavitt, Judith, et al. *Sickness and Health in America: Readings in the History of Medicine and Public Health*, 3rd ed. McGraw-Hill, 1997.

By the Numbers: Etheridge, Elizabeth. *Sentinel for Health: A History of the Centers for Disease Control*. University of California Press, 1992; Furman, Beth. "A Profile of the United States Public Health Service, 1798–1948." Government Printing Office, 1973; Mullan, Fitzhugh. *Plagues and Politics: The Story of the United States Public Health Service*. Basic Books, 1989.

Cadaver Encounters: Coleman, Penny. *Corpses, Coffins and Crypts: A History of Burial*. Henry Holt, 1997; Laderman, Gary. *Rest in Peace: A Cultural History of Death and the Funeral Home In Twen-*

tieth-Century America. Oxford University Press, 2005; Torre, Carlo. "An Exceptional Case of Necrophilia." *The American Journal of Forensic Medicine and Pathology*, 8 (2), 1987; "Remains of ten bodies at Ben Franklin's home." *The London Times*, February 11, 1998; "Man keeps woman's body in freezer." Associated Press, October 28, 2004.

Burial at Sea: "Fisherman hauls up a coffin in net." Associated Press, June 28, 2002; "Burial at sea: Sec. 229.1." Federal Codes and Regulations. National Archives and Records Administration; Barranger, Nicky. "Fantasy coffin attraction." BBC, January 28, 2005; Ad Hoc Committee of the Harvard Medical School to Examine the Definition of Death. "A Definition of Irreversible Coma." *Journal of the American Medical Association*, 1968, vol. 205, no. 6.

Potter's Field: Bergman, Edward F. *Woodlawn Remembers: Cemetery of American History*. North Country Books, 1988; "A Historical Resume of Potter's Field: 1869–1967." NYC Department of Correction, 1967. Olsen, Lise. "Records often are as hard to find as a body." *Seattle-Post*, February 24, 2003.

John Doe: Coates, Robert. *A Street Is Not a Home: Solving America's Homeless Dilemma*. Prometheus Books, 1994; *Medical examiners' and coroners' handbook on death registration*. Centers for Disease Control and Prevention, Department of Health and Human Services (US), 1994; Baden, Michael M. Hennessee, Judith Adler, M.D. *Unnatural Death—Confessions of a Medical Examiner*. Random House, 1989.

Oscar Winners: Redelmeier, Donald, M.D. "Pushing the Envelope: Oscar Winners Live Longer Than Oscar Nominees." *Annals of Internal Medicine*, May 15, 2001, 945; Paster, Zorba, Meltsner, Susan. *The Longevity Code: Your Personal Prescription for a Longer, Sweeter Life*. Clarkson Potter, 2001; Kaufman, J. C. "The cost of the muse: Poets die young." *Death Studies*, 2003, 27 (9): 813–822.

Epitaph: Greene, Janet. *Epitaphs to Remember: Remarkable Inscriptions from New England Gravestones*. Alan C. Hood & Company, 1992; Bergin, Edward. *The Definitive Guide to Underground Humor: Quaint Quotes About Death, Funny Funeral Home Stories and Hilarious Headstone Epitaphs*. Offbeat Publications, 1996. Boot Hill Museum: http://www.boothill.org/.

ACKNOWLEDGMENTS

A giant, gracious thank you to the innumerable librarians who endured my pestering all this time, and for the countless experts in so many fields who took the patience to answer my questions, especially Dr. Michael Baden and Michael Kearl. Many others put forth effort in forming the book through its development, including Ann Rittenberg, Starling Lawrence, Brett Kelly, Michael Larsen, and Antonio Oppi. On the home front, I thank Susan Cummins of the Miami International Book Fair and Mitchell Kaplan of Books and Books, and for e-zine editors Michael Rothenberg and Jonathan Penton for their support. Tom Gilbert of Associated Press and Kenneth Johnson of Library of Congress helped diligently with some of the most demanding art. Through all of it, I thank Ted Mark, my mentor, who showed me how to dismantle the atomic bomb.

I thank Frank Weimann of the Literary Group who believed in this project and placed it in the speed of light. I am grateful to Mauro DiPreta, at Harper-Collins, for his forethought to see the book's possibilities. I especially thank Joelle Yudin, my editor at HarperCollins, for her contagious enthusiasm as she prodded, poked, and pulled the vastness into a coherent form. Every writer should be so fortunate to work with an editor of her caliber. I also thank cover designer Gregg Kulick, production editor Kolt Beringer, interior designer Justin Dodd, Associate Publishers Hope Innelli and Carrie Kania, editorial director David Roth-Ey, and publicist Gilda Squire.

In closing, I am forever appreciative to Susy, my wife, who made possible the clean well-lighted place, and for her knowledge as an RN, ever-ready with impossibly thick, fine-print medical reference books spread open throughout the years. And for my children, Jared, Colette, Michael, Erik, and Joe, who bring me joy.

PHOTOGRAPHIC CREDITS

A

Abatico: Devy, Georges (1887) National Library of Medicine; Abatico/Home Remedy Award: Smith, R.W. (1875) Library of Congress; Abatico/French Periodical Pills: Roberts, George (1845) Library of Congress; Abandonment in Cars: Lee, Russell (1938) Library of Congress; Acordynia: Collier, John (1943) Library of Congress; Air Bags: AP Images; Airshows: Underwood & Underwood Collection/Library of Congress; Alcoholism: New York World-Telegram and the Sun Newspaper Photograph Collection/Library of Congress; Alcoholism/Son and Grace McDaniels: Ronald G. Becker Collection of Charles Eisenmann Photographs, Special Collections Research Center, Syracuse University Library; Alcoholism/Uncle Sam: Flagg, James Montgomery (1917) Library of Congress; Alien Abductions: Corbis; Alligators: Keller, Franz (1875) Library of Congress; Alzheimer's/Audubon: Brady-Handy Photograph Collection (1855) Library of Congress; Ambulance Chasers: Office of War Information (1942) Library of Congress; Amnesia: AP Images; Amnesia/Richard Nobody: BNPS; Amnesia/Electric Shock: Duchenne, Guillaume-Benjamin (1861) National Library of Medicine; Amusement Parks/Human Cannonball: Muller, R. (1879) Library of Congress; Amusement Parks/Crowds Gone Wild: Rea and Sharp, Engraver (1870) Picture Collection, the Branch Libraries, the New York Public Library, Astor, Lenox, and Tilden Foundations; Amusement/Log Fume: Strobridge Lith. Co. (1896) Library of Congress; Anabolic Steroids: Berengario da Carpi, Jacopo (1521) National Library of Medicine; Anorexia: Gibson, Wm. (1888) National Library of Medicine; Anthrax: AP Images; Aphrodisiac/Kiss a Frog: Courtesy A1 Various, Copyright Plant Plant; Aphrodisiac/Spanish Fly: Hines, Lewis Wickes (1912) Library of Congress; Aphrodisiac/Absinthe: *Harper's Weekly,* 27 (Sept 15, 1883) National Library of Medicine; Appliances: Horydezak, Theodor

(1920) Library of Congress; Arsenic: Underwood and Underwood, Washington (1924) Library of Congress; Arsenic/Black Widow/Marie Hilley: AP Images; Auto Racing/Kiddie Division: Delano, Jack (1940) Library of Congress; Auto-castration: Goya, Francisco de (1810) Burstein Collection/Corbis; Autocastration: Jensen, Nicolaus (1471) Surgical Instruments from Antiquity Collection, University of Virginia Health System; Autocastration/Christine Jorgensen: Bettmann/Corbis; Autoerotic Asphyxiation: AP Images; Auto Racing: U.S. District Court of the Western District of Missouri (1930) National Archives and Records Administration of the United States; Avalanche: Frank and Frances Carpenter Collection (1910) Library of Congress.

B

Balloon: Bella C. Landauer Collection (1785) Library of Congress; Barbecues: Corbis; Baseball: New York World-Telegram and the Sun Newspaper Photograph Collection (1949) Library of Congress/Associated Press; Bats: Picture Collection, the Branch Libraries, the New York Public Library, Astor, Lenox, and Tilden Foundations; Bears: Berkeley, Stanley (1878) Picture Collection, the Branch Libraries, the New York Public Library, Astor, Lenox, and Tilden Foundations; Beauty Pageants: New York World-Telegram and the Sun Newspaper Photograph Collection (1952) Library of Congress/Associated Press; Beauty Pageants/Kids: Albertein, Walter (1951) Library of Congress; Beauty Pageants/Christopher Wilder: Bettmann/Corbis; Beaver Fever: Shaw, George (1809) General Research, the New York Public Library, Astor, Lenox, and Tilden Foundations; Bed & Breakfast: Melander and Brother (1876) Library of Congress; Bicycles/Woman on Bicycle: (1869) Library of Congress; Bicycles: Photograph by Eisenmann, N.Y. (1891) Library of Congress; Bingeing: Corbis. Bingeing/Vomitoriums: Mimmo Jodice/Corbis; Black Death/Flea: (July 1859) Picture Collection, the Branch Libraries, the New York Public Library, Astor, Lenox, and Tilden Foundations; Black Death/Spanish Flu: Bettmann/Corbis; Blackouts: New York World-Telegram and the Sun Newspaper Photograph Collection (1965) Library of Congress/Associated Press; Bloodletting: (1561) National Library of Medicine; Body Piercing: AP Images; Boiled and Baked: Shahn, Ben (1936) Library of Congress; Bottoming Out: Corbis; Botulinum Toxin: Corbis. Bowling: New York World-Telegram and the Sun Newspaper Photograph Collection (1936) Library of Congress; Boxing: New York Lith. (1887) Library of Congress; Boxing/Houdini: McManus and Young Collection (1899) Library of Congress; Building Debris/Tampa Skyway Bridge: Corbis, Building Debris/Crumbling Gargoyle: Historic American Buildings Survey (1933) Library of Congress; Bungee Jumping: AP Images; Bungee Jumping/Parkour: Ed Kashi/Corbis; Buried Alive: Eisenbrandt, Christian H. (1843) National Archives and Records Administration of the United States; Buried Alive: Robinson, Henry (1836) Library of Congress.

C

Capital Punishment: Cole, D.S. (1896) Library of Congress; Capital Punishment/Firing squad: War Department (1916) National Archives and Records Administration of the United States; Capital Punishment/Hanging Judge Parker: Library of Congress; Capital Punishment/Electric Chair: Picture Collection, the Branch Libraries, the New York Public Library, Astor, Lenox, and Tilden Foundations; Capital Punishment/Giles: Library of Congress; Carjacking: Roy Morsch/Corbis; Cars: Environmental Protection Agency (1974) National Archives and Records Administration of the United States; Cellphone Etiquette: Franco Vogt/Corbis; Cheerleading: Corbis; Cheerleading/The Pyramid: AP Images; Childbed Fever: Leake, John (1772) National Library of Medicine; Childbed Fever/A Women's Peril: Viardel, Cosme (1673) National Library of Medicine; Chinese Food Syndrome: Corbis. Chinese Food Syndrome/Deadly Delicacies: Jensen, JJPhoto.dk; Chocolate: Advertisement showing a woman eating Owl Brand chocolate (1886) Library of Congress; Choking: Forbes, S.W. (1799) National Library of Medicine; Cockroaches: (1860) Picture Collection, the Branch Libraries, the New York Public Library, Astor, Lenox, and Tilden Foundations; Cockroaches/Typhoid Mary: Bettmann/Corbis; Competitive eating: Lee, Russell (1939) Library of Congress; Compulsive Disorders: Bonn, Phillip (1946) Library of Congress; Compulsive Disorders/Howard Hughes: New York World-Telegram and the Sun Newspaper Photograph Collection (1936) Library of Congress/AP; Co-Sleeping: Rau, William H. (1897) Library of Congress; Crayons: Corbis; Cruise Ships: Bennett, Arnold, Henry W. and Albert A. Berg Collection of English and American Literature, the New York Public Library, Astor, Lenox, and Tilden Foundations; Cruise Ships/Captain Hook: Ellms, Charles (1837) Library of Congress; Cruise Ships/Sultana: Civil War Photograph Collection (1865) Library of Congress; Cults/Jonestown: AP Images; Cults/David Koresh: AP Images; Cults/Ben Yahweh: Bettmann/Corbis; Cults/Order of the Solar Temple: AP Images.

D

Dandy-Walker Syndrome: British Cartoon Collection (1773) Library of Congress; Dating: State Historical Society of Colorado (1910) Library of Congress; Dating/Preppie Murder: AP Images; Deep Fried: Department of Interior (1890) National Archives and Records Administration of the United States; Dental School/Lillian Millicent Entwistle: Bettmann/Corbis; Dildo: John W. Hartman Center for Sales, Advertising and Marketing History; Duke University Rare Book, Manuscript, and Special Collections Library; Dildo: John W. Hartman Center for Sales, Advertising & Marketing History; Duke University Rare Book, Manuscript, and Special Collections Library; Domestic Violence: Coolidge, C. M. (1877) Library of Congress; Dr. Death/Genene Jones: AP Images; Dr.

Death/DR. Donald Harvey: AP Images; Dr. Death/Dr. Larry Ford: AP Images; Dr. Death/Dr. Harold Shipman: AP Images; Drowning: AP Images; Dueling: Print Collection, Miriam and Ira D. Wallach Division of Art, Prints and Photographs, the Branch Libraries, the New York Public Library, Astor, Lenox, and Tilden Foundations; Dueling/Edgar Allen Poe: Sartain, W. (1844) Library of Congress; Dwarfism/Tom Thumb: Ronald G. Becker Collection of Charles Eisenmann Photographs, Special Collections Research Center, Syracuse University Library; Dwarfism/Lucia Zarate: Ronald G. Becker Collection of Charles Eisenmann Photographs, Special Collections Research Center, Syracuse University Library.

E

Earthquake/Split earth: Detroit Publishing Company Photograph Collection (1906) Library of Congress; Earthquake/Evacuation: Department of Defense (1906) National Archives and Records Administration of the United States, Ebola: Corbis; Ebola/Monkey Pox: Corbis; Eccentrics/Langley: AP Images; Ejection: AP Images; Electrocution: (1908) Picture Collection, the Branch Libraries, the New York Public Library, Astor, Lenox, and Tilden Foundations; Electronic Air Freshners: American Medical Association (1912) National Library of Medicine; Electronic Pets: AP Images; Elephantiasis: Ellis, A.G (1921) Siriraj Medical Museum; Elephantiasis: Corbis; Elevators: AP Images; Escalators: Collins, Marjory (1942) Library of Congress; Empire State Building: AP Images; Entrapment/Cribs: Adams, Ansel (1943) Library of Congress; Epidemics: Department of Public Health, Sanitary Division, San Francisco, California (1917) National Library of Medicine; Epidemics/Cholera-George Grantham Bain Collection (1900–1920) Library of Congress; Epidemics/Plaque: Defoe, Daniel (1767) Library of Congress; Euthanasia/Painless: Medieval Hospital (thirteenth century) National Library of Medicine; Euthanasia/Tattoo: BBC.com; Euthanasia/Kevorkian: AP Images; Exercise Equipment: Corbis.

F

Fad Diets: Corbis; Falling Asleep: Reg Charity/Corbis; Falls: Liberman, Howard (1942) Library of Congress; Falls/Man in Barrel: Bettmann/Corbis; Falls/Niagara Falls: Landreth, A. G. (1911) Library of Congress; Fashion/Corset: (1902) Picture Collection, the Branch Libraries, the New York Public Library, Astor, Lenox, and Tilden Foundations; Fashion/Isadora Duncan: Genthe, Arnold (1910) Library of Congress; Fear of Flying: AP Images; Fear of Flying: Office for Emergency Management (1942) National Archives and Records Administration of the United States; Feed and Pet: Clay, Edward William (1840) Library of Congress; Fire Hoses: Costello, Augustine E. (1887) Library of Congress; Fire Hoses/Chicago Fire: Frank Leslie's Illustrated Newspaper (1871 Oct. 28) Library of Congress; Fire Hoses/Triangle Fire: Brown Bros. (1911) Picture Collection, the Branch Libraries, the New York Public Library, Astor, Lenox, and Tilden Foundations; Flesh Eating Virus: (1904) National Library of Medicine; Flying Cows: Bettmann/Corbis; Football: Underwood and Underwood, (1931) Library of Congress; Foreign Bodies: AP Images; Free Rent: AP Images; Free Rent/Earle Nelson: U.S. Department of Justice; Frozen Toilets: McManus-Young Collection (1921) Library of Congress; Frozen Toilets/Worst Cold Snap: Frank Leslie's Illustrated Newspaper, vol. 66, no. 1697 (1888 March) Library of Congress; Furniture: Gottscho, Samuel H. (1932) Library of Congress.

G

Gangs/Gangs of Fat Women: Ronald G. Becker Collection of Charles Eisenmann Photographs, Special; Collections Research Center, Syracuse University Library; Gangs/Hand Signs: Corbis; Gangs/HellcatMaggie: Frank Leslie's Illustrated Newspaper, v. 4, (1857 July 18) Library of Congress; Gangs/Hells Angel: AP Images; Gastric Bypass: Isaac Sprague: Ronald G. Becker Collection of Charles Eisenmann Photographs, Special; Collections Research Center, Syracuse University Library; Geographic Tongue: Center for Disease Control and Prevention; Giants/Robert Wadlow: Ronald G. Becker Collection of Charles Eisenmann Photographs, SpecialCollections Research Center, Syracuse University Library; Gangsters/Gotti: AP Images; Gangsters/Albert Anastasia: AP Images; Gangsters/ Lucky Luciano: AP Images; Gangsters/Richard Kuklinski: Bettmann/Corbis; Going Postal/Mailmen Firing Practice: Underwood and Underwood/Corbis; Going to School: (1931) Library of Congress; Going to School/Young Andrew Golden: Najlah Feanny/Corbis SABA; Golf: George Grantham Bain Collection (1908) Library of Congress; Gone Fishing: Office of War Information (1885) National Archives and Records Administration of the United States; Gone Fishing/Jet Ski: Corbis; Guns: Saturday Evening Post (1912 July 6) Library of Congress.

H

Hair: Guerin, Fritz W. (1902) Library of Congress; Hair/ Jo-Jo Dog-Faced Boy: Ronald G. Becker Collection of Charles Eisenmann Photographs, Special Collections Research Center, Syracuse University Library; Hair/Julia Pastrana: Fortean Picture Library; Halitosis: Corbis; Halitosis: Center for Disease Control and Prevention; Halloween: Rothstein, Arthur (1939) Library of Congress; Halloween Skeleton: Office for Emergency Management (1942) National Archives and Records Administration of the United States; Hang Gliding: Adler, M. (1896) Library of Congress; Hazing: Gianni Dagli Orti/Corbis; Hazing/Boot Camp: AP Images; Hazing/Order of the Illuminati: Corbis; Head and Signs/ School Bus: National Youth Administration (1940) National Archives and Records Administration of the United States; Head and Signs/Guillotine: Corbis; Hiccups: Bettmann/Corbis; Holidays/Xmas Tree: Wright, Wilbur (1900)

Library of Congress; Holidays/W.C. Fields: Bettmann/Corbis; Home Births: Witkowski, Gustave Joseph (1887) National Library of Medicine; Homelessness: Eytinge, Solomon (1876) Library of Congress; Hookworm: Center for Disease Control and Prevention; Hookworm/Ultimate Weight Loss: Corbis; Hoover Dam: Library of Congress; Hoover Dam/Suicide: Bettmann/Corbis; Horse and Buggy: Richards, F. T. (1892) Picture Collection, the Branch Libraries, the New York Public Library, Astor, Lenox, and Tilden Foundations; Hotheads: Boilly, Louis Léopold (1824) National Library of Medicine; Hunting: Cawthon, DeFuniak Springs, Florida (1922) Library of Congress; Hunting/Chai Vang: AP Images; Hurricane: AP Images; Hurricane: Corbis.

I

Ice Cream: Corbis; Ice Cream Man: Collins, Marjory (1942) Library of Congress; Immersion Foot: Army Medical Museum (U.S. 1945) National Library of Medicine; Impotence: Bettmann/Corbis; Independence Day: George Grantham Bain Collection, Library of Congress; Independence Day/Jefferson: Sully, Thomas (1900) Library of Congress; Independence Day/Adams: Dearborn, N. (1814) Library of Congress; Indigestion: Corbis; Insomnia: Blue Lantern Studio/ Corbis; Internet Dating: Corbis.

J

Jailbreak: Wittemann Collection, Library of Congress; Jailbreak/Attica: AP Images; Jaywalking: Posoff, Isadore (1937) WPA Federal Art Project, Library of Congress; Jellyfish: Corbis; Job's Syndrome: Blake, William (1793) Corbis; Juice Extractor/Mulcher: Leaf 191 recto FIGVRE CXXIII from: Le Diverse et Artifiose Machine Corbis; Junk collecting: Office for Emergency Management (1942) National Archives and Records Administration of the United States.

K

Kabuki Syndrome: Jack Fields/Corbis; Kabuki/James Bond: Bettmann/Corbis; Killer Bees: Picture Collection, the Branch Libraries, the New York Public Library, Astor, Lenox, and Tilden Foundations; Kinky Hair Disease: Josef Scaylea/ Corbis; Kissing Disease: Dubois, Albert (1967) Library of Congress.

L

Labor Day: Office of War Information (1942) Library of Congress; Labyrinth Disease: Cieslewicz, Roman (1963) Library of Congress; Labyrinth Disease/Tilt-a-Whirl: Corbis; Latex Sensitivity: Corbis; Laughing: Collier, John (1941) Library of Congress; Laughing/Abbot and Costello: AP Images; Laughing/Arbuckle: Bettmann/Corbis; Laughing/Candy: AP Images; Laughing/Gleason: AP Images; Laughing/Three Stooges: AP Images; Laughing Gas: Netherclift, J. (1830) National Library of Medicine; Laughing Sickness: AP Images; Lawn Darts: John W. Hartman Center for Sales, Advertising and Marketing History; Duke University Rare Book, Manuscript, and Special Collections Library; Laying Tracks: Jackson, William Henry (1880) Library of Congress; Lightning: Corbis; Liposuction: Corbis; Litter Boxes: Putnam, E.D. (1908) Library of Congress; Lockjaw: Bell, C. (1865) National Library of Medicine; Loud Music: National Noise Abatement Council (1941) National Library of Medicine; Loud Music: Belch, W. (1829) National Library of Medicine; Lyme Disease: Center for Disease Control and Prevention.

M

Malls: Environmental Protection Agency (1972) National Archives and Records Administration of the United States; Marathons: Lucas, Charles (1904) Library of Congress; Marijuana: Bettmann/Corbis; Mascots: AP Images; Masturbation: Jalade-Lagand Paris Consideration sur les hernies (1834) National Library of Medicine; Masturbation: Abbey, E. C. (1882) Library of Congress; Mental Deduction: Reisch, Gregor (1525) National Library of Medicine; Meteors: Department of Interior (1871) National Archives and Records Administration of the United States; Microwave Popcorn: Corbis; Microwave: Bettmann/Corbis; Microwave/Frozen Food: William Gottlieb/Corbis; Migraine: Hals, Frans the Younger (1660) National Library of Medicine; Migraine: Delaroche, Paul (1820) Library of Congress; Migraine/Lincoln: Currier and Ives (1865) Library of Congress; Mosquito: U.S. Public Health Service; National Library of Medicine; Mosquito/Jane Mansfield: Hulton-Deutsch Collection/Corbis; Music Business/Sid Vicious: AP Images; Music Business/Kurt Cobain: S.I.N./Corbis; Music Business/Marvin Gaye: AP Images; Music Business/Stephen Foster: Bettmann/Corbis.

N

Narcissism: Boltraffio, Giovanni Antonio; National Gallery Collection and the Trustees of the National Gallery, London/Corbis; Narcissism/Lupe Velez: AP Images; Narcolepsy: Currier, N. (1848) Library of Congress; Narcolepsy: Bubley, Esther (1943) Library of Congress; Needlesticks: Stoll, Sue; National Library of Medicine; Nonstick Pots: Rosener, Ann (1943) Library of Congress; Nuclear Research: Department of Defense (1946) National Archives and Records Administration of the United States; Nuclear Research/Atomic: Nagasaki Medical College (1945) National Library of Medicine.

O

Obesity: Hoblet, C. (1909) Library of Congress; Obesity/Robert Earl Hughes: Bettmann/Corbis; Octopus and Squid:(1805) Bettmann/Corbis; Old Age: Delano, Jack (1941) Library of Congress; Organ Snatchers: Corbis; Oral Sex: Corbis; Outer Space: Silent film *A Trip to the Moon* directed by George Melies (1914) Bettmann/Corbis; Outer Space/Ham: Courtesy NASA; Outlaws: Bettmann/Corbis; Outlaws: Bonnie and Clyde: AP Images; Over-the-Counter (1890) National Library of Medicine; Over-the-Counter/Cocaine Toothache Drops (1890–99) National Library of Medicine; Over-the-Counter/Herbal Bliss: National Library of Medicine.

P

Plastic Making: Environmental Protection Agency (1974) National Archives and Records Administration of the United States; Platform Shoes: Giles Lith. Co. (1886) Library of Congress; Playgrounds: Corbis; Poisonous Spiders: Environmental Protection Agency (1965) National Archives and Records Administration of the United States; Poland's Syndrome: Francesco Lentini: Ronald G. Becker Collection of Charles Eisenmann Photographs, Special Collections Research Center, Syracuse University Library; Poland's Syndrome/Stiles: Ronald G. Becker Collection of Charles Eisenmann Photographs, Special Collections Research Center, Syracuse University Library; Police Training/Isaac Smith: Bettmann/Corbis; Police Training/Police Car: AP Images; Pot Luck Dinners: Turnbull, Laurence (1896) National Library of Medicine; Prostitution: Benard, A. (1790) National Library of Medicine.

Q

Q-Fever: National Photo Company Collection (1909) Library of Congress; Quacks: British Cartoon Collection, Library of Congress; Quacks/Horace Wells: Wood, Wm. (1896) Library of Congress; Quinsy: Farm Security Administration (1935) Library of Congress; Quinsy/Strangler: John Springer Collection/Corbis; Quinsy/Tonsils: Casserio, Giulio (1601) National Library of Medicine.

R

Rabbits: (1889) Picture Collection, the Branch Libraries, the New York Public Library, Astor, Lenox, and Tilden Foundations; Rabbits/Man's Best Friend: Schuler, Earl, WPA Art Program (1941) Library of Congress; Rat Bite Fever: U.S. Food Administration (1918) National Archives and Records Administration of the United States; Rat Bite Fever: (1918) Picture Collection, the Branch Libraries, the New York Public Library, Astor, Lenox, and Tilden Foundations; Raw Meat: Rosner, Ann (1942) Library of Congress; Raw Meat/School Lunch: Collins, Marjory (1942) Library of Congress; Record Breakers: Frank and Frances Carpenter collection (1923) Library of Congress; Record Breakers/ Doug Danger: AP Images; Restaurants: (1953) Library of Congress; Restaurants/Verrazzano: Engraved for Moorés Voyages and Travels (1778) Picture Collection, the Branch Libraries, the New York Public Library, Astor, Lenox, and Tilden Foundations; Restless Leg: Ravenna, Al (1940) Library of Congress; Rice Cakes: AP Images; Riot Acts: Library of Congress; Riot Acts/Slave: Library of Congress; Riot/Vietnam: AP Images; Rodeo: AP Images; Roller Coaster: Vachon, John (1943) Library of Congress; Roller Coaster: Bettmann/Corbis; Roller Coaster/Kiddie Ride: Environmental Protection Agency (1973) National Archives and Records Administration of the United States.

S

Scorpions: Leslie, Frank (1862) Picture Collection, the Branch Libraries, the New York Public Library, Astor, Lenox, and Tilden Foundations; Sea Diving: Environmental Protection Agency (1972) National Archives and Records Administration of the United States; Sea Diving/Diving Dress: Hall, Chauncy (1810) National Archives and Records Administration of the United States; Sea Diving/Barracuda: AP Images; Sea Diving/USS *Indianapolis:* Office of War Information (1943) Library of Congress; Serial/ Panzram: U.S. Dept. of Justice; Serial Killers/Albert Fish: Bettmann/Corbis; Serial/Kemper: Bettmann/Corbis; Serial/Zodiac: Bettmann/Corbis; Serial/Berkowitz: AP Images; Serial/Lucas: AP Images; Serial/Ted Bundy: U.S. Dept of Justice; Serial/John Wayne Gacy: AP

Images; Serial/Ramirez: AP Images; Serial/Rader: AP Images; Sexually Transmitted: Casanova, Giacomo/Mémoires, écrits par lui-même (1872, v. 4.) Library of Congress; Sexually Transmitted/Shame: Humfeville, Foster, Works Progress Administration Federal Art Project (1937) Library of Congress; Sexually Transmitted/Capone: New York World-Telegram and the Sun Newspaper Photograph Collection (1931) Library of Congress; Siamese Twins: Meiser, P.A., Library of Congress; Siamese/Millie & Christine: Ronald G. Becker Collection of Charles Eisenmann Photographs, Special Collections Research Center, Syracuse University Library; Sick Building Syndrome: Bettmann/Corbis; Sidewalk Cafe: AP Images; Sidewalk Cafe: AP Images; Sinkholes: Bettmann/Corbis; Skysurfing: AP Images; Sleep Terror: Fuseli, Henry (1826) National Library of Medicine; Sleepwalkers: Onwhyn, Thomas (1857) National Library of Medicine; Smoking: Rothstein, Arthur (1939) Library of Congress; Snake Handler: Solid Fuels Administration for War (1946) National Archives and Records Administration of the United States; Snake Handler: Gurerro, Joe (June 1915) Picture Collection, the Branch Libraries, the New York Public Library, Astor, Lenox, and Tilden Foundations; Sneezing: Bettmann/Corbis; Sneezing/Cage for Sneezers: Letchworth, William Pryor (1889) National Library of Medicine; Snipers: AP Images; Snowboarding; Corbis; Spectators: National Photo Company Collection (1924) Library of Congress; Sperm Allergy: Corbis; Spontaneous Combustion: Fortean Picture Library; Spontaneous Combustion/Mary Resser: Fortean Picture Library; Spring Break: Bettmann/Corbis; Stage Fright/Carmen Miranda: AP Images; Stage Fright/Irene Clampett: AP Images; Stage Fright/Tiny-Tim: AP Images; Stage Fright/Vic Morrow: John Springer Collection/Corbis; Stage Fright/Margaux Hemingway: Douglas Kirkland/Corbis; Stage Fright/Harrison: Currier, N. (1841) Library of Congress; Stalking/Harris: AP Images; Stampede/Iroquois Theater: AP Images; Stowaway: Corbis; Subways: Inter, R.T. (1904) Picture Collection, the Branch Libraries, the New York Public Library, Astor, Lenox, and Tilden Foundations.

T

Taxis and Trucks: Ford Motor Company (1956) Library of Congress; Thanksgiving: Ferris, Jean Louis Gerome (1910) Library of Congress; Thrift Stores: Lee, Russell (1942) Library of Congress; Thyroid Disease: American Medical Association (1912) National Library of Medicine; Toasters: Theodor Horydczak Collection (1933) Library of Congress; Toilet Time: Mydans, Carl (1935) Library of Congress; Toothache: Tooth Extraction (1892) National Library of Medicine; Tornadoes: Department of Agriculture (1955) National Archives and Records Administration of the United States; Toupees: Ross and Sons (1850) Picture Collection, the Branch Libraries, the New York Public Library, Astor, Lenox, and Tilden Foundations; Train Tracks: Department of the Interior (1942) National Archives and Records Administration of the United States.

U

Umbrellas: Noé, Amédée (1841) National Library of Medicine; Unconsciousness: Department of Defense (1967) National Archives and Records Administration of the United State; Unconsciousness: Environmental Protection Agency (1974) National Archives and Records Administration of the United States; Unisex: Esquirol, Étienne (1834) National Library of Medicine; Unisex/Kork: Ronald G. Becker Collection of Charles Eisenmann Photographs, Special Collections Research Center, Syracuse University Library.

V

Valentine's Day: Department of Interior (1944) National Archives and Records Administration of the United States; Valentine's Day/Clara Harris: AP Images; Valentine's Day/Massacre: AP Images; Vegetarians: (1741) Bettmann/Corbis; Vending Machine: AP Images; Video Games: Corbis; Vigilantes: National Archives and Records Administration of the United States; Volcano: AP Images.

W

War/Revolutionary: Library of Congress; War/Nathan Hale: Pyle, Howard (1880) Picture Collection, the Branch Libraries, the New York Public Library, Astor, Lenox, and Tilden Foundations; War of 1812: Bobbett, Albert (1877) Picture Collection, the Branch Libraries, the New York Public Library, Astor, Lenox, and Tilden Foundations; War-Indians/Custer: Brady-Handy Photograph Collection (1860) Library of Congress Mexican War: Drarke, W.H. (1895) Picture Collection, the Branch Libraries, the New York Public Library, Astor, Lenox, and Tilden Foundations; War/Civil War/Stonewall: Library of Congress; War/Spanish American War: Strobridge Lith. Co., (1899) Library of Congress; War/Young York: Department of Defense; Records of the Office of the Chief Signal Officer (1915–1918) National Archives and Records Administration of the United States; War/Helmet: War Department (1918) National Archives and Records Administration of the United States; War/WWII/Audie Murphy: AP Images; War/Vietnam War: National Archives and Records Administration of the United States; War/Gulf War: AP Images; War/Edwin Starr: Joe La Russo compliments Kyle Artist; Waterbeds: Department of the Interior (1942) National Archives and Records Administration of the United States; Wedding Day: Bell, Curtis (1920) Picture Collection, the Branch Libraries, the New York Public Library, Astor, Lenox, and Tilden Foundations; Wedding/Death of Attila: Bettman/Corbis; Wedding/Glynn Wolfe: AP Images; Westward Expansion/Lewis: Peale, Charles Wilson, Library of Congress; Westward Expansion/Clarke: Peale, Charles Wilson, Library of Congress; Westward Expansion/Orphans: Franzest, Paul (1869) Picture Collection, the Branch Libraries, the New York Public Library, Astor, Lenox, and Tilden Foundations; Westward Expansion/Billy the Kid: AP Images; Westward Expansion/Jesse James: AP Images; Westward Expansion/Wyatt Earp: Department of Defense; Records of the Office of the Chief Signal Officer (1860–1982) National Archives and Records Administration of the United States; Westward Expansion/Wild Bill: Bettmann/Corbis; Working: Palmer, Alfred T. (1941) Library of Congress; Working/Armored Truck: National Photo Company Collection (1930) Library of Congress; Working/Silkwood: AP Images.

X-Y-Z

X-Ray: Corbis; X-Ray/Edison: Photograph by Byron, NYC (1906) Library of Congress; Yawning: Ferrell, John (1942) Library of Congress; Zoofatalism: Max, Gabriel (1908) Picture Collection, the Branch Libraries, the New York Public Library, Astor, Lenox, and Tilden Foundations.

POSTMORTEM

Death Certificate: National Archives and Records Administration of the United States; Unexplained Illness/Ecstasy: Bettmann/Corbis; Fear of Dying/Colonial Tombstone, 1776: Ludwig, Allan, Library of Congress; Cadaver Encounters/ Selected Few: National Library of Medicine; Cadaver Encounters: Keyser, Thomas de (1613) National Library of Medicine; Burial/Platform: Department of Defense (1880) National Archives and Records Administration of the United States; Burial at Sea: National Archives and Records Administration of the United States; Potters Field: New York World-Telegram and the Sun Newspaper Photograph Collection (1915) Library of Congress; Oscar Winners/ Flick: Benjamin K. Edwards Collection (1909) Library of Congress; Colonial Massachusetts Tombstone (1767): Ludwig, Allan, Library of Congress.

EPITAPH

Tombstone (1773): Ludwig, Allan, Library of Congress; Colonial Massachusetts Tombstone Detail (1697): Ludwig, Allan, Library of Congress; Tombstone in Boot Hill Cemetery, Tombstone, Arizona; Lee, Russell, Library of Congress; Tombstone in Boot Hill Cemetery, Tombstone, Arizona/Lynched; Lee, Russell, Library of Congress; Statue in Glass: Horne, Joseph, Library of Congress.